PHILIP'S

STREET ATLAS
North
Yorkshire

D0300587

First published in 2002 by

Philip's, a division of
Octopus Publishing Group Ltd
2–4 Heron Quays, London E14 4JP

First colour edition 2002
Second impression 2002

ISBN 0-540-08144-2

© Philip's 2002

OS Ordnance Survey®

This product includes mapping data licensed
from Ordnance Survey® with the permission
of the Controller of Her Majesty's Stationery
Office. © Crown copyright 2002. All rights
reserved. Licence number 100011710

No part of this publication may be
reproduced, stored in a retrieval system or
transmitted in any form or by any means,
electronic, mechanical, photocopying,
recording or otherwise, without the
permission of the Publishers and the
copyright owner.

To the best of the Publishers' knowledge, the
information in this atlas was correct at the
time of going to press. No responsibility can
be accepted for any errors or their
consequences.

The representation in this atlas of a road,
track or path is no evidence of the existence
of a right of way.

Ordnance Survey and the OS Symbol are
registered trademarks of Ordnance Survey,
the national mapping agency of Great Britain

Printed and bound in Spain
by Cayfosa-Quebecor

Contents

III	**Key to map symbols**	
IV	**Key to map pages**	
VI	**Route planning**	
X	**Administrative and Postcode boundaries**	
1	**Street maps** at 1¼ inches to 1 mile	
208	**Street maps** at 2½ inches to 1 mile	
233	**Street map of York city centre** at 5 inches to 1 mile	
234	**Index** of towns and villages	
238	**Index** of streets, hospitals, industrial estates, railway stations, schools, shopping centres, universities and places of interest	

Digital Data

The exceptionally high-quality mapping found in this atlas is available as digital data in TIFF format, which is easily convertible to other bit mapped (raster) image formats.

The index is also available in digital form as a standard database table. It contains all the details found in the printed index together with the National Grid reference for the map square in which each entry is named.

For further information and to discuss your requirements, please contact Philip's on 020 7531 8439 or george.philip@philips-maps.co.uk

(22a)	**Motorway** with junction number
	Primary route – dual/single carriageway
	A road – dual/single carriageway
	B road – dual/single carriageway
	Minor road – dual/single carriageway
	Other minor road – dual/single carriageway
	Road under construction
	Pedestrianised area
DY7	**Postcode boundaries**
	County and unitary authority boundaries
	Railway
	Railway under construction
	Tramway, miniature railway
	Rural track, private road or narrow road in urban area
	Gate or obstruction to traffic (restrictions may not apply at all times or to all vehicles)
	Path, bridleway, byway open to all traffic, road used as a public path

The representation in this atlas of a road, track or path is no evidence of the existence of a right of way

177
32
229
233
213

Adjoining page indicators
(The colour of the arrow indicates the scale of the adjoining page - see scales below)

The map areas within the pink and blue bands are shown at a larger scale on the page, indicated by the red and blue blocks and arrows

Abbr	Full	Abbr	Full
Acad	**Academy**	Mkt	**Market**
Allot Gdns	**Allotments**	Meml	**Memorial**
Cemy	**Cemetery**	Mon	**Monument**
C Ctr	**Civic Centre**	Mus	**Museum**
CH	**Club House**	Obsy	**Observatory**
Coll	**College**	Pal	**Royal Palace**
Crem	**Crematorium**	PH	**Public House**
Ent	**Enterprise**	Recn Gd	**Recreation Ground**
Ex H	**Exhibition Hall**	Resr	**Reservoir**
Ind Est	**Industrial Estate**	Ret Pk	**Retail Park**
IRB Sta	**Inshore Rescue Boat Station**	Sch	**School**
		Sh Ctr	**Shopping Centre**
Inst	**Institute**	TH	**Town Hall/House**
Ct	**Law Court**	Trad Est	**Trading Estate**
L Ctr	**Leisure Centre**	Univ	**University**
LC	**Level Crossing**	Wks	**Works**
Liby	**Library**	YH	**Youth Hostel**

⇌ Walsall	**Railway station**
⊕	**Private railway station**
▬	**Bus, coach station**
◆	**Ambulance station**
◆	**Coastguard station**
◆	**Fire station**
◆	**Police station**
✚	**Accident and Emergency entrance to hospital**
H	**Hospital**
✛	**Place of worship**
i	**Information Centre** (open all year)
P	**Parking**
P&R	**Park and Ride**
PO	**Post Office**
Å	**Camping site**
⊕	**Caravan site**
▶	**Golf course**
✕	**Picnic site**
Prim Sch	**Important buildings, schools, colleges, universities and hospitals**
River Medway	**Water name**
	River, stream
◀	**Lock, weir**
	Water
	Tidal water
	Woods
	Houses
Church	**Non-Roman antiquity**
ROMAN FORT	**Roman antiquity**

■ The small numbers around the edges of the maps identify the 1 kilometre National Grid lines ■ The dark grey border on the inside edge of some pages indicates that the mapping does not continue onto the adjacent page

The scale of the maps on pages numbered in blue is 3.92 cm to 1 km • 2½ inches to 1 mile • 1: 25344

0	¼	½	¾	1 mile
0	250m	500m	750m	1 kilometre

The scale of the maps on pages numbered in green is 1.96 cm to 1 km • 1¼ inches to 1 mile • 1: 50688

0	¼	½	¾	1 mile
0	250m	500m	750m	1kilometre

The scale of the maps on pages numbered in red is 7.84 cm to 1 km • 5 inches to 1 mile • 1: 12672

0	220 yards	440 yards	660 yards	½ mile
0	125m	250m	375m	½ kilometre

Key to map pages

214 Map pages at 5 inches to 1 mile	
122 Map pages at 2½ inches to 1 mile	**186** Map pages at 1¼ inches to 1 mile

Spennymoor

Bishop Auckland A689

A1 (M)

Newton Aycli

A688

A67

A689

County Durham and Teesside STREET ATLAS

A66

Gainford Piercebridge A66

1 **2** Manfield **3** Darlington Low

Eppleby Hurworth-on-Tees Dinsda

A66 Newsham Croft-on-Te

Melsonby A167

Kirkby Stephen

A685

14 15 **16 17** **18 19** Melsonby **20 21** **22** A167 **23**

Ravenseat Whaw Washfold Moulton North Cowto

Keld Healaugh Reeth **Richmond** Danby Wisk

34 35 **36 37** **38 39** 209 **42 43**

Muker Marrick **40 41** Catterick Bromp

A685 **Catterick Garrison** A1

Kendal Sedbergh Garsdale Head A684 **Askrigg** Redmire Hunton **Northallerton**

A684 **55 56 57** **58 59** **Leyburn** A684 **62 63** **6**

Kirkby Lonsdale A683 **Hawes** West Witton **60 61** Leeming Newby

Thoralby Middleham **Bedale** Wiske

Stone House Stalling Busk Newbiggin Ellingstring Thornton Watlass

77 78 79 **80 81** **82 83** **84 85** Snape **86 87** **8**

Cray Carlton Fearby A6108 Baldersby

Cowan Bridge Buckden **Masham** Grewelthorpe

102 103 **104 105** **106 107** **108 109** **110 111** **112 113** **11**

Burton in Lonsdale **Ingleton** Horton-in-Ribblesdale Arncliffe Kettlewell Swetton **Ripon**

High Bentham Austwick Kilnsey 214

Wray **128 129** **130 131** **132 133** **134 135** **136 137** **138 139** **14**

Langcliffe Malham **Pateley Bridge** Summer Bridge Bishop Monkt

Settle **Grassington** Darley Head **160 161** **16**

Long Preston Airton Burnsall **158 159** Knaresborough

152 153 **154 155** Cracoe **156 157** Blubberhouses 219 220 22

Gargrave Embsay A59 **Harrogate** 222 223

Lancashire STREET ATLAS 216 217 **Skipton 174 175** **176 177** **178 179**

171 **172 173** Addingham Stainburn North Rigton

Barnoldswick **Earby** Cononley A629 Silsden **Ilkley** 218 **Burley in Wharfedale** Otley A659 A659

Chatburn **186 187** Glusburn Menston Guiseley

Clitheroe Trawden Keighley Yeadon

Longridge A6068 **Leeds**

Barton Ribchester **Bradford** M1

Preston A671 Burnley **West Yorkshire STREET ATLAS** Queensbury

Blackburn Halifax Dewsbury Wakefie

Greater Manchester STREET ATLAS

Rawtenstall Mirfield

Coppull Rochdale **Huddersfield** Barnsley

Horwich Bury Heywood Slaithwaite

Bolton Meltham

Wigan Oldham Holmfirth

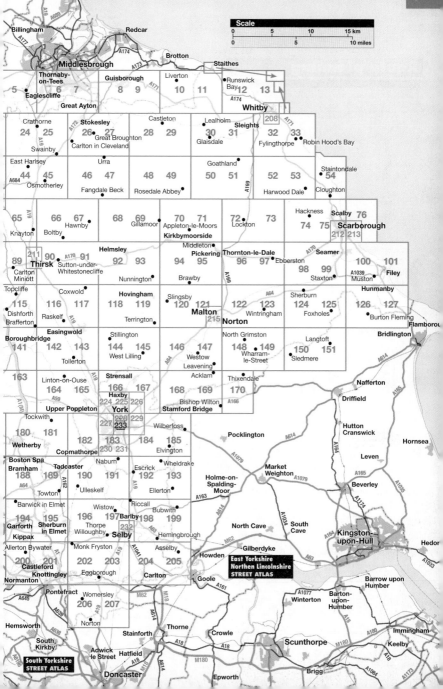

V

Route planning

Scale

0 — 5 — 10 — 15 — 20 km

0 — 5 — 10 miles

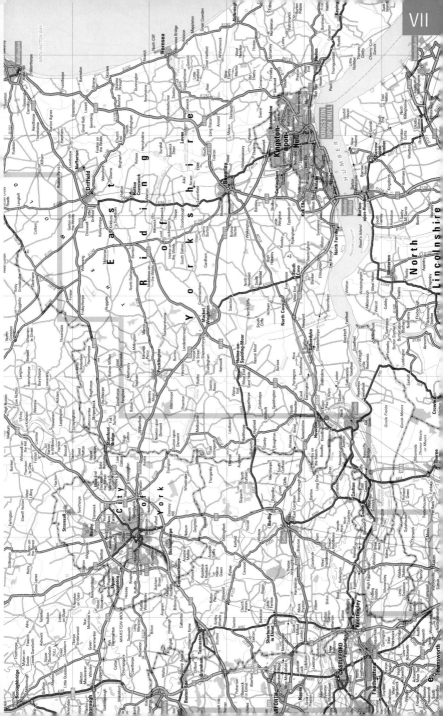

IX

Administrative and Postcode boundaries

X

Counties and unitary authorities

County Durham · Darlington · Redcar and Cleveland · Richmondshire · Cumbria · Lancashire · North Yorkshire · Hambleton · Harrogate · Ryedale · Scarborough · Craven · York · Selby · Leeds · Bradford · Wakefield · East Riding of Yorkshire · Kingston-upon-Hull

Grid references

NY · SD · NZ · OV · TA · OV · SD · SE

Legend

— County and unitary authority boundaries
···· Postcode boundaries
Area covered by this atlas

Scale

0 5 10 15 20 25 30 35 40 km
0 5 10 15 20 25 miles

Place names and postcode areas

CA17 · CA16 · LA10 · LA6 · LA2 · BB7 · DL12 · DL11 · DL8 · DL10 · DL9 · DL7 · DL6 · DL1 · DL2 · DL3 · TS21 · TS18 · TS16 · TS17 · TS15 · TS14 · TS13 · TS12 · TS9 · TS8 · TS7 · TS6 · TS5 · TS4 · TS3 · BD24 · BD23 · BD20 · BD18 · BB8 · BB22 · HG4 · HG3 · HG1 · HG2 · HG5 · YO7 · YO51 · YO61 · YO60 · YO62 · YO21 · YO22 · YO13 · YO18 · YO17 · YO42 · YO31 · YO41 · YO1 · YO32 · YO30 · YO26 · YO23 · YO19 · YO10 · YO24 · YO8 · YO11 · YO12 · YO14 · YO16 · YO25 · LS29 · LS21 · LS22 · LS17 · LS14 · LS15 · LS23 · LS24 · LS25 · LS26 · WF7 · WF8 · WF9 · WF10 · WF11 · DN14 · DN6

Ravenseat · Keld · Muker · Whaw · Newsham · Reeth · Marrick · Marske · Askrigg · Redmire · Leyburn · Bedale · Catterick · Garrison · Richmond · Hunton · West Witton · Middleham · Carlton · Kettlewell · Buckden · Cray · Arncliffe · Kilnsey · Malham · Airton · Gargrave · Long Preston · Settle · Langcliffe · Horton-in-Ribblesdale · Austwick · Ingleton · High Bentham · Wray · Cowan Bridge · Skipton · Embsay · Addingham · Burnsall · Grassington · Cracoe · Barnoldswick · Earby · Glusburn · Sutton · Silsden · Ilkley · Blubberhouses · Darley Head · Pateley Bridge · Summer Bridge · Swetton · Masham · Fearby · Ellingstring · West Tanfield · Ripon · Boroughbridge · Dishforth · Thirsk · Sowerby · Bagby · Coxwold · Easingwold · Tollerton · Sutton-on-the-Forest · Stillington · Crayke · Brandsby · Terrington · Hovingham · Slingsby · Malton · Norton · Westow · Thixendale · Wharram-le-Street · Acklam · Leavening · North Grimston · Wetwang · Huggate · Sherburn · Wintringham · Ebberston · Snainton · Brawby · Pickering · Thornton-le-Dale · Lockton · Rosedale Abbey · Gillamoor · Kirkbymoorside · Helmsley · Nunnington · Harome · Hawnby · Osmotherley · Swainby · Stokesley · Great Ayton · Carlton in Cleveland · Castleton · Lealholm · Sleights · Whitby · Robin Hood's Bay · Runswick Bay · Staithes · Fylingthorpe · Harwood Dale · Goathland · Staintondale · Hackness · Seamer · Scalby · Scarborough · Eastfield · Filey · Hunmanby · Burton Fleming · Langtoft · Sledmere · Foxholes · Cloughton · Wistow · Cawood · Sherburn in Elmet · Tadcaster · Bramham · Boston Spa · Wetherby · Spofforth · Knaresborough · Harrogate · Follifoot · North Rigton · Pannal · Stainburn · Burley in Wharfedale · Garforth · Kippax · Allerton Bywater · Castleford · Pontefract · Knottingley · Normanton · Womersley · Carlton · Goole · Asselby · Barmby · Bubwith · Howden · Selby · Escrick · Skipwith · Naburn · Copmanthorpe · Upper Poppleton · Long Marston · Appleton Roebuck · Ulleskelf · Church Fenton · Riccall · Barlby · Stillingfleet · Thorganby · Wheldrake · Elvington · Dunnington · Stamford Bridge · Wilberfoss · Bishop Wilton · Pocklington · Great Driffield · Nafferton · Hutton Cranswick

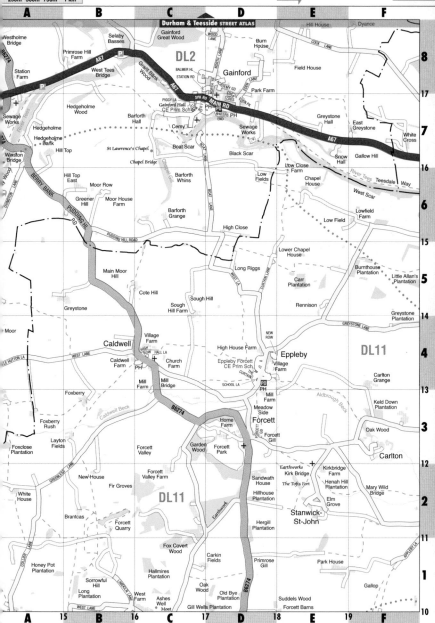

Westholme Bridge
Selaby Basses
Gainford Great Wood
WOOD LANE
Hill House
Dyance

Primrose Hill Farm
A67
DL2
BALMER HL
STATION RD
NORTH LANE
Burn House
COCK LANE
8

Station Farm
West Tees Bridge
Grant Bank Wood
Gainford
Field House
17

Hedgeholme Wood
PIGGY LA
Gainford Hall
CE Prim Sch
SPA RD
ACADEMY GD
EDS
CRES
EDEN PK
Park Farm

Sewage Works
River Tees
Barforth Hall
Cemy
WATERS END
MAIN RD
PH
Greystone Hall
East Greystone
White Cross
7

Hedgeholme
Hedgeholme Bank
Hill Top
St Lawrence's Chapel
Boat Scar
Black Scar
A67
Snow Hall
Gallow Hill
Teesdale Way
16

Winston Bridge
THORNTON LANE
BERRY BANK
Chapel Bridge
Chapel Gill
Barforth Whins
BOAT LANE
Low Fields
Low Close Farm
Chapel House
West Scar
River Tees
6

Hill Top East
Moor Row
Greener Hill
Moor House Farm
PUDDING HILL RD
Barforth Grange
BESS LA
High Close
Lower Chapel House
Lowfield Farm
Low Field
Burnthouse Plantation
Little Allan's Plantation
15

Main Moor Hill
PUDDING HILL ROAD
Long Riggs
CURTAIN LANE
Carr Plantation
Rennison
Greystone Plantation
5

Moor
Greystone
Cote Hill
Sough Hill
Sough Hill Farm
NEW ROW
GREYSTONE LANE
14

LE HUTTON LA
WEST LANE
Caldwell
Village Farm
HIGH ROW
HALL LA
High House Farm
Eppleby Forcett CE Prim Sch
Eppleby
Village Farm
DL11
4

Caldwell Farm
PH
Church Farm
THE CURTAIN
SCHOOL LA
PO
PH
Mill Farm
Carlton Grange
Keld Down Plantation
13

Foxberry
Mill Farm
Mill Bridge
B6274
Caldwell Beck
Meadow Side
Aldbrough Beck
Oak Wood
Carlton
3

Foxberry Rush
Foxclose Plantation
Layton Fields
GREENESS LANE
Forcett Valley
Home Farm
Garden Wood
Forcett Park
Forcett Gill
FORCETT GB
Earthworks
Kirk Bridge
The Tofts Fort
Kirkbridge Farm
Henah Hill Plantation
Mary Wild Bridge
12

White House
New House
Fir Groves
Forcett Valley Farm
DL11
Sandwath House
Hillhouse Plantation
Elm Grove
Stanwick-St-John
2

Brantcas
Forcett Quarry
EARTHWORK
Hergill Plantation
11

COLLIER LANE
Honey Pot Plantation
Sorrowful Hill
TAWNEYS LANE
Fox Covert Wood
Carkin Fields
Primrose Gill
Park House
ASPERTY LA
Gallop
1

Long Plantation
West Farm
WEST LANE
Hallmires Plantation
Ashes Well Moat
Oak Wood
Old Bye Plantation
Gill Wells Plantation
B6274
Suddels Wood
Forcett Barns
10

Scale: 1¼ inches to 1 mile

F6
1 AYRESOME WY
2 WIMBLEDON CL
3 HEADINGLEY CR
4 WHITE HART CR
5 MURRAYFIELD WY
6 BRAMALL LA
7 DEEPDALE WY
8 ANFIELD CT
9 AINTREE CT
10 AVIEMORE CT
11 EPSOM CT
12 ELLAND CT
13 BISLEY CT
14 CHEPSTOW CT
15 KEMPTON CT
16 HICKSTEAD CT
17 MALLORY CT
18 BADMINTON CT
19 TRAFFORD CT

(M) Durham A68, Bishop Auckland
A167 Durham **Durham & Teesside** STREET ATLAS

A   B   C   D   E   F

DL2
DL3

Bottom House Farm
High Faverdale Farm
Holly House Farm
Faverdale
Faverdale Whin
Mount Pleasant

Harrowgate Hill
Sports Ground
Longfield School
Rise Carr Prim Sch
North Cemy
Thompson St

Harrowgate Village
Darlington
CH
Balmoral Rd
Springfield Cty Prim Sch

Whinfield
Quarry
Ellyhill Wood
Ellyhill Farm

1 GLENEAGLES RD
2 CALEDONIAN WY
3 STONEHAVEN WY
4 ROSSWAY
5 TORRANCE DR

Great Burdon
Clarendon Rd
Millbatts Dr

A1150
Close Farm

Cockerton
Superstore
North Rd Prim Sch Trading Estate
Railway Mus
North Road
Industrial Estate
Gurney Pease Prim Sch
Girton Walk
Gresham St
Peterhouse Cl
Augusta Cl
Haughton
Haughton Bridge Red Hall Prim Sch
Haughton Le Skerne
Coombe Drive

DARLINGTON
Sports Ground

Standrop Rd
Woodland Rd
Carmel Road North
Hummersknott
Comp Sch
Abbey
College
Sports Ctr
Arts Ctr Coll
Dolphin Centre
Mag

DL1
The Causeway 1
The Crossway 2
The Stray 3
Heathfield Prim Sch
Lingfield
Allington Way
Yarm Road Industrial Estate

Cleveland St
Cornmill
B6279

Coniscliffe Rd
Coniscliffe Road
A67
Blackwell
Carmel Grove
Cypress
Carmel Road South
A67

Baydale Farm
Baydale Wood
Beck House Farm
Cleasby Lane
Strawgate Grove
PH
Stapleton
Stapleton Manor
Stapleton Grange

Blackwell Bridge
Blackwell Grange
Darlington RFC
Skerne Park
Snipe Lane
CH
Springfield
Stressholme Golf Centre

South Park
Polam Hall School
Marlborough Drive
Grangeside
The Spinney
Junior Sch

Eastbourne
Eastbourne School
St Johns Prim Sch
East Cemy
TA Centre

DL1
Firth Moor
Firth Moor Jun Sch

E1
1 HORNBY CL
2 CROSSFIELD CL
3 SYCAMORE CL
4 MOWBRAY DR
5 ROUNDHILL CL
6 SOUTHFIELD CL
7 DALE CL
8 MALVERN CL
9 GREENSIDE CT
10 COACH LA
11 MANORFIELDS
12 MINSTER WK
13 BRYAN CL
14 LYCH GT
15 THE SABLES
16 CHURCH VW

West Moor Rd
Newstead Farm
Snipe House Farm
Creebeck Farm
Hurworth Moor
High Farm
Pateley Moor Cr
A66
Burma Rd
Hurworth Moor Farm
Hurworth Moor House

Black Banks Farm
Black Banks
Sewage Works
Nag's Head Farm
Oxney Flatts Farm
North Oxen-le-Fields
Blackwell Moor Farm
PH
Green Lane Farm
Butcher House Farm
Roundhill Farm
DL2
Brickyard Farm
Skip Bridge

DL2
Monk End Wood
Croft Road
A167
River Tees
Oxen-le-Fields
Oxneyfield Bridge
Weir
Monk End Farm
Hill Top Farm
Glebe View Farm
Hurworth Place
Eelmfield Rd
Manor Rd
Friars Pardon
Sch
Garden House
Ashfield
Hurworth-on-Tees
The Wayside
Holme Farm
Sanderson Rd
The Oval
Hilton House Farm
Hurworth Rd
Measham Road
Low Hill Bridge

22

4

D1
1 HAWKSWOOD
2 EDEN CL
3 GRANGE AVE
4 HUNTERS CL

For full street detail of Darlington see Philip's
STREET ATLAS of **Co. Durham and Teesside**

27   28   29   30   31

8 17 7 16 6 15 5 14 4 13 3 12 2 11 1 10

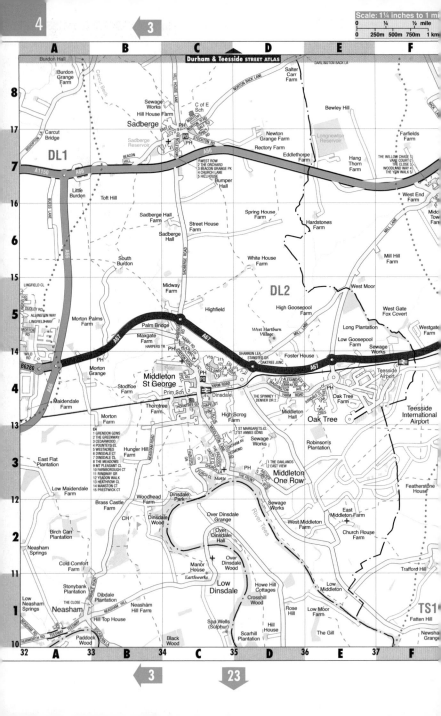

Burdon Hall
Burdon Grange Farm
Carcut Beck
Newton Back Lane
Salter Carr Farm
DARLINGTON BACK LA
8
Sewage Works
C of E Sch
Sadberge
Bewley Hill
Carcut Bridge
Hill House Farm
PH
Sadberge Reservoir
PO
STOCKTON RD
PH
Newton Grange Farm
Longnewton Reservoir
Farfields Farm
17
DL1
BEACON HILL
A66
Rectory Farm
Eddlethorpe Farm
Hang Thorn Farm
THE WILLOW CHASE 1
THE CLOSE 2
THE CLOSE 3
WOODLAND WAY 4
THE YEW WALK 5
7
A1150
1 WEST ROW
2 THE ORCHARD
3 BEACON GRANGE PK
4 CHURCH LANE
5 HILLHOUSE
Bumper Hall
Little Burdon
Toft Hill
BUSES LANE
A66
West End Farm
16
Sadberge Hall Farm
Street House Farm
Spring House Farm
Hardstones Farm
Midd Tow Farm
6
Sadberge Hall
SADBERGE ROAD
White House Farm
MILL LANE
South Burdon
A66
DL2
Mill Hill Farm
15
LINGFIELD CL
Midway Farm
West Moor
DUDLEY RD
ALLINGTON WAY
LINGFIELD WAY
Morton Palms Farm
Highfield
High Goosepool Farm
West Gate Fox Covert
Westgate Farm
5
MORTON
Palm Bridge
A67
West Hartburn Village
Long Plantation
Low Goosepool Farm
Sewage Works
WILD RD
Maxgate Farm
HARPERS TR
PH
SHANNON LEA
STANSTED GR
DAKTREE JUNC
Foster House
A67
Teesside Airport
14
B6280
PH
Morton Grange
Middleton St George
PH
YARM ROAD
2 ALEXANDRA
FARM ROAD
ASHDALE CT
PH
Oak Tree Farm
Teesside International Airport
4
Maidendale Farm
Stodfoe Farm
Prim Sch
Dinsdale
THE SPINNEY 1
DENVER DR 2
Middleton Hall
Oak Tree
Morton Farm
Thorntree Farm
THORNTREE GD
CHAPEL ST
High Scrog Farm
1 ST MARGARETS CL
2 ST ANNES GDNS
13
East Flat Plantation
C4
1 GRENDON GDNS
2 THE GREENWAY
3 CEDARWOOD
4 POUNTEYS CL
5 WESTACRES
6 DINSDALE CT
7 DINSDALE CL
8 THE MEADOWS
9 MT PLEASANT CL
10 FARNBOROUGH CT
11 RINGWAY GR
12 YEADON WALK
13 HEATHROW CL
14 MANSTON CT
15 PRESTWICK CL
Hunger Hill Farm
NEASHAM ROAD
Sewage Works
DESMOND
Robinson's Plantation
Featherstone House
3
Low Maidendale Farm
Woodhead Farm
Motte
PH
1 THE OAKLANDS
2 EAST VIEW
Middleton One Row
Brass Castle Farm
CH
Dinsdale Wood
Dinsdale Park
River Tees
Sewage Works
West Middleton Farm
East Middleton Farm
Church House Farm
12
Birch Carr Plantation
Over Dinsdale Grange
2
Neasham Springs
Cold Comfort Farm
Over Dinsdale Hall
Trafford Hill
Stonybank Plantation
Dibdale Plantation
Manor House
Earthworks
Over Dinsdale Wood
Howe Hill Cottages
Low Middleton
11
Low Neasham Springs
THE CLOSE
Neasham
Neasham Hill Farm
Low Dinsdale
Crosshill Wood
Rose Hill
Low Moor Farm
TS1
HURWORTH RD
TEESDALE
Hill Top House
Paddock Wood
Black Wood
Spa Wells (Sulphur)
Scarhill Plantation
Hill House
The Gill
Fatten Hill
Newsha Grange
1

10

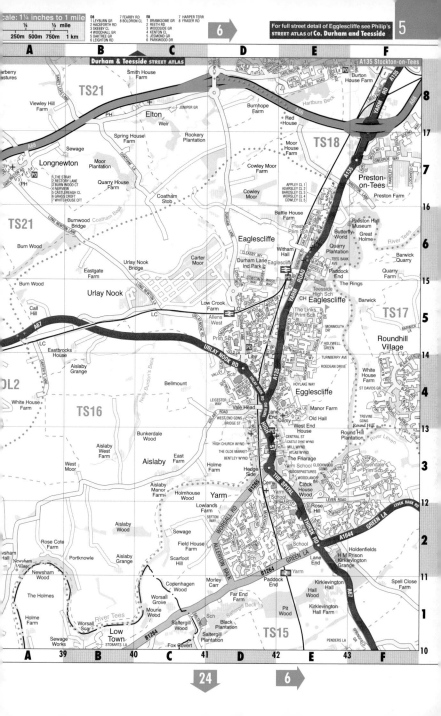

Scale: 1¼ inches to 1 mile

¼   ½ mile

250m 500m 750m   1 km

D8
1 LEYBURN GR
2 HACKFORTH RD
3 SKEEBY CL
4 FAIRVIEW
5 OAKTREE GR
6 LEIGHTON RD

7 FEARBY RD
8 BOLDRON CL

E8
1 BRANKSOME RD
2 REETH RD
3 WOODSIDE GR
4 KENTON CL
5 JESMOND GR
6 PARKWOOD DR

7 HARPER TERR
8 FRASER RD

For full street detail of Egglescliffe see Philip's
STREET ATLAS of Co. Durham and Teesside

5

Durham & Teesside STREET ATLAS

A135 Stockton-on-Tees

TS21

Smith House Farm

Elton

Weir

Juniper Gr

Viewley Hill Farm

Longnewton

1 THE STRAY
2 RECTORY LANE
3 BURN WOOD CT
4 FAIRVIEW
5 CASTLEREAGH CL
6 GRASS CROFT
7 WHITEHOUSE CFT

Spring House Farm

Moor Plantation

Quarry House Farm

Rookery Plantation

Burnhope Farm

Red House

Moor House Farm

Hartburn Beck

Burton House Farm

TS18

Preston-on-Tees

Preston Farm

APPLEBY CL 1
KEARSLEY CL 2
BARDSLEY CL 3
WORSLEY CL 4
COWLEY CL 5

TS21

Burnwood Bridge

Coatham Beck

Eastgate Farm

Coatham Stob

Eaglescliffe

Cowley Moor Farm

Cowley Moor

Preston Prim Sch

Battle House Farm

Witham Hall

Butterfly World

Preston Hall Museum

Great Holme

Quarry Plantation

River Tees

Carter Moor

CLASBY WY

Durham Lane Ind Park

Eaglescliffe

TEES BANK AVE

Paddock End

Barwick Quarry

Quarry Farm

Urlay Nook Bridge

Urlay Nook

Burn Wood

Call Hill

Eastbrooks House

Aislaby Grange

Low Crook Farm

Allens West Prim Sch

Teesside High Sch

The Rings

CH Eaglescliffe

Barwick

TS17

DL2

White House Farm

TS16

Bellmount

Bunkerdale Wood

Aislaby West Farm

East Farm

Aislaby

Leicester Way

Vale Head

Lane End Cemy

Manor End

Old Hall

Monmouth Dr

Holywell Green

Turnberry Ave

Roedean Drive

Hoylake Way

Egglescliffe

White House Farm

ST DAVIDS GR

Roundhill Village

Round Hill

Round Hill Plantation

River Leven

West Moor

Aislaby Manor Farm

Holme Farm

West End Gdns

Bridge St

High Church Wynd

The Olde Market

Bentley Wynd

Central St

Castle Dyke Wynd

Mill Wynd

Atlas Wynd

The Friarage

West End House

Levendale Prim Sch

Holmhouse Wood

Yarm

Hedge Side

Yarm School

Goosepastures

Woodlands

Clockwood Gdns

Rose Cote Farm

Portknowle

Aislaby Wood

Aislaby Grange

Sewage

Field House Farm

Scarfoot Hill

Lowlands Farm

Sefton Way

Yarm School

Cemy

Clock House Wood

Rose Hill

Leven Road

Newsham Village

Newsham Wood

The Holmes

Holme Farm

Worsall Scar

Low Town

STOBARTS LA

Copenhagen Wood

Worsall Grove

Mourie Wood

Saltergill Wood

Saltergill Plantation

Fox Covert

Morley Carr

Far End Farm

Black Plantation

Samsondl Beck

Paddock End

Pit Wood

TS15

Holdenfields

H M Prison Kirklevington Grange

Kirklevington Hall Wood

Kirklevington Hall Farm

Spell Close Farm

PENDERS LA

Sewage Works

River Tees

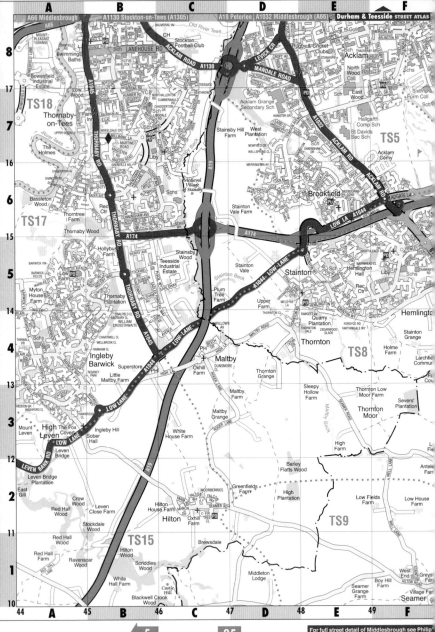

5   25

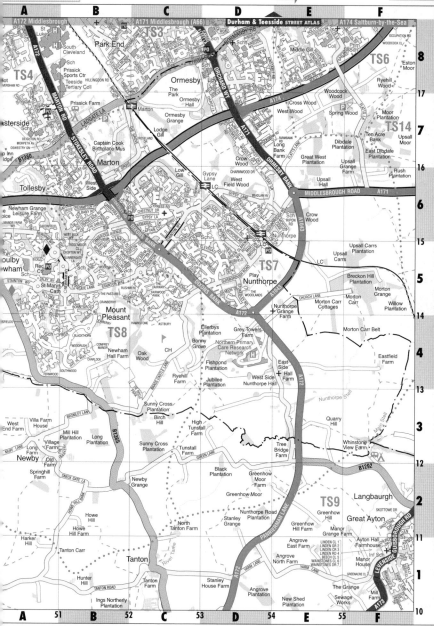

A172 Middlesbrough

A171 Middlesbrough (A66)

Durham & Teesside STREET ATLAS

A174 Saltburn-by-the-Sea

St Lukes

South Cleveland

Park End

TS3

Schs

Middle Gill

Coll

TS6

8

TS4

Prissick Sports Ctr
Teeside Tertiary Coll

HILLINGDON RD

Ormesby

The Park

Ormesby Hall

Cross Wood

Woodcock Wood

Eston Moor

Ryehill Wood

17

Prissick Farm

Ormesby Grange

West Wood

Spring Wood

Moor Plantation

TS14

Captain Cook Birthplace Mus

Lodge Gill

Crow Wood

Long Bank Farm

Dibdale Plantation

Ten Acre Bank

East Dibdale Plantation

Upsall Moor

7

Marton

Great West Plantation

Upsall Grange Farm

Rush Plantation

16

Tollesby

West Side

Low Gill

Gypsy Lane LC

West Field Wood

Upsall Hall

Middlesbrough Road

A171

6

Newham Grange Leisure Farm

GYPSY LANE

Sch

Crow Wood

Upsall Carrs Plantation

15

Rec Ct

Nunthorpe

LC

Upsall Carrs

Breckon Hill Plantation

5

St Marys Cath

The Fairway

TS7

Play Nunthorpe

LC

Morton Grange

Mount Pleasant

The Woodlands

Nunthorpe Grange Farm

Morton Carr Cottages

Morton Carr

Willow Plantation

14

TS8

Newham Hall Farm

Oak Wood

CH

Ellerbys Plantation

Grey Towers Farm

Northern Primary Care Research Network

Morton Carr Belt

4

Bonny Grove

East Side

West Side Nunthorpe Hall

Eastfield Farm

Ryehill Farm

Fishpond Plantation

Jubilee Plantation

13

Sunny Cross Plantation

Birch Hill

High Tunstall Farm

Quarry Hill

Nunthorpe Stell

3

Villa Farm House

Mill Hill Plantation

Long Plantation

Sunny Cross Plantation

Tunstall Farm

GREEN LANE

Tree Bridge Farm

Whinstone View Farm

B1292

12

West End Farm

Village Farm

Newby

Old Farm

Springhill Farm

Newby Grange

Black Plantation

Greenhow Moor Farm

TS9

Langbaurgh

2

Howe Hill

Greenhow Moor

Nunthorpe Road Plantation

Greenhow Hill

Great Ayton

Harker Hill

Howe Hill Farm

North Tanton Farm

Stanley Grange

Greenhow Hill Farm

Manor Grange Farm

Ayton Hall Farmhouse

11

Tanton Carr

Tanton

Angrove East Farm

LINDEN CL 1
LINDEN GR 2
LINDEN CR 3
LINDEN RD 4
BEECH CL 5
WAINSTONES CL 6
WAINSTONES DR 7

Manor House

Hunter Hill

Tanton Farm

Angrove North Farm

YARM LANE

The Grange

Ings Northerly Plantation

TANTON ROAD

Stanley House Farm

Angrove Plantation

New Shed Plantation

Sewage Works

Mill House

A173

1

10

full street detail of Middlesbrough see Philip's
EET ATLAS of **Co. Durham and Teesside**

26
8

Scale: 1¼ inches to 1 mile

0   ¼   ½ mile
0   250m 500m 750m 1 k

Durham & Teesside STREET ATLAS

A2
1 ORCHARD CL
2 BRADLEYS TR
3 CHURCHILL CL
4 SPENCE CT
5 ROWAN DR
6 CENTRAL WY
7 CALIFORNIA GR
8 ROSEBERRY DR
9 OAKLANDS
10 THE HAWTHORNS
11 ROMANY RD
12 WOODBINE CL
13 WHINSTONE VW

For full street detail of Guisborough see Philip's STREET ATLAS of Co. Durham and Teesside

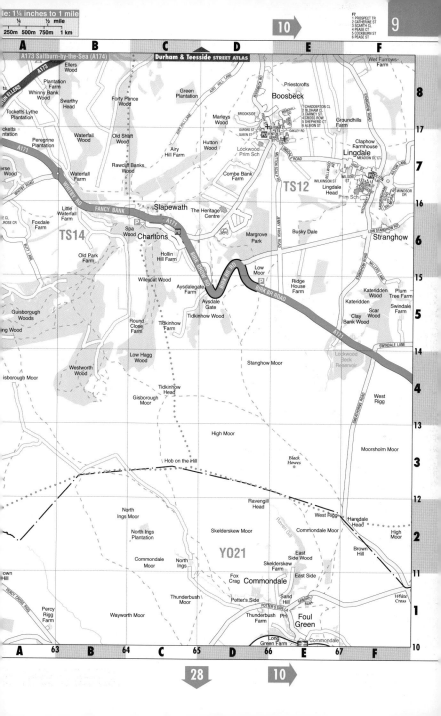

Scale: 1¼ inches to 1 mile

¼ ½ mile
250m 500m 750m 1 km

F7
1 PROSPECT TR
2 CATHERINE ST
3 SCARTH CL
4 PEASE CT
5 COCKBURN ST
6 PEASE ST

Durham & Teesside STREET ATLAS

A173 Saltburn-by-the-Sea (A174)

Wet Furrows Farm

Ellers Wood

Plantation Farm

Whinny Bank Wood

Tocketts Lythe Plantation

Swarthy Head

Forty Pence Wood

Green Plantation

Priestcrofts

Boosbeck

1 CHADDERTON CL
2 OLDHAM CL
3 CARNEY ST
4 CROSS ROW
5 SHEPHERD CT
6 ALBION ST

Groundhills Farm

Marleys Wood

BROOKSIDE

OXFORD ST
QUEEN ST
PO
FENTON ST

OAKLEY RD

Claphow Farmhouse

Lingdale
MEADOW CT.

Peregrine Plantation

Waterfall Wood

Old Shaft Wood

Airy Hill Farm

Hutton Wood

Lockwood Prim Sch

HIGH ST
WILKINSON ST

WILSON ST
PO

KILTON LANE

Lingdale
Head

Lingdale
Prim Sch

WINDSOR DR

horse Wood

Foxdale Farm

Little Waterfall Farm

Waterfall Farm

Rawcliff Banks Wood

Combe Bank Farm

TS12

TS14

FANCY BANK

Slapewath

The Heritage Centre

Margrove Park

Busky Dale

LOW STANGHOW RD

Stranghow

Old Park Farm

Spa Wood

Charltons

PO

Hollin Hill Farm

Wileycat Wood

Aysdalegate Farm

Low Moor

Ridge House Farm

Kateridden Wood

Plum Tree Farm

Guisborough Woods

Round Close Farm

Tidkinhow Farm

Aysdale Gate

Tidkinhow Wood

Clay Bank Wood

Scar Wood

Swindale Farm

ng Wood

Kateridden

SWINDALE LANE

Westworth Wood

Low Hagg Wood

Stanghow Moor

Lockwood Beck Reservoir

isborough Moor

Tidkinhow Head

Gisborough Moor

High Moor

West Rigg

Hob on the Hill

Black Howes

Moorsholm Moor

North Ings Moor

Ravengill Head

West Rigg

Haredale Head

High Moor

North Ings Plantation

Skelderskew Moor

Commondale Moor

Brown Hill

Commondale Moor

North Ings

YO21

East Side Wood

Skelderskew Farm

own Hill

Percy Rigg Farm

Thunderbush Moor

Fox Crag

COMMONDALE

East Side

White Cross

Wayworth Moor

Potter's Side

Sand Hill

Foul Green

Thunderbush Farm PH

Long Green Farm

Commondale

A173

A171

WHITBY ROAD

BIRK BROW RD

BIRK BR ROAD

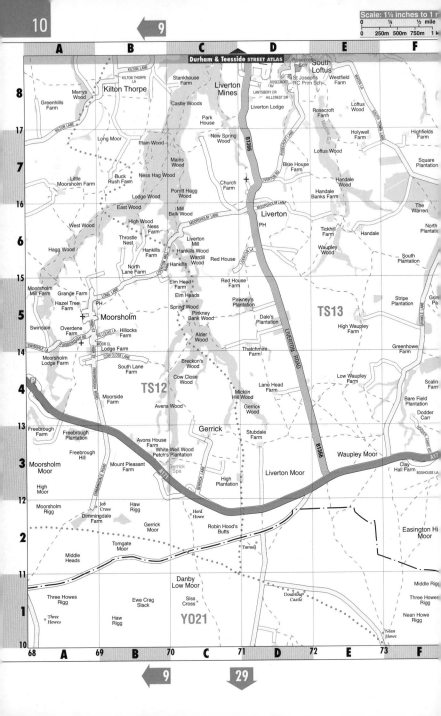

9

Scale: 1¼ inches to 1 r

0   ¼   ½ mile

0   250m 500m 750m   1 k

A **B** **C** **D** **E** **F**

Rosecroft Sch
South Loftus
St Josephs
RC Prim Sch

Kilton Thorpe
KILTON LANE
KILTON THORPE LA
Stankhouse Farm
Liverton Mines
ROSECROFT AV
LANTSBERY DR
HILLCREST DR
Westfield Farm

8

Merrys Wood
Castle Woods
Liverton Lodge
Rosecroft Farm
Loftus Wood

Greenhills Farm
Park House
Holywell Farm
Highfields Farm

KILTON LANE
Long Moor
Plain Wood
New Spring Wood
Loftus Wood
Square Plantation

17

Little Moorsholm Farm
Buck Rush Farm
Mains Wood
Blue House Farm
Handale Wood
The Warren

7

Ness Hag Wood
Church Farm
Handale Banks Farm
North Plantation

Lodge Wood
Pornitt Hagg Wood
Liverton
MOORSHOLM LANE

16

East Wood
Mill Balk Wood
PH
Tickhill Farm
Handale
South Plantation

West Wood
High Wood
Ness Farm
MOORSHOLM LANE
Liverton Mill
Waupley Wood

6

Hagg Wood
Throstle Nest
Hankills Farm
Hankills Wood
Wardill Wood
Red House

Hankills
North Lane Farm
LONG LANE
BENTON MILL

15

Moorsholm Mill Farm
Grange Farm
PH
Elm Head Farm
Red House Farm
Stripe Plantation
Grin Pa

Hazel Tree Farm
Elm Heads
Pinkney's Plantation
TS13

5

Moorsholm
Spring Wood
Pinkney Bank Wood
Dale's Plantation
High Waupley Farm

Swindale
Overdene Farm
Hillocks La
Hillocks Farm
Alder Wood
Greenhowe Farm

SWINDALE LA
HIGH ST
FLISBROUGH RD
MOOR CL
Lodge Farm
COW CLOSE LANE
Thatchmire Farm
Scalin Farm

14

Moorsholm Lodge Farm
South Lane Farm
Breckon's Wood
Lane Head Farm
Bare Field Plantation

P
Moorside Farm
Cow Close Wood
Micklin Hill Wood
Low Waupley Farm
Dodder Carr

4

TS12
Avens Wood
Gerrick Wood

Freebrough Farm
Freebrough Plantation
Avons House Farm
Gerrick
Stubdale Farm
Waupley Moor
Clay Hall Farm

13

Freebrough Hill
White Well Wood
Petch's Plantation
BOGHOUSE LA

Moorsholm Moor
Mount Pleasant Farm
Gerrick Spa
Liverton Moor
A171

3

High Moor
High Plantation

12

Moorsholm Rigg
Job Cross
Haw Rigg
Herd Howe
Easington Hi Moor

Dimmingdale Farm
Gerrick Moor
Robin Hood's Butts

2

Middle Heads
Tomgate Moor
Tumuli

11

Three Howes Rigg
Danby Low Moor
Middle Rigg

1

Three Howes
Ewe Crag Slack
Siss Cross
Doubting Castle
Three Howes Rigg

Haw Rigg
YO21
Nean Howe Rigg

Nean Howe

10

68 A **69** B **70** C **71** D **72** E **73** F

9

29

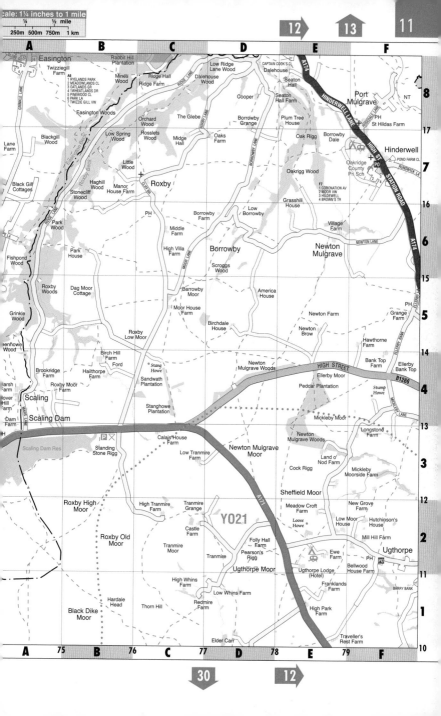

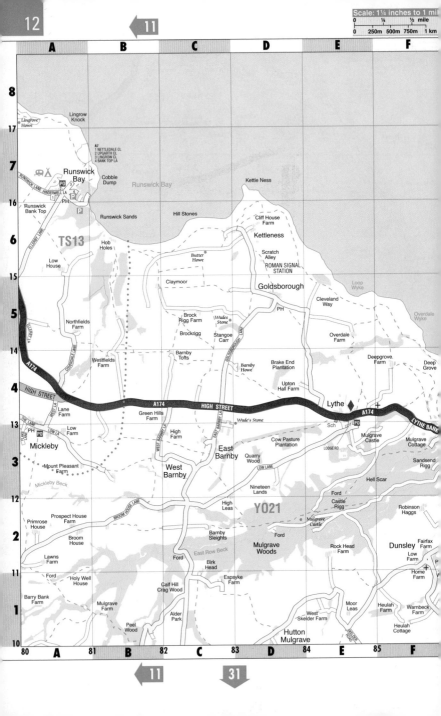

Scale: 1¼ inches to 1 mile
0   ¼   ½   mile
0 250m 500m 750m 1 km

A   B   C   D   E   F

8

17

Lingrow Knock

Lingrove Howe

A7
1 NETTLEDALE GL
2 UPGARTH CL
3 LINGROW CL
4 BANK TOP LA

7

Runswick Bay

Cobble Dump

Runswick Bay

Kettle Ness

RUNSWICK LANE   HINDERWELL LA

PH

16

Runswick Bank Top

P

Runswick Sands

Hill Stones

Cliff House Farm

TS13

Hob Holes

Kettleness

6

Low House

Butter Howe

Scratch Alley

ROMAN SIGNAL STATION

15

Claymoor

Goldsborough

Loop Wyke

ELLERBY LANE

Brock Rigg Farm

Wades Stone

Cleveland Way

PH

Overdale Wyke

5

Northfields Farm

Brockrigg

Stangoe Carr

GOLDSBOROUGH LANE

Overdale Farm

14

ELLERBY LA

Westfields Farm

Barnby Tofts

Barnby Howe

Brake End Plantation

Deepgrove Farm

Deep Grove

4

HIGH STREET

A174

A174   HIGH STREET

Upton Hall Farm

Lythe

A174

LYTHE BANK

WEST BARNBY LA

Lane Farm

Green Hills Farm

Wade's Stone

Sch

P

13

THE LANE

PH   LOW LA

Low Farm

High Farm

Cow Pasture Plantation

LODGE RD

Mulgrave Castle

Mulgrave Cottage

Mickleby

EAST BARNBY LA

East Barnby

Quarry Wood

LOW LANE

Sandsend Rigg

3

Mount Pleasant Farm

West Barnby

Hell Scar

Mickleby Beck

Nineteen Lands

YO21

12

Prospect House Farm

BROOM HOUSE LANE

High Leas

Ford

Castle Rigg

Robinson Haggs

Primrose House

Broom House

Barnby Sleights

Ford

Mulgrave Castle

Mulgrave Woods

Rock Head Farm

Dunsley

Fairfax Farm

2

Lawns Farm

East Row Beck

Low Farm

Home Farm

11

Ford

Holy Well House

Calf Hill Crag Wood

Birk Head

Espsyke Farm

West Skelder Farm

Moor Leas

Heulah Farm

Warnbeck Farm

Barry Bank Farm

Mulgrave Farm

Alder Park

SKELDER RIDGE

Hutton Mulgrave

Heulah Cottage

1

Peel Wood

10

80   A   81   B   82   C   83   D   84   E   85   F

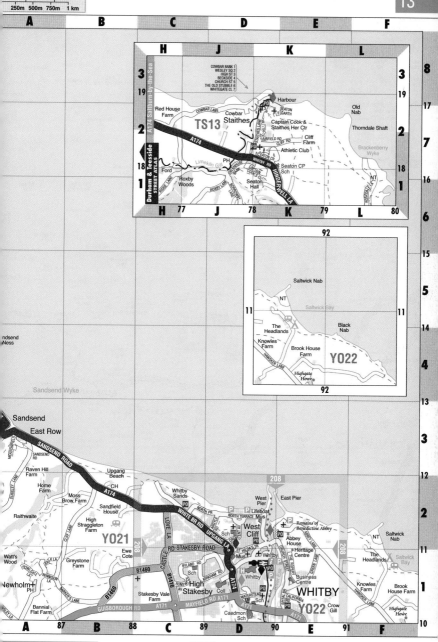

Scale: 1¼ inches to 1 mile

¼   ½ mile

250m 500m 750m 1 km

8
17
7
16
6
15
5
14
4
13
3
12
2
11
1
10

A   B   C   D   E   F

COWBAR BANK 1
WESLEY SQ 2
HIGH ST 3
BECKSIDE 4
CHURCH ST 5
THE OLD STUBBLE 6
WHITEGATE CL 7

H   J   K   L

3
19
2
18
1

Durham & Teesside STREET ATLAS

A174 Saltburn-By-The-Sea

Red House Farm
COWBAR LANE
Cowbar Staithes
A174
Limekiln Gill
PH
FAIRFIELD RD
CLIFF RD
CLIFF RD
SEACON CP
WHITBY RD
BRIDGE LANE
ROXBY LANE
SEATON CP
HINDERWELL LA

TS13

Harbour
SEATON ST BARTH
Captain Cook & Staithes Her Ctr
Cliff Farm
Athletic Club
Seaton CP Sch

Old Nab
Thorndale Shaft
Brackenberry Wyke
NT

Ford
Roxby Woods
Seaton Hall

H 77   J 78   K 79   L 80

92

Saltwick Nab
NT
Saltwick Bay
The Headlands
Knowles Farm
Brook House Farm
Black Nab
YO22
Highgate Howe
HAWSKER LANE

11   11

92

Sandsend Ness

Sandsend Wyke

Sandsend
East Row
SANDSEND ROAD
SANDSEND RD
Raven Hill Farm
Home Farm
Moss Brow Farm
Raithwaite
A174
Upgang Beach
CH
Sandfield House
High Straggleton Farm
YO21
Ewe Cote
Greystone Farm
Watt's Wood
Newholm
PH
Bannial Flat Farm
DUNSLEY LANE
CLIFF LANE
NEWHOLM LA
ROSE LA
BENNISON
MERCER'S LANE
GUISBOROUGH RD
B1460
B1460
CASTLE
STAKESBY ROAD
LOVE LA
RD STAKESBY ROAD
Stakesby Vale Farm
B1460
High Stakesby
RYLAND RD
Coll
RINSWICK RD
Sch
A171
MAYFIELD RD A171
Caedmon Sch
Whitby Sands
NORTH PR
PO
NORTH TERRACE
Sch
WHITE BR RD
UPGANG LANE
West Cliff
Lifeboat Mus
St HILDA'S TER
PO
Mus
Whitby
208
West Pier
East Pier
Remains of Benedictine Abbey
Abbey House
Heritage Centre
Business Centre
PO
WHITBY
YO22
Crow Gill
NT
Saltwick Nab
The Headlands
Saltwick Bay
Knowles Farm
Brook House Farm
Highgate Howe
WATERSTEAD L
HAWSKER LANE
208

208

A 87   B 88   C 89   D 90   E 91   F

For full street detail of the highlighted area see page 208.

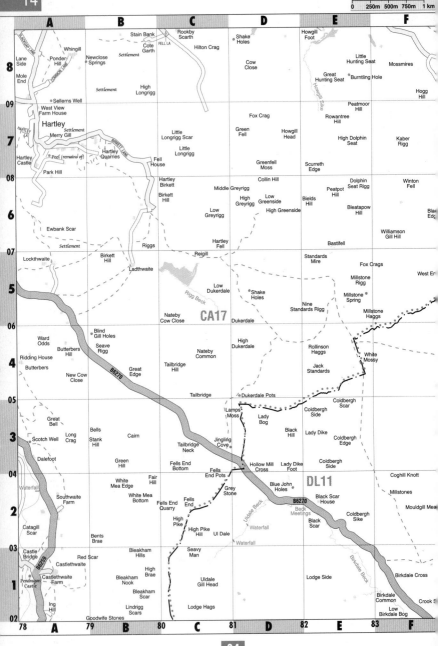

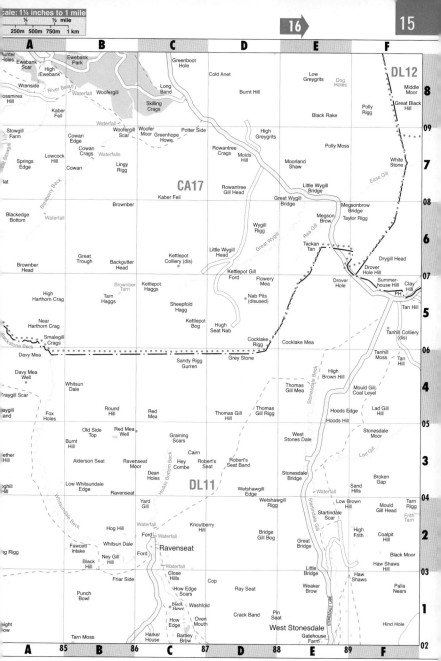

A **B** **C** **D** **E** **F**

DL12

unter Holes
Ewebank Scar
Ewebank Park
Greenboot Hole
Cold Anet
Low Greygrits
Dog Holes
Middle Moor
8

Wrenside
High Ewebank
Long Band
Burnt Hill
Black Rake
Polly Rigg
Great Black Hill

ossmires Hill
River Belah
Woofergill
Skilling Crags
Waterfall

Kaber Fell
Waterfall
Woofer Moor
Potter Side
High Greygrits
Polly Moss
White Stone
09

Stowgill Farm
Cowan Edge
Woofergill Scar
Greenhope Howe
Rowantree Crags
Molds Hill
Moorland Shaw
7

Springs Edge
Lowcock Hill
Cowan Crags
Cowan
Waterfalls
Lingy Rigg
Kaber Fell
CA17
Rowantree Gill Head
Great Wygill Bridge
Little Wygill Bridge
Megsonbrow Bridge
Ease Gill

lat
Blackedge Bottom
Brownber
Waterfall
Wygill Rigg
Megson Brow
Taylor Rigg
08

Brownber Head
Great Trough
Backgutter Head
Kettlepot Colliery (dis)
Little Wygill Head
Great Wygill
Tackan Tan
Drover Hole Hill
Drygill Head
6

High Harthorm Crag
Tarn Haggs
Brownber Tarn
Kettlepot Haggs
Kettlepot Gill Ford
Flowery Mea
Drover Hole
Summer-house Hill
Clay Hill
07

Near Harthorn Crag
Sheepfold Hagg
Nab Pits (disused)
PH
Tan Hill
5

Smalegill Crags
Kettlepot Bog
Hugh Seat Nab
Cocklake Rigg
Cocklake Mea
Tanhill Colliery (dis)

Backstone Beck
Davy Mea
Sandy Rigg Gurren
Grey Stone
Tanhill Moss
Tan Hill
06

Davy Mea Well
Whitsun Dale
Thomas Gill Mea
High Brown Hill
Mould Gill Coal Level
4

raygill and
Fox Holes
Round Hill
Red Mea
Thomas Gill Hill
Thomas Gill Rigg
Hoods Edge
Lad Gill Hill
05

ether Hill
Old Side Top
Red Mea Well
Graining Scars
West Stones Dale
Hoods Hill
Stonesdale Moor
3

oghill Hill
Burnt Hill
Alderson Seat
Ravenseat Moor
Cairn
Hey Combe
Robert's Seat
Robert's Seat Band
Stonesdale Bridge
Broken Gap
Lad Gill

Low Whitsundale Edge
Dean Holes
DL11
Wetshawgill Edge
Waterfall
Sand Hills
04

Ravenseat
Yard Gill
Wetshawgill Rigg
Low Brown Hill
Mould Gill Head
Tarn Rigg
Frith Tarn

g Rigg
Whitsundale Beck
Hog Hill
Waterfall
Knoutberry Hill
Startindale Gill
Startindale Scar
High Frith
Coalpit Hill
2

Fawcett Intake
Whitsun Dale
Ford
Waterfall
Bridge Gill Bog
Great Bridge
Black Moor

Black Hill
Ney Gill Hill
Ford
Ravenseat
Haw Shaws Hill
03

Friar Side
Close Hills
Waterfall
Cop
Ray Seat
Little Bridge
Weaker Brow
Haw Shaws
Palla Nears
1

Punch Bowl
How Edge Scars
Black Howe
Washfold
Crack Band
Pin Seat
Hind Hole

ight ow
Tarn Moss
Harker House
How Edge
Barney Brow
Oven Mouth
West Stonesdale
Gatehouse Farm
STONESDALE LANE
02

A 85 **B** 86 **C** 87 **D** 88 **E** 89 **F**

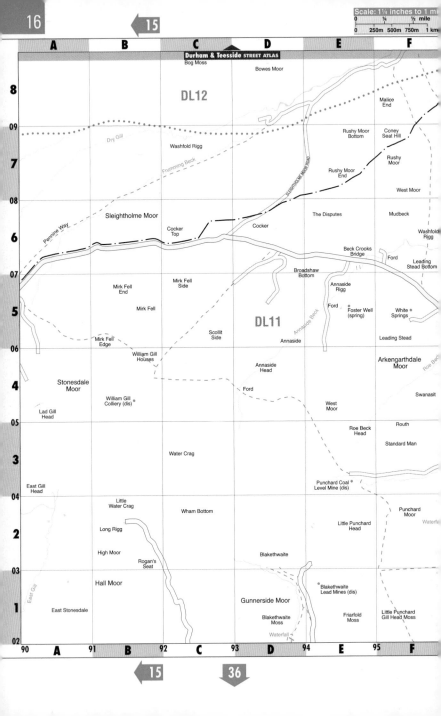

Scale: 1¼ inches to 1 mi

0   ¼   ½   mile
0 250m 500m 750m 1 km

A   B   C   D   E   F

15

DL12

Bog Moss

Bowes Moor

Malice End

8

09

Dry Gill

Washfold Rigg

Rushy Moor Bottom

Coney Seat Hill

7

Frumming Beck

SLEIGHTHOLME MOOR ROAD

Rushy Moor End

Rushy Moor

West Moor

08

Sleightholme Moor

The Disputes

Mudbeck

Washfold Rigg

6

Pennine Way

Cocker Top

Cocker

Beck Crooks Bridge

Ford

Leading Stead Bottom

07

Mirk Fell End

Mirk Fell Side

Broadshaw Bottom

Annaside Rigg

Annaside Beck

5

Mirk Fell

DL11

Ford

Foster Well (spring)

White Springs

06

Mirk Fell Edge

William Gill Houses

Scollit Side

Annaside

Leading Stead

Roe Beck

4

Stonesdale Moor

William Gill Colliery (dis)

Annaside Head

Ford

West Moor

Arkengarthdale Moor

Swanasit

Lad Gill Head

05

Roe Beck Head

Routh

Standard Man

3

Water Crag

East Gill Head

04

Punchard Coal Level Mine (dis)

Punchard Moor

Waterfa

Little Water Crag

Wham Bottom

Little Punchard Head

2

Long Rigg

High Moor

Rogan's Seat

Blakethwaite

Blakethwaite Lead Mines (dis)

East Gill

Hall Moor

Gunnerside Moor

Friarfold Moss

Little Punchard Gill Head Moss

1

East Stonesdale

Blakethwaite Moss

Waterfall

02

90   A   91   B   92   C   93   D   94   E   95   F

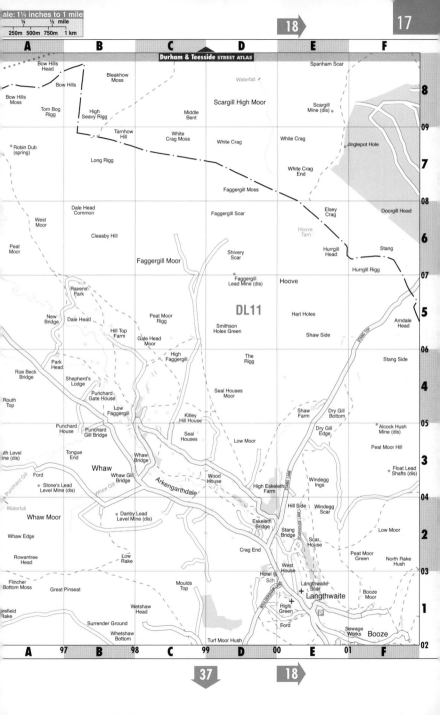

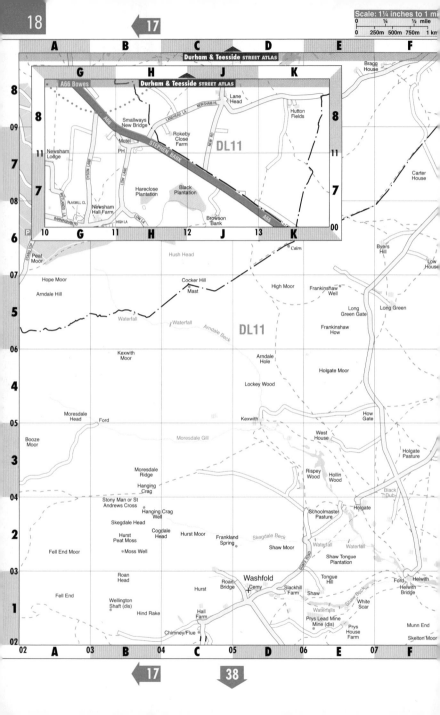

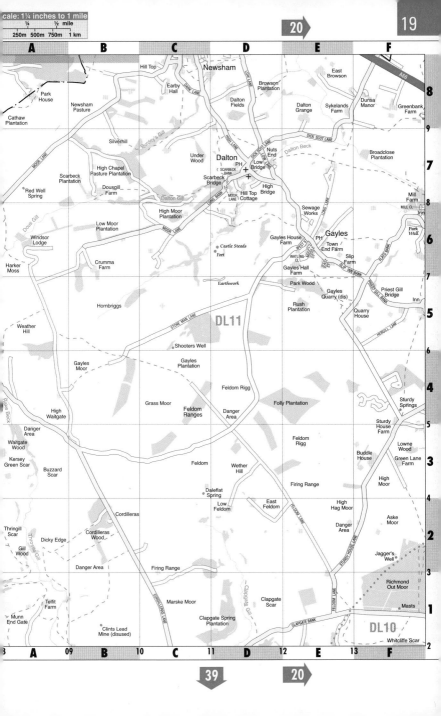

Park House
Cathaw Plantation
Newsham Pasture
Hill Top
Earby Hall
Newsham
Dalton Fields
Browson Plantation
East Browson
Dalton Grange
Sykelands Farm
Dunsa Manor
Greenbank Farm
A66

Silverhill
Burdy's Gill
Under Wood
Dalton
PH
Low Bridge
Nuts End
Dick Scot Lane
Dalton Beck
Broadclose Plantation

Red Well Spring
Scarbeck Plantation
High Chapel Pasture Plantation
Dousgill Farm
Dalton Gill
Scarbeck Bridge
SCARBECK BANK
High Bridge
Mill Farm
MILL CL
Inn

Doug Gill
Low Moor Plantation
High Moor Plantation
LONG BANK
MOOR LANE
Hill Top Cottage
Sewage Works
Gayles
Park Wall

Windsor Lodge
Crumma Farm
Castle Steads
Fort
Gayles House Farm
WEST ST
PH
WATLING CL
Town End Farm
Slip Farm
FELDS PARK

Harker Moss
Gayles Hall Farm
Earthwork
GATES ST
SL CL
INN BANK
Priest Gill Bridge
Inn

Hornbriggs
STONE MAN LANE
DL11
Park Wood
Rush Plantation
Gayles Quarry (dis)
Quarry House
HERGILL LANE

Weather Hill
Shooters Well

Gayles Moor
Gayles Plantation
Flake Beck

High Waitgate
Grass Moor
Feldom Ranges
Feldom Rigg
Danger Area
Folly Plantation
Sturdy Springs
Sturdy House Farm
Lowne Wood

Danger Area
Waitgate Wood
Kersey Green Scar
Buzzard Scar
Feldom
Wether Hill
Feldom Rigg
Firing Range
Buddle House
High Moor
Green Lane Farm

Daleflat Spring
Low Feldom
East Feldom
High Hag Moor
Danger Area
Aske Moor

Thringill Scar
Gill Wood
Dicky Edge
Cordilleras
Cordilleras Wood
FELDOM LANE
Jagger's Well
Richmond Out Moor

Throstle Gill
Danger Area
Firing Range
Marske Moor
DOGGLEAKE LANE
Clapgate Gill
Clapgate Scar
STURDY HOUSE LANE
Masts

Telfit Farm
Munn End Gate
Clints Lead Mine (disused)
Clapgate Spring Plantation
Clapgate Bank
DL10
Whitcliffe Scar

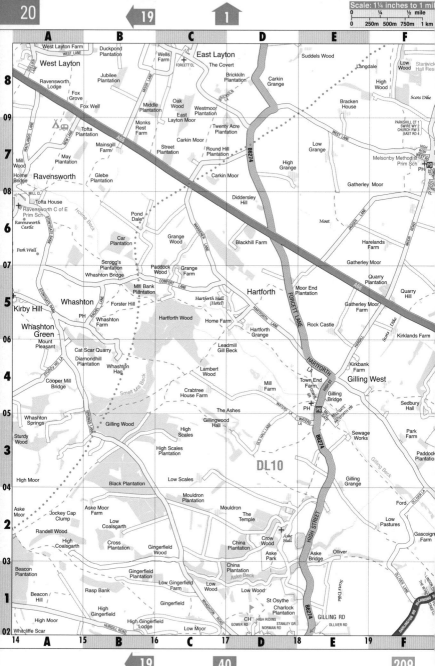

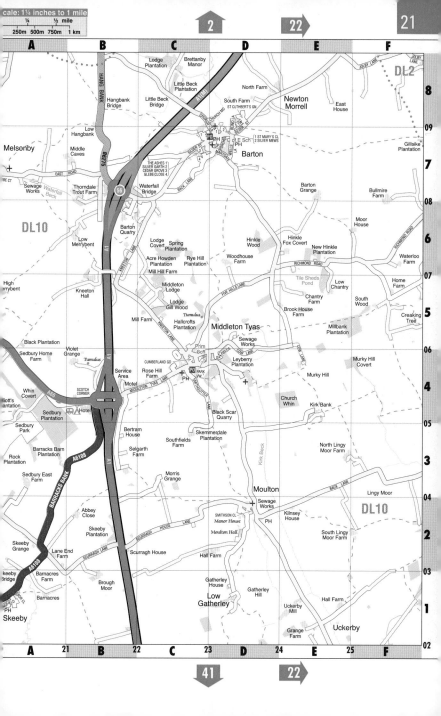

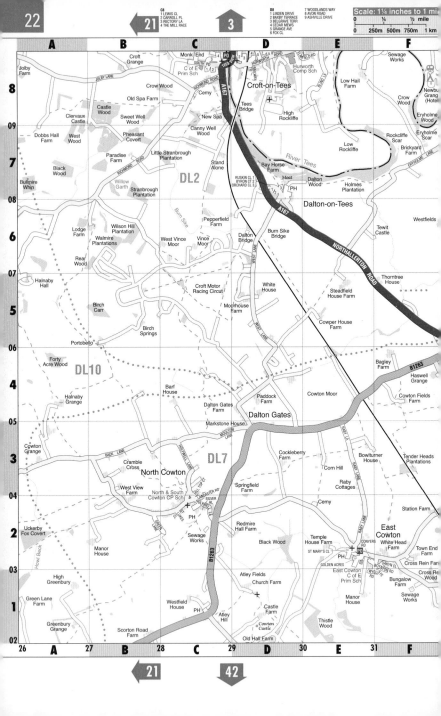

21
3

C8
1 LEWIS CL
2 CARROLL PL
3 RECTORY LA
4 THE MILL RACE

D8
1 LINDEN DRIVE
2 BAXBY TERRACE
3 BELGRAVE TERR
4 CEDAR MEWS
5 GRANGE AVE
6 FOX CL

7 WOODLANDS WAY
8 AVON ROAD
9 ASHVILLE DRIVE

Scale: 1¼ inches to 1 mile
0   ¼   ½ mile
0   250m 500m 750m 1 km

Jolby Farm
Croft Grange
Monk End
JOLBY LANE
Crow Wood
C of E Prim Sch
Cemy
Low Hail Farm
Sewage Works
Newbu Grang (Hotel)
Crow Wood
Old Spa Farm
Castle Wood
Sweet Well Wood
Clervaux Castle
New Spa
Croft-on-Tees
Tees Bridge
Hurworth Comp Sch
Eryholme Wood
Eryholme Scar
Dobbs Hall Farm
West Wood
Pheasant Covert
Canny Well Wood
High Rockliffe
Low Rockliffe
Rockcliffe Scar
Brickyard Farm
Paradise Farm
Little Stranbrough Plantation
RICHMOND ROAD
River Tees
Black Wood
Willow Garth
Stand Alone
DL2
Bay Horse Farm
Dalton Wood
Holmes Plantation
Bullpine Whin
Stranbrough Plantation
RUSKIN CL 1
BYRON CT 2
ORCHARD CL 3
Moat
PH
Dalton-on-Tees
Westfields
Lodge Farm
Wilson Hill Plantation
Burn Sike
Pepperfield Farm
Dalton Bridge
Burn Sike Bridge
NORTHALLERTON ROAD
Tewit Castle
Walmire Plantations
West Vince Moor
Vince Moor
Rear Wood
WEST LANE
Halnaby Hall
White House
Steadfield House Farm
Thorntree House
Croft Motor Racing Circuit
Moorhouse Farm
Cowper House Farm
Birch Carr
Birch Springs
WEST LANE
Portobello
Forty Acre Wood
DL10
Bagley Farm
B1263
Haswell Grange
Barf House
Cowton Moor
Cowton Fields Farm
Halnaby Grange
Dalton Gates Farm
Paddock Farm
Dalton Gates
Markstone House
MUSEUM LANE
Cowton Grange
BACK LANE
Cockleberry Farm
Bowlturner House
Tender Heads Plantations
Cramble Cross
North Cowton
DL7
Corn Hill
Raby Cottages
BABY LA
West View Farm
North & South Cowton CP Sch
Springfield Farm
HOLYWELL LANE
LANCASTER RD
SILVER
Cemy
Station Farm
Uckerby Fox Covert
PICKS
GREEN LANE
PH
Sewage Works
Redmire Hall Farm
Black Wood
Temple House Farm
East Cowton
White Head Farm
Town End Farm
Cross Rein Far
Manor House
ST MARY'S CL
CONVERS RD
PH
GOLDEN ACRES
GAKYN CL
BOYAGON RD
Cross Rein Wood
High Greenbury
B1263
Atley Fields
Church Farm
East Cowton C of E Prim Sch
WYCHE RD
Bungalow Farm
Sewage Works
Green Lane Farm
Westfield House
PH
Castle Farm
Cowton Castle
Manor House
Thistle Wood
Greenbury Grange
Scorton Road Farm
Atley Hill
Old Hall Farm
Howl Beck

21
42

A   B   C   D   E   F
26   27   28   29   30   31
8 09 7 08 6 07 5 06 4 05 3 04 2 03 1 02

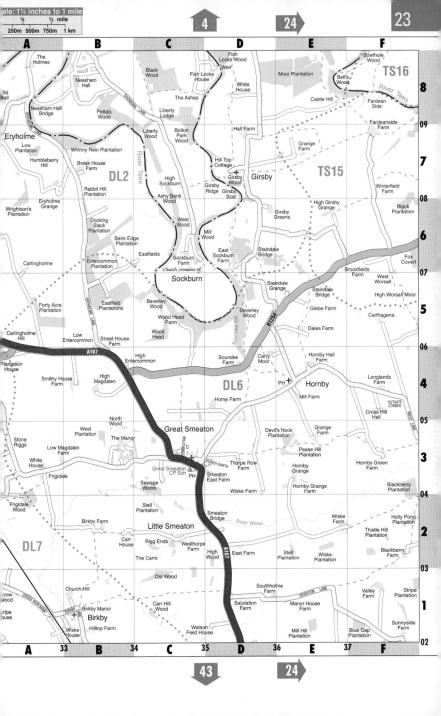

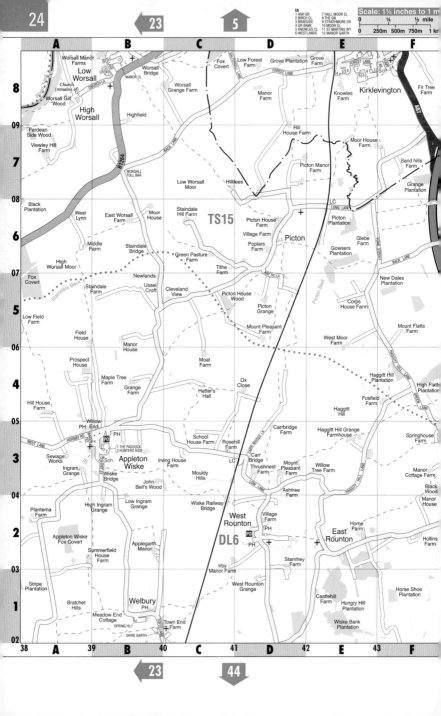

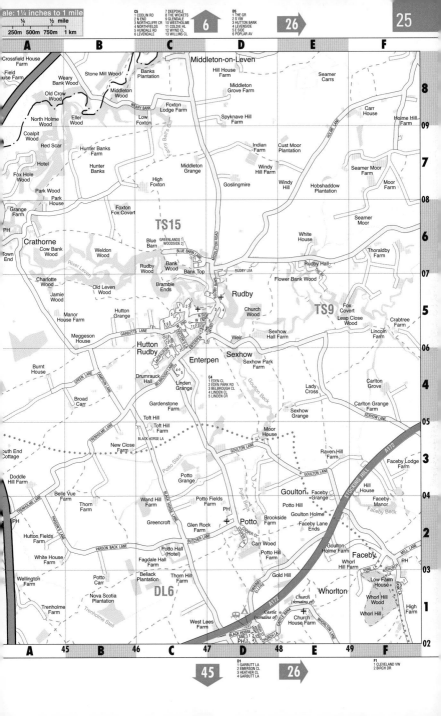

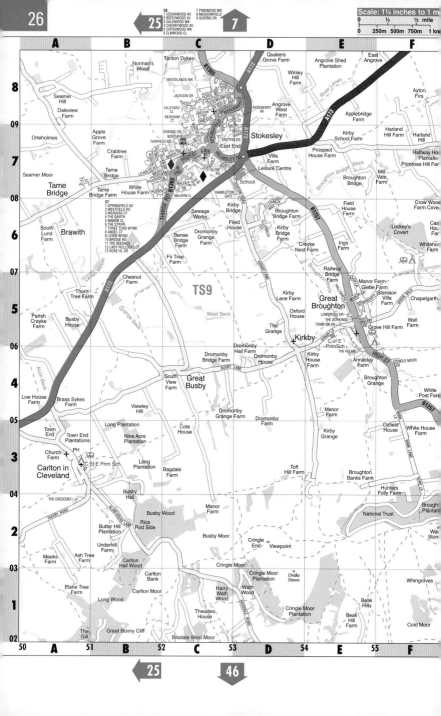

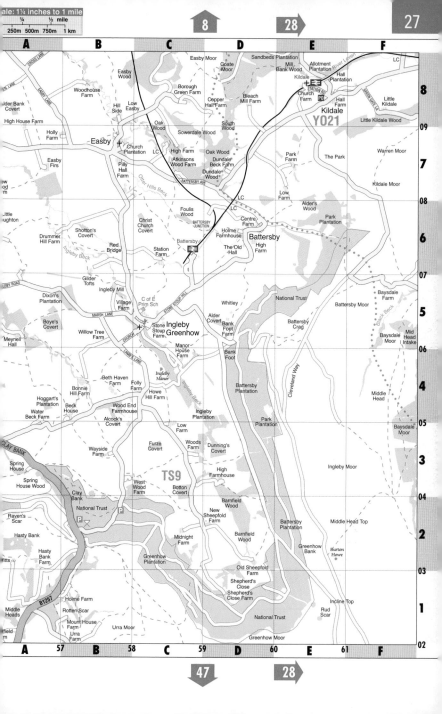

27

9

Scale: 1¼ inches to 1 m

| 0 | ¼ | ½ mile |
| 0 | 250m | 500m | 750m | 1 km |

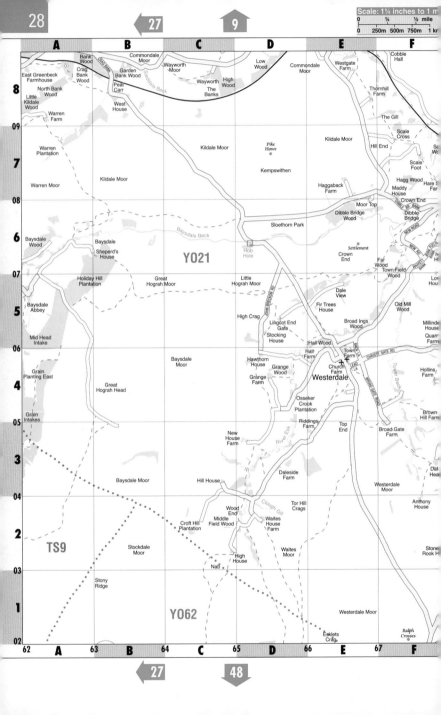

A **B** **C** **D** **E** **F**

Cobble Hall

East Greenbeck Farmhouse
Bank Wood
Crag Bank Wood
Commondale Moor
Wayworth Moor
Low Wood
Commondale Moor
Westgate Farm

North Bank Wood
Garden Bank Wood
Wayworth The Banks
High Wood
Thornhill Farm

8
Little Kildale Wood
Peat Carr
West House

Warren Farm
The Gill

09
Warren Plantation
Kildale Moor
Pike Howe
Kildale Moor
Hill End
Scale Cross
Sc Wo

7
Warren Moor
Kildale Moor
Kempswithen
Scale Foot

Hagg Wood
Hare S Far
Maddy House

Haggaback Farm
Crown End

08
Moor Top
Dibble Bridge Wood
Dibble Bridge

Baysdale Wood
Baysdale
Baysdale Beck
Sloethorn Park

6
Sheperd's House
YO21
Hob Hole
Settlement
Far Wood
Town Field Wood
Lo Hou

07
Holiday Hill Plantation
Great Hograh Moor
Little Hograh Moor
Crown End

Baysdale Abbey
High Crag
Dale View
Fir Trees House
Old Mill Wood

5
Lingcot End Gate
Stocking House
Broad Ings Wood
Millinde House
Quarr Farm

Mid Head Intake
Hall Wood
Town Farm

06
Baysdale Moor
Hawthorn House
Hall Farm
Church Farm
Westerdale
Hollins Farm

4
Grain Planting East
Grange Wood
Grange Farm

Great Hograh Head
Osseker Crook Plantation
Brown Hill Farm

05
Grain Intakes
Riddings Farm
Top End
Broad Gate Farm

New House Farm
River Esk
Dal Hea

3
Baysdale Moor
Hill House
Daleside Farm
Westerdale Moor
Anthony House

04
Wood End
Waites House Farm
Tor Hill Crags

Croft Hill Plantation
Middle Field Wood

2
TS9
Stockdale Moor
Clough Gill
Waites Moor
Stone Rook H

High House
Nab

03
Stony Ridge

1
YO62
Westerdale Moor
Ralph Crosses

Esklets Crag

02
62 **A** 63 **B** 64 **C** 65 **D** 66 **E** 67 **F**

27
48

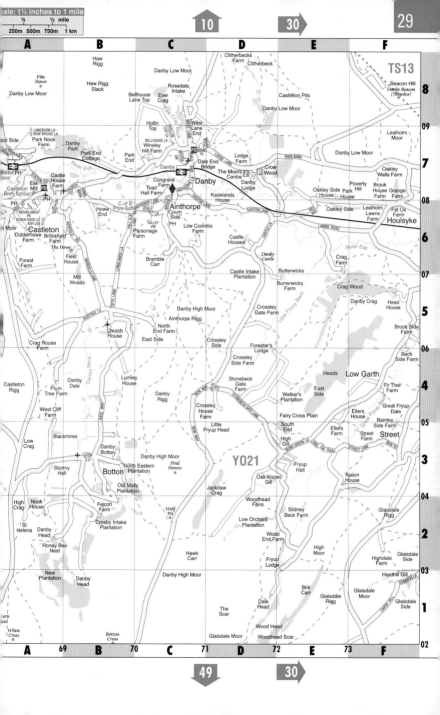

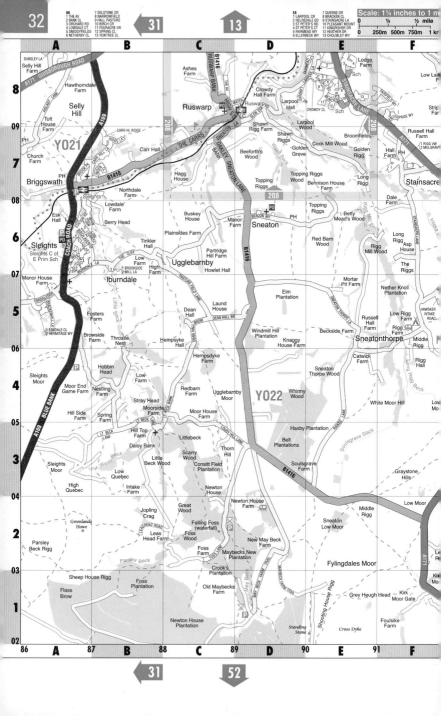

Scale: 1¼ inches to 1 mile

¼   ½ mile

250m 500m 750m 1 km

Scale: 1¼ inches to 1 m

0   ¼   ½ mile
0 250m 500m 750m 1 km

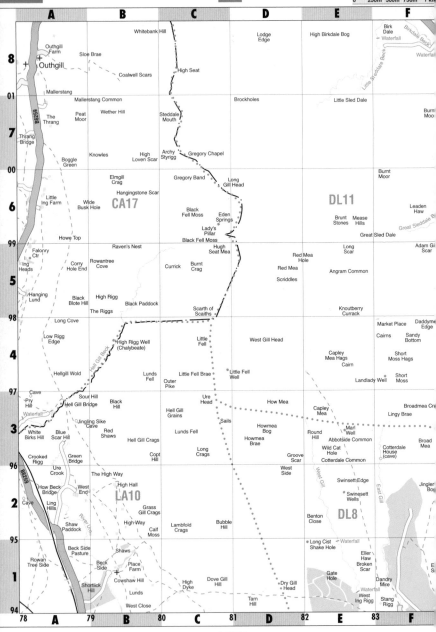

	A	B	C	D	E	F

8

Outhgill Farm
Outhgill
Sloe Brae
Coalwell Scars
Whitebank Hill
High Seat
Lodge Edge
High Birkdale Bog
Birk Dale Waterfall
Little Steddale Beck
Birkdale Beck
Waterfall

01

Mallerstang
Mallerstang Common
Peat Moor
Wether Hill
Steddale Mouth
Brockholes
Little Sled Dale
Burnt Moo

7

The Thrang
Thrang Bridge

00

Knowles
High Loven Scar
Archy Styrigg
Gregory Chapel
Boggle Green

Little Ing Farm
Elmgill Crag
Hangingstone Scar
CA17
Gregory Band
Long Gill Head
Burnt Moor

6

Wide Busk Hole
Black Fell Moss
Eden Springs
Leaden Haw

Brunt Stones
Mease Hills
Great Sledale B

Howe Top
Lady's Pillar
Black Fell Moss
Great Sled Dale
DL11

99

Falorny Ctr
Ing Heads
Raven's Nest
Hugh Seat Mea
Red Mea Hole
Long Scar
Adam Gi Scar

Corry Hole End
Rowantree Cove
Currick
Burnt Crag
Red Mea
Angram Common

5

Hanging Lund
Black Blote Hill
High Rigg
Black Paddock
Scriddles

The Riggs
Knoutberry Currack

98

Long Cove
High Rigg Well (Chalybeate)
Little Fell
West Gill Head
Market Place
Cairns
Sandy Bottom
Daddyme Edge

4

Low Rigg Edge
Hell Gill Beck
Lunds Fell
Little Fell Brae
Little Fell Well
Capley Mea Hags Cairn
Short Moss Hags

Hellgill Wold
Outer Pike
Landlady Well
Short Moss

97

Cave
Pry Hill
Waterfall
Sour Hill
Hell Gill Bridge
Black Hill
Ure Head
How Mea
Capley Mea
Broadmea Cra
Lingy Brae

3

White Birks Hill
Jingling Sike Cave
Red Shaws
Hell Gill Grains
Sails
Lunds Fell
Howmea Bog
Howmea Brae
Round Hill
Marl Well
Abbotside Common
Broad Mea

Crooked Rigg
Green Bridge
Hell Gill Crags
Copt Hill
Long Crags
Groove Scar
Wild Cat Hole
Cotterdale Common
Cotterdale House (cave)

96

B6259
Ure Crook
How Beck Bridge
LA10
The High Way
High Hall
West Side
West Gill
Swinsett Edge

2

Cave
Ling Hills
West End
Grass Gill Crags
Lambfold Crags
Bubble Hill
Swinesett Wells
DL8
Jingl Bo

River Ure
High Way
Calf Moss
Benton Close
East Gill

95

Shaw Paddock
Beck Side Pasture
Shaws
Long Cist Shake Hole
Waterfall
Eller Haw Broken Scar

1

Rowan Tree Side
Beck Side
Place Farm
Cowshaw Hill
High Dyke
Dove Gill Hill
Dry Gill Head
Gate Hole
Waterfall
West Ing Rigg
Dandry Mire
E S

Shortlick Hill
Lunds
West Close
Tarn Hill
Stang Rigg

B6259

78	A	79	B	80	C	81	D	82	E	83	F

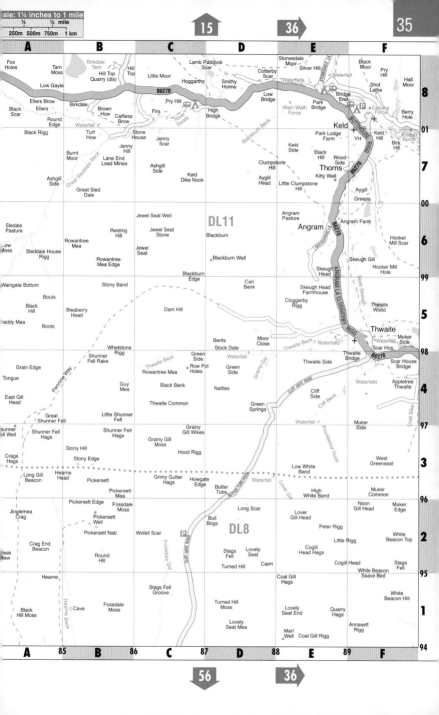

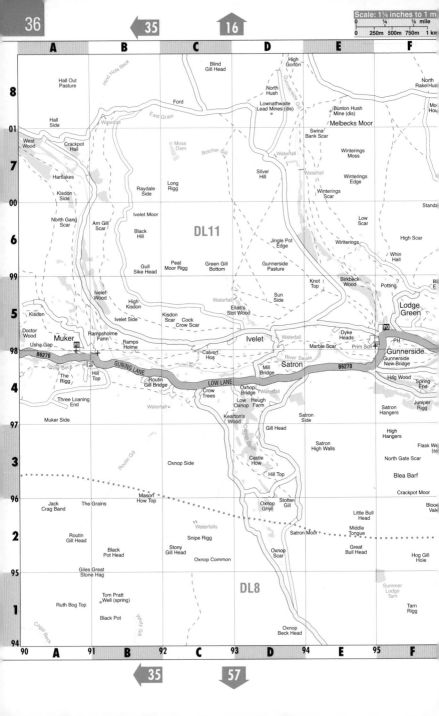

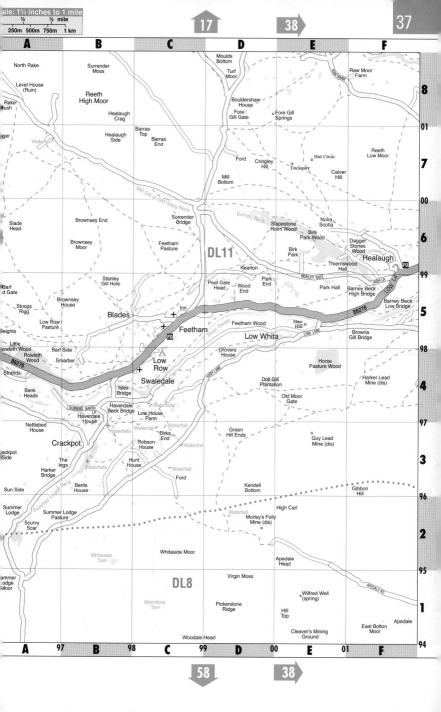

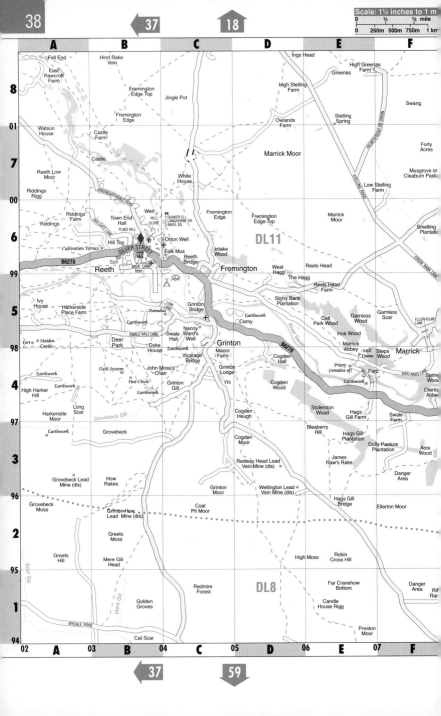

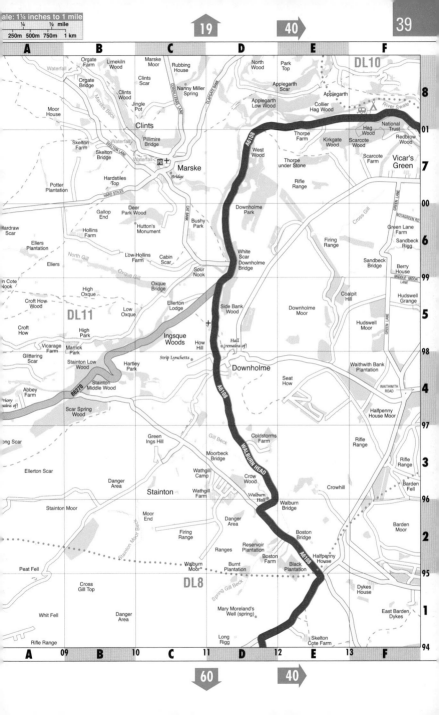

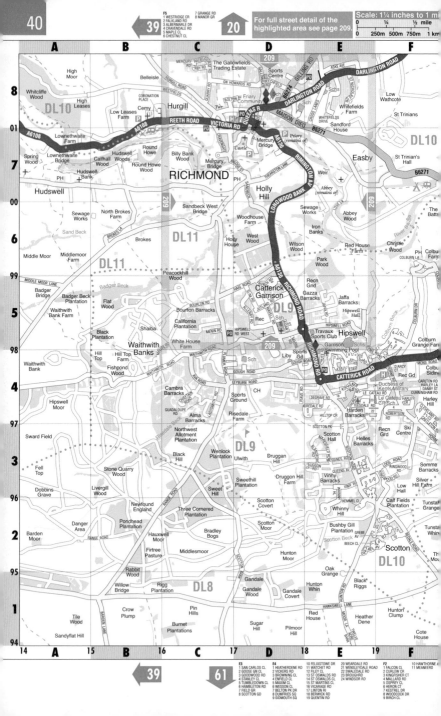

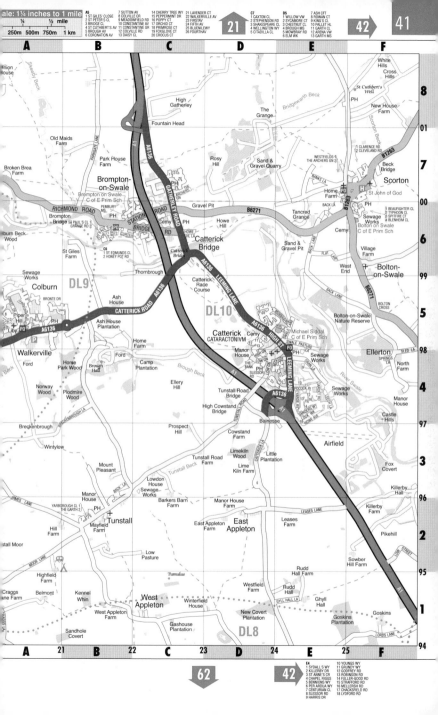

A5
1 ST GILES CLOSE
2 ST PETER'S CL
3 BRIDGE CL
4 ST CUTHBERT'S AV
5 BROUGH AV
6 CORONATION AV

7 SUTTON AV
8 COLVILLE DR
9 MEADOWFIELD DR
10 CONSTANTINE AV
11 CONSTANTINE GR
12 COLVILLE RD
13 DAISY CL

14 CHERRY TREE WY
15 PEPPERMINT DR
16 POPPY CT
17 ORCHID CT
18 PRIMROSE CT
19 FOXGLOVE CT
20 CROCUS CT

21 LAVENDER CT
22 WALKERVILLE AV
23 FIRSTAV
24 FIFTH AV
25 BLUEBELL EWY
26 FOURTH AV

C7
1 CAXTON CL
2 STEPHENSON RD
3 SHAKESPEARE CL
4 WELLINGTON WY
5 CITADILLA CL

D5
1 WILLOW VW
2 SYCAMORE CT
3 CHESTNUT CL
4 BROUGH MS
5 MOWBRAY RD
6 ELM WK

7 ASH CFT
8 ROWAN CT
9 KING'S CL
10 PALLET HL
11 GARTH CL
12 ARENA VW
13 GARTH MS

E4
1 SYDALL S WY
2 KILLERBY DR
3 ST ANNE'S CR
4 CHAPEL RIGGS
5 BENNIONS WY
6 PER ARDUA WY
7 CENTURIAN CL
8 SLESSOR RD
9 HARRIS DR

10 YOUNGS WY
11 GRUNDY WY
12 GODFREY RD
13 ROBINSON RD
14 FULLER-GOOD RD
15 STRAFFORD RD
16 MELLERSH RD
17 CHACKSFIELD RD
18 LYDFORD RD

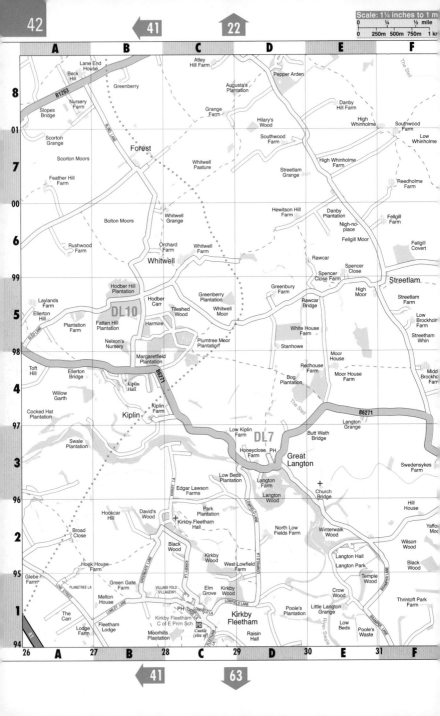

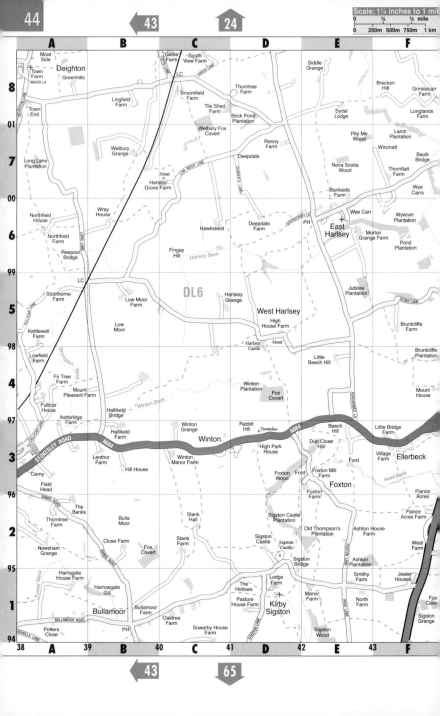

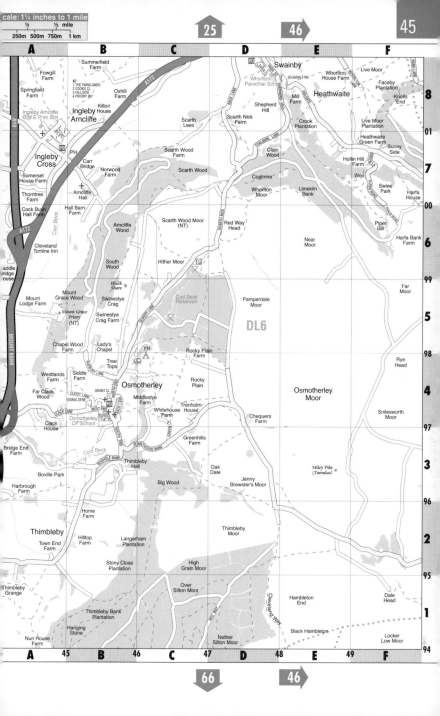

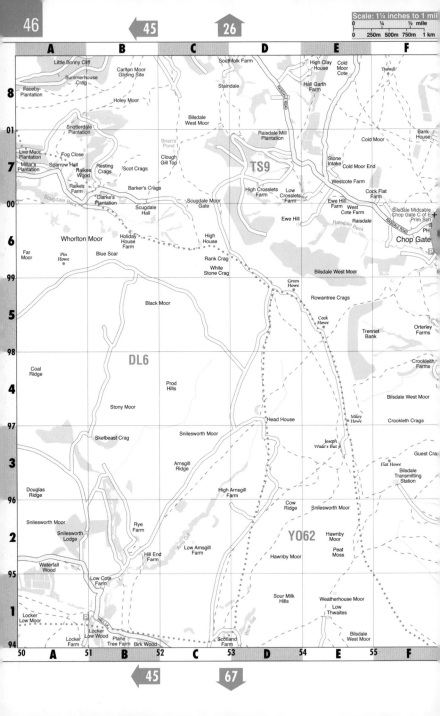

Scale: 1¼ inches to 1 mile

0   ¼   ½   mile
0 250m 500m 750m 1 km

8

01

7

00

6

99

5

98

4

97

3

96

2

95

1

94

A   B   C   D   E   F

Little Bonny Cliff
Summerhouse Crag
Faceby Plantation
Carlton Moor Gliding Site
Holey Moor
Southfolk Farm
Staindale
High Clay House
Cold Moor Cote
Hall Garth Farm
Tumuli

Snotterdale Plantation
Bilsdale West Moor
Raisdale Mill Plantation
Cold Moor
Bank House

Live Moor Plantation
Fog Close
Brian's Pond
Clough Gill Top
Stone Intake
Cold Moor End

Millar's Plantation
Sparrow Hall
Resting Crags
Scot Crags
TS9
Westcote Farm
Cock Flat Farm

Raikes Wood
Raikes Farm
Barker's Crags
High Crosslets Farm
Low Crosslets Farm
Ewe Hill Farm
West Cote Farm
Bilsdale Midcable
Chop Gate C of E Prim Sch

Clarke's Plantation
Scugdale Hall
Scugdale Moor Gate
Ewe Hill
Raisdale
Raisdale Beck
PH
Chop Gate

Wholrton Moor
Holiday House Farm
High House
P

Far Moor
Pin Howe
Blue Scar
Rank Crag
White Stone Crag
Bilsdale West Moor

Black Moor
Green Howe
Rowantree Crags

DL6
Cock Howe
Trennet Bank
Orterley Farms

Coal Ridge
Prod Hills
Crookleith Farms

Stony Moor
Bilsdale West Moor

Skelbeast Crag
Snilesworth Moor
Head House
Miley Howe
Crookleth Crags

Arnsgill Ridge
Joseph Wade's Hut
Guest Carr
Flat Howe
Bilsdale Transmitting Station

Douglas Ridge
High Arnsgill Farm
Cow Ridge
Snilesworth Moor

Snilesworth Moor
Rye Farm
Low Arnsgill Farm
YO62
Hawnby Moor
Peat Moss

Snilesworth Lodge
Hill End Farm
Hawnby Moor

Waterfall Wood
Low Cote Farm
Sour Milk Hills
Weatherhouse Moor
Low Thwaites

Locker Low Moor
Locker Farm
Plane Tree Farm
Birk Wood
Scotland Farm
Bilsdale West Moor
P

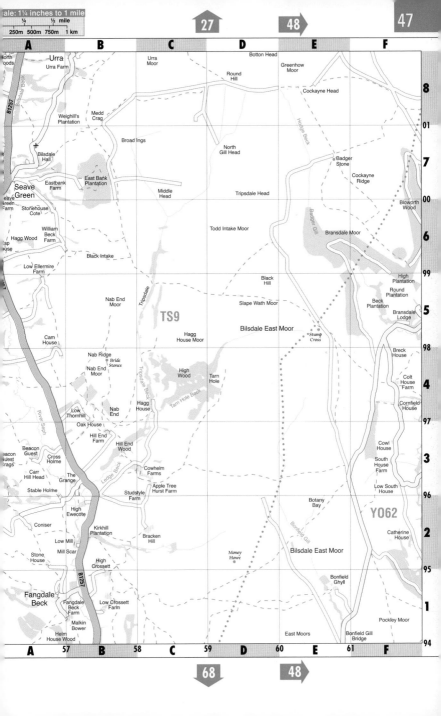

A   B   C   D   E   F

North
Woods

Urra
Urra Farm

Urra
Moor

Botton Head

Greenhow
Moor

Cockayne Head

8

Round
Hill

01

B1257

Bilsdale Beck

Weighill's
Plantation

Medd
Crag

Broad Ings

North
Gill Head

Hodge Beck

Badger
Stone

Cockayne
Ridge

7

Bilsdale
Hall

Seave
Green

Eastbank
Farm

East Bank
Plantation

Middle
Head

Tripsdale Head

00

Bloworth
Wood

Seave
Green
Farm

Stonehouse
Cote

William
Beck
Farm

Badger Gill

Bransdale Moor

6

Hagg Wood

Todd Intake Moor

sp
ouse

Black Intake

Low Ellermire
Farm

High
Plantation

99

Nab End
Moor

Tripsdale

Black
Hill

Round
Plantation

Beck
Plantation

Bransdale
Lodge

5

TS9

Slape Wath Moor

Bilsdale East Moor

Cam
House

Hagg
House Moor

Stump
Cross

Breck
House

98

Nab Ridge
Bride
Stones

Nab End
Moor

High
Wood

Tarn
Hole

Colt
House
Farm

4

Tripsdale Beck

Tarn Hole Beck

Hagg
House

Cornfield
House

97

Low
Thornhill

Nab
End

Oak House

River Seph

Hill End
Farm

Cowl
House

3

Beacon
Guest
rags

Cross
Holme

Hill End
Wood

Cowhelm
Farms

South
House
Farm

Carr
Hill Head

The
Grange

Ledge Beck

Apple Tree
Hurst Farm

Low South
House

96

Stable Holme

Studstyle
Farm

Botany
Bay

YO62

High
Ewecote

Coniser

Kirkhill
Plantation

Bracken
Hill

Bonfield Gill

Catherine
House

2

Low Mill

Mill Scar

Money
Howe

Bilsdale East Moor

95

Stone
House

High
Crossett

**Fangdale
Beck**

B1257

Fangdale
Beck
Farm

Low Crossett
Farm

Bonfield
Ghyll

1

Malkin
Bower

Pockley Moor

Helm
House Wood

East Moors

Bonfield Gill
Bridge

94

A   57   B   58   C   59   D   60   E   61   F

Scale: 1¼ inches to 1 m

0   ¼   ½ mile
0   250m 500m 750m 1 km

A **B** **C** **D** **E** **F**

YO21

P

Rosed..
Head..

Middle Head

High
Hill Top

Flat
Howe

8

Dale Head

01

Farndale Moor

Blakey
Gill Head

7

Carr
Wood

Oak Beck Head

Farndale Moor

Elm
House

Ash
House

Spring
House

Blakey
Howe

00

Cammon
Stone

The
Lion

YO62

Sorley Wood

Lendersfield
House

NT

Round
Crag

6

Spout
House

Esk
House

Oak
Beck
Wood

NT
Sikehill
Wood

High Blakey Moor

Ewe
Hill

Blakey Gill

Bloworth
Wood

Fox Hole
Crag

Wether
Hill

Hill
Houses

Cockham Cross
(remains of)

Long
Causeway

Dick Wood

Birch
Plantation

Bransdale Moor

Frost Hall

Lady
Green

Oak House

Bloworth Slack

Gimmer
Bank
Wood

Bloworth
Wood

Hollins
Farm

Head
House
Farm

Crow
Wood

5

Three
Howes

Eller
House

River Dove

DALESIDE ROAD

NT
Hall Wood

Hanging
Bank Wood

North Gill
House

Cockayne

Cow Sike

Shotton
Hill

Hall Farm

98

Toad Hole

Ouse
Gill Head

Penny
Hill Crag

Broom Hill

Church
Houses
Farm

Long Lane

Lodge
Farm

Smout
House
Farm

Dickon
Howe

Farndale

MACKENBRIDGE LANE

Woodstock
Bower

4

Yoad
House

WESTSIDE ROAD

Wilson
House

Monket
House

THORN INTH LA

CROSS LA

**Church
Houses**

MILL LANE

DALESIDE

YO79

MONKET HO BANK

Monket
House Crags

DALESIDE ROAD

Bragg
Farm

Spout
House

West Gill Head

Bitchagreen

New Ban
Crag

97

Bransdale

Shaw Ridge

Hazel
House

Hawthorn
Crag

Horn
Ridge

Ridge
House

Cote
Hill

3

Groat Hill

West Gill Beck

Horn
End Crag

Toad
Hole

Oak Cragg

Beck Lane

96

Barker
Plantation

Ouse Gill

Double
Crag

Horn End
Cottages

Crow
Wood

Dove Bank
Wood

2

Horn
End

P

Stocking
Crags

Hodge Beck

Lidmoor
Farms

Low
Wood

Moor House
Farm

BAXBECK ROAD

Garnets
Crag

Keysbeck

Low Mill

Kneysbeck

GREEN LANE

WASTE LA

DALESIDE RD

River Dove

Holly
Bush
Farm

95

Stork House

Cross
Plantation

MILL LANE

Olive
House

Tenter

Rawse
Syke

1

94

62   **A**   **63**   **B**   **64**   **C**   **65**   **D**   **66**   **E**   **67**   **F**

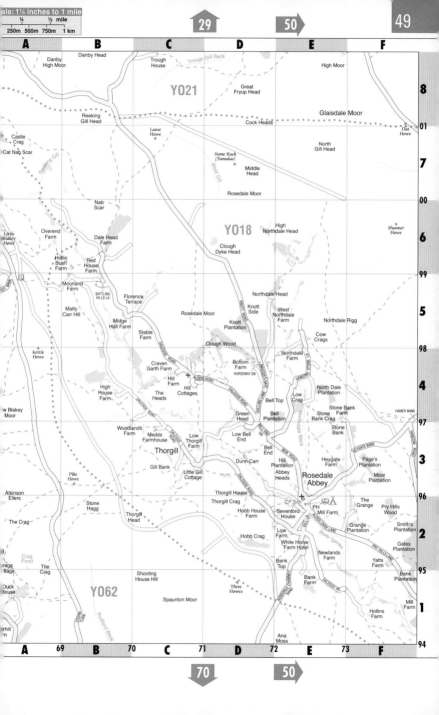

Scale: 1¼ inches to 1 m

Glaisdale Head

Nab Rigg

Traverse Moor

Winter Gill

Y021

Egton High Moor

Middle Heads

Brown Hill

Murk Mi Moor

Three Howes

Pike Hill Moss

Y022

Yarlsey Moss

Wheeldale Gill

Upper Heads

Peat Moss

Coster Gill

Wheeldale Plantation

Bluewath Beck

White Moor

Wheeldale Howe

Blue Man-i'-th'-Moss

Wheeldale Gill

Raven Stones

Scar End

Turnhill Rigg

Rutmoor Head

Black Moor Rigg

Hamer Moor

Crook Beck Rigg

Owlet Moor

Y018

Wheeldale Moor

Hamer Bridge

Row Mires Rigg

Low Hamer

Higher Row Mires

Howth Rigg

Lower Row Mires

Middle Rigg

Black Rigg Beck

Hartoft Moor

Hartoft Rigg

Dukes Lea Farm

White House

Ford

Russell's Wood

Middleton Moor

Rutmoor Beck

Black Rigg

High Wind Hill

Low Wind Hill

Low Wind Hill Farm

Allotment Plantation

Ford

Ramsden Head

Allotment Farm

Rock House Farm

Heads House Farm

St James Farm

Leaf Howe Hill

Cropton Forest

Craven Farm

Dyke House Farm

Rock House Wood

Ford

Head House Wood

Low Muffles

Wrelton Moor

Leaf Howe

Low Leaf Howe House

Mauley Cross

Old Wive Well

Hartoft Beck

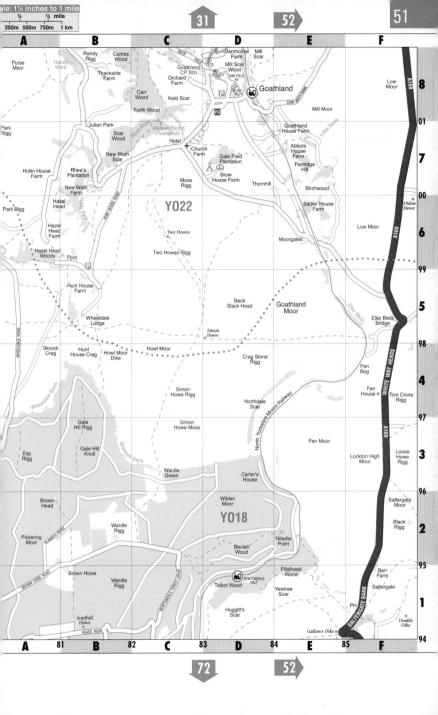

A   B   C   D   E   F

Purse Moor

Randy Mere

Randy Rigg
Combs Wood
Thackside Farm

Park Rigg

Julian Park

Carr Wood

Keld Scar

Forth Wood

Goathland CP Sch
Orchard Farm
Darnholme Farm
Mill Scar Wood
Mill Scar
OAK FIELD AV

Goathland

Mill Moor

Low Moor

A169

8

01

Scar Wood

Malliyan Spout (waterfall)

Hotel

Church Farm

New Wath Scar

Hollin House Farm
Rhea's Plantation

New Wath Farm

Hazel Head

Park Rigg

Hazel Head Farm

Hazel Head Woods

Ford

Nelly Ayre Foss

Howl House Road

YO22

Two Howes

Two Howes Rigg

Gale Field Plantation
Brow House Farm

Moss Rigg

Thornhill

Goathland House Farm
Abbots House Farm
Partridge Hill

Birchwood

Sadler House Farm

Little Beck

COW WEST BANK

Goathland House Farm

Low Moor

Widow Howe

A169

7

00

6

99

Hunt House Farm

Wheeldale Lodge

Beck Slack Head

Goathland Moor

Moorgates

Eller Beck

Eller Beck Bridge

5

WHEELDALE ROAD

Skivick Crag

Hunt House Crag

Howl Moor Dike

Howl Moor

Simon Howe

Crag Stone Rigg

Fen Bog

WHITE WAY HEADS

98

Simon Howe Rigg

Northdale Scar

North Yorkshire Moors Railway

Fen House

Tom Cross Rigg

4

Gale Hill Rigg

Esp Rigg

Gale Hill Knoll

Simon Howe Moss

Fen Moor

A169

Lockton High Moor

Loose Howe Rigg

97

3

Blawath Beck

Wheeldale Beck

Wardle Green

Carter's House

96

Brown Head

Pickering Moor

Wardle Rigg

Wilden Moor

YO18

Saltergate Moor

Black Rigg

2

BLAWATH ROAD

Beulah Wood

Needle Point

Brown Howe

Wardle Rigg

NEWTONDALE FOREST DRIVE

Talbot Wood

NEWTONDALE HALT

Pifelhead Wood

Yewtree Scar

Barr Farm

Saltergate

95

1

Scarffhill Howe

HEADS ROAD

BROWN HOWE ROAD

Huggitt's Scar

Gallows Dike

PH

SALTERGATE BANK

Double Dike

94

A   81   B   82   C   83   D   84   E   85   F

Scale: 1¼ inches to 1 mile

York Cross
Whinstone Ridge
York Cross Rigg
Newton House Plantation
Bracken Hill
Ling Hill Plantation
Biller Howe Dale
Biller Howe
Dobbiner Head
Foster Howes
Sneaton High Moor
Pike Hill
Blea Hill Rigg
Biller Howe Farm
YO22
Foster Howes Rigg
Cock Lake Side
Blea Hill Howe
Biller Howe
Widow Howe Moor
Ann's Cross on Tumulus
Biller Howe Turf Rigg
Widow Howe Rigg
Louven Howe Side
Green Swang
Fylingdales Moor
Shuny Sike
Stony Leas
Burn Howe Duck Pond
Burn Howe
Louven Howe
High Moor
Burn Howe Rigg
Little Eller Beck
Lilla Howe
YO13
Eller Beck
Lilla Rigg
YO18
Snod Hill
High Woof Howe
Stony Rigg
Loose Howe Rigg
Worm Sike Rigg
Derwent Head Rigg
Woof Howe Grain
Lockton High Moor
Low Woof Howe
Barley Carr F
Grey Stones
May Moss
Becken Howe
Moors Rigg
Langdale Forest
Nab Farm
Allerston High Moor
Water Flash
Malo Cross
Little Grain Noddle
Whinney Nab
Blakey Rigg
Black Holes
Long Grain
Hazelhead Moor
Black Noddle
Long Side
Stone Hill Heads
Thorn Hill Head
Maw Rigg

Scale: 1¼ inches to 1 mile

¼   ½ mile
250m 500m 750m 1 km

A   **B**   **C**   **D**   **E**   **F**

Kirk Moor

Hogarth Hill Farm

Oxbank Wood

How Dale

Howdale Farm

Robin Hood's Butts

National Trust

8

Evan Howe

Ox Pasture Wood

Spring Hill

Thorney Brow

Brow Moor

ROBIN HOOD'S RD

CRAG HL

Spring Hill Farm

Y022

Howdale Moor

P

Beacon Howes

Church Farm

01

Low Flask Farm

SCARBOROUGH ROAD

MAIN RD/CHURCH RD

wn Rigg Moor

A171

Cook House Farm

BLACKSMITH HILL

Green Dike

7

Bungalow Farm

PH

Stoney Marl Howes

Pye Rigg End

Brown Rigg

Wragby Farm

P

Stony Marl Moor

Helwath Grain Side

Pye Rigg Howe

Wellfield Farm

Jugger Howes

Brown Rigg Beck

Wragby Wood

Staintondale Moor

00

High Moor

Jugger Howe Moor

Helwath Bridge

Pye Rigg

Rudda Howe

RUDDA ROAD

6

Helwath Beck

Penny Howe

Pye Rigg Slack

Jugger Howe Beck

Y013

A171

Brown Rigg

HELWATH ROAD

GALLOW HOWE WHITE ROAD

BROWN RIGG ROAD

99

Burn Howe Moor

Harwood Dale Forest

Falcon Inn

5

Bloody Beck

Three Howes

STURDY DALE

98

Lownorth Moor

Hallow Rigg

Teydale Farm

Pike Rigg

Castlebeck Farm

Scar Wood

Hardhurst Howes

4

Riverhead Farm

Park Hill Farm

Castlebeck Wood

Cowgate Rigg

Standingstones Rigg

97

Barley Carr Tongue

Moss Gill Slack

Ford

Chapel Farm

Cowgate Slack

High Seat

St Margaret's Church

Moor Cottage Farm

3

Harwood Dale Moor

Weir

Ford

Brooklands Farm

arley Slack

Nettlehead Wood

Keasbeck Farm

MOOR END ROAD

Key Head

PH

Crosses Farm

School Hill Farm

Keasbeck Hill Farm

96

Ford

Murk Head

Harwood Dale

Grange Wood

LOWNORTH ROAD

High Langdale End

Morra Head Wood

Murk Head Farm

Murk Head Wood

Grange Farm

WELL LANE

2

Stony Wood

Flat Wood

Lownorth Beck

Hardwick Farm

Thirley Cote Farm

WEST SIDE ROAD

Hagg Wood

LOWNORTH ROAD

LITTLE BECK

REASTY ROAD

Burgate Farm

Langdale Rigg End

Hingles Wood

Lownorth Plantation

West Syme

95

SUTR GATE

Warsman Head

Viewpoint

Barns Cliff End

Merry Wood

Breckenhurst Farm

Pits Wood

REASTY HILL

1

Langdale Rigg

Barns Cliff

Silpho Moor

P

Swarth Howe

A   93   **B**   94   **C**   95   **D**   96   **E**   97   **F**   94

A B C D E F

02
Old Peak or
South Cheek
Ravenscar

8
THE DELL
RAVENSCAR
STATION ROAD
NT
CLIFF RD
Blea Wyke
Point
Church Rd
Farm
CATON RD
CHURCH ROAD
RAVEN HALL RD
Common
Cliff

01

7
Bent Rigg
Farm
Bent
Rigg

Danesdale
Farm
Bell Hill
Farm
BENT RIGG LANE
WAR DIKE LANE

00
Rudda
RUDDA RD
Grange
Farm

6
Sandybed
Wood
Prospect
House Farm

99
Church Farm
TOFTA ROAD
Meeting
House Farm
White
Hall Farm
Petard
Point
Cleveland Way

5
Tofta
Farm
Bees
Nest Farm
Plane
Tree Farm
PRIOR WATH RD
BINDER RIGG RD
Island
Farm
Shire Horse
Farm
Rigg
Hall
Rigg Hall
Farm
Staintondale
PH
Shirehorse
Centre

98
Crowdon
PRIOR
WATH RD
Quarry
Farm
North Bridge
End
White House
Farm

4
Thorny Beck
Hunter
Howe
Wyke
Lodge
Bridge
Farm
DOWNDALE ROAD
Whitestone
Farm
A171
Cloughton
Moor House
Hayburn Beck
Farm
HODGSON HILL
Redhouse
Farm
Hayburn
Wyke

97
Standingstones
Rigg
Hodgson Moor
Plantation
RINGING KELD HILL
Cloughton
Moor
Nab
End
National
Trust
Hayburn
Wyke Hotel
YO13
CAYWOOD HILL

3
Linglands Farm
Cloughton
Woods
The
Hulleys
Newlands
Farm

96
Tongue Field
Plantation
MOOR END RD
Rockwood
Farm
Gowland
Farm
A171
Cloughton
Plantations
Stone Dale
Plantation
Caywood
Plantation
Rodger
Trod
Sycarham
Wood
PRATT LANE

2
Spring House
Farm
GOWLAND LANE
Cloughton
Newlands
Little
Moor Road
Greystone
Farm
Middle
Part Farm
Sycarham
Farm
SALT PANS ROAD
HOOD LANE
Cloughton
Wyke

95
Ellis
Close
Farm
Cloughton
Woods
Ripley's
Farm
HOLM HL WHITE WAY WEST
Little Moor
Moorside
Farm
Court Green
Farm
NEWLANDS LA
Hundale Point

1
Thirley Beck
Farm
Beck Syme
THIRLEY DALE ROAD
RIPLEY'S
RD
RIPLEY'S ROAD
Cloughton
Green
Farming
PO
1 COURT GREEN CL
2 LOCKWOOD CH
Court Green CL
Cleveland Way

Surgate Brow
Plantation
LT MOOR CL 1
MOOR LA 2
BECK LA 3
PH
STATION LA
LINTON CL
Cloughton
Fields Farm
Long Nab

94
A 98 B 99 C 00 D 01 E 02 F 03

53 75

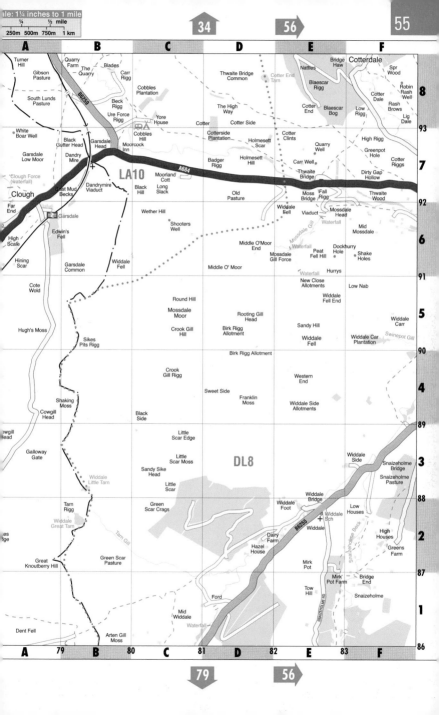

A   B   C   D   E   F

Turner Hill

Gibson Pasture

Quarry Farm   Blades
The Quarry   Carr Rigg

Cobbles Plantation

Thwaite Bridge Common

Cotter End Tarn

Nattles

Bridge Haw   Cotterdale

Spr Wood

Robin Rash Well

8

South Lunds Pasture

B6259

Beck Rigg

Ure Force Rigg

Yore House

The High Way

Cotter

Cotter Side

Blaescar Rigg

Cotter End   Blaescar Bog

Cotter Dale   Low Rigg

Rash Brows

Lig Dale

White Boar Well

Black Gutter Head   Garsdale Head

Dandry Mire

Moorcock Inn

Cobbles Hill

Cotterside Plantation

Cotter   Holmesett Scar

Cotter Clints

Quarry Well

High Rigg

Greenpot Hole

Cotter Riggs

93

Garsdale Low Moor

LA10

A684

Moorland Cott

Badger Rigg

Holmesett Hill

Carr Well

Thwaite Bridge

Dirty Gap Hollow

7

Clough Force (Waterfall)

Clough

East Mud Becks

Dandrymire Viaduct

Black Hill   Long Slack

Old Pasture

Moss Bridge   Fall Rigg

Thwaite Wood

92

Far End

Garsdale

Widdale Fell

Viaduct   Mossdale Head

Mid Mossdale

High Scale

Edwin's Fell

Wether Hill

Shooters Well

Waterfall

6

Hining Scar

Garsdale Common

Widdale Fell

Middle O'Moor End

Mossdale Gill Force

Middle O' Moor

Waterfall

Mossdale Gill

Peat Fell Hill

Dockhurry Hole

Shake Holes

Cote Wold

Waterfall

Hurrys

91

Hugh's Moss

Sikes Pits Rigg

Round Hill

Mossdale Moor

Crook Gill Hill

Rooting Gill Head

Birk Rigg Allotment

New Close Allotments

Widdale Fell End

Sandy Hill

Widdale Fell

Low Nab

Widdale Carr

Widdale Car Plantation

Swinepot Gill

5

Birk Rigg Allotment

90

Crook Gill Rigg

Sweet Side

Franklin Moss

Western End

Widdale Side Allotments

4

Shaking Moss

Cowgill Head

owgill lead

Galloway Gate

Black Side

Little Scar Edge

Little Scar Moss

Sandy Sike Head

Little Scar

DL8

Widdale Side

89

Snaizeholme Bridge

Snaizeholme Pasture

3

Widdale Little Tarn

Tarn Rigg

Widdale Great Tarn

es ge

Great Knoutberry Hill

Green Scar Crags

Green Scar Pasture

Tarn Gill

Widdale Foot

Widdale Bridge

Widdale

Dairy Farm

Hazel House

Widdale Sch

Low Houses

High Houses

Greens Farm

88

2

Mirk Pot

B6255

Snaizeholme Beck

Mirk Pot Farm

Bridge End

Snaizeholme

87

Dent Fell

Arten Gill Moss

Mid Widdale

Waterfall

Ford

Tow Hill

SNAIZEHOLME RD

1

86

A   B   79   80   C   81   D   82   E   83   F

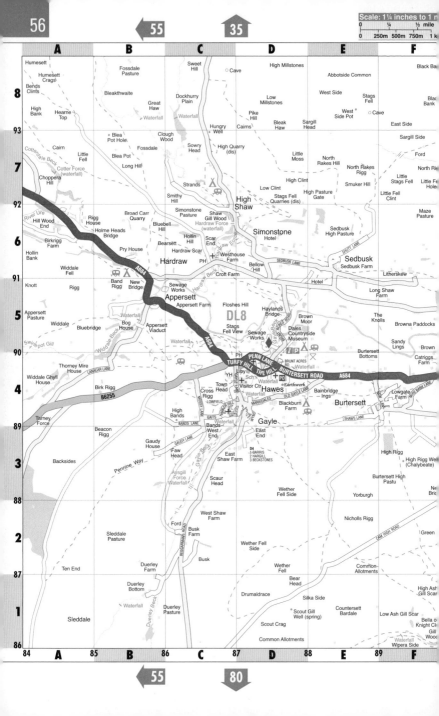

Scale: 1¼ inches to 1 r

0   ¼   ½ mile

0   250m   500m   750m   1 k

8

Hurnesett

Humesett Crags

Bends Clints

High Bank

Hearne Top

Fossdale Pasture

Bleakthwaite

Great Haw

Waterfall

Sweet Hill

Cave

Dockhurry Plain

Waterfall

Hungry Well

High Millstones

Abbotside Common

West Side

Low Millstones

Pike Hill

Bleak Haw

Sargill Head

Stags Fell

West Side Pot

East Side

Cave

Black Ba

Blac Bank

93

Cotterdale Beck

Cairn

Little Fell

Blea Pot

Choppera Hill

Blea Pot Hole

Fossdale

Long Hill

Clough Wood

Sowry Head

Strands

High Quarry (dis)

Cairns

Little Moss

Low Clint

High Clint

North Rakes Hill

North Rakes Rigg

Smuker Hill

Sargill Side

Ford

Little Stags Fell

Little Fe Hole

North Ri

7

Cotter Force (waterfall)

Hill Wood End

River Ure

Rigg House

Smithy Hill

Simonstone Pasture

Bluebell Hill

Broad Carr Quarry

Shaw Gill Wood

Hardraw Force (waterfall)

Scar End

High Shaw

Stags Fell Quarries (dis)

High Pasture Gate

High Clint

Sedbusk High Pasture

Little Fell Clint

Maze Pasture

92

Birkrigg Farm

Holme Heads Bridge

Pry House

Bearsett

Hollin Hill

Hardraw Scar

Hardraw

PH

Westhouse Farm

Simonstone Hotel

Bellow Hill

SEDBUSK LANE

Sedbusk Farm

Sedbusk

Litherskew

6

Hollin Bank

Widdale Fell

Knott

Rigg

Band Rigg

New Bridge

A684

Croft Farm

Hardraw Beck

Hotel

Long Shaw Farm

91

Appersett Pasture

Widdale

Bluebridge

Bog House

Waterfall

Appersett

Appersett Farm

Appersett Viaduct

Sewage Works

Floshes Hill

Haylands Bridge

Brown Moor

DL8

Dales Countryside Museum

The Knolls

Browna Paddocks

Sandy Lings

Brown

5

Swinpot Gill

Thorney Mire House

Widdale Ghyll House

LANACAR LANE

Waterfall

Stags Fell View

Sewage Works

TURFY HILL

PENN LANE

THE HILL

BRUNT ACRES

BURTERSETT ROAD

Earthwork

A684

Catriggs Farm

Burtersett Bottoms

90

Birk Rigg

B6255

Tarney Force

Beacon Rigg

High Bands

Cross Rigg

Town Head

YH

Visitor Ctr

Hawes

LOWFIELD

Sch

Waterfall

MARKET PL

Gayle

Bainbridge Ings

Blackburn Farm

Burtersett

SHAWS LANE

Lowgate Farm

BANK LANE

4

Backsides

Gaudy House

Faw Head

GAUDY LANE

BANDS LANE

Bands West End

East Shaw Farm

East End

D4
1 BARRIS
2 HARGILL
3 BECKSTONES

High Rigg

High Rigg Well (Chalybeate)

Burtersett High Pastu

Ne Bri

3

Pennine Way

Aysgill Force Waterfall

Scaur Head

Wether Fell Side

Yorburgh

Nicholls Rigg

88

Ten End

Sleddale Pasture

Duerley Farm

Ford

BRACKENHALL ROAD

Busk Farm

West Shaw Farm

Busk

Wether Fell Side

Wether Fell

CAM HIGH ROAD

Common Allotments

Green

2

Sleddale

Duerley Bottom

Waterfall

Duerley Pasture

Duerley Beck

Bear Head

Drumaldrace

Silka Side

Scout Gill Well (spring)

Scout Crag

Common Allotments

Countersett Bardale

Low Ash Gill Scar

High Ash Gill Scar

Bella o Knight Cl

Gill Wood

Waterfall

Wipera Side

1

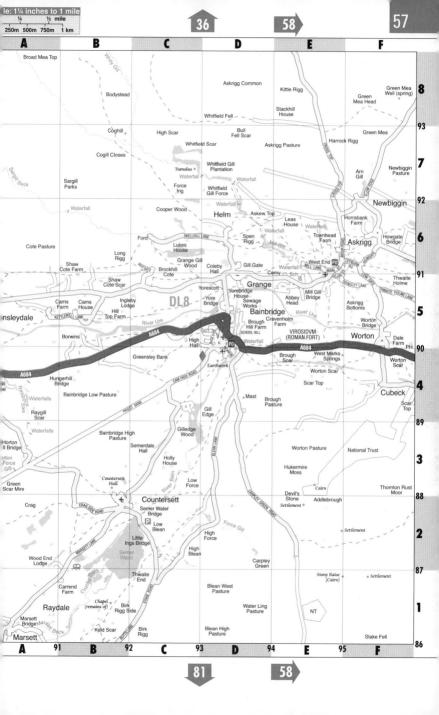

A   B   C   D   E   F

8

Broad Mea Top

Whitby Gill

Askrigg Common
Kittle Rigg

Green Mea
Well (spring)

Bodystead

Whitfield Fell

Stackhill
House

Green
Mea Head

93

Sargill Beck

Coghill

High Scar

Whitfield Scar

Bull
Fell Scar

Askrigg Pasture

Green Mea

Harrock Rigg

CROSS TOP

7

Cogill Closes

Tumulus
Waterfall

Whitfield Gill
Plantation
Waterfall

Arn
Gill

Newbiggin
Pasture

Sargill
Parks

Force
Ing

Whitfield
Gill Force

92

Waterfall

Cooper Wood

Helm

Askew Top

Waterfall

Newbiggin

Horrabank
Farm

Askrigg

6

Cote Pasture

Ford

SKELLGILL LANE

Lukes
House

Leas
House
Spen
Rigg

Waterfall

Mill Gill

Townhead
Farm

West End PO

Howgate
Bridge

Thwaite
Holme

Long
Rigg

Grange Gill
Wood

Gill Gate

Waterfall

LEYBURN

91

Shaw
Cote Farm

REDGATE

Brockhill
Cote

Coleby
Hall

Cemy Sch

MILL LANE
MAIN

PRINGLEY LANE

LOW ROAD

THWAITE HOLME LANE

Shaw
Cote Scar

Yorescott

Grange

Yorebridge
House
Sewage
Works

Abbey
Head

Mill Gill
Bridge

Askrigg
Bottoms

Cams
Farm
Cams
House

Ingleby
Lodge

Yore
Bridge

Bainbridge

Brough
Cravenholm
Farm

Worton
Bridge

5

nsleydale

KETTLEWELL LANE

Hill
Top Farm

DL8

River Ure

SCHOOL HILL

VIROSIDVM
(ROMAN FORT)

River Ure

Worton

Dale
Farm PH

Borwins

A684

High
Hall

PO

Waterfall

A684

Brough
Scar

West Marks
Springs

Worton
Scar

90

Hungerhill
Bridge

Greensley Bank

Earthwork

CAM HIGH ROAD

Worton Scar

Scar Top

Cubeck

4

A684

Raydale Beck

Bainbridge Low Pasture

PRIEST BANK

Mast

Brough
Pasture

Scar
Top

89

Waterfalls

Raygill
Scar

Bainbridge High
Pasture

Gilledge
Wood

Gill
Edge

Horton
ll Bridge

Waterfalls

Semerdale
Hall

BLEAN LANE

Worton Pasture

National Trust

3

orton
Force
Gill

Holly
House

River Bain

Low
Force

Hukermire
Moss

CARPLEY GREEN ROAD

Thornton Rust
Moor

Green
Scar Mire

Countersett
Hall

Cairn

Devil's
Stone
Settlement

Addlebrough

88

Crag

CRAG SIDE ROAD

Countersett

Semer Water
Bridge

P Low
Blean

Force Gill

Settlement

2

MARSETT LANE

Little
Ings Bridge

Semer
Water

High
Force

Carpley
Green

Stony Raise
(Cairn)

Settlement

87

Wood End
Lodge

Crooked Beck

Thwaite
End

High
Blean

Blean West
Pasture

Carrend
Farm

Chapel
(remains of)

Birk
Rigg Side

Water Ling
Pasture

NT

1

Marsett
Bridge

Marsett Beck

Raydale

WHITESIDE

Keld Scar

Birk
Rigg

Blean High
Pasture

Stake Fell

Marsett

86

A   91   B   92   C   93   D   94   E   95   F

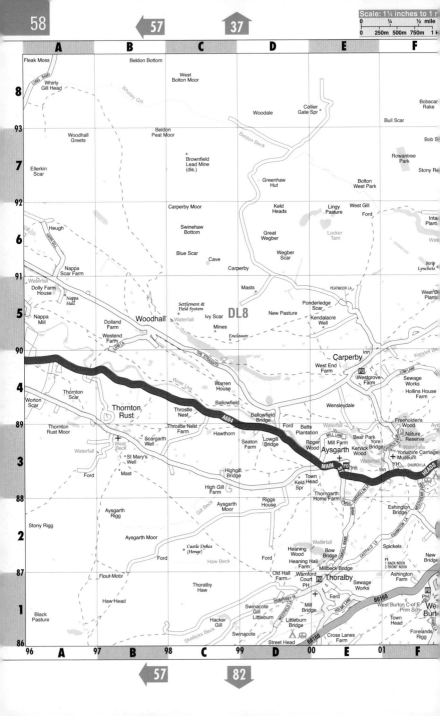

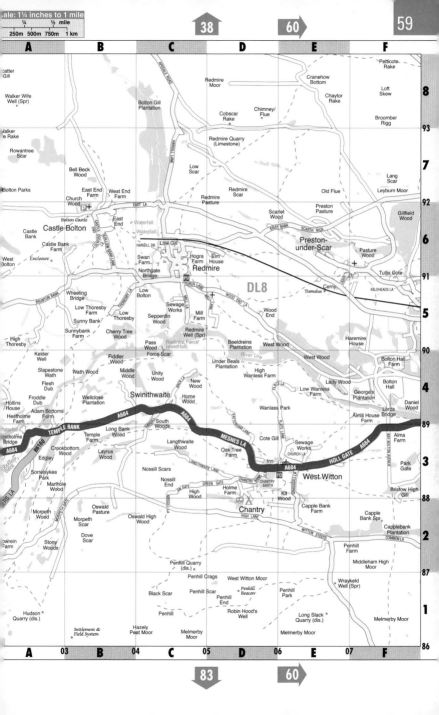

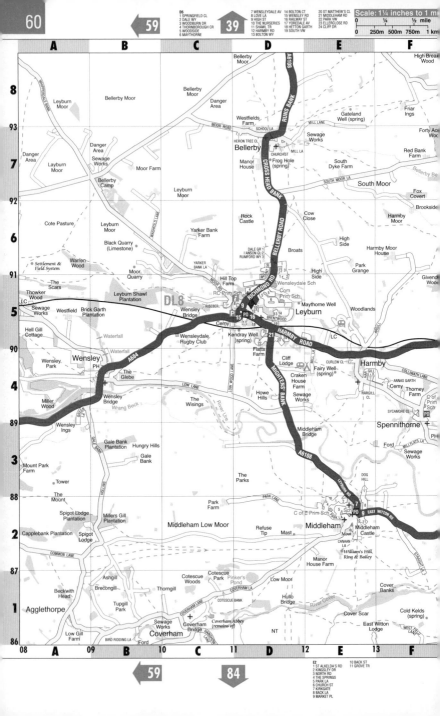

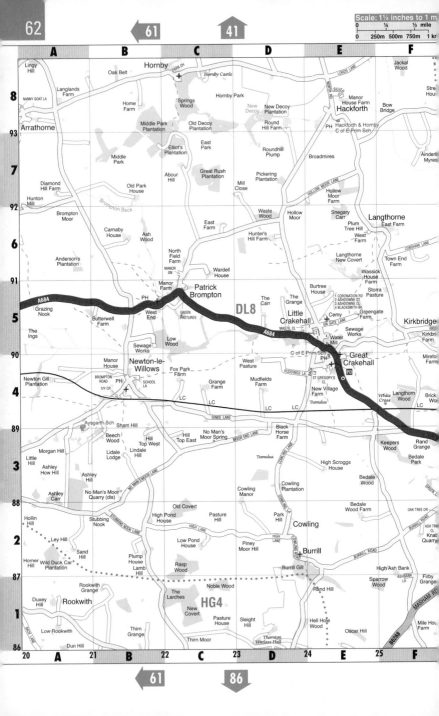

Pheasant Hill
Moor Hills
The Bog
Great Fencote
Penwell House
Mill Beck
Fleetham Wood
Crow Wood
Bramper Farm
Thrincroft Ings
Halliken Bridge

LOW STREET
TICKERGATE LANE
Holtby Grange
Little Fencote
THE GREENWAYS
Fencote Park
Scruton Bridge
Scruton Grange
Hill Top

CHAPEL GARTH

Gunhill Plantation
HERGILL LA
FLEETHAM LA

Sand Hill
Carr Hill
Warren House
Stud Farm
CRANK LANE

Scruton
THE PARKLANDS
COMMON LA
PEACOCK'S CL
GRANGE CL E
Sewage Works
Sewage Works
Swale Bridge

Holtby Hall
Holby Park
BEECH 'CC'
PH
Morton Flatts
Morton Bridge

Novice Wood
Bingley's Wood
Little Holtby
Low Leases Farm
West House Farm
MEADOW DR
MEADOW CT
Glebe Barn
LC

bshaw Farm
Leases Grange
Carriage Road Plantation
Swalefields

Leases Grange Farm
Hillcrest Farm
Fox Covert Plantation
Moor House Farm
Ham Hall
LC
Field House
A684
Cross Lanes Farm

Leases Bridge Quarry (dis)
Thoroughway House
Roughley Corner
Holmfield Farm
Grimescar Farm
Spring House

Crakehall Ings
Conygarth Hill
Pit (dis)
GLEBE SQ
LOWLANDS DR
ASHLANDS DR
Blow Houses
Gravel Pit
Sewage Works
DL7

POTLANDS 1
HARKNESS CL 2
HARKNESS DR 3
GRANGE AV 4
FREEMANS WY 5
Leeming Bar

Aiskew Grange
Micklebrack
C of E Sch
Leeming Bridge
Leeming
CP Sch

Sand Hill
Motel
Mill Farm
Far Wood
PH
PO
Airfield
Sewage Works

A3
1 BACK LA
2 EMGATE
3 THE WYND
4 MARKET PL
5 BRIDGE ST
6 SOUTH END AV
7 HARBOUR VW

Leeming Lodge
Clapham Lodge

ry Bowes Wood
Rectory Wood
Aiskew
LC
A684
Cowfold Grange
Bromakin Farm
RAF Leeming CP Sch

CH
Bedale Hall
Mus
DL8
Open Farm
Aiskew Farm
Floodbridge Farm
Bromaking Grange
Londonderry
Crosby Farm
Gatenby Wood
The Poplars

BEDALE
Flood Bridge
PH
WIGHTFIELD LANE

Springfield Farm
Southlands Farm
Bridge Grange Farm
B6285
Charcoal Plantation
Exelby
LEEMING LA

Manley Farm
Cob Castle
Lord's Moor Plantation
PH
Low Grange
High Grange
Crow Wood
Crow Wood
Smearholme

B2
1 BROOKSIDE AV
2 BROOKSIDE CL
3 STAPLETON CL
4 EASBY CL
5 VASEY CL
6 BERESFORD CL
7 NATTRASS WK
8 BOWE CR

Firby
Christ's Hospital
Lord's Moor Farm
James's Plantation
Bracken Hills
Conquers Hill
THEAKSTON HARGILL
Theakston Grange

WYCAR
OAK TREE CL
QUEEN ANNE'S CT
QUEEN ANNE'S DR
HARBOUR RI
THE COURT
OAK TREE RD
ASH TREE RD
SYCAMORE DR
10 GRANGE CL
11 KENDREW C
12 TOM HALL CTL
13 PINEWOOD GR
14 BEECHWOOD CL
15 GLEBE CL
16 BENKHILL DR
17 MOWBRAY CR
18 FITZALAN RD
19 GRANGE RD
20 MEADOW GR
21 PARKER DR
22 HIRD AV

B3
1 HERON CL
2 INGS VW
3 KINGFISHER DR
4 SPRUCE GILL AV
5 SPRUCE GILL DR
6 WILLOW DR
7 CHERRY GR
8 BIELBY CL
9 MEADOWFIELD
10 HOLLY RD
11 HAXEL CT
12 NEWSTEADS
13 THE CRESCENT
14 BADGER HILL DR
15 FOX COVERT CL
16 OTTERBECK WY

D4
1 MILLFIELD CL
2 ST JOHN'S RD
3 ST JOHN'S CR
4 NEWTON CR
5 PROSPECT WY
6 HARGILL LA

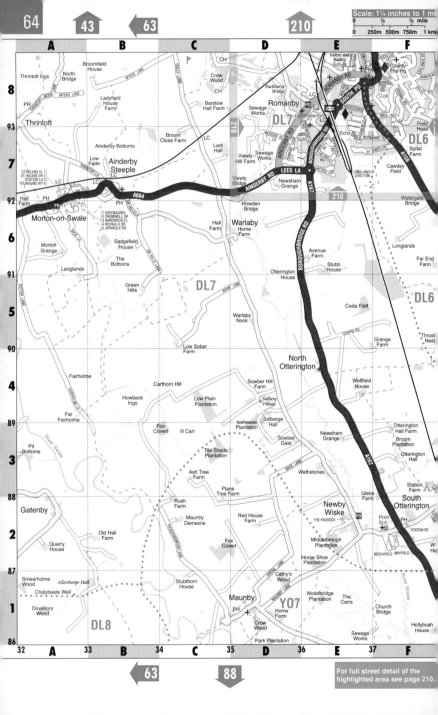

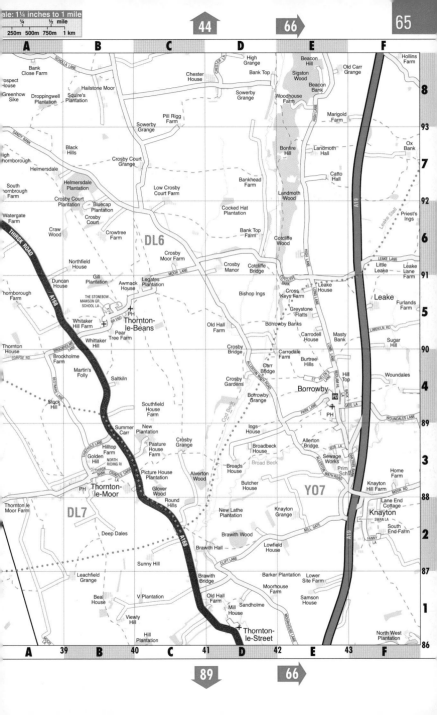

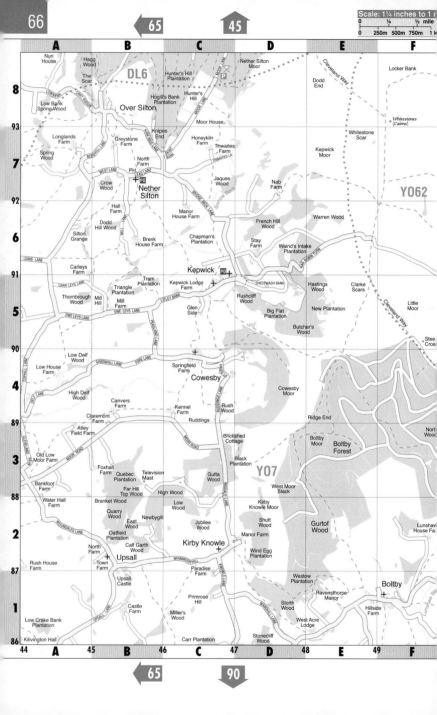

A **B** **C** **D** **E** **F**

Nun House
Hagg Wood
The Scar
DL6
Hunter's Hill Plantation
Nether Silton Moor

MOOR LANE

Dodd End
Cleveland Way
Locker Bank

8

Low Bank Spring-Wood
LOW BANK
CART HOUSE
Over Silton
Hugill's Bank Plantation
Hunter's Hill

Moor House

Whitestones (Cairns)

Whitestone Scar
Whitestone Scar

93

Longlands Farm
Greystone Farm
Knipes End
Honeykiln Farm
Thwaites Farm
THWAITES LA

Kepwick Moor

7

Spring Wood
BENDELL LANE
North Farm
WEST LANE
HEAD LANE
SHORT BANK
Jaques Wood
Nab Farm

Y062

92

Crow Wood
PH
PO
Nether Silton

BRIDGE BECK LANE
SKYROW BECK

French Hill Wood
Warren Wood

Hall Farm
Manor House Farm
MILL LANE

6

Silton Grange
Dodd Hill Wood
Brenk House Farm
Chapman's Plantation
Stay Farm
Waind's Intake Plantation
BAY ROBIN LANE

LEAKE LANE
Carleys Farm
Kepwick
PO
Hastings Wood
Clarke Scars

91

CARR LEYS LANE
Tram Plantation
Kepwick Lodge Farm
SHEEPWASH BANK
Rushcliff Wood
New Plantation
Cleveland Way

Thornbrough Wood
Triangle Plantation
Mill Hill
Mill Farm
LITLEY BANK
Glen Side
Big Flat Plantation
Little Moor

5

EWE LEYS LANE
Ewe Leys Lane
Butcher's Wood
Stee Cross

PICKLAND LANE

90

Low Delf Wood
GREENHILL LANE
FORE LANE
Springfield Farm

4

Low House Farm
High Delf Wood
Cowesby
Cowesby Moor
Ridge End

DELF LANE
Canvers Farm
Kennel Farm
Rush Wood

Claremont Farm
Ruddings
Boltby Moor
Boltby Forest
Nort Wood

89

Atley Field Farm

CLEVELAND LANE
Old Low Moor Farm
MOOR LANE
Brickshed Cottage
MOOR ROAD

3

Bankfoot Farm
Foxhall Farm
Quebec Plantation
Television Mast
Black Plantation
Y07

Gutta Wood
West Moor Slack

88

Water Hall Farm
Branket Wood
Quarry Wood
High Wood
Low Wood
Kirby Knowle Moor
Gurtof Wood
Lunshav House Fa

WOUNDALES LANE
East Wood
Newbygill

2

North Farm
Oatfield Plantation
Call Garth Wood
Jubilee Wood
Shutt Wood

Rush House Farm
Town Farm
Upsall
INGLEBY LANE
Kirby Knowle
Manor Farm
Wind Egg Plantation

87

Upsall Castle
WHINMOORHILL
Paradise Farm
KNOWLE LANE
Westow Plantation
Ravensthorpe Manor
Boltby

UPSALL LANE

1

Low Crake Bank Plantation
Castle Farm
Miller's Wood
Primrose Hill
Storth Wood
WANDALE LANE
West Acre Lodge
Hillside Farm
Lunshav Ba

86

Killvington Hall
Carr Plantation
Stonecliff Wood

44 **A** 45 **B** 46 **C** 47 **D** 48 **E** 49 **F**

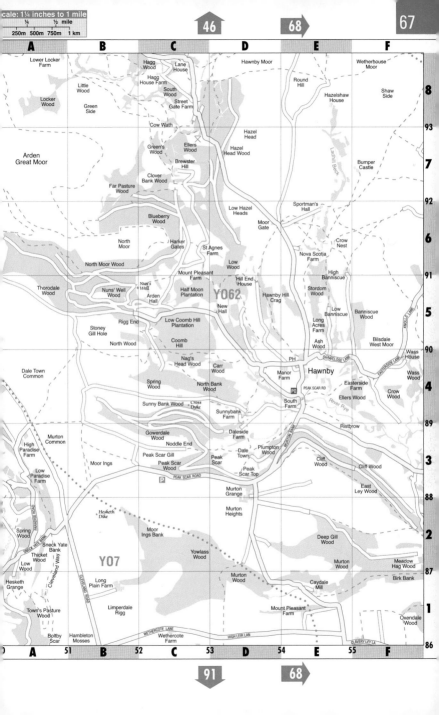

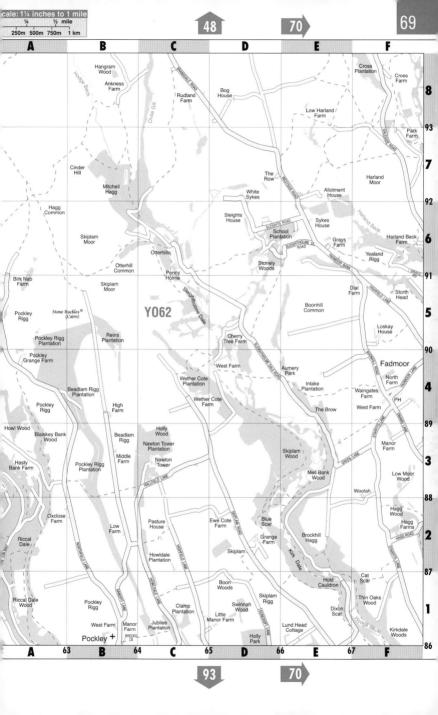

A   B   C   D   E   F

Hangram Wood
Ankness Farm
Rudland Farm
Bog House
Cross Plantation
Cross Farm
8
Low Harland Farm
Park Farm
93
Cinder Hill
Mitchell Hagg
The Row
White Sykes
Allotment House
Harland Moor
7
Hagg Common
Sleights House
Sykes House
Harland Beck
92
Skiplam Moor
School Plantation
Grays Farm
Harland Beck Farm
6
Otterhills
Stonely Woods
Yealand Rigg
Otterhill Common
Penny Holme
Birk Nab Farm
Dial Farm
Storth Head
91
Pockley Rigg
Skiplam Moor
Stone Ruckles (Cairn)
YO62
Boonhill Common
5
Pockley Rigg Plantation
Reins Plantation
Cherry Tree Farm
Loskay House
90
Pockley Grange Farm
West Farm
Aumery Park
Fadmoor
North Farm
Beadlam Rigg Plantation
Wether Cote Plantation
Intake Plantation
Waingates Farm
4
Pockley Rigg
High Farm
Wether Cote Farm
The Brow
West Farm
PH
89
Howl Wood
Blaiskey Bank Wood
Beadlam Rigg
Holly Wood
Nawton Tower Plantation
Skiplam Wood
Manor Farm
3
Hasty Bank Farm
Pockley Rigg Plantation
Middle Farm
Nawton Tower
Mell Bank Wood
Low Moor Wood
Woolah
88
Oxclose Farm
Low Farm
Pasture House
Ewe Cote Farm
Blue Scar
Brockhill Hagg
Hagg Wood
Hagg Farms
2
Riccal Dale
Howldale Plantation
Skiplam
Grange Farm
Cat Scar
87
Riccal Dale Wood
Pockley Rigg
Clamp Plantation
Boon Woods
Swinnah Wood
Skiplam Rigg
Hold Cauldron
Thin Oaks Wood
Dixon Scar
Kirkdale Woods
1
West Farm
Manor Farm
Pockley
Jubilee Plantation
Little Manor Farm
Holly Park
Lund Head Cottage
86

A   63   B   64   C   65   D   66   E   67   F

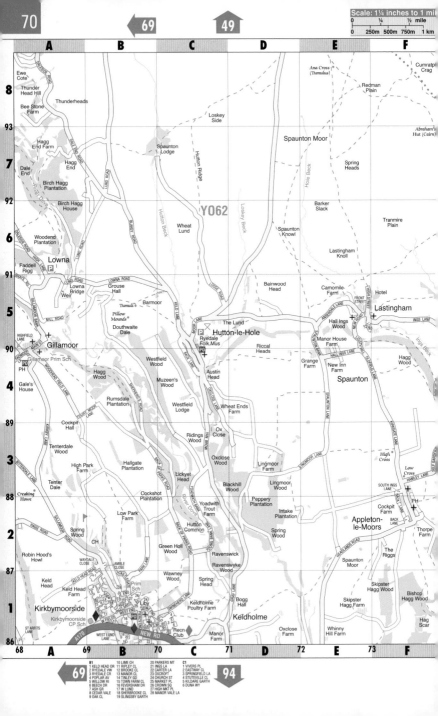

Scale: 1¼ inches to 1 mi

0   ¼   ½ mile
0 250m 500m 750m 1 km

A **B** **C** **D** **E** **F**

8

Ewe
Cote
Thunder
Head Hill
Bee Stone
Farm

Thunderheads

Ana Cross
(Tumulus)

Redman
Plain

Cumratp
Crag

93

Loskey
Side

Spaunton Moor

Abraham's
Hut (Cairn)

7

Hagg
End Farm
Dale
End
Birch Hagg
Plantation

Hagg
End

Spaunton
Lodge

Hutton Ridge

Spring
Heads

92

Birch Hagg
House

Woodend
Plantation

YO62

Wheat
Lund

Hole Beck

Loskey Beck

Barker
Slack

Spaunton
Knowl

Lastingham
Knoll

Tranmire
Plain

6

Lowna

Faddell
Rigg

Lowna
Bridge
Weir

Lowna Road

Grouse
Hall

Bainwood
Head

Camomile
Farm

Hotel

91

Barmoor

Tumuli

Pillow
Mounds

Douthwaite
Dale

The Lund

Ryedale
Folk Mus.

Hutton-le-Hole

Hall Ings
Wood

Lastingham

5

Highfield
Lane
Gillamoor

Manor House
Farm

Hagg
Wood

90

Gillamoor Prim Sch
PH

Westfield
Wood

Hagg
Wood

Muzeen's
Wood

Riccal
Heads

Grange
Farm

New Inn
Farm

Spaunton

4

Gale's
House

Rumsdale
Plantation

Westfield
Lodge

Austin
Head

Wheat Ends
Farm

89

Cockpit
Hall

Tenterdale
Wood

High Park
Farm

Hallgate
Plantation

Ridings
Wood

Ox
Close

Oxclose
Wood

Lingmoor
Farm

High
Cross

Low
Cross

3

Tenter
Dale

Lickyet
Head

Blackhill
Wood

Lingmoor
Wood

Peppery
Plantation

Cockpit
Farm

88

Creaking
Howe

Cockshot
Plantation

Yoadwith
Trout
Farm

Intake
Plantation

PH

Appleton-
le-Moors

Thorpe
Farm

2

Robin Hood's
Howl

Spring
Wood

CH

Low Park
Farm

Hutton
Common

Green Holl
Wood

Ravenswick

Spring
Wood

Spaunton
Moor

The
Riggs

87

Keld
Head

Keld Head
Farm

Wawney
Wood

Ravenswyke
Wood

Spring
Head

Skipster
Hagg Wood

Bishop
Hagg Wood

1

Kirkbymoorside

Prim
Sch

Keldholme
Poultry Farm

Bogg
Hall

Keldholme

Skipster
Hagg
Farm

Hag
Scar

86

Kirkbymoorside CP Sch
ST ARITS
LANE

A170
NEW RD

Recn
Club

Manor
Farm

Oxclose
Farm

Whinny
Hill Farm

68 **A** **69** **B** **70** **C** **71** **D** **72** **E** **73** **F**

B1
1 KELD HEAD DR
2 RYEDALE VW
3 RYEDALE CR
4 POPLAR AV
5 WILLOW RI
6 BEECH DR
7 ASH GR
8 CEDAR VALE
9 OAK CL
10 LIME CH
11 RIPLEY CL
12 BROOKE CL
13 MANOR CL
14 TINLEY GD
15 TOWN FARM CL
16 FEVERSHAM DR
17 W LUND
18 SHERBROOKE CL
19 SLINGSBY GARTH
20 PARKERS MT
21 INGS LA
22 CARTER LA
23 OXCROFT
24 CHURCH ST
25 MARKET PL
26 CROWN SQ
27 HIGH MKT PL
28 MANOR VALE LA
C1
1 VIVERS PL
2 EASTWAY CL
3 SPRINGFIELD LA
4 STUTTVILLE CL
5 KILDARE GARTH
6 DUNA WY

A B C D E F

8

Raindale Head Farm
Raindale Head
Scarfhill Rigg
Raper's Farm
Levisham Moor
Hole of Horcum
Horcum Wood
NT

Low Over Blow
Gallock Hill
West Side Brow
Seavy Pond
Low Horcum

93

Middle Head
Wethead Rigg
Skelton Tower
Levisham Moor
Little Marlit Head
Lockton Low Moo

Low Raindale
West Side Brow
Marfit Head

7

Taylor Hill
Yorfalls Wood
Far Black Rigg
First Rigg
Black Howe Rigg
Great Mar Head Sla

East Toft Dike

92

Stony Moor
Levisham Moor
Rhumbard Snout Wood
Dundale Rigg
Horness Rigg
High Horcum Farm
Lower Marfit Head Slack

Raindale Scar
Dundale Pond

6

Chilton Saintoft Farm
Boonhill Farm
Grove House
Braygate Balk
Warren Farm
Smeffell Rigg
Hi Ho Fa

91

Black Howe
Rawcliff Road
LC
Levisham Station
LT Field La
PH
PO
Levisham
High Horcum Farm
Mount Pleasant Farm
Pasture Rigg

Newton-on-Rawcliffe
PH
East Side
Manor Farm
Braygate La

5

Melrose Farm
Chapel Farm
Levisham Wood
YO18
Low Stead Farm
Levisham Mill Farm
Rus Hea

Keld Farm
Cemy
Mill Bank Road

90

East Brow Farm
East Brow Wood
Rowl Wood
PO
BACK LA
Green Dale

Keldlands
East Brow House
HUDGIN LA
Lockton
Thwaite Head

4

Keldlands Farm
Howlgate Nab
Thwaite Wood
Holm Woods

Haugh Rigg Farm
Lydds House
Levisham Wood
Hagg Wood
Staindale Lodge
Clenfield Rigg

89

Glebe Farm
Howlgate Farm
High Wood
High Dalby House

Keldgate Road
Lydds Farm
RUDDINGS ROAD
CROSSDALE RD
PH

3

Yatts Farm
Little Dale Rigg
Farwath Hill Top
Farfields
Fox & Rabbit Farm
Sneverda Rigg

Crown Wood
Ness Head
Farwath

88

Blansby Park Wood
High Plantation
Low Wood
Visitor Centre

Gundale Wood
Oak Tree Farm
Square Wood
Black Plantation
Nut Wood
Low Dalt

2

East Hambleton Farm
High Blansby
Blansby Park

Haugh Wood
Spring Wood
High Kingthorpe
Upper Dalby Wood

87

Southview Farm
West Farm
Blansby Park Wood
Low Dalby Wood

1

New Hambleton Farm
Yatts Brow Farm
Blansby Park Farm
High Kingthorpe
East Kingthorpe Farm
Pexton Moor

Wailes Hagg Wood
Blansby Park Wood
Common Plantation

Newbridge Quarry

86

80 A 81 B 82 C 83 D 84 E 85 F

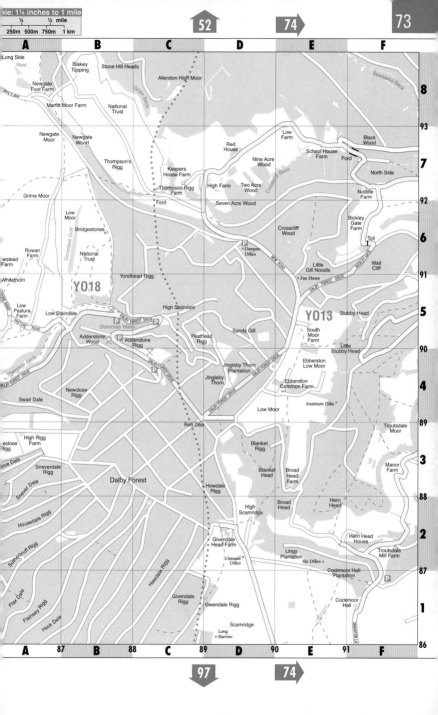

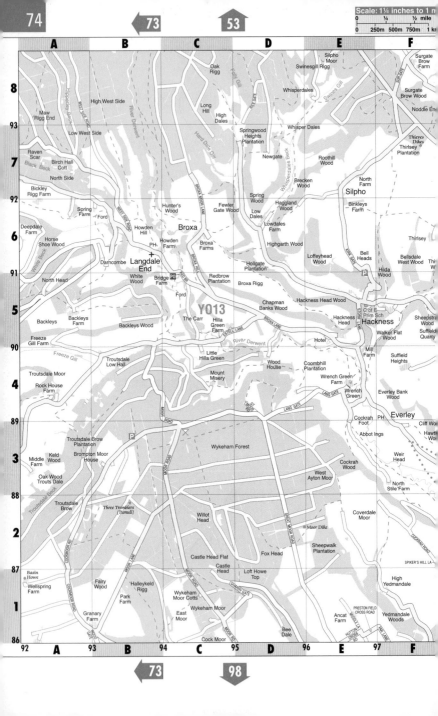

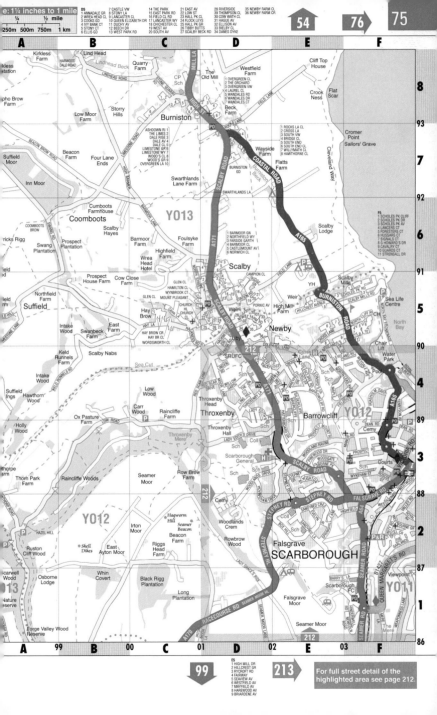

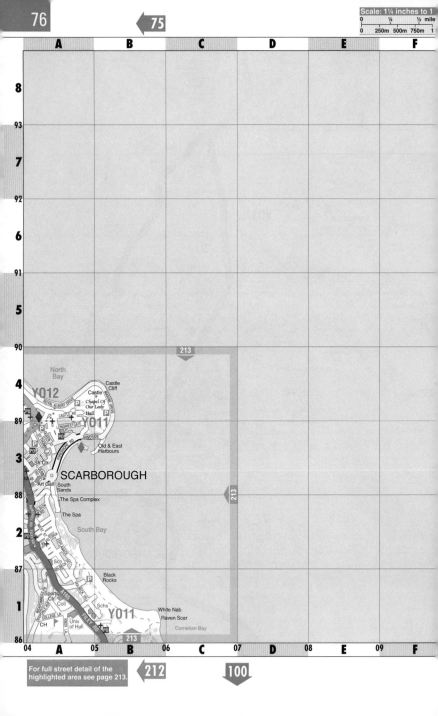

Scale: 1¼ inches to 1

0   ¼   ½ mile

0   250m 500m 750m 1

A   B   C   D   E   F

8

93

7

92

6

91

5

90

213

North Bay

4

YO12

Castle Cliff

ROYAL ALBERT DRIVE

Castle

Chapel Of Our Lady

CASTLE RD

Hall

89

LONGWESTGATE

YO11

Sch

SANDSIDE

PO

3

FORESHORE RD

Sh Ctr

Old & East Harbours

Mus

SCARBOROUGH

Art Gall

South Sands

88

The Spa Complex

The Spa

2

South Bay

87

Black Rocks

Coll

Sports Ctr

Coll

COLLEGE LA

Schs

1

YO11

White Nab

Raven Scar

CH

KING ST

FALE RD

Univ of Hull

PO

Cornelian Bay

86

213

04   A   05   B   06   C   07   D   08   E   09   F

For full street detail of the highlighted area see page 213.

212

100

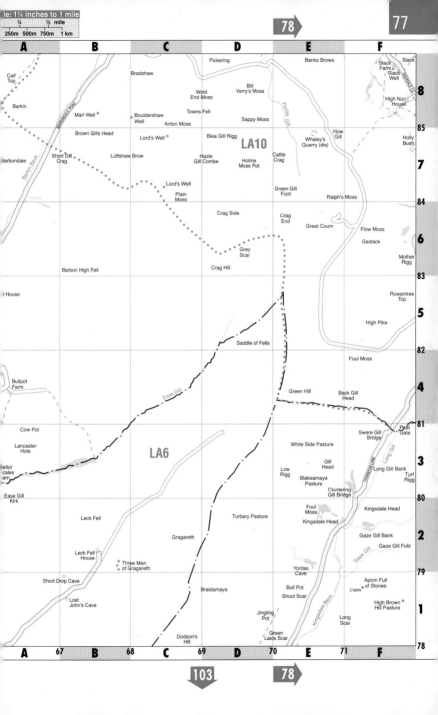

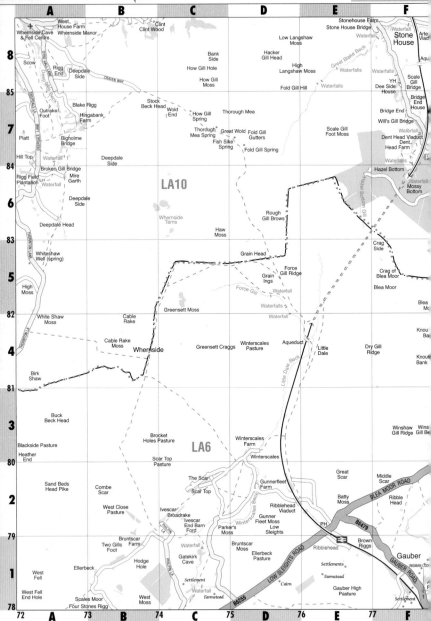

Scale: 1¼ inches to 1 r

0   ¼   ½ mile
0   250m 500m 750m 1 k

A   B   C   D   E   F

West House Farm
Whernside Cave & Fell Centre
Whernside Manor
Clint
Clint Wood

Stonehouse Farm
Stone House Bridge
Stone House
Waterfall
Arte
Viad

8

Scow
Rigg End
Deepdale Side

Bank Side
How Gill Hole
How Gill Moss

Hacker Gill Head
Low Langshaw Moss
High Langshaw Moss

Great Blake Beck
Waterfalls
Waterfalls
Aqu

CRAVEN WAY

Fold Gill Hill

Waterfalls

YH Dee Side House
Scale Gill Bridge

85

Outrake Foot
Blake Rigg
Hingabank Farm

Stock Beck Head
Wold End
How Gill Spring

Thorough Mea

Fold Gill Gutters

Scale Gill Foot Moss

Bridge End
Bridge End House
Will's Gill Bridge

7

Platt
Bigholme Bridge

Thorough Mea Spring
Fish Sike Spring
Great Wold
Fold Gill Spring

Waterfall
Dent Head Viaduct
Dent Head Farm

Hill Top
Waterfall
Broken Gill Bridge
Mire Garth
Deepdale Side

Waterfalls

84

Rigg Field Plantation
Waterfall

Deepdale Side

LA10

Hazel Bottom

Mossy Bottom
Waterfall

6

Deepdale Head

Whernside Tarns

Haw Moss

Rough Gill Brows

Great Bottom Gill

Crag Side

83

Whiteshaw Well (spring)

Grain Head

Force Gill Ridge

Crag of Blea Moor
Blea Moor

Blea Mo

5

High Moss

Grain Ings

Force Gill
Waterfall

Blea Moor

White Shaw Moss

Cable Rake

Greensett Moss

Waterfalls

Waterfall

82

THORNTON LANE

Cable Rake Moss

Whernside

Greensett Craggs
Winterscales Pasture

Aqueduct

Little Dale

Dry Gill Ridge

Knou Ba

4

Birk Shaw

Little Dale Beck

Knou Bank

81

Buck Beck Head

Brocket Holes Pasture

Winterscales Farm

Winterscales Beck

Winshaw Gill Ridge
Wins Gill B

3

Blackside Pasture
Heather End

LA6

Scar Top Pasture

Winterscales

Great Scar

Middle Scar

BLEA MOOR ROAD

80

Sand Beds Head Pike
Combe Scar

The Scar
Scar Top

Gunnerfleet Farm

Batty Moss

Ribble Head

2

West Close Pasture

Ivescar Broadrake

Ribblehead Viaduct
Gunner Fleet Moss
Low Sleights

PH
B6479

Ivescar End Barn Ford
Parker's Moss

LOW SLEIGHTS ROAD

Brown Riggs

Gauber

GAUBER ROAD

79

Bruntscar Farm
Two Gills Foot

PHILPIN LA

Bruntscar Moss
Ellerbeck Pasture

Ribblehead

Settlements

INGMAN LO

1

West Fell

Ellerbeck
Hodge Hole

Gatekirk Cave

Farmstead

Gauber High Pasture

Waterfall

Settlement

West Fell End Hole

Scales Moor
Four Stones Rigg

Settlement
West Moss

Waterfall
Farmstead

Cairn

B6255

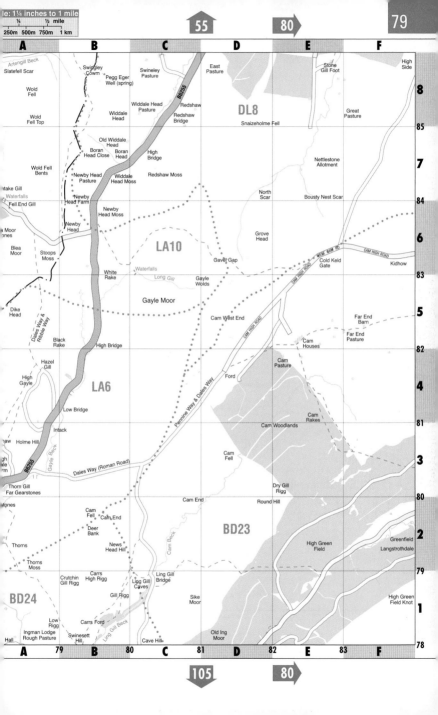

A **B** **C** **D** **E** **F**

Artengill Beck
Slatefell Scar

Swiggley Cowm
Pegg Eger Well (spring)

Swineley Pasture

East Pasture

Stone Gill Foot

High Side

Wold Fell

Widdale Head Pasture

Redshaw

DL8

8

Wold Fell Top

Widdale Head

Redshaw Bridge

Great Pasture

Snaizeholme Fell

85

Old Widdale Head

Boran Head Close

Boran Head

High Bridge

7

Wold Fell Bents

Newby Head Pasture

Widdale Head Moss

Redshaw Moss

Nettlestone Allotment

ntake Gill
Waterfalls
Fell End Gill

Newby Head Farm

North Scar

Bousty Nest Scar

84

Newby Head Moss

a Moor
ones

Newby Head

LA10

Grove Head

WEIR DAM RD

CAM HIGH ROAD

6

Blea Moor

Stoops Moss

White Rake

Waterfalls

Long Gill

Gavel Gap

Cold Keld Gate

Kidhow

83

CAM TIBET ROAD

Gayle Wolds

Dike Head

Gayle Moor

Cam West End

Far End Barn

5

Far End Pasture

Black Rake

High Bridge

Cam Houses

82

Dales Way & Ribble Way

Hazel Gill

Cam Pasture

High Gayle

LA6

Ford

4

Low Bridge

Cam Rakes

81

Pennine Way & Dales Way

Cam Woodlands

Intack

Holme Hill

Gayle Beck

Cam Fell

B6255

gh
le
rm

Dales Way (Roman Road)

3

Thorn Gill
Far Gearstones

Dry Gill Rigg

80

tones

Cam Fell

Cam End

Cam End

Round Hill

BD23

Deer Bank

2

High Green Field

Greenfield

Langstrothdale

Thorns

News Head Hill

Cam Beck

79

Thorns Moss

Crutchin Gill Rigg

Carrs High Rigg

Ling Gill Bridge

Ling Gill Caves

Sike Moor

BD24

Gill Rigg

High Green Field Knot

1

Low Rigg

Carrs Ford

Ling Gill Beck

Ingman Lodge Rough Pasture

Hall

Swinesett Hill

Cave Hill

Old Ing Moor

78

A 79 **B** 80 **C** 81 **D** 82 **E** 83 **F**

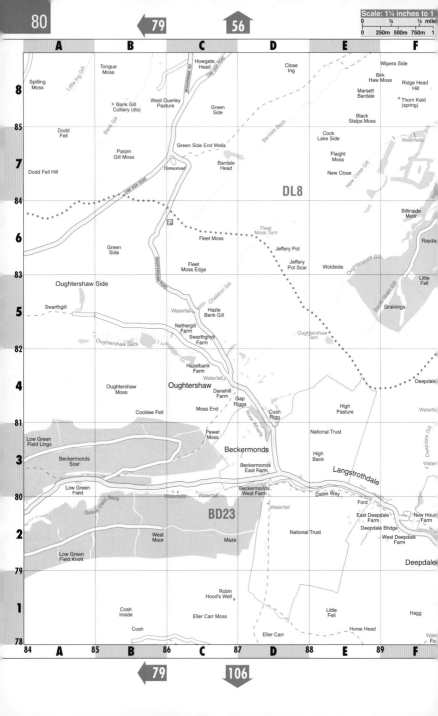

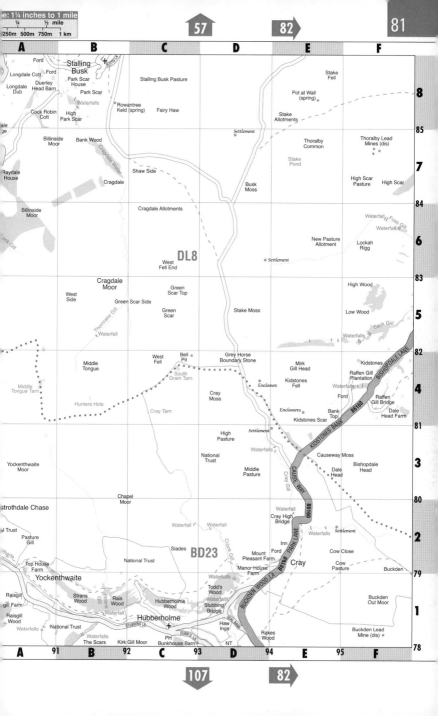

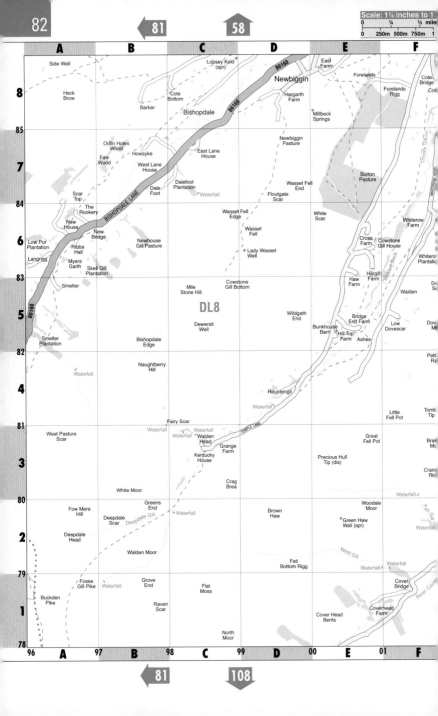

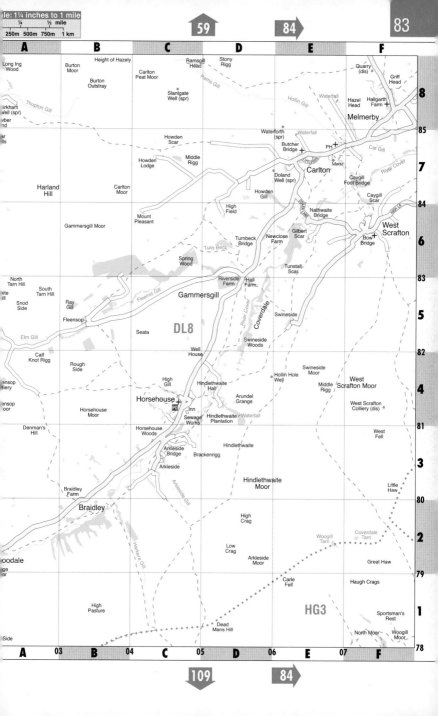

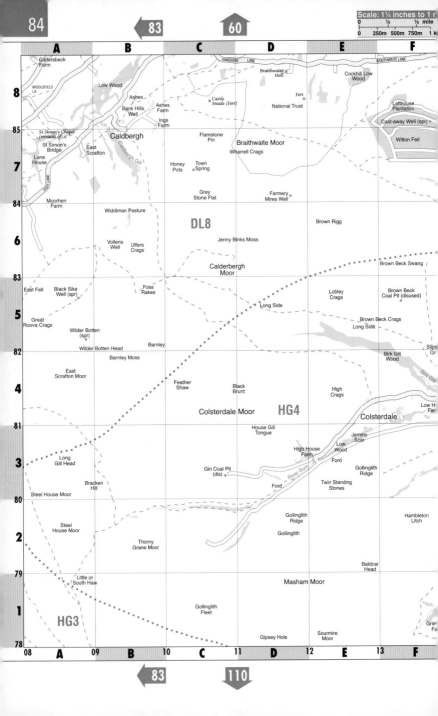

Scale: 1¼ inches to 1 r

| 0 | ¼ | ½ mile |
| 0 | 250m | 500m | 750m | 1 k |

A   **B**   **C**   **D**   **E**   **F**

HANGHOW LANE

BRAITHWAITE LANE

Gildersbeck Farm

Low Wood

MIDDLEFIELD LA

Ashes

Bank Hills Well

Ashes Farm

Braithwaite Hall

Fort

National Trust

Cockhill Low Wood

Lofthouse Plantation

Cast-away Well (spr)

Witton Fell

8

Castle Steads (Fort)

Ings Farm

85

St Simon's Chapel (remains of)

Caldbergh

Flamstone Pin

Braithwaite Moor

Wharrell Crags

St Simon's Bridge

Lane House

East Scrafton

Caldbergh Gill

7

Honey Pots

Town Spring

Grey Stone Flat

Farmery Mires Well

84

Moorhen Farm

HIGH LANE

Widdiman Pasture

DL8

Brown Rigg

6

Vollens Well

Ulfers Crags

Jenny Binks Moss

Calderbergh Moor

Brown Beck Swang

83

East Fell

Black Sike Well (spr)

Foss Rakes

Long Side

Lobley Crags

Brown Beck Coal Pit (disused)

5

Great Roova Crags

Wilder Botten (spr)

Brown Beck Crags

Long Side

Wilder Botten Head

Barnley

Birk Gill Wood

Slips Cr

82

Barnley Moss

East Scrafton Moor

Feather Shaw

Black Brunt

High Crags

Low H Far

4

Colsterdale Moor

HG4

Colsterdale

81

House Gill Tongue

Jemmy Scar

Long Gill Head

High House Farm

Low Wood

Ford

Gollinglith Ridge

3

Bracken Hill

Gin Coal Pit (dis)

Ford

River Burn

Twin Standing Stones

Steel House Moor

80

Steel House Moor

Gollinglith Ridge

Hambleton Litch

2

Thorny Grane Moor

Gollinglith

79

Little or South Haw

Baldcar Head

Masham Moor

1

HG3

Gollinglith Fleet

Gipsey Hole

Sourmire Moor

Grim Fe

78

08   **A**   **09**   **B**   **10**   **C**   **11**   **D**   **12**   **E**   **13**   **F**

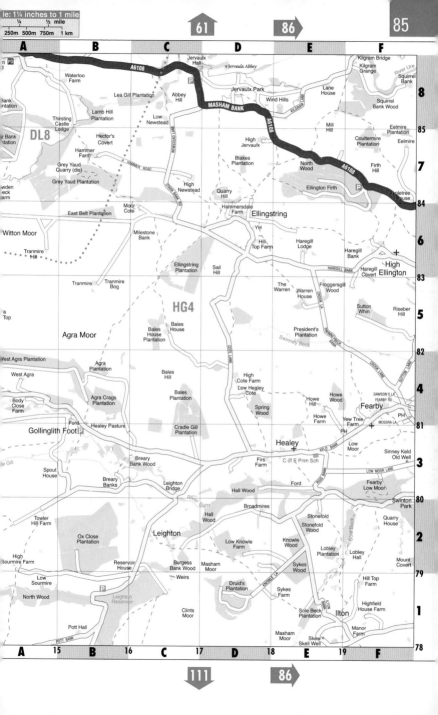

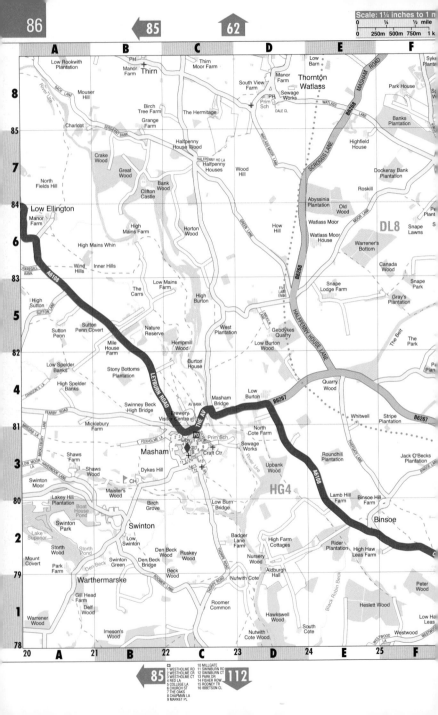

Scale: 1¼ inches to 1 mile

0   ¼   ½   mile
0   250m   500m   750m   1 k

A   B   C   D   E   F

8
85
7
84
6
83
5
82
4
81
3
80
2
79
1
78

Low Rookwith Plantation
PH
Manor Farm
Thirn
Thirn Moor Farm
Park House
Syke Plant
Mouser Hill
South View Farm
Manor Farm
Thornton Watlass
Low Barn
Banks Plantation
Birch Tree Farm
The Hermitage
PH
Prim Sch
DALE CL
Highfield House
Charlcot
SERGEANT BANK
Grange Farm
Halfpenny House Wood
Sewage Works
WATLASS LANE
B6268
MASHAM ROAD
Dockeray Bank Plantation
Crake Wood
Great Wood
Halfpenny Ho
Halfpenny Houses
HALFPENNY HO LA
Wood Hill
SCROGGS LANE
Roskill
North Fields Hill
Clifton Castle
Bank Wood
Horton Wood
How Hill
Abyssinia Plantation
Old Wood
MOOR LANE
DL8
Snape Plant
Low Ellington
Manor Farm
High Mains Farm
GREEN LANE
Watlass Moor
Watlass Moor House
Snape Lawns
HAREGILL BANK
A6108
High Mains Whin
Inner Hills
Warrener's Bottom
Canada Wood
Snape Park
Wind Hills
The Carrs
Low Mains Farm
FIVE LANE ENDS
B6268
Snape Lodge Farm
Gray's Plantation
High Sutton
SUTTON LA
High Burton
LANE HEAD
Gebdykes Quarry
HALFPENNY HOUSE LANE
The Belt
The Park
Sutton Penn
Sutton Penn Covert
Nature Reserve
West Plantation
Low Burton Wood
DAWSON'S LA
Mile House Farm
Hempmill Wood
Burton House
Quarry Wood
Pa Pla
Low Spelder Banks
Stony Bottoms Plantation
LEYBURN ROAD
Low Burton
B6267
B6267
High Spelder Banks
Swinney Beck High Bridge
Masham Bridge
Low Burton
Whitwell
Stripe Plantation
FEARBY ROAD
Micklebury Farm
THE AV
AV BANK
Brewery Visitor Centre
FOXHOLME LA
Prim Sch
North Cote Farm
Roundhill Plantation
Jack O'Becks Plantation
MONGOSA LA
Shaws Farm
Shaws Wood
Masham
Craft Ctr
Libry
Sewage Works
Upbank Wood
A6108
Lamb Hill Farm
Binsoe Hill Farm
LOW MOOR LA
WESTHOLME LANE
CH
Dykes Hill
Maister's Wood
River Ure
HG4
Binsoe
Lakey Hill Plantation
Boat House Pond
Birch Grove
Low Burn Bridge
Rider Plantation
High Haw Leas Farm
Swinton Park
Storth Wood
Storth Pond
Swinton
Low Swinton
Den Beck Wood
Ruskew Wood
Badger Lane Farm
High Farm Cottages
Lake Superior
Den Beck
Swinton Green
Den Beck Bridge
THORPE ROAD
Beck Wood
Nursery Wood
Aldburgh Hall
Peter Wood
Mount Covert
Park Farm
Warthermarske
ROOMER LANE
Nutwith Cote
Black Robin Beck
Heslett Wood
Low Ha Leas
Gill Head Farm
Delf Wood
Roomer Common
Hawkswell Wood
South Cote
WESTWOOD LA
Westwood
Warrener Wood
Imeson's Wood
Nutwith Cote Wood

20   A   21   B   22   C   23   D   24   E   25   F

C3
1 WESTHOLME RD
2 WESTHOLME CR
3 WESTHOLME CT
4 RED LA
5 COLLEGE LA
6 CHURCH ST
7 THE OAKS
8 CHAPMAN LA
9 MARKET PL
10 MILLGATE
11 SWINBURN RD
12 SWINBURN CT
13 PARK DR
14 FISHER ROW
15 RODNEY TR
16 IBBETSON CL

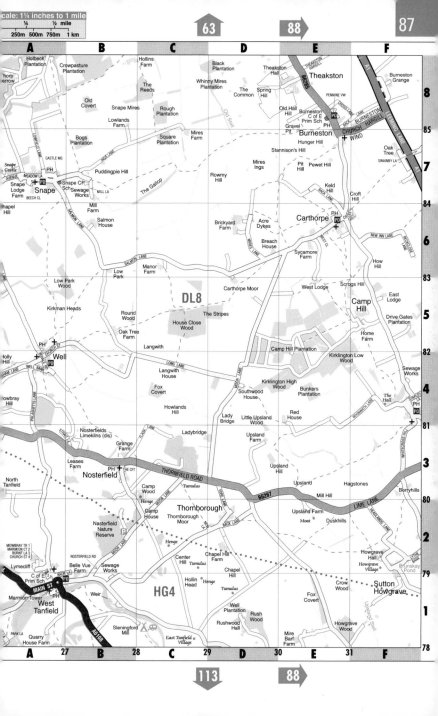

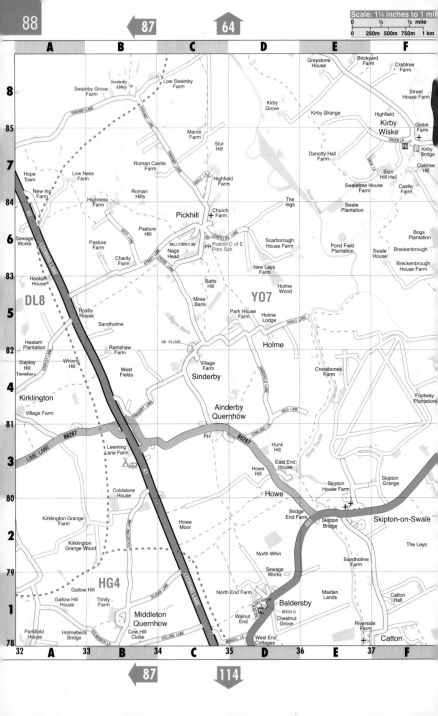

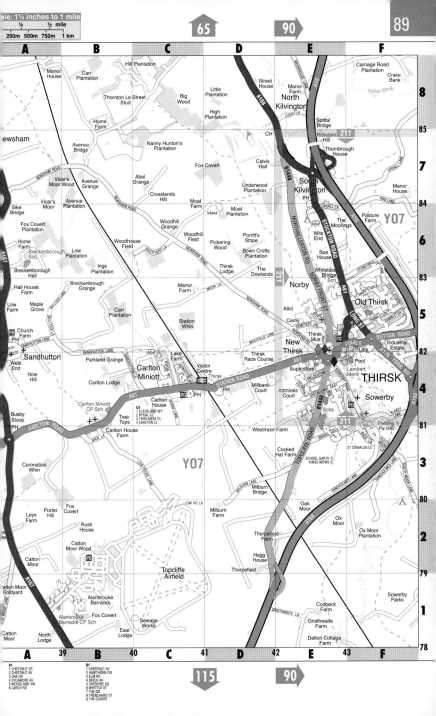

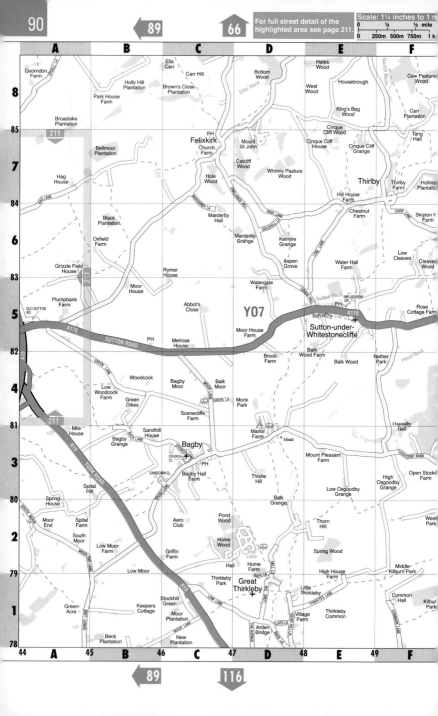

90 ← 89 66

For full street detail of the
highlighted area see page 211.

Scale: 1¼ inches to 1 m

0   ¼   ½ mile
0 250m 500m 750m 1 k

A   **B**   **C**   **D**   **E**   **F**

8

Quordon Farm

Holly Hill Plantation

Park House Farm

Ella Carr

Carr Hill

Brown's Close Plantation

Bottom Wood

Hales Wood

West Wood

Housebrough

Cow Pasture Wood

King's Bog Wood

Carr Plantation

Eller Beck

Gundil Beck

85

211

Broadsike Plantation

Bellmoor Plantation

Felixkirk

PH

Church Farm

Mount St John

Catcliff Wood

Cinque Cliff Wood

Cinque Cliff House

Cinque Cliff Grange

Tang Hall

7

Hag House

Black Plantation

Hole Wood

Marderby Hall

Whinny Pasture Wood

Thirlby

Thirlby Farm

Hollins Plantatio

84

BACK LANE

MARDERBY LA

DRELOWS HILL

HIGH LANE

GOLDHILL LA

Hill House Farm

Chestnut Farm

Skipton H Farm

CARR LANE

6

Oxfield Farm

Marderby Grange

Kelmire Grange

Low Cleaves

Cleaves Wood

83

Grizzle Field House

211

Plumpbank Farm

Moor House

Rymer House

Aspen Grove

Water Hall Farm

Watergate Farm

Y07

Sutton Beck

Hood Beck

MELBOURNE DR

PH

Rose Cottage Farm

5

OLD SUTTON RD

Abbot's Close

Moor House Farm

GRASS HILL

Sutton-under-Whitestonecliffe

School

A170

82

A19

A170

SUTTON ROAD

PH

Melrose House

Brook Farm

Balk Wood Farm

Balk Wood

Nether Park

4

211

GREEN LANE

Low Woodcock Farm

Woodcock

Green Dikes

Bagby Moor

MOOR LANE

GREEN LA

Balk Moor

Monk Park

Osgoodby Hall

81

Scenecliffe Farm

Mile House

BACK LANE

Sandhill House

Bagby Grange

Bagby

CHURCH CL

PH

Manor Farm

Moat

Mount Pleasant Farm

OSGOODBY BANK

High Osgoodby Grange

Open Stocki

3

YORK ROAD

SANDOWN CL

BAGBY LANE

Bagby Hall Farm

Thistle Hill

Low Osgoodby Grange

80

Spital Hill

Spring House

Moor End

Spital Farm

Aero Club

Pond Wood

Balk Grange

Thorn Hill

West Park

2

A19

SOUTH MOOR

MOOR END LANE

South Moor Farm

Low Moor Farm

Griffin Farm

Home Wood

Hall

The Lake

Home Farm

MILL LANE

Spring Wood

High House Farm

Middle Kilburn Park

79

Low Moor

Thirkleby Park

LOW LANE

Great Thirkleby

BACK LANE

Little Thirkleby

THWAITES LANE

High House Farm

Common Hall

Kilbur Park

1

SANDY LANE

Green Acre

Keepers Cottage

Stockhill Green

Moor Plantation

MOOR LANE

THE AVENUE

Arden Bridge

BACK LA

FLATS LA

VICAR HILL LA

Village Farm

Thirkleby Common

COMMON LANE

78

Beck Plantation

New Plantation

44   **A**   **45**   **B**   **46**   **C**   **47**   **D**   **48**   **E**   **49**   **F**

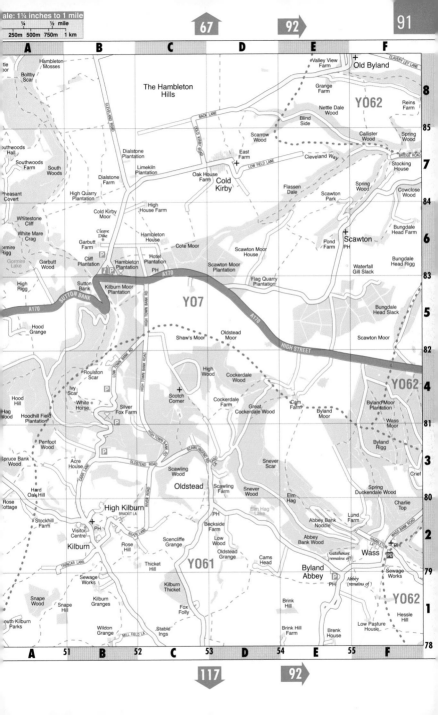

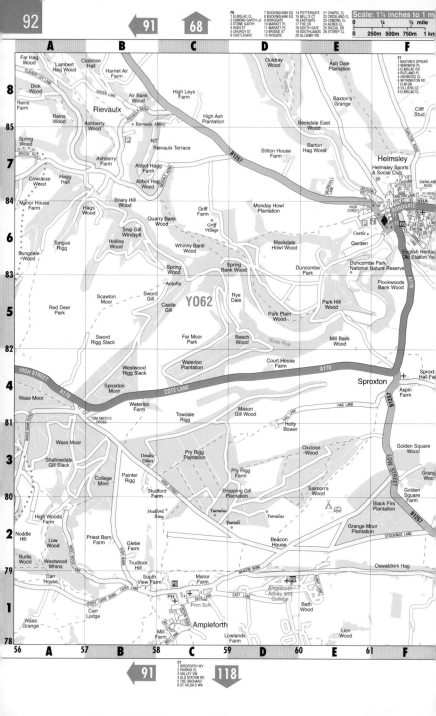

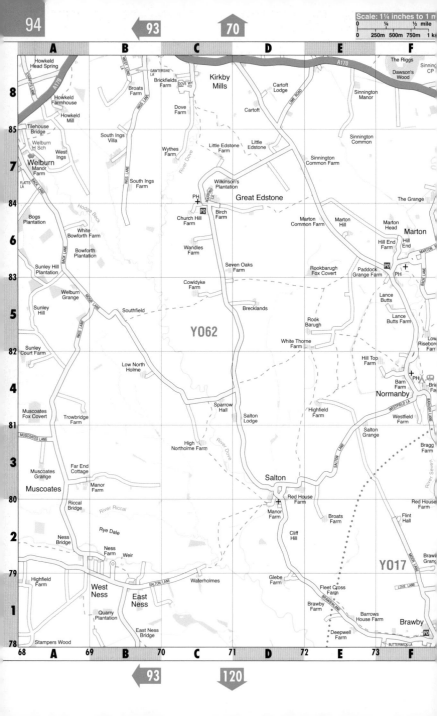

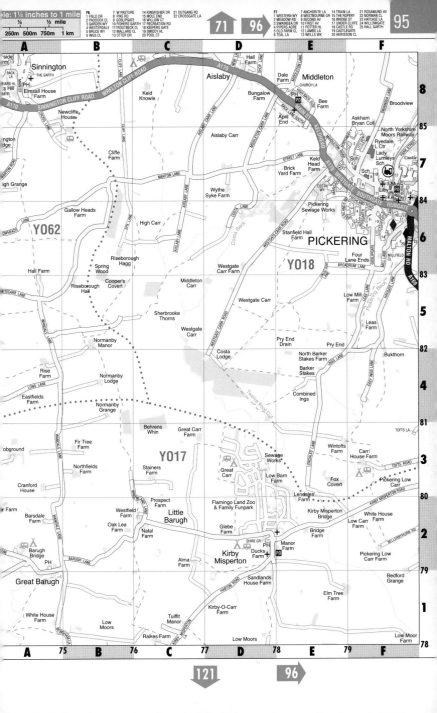

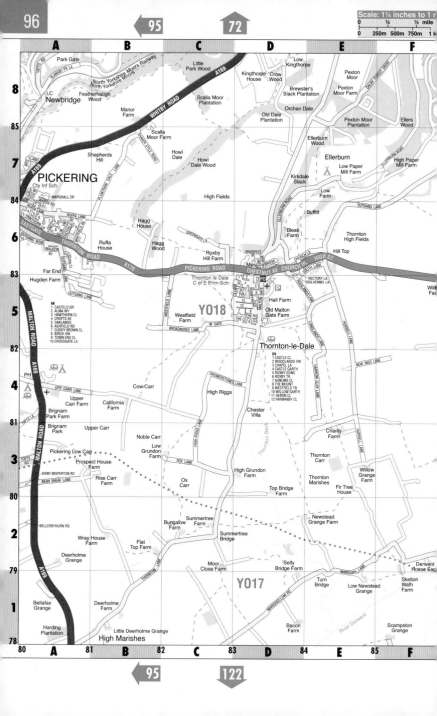

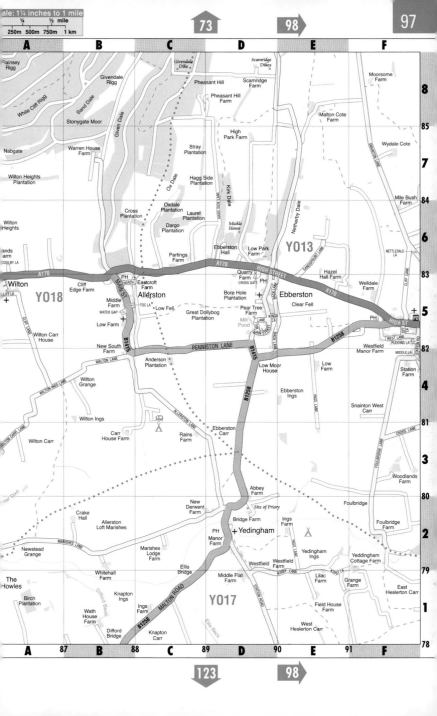

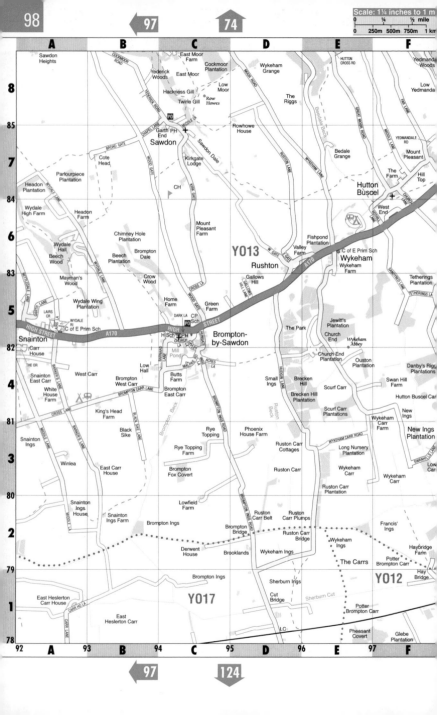

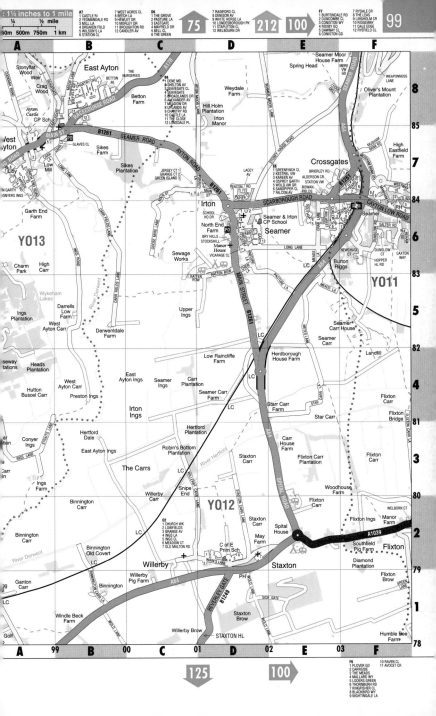

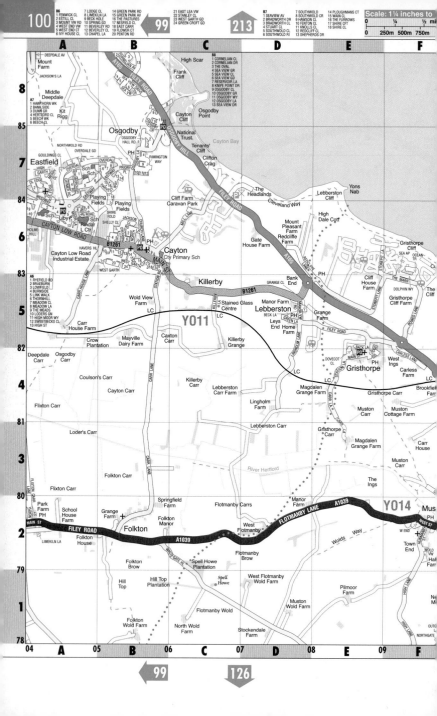

Scale: 1¼ inches to 1 mile

¼ ½ mile

250m 500m 750m 1 km

A B C D E F

8

85

7

84

6

83

Wyke

5

82

7

84

house
nd

Club
Point

North
Cliff

A4
1 COPSE HL
2 HAZEL RD
3 ROWAN AV
4 WIDGEON CL
5 SNIPE CL
6 HERON CT
7 CYGNET CL
8 MALLARD CL
9 SHELDRAKE CL

Cleveland Way

wbiggin

Filey
Field

wbiggin
rm West

CHERRY TREE DR.

PINEWOOD
AV

Filey Spa

North Cliff
City Park

Filey Brigg
Nature Reserve

4

81

RBOROUGH ROAD

PLANE TREE
WY

WOODALE

Filey
Sands

Y014

rayke
se Farm

Nature
Reserve

North Cliff
City Park

Lifeboat
Station

B3
1 THE CROFT
2 ASHLEY CT
3 QUEEN'S TR
4 LAUNDRY RD
5 CHURCH ST
6 ST OSWALDS CT
7 RAVINE TOP
8 BIRCH CL
9 GARLTON RD
10 VICTORIA AV
11 NORMAN CR
12 WEST RD
13 PROVIDENCE PL
14 QUEEN ST
15 REYNOLDS ST
16 MARINER'S TR
17 WHITKIRK PL
18 WHISTON DR

19 LINTON CL
20 STATION AV
21 GRANVILLE RD
22 CROMWELL AV
23 CLAREMONT
24 MITFORD ST
25 CLIFFORD'S TR
26 THE AVENUE
27 CHAPEL ST
28 UNION ST
29 RAINCLIFFE AV
30 HOPE ST
31 MURRAY ST
32 CARGATE HL
33 BELLE VUE CR
34 BELLE VUE ST
35 JOHN ST
36 WELFORD RD

37 WEST VALE
38 RUTLAND ST
39 HINDLE DR
40 FLOWER GARTH
41 HALLAM CL
42 ST JOHN'S AV
43 BROOKLANDS
44 BROOKLANDS CL
45 DORAN CL
46 PADBURY CL
47 CLARENCE AV
48 SOUTHDENE
49 COOPER RD
50 PADBURY AV
51 SOUTH CR CL
52 MELVILLE TR
53 CRESCENT HL
54 SOUTH CR AV

FILEY

Library

Sun Lounge
Theatre

EW DR
WOOD DR
WOOD AV
SALL CL
SETT AV
URN PL

Beacon
Hill

Swimming
Pool

Filey School

3

80

Cemy

Allison
Field
Farm

Mill
Farm

Muston
Grange

CH

Muston
Sands

Filey Bay

2

79

North
Moor

Lowfield
Farm

Filey Golf Club

Moor
arm

The
Dams

SOUTH CLIFF

PH

1 BACK SEA VW
2 THE CLOSE
3 HAWTHORN WY

Hunmanby
Sands

1

78

VW

PH

LC

HIGHLANDS CL
PRIMROSE DR
PRIMROSE
VALLEY RD

LAKESIDE

Primrose
Valley

A 11 B 12 C 13 D 14 E 15 F

PIPER CL
EW DR
WOOD DR
WOOD AV
SALL CL
SETT AV
URN PL
EN PL

10 RIVELIN WY
11 FEWSTON CL
12 COLLINGHAM WY
13 WASHBURN CL
14 WHARNCLIFFE PL
15 WIDHOPE WY
16 EWDEN CL

B4
1 LARCH GR
2 WILLOW CL
3 CEDAR GR
4 GROVE HILL RD
5 HORNDALE RD
6 THORN TREE AV
7 ALMOND CL
8 ARNDALE WY
9 CHURCH CLIFF DR

10 ELM CL
11 ALMOND GR
12 ASH GR
13 ASH RD
14 GROVE RD
15 THE GARDENS
16 THE CROFT
17 RAVINE HL
18 CHURCH CL

Scale: 1¼ inches to 1 mile
0   ¼   ½ mile
0 250m 500m 750m 1

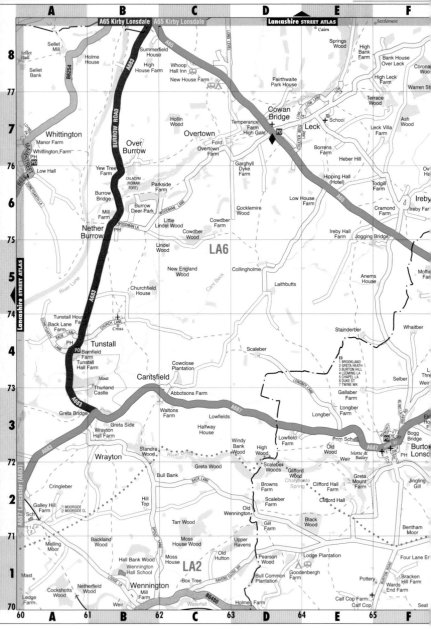

A65 Kirby Lonsdale   A65 Kirby Lonsdale

Sellet Hall
Sellet Mill
Holme House
Summerfield House
Whoop Hall Inn
High House Farm
New House Farm
Springs Wood
Cairn
Settlement
High Bank Farm
Bank House Over Leck
Corona Woo
Sellet Bank
High Leck Farm
Warren St

Whittington
Manor Farm
Whittington Farm
Low Hall
PH
PO
Over Burrow
Hollin Wood
Overtown
Temperance Farm High Gale
Cowan Bridge
Leck
School
PO
Terrace Wood
Ash Wood
Borrens Farm
Leck Villa Farm
Heber Hill

Yew Tree Farm
Burrow Bridge
CALADVM (ROMAN FORT)
Parkside Farm
Ford
Overtown Farm
Garghyll Dyke Farm
Fairthwaite Park House
Hipping Hall (Hotel)
Todgill Farm
Ireby
Ov Ha
Ireby Far

Mill Farm
Burrow Deer Park
WOODMAN LANE
Little Lindel Wood
Cowber Farm
Cockwberr Wood
Cocklemire Wood
Low House Farm
Cramond Farm

Nether Burrow
PH
WOODMAN LA
Cowdber Wood
Lindel Wood
Ireby Hall Farm
Jogging Bridge

New England Wood
LA6
Collingholme
Laithbutts
Anems House
Moffie Far

River Lune
Churchfield House
Carr Back
Stainderber
Whaitber

Tunstall House Farm
Back Lane Cross
CHURCH LANE
BACK LANE
PH
Tunstall
PO
Barnfield Farm
Tunstall Hall Farm
Moat
Thurland Castle
Cowclose Plantation
Cantsfield
Abbotsons Farm
Scaleber
E3
1 BROOKLAND
2 GRETA HEATH
3 BURTON HILL
4 LEEMING LA
5 CHAPEL LA
6 DUKE ST
7 TWINE WK
Selber
L
Thre
Weir

Greta Bridge
Greta Side
Wrayton Hall Farm
Waltons Farm
Lowfields
Halfway House
A687
Longber
Gallaber Farm
Longber Farm
Bogg Bridge
PH
Burto
Lonso

A683
Wrayton
Standra Wood
River Greta
Greta Wood
Windy Bank Wood
High Wood
Lowfield Farm
Old Wood
Prim Sch
Motte & Bailey
Weir
Greta Mount Farm
Jingling Gill

Cringleber
Galley Hill Farm
Sch
1 MOORSIDE
2 MOORSIDE CL
Bull Bank
BACK LANE
Hill Top
Scalebee Woods
Browns Farm
Clifford Wood
Chalybeate Spring
Scaleber Farm
Clifford Hall Farm
Clifford Hall
Black Wood

Melling Moor
Mast
Backland Wood
Tarr Wood
Moss House Wood
Moss House
LA2
Old Wennington
Upper Ravens
Gill Farm
Pearson Wood
Old Hutton
Box Tree
Bull Common Plantation
Lodge Plantation
Goodenbergh
Bentham Moor
Four Lane Er
Wards End Farm
Bracken Hill Farm
Pottery

Ledge Farm
Cockshotts Wood
Netherfield Wood
Wennington Hall School
Wennington Mill Farm
Weir
B6480
Waterfall
RAVENS GORE RD
Holmes Farm
Calf Cop Farm
Calf Cop
Seat

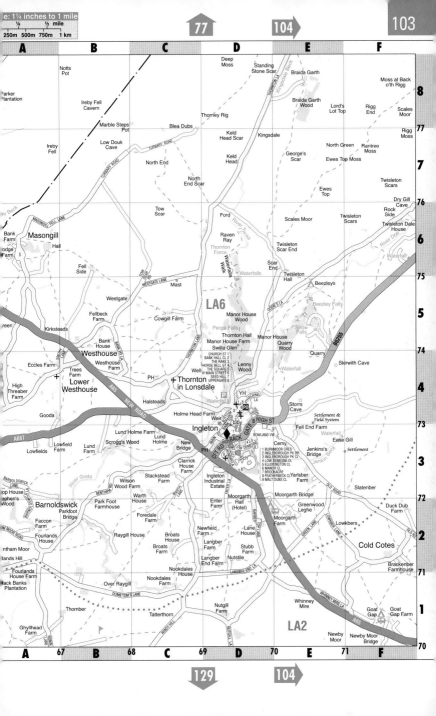

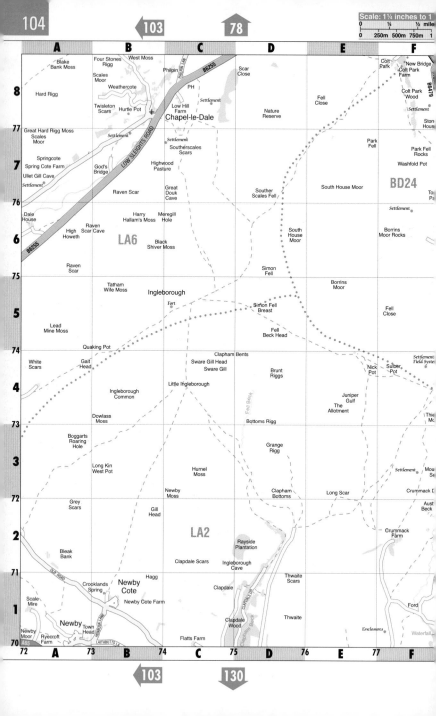

103
78

Scale: 1¼ inches to 1 mile

0   ¼   ½ mile

0 250m 500m 750m 1

A · **B** · **C** · **D** · **E** · **F**

Blake Bank Moss
Four Stones Rigg
West Moss
Philpin
B6255
Scar Close
Colt Park
New Bridge
Colt Park Farm
B6479

8
Hard Rigg
Scales Moor
Weathercote
PH
Fell Close
Colt Park Wood
Settlement
Ston Hous

Twisleton Scars
Hurtle Pot
Low Hill Farm
Chapel-le-Dale
Nature Reserve

77
Great Hard Rigg Moss
Scales Moor
Settlement
Southerscales Scars
Park Fell
Park Fell Rocks
Washfold Pot

Springcote
Spring Cote Farm
Ullet Gill Cave
Settlement
God's Bridge
Highwood Pasture
Souther Scales Fell
South House Moor
BD24

7

76
Raven Scar
Great Douk Cave
To Pe

Dale House
Harry Hallam's Moss
Meregill Hole
South House Moor
Settlement
Borrins Moor Rocks

6
High Howeth
Raven Scar Cave
LA6
Black Shiver Moss

Raven Scar
Simon Fell

75
Tatham Wife Moss
Ingleborough
Fort
Simon Fell Breast
Borrins Moor
Fell Close

5
Lead Mine Moss
Fell Beck Head

74
Quaking Pot
Gait Head
Clapham Bents
Sware Gill Head
Sware Gill
Nick Pot
Sulber Pot
Settlement
Field Syste

White Scars
Little Ingleborough
Brunt Riggs

4
Ingleborough Common
Juniper Gulf
The Allotment
Thie Mc

Dowlass Moss
Bottoms Rigg

73
Boggarts Roaring Hole
Fell Beck

3
Long Kin West Pot
Hurnel Moss
Grange Rigg
Settlement
Mou Se

Newby Moss
Clapham Bottoms
Long Scar
Crummack D

72
Grey Scars
Gill Head
Aust Beck

2
Bleak Bank
LA2
Rayside Plantation
Ingleborough Cave
Crummack Farm

Clapdale Scars

71
Hagg
Clapdale
Thwaite Scars

Crooklands Spring
Newby Cote
Newby Cote Farm
Clapdale Wood
Thwaite
Ford

1
Scale Mire
Clapham Beck

Newby
Town Head
Waterfall

70
Newby Moor
Ryecroft Farm
Flatts Farm
Enclosures

A86
OLD ROAD
LAITHBUTTS LA

72 **A** · **73** **B** · **74** **C** · **75** **D** · **76** **E** · **77** **F**

103
130

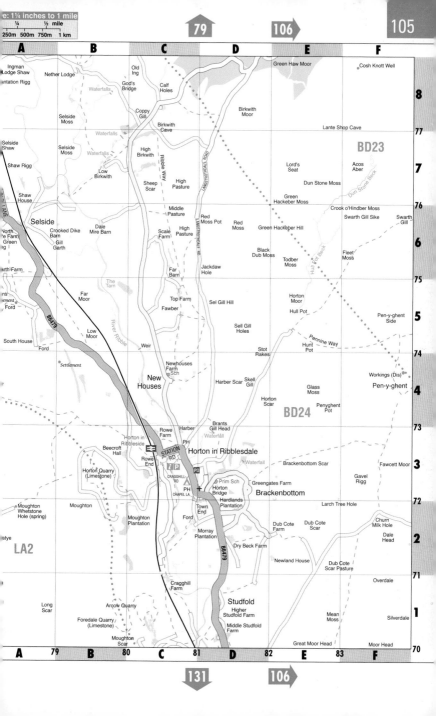

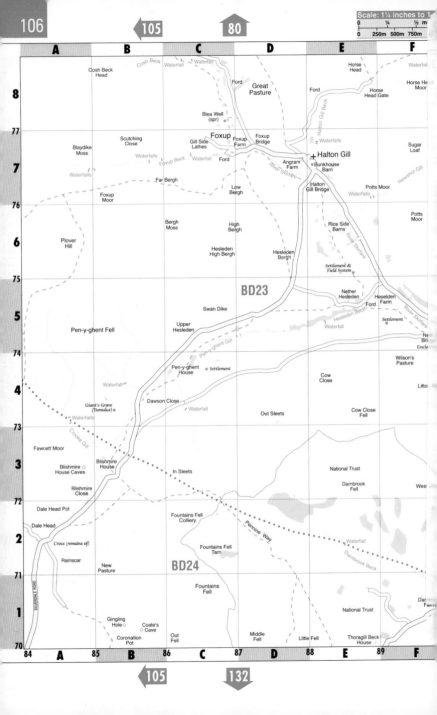

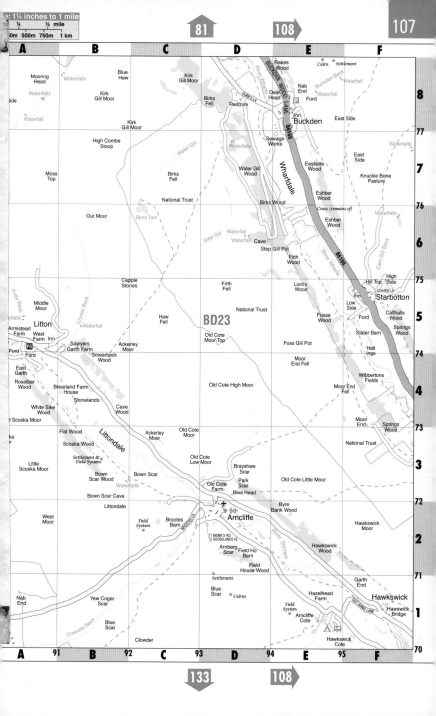

Scale: 1¼ inches to 1 mile

¼   ½ mile
250m 500m 750m 1 km

A   B   C   D   E   F

8

Mooring
Head

Waterfalls

Blue
Haw

Kirk
Gill Moor

Kirk
Gill Moor

Waterfalls

Kirk
Gill Moor

Waterfall

Birks
Fell

Redmire

DUBBS LA

BUCKDEN WOOD LANE

River Wharfe

Rakes
Wood

Cairn

Settlement

Nab
End

Buckden Beck

Waterfall

Dale
Head

Ford

East Side

77

Inn

Buckden

B6160

High Combe
Stoop

Kirk
Gill Moor

Water Gill

Birks
Fell

Birks
Fell

Waterfalls

Water Gill
Wood

Sewage
Works

Eastside
Wood

East
Side

7

Moss
Top

National Trust

Birks Wood

Wharfdale

Eshber
Wood

Knuckle Bone
Pasture

Out Moor

Birks Tarn

Waterfalls

Cross (remains of)

Eshber
Wood

76

Step Gill

Waterfall

Waterfall

Cave

Step Gill Pot

Firth
Wood

River Wharfe

B6160

Cam Gill Beck

Waterfalls

6

Potts Beck

Capple
Stones

Crystal Beck

Firth
Fell

Lord's
Wood

Hill Top

High
Side

75

Waterfalls

Middle
Moor

Litton

Waterfall

Haw
Fell

National Trust

Fosse
Wood

COATES LA

Starbotton

Inn

Low
Side

Ford

Calfhalls
Wood

5

Armistead
Farm

West
Farm

Inn

Sawyers
Garth Farm

Ackerley
Moor

Old Cote
Moor Top

Foss Gill Pot

Springs
Wood

Slater Barn

BD23

PO

Ford

Ford

Smearbeck
Wood

Moor
End Fell

Hall
Ings

74

East
Garth

Roselber
Wood

Brearland Farm
House

Stonelands

Cave
Wood

Old Cote High Moor

Moor End
Fell

Wibbertons
Fields

4

White Sike
Wood

West Scoska Moor

Littondale

Flat Wood

Ackerley
Moor

Old Cote
Moor

Moor
End

Springs
Wood

73

Scoska Wood

Little
Scoska Moor

Settlement &
Field System

Bown
Scar Wood

Bown Scar

Old Cote
Low Moor

Brayshaw
Scar

National Trust

3

Little
Scoska Moor

Waterfalls

Park
Scar

Blea Head

Old Cote Little Moor

Bown Scar Cave

Littondale

Old Cote
Farm

Byre
Bank Wood

72

West
Moor

Field
System

Brootes
Barn

BROTES LA

Sch

Arncliffe

River Skirfare

Hawkswick
Moor

2

1 MONK'S RD
2 GOOSELANDS HL

Arnberg
Scar

Field Ho
Barn

Hawkswick
Wood

Field
House Wood

71

Nab
End

Yew Cogar
Scar

Settlement

Blue
Scar

Cairns

Field
System

Arncliffe
Cote

Hazelhead
Farm

OUT GANG LANE

Garth
End

Hawkswick

Hawswick
Bridge

1

Blue
Scar

Cowside Beck

Clowder

Hawkswick
Cote

70

A   B   C   D   E   F

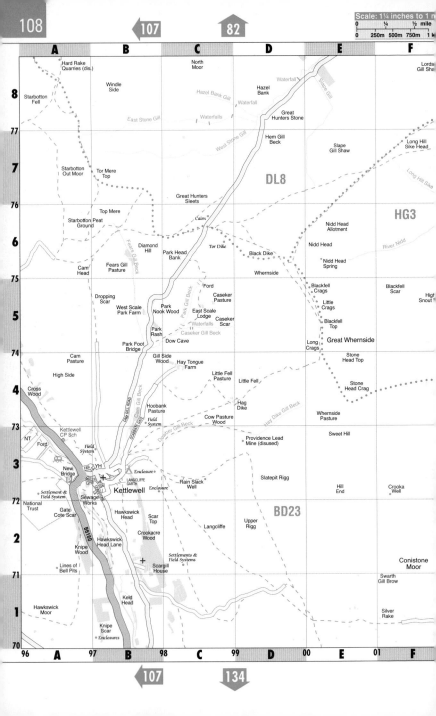

A B C D E F

L8

8

Little Whernside

Lodge Pasture

How Gill

Edge Tops

Carle Fell Side

Raydale Knotts

High Pasture

Carle Side

High Woodale

Scar Plantation

Weirs

77

Angram Pasture

Scar House Reservoir

Woodale Scar

Weir

Tower

Angram Reservoir

Haden Carr Pasture

Woodale Moss

7

Angram Low Pasture

Brown Hill

Scar House Pasture

IN MOOR LANE

Weir

Side Allotment

Scar House Moss

76

Weir

Wising Gill Crags

Kay Head Allotment

Stone Beck

Waterfall

Maiden Gill Allotment

Cocklake

Moor Allotments

6

Clack Gill Beck

75

Lodge Moor

Nab End

Waterfall

Maiden Gill Crags

Key Head

Armathwaite

Low Riggs

Red Scar

East Gill Dike

HG3

High Riggs

5

Aygill Beck

West Gill Dike

Low West Moor

West End Lathe

74

Aygill Pike

Far Pasture

West End

Hard Gap

Riggs Moor

Staining Gill Beck

Sandy Sikes Gill

Riggs Moor

How Stean Beck

Wising Gill

4

73

Blake Hill

High West Moor

Staining Gill Intake

Flaystones

Whey Crags

BD23

Great Blowing Gill Beck

Stott Crags

3

High West Moor

Stock Ridge

Black Hill Drive

Waterfall

Waterfall

72

Mossdale Beck

Straight Stean Beck

White Stean Well

Great Scar

Stock Ridge Bottom

Stone Butts Drive

Sandy Gate

Waterfall

Red Scars

Acoras Scar

Oliver Scar

Blackstean Gill

Green Grooves Gill

Stean Moor

West Gill

Peat Moor Butts (Grouse)

2

Friar Hood Gill

Peat Moor Drive

71

Meugher

Great Stangate

Moss Drive

1

dale

70

A 03 B 04 C 05 D 06 E 07 F

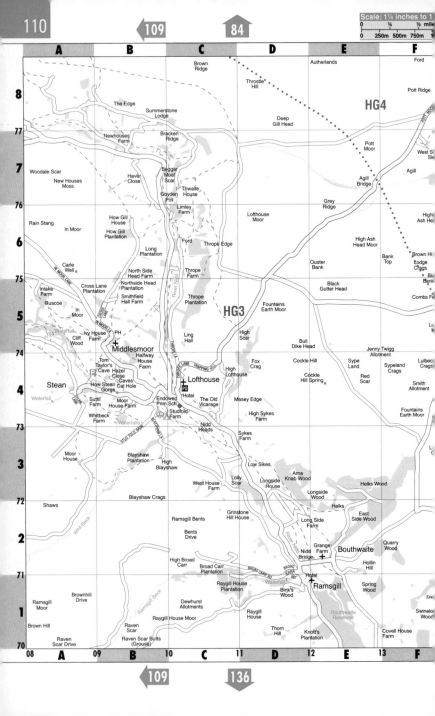

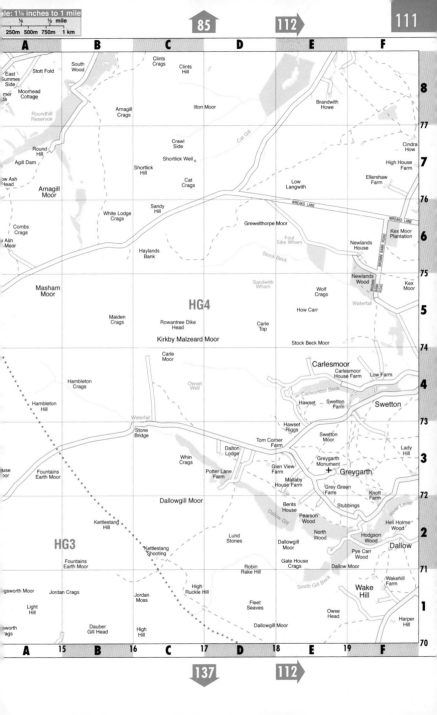

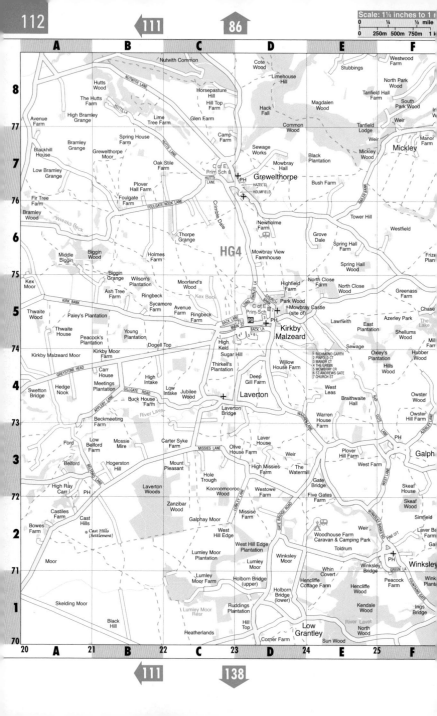

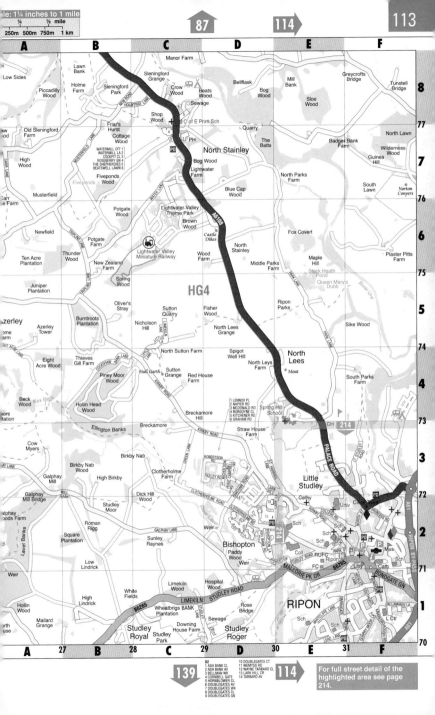

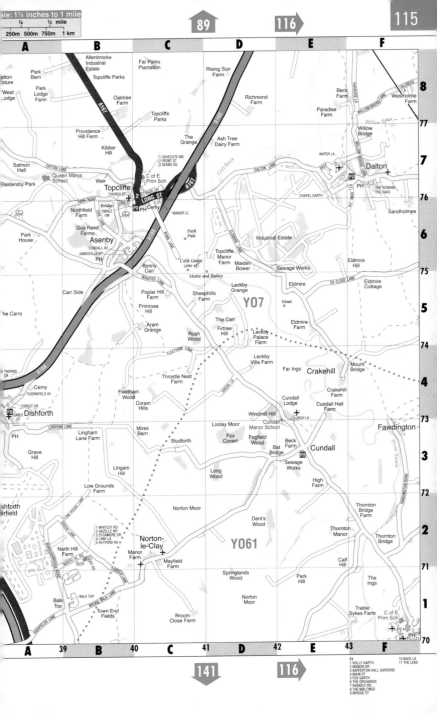

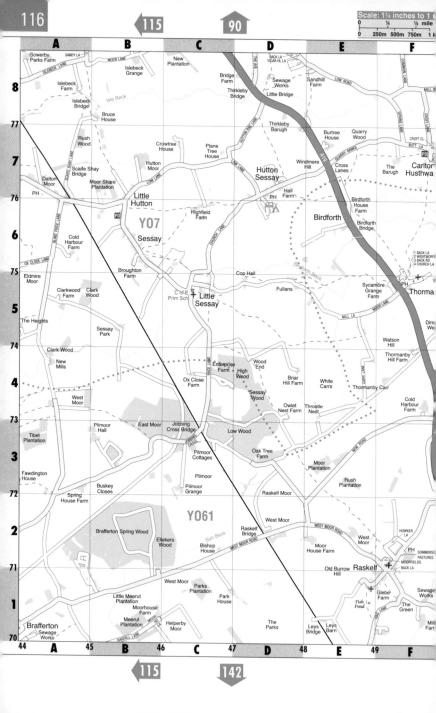

115
90

Scale: 1¼ inches to 1 mile

0   ¼   ½ mile
0   250m 500m 750m 1 k

A **B** **C** **D** **E** **F**

Sowerby Parks Farm
SANDY LA
MOOR LANE
ISLEBECK LANE
New Plantation
BACK LA
VICAR HL LA
COMMON LANE
MILL

Islebeck Farm
Islebeck Grange
Bridge Farm
Thirkleby Bridge
Sewage Works
Sandhill Farm
LOW ROAD
SPRING RD
CROFT CL

8

Islebeck Bridge
Isle Beck
Little Bridge
Thirkleby Barugh
Burtree House
Quarry Wood
CROFT CL
BUTT RD

Bruce House

77

Rush Wood
Crowtree House
Plane Tree House
Windmere Hill
Cross Lanes
The Barugh
Carlton Husthwa

7

Scaife Shay Bridge
SCAIFE SHAY LANE
LOW LANE
Hutton Moor
LOW ROAD
Hutton Sessay
QUARRY BANKS
Birdforth House Farm

Dalton Moor
PH
Moor Share Plantation
Hall Farm
PH
Birdforth
Birdforth Bridge

76

BLIND PIECE LANE
Little Hutton
PO
Highfield Farm
1 BACK LA
2 WENTWORT
3 BACK RD
4 CHURCH LA

6

Cold Harbour Farm
Y07
Sessay
CHURCH LANE
PH
Thorma

OX CLOSE LANE

75

Eldmire Moor
Broughton Farm
C of E Prim Sch
Cop Hall
Birdforth Beck
Sycamore Grange Farm
PH

Clarkwood Farm
Clark Wood
+ Little Sessay
Fullans
MILL LA
MOOR LANE

The Heights

5

Sessay Park
Dim We

74

Clark Wood
Enterprise Farm
Wood End
Watson Hill
Thormanby Hill Farm

New Mills
RACE LANE
High Wood
Briar Hill Farm
White Carrs
Thormanby Carr

4

West Moor
Ox Close Farm
Sessay Wood
CARR LANE
Cold Harbour Farm

73

Tibet Plantation
Pilmoor Hall
East Moor
Jobbing Cross Bridge
Low Wood
Owlet Nest Farm
Throstle Nest

3

Fawdington House
Pilmoor Cottages
Oak Tree Farm
Moor Plantation
NEW ROAD

Buskey Closes
Spring House Farm
Pilmoor
Rush Plantation

72

Pilmoor Grange
Raskelf Moor

Y61
Brafferton Spring Wood
Ellekers Wood
Sun Beck
Raskelf Bridge
West Moor
WEST MOOR ROAD
West Moor
HOWKER LA

2

Bishop House
WEST MOOR ROAD
Moor House Farm
PH
SOMMERS
PASTURES
MOORFIELDS
BACK LA

71

West Moor
Parks Plantation
Old Burrow Hill
Raskelf

1

Little Meerut Plantation
Moorhouse Farm
Park House
Glebe Farm
Sewage Works

Meerut Plantation
Helperby Moor
Fish Pond
The Green

Brafferton
Sewage Works
The Parks
Leys Bridge
Leys Barn
Mill Far

70

A 44 **B** 45 **C** 46 **D** 47 **E** 48 **F** 49

RAGHILL LANE

115
142

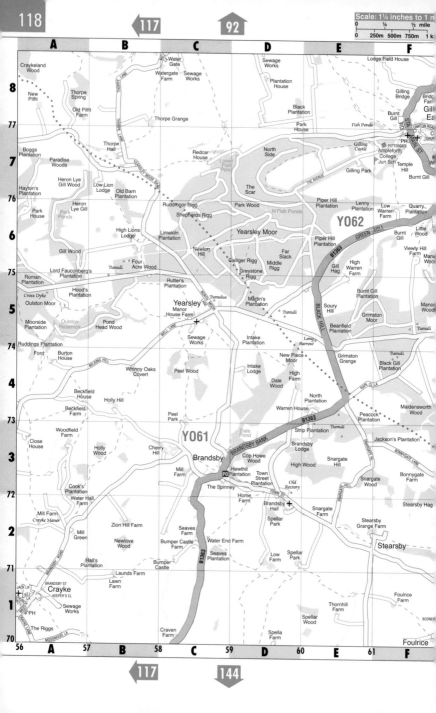

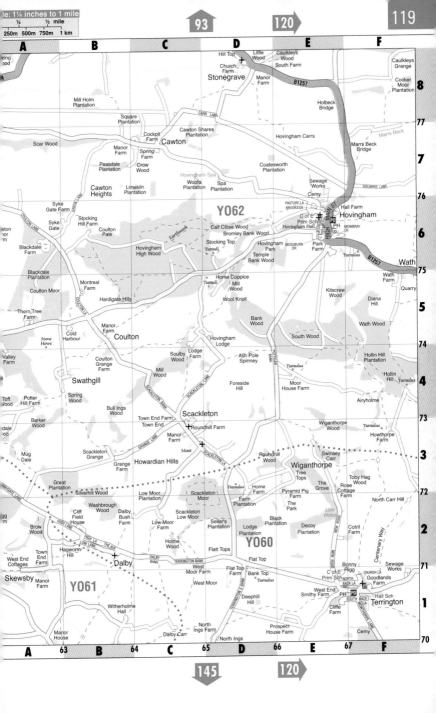

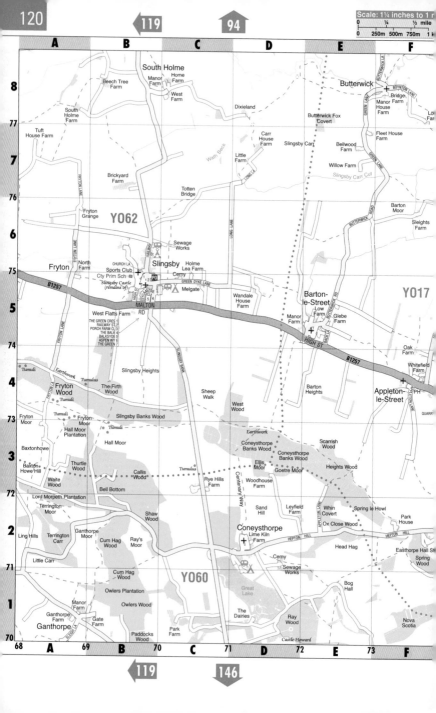

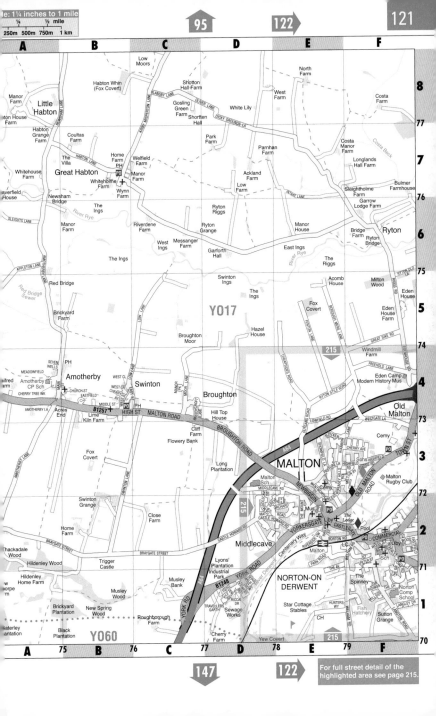

Scale: 1¼ inches to 1 m

0   ¼   ½ mile
0   250m 500m 750m   1 k

8

Low Bellafax Grange

White House Farm

The Riggs

Holme Farm

The Firs

High Carr

Redcarr Plantatio

Golden Square

Sheepfoot Grange

Riggs Barn

The Howles

Low Marishes

Wath Farm

High Carr Plantation

77

Middle Farm

MARISHES LOW ROAD

Marishes

Low Moor Farm

Middle Farm

Middle Plantation

7

Grove House Farm

Howe Bridge Farm

Rillington Low Moor

Elm Farm

Sleights Farm

SOUTHING ROAD

North Ings

Newstead Farm

BACK

Howe Bridge

Abbey Farm

Lambert's Plantation

LOW MOOR'S LA

76

Abbotts Farm

Ryton Ings

West Wykeham Ings

South Ings

Lilac Farm

LC

Americ Plantati

A169

Castle Ings

Rye Mouth

Breckney Farm

The Breckneys

Ivy Lea Farm

LC

6

Howe Farm

Wykeham

Wykeham Farm

East Wykeham Ings

Fox Covert

Manor Farm

The Howes

BRECKNEY LA

LC

Edge Plantation

Old Malton Moor

HOWE ROAD

Willow Farm

LONG MOOR LANE

75

Edenhouse Plantation

WYKEHAM ROAD

West Moor

Hawk Plantation

Villa Farm

LC

Sewage Works

Park Farm

Rillington Manor

Rillington

Long Ings

The Carrs

MANOR VW 1
SLEDGATE GARTH 2
SOUTHLEA 3
MEADOW CT 4
SAXON DR 5
WOODLANDS AV 6
WOODLANDS GR 7

PH

SCARBOROUGH

DELGATE

Old Malton Moor

Black Wood

Espersykes

Ruston Plantation

Church Farm

PO

LONG PINE

CP School

Cemy

Outgar Plantati

74

215

RABBIT LANE

Scagglethorpe Ings

LC

SCAGGLETHORPE LANE

Moor Farm

Scagglethorpe Grange

West Field

MALTON ROAD A64 WESTGA

COLLINGERS LA

Church Farm

4

EDENHOUSE RD

WISE HOUSE LANE

Wyse House

Rixt Woods

Settrington Ings

Scagglethorpe Moor

Marr House

Acuba Farm

Five Beeches

Laurel Farm

Bassett House

A84

Barr Farm

A64

Marr Whin

Willow Farm

Under Brow Farm

Thorpe Bassett Wold

Spring Farm

73

LASCELLES LANE

Abbey Ings

Fish Ponds

Villa Farm

Norton Parks

Beck House

Manor Farm

PH

Scagglethorpe Brow

Thorpe Bassett Wold

3

Quarry Farm

SCARBOROUGH ROAD

Scagglethorpe Bridge

Brambling Fields

Beech Tree Farm

Brow Farm

SOUTHFIELD

Scagglethorpe

Brow Farm

72

B1248

215

Priorpot Bridge

Norton Grove Stud

Whinflower Hall

BELL PIECE LA

HIGHFIELD

Ebor House

Thorpe Bassett Wold

2

Norton Grove Industrial Estate

The Moor

The Holms

SEWERS LANE

BEAGONS LANE

HIGHFIELD LA

Crosscliffe Farm

Many Thorns Farm

Settrington Beck

MIDDLETON CL

Settrington Cliffs

THORPE BASSETT LANE

71

RYEDALE CL

Centenary Way

Elm Tree Farm

COOK GARTH

MOOR LA

TOWN ST

CHAPEL RD

C of E Prim School

Cinquefoil Hill

Shepherdess Plantation

Town Wold

HIGH STF

Wol House

1

B1248

BEVERLEY ROAD

Westfield Farm

Settrington Plantation

Town Green Farm

SCARLET BALK LANE

BACK LANE

Cemy

Settrington

Cemy

HOWE CLIFFE LANE

Wardale

70

215

Gallops

Scarlet Balk Plantation

LANGTON LA

Rectory Farm

Settrington House

Y017

For full street detail of the highlighted area see page 215.

A   81   B   82   C   83   D   84   E   85   F

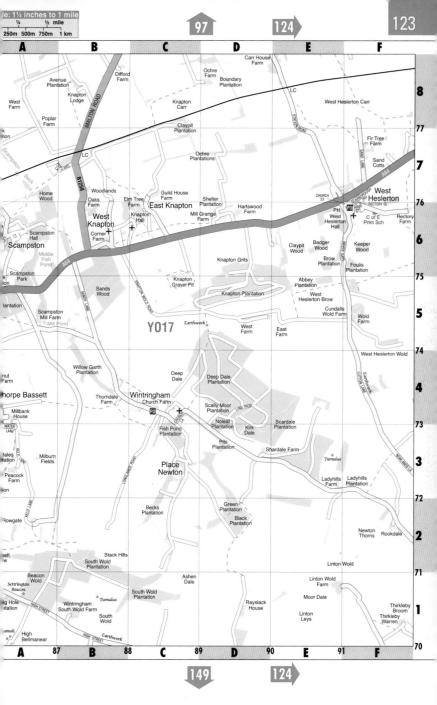

A   B   C   D   E   F

Avenue Plantation
West Farm
Poplar Farm
Knapton Lodge
Difford Farm
Ochre Farm
Boundary Plantation
Carr House Farm
Knapton Carr
Claypit Plantation
West Heslerton Carr

8

77

LC
MALTON ROAD
B1258
LC

Ochre Plantations
Fir Tree Farm
Sand Cotts

7

A64
SAND LANE

Home Wood
Woodlands
Oaks Farm
Elm Tree Farm
Guild House Farm
Shelter Plantation
Hartswood Farm
CHURCH ST
West Heslerton

76

West Knapton
East Knapton
Knapton Hall
Mill Grange Farm
PH
West Heslerton Hall
PO HIGH
C of E Prim Sch
Rectory Farm
RECTORY DL

Scampston Hall
Corner Farm
Claypit Wood
Badger Wood
Brow Plantation
Keeper Wood
Foulis Plantation

6

Scampston
Middle Fish Pond
Knapton Grits

Scampston Park
Knapton Gravel-Pit
Abbey Plantation
West Heslerton Brow

75

lantation
Sands Wood
Knapton Plantation
Cundalls Wold Farm
Wold Farm

5

YO17
Earthwork
West Farm
East Farm
West Heslerton Wold

74

Willow Garth Plantation
Deep Dale
Deep Dale Plantation
LUTTON LANE
Earthwork

4

horpe Bassett
Thorndale Farm
Wintringham
Church Farm
PO
Scally Moor Plantation
LING TROD

73

Millbank House
WATER LANE
Fish Pond Plantation
Noleat Plantation
Kirk Dale
Scardale Plantation
BERGATE CLA

Milburn Fields
Pits Plantation
Shardale Farm
Tumulus

3

KELD LANE
dales ation
Peacock Farm
LONGLANDS ROAD
Place Newton
CHURCH
Ladyhills Farm
Ladyhills Plantation

72

Rowgate
Becks Plantation
Green Plantation
Black Plantation
Newton Thorns
Rookdale

2

Stack Hills
South Wold Plantation
Ashen Dale
Linton Wold

71

sett w
Beacon Wold
Settrington Beacon
Tumulus
South Wold Plantation
Rayslack House
Linton Wold Farm
Moor Dale
Thirkleby Broom

1

g Hole lation
HIGH STREET
Wintringham South Wold Farm
South Wold
Linton Leys
Thirkleby Warren

umuli
High Bellmanear
HIGH STREET
Earthwork

70

A   87   B   88   C   89   D   90   E   91   F

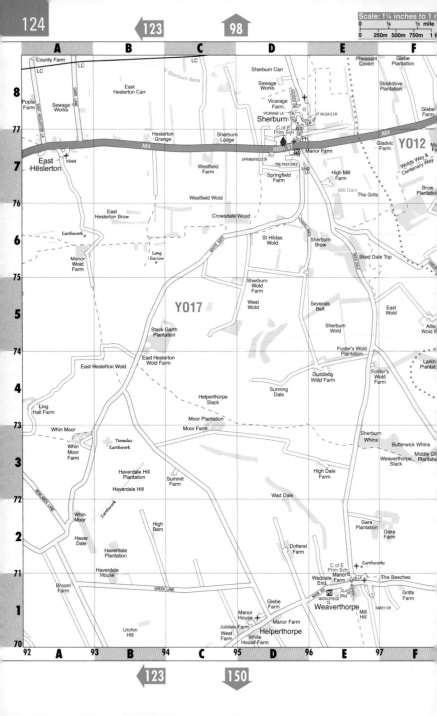

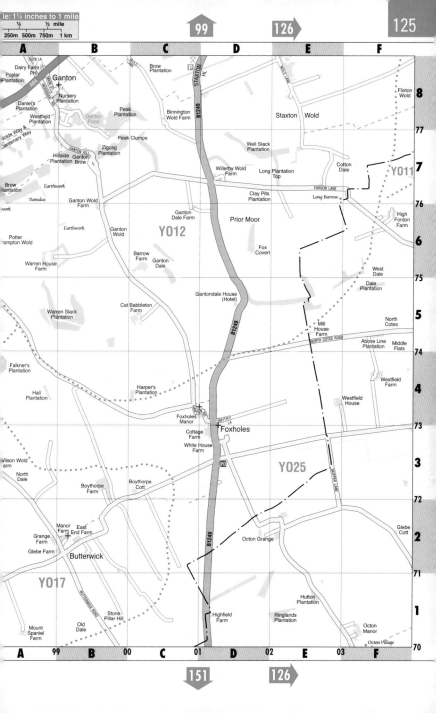

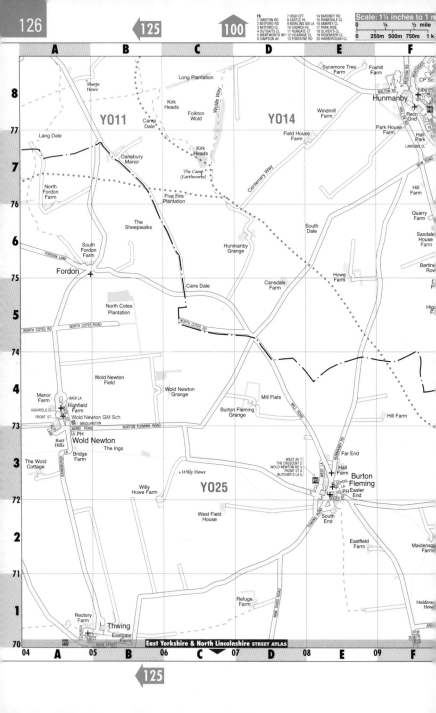

126

125

100

1 OWSTON RD
2 MITFORD RD
3 MITFORD CL
4 OUTGAITS CL
5 WENTWORTH WY
6 SIMPSON AV

7 HIGH CFT
8 CASTLE HL
9 BOWLING GN LA
10 CHURCH HL
11 HUNGATE CT
12 VICARAGE CL
13 FONTAYNE RD

14 BARDNEY RD
15 ROWEDALE CL
16 AMBREY CL
17 PARK RISE
18 OLIVER'S CL
19 ROSEMOOR CL
20 HARBOROUGH CL

Scale: 1¼ inches to 1 m

0   ¼   ½ mile
0   250m 500m 750m 1 k

Sycamore Tree Farm
Foxhill Farm
CP Sc
Liby STO
MALTON RD
Hunmanby
PO
Recn Gnd

Long Plantation

Sharpe Howe

Kirk Heads
Folkton Wold

Wolds Way

Y014

Windmill Farm

Park House Farm

Hall Park

LAWSONS CL

Y011

Camp Dale

Lang Dale

Kirk Heads

Field House Farm

Hill Farm

North Fordon Farm

Danebury Manor

The Camp (Earthworks)

Centenary Way

Quarry Farm

Saxdale House Farm

Five Firs Plantation

Bartine Row

The Sheepwalks

Hunmanby Grange

South Dale

South Fordon Farm

FORDON LANE

Fordon

Cans Dale

Cansdale Farm

Howe Farm

Hig F

D F

North Cotes Plantation

NORTH COTES RD

NORTH COTES ROAD

NORTH COTES RD

Wold Newton Field

Wold Newton Grange

Mill Flats

WEST ROAD

Hill Farm

Manor Farm

BACK LA

Highfield Farm

HIGHFIELD CL

FRONT ST

Wold Newton GM Sch

BRIDLINGTON

LAKING ROAD

BURTON FLEMING ROAD

Burton Fleming Grange

Far End

Butt Hills

Wold Newton

LA PH

The Ings

WEST LA

Hall Farm

SCHOOL LA

Burton Fleming

The Wold Cottage

Bridge Farm

WEST AV 1
THE CRESCENT 2
WOLD NEWTON RD 3
FRONT ST 4
BUTCHER S LA 5

PO

Easter End

SCARBOROUGH LA

Willy Howe Farm

Willy Howe

Y025

SOUTH ST

South End

NINE DIKES ROAD

THWING ROAD

West Field House

Eastfield Farm

Maidens Farm

HUNMANBY ROAD

Refuge Farm

Maidens Howe

Rectory Farm

Thwing

Eastgate Farm

CHURCH LA

MAIN STREET

PO

A8
1 WRANGHAM DR
2 LENNOX CL
3 BURLYN RD
4 CHERRY RD
5 HAWKE GARTH
6 MANOR GD
7 CECIL RD
8 HOWES RD
9 WATSON CL
10 HAMERTON RD
11 HAMERTON CL
12 GRIMSTON RD
13 STRICKLAND RD
14 PERCY RD
15 HAVERCROFT RD
16 COWLINGS CL

101

East Yorkshire & North Lincolnshire STREET ATLAS

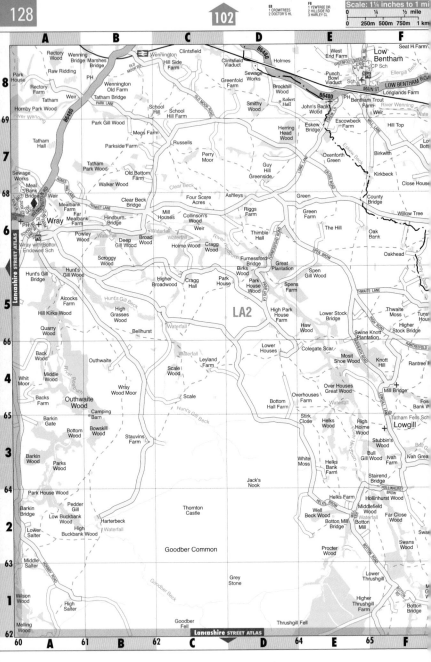

Rectory Wood
Wenning Marshes
Wennington Bridge
Wennington
Clintsfield
Clintsfield Viaduct
Holmes
Punch Bowl Viaduct
West End Farm
Low Bentham
Seat H. Farm
Greenfoothole
CP Sch
Ellergill Fm
LOW BENTHAM ROAD
Raw Ridding
PH
Wennington Old Farm
Hill Side Farm
Greenfold Farm
Sewage Works
Brockhill Wood
B6480
Bentham Trout Farm
Longlands Farm
River Wenning
Wate
Park House
Rectory Farm
Tatham
Weir
Tatham Bridge
PARK LANE
School Hill
School Hill Farm
Smithy Wood
Robert Hall
John's Bank Wood
PH
Weir
Hill Top

8

Hornby Park Wood
River Wenning
B6480
Park Gill Wood
Megs Farm
Russells
Herring Head Wood
Eskew Bridge
Escowbeck Farm
Eskew Beck

69

Tatham Hall
Parkside Farm
Perry Moor
Guy Hill Greenside
Oxenforth Green
Green
Birkwith
Kirkbeck
Lo
Bott
Close House

7

Sewage Works
Meal Bank Bridge
Weir
Tatham Park Wood
Old Bottom Farm
Clear Beck
Ashleys
Green
Green Farm
County Bridge
Willow Tree

68

PH
Wray
Mealbank Farm
Far Mealbank Farm
HINKLET LANE
Clear Beck Bridge
Hindburn Bridge
Mill Houses
Collinson's Wood
Four Scare Acres
Riggs Farm
Weir
Thimble Wood
The Hill
Oak Bank
Oakhead

6

Wray with Botton Endowed Sch
Powley Wood
Waterfall
Deep Gill Wood
Broad Wood
Holme Wood
Cragg Wood
Furnessford Bridge
Birks Wood
Great Plantation
Spen Gill Wood
OPEN ROAD

Scroggy Wood
Higher Broadwood
Cragg Hall
Park House
Park House Wood
Spens Farm
THWAITE LANE

Hunt's Gill Bridge
Hunt's Gill Wood
Hunt's Gill Beck
High Grasses Wood
LA2
High Park House Farm
Lower Stock Bridge
Thwaite Moss
Tuns Hous

5

Alcocks Farm
Hill Kirks Wood
Bellhurst
Haw Wood
Swine Knott Plantation
Higher Stock Bridge
HARTREFIELD

Quarry Wood
Waterfall
Lower Houses
Colegate Scar
Mosit Shoe Wood
Knott Hill
Rantree

66

Back Wood
Outhwaite
Scale Wood
Leyland Farm
Over Houses Great Wood
Mill Bridge
Fos

4

Whit Moor
Middle Wood
Wray Wood Moor
Scale
Overhouses Farm
Waterfall
High Holme Wood
Tatham Fells Sch
Bank W

Backs Farm
Outhwaite Wood
Camping Barn
Hunt's Gill Beck
Bottom Hall Farm
Stirk Close
Helks Wood
Lowgill

65

Barkin Gate
Bottom Wood
Bowskill Wood
Stauvins Farm
White Moss
Helks Bank Wood
Stubbin's Wood
Bull Gill Wood
Ivah Farm
Ivah Grea

3

Barkin Wood
Parks Wood
Jack's Nook
Stairend Bridge
HOLLINHURST BROW

64

Park House Wood
Pedder Gill
Thornton Castle
Helks Farm
Hollinhurst Wood
Far Close Wood

Barkin Bridge
Low Buckbank Wood
Harterbeck
Waterfall
Well Beck Wood
Middlefield Wood
Waterfall
Swa

2

Lower Salter
High Buckbank Wood
Botton Mill Bridge
Botton Mill
Swans Wood

Middle Salter
Goodber Common
Procter Wood

63

Wilson Wood
High Salter
Goodber Beck
Grey Stone
Lower Thrushgill
M
G
V

1

Melling Wood
Goodber Fell
Goodber Fell
Thrushgill Fell
Higher Thrushgill Farm
Botton Bridge

62

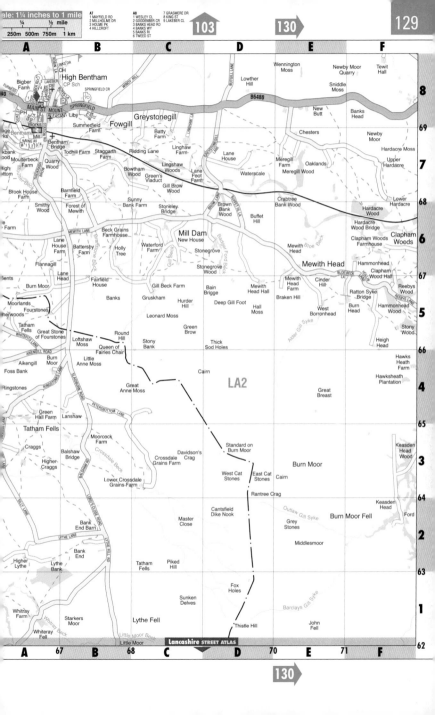

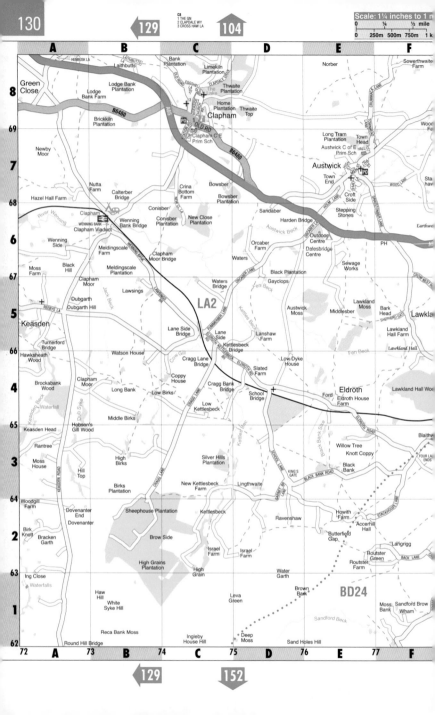

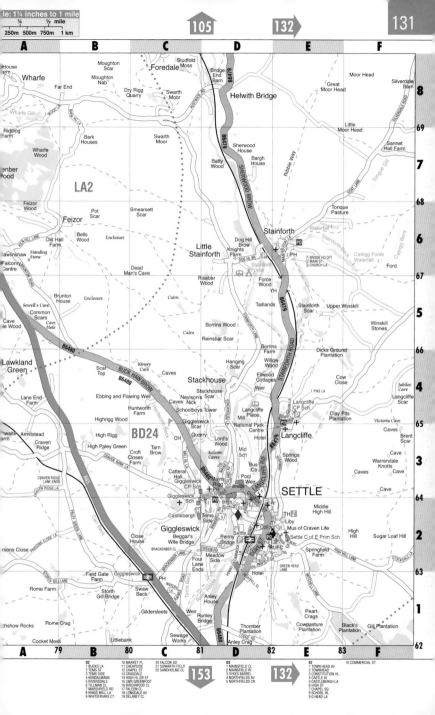

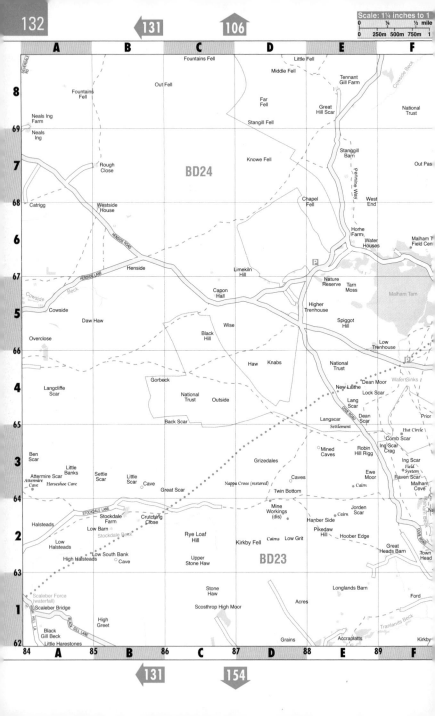

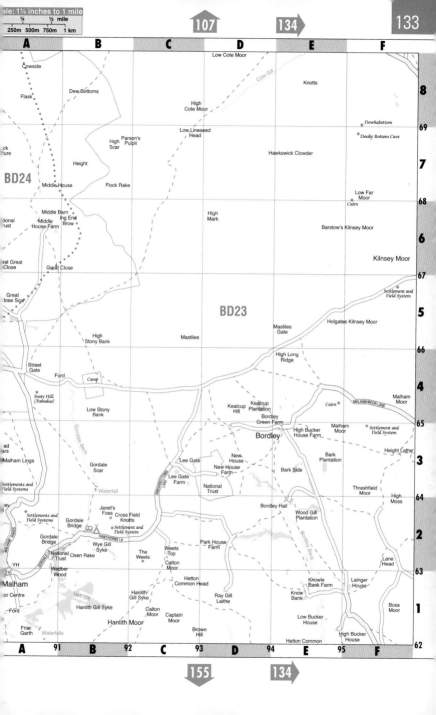

A   B   C   D   E   F

Low Cote Moor

Cowside
Cote Gill
Knotts
Flask

8

Dew Bottoms

High
Cote Moor

Low Lineseed
Head

Dowkabottom
69

Parson's
Pulpit
High
Scar

Douky Bottom Cave

ck
ture

Hawkswick Clowder

BD24

Height

7

Middle House

Flock Rake

Low Far
Moor
Cairn
68

ional
rust

Middle Barn
Ing End
Brow
Middle
House Farm

High
Mark

Barstow's Kilnsey Moor

6

st Great
Close

Kilnsey Moor

Great Close

67

Great
lose Scar

Settlement and
Field System

5

BD23

Holgates Kilnsey Moor

High
Stony Bank

Mastiles

Mastiles
Gate

66

High Long
Ridge

Street
Gate

Ford

Camp

4

Seaty Hill
(Tumulus)

Low Stony
Bank

Kealcup
Hill

Kealcup
Plantation

Cairn

MALHAM MOOR LANE

Malham
Moor

ad
ars

Bordley
Green Farm

Malham
Moor
65

Settlement and
Field System

Malham Lings

Gordale Back

Mastiles

High Bucker
House Farm

Bordley

Height Lathe

ttlements and
Field Systems

Lee Gate

New
House

Bark
Plantation

3

ey

Gordale Scar

Lee Gate
Farm

New House
Farm

Bark Side

Threshfield
Moor

High
Moss

Waterfall

National
Trust

64

Settlements and
Field Systems

Janet's
Foss

Cross Field
Knotts

Bordley Hall

Wood Gill
Plantation

2

Gordale
Bridge

Settlement and
Field System

HAWTHORNS LA

MALHAM LINGS

Gordale
Bridge

Wye Gill
Syke

Park House
Farm

Lane
Head

National
Trust

Oxen Rake

The
Weets

Weets
Top

Knowle
Bank Farm

Lainger
House

Boss
Moor

YH

Wedber
Wood

Calton
Moor

Know
Bank

1

Malham

or Centre

Hetton
Common Head

Low Bucker
House

Ford

Hanlith
Gill Syke

Ray Gill
Laithe

High Bucker
House

Friar
Garth

Hanlith Gill Syke

Calton
Moor

Captain
Moor

Hetton Common

62

Waterfalls

Hanlith Moor

Brown
Hill

Hell Gill

Bordley Beck

Scale: 1¼ inches to 1

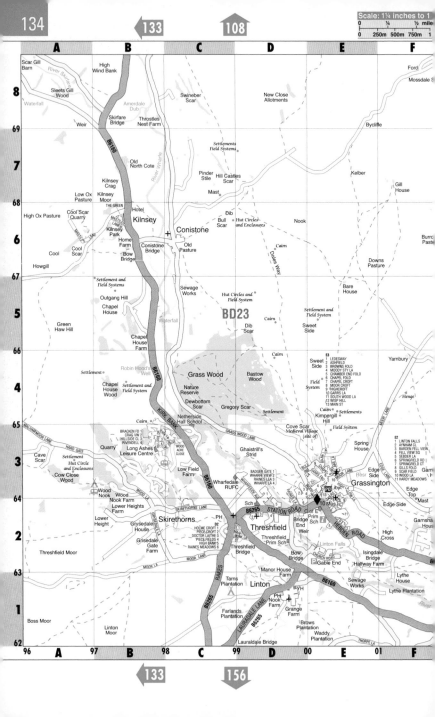

A   B   C   D   E   F

Scar Gill Barn
River Skirfare
High Wind Bank
Ford
Mossdale

Sleets Gill Wood
8
Swineber Scar
New Close Allotments

Waterfall
Amerdale Dub
Bycliffe

69
Skirfare Bridge
Throstles Nest Farm
Settlements Field Systems

Weir
Old North Cote
River Wharfe

7
Pinder Stile
Hill Castles Scar
Kelber

Kilnsey Crag
Mast
Gill House

Low Ox Pasture
Kilnsey Moor
THE GREEN
Hotel

68
High Ox Pasture
Cool Scar Quarry
Kilnsey Park
MASTILES
MASTILES LANE
Kilnsey
Conistone
Dib Bull Scar
Hut Circles and Enclosures
Nook
Burre Paste

6
Cool
Cool Scar
MASTILES LANE
Home Farm
Conistone Bridge
Old Pasture
Cairn
Downs Pasture

Howgill
Bow Bridge
Bare House

67
Settlement and Field Systems
Dales Way

5
Outgang Hill
Chapel House
Sewage Works
Hut Circles and Field System
Cairn
Settlement and Field System
Sweet Side

Green Haw Hill
BD23
Cairn

66
Chapel House Farm
Waterfall
Dib Scar
Cairn
Sweet Side
E3
1 LEDESWAY
2 ASHFIELD
3 BROWNS FOLD
4 MOODY STY LA
5 CHAMBER END FOLD
6 CHAPEL FOLD
7 MOOR CROFT
8 HIGHCROFT
9 GARRS LA
10 GARRS LA
11 SOUTH WOOD LA
12 WISP HILL
13 MAIN ST
Yarnbury

4
Chapel House Wood
Settlement and Field System
Grass Wood
Bastow Wood
Field System
Henge

Nature Reserve
Dewbottom Scar
Gregory Scar
Settlement
Cairn
Kimpergill Hill
Settlements
Field System

65
Cairns
Netherside Hall School
GRASS WOOD LANE
Cove Scar Medieval Village (site of)
Spring House
E2
1 LINTON FALLS
2 AYNHAM CL
3 BARDEN FELL VIEW
4 FELL VIEW SQ
5 SEEBER LA
6 SPRINGFIELD RD
7 SPRINGFIELD CT
8 GILLS FOLD
9 SCAR FIELD
10 WOOD LA
11 HARDY MEADOWS

3
Cave Scar
Settlement Hut Circle and Enclosures
BRACKEN FD 1
CRAG VW 2
HILLSIDE CL 3
RIVENDELL 4
Long Ashes Leisure Centre
WOOD ACRE CLOSE
Ghaistrill's Strid
Edge Side
Grassington
Edge Top
Mast

Cow Close Wood
Quarry
Low Field Farm
Wharfedale RUFC
BADGER GATE 1
WHARFE VIEW 2
RAINES LEA 3
WHARFE LA 4
Lib
Mus
Edge Side

64
Wood Nook
Nook Farm
Lower Heights Farm
WOOD LA
SKIRETHORNS LANE
Sch
B6265
STATION ROAD
Prim Sch
WEBB LA
HEBDEN ROAD

2
Lower Height
Grysedale House
Skirethorns
PH
Threshfield
D2
HOLME CROFT 1
PIECE CROFT 2
DOCTOR LAITHE 3
PIECE FIELDS 4
HIGH BANKS 5
RAINES MEADOWS 6
Threshfield Prim Sch
End
Prim Sch
Weir
High Cross
Garnsha House

Grisedale Gate Farm
MOOR LANE
Threshfield Bridge
Bow Bridge
Gable End
Isingdale Bridge
Halfway Farm
Lythe House

63
Threshfield Moor
RAKES
MOOR LA
Tarns Plantation
Manor House Farm
CHURCH ROAD
B6160
Sewage Works
Lythe Plantation

1
Boss Moor
Linton Moor
LAURADALE LANE
B6265
Linton
Farlands Plantation
PH
Nook Farm
Grange Farm
YH
Brows Plantation
Waddy Plantation
River
THORPE LA

62
Lauradale Bridge

96   A   97   B   98   C   99   D   00   E   01   F

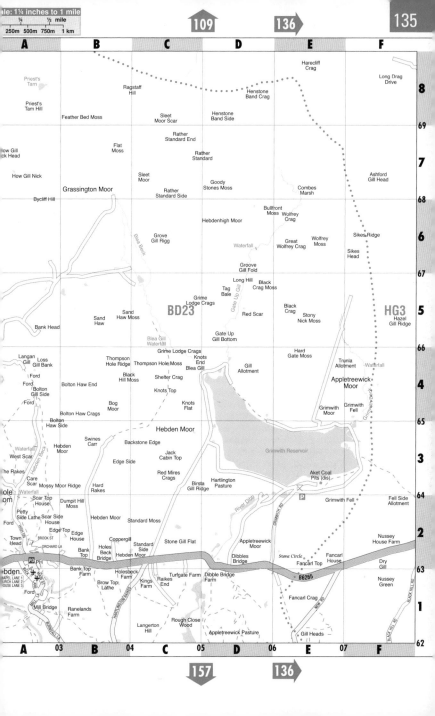

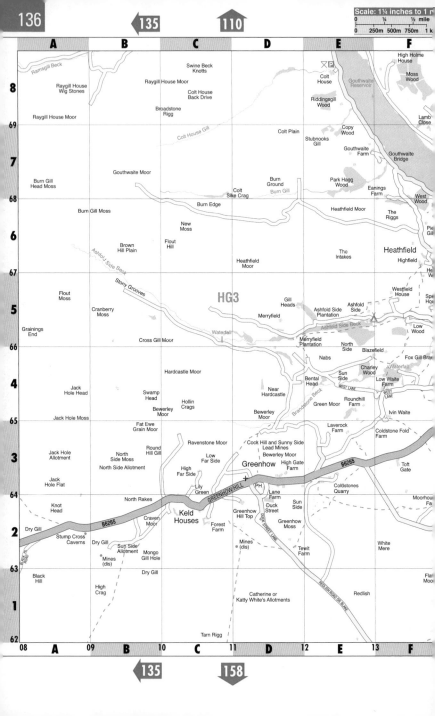

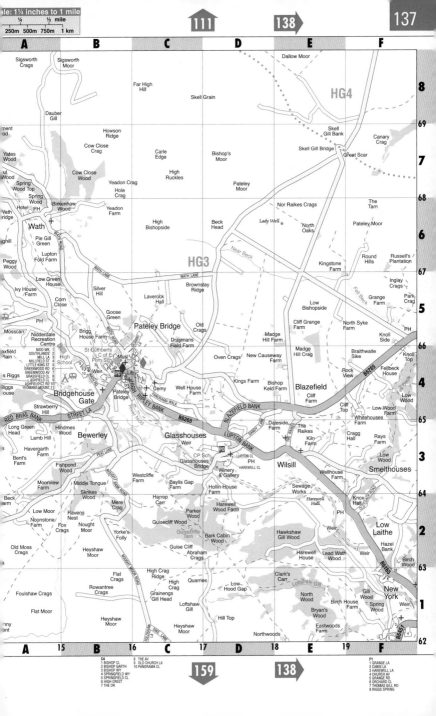

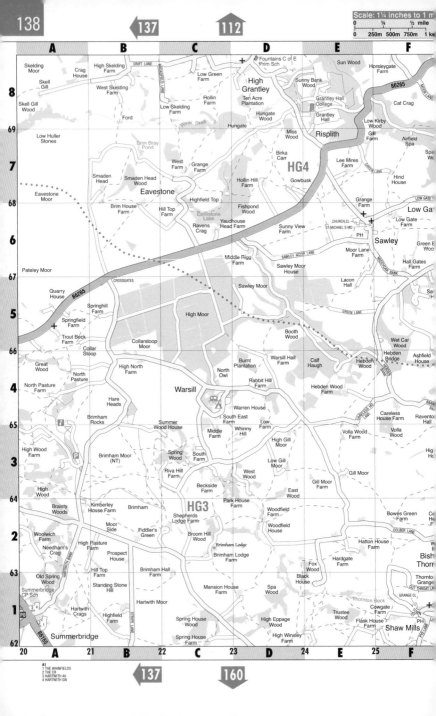

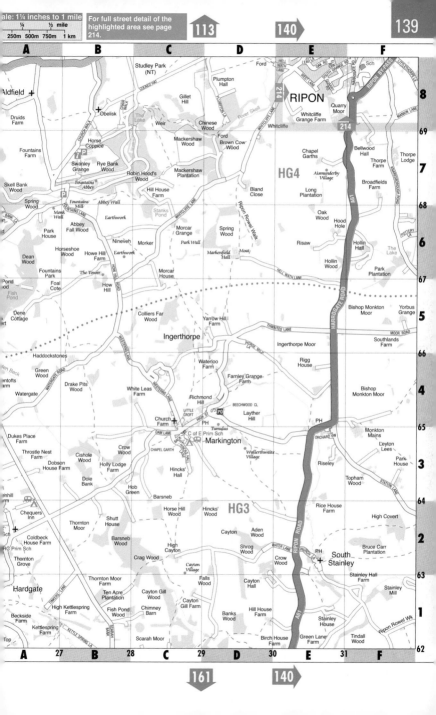

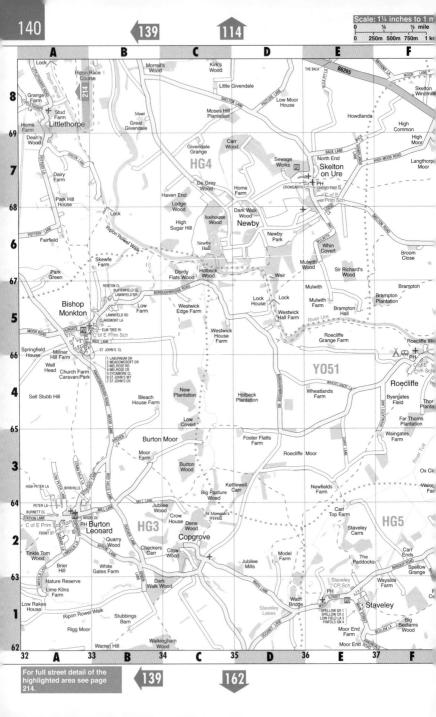

Lock
Ripon Race Course
214
Morrell's Wood
Kirk's Wood
Little Givendale
THE BALK
B6265
MOOR LANE
ANTHONY LA
Skelton Windmill

8

Grange Farm
LIDLETHORPE CLOSE
Ripon Canal
Stud Farm
Littlethorpe
Moat
Great Givendale
Moses Hill Plantation
SKELTON LANE
PASTURE LANE
Low Moor House
Howlands
BLEA BECK
High Common
High Moor

69

Home Farm
Dean's Wood
Givendale Grange
Carr Wood
De Grey Wood
HG4
Sewage Works
North End
Skelton on Ure
PH
CHERRYTREE CL
CROWGARTH
C of E Prim Sch
BACK LANE
HIGH MOOR ROAD
Langthorpe Moor
High Moor

7

POTTERY LANE
GREEN LANE
Dairy Farm
Park Hill House
Lock
Haven End
Lodge Wood
Home Farm
Icehouse Wood
Dark Walk Wood
Newby
SKELTON ROAD

68

POTTERY LANE
Fairfield
Ripon Rowel Walk
High Sugar Hill
Newby Hall
Newby Park
Mulwith Wood
Whin Covert
Sir Richard's Wood
MULWITH
LONNE LA
Broom Close

6

Park Green
Skewfe Farm
Dordy Flats Wood
Holbeck Wood
Weir
Mulwith
Mulwith Farm
Brampton
Brampton Plantation

67

Bishop Monkton
RENTON CL
BUTTERFIELD CL
LAWNFIELD DR
Low Farm
BOROUGHBRIDGE ROAD
Westwick Edge Farm
Lock House
Lock
Westwick Hall Farm
River Ure
Brampton Hall
Roecliffe

5

MOOR ROAD
HUNGATE
LAWNFIELD RD
CLAREMONT LA
C of E Prim Sch
ELM TREE RI
KINGS LANE
Westwick House Farm
Roecliffe Grange Farm
Roecliffe W
PH

Springfield House
Millner Hill Farm
St JOHN'S LANE
ST JOHN'S CL
1 LABURNUM DR
2 MEADOWCROFT DR
3 MELROSE RD
4 MELROSE DR
5 SYCAMORE CL
6 ST JOHN'S WY
7 ST JOHN'S CR
New Plantation
Holbeck Plantation
BOROUGHBRIDGE RD
Wheatlands Farm
WHEATLANDS LA
Y051
C of E Prim Sch

66

Well Head
Church Farm Caravan Park
Bleach House Farm
Roecliffe
Byergates Field
Thor Planta

4

Sell Stubb Hill
KNARESBOROUGH ROAD
MOOR LANE
Low Covert
Burton Moor
Moor Farm
Burton Wood
Foster Flatts Farm
Roecliffe Moor
Far Thorns Plantation
Waingates Farm

65

ARCHER LA
RED FIELD LANE
Kettlewell Carr
Newfields Farm
CARR LANE
River Tutt
Ox Clk

3

High Peter La
PETER LA
BIRKHILLS
LONG LANE
Big Pasture Wood
Weing Far

64

BURNETT CL
PETER LA
STATION LANE
MILL LANE
WIGBY CL
Jubilee Wood
Crow House
MILL LANE
St Mongan's Well
Carr Top Farm
Staveley Carrs
HG5

2

C of E Prim Sch
FRONT ST
PH
Burton Leonard
HG3
Quarry Wood
Checkers Carr
APRON LANE
GREEN LANE
Dene Wood
Copgrove
Jubilee Mills
Model Farm
The Paddocks
Carr Ends
Spellow Grange

Tinkle Tom Wood
Brier Hill
White Gates Farm
Crow Wood
Dark Walk Wood
WATH LANE
Staveley CP Sch
PH
Wayside Farm
MINSKIP ROAD
Ce

63

Nature Reserve
Lime Kilns Farm
Ripon Rowel Walk
Stubbings Barn
Walkingham Hill
Staveley Lakes
Wath Bridge
SPELLOW GR 1
SPELLOW CR 2
LOW FIELD LA 3
PINFOLD GN 4
MAIN STREET
Staveley
PH
Big Bedlams Wood
BEDLAM LA

1

Low Rakes House
Rigg Moor
Warren Hill
OCCANEY LANE
Moor End Farm
Moor End
DINSDALE LA

62

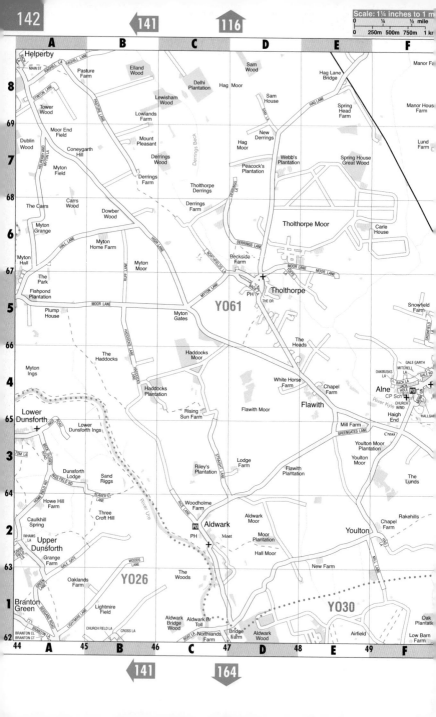

Scale: 1¼ inches to 1 m

0   ¼   ½ mile
0 250m 500m 750m 1 kr

Column A

Helperby
MAIN ST
RAEHILL LA
STINTON LANE
Tower Wood
Moor End Field
Dublin Wood
Coneygarth Hill
Myton Field
The Cairs
Carrs Wood
Myton Grange
HALL LANE
Myton Home Farm
Myton Hall
The Park
Fishpond Plantation
Plump House
MOOR LANE
Myton Ings
Lower Dunsforth
Lower Dunsforth Ings
Dunsforth Lodge
Sand Riggs
Howe Hill Farm
Caulkhill Spring
Upper Dunsforth
INHAMS LA
Grange Farm
GALE GATE
Oaklands Farm
YO26
Branton Green
BRANTON ROAD
LIGHTMIRE LANE
Lightmire Field
BRANTON CL
BRANTON CT
GREEN LANE
INGHAMS ROAD
HOME FIELD RD
BILTON GREEN ROAD
CAULK FIELD LA
WOODS LANE
CHURCH FIELD LA
CROSS LA

Column B

Pasture Farm
Elland Wood
Lewisham Wood
Lowlands Farm
Mount Pleasant
Derrings Wood
PASTURE LANE
Derrings Farm
Dowber Wood
The Haddocks
RIVER LANE
HIGH LANE
HADDOCKS LANE
Haddocks Plantation
Three Croft Hill
SCALBER'S LANE
The Woods
WOODS LANE

Column C

Delhi Plantation
Hag Moor
DERRINGS BECK
Tholthorpe Derrings
Derrings Farm
DERRINGS
Myton Moor
NORTH FIELDS LA
Haddocks Moor
MYTON LANE
Myton Gates
Rising Sun Farm
Riley's Plantation
STRAIGHT LANE
ROG LANE
Woodholme Farm
Aldwark
PO
PH
Moat
The Woods
Aldwark Bridge Wood
Aldwark Br Toll
BOAT LA
Northlands Farm
Bridge Farm

Column D

Sam Wood
Hag Moor
Sam House
New Derrings
Hag Moor
Peacock's Plantation
Webb's Plantation
DERRINGS LANE
Beckside Farm
+ BACK LA
Tholthorpe
PH
THE OR
YO61
The Heads
White Horse Farm
Flawith Moor
Flawith
Lodge Farm
Flawith Plantation
Aldwark Moor
Moor Plantation
Hall Moor
New Farm
Aldwark Wood
YO30

Column E

Hag Lane Bridge
HAG LANE
Spring Head Farm
Spring House Great Wood
SAM LA
Tholthorpe Moor
Carle House
Snowfield Farm
GALE GARTH
MITCHELL LA
OAKBUSKS LA
BACK LA
Alne
JACK HOLE
CP Sch
CHURCH WIND
River Kyle
Haigh End
Cross
Mill Farm
GREENGATES LANE
Youlton Moor Plantation
Youlton Moor
The Lunds
Youlton
Chapel Farm
Rakehills
MILL LANE
Airfield

Column F

Manor Fa
Manor House Farm
Lund Farm
Chapel Farm
GALE RD
HALLGAR
Oak Plantatic
Low Barn Farm

Left margin numbers: 8, 69, 7, 68, 6, 67, 5, 66, 4, 65, 3, 64, 2, 63, 1, 62

Bottom axis: 44 A 45 B 46 C 47 D 48 E 49 F

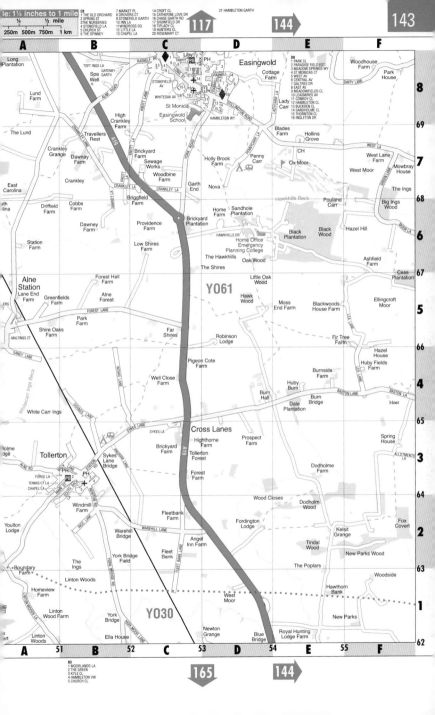

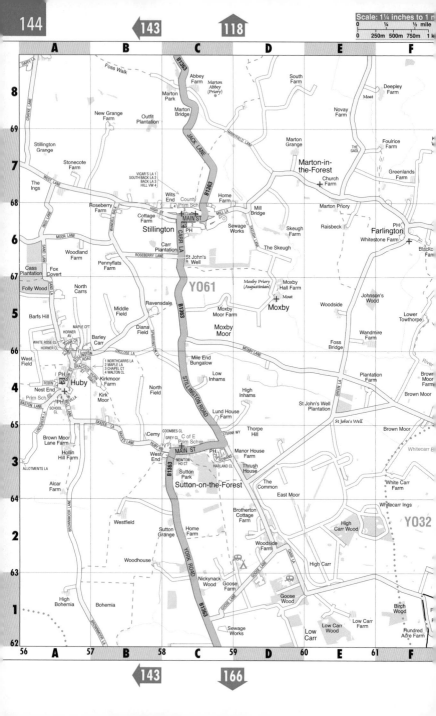

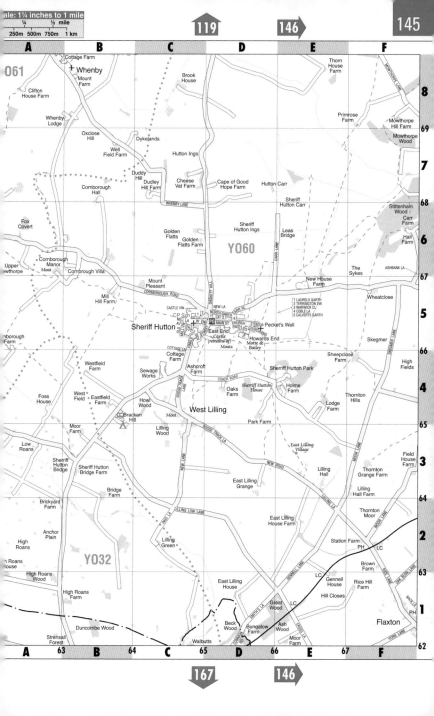

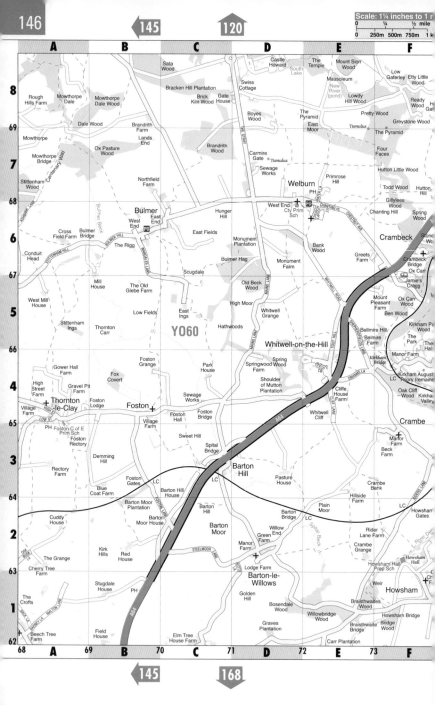

A **B** **C** **D** **E** **F**

8

Sata Wood

Castle Howard

The Temple

Mount Sion Wood

Low Gateley   Etty Little Wood

Rough Hills Farm

Mowthorpe Dale

Mowthorpe Dale Wood

Bracken Hill Plantation

Brick Kiln Wood

Gate House

Swiss Cottage

South Lake

Mausoleum

New River (pond)

Lowdy Hill Wood

Pretty Wood

Ready Wood   Hag

69

Dale Wood

Brandrith Farm

Lands End

Boyes Wood

The Pyramid

East Moor

Tumulus

Greystone Wood

Mowthorpe

Ox Pasture Wood

Brandrith Wood

The Pyramid

Four Faces

7

Mowthorpe Bridge

Northfield Farm

Carmire Gate

Sewage Works

Tumulus

Hutton Little Wood

Stittenham Wood

Centenary Way

Welburn

Primrose Hill

Todd Wood

Hutton Hill

68

Bulmer

West End   East End

Hunger Hill

West End   Cty Prim Sch

PH

Chanting Hil

Gillylees Wood

Chanting Hill

Spring Wood

Bulmer Beck

West End   PO

Cross Field Farm

Bulmer Bridge

The Rigg

East Fields

Monument Plantation

Bank Wood

Greets Farm

Crambeck

Stone Wo

6

Conduit Head

Bulmer Hag

Monument Farm

Crambeck Bridge

Ox Pasture

Jamie's Cragg

67

West Mill House

Mill House

The Old Glebe Farm

Scugdale

Old Beck Wood

Mount Pleasant Farm

Ox Carr Wood

Ben Wood

Kirkham Pa Wood

5

Stittenham Ings

Thornton Carr

Low Fields

East Ings

High Moor

Whitwell Grange

Hathwoods

Bellmire Hill

Belmire

The Park

The Hal

66

YO60

Whitwell-on-the-Hill

Kirkham Bridge

Manor Farm

Kirkham August Priory (remain

4

Gower Hall Farm

Foston Grange

Park House

Springwood Wood Farm

Spring

Shoulder of Mutton Plantation

Cliffe House Farm

LC

Oak Cliff Wood

Kirkha Valley

High Street Farm

Gravel Pit Farm

Fox Covert

Thornton le-Clay

Foston Lodge

Foston

Sewage Works

Whitwell Cliff

Crambe

65

Village Farm

PH

Foston C of E Prim Sch

Foston Rectory

Village Farm

Foston Hall

Foston Bridge

Sweet Hill

Manor Farm

Beck Farm

3

Rectory Farm

Demming Hill

Spital Bridge

Barton Hill

Pasture House

Crambe Bank

Hillside Farm

LC

64

Blue Coat Farm

Foston Gates

LC

Barton Hill House

Barton Hill

LC

Plain Moor

Barton Bridge

LC

Howsham Gates

2

Cuddy House

Kirk Hills

Red House

Barton Moor Plantation

Barton Moor House

Barton Moor

Manor Farm

Willow End

Green Farm

Spital Beck

Rider Lane Farm

Crambe Grange

Howsham Hall

63

The Grange

Cherry Tree Farm

STEELMOOR LANE

Lodge Farm

Barton-le-Willows

Howsham Hall Prep Sch

Howsham

1

The Crofts

Stugdale House

PH

Field House

Golden Hill

Bosendale Wood

Willowbridge Wood

Graves Plantation

Weir

Braithwaites Wood

Braithwaite Bridge Wood

Howsham Bridge

62

Beech Tree Farm

Elm Tree House Farm

Carr Plantation

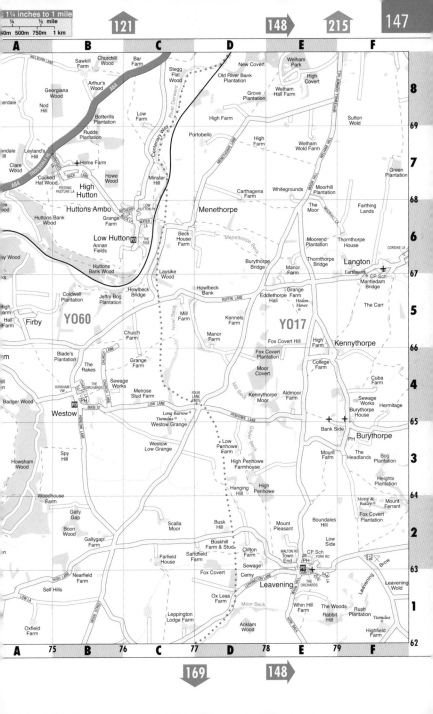

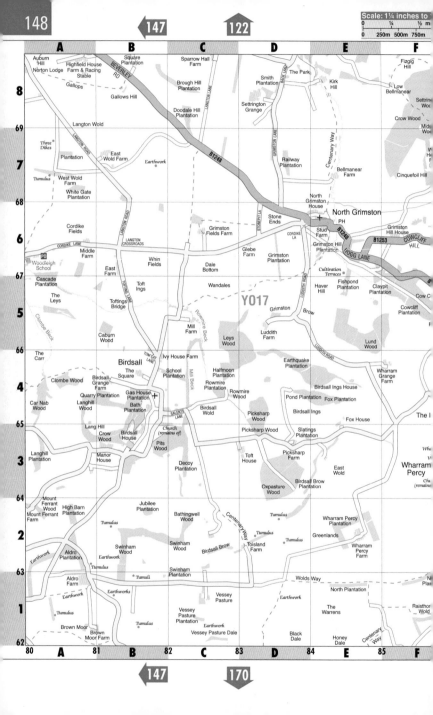

Scale: 1¼ inches to 1 mile
¼ ½ mile
250m 500m 750m 1 km

A 87 **B** 88 **C** 89 **D** 90 **E** 91 **F**

Screed Plantation

Wold Barn

Nine Springs Dale

uggleby Dale Plantation

r's n

8

High Mowthorpe Plantation

Earthwork

HIGH STREET

WOLD ROAD

Kirby Wold Farm

High Mowthorpe Farm

Tumuli

Duggleby Wold

Wold Top Farm

69

7

High Mowthorpe

High Mowthorpe Plantation

LOW ROAD

68

Duggleby Wold

Duggleby

Old Tillage Farm

East End

Dollyth Howe

Manor Farm

B1253 HIGH STREET

Mowthorpe Wold

Kirby Grindalythe

Cromwell Hill

Squirrel Hall Farm

6

BROAD BALK (PUBLIC)

Sewage Works

PO

Home Farm

Highbury Farm

West End Farm

Medieval Village of Mowthorpe

Low Mowthorpe Farm

Kirby Plantation

67

West End

Duggleby Howe

Low Mowthorpe

BROAD BALK

WATER NEW RD

Oakhill Springs

Y017

Crook Plantation

Gelding Pit (spring)

5

Manor Farm

STONEPIT BALK

Oak Hill

B1253

KIRBY LANE

66

Wharram le Street

WOLDS WAY

Low Mowthorpe

Crowtree Slack

Earthwork

STONEPIT HILL

4

Wold Plantation

Wold Farm

Wharram Wold Farm

Kirby Grange

Gallop Plantation

Marramatte

Marramatte Farm

WY...

B1253

MILL LANE

65

Bella Farm

North Wold Farm

entenary Way

P

Canada

Tumulus

Towthorpe Plantation

3

Wood

B1248

Tumulus

Towthorpe Plantation

Mill Farm

64

Wharram Percy Wold

Tumuli

Tumulus

Towthorpe Wold

Outfield Plantation

Towthorpe Dale

2

Tunnel Plantation

ulus

Fairy Stones

Fairy Dale

Mowthorpe Dale

Middle Hill

Y025

Kirk Hill

Burdale North Wold

Towthorpe Village

63

William Dale

Burdale Warren Middle Dale

Burdale House Farm

Whay Dale

Ling Farm

Towthorpe

Low Side

Towthorpe Field

York Dale

B1251

1

York Earthwork

York Bank

62

A 87 **B** 88 **C** 89 **D** 90 **E** 91 **F**

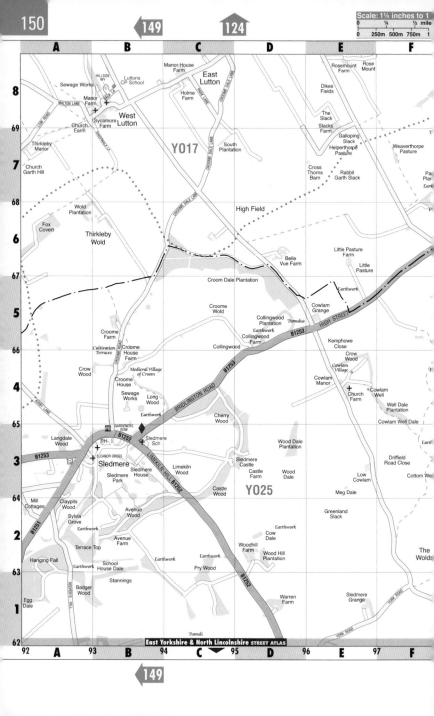

8

Sewage Works

HILLSIDE WY

Luttons CP School

Manor House Farm

East Lutton

Rosemount Farm

Rose Mount

Manor Farm

Holme Farm

Dikes Fields

69

West Lutton

Church Farm

Sycamore Farm

Thirkleby Manor

MALTON LANE

LOW ROAD

BACK LA

GROOME DALE LANE

HORN LANE

The Slack

Slacks Farm

Galloping Slack

Helperthorpe Pasture

Weaverthorpe Pasture

YO17

South Plantation

7

Church Garth Hill

Cross Thorns Barn

Rabbit Garth Slack

Pa Plar Ear

68

Wold Plantation

GROOME DALE LANE

High Field

P

Fox Covert

Thirkleby Wold

6

Belle Vue Farm

Little Pasture Farm

Little Pasture

67

Croom Dale Plantation

Earthwork

P

5

Croome Farm

Croome Wold

Collingwood Plantation

Tumulus

Cowlam Grange

HIGH STREET

Cultivation Terraces

Croome House Farm

Earthwork

Collingwood Farm

B1253

Kemphowe Close

Crow Wood

66

GROOME DALE

Collingwood

Cowlam Village

Crow Wood

Medieval Village of Croom

B1253

Cowlam Manor

4

Croome House

Long Wood

BRIDLINGTON ROAD

Church Farm

Cowlam Well

Well Dale Plantation

Sewage Works

Earthwork

Cherry Wood

Cowlam Well Dale

65

PO

GARDENERS ROW

Wood Dale Plantation

Earth

Langdale Wood

PH

B1252

Sledmere Sch

Wood Dale

Driffield Road Close

Cottom We

3

B1253

P

ELEANOR CROSS

Sledmere

Sledmere Park

Sledmere House

LIMEKILN HILL B1252

Limekiln Wood

Sledmere Castle

Castle Farm

Low Cowlam

YO25

64

Mill Cottages

Claypits Wood

Sylvia Grove

Avenue Wood

Castle Wood

Meg Dale

Greenland Slack

B1251

Earthwork

2

Terrace Top

Avenue Farm

Earthwork

Cow Dale

Earthwork

Woodhill Farm

Wood Hill Plantation

The Wolds

63

Hanging Fall

Earthwork

School House Dale

Earthwork

Pry Wood

KEEPER'S HILL

1

Egg Dale

Badger Wood

Stannings

Warren Farm

Sledmere Grange

YORK ROAD

62

92   A   93   B   94   C   95   D   96   E   97   F

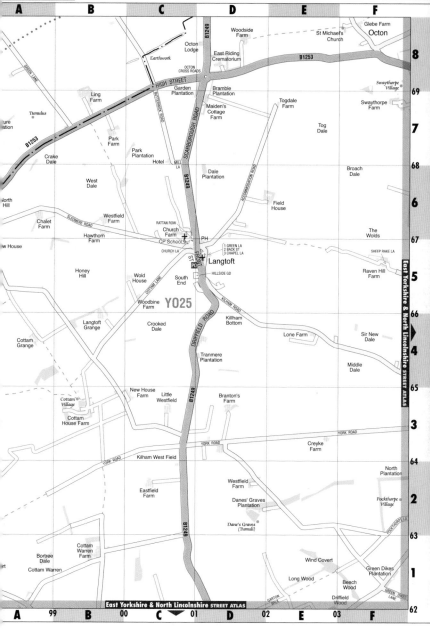

Scale: 1¼ inches to 1 mile
¼   ½ mile
250m 500m 750m 1 km

| A | B | C | D | E | F |

8

Glebe Farm
Octon

Woodside Farm

St Michael's Church

B1253

Octon Lodge

Earthwork

East Riding Crematorium

OCTON CROSS ROADS

69

Swaythorpe Village

HIGH STREET

Ling Farm

Garden Plantation

Bramble Plantation

Togdale Farm

Swaythorpe Farm

Tumulus

Tog Dale

7

...ture ...ation

B1253

Park Farm

Maiden's Cottage Farm

Crake Dale

Park Plantation

Hotel

Dale Plantation

Broach Dale

68

West Dale

North Hill

Chalet Farm

Westfield Farm

Field House

6

SLEDMERE ROAD

Hawthorn Farm

RATTAN ROW

Church Farm

CP School

PH

The Wolds

67

...w House

CHURCH LA

Langtoft

1 GREEN LA
2 BACK ST
3 CHAPEL LA

SHEEP RAKE LA

Honey Hill

Wold House

South End

HILLSIDE GD

Raven Hill Farm

5

YO25

Woodbine Farm

KILHAM ROAD

66

Langtoft Grange

Crooked Dale

Killham Bottom

Lone Farm

Sir New Dale

Cottam Grange

DRIFFIELD ROAD

Tranmere Plantation

Middle Dale

4

65

Cottam Village

New House Farm

Little Westfield

Branton's Farm

Cottam House Farm

YORK ROAD

3

YORK ROAD

Creyke Farm

64

Kilham West Field

North Plantation

Eastfield Farm

Westfield Farm

Danes' Graves Plantation

Packthorpe Village

2

Dane's Graves (Tumuli)

63

Cottam Warren Farm

Bortree Dale

Cottam Warren

Wind Covert

Green Dikes Plantation

1

Long Wood

Beech Wood

Driffield Wood

62

| A | 99 | B | 00 | C | 01 | D | 02 | E | 03 | F |

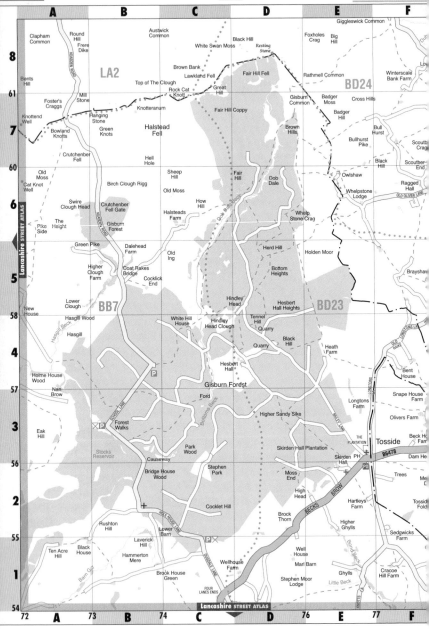

130

A **B** **C** **D** **E** **F**

Lancashire STREET ATLAS

Giggleswick Common

Clapham Common

Round Hill
Frere Dike

Austwick Common

Black Hill
White Swan Moss

Resting Stone

Foxholes Crag
Big Hill

8

Bents Hill

LA2

Brown Bank

Lawkland Fell
Top of The Clough

Fair Hill Fell

Rathmell Common

BD24

Winterscale Bank Farm

Foster's Craggs

Mill Stone

Rock Cat Knott

Great Hill

Gisburn Common

Badger Moss

Cross Hills

61

Knottend Well

Hanging Stone

Knotteranum

Fair Hill Coppy

Badger Hill

Bullhurst Pike

Bull Hurst

Scoutb Crag

Bowland Knots

Green Knots

Halstead Fell

Brown Hills

Scouther End

7

Crutchenber Fell

Hell Hole

Black Hill

60

Old Moss

Sheep Hill

Fair Hill

Dob Dale

Owlshaw

Ragged Hall

Cat Knot Well

Birch Clough Rigg

Old Moss

How Hill

Whelpstone Lodge

OLD OLIVER LANE

Swire Clough Head

Crutchenber Fell Gate

Halsteads Farm

Whelp Stone Crag

Holden Moor

Brayshaw

6

Pike Side

The Height

Gisburn Forest

Herd Hill

Green Pike

Dalehead Farm

Old Ing

Bottom Heights

BD23

5

Higher Clough Farm

Coat Rakes Bridge

Cocklick End

Hindley Head

Hesbert Hall Heights

Lower Clough

BB7

White Hill House

Hindley Head Clough

Tennel Hill Quarry

New House

Hasgill Wood

Quarry

Black Hill

Heath Farm

58

Hasgill

Hesbert Hall

Quarry

Bent House

Holme House Wood

Nan Brow

P

Gisburn Forest

Ford

Higher Sandy Sike

Longtons Farm

Snape House Farm

57

Eak Hill

P

Forest Walks

Park Wood

Skirden Hall Plantation

THE PLANTATION

Olivers Farm

Tosside

Beck H Farm

3

Stocks Reservoir

Causeway

Stephen Park

Skirden Hall

Skirden PH

B6478

Dam He

Trees

Me

Bridge House Wood

Cocklet Hill

Moss End

High Head

Hartleys Farm

Tossid Fold

2

Rushton Hill

Lower Barn

Brock Thorn

Higher Ghylls

Sedgwicks

55

Ten Acre Hill

Black House

Laverick Hill

Hammerton Mere

P

Wellhouse Farm

Well House

Marl Barn

Ghylls

Little Beck

Cracoe Hill Farm

1

Barn Gill

Brook House Green

FOUR LANES ENDS

Stephen Moor Lodge

Bond Beck

KIRKBY

54

A **72** **B** **73** **74** **C** **D** **76** **E** **77** **F**

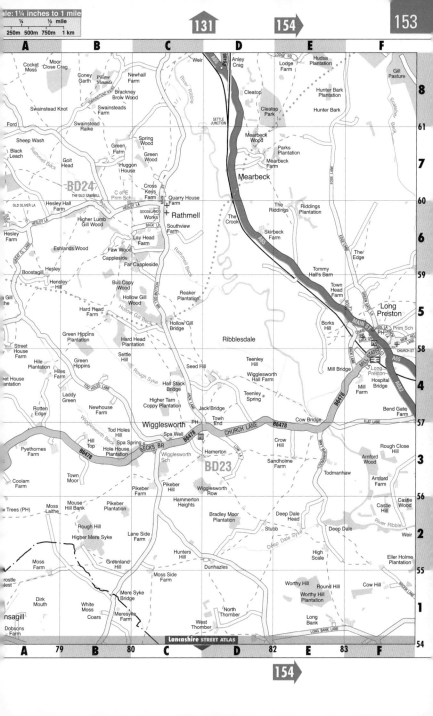

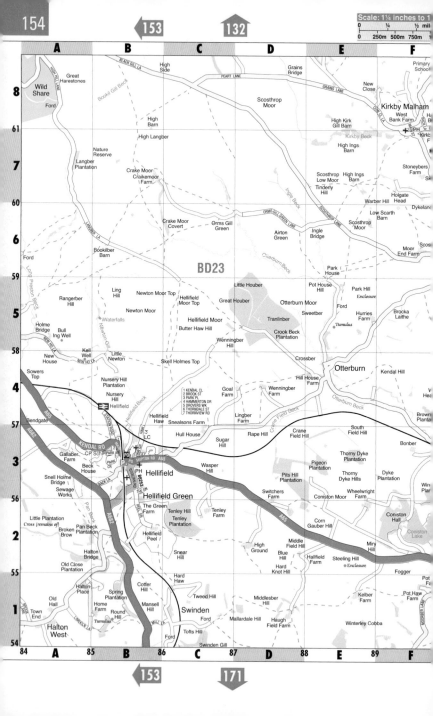

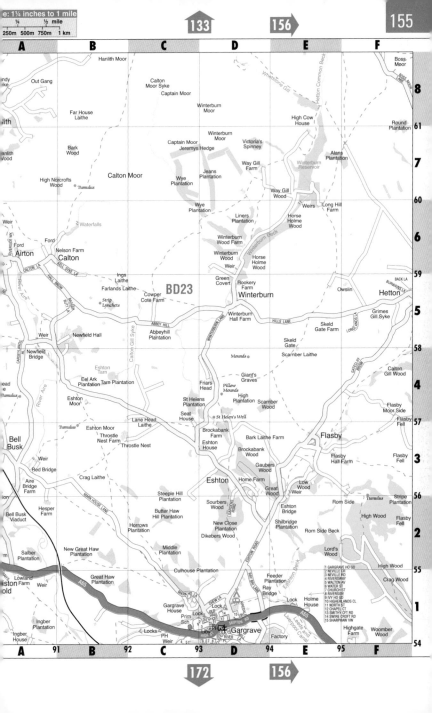

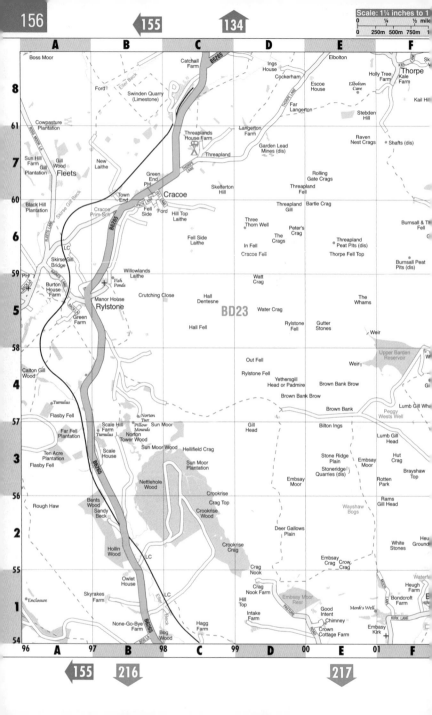

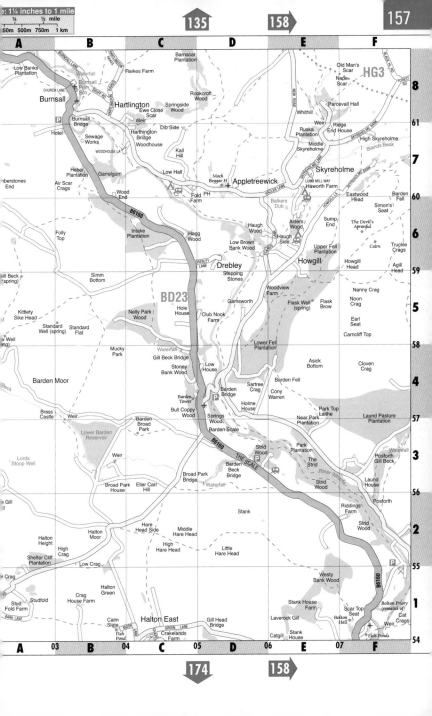

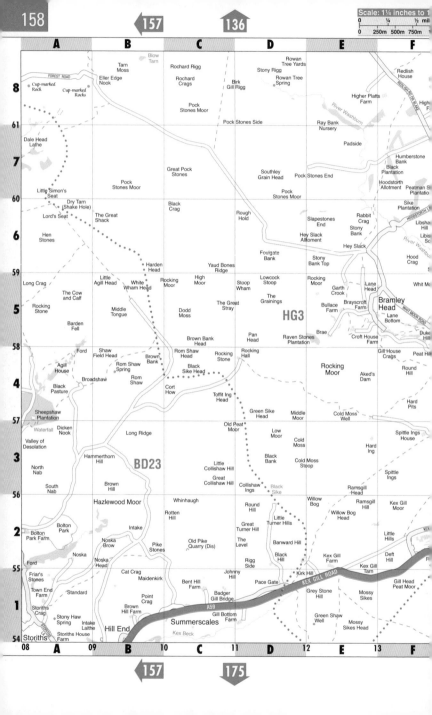

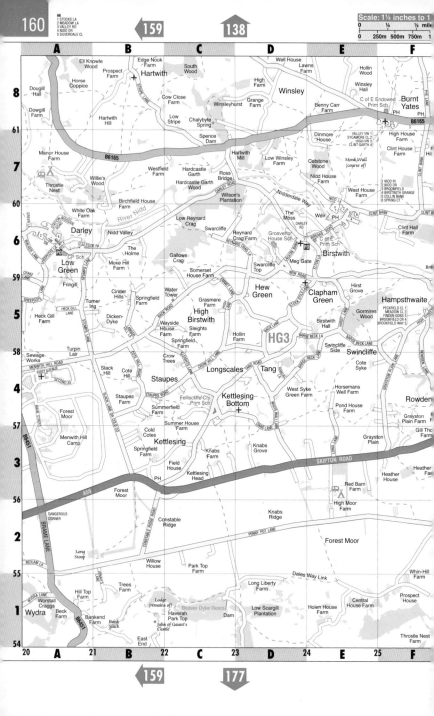

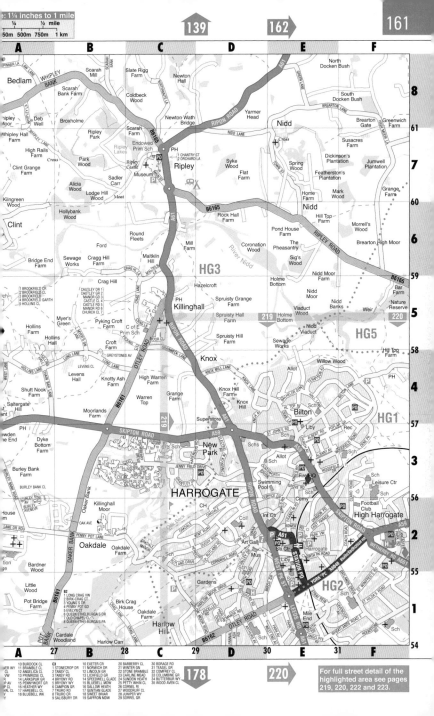

Scale: 1¼ inches to 1 mile

161
140

| A | B | C | D | E | F |

8

Hill Top Farm
Simon Slack Wood
Rigg Moor Plantation
Walkingham Wood
Warren Covert
Warren Farm
Walkingham Hill Farm
Occaney
OCCANEY LA
Hollins Hill
The Moor
ARKENDALE ROAD
Loftus Hill

HG3

Seed Field Covert
Anthony Covert
Shaw Bridge
Low Hall
Loftus Hill Fox Covert

61

PH
Brearton
Scarr Beck Plantation
Low Moor
WARREN LANE
Branton Court
Farnham
Low Hall Farm
Ferrensby Moor
PH
Ferrensby
WILLOW GARTH

7

Brearton Moor
Dovecote Carr
LOW MOOR LANE
The Mires
PH
FARNHAM LANE
Ferrensby Lodge
Poplars Farm

Low Moor
STANG LANE
Sunnyside Farm
Throstle Nest Farm
Sandy Bank Farm

60

Lingerfield Prim Sch
LOW MOOR LANE
Hillside Farm
Hydale Farm
Gravel Pit
Rabbit Hill
Gibbet Hill
Gibbet Farm
Far Andrew Hill

CHANTRY LA
PO
Port Arthur Farm
POPLAR GN
Lingerfield
Lingerfield Farm

6

Old Hall
MANOR DR
PH
SMITHY LA
Scotton
Preston Farm
Market Flat
HG5
Gravel Pit
CH
Sand Hills
Near Andrew Hill

HAVIKIL PK
SCOTTON CT
Preston House
Coney Garth
Gravel Pit
Hopewell House

59

HAVIKIL LA
MIRE SYKE LANE
HIGH MOOR LA
Low Preston Covert
Scriven
BAR LANE
HAZELHEADS LA

B6165
RIPLEY ROAD
Weir
SCOTTON GR
High Wood
THE GABLES
GREENGATE DR
GREENGATE LA
HAZELHEADS LA
221
Hay-a-

5

P
220
Appleby Carr
Park Corner Farm
Low Wood
Guiseley Hill
PARK GR
WATER LA
Meadowside CP Sch
Hall Farm

58

River Nidd
Scotten Banks
Gates Wood
THE LANDS
Weir
Hall Farm

Spring Wood
Long Plantation
The Parks
Fox Wood
Sch
HAY-A-PARK LANE
LC

4

BILTON LANE
Bilton Spa
Bilton Hall
Conyngham Hall
Jun Sch
Knaresborough
Inf Sch
KNARESBOROUGH
Sch
Highfield Farm

HG1

57

Longlands Farm
College
BOGS LANE
Forest Head
CH
Belmont Wood
Castle Mus
Swimming Pool
Sch
EASTFIELD
Manse Farm
A59
YORK ROAD
Sewage Works

3

Starbeck
Springwater Sch
Mother Shipton's Cave
Dropping Well
HG5
MANSE
St Robert's Cave
HG5
221

56

Liby
Starbeck
Baths
Gallow Hill
CASS
HG5
Stone Face Farm
South Ings
PO
Goldsborough Mill Farm
MILL RD

HG2

LC
FAIRFAX DR
FOREST MOOR RD
Calcutt
Thistle Hill
B6163
Guys Crag

2

Woodlands
OP Sch
Forest Moor
Thistle Hill
Birkham Wood
WETHERBY RD

55

Cemetery
Brick Kiln Plantation
Simon Knoll
A658
Tickhill Wood
Tickhill Farm
B6164

1

WETHERBY ROAD
A661
Showground
HG3
Rudfarlington Farm
221
Low Grange
Abraham's Whin
Scalibar Farm
KNARES

54

CH
Crimple
CRIMPLE LA
RUDDING LA
COLLIN'S HL
Plompton Hall
Plompton Hall

| A | B | C | D | E | F |
| 32 | 33 | 34 | 35 | 36 | 37 |

For full street detail of the highlighted area see pages 220 and 221.

161
179

Scale: 1¼ inches to 1 mile
¼   ½ mile
250m 500m 750m 1 km

A   **B**   **C**   **D**   **E**   **F**

8

Barnkiln Wood

Marton Lane

A168

The Carr

LEGRAM RD
PRIESTCARR LA
LEGRAM LA

Marton Wood

Grassgills Farm

High Field

Low Farm

B6265

CARR SIDE ROAD

61

Field Lane

HOLGATE BANK

Hazel Head

PH

Arkendale

Bougham Farm

LONGLANDS FIELD RD
BOWCARR LA
MICKLEDALE LA
MOOR LA

Woodside Farm

Great Ouseburn Moor

Marton Cottage Farm

The Dale

Brunsell Hill

Mar Head

MANOR PK
REINS
HL BANK

Holly Bank Farm

Ninevah Farm

SPITLANDS LANE

Marton Moor

Moor Farm

MAR HEAD BALK

7

Arkendale Moor

Carr Plantation

North Kills

CLARETON LA

Thornbar Farm

South Farm

MOOR LANE

Great Ouseburn Moor

Lylands Wood

Cherry Hill

Lylands Farm

60

Parsons Closes

Clareton Field

Shepherds Wood

Sand Hill

Walls Close House

Hollin Hill

Broadfield Wood

West Sleeper Farm

Clareton Moor Farm

CLARETON LANE
LINGER LA

Claro Field

Bog Plantation

6

Clareton Moor

THIRTY ACRE MOOR LANE

Clarenton Hill

LINGER LANE

Mill Field

Decoy Plantation

Far Park

High Fish Pond

Agar's Plantation

Oxclose Farm

Fair View Farm

Low Farm

59

PH

Coneythorpe

GREEN LA

Tate's Plantation

A168

Middle Fish Pond

Lower Fish Pond

Gate Hill

Cherry Hill

High Farm

Burtree Flats

STARRA FIELD LANE

Brown Moor

Spring Bank Farm

Mill Hill

HG5

WEST LANE

5

Castle Farm

HAY-A-PARK LA
SHORTSILL LA
YORK ROAD

Oakheads Hill

Allerton Park

Willow Hole

YO26

WEST LANE

58

Flaxby

SHORTSILL LA

Flaxby Moor

Allerton Mauleverer

Long Plantation

Clockhill Farm

Manor Farm

BRAKER LANE

4

Balfe Hill

A59

Flaxby Covert

Allerton Grange

47

Holly Cott

NEW ROAD

Rainshaw Farm

CLOCKHILL FIELD LANE

57

K ROAD

Sand Hill

Spring Wood

Flaxby Moor Farm

Allerton Moor

Middle Plantation

PH

High Grange Farm

Hopperton Plantation

A59

Goldsborough Fields

Burial Gd

SPOFON RD

Low Farm

Bayram Hill

New Inn Farm

Low Plantation

HOPPERTON FIELD LANE

Walker Farm

Hopperton

Gelsthorpe Farm

SCATE MOOR LANE

Scate Moor

3

PRINCESS MEAD CL
WOODLANDS CL

Goldsborough H Court

CHURCH STREET

Goldsborough Moor

Green Dick Wood

A168

GREY THORN LANE

Grange Farm

Gelsthorpe Moor

LC

Little Scate Moor Wood

56

oldsborough

sborough Park

Leys Pond

Parsonage Wood

Beatmire Well (spring)

Old Forest Farm

Poulter's Plantation

WHIXLEY LANE

Great Scate Moor Wood

Cattal Grange

2

Pikeshaw Wood

Oatland Farm

Langshawe Wood

Northlands Farm

55

Great Wood

Ribston Lodge

Ribston Big Wood

LS22

New Forest Farm

Hollin Hill
Cranberry Carr

Hamley Hill

1

High Wood

Brickhill Wood

Highfield Farm

Whixley Lane End

Nursery Hill Cottage

A1(M)

HORN HILL

Park House

Pessac Plantation

54

A   39   **B**   40   **C**   41   **D**   42   **E**   43   **F**

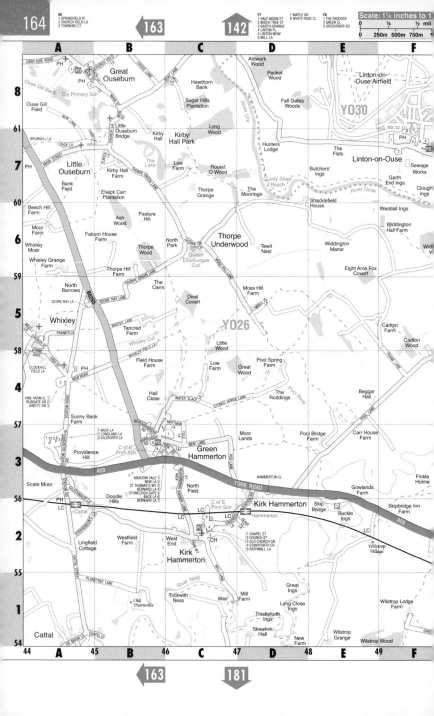

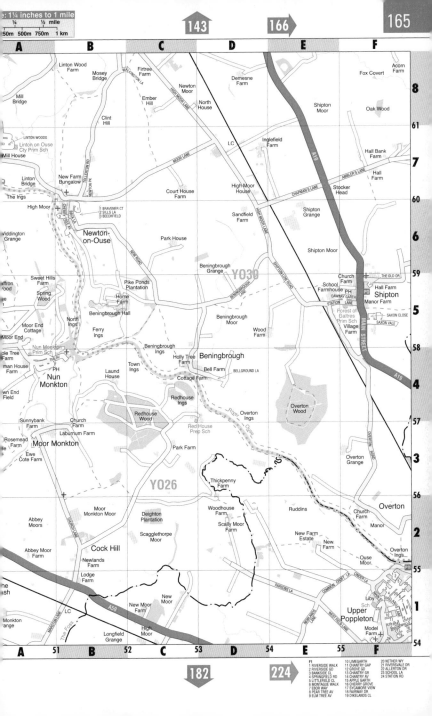

F1
1 RIVERSIDE WALK
2 RIVERSIDE GD
3 BANKSIDE CL
4 SPRINGFIELD RD
5 LITTLEFIELD CL
6 MONTAGUE WALK
7 EBOR WAY
8 PEAR TREE AV
9 ELM TREE AV
10 LIMEGARTH
11 CHANTRY GAP
12 GROVE GD
13 CHANTRY GR
14 CHANTRY AV
15 APPLE GARTH
16 CHERRY GROVE
17 SYCAMORE VIEW
18 FAIRWAY DR
19 DIKELANDS CL
20 NETHER WY
21 RIVERSVALE DR
22 ALLERTON DR
23 SCHOOL LA
24 STATION RD

E5
1 VILLAGE GARTH
2 LONGCROFT
3 RIPLEY GR
4 SOUTHLANDS
5 THE AVENUE
6 REDWOOD DR
7 MULBERRY DR
8 ASH LA
9 ELM END
10 COPPICE CL
11 LITTLE LA
12 HAWTHORN AV
13 BIRCH LA
14 FLETCHER CT
15 ST MARY'S CL
16 SANDY LA
17 CHURCH LA
18 BROAD OAK LA
19 WESTFIELD PL
20 WESTFIELD RD
21 WESTFIELD CL
22 ST NICHOLAS WY
23 PLANTATION WY
24 MIDDLE BANKS
25 HORNSEY GARTH
26 GLEBE WY
27 FOREST CL
28 CHURCHFIELD DR
29 SANDYLAND
30 HEADLAND CL
31 WANDHILL
32 KENILDY DR
33 ABELTON GR
34 ORCHARD PADDOCK

For full street detail of the highlighted area see pages 224 and 225.

D5
1 CASTLE CL
2 WINDSOR DR
3 TOWN END GDNS
4 STEEPLE CL
5 HAREWOOD CL
6 DELAMERE CL
7 ETON DR
8 SAXFORD WAY
9 CANTERBURY CL
10 HAMBLETON VW
11 BACK LANE
12 WESTFIELD GR
13 BURRILL DR
14 TWIN PIKE WAY
15 STABLER CL
16 HELMSLEY GR
17 CORNER CL
18 LANCAR CL
19 WATERINGS
20 BUTTERS CL
21 CORBAN WY
22 BUTT HILL

F5
1 FARNDALE CL
2 SANDHOLME
3 NEWDALE
4 KELDALE
5 NORTHCROFT
6 RUSHWOOD CL
7 LANSDOWN WY
8 SCRIVEN GR
9 WOODCOCK CL
10 FALCON CL
11 MALLARD WY
12 HALL RISE
13 FOLKS CL
14 OLD COPPICE
15 NEW FORGE CT
16 CHATSWORTH DR
17 RIVERSDALE
18 NETHERWINDINGS
19 THORNHILLS
20 GAR
21 LANB
22 LANB

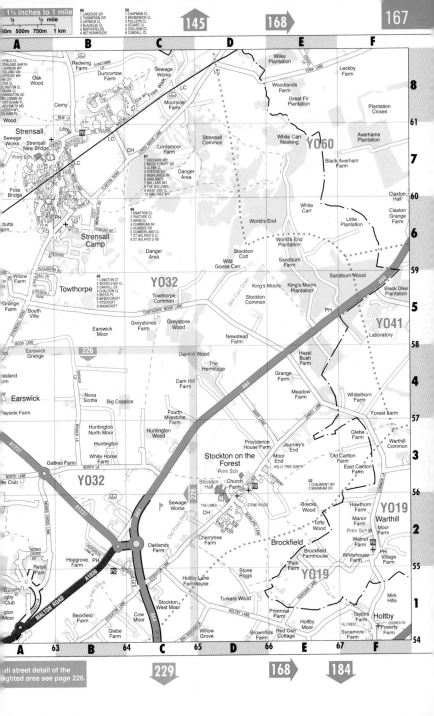

167
146

Scale: 1¼ inches to 1
0   ¼   ½ mile
0   250m 500m 750m   1

A **B** **C** **D** **E** **F**

8
Glebe Farm
SANDY LANE
SANDY LANE
The Brecks
Harton Lodge Farm
Harton
Sewage Works
Brough Plantation
Barnby Plantation
Old Oak Wood
Paradise Farm
Sewage Works
Harton Moor
Harton Lodge Plantation
Deer Dales
Brown Gates
Peas Hill

61
White Averham
Bossall
Bossall Hall Moat
Barnby House
Scrayingham

7
Lobster House Farm
Vicarage Farm
Sand Hills
Mount Pleasant Farm
Craw Kell
YO60
Milner Farms
The Evers
Sewage Works
KIRK BALK LANE
Claxton
Belle Vue Farm
Bell Closes
West Belt Wood
Bridge End Farm
Lobster House

60
Claxton Moor
Johnsons Farm
Kissthorn Farm
Bossall Wood
East Belt Wood
South Farm

6
Claxton Ings
Common Moor
Whey Carr
Pasture Farm
Woodhouse Farm
Bridge End Fields

59
Whey Carr Plantation
Sand Hutton
Aldby Field Farm
Sinkinson House Farm
Aldby Park

5
Gravel Pit Farm
Whey Carr Farm
Sand Hutton C of E Prim Sch
Pine Top
Whey Carr
Low Moor Farm
Weir

58
White Syke Farm
White Sike Plantation
Weed Hill Plantation
Home Farm
Whitehills Wood
Beech Farm
Buttercrambe
Home Farm
Spring

4
Sand Hutton Common
The Carr
Grange Wood
Buttercrambe Moor Strip
Buttercrambe Moor
Stubbs Wood
Bank Farm
Barlam Beck

Upper Helmsley Common
Scrogs Wood
Buttercrambe Moor Wood
Birk Wood
Ellers Farm

57
Gallops
Common Farm
Upper Helmsley
Moor Wood
Birk House Farm

3
Edge of the Wood
Home Farm
Park Woods
Low Moor
Wood End Cottage
YO41
Bleach Farm
Helmsley Hills
NORTHGATE LANE
Cakies Wood
Grange Farm
Burtonfield Hall
Flawith Carr
Low Burtonfields Farm

56
Forest House Farm
Rise Wood
Hall Farm
Primrose Hill Farm
MAIN STREET

2
YO19
Ivy House Farm
PH
Fox Farm
Meadow Side
Gate Helmsley Common
Manor Farm
Sewage
STAMFORD BRIDGE WEST
A166
CLOVERLEY CL
WILLOW CT
LOWGLADE
PO
WHITEROSE DR
Stamford Bridge
D1
1 HAROLDS WY
2 NORSEWAY
3 HARDRADA WY

55
Scoreby Grange
Gate Helmsley
Scoreby Farmhouse
CHERRY PADDOCK
OTTERWOOD PADDOCK
BEAGLE SPINNEY
Bell Ings
FORESTERS WK
Brown Moor
Beechwood House

1
Hendwick Hall Farm
Minster Way
Smackdam Bridge
Millsike Bridge
Millsike Beck
White House Farm
COWL GATE
HIGH CATTON ROAD
Fairfield Farm

54
High Catton Grange

68 **A** **69** **B** **70** **C** **71** **D** **72** **E** **73** **F**

167
185

D2
1 BRIDLINGTON RD
2 DERWENT CL
3 DANESWELL CL
4 BURTON FIELDS RD
5 GARROWBY VW
6 KINGSWAY
7 DARLEY CL
8 WHARTON RD
9 ST JOHN'S RD
10 CHURCH LA
11 EGREMONT CL
12 BURTON FIELDS CL
13 HEATHER BANK
14 TOSTIG CL
15 FAIRFAX
16 SCHOOL CL
17 ROMAN AV N
18 GODWINSWAY
19 BUTTS CL
20 VIKING CL
21 MIDGLEY CL
22 BROWN MOOR
23 FURLONG RD

: 1¼ inches to 1 mile

| ¼ | ½ | mile |

50m 500m 750m 1 km

147

170

169

A   B   C   D   E   F

YO60

The Farm

Whitecarr Beck

Plaster Pitts Farm

"Hanging Cliffs"

Poplar Farm

Ivy House Farm

Leppington Wood

Acklam Lodge

Wood Farm

Acklam
Acklam Wold Farm
PH
Highfield
Penty Farm
Wood
Beckhouse Farm

Spring Head

Manor Farm

Acklam Wold

Deepdale Spring

Deep Dale

Leppington

Manor Farm

Motte & Bailey

Pasture Hill Farm

8

Low Field

ACRES LANE

Cruntield lane

Scrayingham Grange

Buskhill Plantation

Busk High Farm

YO17

High Sleights Farm

Back Warren Plantation

61

KIRK GATES

Leppington Beck

Dennings Plantation

Denn Ings

High Farm

Acklam Ings

7

Wheathills Farm

Swallowpits Beck

Rush Hill

Low Farm

Barthorpe Lodge Farm

Barthorpe Grange

Bottoms Head

Lower Sleights Farm

60

Pasture Farm

BLEABERRY LANE

Far Hillside Plantation

Baffham Plantation

6

Howl Beck

The Leys

West Wood

Bugthorpe Grange

Thoralby Hall

Stubb's Plantation

Beck Plantation

Glider Beck

Gorman Castle

Baffham Farm

East Ings

Salamanca Beck

Pasture Farm

Glebe Farm

59

YO41

High Pasture Hill

Grange Plantation

Haybridge Mill Farm

Moat

Moat Farm

Church Farm

Moat

Longhowes Plantation

Primrose Farm

Primrose Hill

BURTHORPE LA TOWN E

5

Bugthorpe

PO

HIGH ROW
Lilac Farm

58

Manor House
PO

DOE PK LA

Haybridge Mill Farm

Corner Farm

Barf Plantation

Home Farm

Minnees Plantation

Garden Plantation

Preserve Plantation

Garrowby Hall

Cheesecake House

4

benbeck

West Croft Farm

Broad Ings

West Ings

Keldsike Plantation

Crow Wood

Bluepaling Plantation

Old Wood

Ash Plantation

57

Poplar Farm

Brickyard Farm

Clayhill Plantation

Garrowby Lodge

GARROWBY STREET

Garrowby Hill Plantation

GARROWBY HL

3

A166

CLAY HILL

Jubilee Plantation

A166

Kitty Hill (Tumuli)

Lodge Farm

Kitty Hill

Garrowby Hill

North Hill

North Field

Rush Plantation

56

Clay Farm

Manor Farm

Awnhams Bridge

VALE CR

on

GRANGE CL

Glebe Farm

Manor Farm

Manor House Farm

East Farm

Fox Covert

Bishop Wilton

2

orner Farm

Yew Tree Farm

Youlthorpe

WHITE CROSS WY
HOLLY CL

YO42

Sch

Moat

PH

Prison

Pasture Farm

Youlthorpe Pasture Hill Farm

Providence Farm

Willow Tree Farm

Gowthorpe Farm

Grange Farm

Cautley Farm

PARK LA CL

55

Airstrip (Disused)

Industrial Estate

COMMON LA

Tynewood Farm

Gowthorpe

Belthorpe Whin

High Belthorpe

BELTHORPE LANE

BOLTON RD

1

East Yorkshire & North Lincolnshire STREET ATLAS

A   75   B   76   C   77   D   78   E   79   F   54

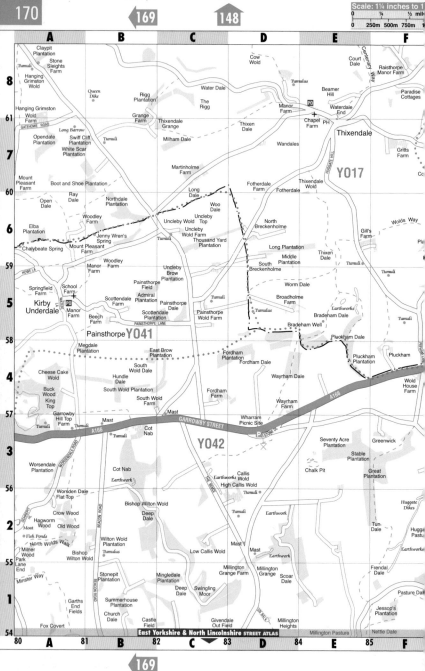

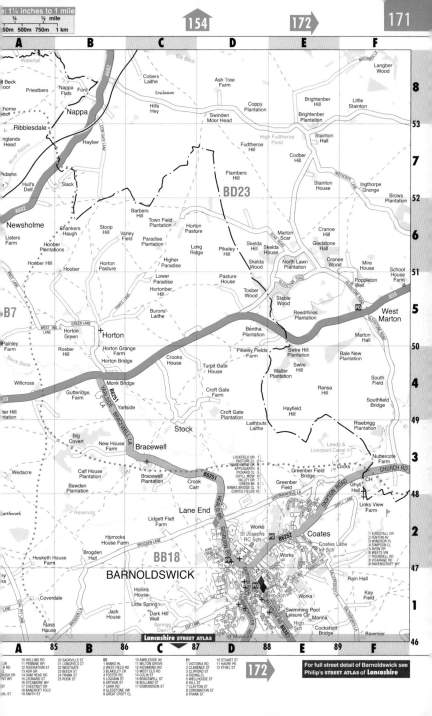

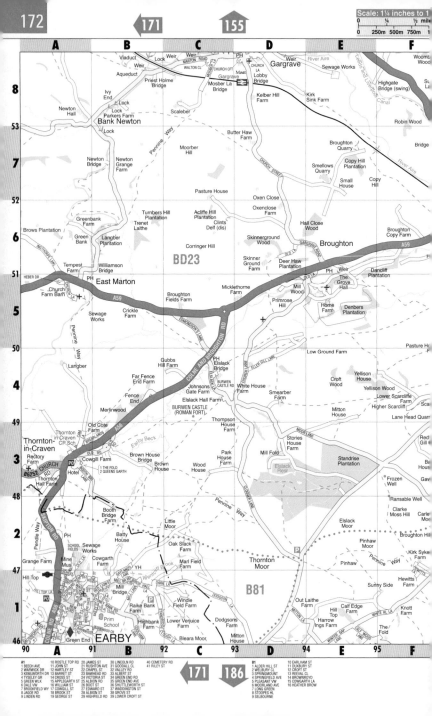

A   B   C   D   E   F

8

53

7

52

6

51

5

50

4

49

3

48

2

47

1

46

Woomby Wood

St Helens

Highgate Bridge (swing)

Robin Wood

Bridge

River Aire

Gargrave

Sewage Works

Weir

River Aire

Kirk Sink Farm

Kelber Hill Farm

Butter Haw Farm

Broughton Quarry

Smellows Quarry

Copy Hill Plantation

Small House

Copy Hill

CHURCH STREET

Pasture House

Oxen Close

Oxenclose Farm

Hall Close Wood

Broughton Copy Farm

A59

Tumbers Hill Plantation

Acliffe Hill Plantation

Clints Delf (dis)

Skinnerground Wood

Greenbank Wood

Trenet Laithe

Corringer Hill

Skinner Ground Farm

Deer Haw Plantation

Broughton

BD23

Denbers Plantation

Dancliff Plantation

Green Bank

Langber Plantation

Williamson Farm

Tempest Farm

East Marton

Broughton Fields Farm

Micklethorne Farm

Mill Wood

The Grove Hall

GARGRAVE ROAD

OLD LA

HEBER DR

Church Farm Barn

PH

A59

Crickle Farm

Primrose Hill

Home Farm

Sewage Works

EDMONDSONS LANE

Pennine Way

Langber

Gubbs Hill Farm

Far Fence End Farm

Elslack Bridge

PH

Burwen Castle Farm

White House Farm

Smearber Farm

Low Ground Farm

Pasture Ho

Croft Wood

Yellison House

Yellison Wood

COLNE AND BROUGHTON RD

ELLERE GILL LANE

Fence End

Johnsons Gate Farm

Elslack Hall Farm

BURWEN CASTLE (ROMAN FORT)

Lower Scarcliffe Farm

Higher Scarcliff

Scar

Lane Head Quarr

Merlinwood

Old Cote Farm

Thornton-in-Craven

Thornton in Craven CP Sch

Thompson House Farm

Mitton House

MOOR LANE

Red Gill

Rectory Farm

B6252

CHURCH RD

Cowgill Farm

PO

OLD RD

1 THE FOLD
2 QUEENS GARTH

Brown House Bridge

Brown House

Wood House

Park House Farm

Mill Fold

Stories House Farm

Standrise Plantation

Ho

Bei

Hotel

Thornton Hall Farm

Earby Beck

Elslack Resr

Frozen Well

SKIPTON RD

Pendle Way

Booth Bridge Farm

Little Moor

Pennine Way

Ransable Well

Clarke Moss Hill

Carle

Grange Farm

PH

Batty House

Oak Slack Farm

Thornton Moor

Elslack Moor

Broughton Hill

Kirk Syke

Hill Top

SCHOOL FIELDS

Sewage Works

Cowgarth Farm

Marl Field Farm

B81

Pinhaw Moor

Pennine Way

Pinhaw

Sunny Side

Hewitts Farm

PITTS

Mine Mus

YH

Wentworth Brook

Mill Bridge

DALE VIEW

GALLABER

Windle Field Farm

DODGSON

Out Laithe Farm

Calf Edge Farm

Knott Farm

Prim School

Raike Bank Farm

Hirbank Farm

Lower Verjuice Farm

Dodgsons Farm

Hill Top Harrow Ings Farm

WINTER GAP LANE

WHITE HL LA

The Fold

Green End

EARBY

Bleara Moor

Mitton House

OLD RD

A   B   C   D   E   F

← 171   ↓ 186

A1
1 BEECH AVE
2 WARWICK DR
3 KENILWORTH DR
4 TYSELEY GR
5 GREEN WLK
6 DALE VW
7 BROOKFIELD WY
8 JAGOE RD
9 LINDEN RD
10 ROSTLE TOP RD
11 JOHN ST
12 HARTLEY ST
13 BARRET ST
14 CROSS ST
15 APPLEGARTH ST
16 WILLIAM ST
17 COWGILL ST
18 BROOK ST
19 GEORGE ST
20 JAMES ST
21 RUSHTON AVE
22 CHAPEL ST
23 BANKHEAD RD
24 VICTORIA ST
25 ALBION RD
26 BOOT ST
27 EDWARD ST
28 ALBION ST
29 HIGHFIELD RD
30 LINCOLN RD
31 GOODALL CL
32 VALLEY RD
33 ALBERT ST
34 GREEN END RD
35 GREEN END AVE
36 SHUTTLEWORTH ST
37 WADDINGTON ST
38 GROVE ST
39 LOWER CROFT ST
40 CEMETERY RD
41 RILEY ST

B1
1 ALDER HILL ST
2 WELBURY CL
3 SPRINGMOUNT
4 SPRINGFIELD AVE
5 PLEASANT VW
6 MOORLAND AVE
7 LONG GREEN
8 STOOPES HL
9 SELBOURNE
10 EARLHAM ST
11 DUXBURY ST
12 CROFT ST
13 REVIVAL CL
14 BROWNROYD
15 COWGARTH LA
16 HEATHER BROW

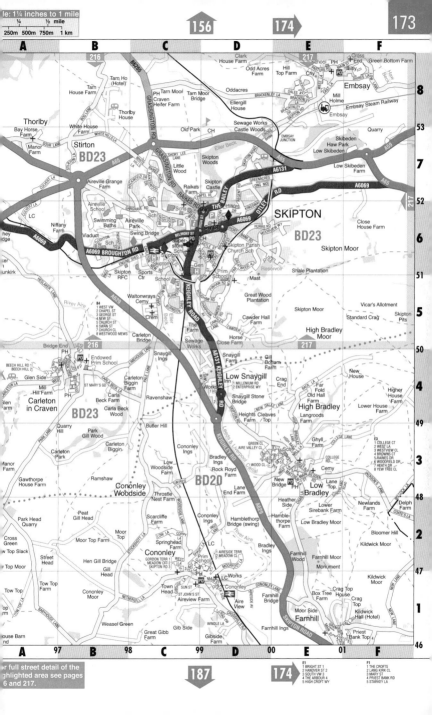

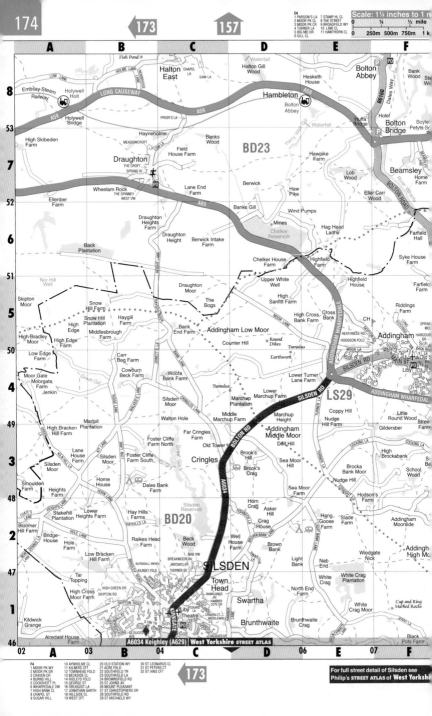

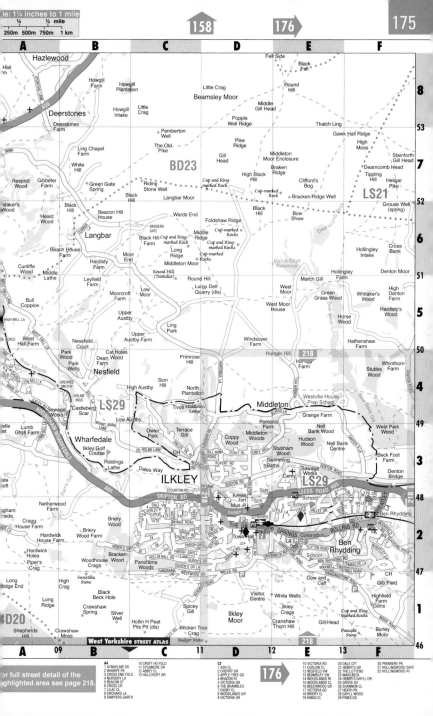

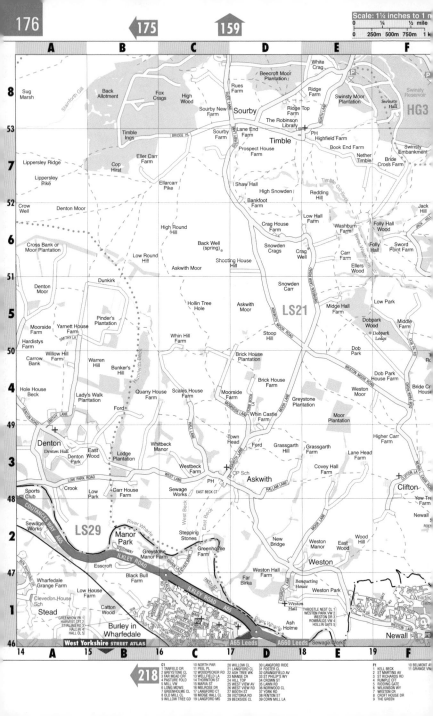

ale: 1¼ inches to 1 mile

¼   ½   mile
250m 500m 750m 1 km

A B C D E F

8

Watson House Farm
HSON'S LANE
B6451
PH
Watson Lane Farm
Brown Bank
BRAIME LA
WATSON'S LANE
BROWN LANE ROAD
Whistle House
Bland Hill Farm
Sandwith Moor
Scargill Reservoir
Sandwith Hills
Scargill Pasture
Ten Acre Reservoir
Springhill Farm
Moor Park Farm

53

BROAD DUBB ROAD
BROAD DUBB ROAD
Cooper House Farm
Brat Ridge
Sandwith Moor
HG3
NORWOOD LANE
Phoenix Farm

7

Scow Hall Farm
BRAT LA
Paddock Hill
ud Lane Farm
Hambleton House Farm
TOP LANE
Bratt Farm
Almias Cliff
P
Sandwith Moor
Stainburn Moor
Crimple Head Farm
Shawfield Head Farm
B6161
OTLEY ROAD

52

Brass Castle
Norwood Edge Plantation
Hunter's Stones
Lanshaw Farm
Lanshaw Moor
Briscoerigg Farm
BRISCOE RIDGE LANE

6

Warren Plantation
NORWOOD BOTTOM LA
Prospecthouse Farm
Lindley Moor
Highfield Farm
Briscoerigg

51

Norwood Bottom
B6451
Norwood Hall
Wood Top Farm
Buttoner House Farm
Napes Hill
Moorside Farm

5

Viaduct
Farnley Moor
Rose Tree Farm
Lindley Wood
Lindley Wood Farm
Springs Wood
Lindley Hall Farm
Lindley Wood Resr
Beckbottom Farm
B6161
Moorside Bridge
NEW LANE
GREENHILL LANE
Staniston Hill
Gillcroft Farm
BRAITHORNE LANE

50

4

Crag Farm
ey
Crag Plantation
Oxmires Hill
Quarry Hill
Yew Tree Farm
Pear Tree Farm
Lindley Green Farm
Lindley Bridge
Lindley
NEW WHIN LANE
COACH LANE
GILL LANE
Hill Top Farm
Robins Hill
Gayle Farm
GALE LA
Braythorn
Townend Farm
LOW LANE
Home Farm
Stainburn
LS17

49

3

addockstones Farm
Carr Side
Farnley
C of E Prim Sch
Elsingbottom Farm
CINDER LA
West End Farm
Stainburn Bank
Low Bank
Woodbottom Farm
CHURCH LANE
Fir Tree Farm
Bailey's Whins
Bogridge Farm

48

Mount Pleasant Farm
MANROYD
Copmanroyd Farm
B6451
FARNLEY LA
Creamery Farm
Home Farm
Farnley Hall
Lake Plantation
Farnley Lake
LS21
Fishpool
LEATHLEY LANE
Leathley Grange
Leathley Farm
Leathley Moor
Hilltop Farm
STAINBURN LANE
Hold Gills
RIFFA LANE
North Field
Castley Moor
Riffa Wood

2

The Whartons Prim Sch
Otley Plantation
Farnley Park
FARNLEY PARK
East Park
Hasling Hall Farm
Low End
Barks Hill
Leathley
HALL LANE
SCALE LA
Hartmires
Leafield Bank
Riffa Farm
Riffa Beck Farm
A658

47

1

Prince Henry's Gram Sch
RIVERSIDE AV
The Sandbeds
River Wharfe
Sewage Works
Leathley Bridge
Leathley LANE
Leathley Hall
Leathley Park or Hartmires
Leathley Field
Crosby Close
Riffa Beck
A658 Bradford

West Yorkshire STREET ATLAS

46

A 21 B 22 C 23 D 24 E 25 F

NBECK AV
NBECK CL
RSIDE DR
RSIDE PK
NER CR
ELSTAN LA
PENDALE RI
ECROFT RD

10 NEWALL HALL PK
11 OATLANDS DR

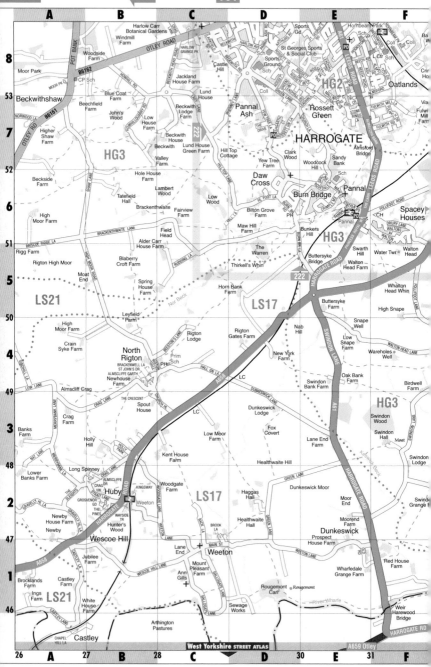

E6
1 CLIVE RD
2 CASTLE CL
3 BEECH LA
4 CANBY LA
5 CHURCH HL
6 MILL CL

7 MANOR GARTH
8 SCHOOL LA
9 CHURCH CL

A B C D E F

8

Crimple Valley
Golf Course
HG2
Mill
Hill Wood
Weir
Quarry
Wood
Home
Farm
Square
Wood
Long Plantation
Follifoot
Ridge
Follifoot
Ridge Farm
Crimple
Farm
Rudding
Dower
The
Carrs
Rudding Park
Golf Course
Fox
Covert
Park
Wood
CH
Low
Wood
PH
Follifoot
HG3
The Whins
Oak
Wood
Leaconfield
Plantation
Quarry
Wood
Haggs
Wood

Duck Nest
Farm
Brown
Hill
Brown Hill
Wood
Spofforth Moor
Haggs
Farm
Haggs Road
Farm
Spa Bottom
Farm
Lodge
Wood
Parkin's
Wood
Alder Wood
223

Wingate
Farm
Plompton
Park
Plompton
Rocks
Plompton
Square
The Warren
Braham
Hall
Aketon
Lodge
Cherry Tree
Farm
Aketon Villa
Farm
CH
Manor
Farm
Spofforth Moor
Golf Course
Shaw
Bridge
Hell
Hole
Spofforth
Castle
Lodge
Farm
Cup and Ring
marked Boulder
Low Lane
Bridge

Plompton
High Grange
Loxley
Farm
Braham
Wood
Throstle
Nest Farm
Beech
Hill
53
HG5
York
Hill
Swainthornes
Wood
Sewage
Works
Grosper
Farm
52
Hill Top
House
Newsholme
Farm
6
Prim'r
Sch
PH Spofforth
51
E5
1 CASTLE INGS
2 CHAPEL LA
3 WHITE HORSE MS
4 PARK LANDS
5 EAST PK RD
6 PARK MOUNT
7 PARK HO GN
Red
Hill
Spofforth
Hall
5
7

HG3
Hillside
Farm
Hill
p Hall
North
Wood
Cemy
Low Hall
East
Plantation
Parks
Farm
Cocked
Hat Whin
Sunrise
Farm
Park
House
Farm
Dale
Wood
Fox Heads
Farm
Spofforth
Park
Royal Oak
Plantation
Home
Farm
Stockeld
Grange
Farm
50
Prim'r
Sch
Kirkby Overblow
PH
FOLLIFOOT LA
Ingham
Whinn
High
Park Farm
Bowrake
Farm
Whin Lane
Farm
Stockfield Park House
Pigeon
Cote Wood
Bathing
Well Wood
4
Bowrake
Farm
Stockeld Park
49
Stainburn
Hill
Lund
Head
Addlethorpe
Grange
Addlethorpe
Wood
LS22
Sicklinghall
Sicklinghall
Wood
Skerry Grange
Farm
Spring
Wood
SICKLINGHALL RD
3
Barrowby
Punch Bowl
Coverts
PH
Sicklinghall
CP Sch
THE CR
Linton
Springs
(Hotel)
48
Barrowby
Grange
Beck View
Farm
Hill
Croft
Farm
Sicklinghall
House
Devonshire
Whin
Linton
Spring
Farm
Devonshire
Wood
2
Low Barrowby
Todd
Hill
Morcar Hill
Farm
Clap
Gate
Cliff
Top
Kearby Town
End
Paddock
House Farm
West
Plantation
47
Swindon
armhouse
Spring
Moor
Netherby
Bodrum
Hill
Owl
Head
Manor
Farm
Chapel
Hill
Bank
Hill
Carlshead
House
Old Wives'
Wood
Wood Hall
(Hotel)
Lime Kiln
Wood
Beech End
Cow
Wood
1
Sewage
Works
The
Fitts
LS17
Netherby Deep
Back
Water
Carlton
Hill
Spring
Wood
Ox
Close
Carlston
Hill
Carlstonhill
Farm
Carthick
Wood
West Yorkshire STREET ATLAS
46

For full street detail of the
highlighted area see pages
222 and 223.

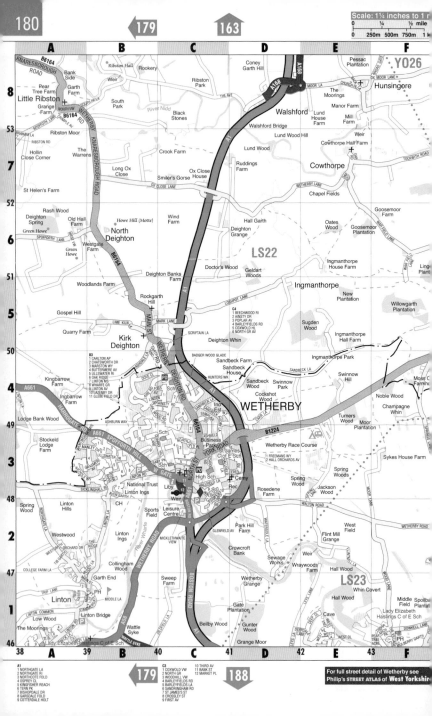

Scale: 1¼ inches to 1 r

0 ¼ ½ mile
0 250m 500m 750m 1 k

A **B** **C** **D** **E** **F**

KNARESBOROUGH ROAD
B6164
Ribston Hall
Rookery
Coney Garth Hill
Pessac Plantation
OX MOOR LANE
Y026

8

Bank Side
Garth Farm
Ribston Park
MOOR LA
The Moorings
Manor Farm
Hunsingore

Pear Tree Farm
Little Ribston
South Park
The AVE
Walshford
Lund House Farm
Mill Farm

Grange Farm
B6164
River Nidd
Black Stones
Walshford Bridge
Lund Wood Hill

BRAHAM LA
Ribston Moor
RIBSTON RD
Crook Farm
Lund Wood
Cowthorpe Hall Farm
Weir

53

Hollin Close Corner
The Warrens
Long Ox Close
Ox Close House
Ruddings Farm
Cowthorpe
TOCKWITH RD

7

St Helen's Farm
Smiler's Gorse
OX CLOSE LANE
Chapel Fields
WETHERBY LANE

52

Rash Wood
Deighton Spring
Old Hall Farm
Howe Hill (Motte)
Wind Farm
Hall Garth
Deighton Grange
Goosemoor Farm
Goosemoor Plantation

Green Howe
SPOFFORTH LANE
North Deighton
LS22
Oates Wood
Ingmanthorpe House Farm

6

Green Howe
Westgate Farm
B6164
Doctor's Wood
Geldart Woods
Ingmanthorpe
New Plantation

51

Woodlands Farm
Deighton Banks Farm
A1
LOBSPOT LANE
Willowgarth Plantation

Gospel Hill
Rockgarth Hill
Ingmanthorpe Hall Farm

5

LIME KILN
MARK LANE
C4
1 BEECHWOOD RI
2 AINSTY DR
3 POPLAR AV
4 BARLEYFIELDS RD
5 COXWOLD HL
6 NORTH GR AV
Sugden Wood

Quarry Farm
Kirk Deighton
SCRIFTAIN LA
Deighton Whin

50

83
1 CARLTON AP
2 CHATSWORTH DR
3 MARSTON WY
4 BUTTERMERE AV
5 ULLSWATER RI
6 OAK RIDGE
7 LINTON MS
8 WHARFE GR
9 LINTON AV
10 LADEMPY DR
11 GLEBE FIELD DR
BADGER WOOD GLADE
Sandbeck Farm
Sandbeck House
Ingmanthorpe Park
SANDBECK LA
Swinnow Hill
Moss C
Farmho

Kingbarrow Farm
HUNTERS WK
Sandbeck Wood
Swinnow Park
Noble Wood
Champagne Whin

4

A661
A1
Ingbarrow Farm
Cockshot Wood
WETHERBY
Turners Wood
Moor Plantation

Lodge Bank Wood
HARROGATE RD
ASHBURN WAY
Ind Est
B1224
Wetherby Race Course
Sykes House Farm

49

Stockeld Lodge Farm
A667
SPOFFORTH HILL
Sch
YORK ROAD
Ashfield Business Park
1 FREEMANS WY
2 HALL ORCHARDS AV
Spring Woods

3

Spring Wood
Linton Hills
Sch
High Sch
St James C of E Sch
Cemy
Rec
Rosedene Farm
Spring Wood
Jackson Wood

48

Westwood
National Trust
Linton Ings
Liby
Weir
Park Hill Farm
Flint Mill Grange
West Field
WETHERBY ROAD

2

Spring Wood
Linton Ings
Sports Field
Leisure Centre
Micklethwaite View
GLENFIELD AV
Crowcroft Bank
Weir
Wraywoods Farm
Hall Wood

47

COLLEGE FARM LA
Collingham Wood
Sweep Farm
BOSTON ROAD
Sewage Works
Wetherby Grange
LS23
Whin Covert

Linton
Garth End
MIDDLE LA
PH
Gate Plantation
Hall Wood
Middle Field
Spoilba Plantat

1

Linton Common
Low Wood
Linton Bridge
Wattle Syke
Beilby Wood
Gunter Wood
Cave
Lady Elizabeth Hastings C of E

The Moorings
Lady Elizabeth Hastings C of E Sch
WATTLE SYKE
Grange Moor
WEST DL
PH

46

A **B** **C** **D** **E** **F**
38 39 40 41 42 43

A1
1 NORTHGATE LA
2 NORTHGATE RI
3 NORTHCOTE FOLD
4 OSPREY CL
5 KINGFISHER REACH
6 TERN PK
7 BISHOPDALE DR
8 GARSDALE FOLD
9 COTTERDALE HOLT

C3
1 COXWOLD VW
2 NORTH GR
3 WOODHILL VW
4 BARLEYFIELDS RD
5 BARLEYFIELDS LA
6 SANDRINGHAM RD
7 ST JAMES ST
8 CROSSLEY ST
9 FIRST AV

10 THIRD AV
11 BANK ST
12 MARKET PL

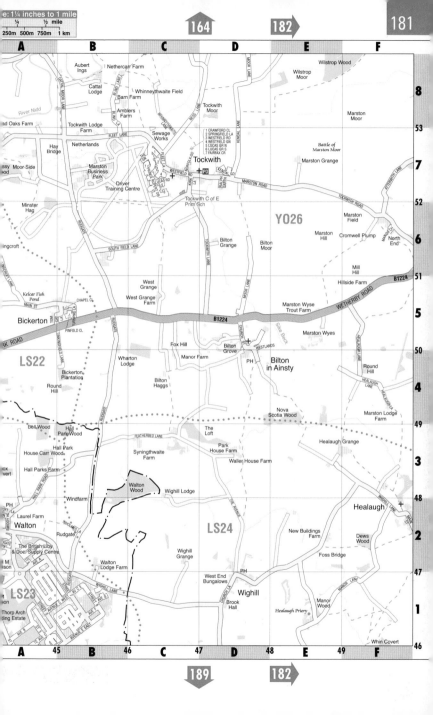

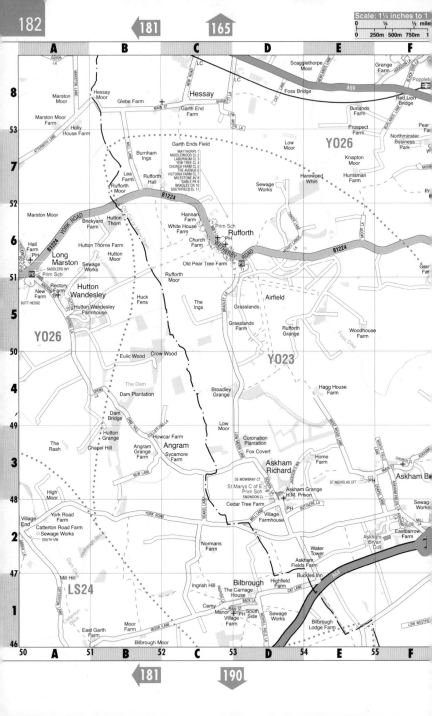

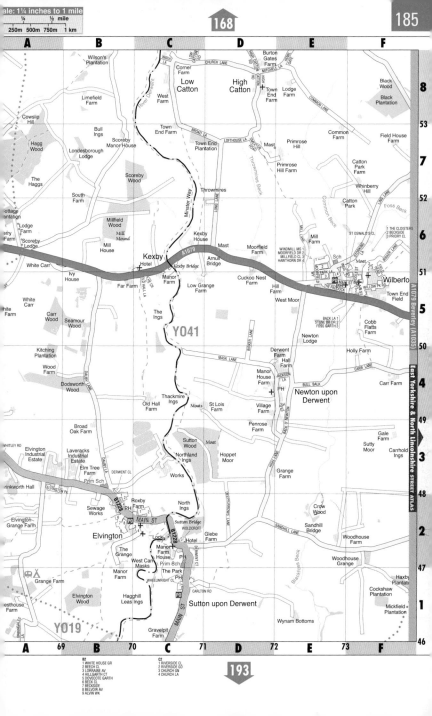

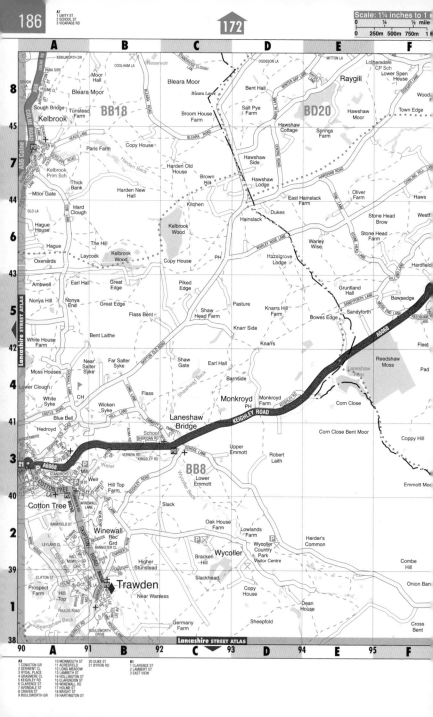

172

Lancashire STREET ATLAS

KENILWORTH DR
PARK SIDE
Moor Hall
COOLHAM LA
Reservoir
STAINCLIFFE CLOUGH LA
Bleara Moor
DODGSON LA
MITTON LA
Lothersdale
CP Sch
Lower Spen House
SKIPTON RD
Wood

8

Bleara Moor
Bleara Lane
Bent Hall
Salt Pye Farm
WINTER GAP LANE
Raygill
BD20
Hawshaw Moor
Town End

Sough Bridge
Tunstead House
Kelbrook
BB18
Broom House Farm
Hawshaw Cottage
COLNE ROAD
Springs Farm

45
SOUGH
COLNE ROAD
HOLME LA
HEADS LANE
BLEARA ROAD
BLEARA RD
Hawshaw Side
Hawshaw Lodge
HANGING ROAD

7
A56 Colne
Kelbrook Prim Sch
Paris Farm
Copy House
Harden Old House
Brown Hill
Hawshaw Side
Hawshaw Lodge
Oliver Farm
Haws
DOVE LANE
COLNE ROAD
Harden Beck

44
Thick Bank
Harden New Hall
Kitchen
East Hainslack Farm
Stone Head Brow
Westf
Moor Gate
OLD LA
COLNE LANE

6
Hard Clough
Hainslack
Dukes
WARLEY WISE LANE
Stone Head Farm
Hardfield
Hague House
Kelbrook Wood
Warley Wise
Hague
The Hill
Laycock
Copy House
PH
Hazelgrove Lodge
STONE HEAD LANE
HILL

43
Oxenards
Kelbrook Wood
Copy House

5
Ambwell
Earl Hall
Great Edge
Piked Edge
Pasture
Knarrs Hill Farm
Gruntland Hall
Bawsedge
Nonya Hill
Nonya End
Great Edge
Shaw Head Farm
Bowes Edge
Sandyforth
A6068
SANDYFORTH LANE
MOSS END LANE
REEDSHAW LANE
Flass Bent
Knarr Side

42
White House Farm
Bent Laithe
Knarrs
Laneshaw River
Reedshaw Moss
Fleet
Pad

4
Moss Houses
Lower Clough
Near Salter Syke
Far Salter Syke
Shaw Gate
Earl Hall
Barnside
Corn Close
LONG LANE
SKIPTON OLD ROAD
Shawhead Beck
KEIGHLEY RD

White Syke
CH
Wicken Syke
Flass
HILL LANE
Monkroyd Farm
Monkroyd
PH
Corn Close Bent Moor
Coppy Hill

41
CASTLE ROAD
Blue Bell
Laneshaw Bridge
EMMOTT LANE
KEIGHLEY ROAD
Hedroyd
ALMA RD
School
SHERIDAN RD
WINDERMERE

3
Sch
A6068
STANDROYD
Mill
Weir
VERNON RD
KINGSLEY RD
SCHOOL LANE
Upper Emmott
Robert Laith
COTTON TREE LA
MOYROYD LANE
PO

40
COTTON TREE
B6251
Cotton Tree
Hill Top Farm
BB8
Lower Emmott
Emmott Moo
BANKFIELD ST
WINEWALL LANE
NEW ROAD
Slack
Wycoller Beck

2
Winewall
Rec Grd
BANNISTER CL
CARRIER'S RD
Higher Stunstead
Oak House Farm
Bracken Hill
Wycoller
Lowlands Farm
Wycoller Country Park Visitor Centre
Herder's Common
Combe Hill
LEYLAND CL
HALL MDWS
SKIPTON ROAD

39
CLIFTON ST
Slackhead
Onion Ban
Prospect Farm
Hill Top
Near Wanless
Copy House
Dean House
COLNE RD

1
Trawden
Germany Farm
Sheepfold
Cross Bent
FOULDS ROAD
Beardshaw Beck
BOULSWORTH DRIVE

38

90   A   91   B   92   C   93   D   94   E   95   F

A3
1 CONISTON GR
2 DERWENT CL
3 RYDAL PLACE
4 GRASMERE CL
5 KEIGHLEY RD
6 CLARENCE ST
7 AVONDALE ST
8 CRAVEN ST
9 BOULSWORTH GR

10 MONMOUTH ST
11 ACRESFIELD
12 LONG MEADOW
13 LAMBETH ST
14 HOLLINGTON ST
15 CLARENDON ST
16 WINEWALL RD
17 HOLME ST
18 BRIGHT ST
19 HARTINGTON ST

20 DUKE ST
21 BYRON RD

B1
1 CLARENCE ST
2 LAMBERT ST
3 EAST VIEW

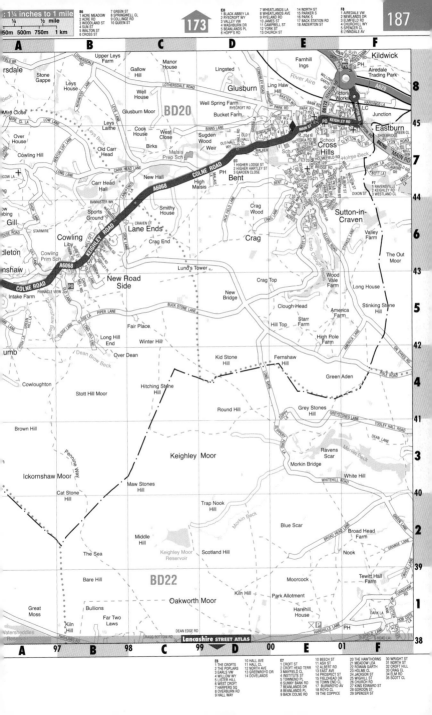

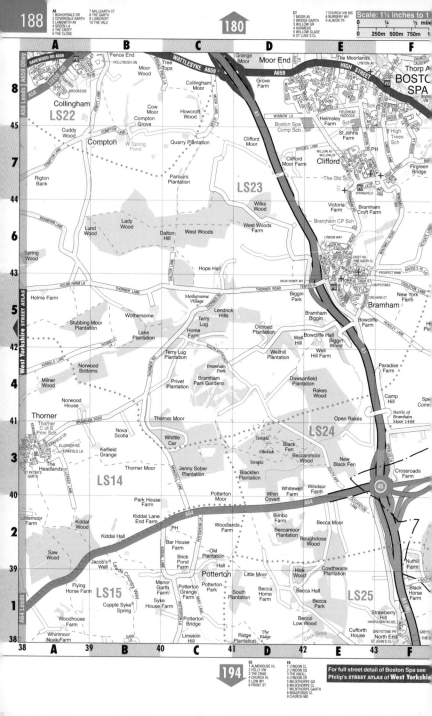

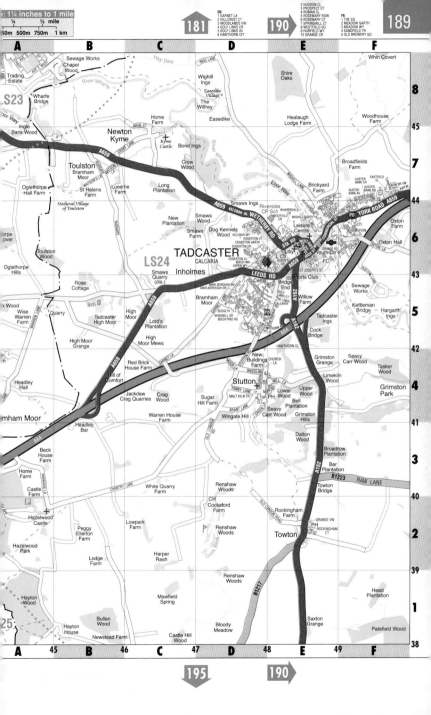

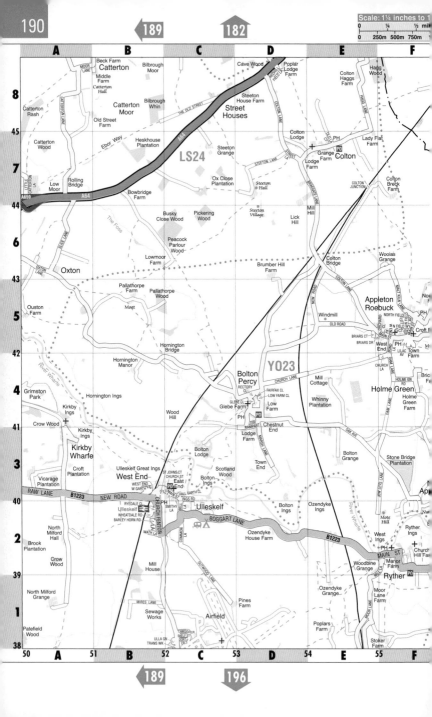

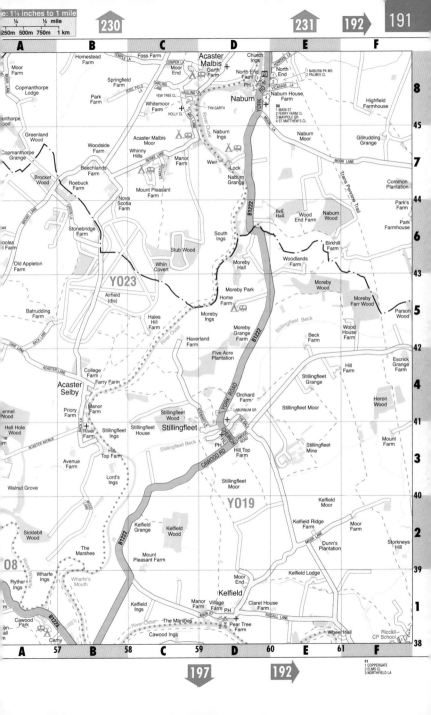

Scale: 1¼ inches to 1 mile
0 ¼ ½ mile
0 250m 500m 750m 1

8
45
7
44
6
43
5
42
4
41
3
40
2
39
1
38

A 62 B 63 C 64 D 65 E 66 F 67

THE CRANBROOKS 1
MOOR CL 2
BRAITHEGAYTE 3
RUFFHAMS CL 4
DERWENT DR 5
RAKER CL 6
HARCOURT CL 7
WALKER LA 8
DYKELANDS CL 9
LOW WELL PK 10

Sparrow Hall Farm
Hagg Wood
Low Well Farm
Wheldrake
Kirk's Rein
Gothic House Farm
West Plantation
Wigman Wood
Wigman Hall
Brick Farm
BENJY LANE
Tile Farm
Millfield
Rush Farm
Primrose Farm
Wincover Farm
Pasture Farm
Deighton
FORGE LA
SWAN FARM CT
Swan Farm
SWAN CL
Sheepwalk Farm
NEW ROAD
Long Wood
North Selby Mine
Wharren House Farm
Lacy Bottom Wood
The Bottoms
Orchard Farm
South End
Moat
PH
Spring House Farm
Spring Wood
Chequer Hall
Wheldrake Wrayst
WELDRAKE LANE
Wheldrake Grange
Mill Hill Farm
Crab Tree Farm
DOWER CHASE
1 DOWER CHASE
2 SOUTHLANDS CL
3 ESCRICK CT
4 WOODLANDS
5 ESCRICK PK GD
DOWER PK
The Carrs
Gravel Pitt Hill
Gilbertson's Wood
Glebe Farm
Escrick
PO
PH
Gashouse Plantation
WHELDRAKE LANE
Tileshed Farm
Common Bottom Farm
COMMON
Escrick C of E Prim Sch
Bridge Farm
Millfield Plantation
Common Bottom Wood
Moons Plantation
Kennel Plantation
YO19
Grey Reins
Common Farm
SOUTHMOOR
Queen Margarets School
Escrick Park
Manor Farm
Old Road Plantation
Fox Covert Plantation
Escrick Park Home Farm
Mount Pleasant Farm
Dogs Leg Wood
Horn Farm
Harrop's Plantation
Aviary Plantation
Whinchat Hall
Low Cover Wood
West Grange
ROTH HILL LANE
Works
Duck Hole Plantation
West End
Park Farm
Menagerie Farm
Hackings Wood
Bridge Farm
Thornhill Farm
Manor Wood
Thorganby Lodge
Glade Farm
Hunt Pease Carrs
BLADE ROAD
Common Wood
Crook Moor
Sheds Bell Farm
Hollicarrs Wood
Field House Farm
Manor Farm
West End Farm
HOLLICARRS CL
Hart Nooking
Charity Farm
Broomhill Plantation
DERRY LANE
Duffield V
Rainbows End
Nightingale Wood
YO8
Danes Hills (Tumuli)
Red Moors
Approach Farm
Black Tom Hill
Rider's Plantation
Little Skipwith
Hill Farm
Crook Moor
Redmoor Farm
Scorce Bridge
A19
Anne's Plantation
Church Farm
Park Farm
School Farm
PH
Town End
Little Common
Skipwith
Plantation House
COMMON BLACKWOOD ROAD
Moat
Bluebell Farm
PO
Peel Hall Farm
The Ings
South Moor Hill
South Moor

A1
1 MILL LA
2 HOLMES DR
3 CHAPEL LA
4 CHAPEL WK
5 PINFOLD CL

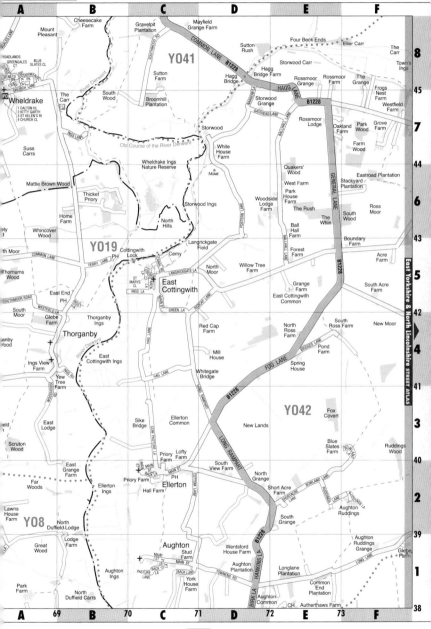

A   B   C   D   E   F

Mount
Pleasant

Cheesecake
Farm

Gravelpit
Plantation

Mayfield
Grange Farm

Four Beck Ends

Eller Carr

The
Carr

Town's
Ings

8

ROADLANDS
GREENGALES
CT   BLUE
SLATES CL

Sutton
Rush

Storwood Carr

Common Lane   B1228

YO41

Hagg
Bridge Farm

Rossmoor
Grange

Rossmoor
Farm

The
Grange

Frogs
Nest
Farm

The
Carr   P

Sutton
Farm

Hagg
Bridge

Hagg Lane   B1228

Westfield
Farm

45

Wheeldrake

1 DALTON HL
2 KITTY GARTH
3 ST HELEN'S RI
4 CHURCH RI

South
Wood

Broomhill
Plantation

Storwood
Grange

GATEHEAD LANE

Rossmoor
Lodge

Oakland
Farm

Park
Wood

Grove
Farm

7

Storwood

White
House
Farm

Farm
Wood

River Derwent

Ings Lane

Old Course of the River Derwent

Suss
Carrs

Wheeldrake Ings
Nature Reserve

Moat

Quakers'
Wood

Eastroad Plantation

Stackyard
Plantation

44

Mattie Brown Wood

Thicket
Priory

Storwood Ings

West Farm

Park
House
Farm

Ross
Moor

6

th Moor

Common Lane

Thornums
Wood

Home
Farm

Whincover
Wood

North
Hills

Langrickgate
Field

Woodside
Lodge
Farm

The Rush

Ball
Farm

Ball
Farm

The
Whin

South
Wood

Boundary
Farm

43

YO19

Cottingwith
Lock

Ferry Lane

PH

Cemy

North
Moor

Willow Tree
Farm

POTTERY LANE

BALLHALL LANE

Forest
Farm

Acre
Farm

5

Thornums
Wood

St Marys
CL

East
Cottingwith

Langrickgate La

BACK LANE

INGS LA

Grange
Farm

East Cottingwith
Common

South
Ross
Farm

South Acre
Farm

42

South
Moor

East End

PH

SOUTHMOOR ROAD

WESTFIELD LA

Glebe
Farm

Thorganby Ings

Green La

Red Cap
Farm

North
Ross
Farm

Pond
Farm

New Moor

4

anby
ood

Thorganby

River Derwent

East
Cottingwith Ings

HAG LANE

Mill
House

Whitegate
Bridge

Spring
House

Fog Lane   B1228

Bridges Lane

41

Ings View
Farm

Yew Tree
Farm

INGS RD

Sike
Bridge

Ellerton
Common

Long Rampart

New Lands

YO42

Fox
Covert

Blue
Slates
Farm

Ruddings
Wood

3

field

East
Lodge

Priory
Farm

Lofty
Farm

South
View Farm

B1228

BOG LANE

40

Scruton
Wood

East
Grange
Farm

COW PASTURE LA

Priory Farm

MAIN
ST

BACK LA

PH
Ellerton

Hall Farm

South
Grange

Short Acre
Farm

Rowland Lane

Ruddings Lane

Aughton
Ruddings

2

Lawns
House
Farm

YO8

North
Duffield Lodge

Ellerton Ings

Lodge
Farm

South
Grange

Aughton
Plantation

Aughton
Ruddings
Grange

Long Lane

Glebe
Farm

39

Great
Wood

Aughton
Stud
Farm

MAIN ST

BACK LANE

Wentsford
House Farm

Hankin's La

Longlane
Plantation

1

Park
Farm

North
Duffield Carrs

Aughton Ings

PASTURE
LANE

York
House
Farm

Birk La

TOWNEND RD

Aughton
Plantation

Aughton
Common

CH

Common
End
Plantation

Autherthaws Farm

38

A   69   B   70   C   71   D   72   E   73   F

A **B** **C** **D** **E** **F**

8

37

LS15

7

36

6

35

5

LS25

4

34

33

3

2

LS26

32

GARFORTH

31

1

30

38 **A** **39** **B** **40** **C** **41** **D** **42** **E** **43** **F**

A1
1 WHITECLIFFE RD
2 LOWTHER DR
3 LOWTHER CR
4 CHURCH CL
5 SMEATON GR
6 THE PLEASANCE
7 WOODLAND GR
8 WOODLAND CR
9 WOODLAND AV
10 SPRINGWELL RD
11 SPRINGWELL AV
12 THE DR
13 SCOTT CL
14 ST MARY'S AV
15 PRIMROSE HL DR
16 PRIMROSE HL GR

For full street detail of Garforth see
Philip's STREET ATLAS of West Yorksh

Scale: 1¼ inches to 1 mile
¼   ½ mile
250m 500m 750m 1 km

Column A

Hayton Wood
South Dyke
The Rein
Woodhouse Grange
LANE
B1217
Lotherton Farm
HUTTON COPLEY LA
Bird Garden
Lotherton Hall
COPLEY LANE
Bragdale
Coburnhill Wood
Scott's Wood
Weet Wood
Ringhay Wood
Near Fox Covert
Longroyd Wood
Daniel Hartly's Wood
Hill Top
PH
Sch
Hartly Wood
Hartly Wood
GARDEN VILLAGE
New Mickfield
Highroyds Wood
Castle Hills
SUNNYBANK RD
Newtown Farm
A1(M)
field Plantation
Micklefield Plantation
ROAD A63
Beacon Plantation
ld on
Ledston Park
Wellington Plantation
g Plantation

Column B

Castle Hill Wood
Lowlead Farm
Crow Hill
Lead Mill Farm
Lead Hall Farm
B1217
OAK LA
The Crooked Billet PH
West Field
COLDHILL LANE
Coldhill Pond
Coldhill Farm
Far Fox Covert
Middle Fox Covert
Huddleston Hall
Old Wood
Huddleston Old Wood
Old Wood
Newthorpe Barrack
Newthorpe Quarry
Hill House Farm
Grange Farm
HALL LANE
LC
HIGHFIELD LANE
Whitecoat Plantation
The Boot & Shoe Inn
B1222
Pointer Farm
Hundred Acre Plantation
Peckfield Lodge
Hundred Acre Plantation
Scat House Farm
PARK LA
Hill Top Farm
Dale Plantation
Selby Fork
Street Close Plantation

Column C

Castle Hill Farm
WALNUT CL
Saxton
Saxton Lane
SCARTHINGWELL CR
Saxton CH
Sch
Manor Farm
DACRE CT
Top End
Plough Farm
PH
Headwell Farm
Old Headwell
HEADWELL LANE
Saxton Field
COLDHILL LANE
Garlic Flats
OLDGATE LANE
Oldgate Farm
COLDHILL LANE
Mile Hill
MILE HILL
COLDHILL LANE
LS25
Low Grange
Gorse Bridge Farm
B1222
GORSE LANE
Newthorpe
The New Inn
STEETON WY
WHIN LANE
WHITECOTE LANE
Steeton Hall Heritage Centre
Westfield Farm
WESTFIELD CL
WESTFIELD LANE
Orchard Farm
Lumby
Mulberry Farm
RED HILL LA
Hall Farm
Well Farm
Lumby Hall

Column D

Battlefield 1461
DOTCHERS LANE
HEADWELL LANE
SCARTHINGWELL LANE
SAXTON LANE
LS24
Ash Tree Inn
Laurel Grove
Stream Farm
Mile Hill
Beck Farm
HIGHFIELD LANE
BUTTS LANE
WHIN LANE

Column E

Scarthingwell Golf Course
Whithill Field
A162
Scarthingwell
Scarthingwell Farm
Scarthingwell Park
Orchard End
Quarry Farm
ASH TREE GARTH
ORCHARD
MAIN ST
Wood End
Sherburn in Elmet
Stream Dike
ELLARFIELD LA
FINKLE HILL
PH
ELIZABETH
RUDSTONE GR
Hall Garth
Church Farm
KIRKGATE
CHURCH
CHURCH HL
ATHELSTANE CT
CROFT
EVERSLEY GARTH CR
PROSPECT AV
HIGH TREES CT
BEECHWOOD CFT
BEECHWOOD CR
BEECHWOOD GLADE
Sch
EVERSLEY
WEST VW
Mill Dike
Low Grange
HIGHFIELD GN
Prospect Farm
Home Farm
South Milford
WOODLANDS
THE NOOK
PO
PH
Westfield Farm
SAND LA
WAIN GRO
WAIN GATE
RD
LEGION RD
South Milford
Orchard Lane
Old Quarry Lane
CASS LANE

Column F

Patefield Wood
Carr Wood
Old Hall Farm
CH
Scarthingwell CH
COMMON ROAD
Barkston Moor
Ivy Hall Farm
ORCHARD LA
Barkston Ash
BACK
Sawyer Wells Farm
Manor Farm
Spital Moor
A162
SPRINGFIELD CT
HARDWTH AV
MEADOW
LADY
MOOR LA
EAST MEADOW
PASTURE WY
PASTURE CL
MANOR WK
ANGUS DR
Sch
EAST
PLUMPTON
Prospect Farm
A162
MILL LA
BURLEY CR
CAWDEL WY
The Spinney
INGTHORNS LANE
LONG HEADS LA

Grid references (right edge, top to bottom): 8, 37, 7, 36, 6, 35, 5, 34, 4, 33, 3, 32, 2, 31, 1, 30

Grid references (bottom, left to right): 45, 46, 47, 48, 49

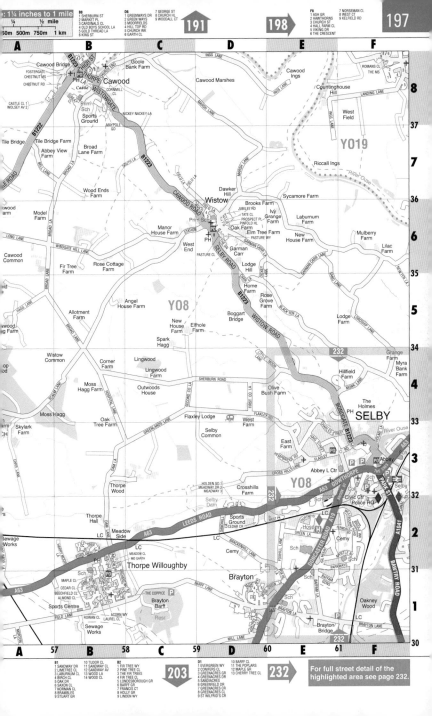

191

198

197

B8
1 SHERBURN ST
2 MARKET PL
3 CARDINALS CL
4 OLD BOYS SCHOOL LA
5 GOLD THREAD LA
6 KING ST

D6
1 GREENWAYS DR
2 GREEN WAYS
3 MOORFIELDS
4 HILL TOP RD
5 CHURCH WK
6 GARTH CL

7 GEORGE ST
8 CHURCH HL
9 WOODALL CT

F8
1 ASH GR
2 HAWTHORNS
3 CHURCH ST
4 HALL FARM CL
5 VIKING DR
6 THE CRESCENT

7 NORSEMAN CL
8 WEST CT
9 KELFIELD RD

Cawood Bridge
FOSTERGATE
Chestnut Ms
HIGH ST
Cawood
Castle
WISTOWGATE
THORPE LA
Prim Sch
CASTLE CL 1
WOLSEY AV 2
Chestnut Rd
CORNMILL LA
Goole Bank Farm
Cawood Marshes
Cawood Ings
ROMANS CL
THE MS
Countinghouse Hill
LANDING LANE
Tile Bridge
B1222
Tile Bridge Farm
Abbey View Farm
Broad Lane Farm
BROAD LA
BELL LANE
SOUTH LA
B1223
NICKEY NACKEY LA
Sports Ground
MAYPOLE GD
West Field
INGS LANE
INGS LANE
Y019
Riccall Ings
River Ouse
wood Farm
Model Farm
LONG LANE
BROAD LA
Wood Ends Farm
CAWOOD ROAD
FIELD LA
B1223
Dawker Hill
JUBILEE RD
TATE CL
Brooks Farm
Ivy Grange Farm
Sycamore Farm
Laburnum Farm
Mulberry Farm
Cawood Common
BRIDGE LANE
BROAD LANE
WINDGATE HILL LANE
Fir Tree Farm
Rose Cottage Farm
Manor House Farm
West End
STATION RD
Wistow
Prim Sch
PO
PH
Oak Lane
PROSPECT PL
PINFOLD HL
Elm Tree Farm
PASTURE WY
New House Farm
GARMAN CARR LA
LILAC Farm
INKER LA
Cawood Common
ld
wood agg Farm
HAGG LANE
BROAD LANE
Allotment Farm
Angel House Farm
Y08
New House Farm
Elfhole Farm
PASTURE LA
Garman Carr
SELBY ROAD
Lodge Hill
Home Farm
Rose Grove Farm
B1223
GARMAN CARR LANE
SAND LANE
Lodge Farm
LONGHEDGE LANE
Wistow Common
Corner Farm
Lingwood
Lingwood Farm
Spark Hagg
Boggart Bridge
WISTOW ROAD
BLACK FEN LA
232
Grange Farm
Myra Bank Farm
op
ood
Moss Hagg
Moss Hagg Farm
HOSPITAL LANE
Outwoods House
Oak Tree Farm
SECOND CO LA
SHERBURN ROAD
FIRST CO LA
Olive Bush Farm
Hillfield Farm
MONK LANE
The Holmes
Skylark Farm
DAIR LANE
GREENLANDS LANE
Flaxley Lodge
FLAXLEY HL
West Farm
Selby Common
SELBY
River Ouse
East Farm
HEMINGBRO RD
CHARLES STREET
PO
Abbey
arm
H
Thorpe Wood
HOLDEN GD 1
MEADWAY DR 2
MEADWAY 3
Crosshills Farm
Y08
CROSS HILLS LANE
FLAXLEY
Abbey L Ctr
GOWTHORPE
B1223
Col
Selby
PARK ST
Civic Ctr
Police HQ
Sch
232
Thorpe Hall
OAK LANE
Meadow Side
A63
LEEDS ROAD
Selby Dam
Sports Ground
CEDAR CR
West PK
LC
Hosp
Cemy
GREEN LA
Sch
A63
Sewage Works
LC
MEADOW CL
MD GARTH
Thorpe Willoughby
TREE
PH
LC
BRACKENMILL LANE
Cemy
MYRTLE AV
Brayton
BARLOW
PARKWAYS
Oakney Wood
A1041
BAWTRY ROAD
MAPLE CL
CEDAR CL
BEECHFIELD CL
ALMOND CL
Sch
PO
Sports Centre
THE COPPICE
Brayton Barff
Resr
ROWAN CL
ACORN WY
LAUREL CL
FIELD LANE
BRAYTON LA
Sch
BARFF LANE
MILL LANE
Brayton Bridge
BRAYTON LANE
LC
232

203

232

B1
1 SANDWAY DR
2 LIMETREE CL
3 LABURNUM CL
4 BIRCH CL
5 OAK DR
6 SAXON CL
7 NORMAN CL
8 BRAMBLES
9 STUART GR

10 TUDOR CL
11 SANDWAY CL
12 SANDWAY AV
13 WOOD LA
14 WOOD CL

B2
1 FIR TREE WY
2 PINE TREE CL
3 THE FIR TREES
4 FIR TREE CL
5 LONDESBOROUGH GR
6 BARFF GR
7 FRANCIS CT
8 HOLLY GR
9 LINDEN WY

D1
1 EVERGREEN WY
2 CONIFERS CL
3 GREENACRES DR
4 GREENACRES OR
5 SANDIACRES
6 GRENFIELD DR
7 GREENACRES CL
8 GREENACRES CL
9 ST WILFRID'S CR

10 BARFF CL
11 THE POPLARS
12 MAPLE GR
13 CHERRY TREE CL

For full street detail of the highlighted area see page 232.

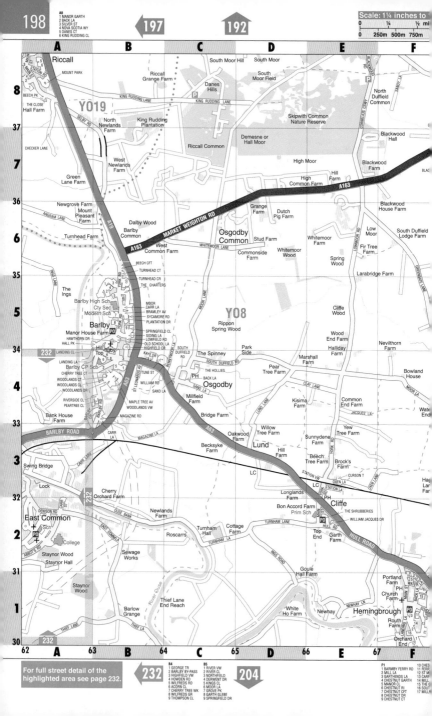

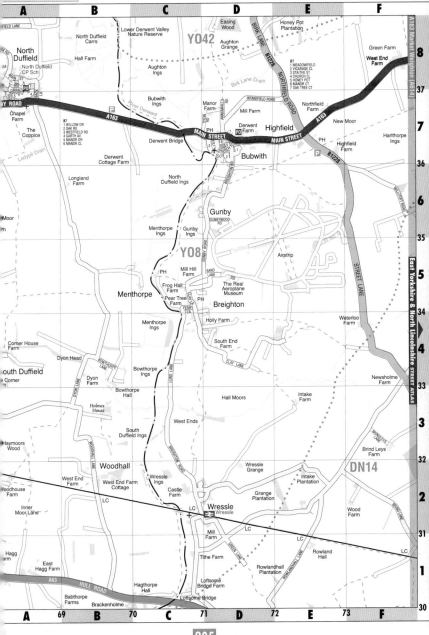

le: 1¼ inches to 1 mile

¼   ½ mile
250m 500m 750m 1 km

A   B   C   D   E   F

North Duffield Lane
North Duffield
North Duffield CP Sch
EA
PO

Chapel Farm
The Coppice

Lower Derwent Valley Nature Reserve
North Duffield Carrs
Hall Farm
Aughton Ings

Easing Wood
YO42
Aughton Grange

Honey Pot Plantation
Green Farm
West End Farm

BIRK LANE
NORTHFIELD ROAD
B1228

8
37

River Derwent
A163
Y ROAD

Bubwith Ings
Manor Farm
INTAKEFIELD ROAD
Mill Farm
Northfield Farm
A163
New Moor

D7
1 MEADOWFIELD
2 VICARAGE CL
3 STAITHE ST
4 CHURCH CL
5 HONEY POT
6 MANOR CT
7 OAK TREE CT

MAIN STREET
PH
Derwent PO
Highfield
MAIN STREET
PH
Highfield Farm
Harthorpe Ings

7

#7
1 WILLOW DR
2 OAK RD
3 WESTFIELD RD
4 GARTH AV
5 MANOR DR
6 MANOR CL

Derwent Bridge
Church Sch
Bubwith

B1228

36

Ladypit Drain

Derwent Cottage Farm
North Duffield Ings

BREIGHTON RD
WILTOFT ROAD

6

Longland Farm

Gunby

35

Moor
th

Menthorpe Ings
Gunby Ings
GUNBYWOOD RD
GRANBY ROAD
YO8

Airstrip

STREET LANE

5
34

PH
Mill Hill Farm
SAND LANE
The Real Aeroplane Museum

Menthorpe
Frog Hall Farm
Pear Tree Farm
PH
FERRY LA
Breighton

Waterloo Farm

Menthorpe Ings
Holly Farm

LUND LANE

4
33

Corner House Farm
Dyon Head
BOWTHORPE LANE
DYON AV
Dyon Farm
Bowthorpe Ings
Bowthorpe Hall

South End Farm
CLAY LANE

Newsholme Farm

uth Duffield
Corner
m

Holmes House
South Duffield Ings

Hall Moors
Intake Farm

3
32

Haymoors Wood

BREIGHTON ROAD
WOODHALL LANE

West Ends

Brind Leys Farm
DN14

oodhouse Farm

Woodhall
West End Farm
West End Farm Cottage
LC
Wressle Ings
Castle Farm
Wressle Grange
Intake Plantation
BUSK LANE

2

Inner Moor Lane

LC
Wressle
Wressle
LC
Grange Plantation
Wood Farm

31

Hagg
arm

East Hagg Farm
Babthorpe Farms
Brackenholme

Mill Farm
Tithe Farm
GREEN LANE
Loftsome Bridge Farm
Loftsome Bridge

Rowlandhall Plantation
ROWLANDHALL LANE
Rowland Hall
BUSK LANE
LC

1

A63
HULL ROAD
Hagthorpe Hall

30

For full street detail of Castleford see Philip's STREET ATLAS of West Yorkshire

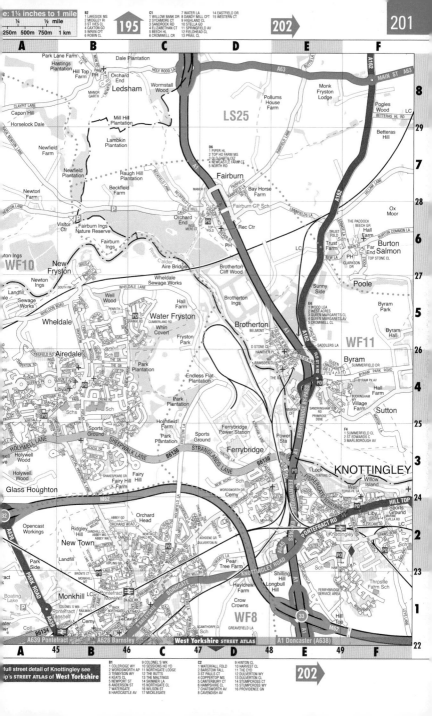

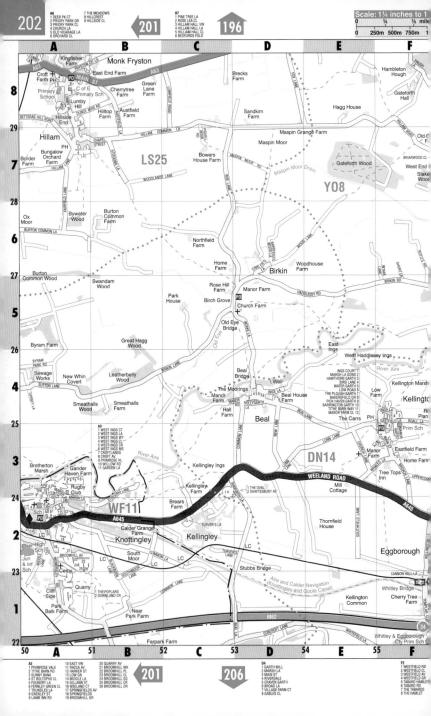

A6
1 DEER PK CT
2 PRIORY PARK GR
3 PRIORY PARK CL
4 CHURCH LA
5 OLD VICARAGE LA
6 ORCHARD CL
7 THE MEADOWS
8 HILLCREST
9 HILLSIDE CL

A7
1 PINE TREE LA
2 ROSE LEA CL
3 HILLAM HALL VW
4 HILLAM HALL LA
5 HILLAM HALL CL
6 BEDFORDS FOLD

Scale: 1¼ inches to 1
0   ¼   ½ mile
0   250m 500m 750m 1

Monk Fryston

Kingfisher Farm
Croft Farm PH
East End Farm
Primary School
C of E Primary Sch
Cherrytree Farm
Green Lane Farm
Brecks Farm
Hambleton Hough
Gateforth Hall

Lumby Hill
Hilltop Farm
Austfield Farm
Sandkim Farm
Hagg House

Hillside End
Hillam
Maspin Grange Farm
Maspin Moor
Old C

Border Farm
Bungalow Orchard Farm
Bowers House Farm

LS25
Gateforth Wood
YO8
West End
Stake Wood
BRIARWOOD CL

Ox Moor
Bywater Wood
Burton Common Farm
Northfield Farm
Maspin Moor Drain

Burton Common Wood
Swandam Wood
Home Farm
Woodhouse Farm
Birkin

Park House
Rose Hill Farm
Birch Grove
Manor Farm
Church Farm

Byram Farm
Great Hagg Wood
Old Eye Bridge
East Ings
West Haddlesey Ings
River Aire

Sewage Works
New Whin Covert
Leatherbelly Wood
Beal Bridges
Weir
The Moorings
Kellington Marsh
Low Farm
Kellington

Smeathalls Wood
Smeathalls Farm
Manor Farm
Beal House Farm
Hollygarth
Hall Farm
Beal
The Carrs
Manor Farm
Eastfield Farm
Home Farm

A3
1 WEST INGS CT
2 WEST INGS LA
3 WEST INGS WY
4 WEST INGS CL
5 WEST INGS CR
6 WEST INGS MS
7 CROFTLANDS
8 CROFT AV
9 PRIMROSE HL
10 WILLOW RD
11 GARDEN LA

INGS COURT 1
MARSH LA GDNS 2
HAWTHORN GARTH 3
BIRD LANE 4
WATER GARTH 5
LOW ROAD 6
THE PLOUGH GARTH 7
BAKERSFIELD DR 8
PICK HAVEN GARTH 9
BARRINGTON GARTH 10
TITHE BARN WAY 11
MANOR FARM CL 12

Brotherton Marsh
Gander Haven Farm
Rugby Club
Kellingley Ings
DN14

River Aire
WF11
Kellingley Farm
Brears Farm
1 THE OVAL
2 SHAFTESBURY AV
Tree Tops Inn
Mill Cottage

High Sch
Jun & Inf Sch
Cemy
A645
Calder Grange Farm
Knottigley
Kellingley
South Moor
Thornfield House
Eggborough

Cliff Side
Quarry
1 THE POPLARS
2 DOWNLAND CR
Near Park Farm
Stubbs Bridge
Aire and Calder Navigation
(Knottingley and Goole Canal)
Whitley Bridge
Cherry Tree Farm

Park Balk Farm
M62
Farpark Farm
Kellington Common
Whitley & Eggborough Cty Prim Sch
34

A2
1 PRIMROSE VALE
2 TITHE BARN RD
3 SUNNY BANK
4 ST BOLTOPHS CL
5 FOUNDRY LA
6 FERNLEY GREEN CL
7 TRUNDLES LA
8 GRENLEY ST
9 LAMB INN RD
10 EAST VW
11 RACCA AV
12 HARKER ST
13 LOW GN
14 MIDDLE LA
15 GILLANN ST
16 WEELAND CT
17 SPRINGFIELDS AV
18 SPRINGFIELDS
19 BROOMHILL GR
20 QUARRY AV
21 BROOMHILL WK
22 BROOMHILL PL
23 BROOMHILL CL
24 BROOMHILL SQ
25 BROOMHILL CR
26 BROOMHILL DR

D4
1 GARTH MILL
2 MARSH LA
3 MAIN ST
4 RIVERDALE
5 CRAVEN GARTH
6 BROAD LA
7 VILLAGE FARM CT
8 GABLES CL

F2
1 WESTFIELD RD
2 WESTFIELD CL
3 WESTFIELD AV
4 WESTFIELD GR
5 TABARD HAMLET
6 TABARD RD
7 THE TABARDS
8 THE HAMLET

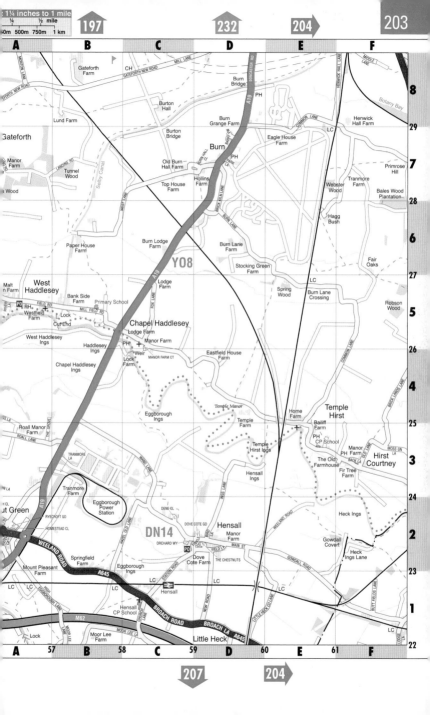

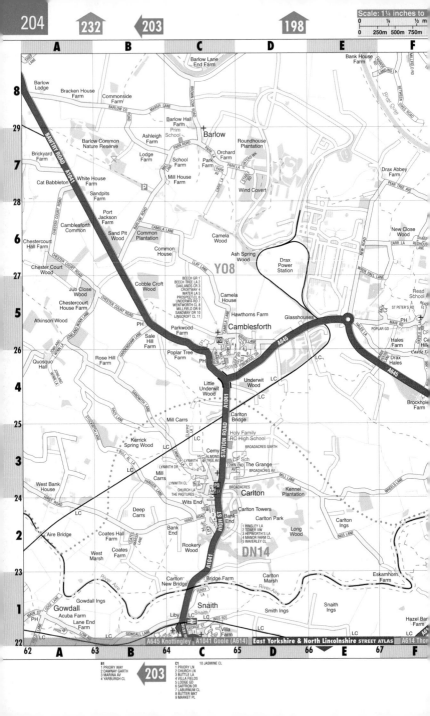

A   B   C   D   E   F

8
Barlow
Lodge
Bracken House
Farm
Commonside
Farm
Barlow Lane
End Farm
Bank House
Farm

MARSH LANE

BARLOW CO

29
Barlow Hall
Farm
Prim
School
Barlow
Roundhouse
Plantation
Drax Abbey
Farm

BANTUFF ROAD A1041

Ashleigh
Farm
Lodge
Farm
Orchard
Farm

7
Brickyard
Farm
Barlow Common
Nature Reserve
School Lane
Park
Farm

Cat Babbleton
White House
Farm
Mill House
Farm
Wind Covert

28
Sandpits
Farm
Port
Jackson
Farm

6
Chestercourt
Hall Farm
Camblesforth
Common
Sand Pit
Wood
Common
Plantation
Camela
Wood
New Close
Wood

CAMELA LANE

CHESTER COURT ROAD

Common
House
Ash Spring
Wood
Drax
Power
Station

Y08

27
Chester Court
Wood
Cobble Croft
Wood
BEECH GR 1
BEECH TREE LA 2
OAKLANDS CR 3
CROFTWAY 4
WATER LA 5
PROSPECT CL 6
UNDERWIT RD 7
WENTWORTH CL 8
MILLFIELD DR 9
SANDWAY DR 10
LINGCROFT CL 11
Camela
House
Read
School

5
Jub Close
Wood
Chestercourt
House Farm
Parkwood
Farm
Hawthorns Farm
Glasshouses

CHESTER COURT ROAD

Atkinson Wood

PH

Camblesforth
Hales
Farm
Drax
Hales

A645

26
Quosquo
Hall
Rose Hill
Farm
Sale
Hill
Farm
Poplar Tree
Farm

PH

LC.

4
West Bank
House
Kerrick
Spring Wood
Little
Underwit
Wood
Underwit
Wood
Brockhole
Farm

A1041

Mill Carrs
Carlton
Bridge

25
Mill Carrs
Holy Family
RC High School
BROADACRES GARTH
Cemy
CARLTON ROAD

3
West Bank
House
Mill
Carrs
LYNWITH DR
CP Sch
The Grange
BROADACRES AV
Kennel
Plantation

HARKER LANE

LYNWITH CL
Carlton

24
Deep
Carrs
CHURCH LANE
THE PASTURES
Wits End
BROADACRES
Carlton Towers
Carlton Park
Carlton
Ings

HIRST ROAD

2
Aire Bridge
Coates Hall
Farm
Bank
End
Bank
End
1 HINGLEY LA
2 TOWER VW
3 HEPWORTH'S LA
4 MANOR FARM CL
5 WAVERLEY CL
Long
Wood

West
Marsh
Coates
Farm
Rookery
Wood

DN14

HIGH ST

23
Carlton
New Bridge
Bridge Farm
Carlton
Marsh
Eskamhorn
Farm

River Aire

River Aire

1
Gowdall
Gowdall Ings
Acuba Farm
Lane End
Farm
Snaith
Snaith
Ings
Hazel Bar
Farm

PH

Liby
Villa
Farm
Smith Ings

GOWDALL LANE

22
A645 Knottingley | A1041 Goole (A614) | East Yorkshire & North Lincolnshire STREET ATLAS | A614 Thor

62   A   63   B   64   C   65   D   66   E   67   F

B1
1 PRIORY WAY
2 DAWNAY GARTH
3 MARINA AV
4 YARBURGH CL

C1
1 PRIORY LN
2 CHURCH LN
3 BUTTLE LA
4 VILLA FIELDS
5 LODGE GD
6 SAFFRON DR
7 LABURNUM CL
8 BUTTER MKT
9 MARKET PL
10 JASMINE CL

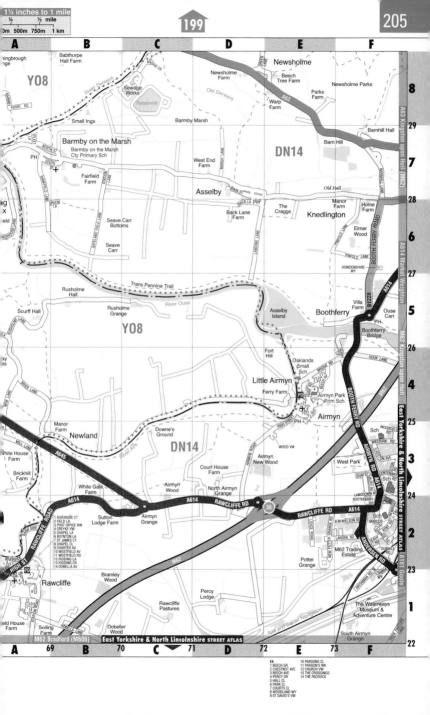

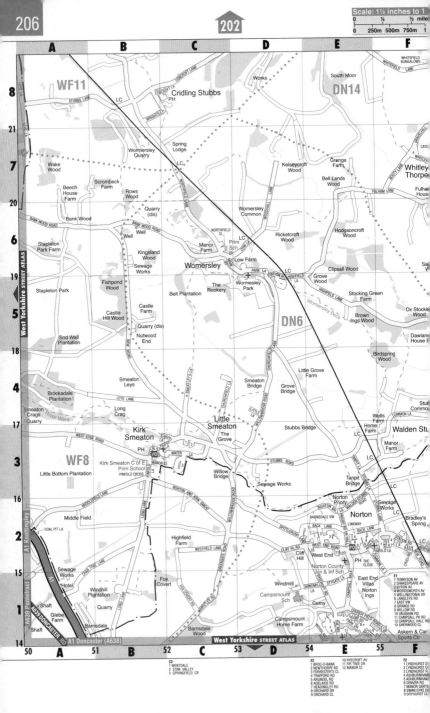

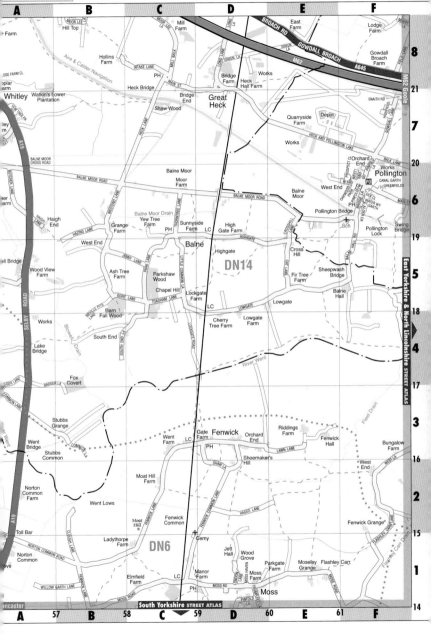

: 1¼ inches to 1 mile

¼   ½   mile

50m 500m 750m 1 km

A   **B**   **C**   **D**   **E**   **F**

Farm

Moor Lee La
Hill Top

Mill
Farm

East
Farm

BROACH RD

GOWDALL BROACH

Lodge
Farm

MENWELL LA

8

Hollins
Farm

Aire & Calder Navigation

INTAKE LANE

MILL RISE

MOOR LEE

LONG LA

LONG LA

GREEN LA

GREEN LANE

A645

M62

M62 Goole

EAST FIELD

21

College Farm Cl
Poplar
Farm

Whitley

Watkin's Lower
Plantation

PH

Heck Bridge

MAIN ST

Bridge
End

Bridge
Farm

Heck
Hall Farm

Works

Works

Gowdall
Broach
Farm

ley
ey

YEW TREE PK

A19

Shaw Wood

Bridge
End

Great Heck

Quarryside
Farm

Depot

SNAITH RD

7

er
arm

BADGER LANE

BALNE MOOR
CROSS ROAD

BALNE MOOR ROAD

Balne Moor

Moor
Farm

BALNE MOOR ROAD

HECK AND POLLINGTON LAKE

Works

Balne
Moor

West End

BALK LANE

Orchard
End

Works

Pollington

CANAL GARTH

GREENFIELDS

PO

6

20

ll Bridge

HAGUE
LANE

Haigh
End

HAXING LANE

WESTFIELD LANE

Grange
Farm

Balne Moor Drain

Yew Tree
Farm

PH

Sunnyside
Farm

LC

High
Gate Farm

HIGHGATE

Pollington Bridge

Sch

Pollington
Lock

Swing
Bridge

GARNSWORTH RD

Wood View
Farm

West End

Balné

Highgate

DN14

Cross
Hill

CARR LANE

OAT LANE

Fir Tree
Farm

Sheepwash
Bridge

Balne
Hall

East Yorkshire & North Lincolnshire STREET ATLAS

19

5

Ash Tree
Farm

Parkshaw
Wood

Chapel Hill

JENNY LANE

GORE LANE

UGHAM LANE

Lockgate
Farm

LC

Cherry
Tree Farm

Lowgate

Lowgate
Farm

MAIN RD

18

Works

MOXLEY PITS LANE

Barn
Fall Wood

Blowell Drain

South End

SOUTH END LA

LOCKGATE ROAD

LC

River Went

Fleet Drain

4

Lake
Bridge

BADGER LANE

Fox
Covert

17

COMMON LANE

Stubbs
Grange

COMMON LA

Went
Farm

Gate
Farm

LC

Fenwick

PH

Orchard
End

Riddings
Farm

LAWN LANE

Fenwick
Hall

West
End

WEST LA

Bungalow
Farm

3

Went
Bridge

Stubbs
Common

Moat Hill
Farm

Shoemaker's
Hill

SHAW LA

16

Norton
Common
Farm

Went Lows

Moat
Hill

Fenwick
Common

FENWICK COMMON LANE

HAGGS LANE

2

A19

Toll Bar

GLASGOW LANE

NORTON COMMON ROAD

Ladythorpe
Farm

DN6

Cemy

Jeff
Hall

Wood
Grove

MOSS HAVEN

Parkgate
Farm

Moseley
Grange

Flashley Carr

FLASHLEY CARR LANE

15

rove

Norton
Common

Elmfield
Farm

WILLOW GARTH LANE

MOSS ROAD

LC

Manor
Farm

PH

LONDON LANE

MOSS RD

Moss
Farm

PINFOLD LA

Moss

MOSS ROAD

Fenwick Grange

1

A   57   **B**   58   **C**   59   **D**   60   **E**   61   **F**

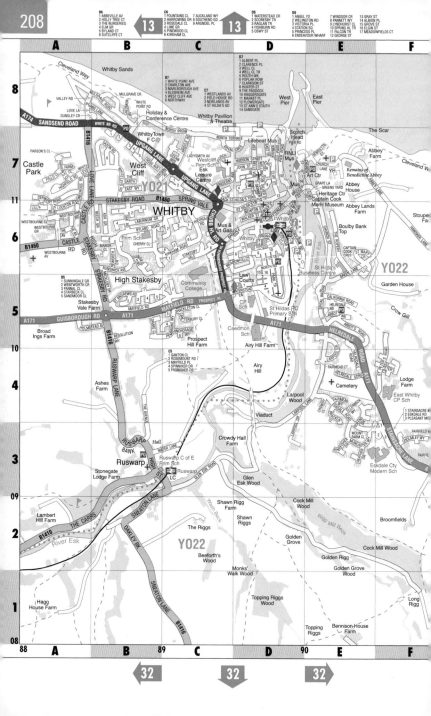

B6
1 ABBEVILLE AV
2 HOLLY TREE CT
3 THE NURSERIES
4 ELM GR
5 BYLAND CT
6 SUTCLIFFE CT

C6
1 FOUNTAINS CL
2 HARROWING DR
3 ROSEDALE CL
4 LIME GR
5 PINEWOOD CL
6 KIRKHAM CL

C7
1 AUCKLAND WY
2 SCORESBY TR
3 SOUTHEND GD
4 ARUNDEL PL

D5
1 WATERSTEAD CR
2 SCORESBY TR
3 RAGLAN TR
4 FISHBURN RD
5 OWSY ST

D6
1 ANGEL YD
2 WELINGTON RD
3 VICTORIA PL
4 STATION SQ
5 PRINCESS PL
6 ENDEAVOUR WHARF

7 WINDSOR CR
8 PANNETT WY
9 LYNDHURST CL
10 SPRING HL TR
11 FALCON TN
12 GEORGE ST

13 GRAY ST
14 GREENS YARD
15 GROVE ST
16 ELGIN ST
17 MEADOWFIELDS CT

D7
1 ALBERT PL
2 CLARENCE PL
3 WELL CL
4 WELL CL TN
5 ROUTH WK
6 POPLAR ROW
7 CLARKSON ST
8 HUNTER ST
9 THE PADDOCK
10 HAGGERSGATE
11 MARKET PL
12 FLOWERGATE
13 ST ANN'S STAITH
14 SANDGATE

B7
1 WHITE POINT AVE
2 CHARLTON AVE
3 MARLBOROUGH AVE
4 BLENHEIM AVE
5 WEST CLIFF AVE
6 NORTHWAY

C7
1 WESTLANDS AV
2 FIELD HOUSE RD
3 NEWLANDS AV
4 ST HILDA'S GD

B5
1 SUNNINGALE GR
2 WENTWORTH CR
3 PANNAL CL
4 STARBECK CL
5 SANDMOOR CL

C5
1 GANTON CL
2 ROSEMOUNT RD
3 MAYFIELD PL
4 SPINNIKER DR
5 FROBISHER DR

1 STAINSACRE
2 ESKDALE RD
3 PLEASANT MO

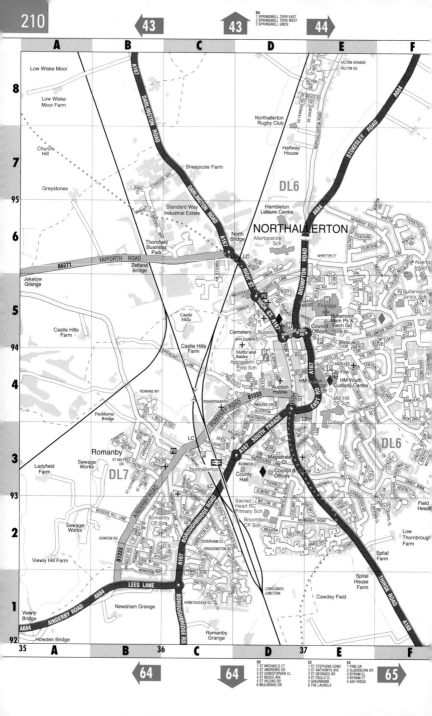

43 43 44

NORTHALLERTON

DL6

DL7

DL6

D2
1 ST MICHAELS CT
2 ST ANDREWS GR
3 ST CHRISTOPHER CL
4 ST BEDES AVE
5 ST HILDAS RD
6 MULGRAVE DR

E2
1 ST STEPHENS GDNS
2 ST ANTHONYS AVE
3 ST GEORGES GR
4 ST PAULS CL
5 GREENBANK
6 THE LAURELS

E3
1 PINE GR
2 SLADEBURN DR
3 BYRAM CL
4 BYRAM CT
5 ASH RIDGE

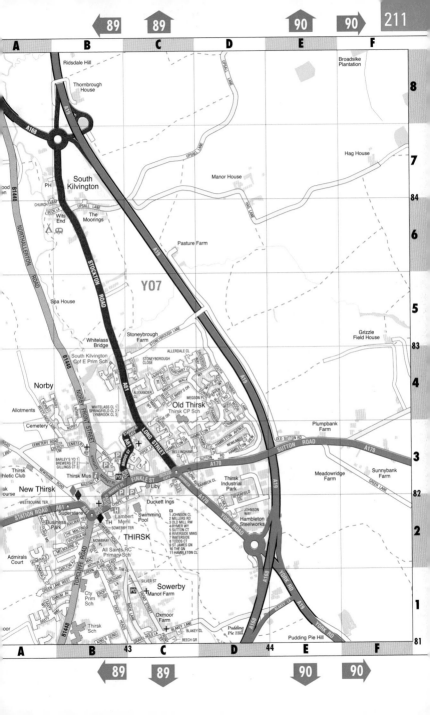

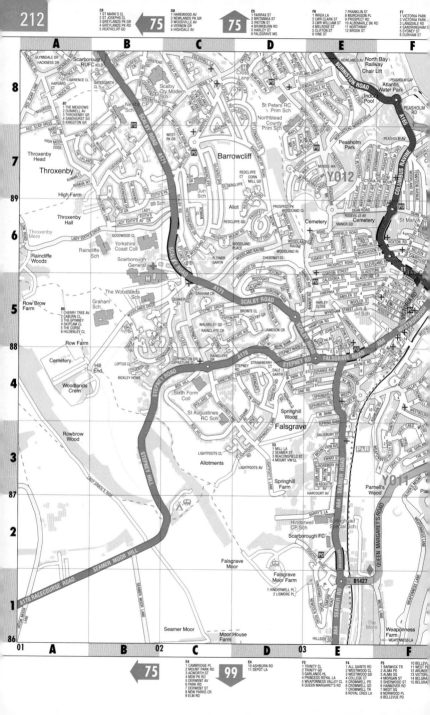

C8
1 ST MARK'S CL
2 ST JOSEPHS CL
3 GREYLANDS PK GR
4 GREYLANDS PK RD
5 HEATHCLIFF GD

D8
1 HAREWOOD AV
2 NEWLANDS PK GR
3 WOODVILLE AV
4 BRINKBURN RD
5 HIGHDALE AV

E5
1 FAIRFAX ST
2 BRITANNIA ST
3 IRETON ST
4 BRINKBURN RD
5 HARLEY ST
6 FALSGRAVE MS

F6
1 WREA LA
2 LWR CLARK ST
3 PROSPECT RD
4 MELROSE ST
5 CLIFTON ST
6 VINE ST

7 FRANKLIN ST
8 MURCHISON PL
9 PROSPECT RD
10 ALBEMARLE BK RD
11 NORTHWAY
12 BROOK ST

F7
1 VICTORIA PARK
2 VICTORIA ROAD
3 LANGDALE ST
4 SANDRINGHAM ST
5 SYDNEY ST
6 DURHAM ST

E4
1 CAMBRIDGE PL
2 MOUNT PARK RD
3 ACWORTH ST
4 NEW PK RD
5 DERWENT AV
6 PARK RD
7 DERWENT ST
8 NEW PARKS CR
9 ELM RD

E4
10 ASHBURN RD
11 DEPOT LA

F3
1 TRINITY CL
2 TRINITY GD
3 GARLANDS HL
4 PRINCESS ROYAL LA
5 WEAPONNESS VALLEY CL
6 QUEEN MARGARET'S RD

F4
1 ALL SAINTS RD
2 WESTWOOD CL
3 WESTWOOD GD
4 COLLEGE CT
5 CROMWELL PD
6 CROMWELL GD
7 CROMWELL TR
8 ROYAL CRES LA

F5
1 BARWICK TR
2 ALMA PD
3 ALMA SQ
4 MORGAN ST
5 SHERWOOD ST
6 HANNOVER RD
7 WEST SQ
8 NORWOOD PL
9 BELLEVUE PL

10 BELLEVUE
11 WEST PL
12 ARUNDEL
13 VICTORIA
14 BELGRAVE
15 BELGRAVE

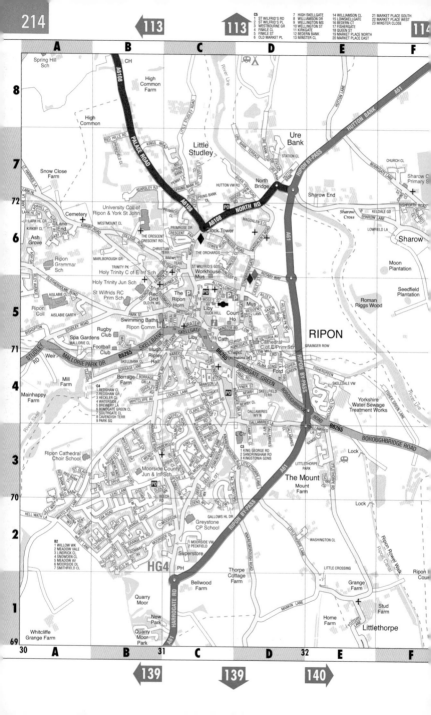

C5
1 ST WILFRID'S RD
2 ST WILFRID'S PL
3 WESTBOURNE GR
4 FINKLE CL
5 FINKLE ST
6 OLD MARKET PL

7 HIGH SKELLGATE
8 WILLIAMSON DR
9 WELLINGTON MS
10 WELLINGTON ST
11 KIRKGATE
12 BEDERN BANK
13 MINSTER CL

14 WILLIAMSON CL
15 LOWSKELLGATE
16 BEDERN CT
17 FISHERGATE
18 QUEEN ST
19 MARKET PLACE NORTH
20 MARKET PLACE EAST

21 MARKET PLACE SOUTH
22 MARKET PLACE WEST
23 MINSTER CLOSE

RIPON

Spring Hill Sch

CH

High Common Farm

River Ure

Ure Bank

High Common

Little Studley

Sharow C Primary Sch

Snow Close Farm

North Bridge

Sharow End

CHURCH CL

Cemetery

University Coll of Ripon & York St John

Clock Tower

Sharow Cross

Sharow

Ash Grove

WESTMOUNT CL

Moon Plantation

Ripon Grammar Sch

The Crescent

St Wilfrid's GdS

Seedfield Plantation

Holy Trinity C of E Inf Sch

Workhouse Mus

Roman Riggs Wood

Holy Trinity Jun Sch

St Wilfrids RC Prim Sch

The Ripon Horn

Mus

RIPON

Ripon Coll

AISLABIE GARTH

Swimming Baths

Duck Hill

Court Ho

Ripon Comm

Liby

Cath

Grainger Row

Spa Gardens

Football Club

Hugh Ripley Hall

B6265

FISHERGREEN

Ripon Cathedral C of E Prim Sch

Mill Farm

Borrage Farm

BONDGATE GREEN

SKELDALE VW

Yorkshire Water Sewage Treatment Works

Mainhappy Farm

River Skell

D4
1 REDSHAW CL
2 REDSHAW GR
3 HECKLER CL
4 WATERSIDE
5 BREWERY LA
6 BONDGATE GREEN CL
7 SOUTHGATE CL
8 CAVENDISH TERR
9 PARK SQ

B6265

BOROUGHBRIDGE ROAD

Ripon Cathedral Choir School

C3
1 KING GEORGE RD
2 SANDRINGHAM RD
3 KINGSTONIA GDNS

Moorside County Jun & Inf Sch

Ctr

Lock

The Mount

Mount Farm

Greystone CP School

RIPON BY-PASS

Lock

B2
1 WILLOW WK
2 MEADOW VALE
3 LINDRICK CL
4 SNOWDEN CL
5 MEADOW AV
6 MOORSIDE CL
7 SMITHFIELD CL

Superstore

WASHINGTON CL

Ripon Rowel Walk

River Canal

HG4

PH

Thorpe Cottage Farm

LITTLE CROSSING

Ripon Cour

Bellwood Farm

Quarry Moor

Grange Farm

New Park

HARROGATE ROAD

Home Farm

Stud Farm

Quarry Moor Park

A61

MARION LANE

Littlethorpe

Whitcliffe Grange Farm

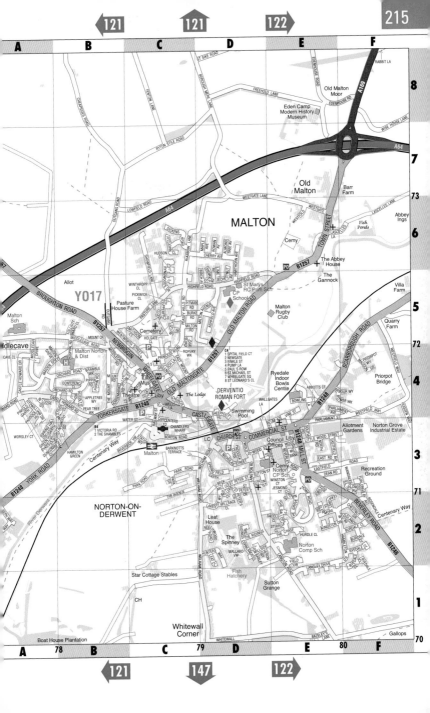

172 156

14 G

F4
1 PARK ST
2 PRIMROSE HL
3 VICTORIA TR
4 HALLAM'S YD
5 THE PINFOLD
6 BACK O THE BECK

7 WATSON'S HO
8 CANAL YD
9 BAY HORSE YD
10 VICTORIA ST
11 SHEEP ST
12 DEVONSHIRE PL
13 COACH ST YD

D3
1 SAWLEY ST
2 CLITHEROE ST
3 THORNTON ST
4 PENDLE ST
5 GREENFIELD ST
6 RUSKIN AVE
7 NIFFANY GDNS
8 STATION VW

E3
1 AIREDALE MS
2 GLYNWED CT
3 ELLER MS

E4
1 ROOKWOOD CL
2 BELLEVUE TERR
3 BELGRA. ST

F3
1 CLIFFORD ST
2 HIRDS YD
3 CARLETON ST
4 CHURCH ST
5 UNION TR
6 CUMBERLAND ST
7 SOUTHFIELD TR
8 LINTON CT
9 THANET'S CT

10 PEMBRO
11 BENNETT

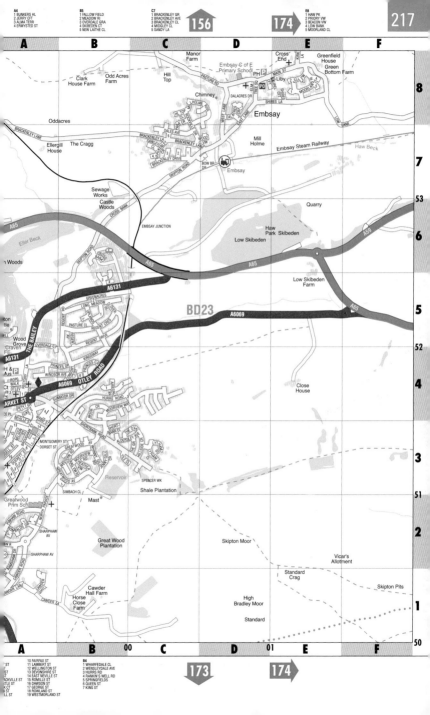

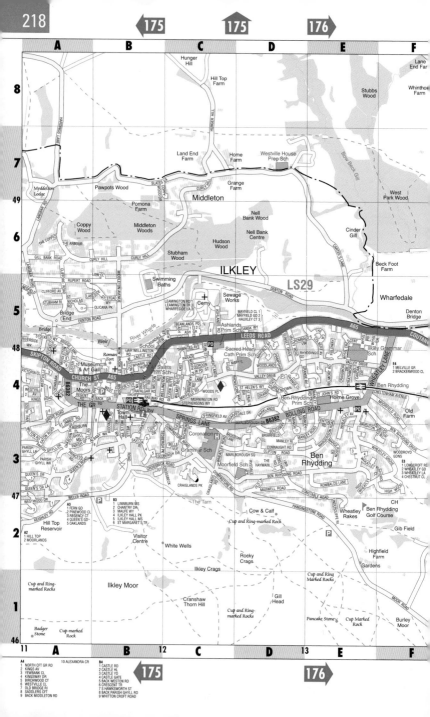

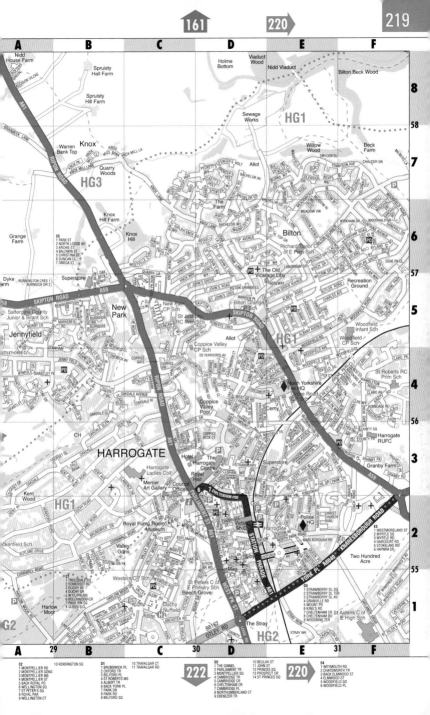

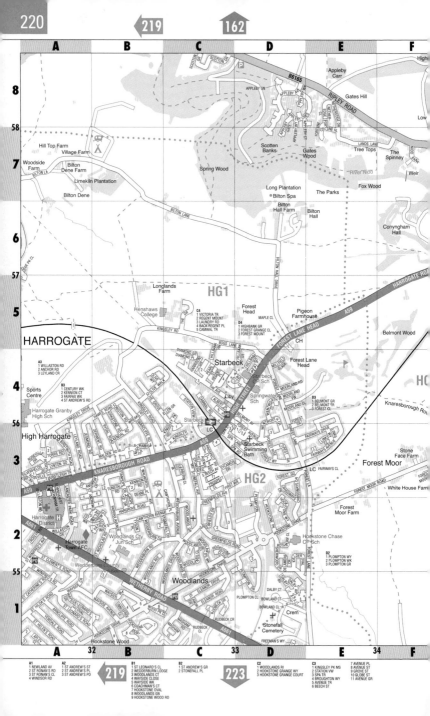

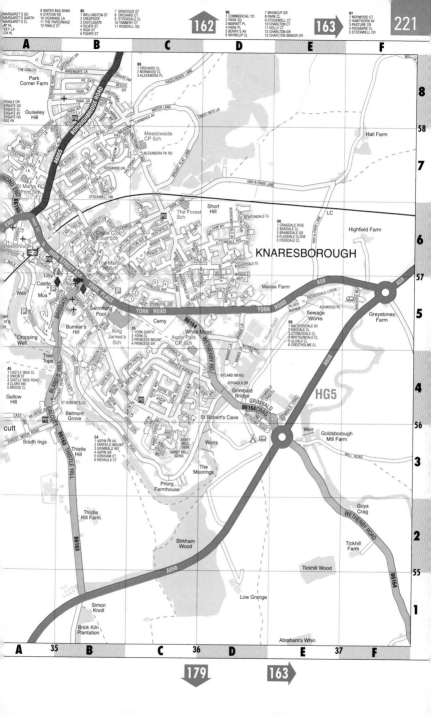

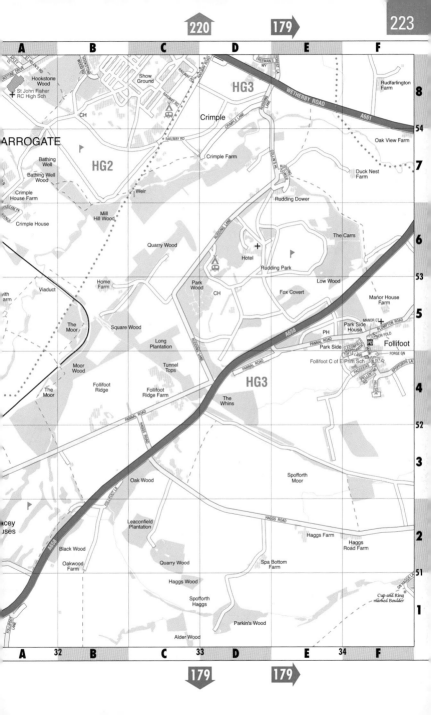

8
54
7
6
53
5
52
4
3
2
51
1

A 32 B C 33 D E 34 F

ARROGATE

HG2

HG3

HG3

HG3

Hookstone Wood
St John Fisher RC High Sch
CH
Show Ground
Crimple
HG3
Rudfarlington Farm
Oak View Farm

Bathing Well
Bathing Well Wood
Crimple House Farm
Crimple House
Weir
Mill Hill Wood
Crimple Farm
Railway RD
Crimple Lane
Rudding Dower
Duck Nest Farm

Quarry Wood
Home Farm
Hotel
Rudding Park
The Carrs
Low Wood
Manor House Farm

with arm
Viaduct
The Moor
Square Wood
Park Wood
CH
Fox Covert
Park Side House
PH
Park Side
Follifoot
Follifoot C of E Prim Sch

Long Plantation
Moor Wood
Tunnel Tops
Follifoot Ridge
Follifoot Ridge Farm
The Whins
HG3

The Moor

Oak Wood
Spofforth Moor

Leaconfield Plantation
Haggs Road
Haggs Farm
Haggs Road Farm

cey uses
Black Wood
Oakwood Farm
Quarry Wood
Haggs Wood
Spofforth Haggs
Spa Bottom Farm

Parkin's Wood
Alder Wood
Cup and Ring marked Boulder

A661
A658
A658
A661

Wetherby Road
Pannal Road
Pannal Road
Haggs Road
Rudding Lane
Follifoot Lane
Follifoot Lane

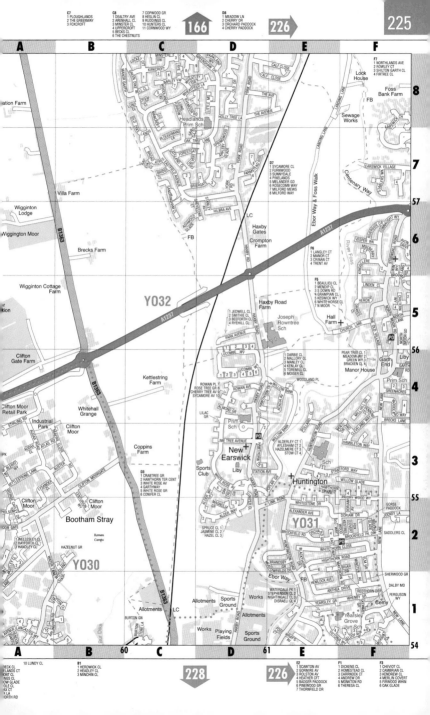

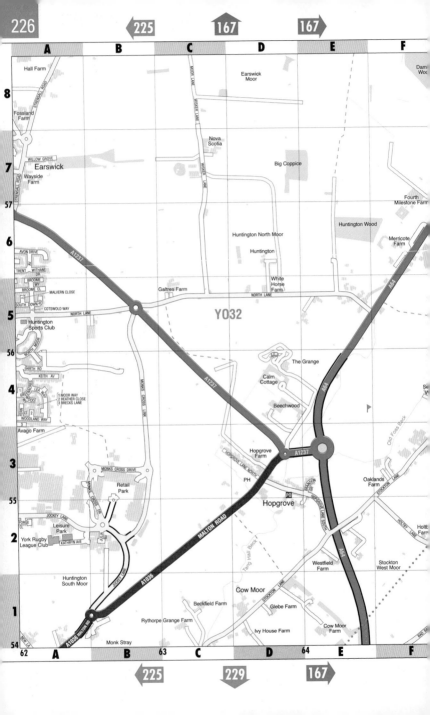

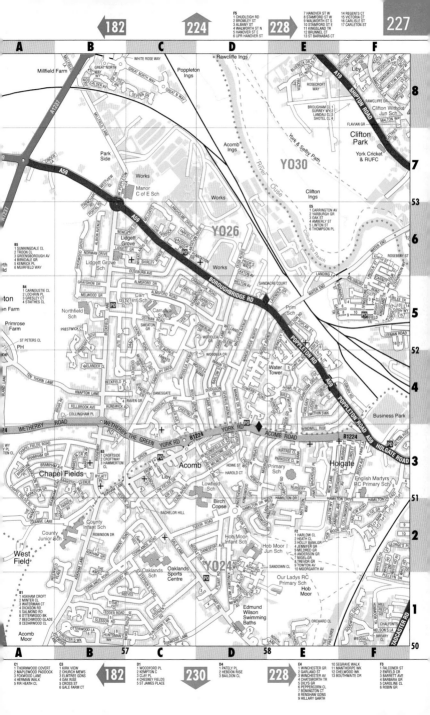

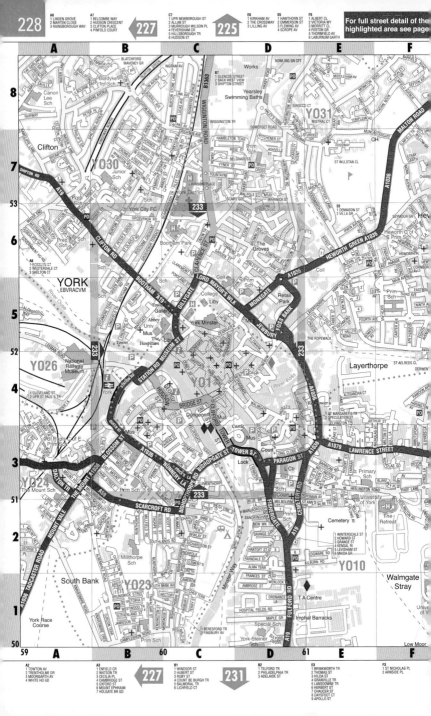

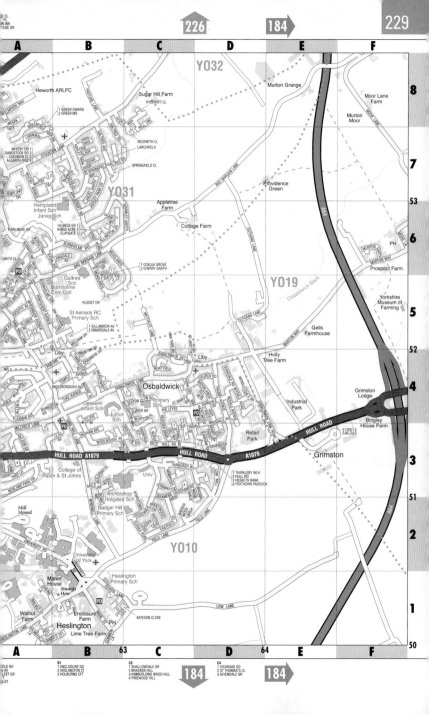

C8
1 HINTON AV
2 LYDHAM CT
3 MARTIN CHEESEMAN CT
4 CRANFIELD PL

D8
1 FARMLANDS RD
2 DRINGFIELD CL
3 HERDSMAN RD
4 SANDCROFT CL
5 DEEPDALE

E8
1 TURNMIRE RD
2 SOUTHFIELD CR
3 MEADOW CT
4 THE PASTURES
5 ST HELEN'S RD

F8
1 KENSINGTON CL
2 REGENCY MS

A3
1 LARKFIELD CL
2 HORSEMAN CL
3 LYNWOOD AV
4 LYNWOOD VW

B1
1 SADDLERS CL
2 FARRIERS CFT
3 WAGGONERS DR
4 POTTERS DR
5 WAINERS CL
6 MILLERS CFT
7 LORINERS DR
8 GARDENERS CL

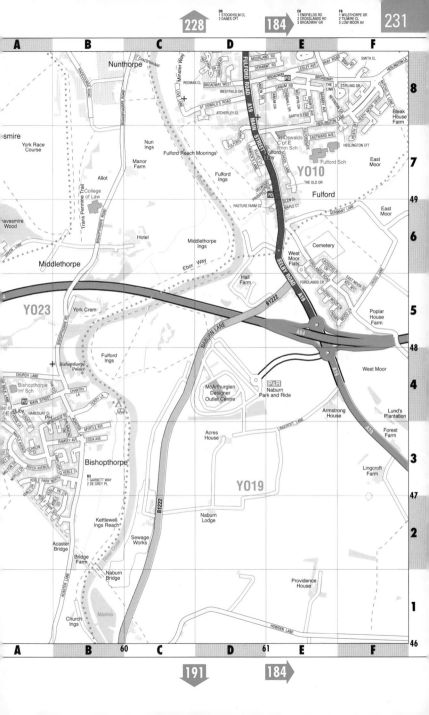

C5
1 YORK ST
2 HARPER ST
3 DOUGLAS ST
4 RAINCLIFFE ST
5 LONDESBOROUGH ST
6 HILDA ST

7 PORTHOLME CR
8 SOUTH PAR
9 TURNERS SQ
10 AUDUS ST
11 MARKET PL

D5
1 MICKLEGATE
2 WREN LA
3 CHURCH HL
4 CHURCH LA

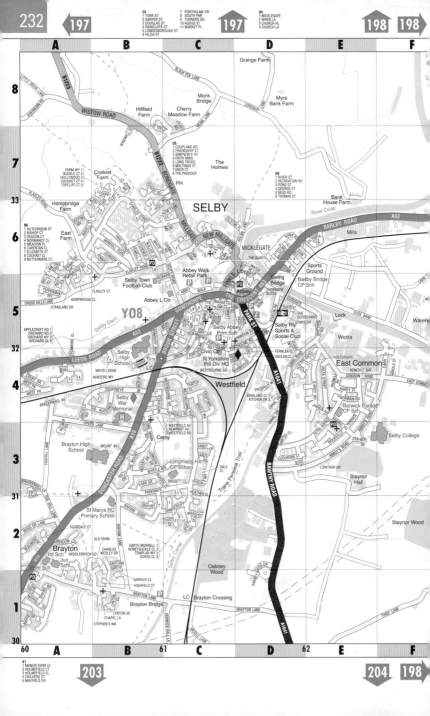

Grange Farm

Monk
Bridge

Myra
Bank Farm

WISTOW ROAD
B1223

Hillfield
Farm

Cherry
Meadow Farm

8

Cockret
Farm

C6
1 COUPLAND RD
2 FRIENDSHIP CT
3 SIMPSON'S YD
4 FRITH MWS
5 LONG TROODS
6 MALTINGS CT
7 EBOR CT
8 THE PADDOCK

The
Holmes

7

D6
1 RIVER ST
2 RECREATION RD
3 POND ST
4 GEORGE ST
5 NESS RD
6 THOMAS ST

Bank
House Farm

River Ouse

A63

BARLBY ROAD

33

Hempbridge
Farm

SELBY

Mills

B6
1 HUTCHINSON ST
2 BISHOP CT
3 DEACON CT
4 NORMANDY CL
5 MEADOW CL
6 CARENTAN CL
7 ELIZABETH CT
8 COCKRET CL
9 BUTTERMERE CL

East
Farm

NEW MILLGATE

MICKLEGATE

The Quay

6

Sports
Ground

Barlby Bridge
CP Sch

Selby Town
Football Club

Abbey Walk
Retail Park

Swing
Bridge

THORGONIN
BLDGS

Selby

Lock

Ouse Bank

HEMPBRIDGE CL

Abbey L Ctr

THE CRESCENT

Abbey

Selby Rly
Sports &
Social Club

Works

Wareh

CROSS HILLS LANE

STANILAND DR

GOWTHORPE

Selby Darn

YO8

Selby Abbey
Prim Sch

5

APPLECROFT RD 1
ORCHARD RD 2
ORCHARD WY 3
ORCHARD CL 4

LEEDS ROAD

A63

Coll

Civic Ctr

N Yorkshire
Pol Div HQ

FERNLEA CL

ASHLEA CL

FOSTERGATE

East Common

EAST COMM

32

Selby
High
School

WHITE LODGE

HUNTERS WY

LC

WESTBOURNE SQ

Westfield

BENEDICT AVE

DENISON
ROAD

4

WEST PK

BRACKENHILL LA

COURTNEYS

Selby War
Memorial

H

Cemy

FERNDALE RD

1 WESTFIELD AV
2 NEWPORT AV
3 WESTFIELD RD

Westfield

HATCH

A19

PROSPECT RD

KIRKLAND CL 1
KITCHEN DR 2

A1041

HARDY ST

GERMAIN RD

Barwick Parade
CP Sch

Selby College

DONCASTER ROAD

MOUNT AV

SANDY

PO

STAYNOR

3

Brayton High
School

Longmans Hill
CP School

DALE
CL

Selby Canal

Trans Pennine Trail

LOWTHER DR

Staynor
Hall

BRACKENHILL LA

Myrtle Ave

BASSETT CL

RYEDALE

HEATHER CL

31

BRIG
CLWN

St Marys RC
Primary School

BATEMAN GDNS

BRYONY CT

DANESBOROUGH

THISTLE

Staynor Wood

MOSS DR LANE

SCARDALE CT

OLD FARM

GARTH MORRELL 1
HONEYSUCKLE CL 2
TEMPLAR WY 3
GORSE CL 4

Oakney
Wood

2

Brayton
Inf Sch

CHARLES
WESLEY DR

MIDDLEBROOK GD

BARTONS
GARTH

Jun
Sch

GARRICK CL
HIGHFIELD CT

BAWTRY ROAD

THIEF LANE

PO

Prim Sch

LYNTON

Brayton Bridge

LC Brayton Crossing

1

LYNTON GD
CHAPEL LA
STEPHEN'S WK

Brayton Lane

MIDDLE LANE

30

60 A B 61 C D 62 E F

A1
1 MANOR FARM CL
2 HOLMEFIELD CT
3 HOLMEFIELD CL
4 CHILVERS CT
5 MAYFIELD DR

203 204 198

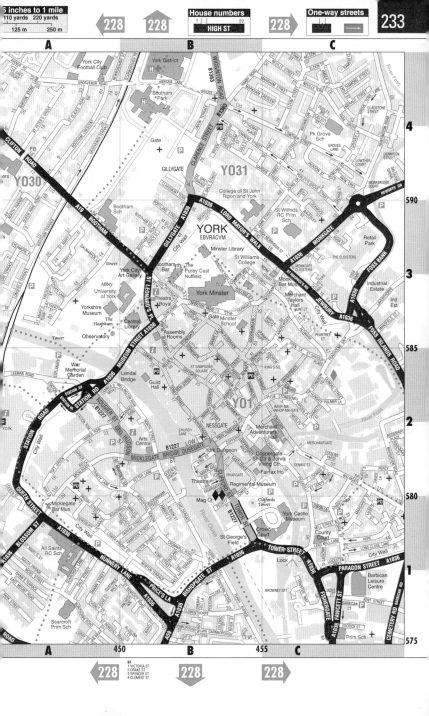

Index

Church Rd 🄶 Beckenham BR2.........**53** C6

Place name	Location number	Locality, town or village	Postcode district	Page and grid square
May be abbreviated on the map	Present when a number indicates the place's position in a crowded area of mapping	Shown when more than one place has the same name	District for the indexed place	Page number and grid reference for the stand mapping

Public and commercial buildings are highlighted in magenta. Places of interest are highlighted in blue with a star⋆

Abbreviations used in the index

Acad	Academy	Comm	Common	Gd	Ground	L	Leisure	Prom	Prom
App	Approach	Cott	Cottage	Gdn	Garden	La	Lane	Rd	Road
Arc	Arcade	Cres	Crescent	Gn	Green	Liby	Library	Recn	Recreati
Ave	Avenue	Cswy	Causeway	Gr	Grove	Mdw	Meadow	Ret	Retail
Bglw	Bungalow	Ct	Court	H	Hall	Memi	Memorial	Sh	Shopping
Bldg	Building	Ctr	Centre	Ho	House	Mkt	Market	Sq	Square
Bsns, Bus	Business	Ctry	Country	Hospl	Hospital	Mus	Museum	St	Street
Bvd	Boulevard	Cty	County	HQ	Headquarters	Orch	Orchard	Sta	Station
Cath	Cathedral	Dr	Drive	Hts	Heights	Pal	Palace	Terr	Terrace
Cir	Circus	Dro	Drove	Ind	Industrial	Par	Parade	TH	Town Hall
Cl	Close	Ed	Education	Inst	Institute	Pas	Passage	Univ	University
Cnr	Corner	Emb	Embankment	Int	International	Pk	Park	Wk, Wlk	Walk
Coll	College	Est	Estate	Intc	Interchange	Pl	Place	Wr	Water
Com	Community	Ex	Exhibition	Junc	Junction	Prec	Precinct	Yd	Yard

Index of localities, towns and villages

A

Aberford 194 F7
Acaster Malbis 191 D8
Acaster Selby 191 B4
Acklam 169 E8
Acklam 6 E8
Acomb 227 C3
Addingham 174 F5
Agglethorpe 60 A1
Ainderby Quernhow ..88 C4
Ainderby Steeple 64 B7
Ainthorpe 29 C6
Aire View 173 D1
Airedale 201 B4
Airmyn 205 E4
Airton 155 A6
Airy Hill 208 D4
Aiskew 63 A3
Aislaby 5 C3
Aislaby 31 F7
Aislaby 95 D8
Aldborough 141 C5
Aldbrough St John 2 A2
Aldfield 139 A8
Aldwark 142 C2
Allerston 97 C5
Allerton Bywater ...200 D6
Allerton Mauleverer ..163 E4
Alne 142 F4
Alne Station 143 A5
Amotherby 121 B4
Ampleforth 92 C1
Angram 182 C3
Angram 35 E6
Appersett 56 C5
Appleton Roebuck ...190 F5
Appleton Wiske 24 B3
Appleton-le-Moors ...70 F2
Appleton-le-Street ..120 F4
Appletreewick 157 D7
Archdeacon Newton ...2 F7
Arkendale 163 B8
Arncliffe 107 D2
Arrathorne 62 A8
Asenby 115 B6
Askham Bryan 182 F3
Askham Richard 182 D3
Askrigg 57 F6

B

Askwith 176 D3
Asselby 205 D7
Aughton 193 C1
Austwick 130 E7
Aysgarth 58 E3
Azerley 113 A5

B

Bagby 90 C3
Bainbridge 57 D5
Baldersby 88 D1
Baldersby St James ..114 E8
Balne 207 C5
Bank Newton 172 B8
Barden 61 A8
Barden-le-Street ...120 C5
Barkston Ash 195 F7
Barlby 198 B5
Barlow 204 C7
Barmby on the Marsh .205 B7
Barnoldswick 171 D1
Barnoldswick 103 A2
Barrowcliff 212 D7
Barton 21 D7
Barton Hill 146 D3
Barton-le-Street ...120 C5
Barton-le-Willows .146 D1
Barwick in Elmet ..194 B8
Battersby 27 D6
Beadlam 93 C7
Beal 202 D4
Beamsley 174 F7
Beckermonds 80 D3
Beckwithshaw 178 A7
Bedale 63 B2
Bedlam 161 A8
Bell Busk 155 A3
Bellerby 60 D7
Ben Rhydding 218 E3
Beningbrough 165 D4
Bent 187 D7
Beverley 137 B3
Bickerton 181 A5
Biggin 196 E5
Bilbrough 182 D1
Bilton 219 E6
Bilton in Ainsty ...181 E4
Binsoe 86 F2
Birdforth 116 E6

B

Birdsall 148 B4
Birkby 23 B1
Birkin 202 D6
Birstwith 160 E6
Bishop Monkton ...140 A5
Bishop Thornton ..138 F2
Bishop Wilton 169 F2
Bishopthorpe 231 B3
Bishopton 113 D2
Black Banks 3 D2
Blackwell 3 B4
Blades 37 B5
Blazefield 137 E4
Blubberhouses 159 D2
Boltby 66 F1
Bolton Abbey 174 E8
Bolton Bridge 174 F8
Bolton Percy 190 D4
Bolton-on-Swale ...41 F6
Boosbeck 9 E8
Bootham Stray 225 B2
Boothferry 205 F5
Booze 17 F1
Bordley 133 D3
Boroughbridge ...141 C5
Borrowby 11 D6
Borrowby 65 E4
Bossall 168 D7
Boston Spa 188 F8
Botton 29 B3
Bouthwaite 110 E2
Bracewell 171 C3
Brackenbottom 105 C3
Brafferton 116 A1
Braidley 83 B2
Bramham 188 F5
Brandsby 118 C3
Branksome 2 F6
Branton Green 142 A1
Brawby 94 F1
Brawith 26 A6
Braythorn 177 E4
Brayton 232 A2
Brearton 162 A7
Breighton 199 D5
Bridge Hewick 114 B1
Bridgehouse Gate ..137 B4
Briggswath 32 B7
Briscoerigg 177 F5
Brockfield 167 E2

B

Brompton 43 F3
Brompton-by-Sawdon ..98 C5
Brompton-on-Swale ..41 B7
Brookfield 6 E6
Brotherton 201 D5
Broughton 121 D4
Broughton 172 E6
Broxa 74 C6
Brunthwaite 174 D1
Bubwith 199 D7
Buckden 107 E8
Bugthorpe 169 D4
Bullamoor 44 B1
Bulmer 146 B6
Burley in Wharfedale ..176 B1
Burn 203 D7
Burn Bridge 222 D3
Burneston 87 E7
Burniston 75 C8
Burnsall 157 B8
Burnt Yates 160 F8
Burrill 62 E2
Burtersett 56 E4
Burton Fleming ..126 E3
Burton in Lonsdale ..102 F3
Burton Leonard ...140 B2
Burton Salmon ...201 F6
Burythorpe 147 F3
Buttercrambe 168 F5
Butterwick 120 E8
Butterwick 125 B2
Byland Abbey 91 E1
Byram 201 F64

C

Calcutt 221 A3
Caldbergh 84 B7
Caldwell 1 B4
Calton 155 B6
Camblesforth 204 D5
Camp Hill 87 F5
Cantsfield 102 B4
Carlbury 2 B7
Carlesmoor 111 E4
Carleton in Craven ..173 A4
Carlton 1 F3
Carlton 204 D3
Carlton 83 E7

C

Carlton
Carlton Husthwaite ....
Carlton in Cleveland ....
Carlton Miniott ....
Carperby ....
Carthorpe ....
Castle Bolton ....
Castleford ....
Castleton ....
Castley ....
Cattal ....
Catterick ....
Catterick Bridge ....
Catterick Garrison ....
Catterton ....
Catton ....
Cawood ....
Cawthorne ....
Cawton ....
Cayton ....
Chantry ....
Chapel Fields ....
Chapel Haddlesey ....
Chapel-le-Dale ....
Charltons ....
Chop Gate ....
Church Fenton ....
Church Houses ....
Clapham ....
Clapham Green ....
Claxton ....
Cleasby ....
Cliffe ....
Cliffe ....
Clifford ....
Clifton ....
Clifton ....
Clifton Park ....
Clint ....
Clints ....
Clough ....
Cloughton ....
Cloughton Newlands ....
Coates ....
Cobby Syke ....
Cock Hill ....
Cockayne ....
Cockerton ....
Colburn ....
Cold Cotes ....

d Kirby 91 D7
ingham 188 A8
sterdale 84 E4
on 190 E7
mondale 9 D1
eysthorpe 120 D2
eythorpe 163 A5
iston Cold 155 A1
istone 134 C6
onley 173 C2
onley Woodside 173 C3
stable Burton 61 C5
mboots 75 B6
grove 140 C2
manthorpe 230 B2
t Hewick 114 C2
erdale 55 F8
on Tree 186 A2
lby Newham 7 A5
lton 119 B5
ntersett 57 C2
erham 60 C1
van Bridge 102 D7
esby 66 C4
wling 62 D2
wling 187 B6
wthorpe 180 E7
wold 117 D8
ckpot 37 B3
coe 156 C7
g 187 D6
kehill 115 E4
nbe 146 F3
nbeck 146 F6
thorne 25 A6
y 81 E2
yke 118 A1
lling Stubbs 206 C8
nple 223 D8
gles 174 C3
ckey Hill 184 A1
t-on-Tees 22 D8
oton 71 B4
sby Court 65 B6
ss Hills 187 E7
ss Lanes 143 D3
ssgates 99 E7
wdon 54 A4
eck 57 F4
dall 115 E3
syke 200 E3
re 159 F7
re Banks 159 F8
by 119 B2
sbridge Centre 130 E6
ow 111 F2
on 19 D7
on 115 F7
on Gates 22 D4
on-on-Tees 22 E6
by 29 C7
by Wiske 43 C5
ey 160 A6
ington 3 E6
v Cross 222 B3
pdale 80 F2
rstones 175 B8
ghton 44 A8
ghton 192 A7
ton 176 A3
nforth 115 A4
wnholme 39 D4
ughton 174 B7
k 204 F5
oley 157 D6
ghouses 230 E8
gleby 149 B6
keswick 178 E2
nington 184 F7
sley 12 F2
lescliffe 5 E5
by 172 B1
swick 226 A7
by 27 B7
by 209 F5
ngton 11 A8
ngwold 143 D8
Appleton 41 D2
Ayton 99 B8
Barnby 12 C3
Common 232 E4
Cottingwith 193 C5
Cowton 22 F2
Garforth 194 E4
Harlsey 44 E6
Hauxwell 61 D8
Heslerton 124 A7
Knapton 123 C6
Layton 20 C8
Lutton 150 C8
Marton 172 B6
East Ness 94 B1
East Newton 93 C2
East Rounton 24 E2
East Row 13 A3
East Witton 61 A1
Eastbourne 3 E4
Eastburn 187 F7
Eastby 156 F1
Easterside 7 A7
Eastfield 100 A7
Eavestone 138 B7
Ebberston 97 E5
Eggborough 202 F2
Egglescliffe 5 E4
Egton 31 B5
Egton Bridge 31 A4
Eldroth 130 E4
Ellerbeck 44 F3
Ellerburn 96 E7
Ellerton 193 C2
Ellerton 41 F4
Ellingstring 85 D6
Elton 5 C8
Elvington 185 B2
Embsay 217 D8
Enterpen 25 C4
Eppleby 1 E4
Eryholme 23 A7
Escrick 192 B5
Eshton 155 D3
Everley 74 F4
Exelby 63 D1

F

Faceby 25 F2
Fadmoor 69 F4
Fairburn 201 D7
Falsgrave 212 D3
Fangdale Beck 47 A1
Farlington 144 F6
Farnham 162 D7
Farnhill 173 E1
Farnley 177 B2
Faverdale 3 B8
Fawdington 115 F3
Fearby 85 F4
Feetham 37 C5
Feizor 131 B6
Felixkirk 90 C7
Fenwick 207 D3
Ferrensby 162 F7
Ferrybridge 201 D3
Fewston 159 F1
Fewston Bents 159 F1
Filey 101 C3
Finghall 61 D4
Firby 63 A1
Firby 147 A5
Firth Moor 3 F4
Fishpool 177 C2
Flasby 155 E3
Flawith 142 E4
Flaxby 163 B4
Flaxton 145 F1
Fleets 156 A7
Flixton 99 F2
Folkton 100 B2
Follifoot 223 F5
Forcett 1 D3
Fordon 126 A6
Foredale 131 C8
Forest 42 B7
Forest Moor 220 F3
Foston 146 B4
Foul Green 9 E1
Foulrice 118 F1
Fowgill 129 B8
Foxholes 125 D3
Foxton 44 E3
Foxup 106 C7
Fremington 38 D6
Fryton 120 A6
Fulford 231 E7
Full Sutton 169 A2
Fylingthorpe 33 B3

G

Gainford 1 D8
Galphay 112 F3
Gammersgill 83 C5
Ganthorpe 120 A1
Ganton 125 A8
Garforth 194 C4
Gargrave 155 D1
Garriston 61 B7
Gate Helmsley 168 B2
Gateforth 203 A7
Gatenby 64 A2
Gauber 78 F1
Gayle 56 D4
Gayles 19 E6
Gerrick 10 C3
Giggleswick 131 C2
Gill 187 A6
Gillamoor 70 A5
Gilling East 118 F8
Gilling West 20 E4
Girsby 23 D7
Glaisdale 30 D4
Glass Houghton 201 A3
Glasshouses 137 C3
Glusburn 187 D8
Goathland 51 E8
Goldsborough 163 A2
Goldsborough 12 D5
Gollinglith Foot 85 B3
Goulton 25 E3
Gowdall 204 A1
Gowthorpe 169 C1
Grafton 141 D2
Grange 57 D5
Grassington 134 E3
Great Ayton 7 F2
Great Barugh 95 A1
Great Broughton 26 E5
Great Burdon 3 F8
Great Busby 26 C4
Great Crakehall 62 E4
Great Edstone 94 C7
Great Fencote 63 C8
Great Habton 121 B7
Great Heck 207 D7
Great Langton 42 D3
Great Ouseburn 164 B8
Great Preston 200 C8
Great Smeaton 23 C3
Great Thirkleby 90 D1
Green Close 130 A8
Green Hammerton 164 C3
Green Hill 194 F8
Greenhow 136 D3
Grewelthorpe 112 D7
Greygarth 111 F3
Greystonegill 129 C8
Grimston 229 E3
Grindale 127 D2
Grinton 38 C5
Gristhorpe 100 E4
Grosmont 31 D3
Grunsagill 153 A1
Guisborough 8 D7
Gunby 199 D6
Gunnerside 36 F4

H

Hackforth 62 E8
Hackness 74 F5
Hall Garth 184 F6
Halton East 174 C8
Halton Gill 106 E7
Halton West 154 A1
Hambleton 174 D8
Hambleton 196 F1
Hampsthwaite 160 F5
Hanlith 155 A8
Hardgate 139 A1
Hardraw 56 C6
Harlow Hill 222 A8
Harmby 60 E4
Harome 93 C4
Harrogate 219 D1
Harrowgate Hill 3 C8
Harrowgate Village 3 E8
Hartforth 20 D5
Hartley 14 A7
Hartlington 157 C8
Harton 168 C8
Hartwith 160 B8
Haughton Le Skerne 3 F6
Hawes 56 D4
Hawkswick 107 F1
Hawnby 67 E4
Hazlewood 175 A8
Healaugh 182 A2
Healaugh 37 F6
Healey 85 E3
Heathfield 136 F6
Heathwaite 45 E8
Hebden 135 A1
Hellifield 154 B3
Hellifield Green 154 B3
Helm 57 D6
Helmsley 92 F7
Helperby 142 A8
Helperthorpe 124 D1
Helwith Bridge 131 D8
Hemingbrough 198 F1
Hemlington 6 F4
Hensall 203 D2
Heslington 229 B1
Hessay 182 C8
Hetton 155 F5
Hew Green 160 D5
Heworth 228 F6
Heyshaw 159 D8
High Bentham 129 B8
High Birstwith 160 D5
High Bradley 173 E4
High Catton 185 D8
High Coniscliffe 2 C6
High Ellington 85 F6
High Grantley 138 D8
High Harrogate 220 A3
High Hawsker 33 B6
High Hutton 147 B7
High Kilburn 91 B2
High Leven 6 A3
High Marishes 96 B1
High Mowthorpe 149 D7
High Shaw 56 D7
High Stakesby 208 B5
High Worsall 24 A8
Highfield 199 E7
Hillam 202 A7
Hilton 6 C2
Hinderwell 11 F7
Hipswell 209 F1
Hirst Courtney 203 F3
Hole Bottom 135 A3
Holgate 227 F3
Hollinthorpe 194 A2
Holly Hill 209 B5
Holme 88 D5
Holme Green 190 F4
Holtby 167 F1
Hopetown 200 C2
Hopgrove 226 D2
Hopperton 163 E3
Hornby 23 E4
Hornby 62 B8
Horsehouse 83 C4
Horton 171 B5
Horton in Ribblesdale 105 C3
Houlsyke 29 F6
Hovingham 119 F6
Howe 88 E3
Howgill 157 E6
Howsham 146 F1
Hubberholme 81 C1
Huby 144 A4
Huby 178 B2
Hudswell 40 A7
Hummersknott 3 A5
Hunmanby 126 F8
Hunsingore 180 F8
Huntington 225 E3
Hunton 61 E7
Hurgill 209 A7
Hurworth Place 3 D1
Hurworth-on-Tees 3 E1
Hut Green 203 A2
Hutton Bonville 43 C7
Hutton Buscel 98 E7
Hutton Conyers 114 A4
Hutton Gate 8 D6
Hutton Hang 61 D3
Hutton Mulgrave 12 D1
Hutton Rudby 25 C5
Hutton Sessay 116 D7
Hutton Village 8 E4
Hutton Wandesley 182 A5
Hutton-le-Hole 70 C5
Huttons Ambo 147 B6

I

Ickornshaw 187 A6
Ilkley 218 B4
Ilton 85 E1
Ingerthorpe 139 C5
Ingleby Arncliffe 45 B8
Ingleby Barwick 6 B4
Ingleby Cross 45 A7
Ingleby Greenhow 27 C5
Ingleton 103 D3
Ingmanthorpe 180 E5
Inholmes 189 C6
Ireby 102 F6
Irton 99 D6
Ivelet 36 D5

J

Jennyfield 219 A5
Junction 187 F8

K

Keasden 130 A5
Kelbrook 186 A8
Keld 35 E8
Keld Houses 136 C2
Keldholme 70 D1
Kelfield 191 D1
Kellingley 202 C2
Kellington 202 F4
Kennythorpe 147 F5
Kepwick 66 C6
Kettleness 12 D6
Kettlesing 160 C3
Kettlesing Bottom 160 D4
Kettlewell 108 B3
Kexby 185 C6
Key Green 31 A3
Kilburn 91 B2
Kildale 27 E8
Kildwick 187 F8
Killerby 100 C5
Killinghall 161 C5
Kilnsey 134 B6
Kilton Thorpe 10 B8
Kiplin 42 B4
Kippax 194 E1
Kirby Grindalythe 149 E6
Kirby Hill 20 A5
Kirby Knowle 66 C2
Kirby Misperton 95 D2
Kirby Sigston 44 D1
Kirby Underdale 170 A5
Kirby Wiske 88 F8
Kirk Deighton 180 B5
Kirk Hammerton 164 C2
Kirk Smeaton 206 B3
Kirkbridge 62 F5
Kirkby 26 D5
Kirkby Fleetham 42 D1
Kirkby Hill 141 B7
Kirkby Malham 154 F8
Kirkby Malzeard 112 D5
Kirkby Mills 94 C8
Kirkby Overblow 179 A4
Kirkby Wharfe 190 A3
Kirkbymoorside 70 B1
Kirkham 147 A4
Kirklevington 24 F8
Kirklington 88 A4
Knapton 227 A5
Knaresborough 221 A6
Knavesmire 230 F7
Knayton 65 F2
Knedlington 205 F6
Knottingley 201 F3
Knottingley 202 B2
Knox 219 B7

L

Lane End 171 C2
Lane Ends 187 C6
Laneshaw Bridge 186 C4
Langbar 175 B6
Langbaurgh 7 F2
Langcliffe 131 E3
Langthorne 62 F6
Langthorpe 141 A6
Langthwaite 17 E1
Langtoft 151 D5
Langton 147 F6
Lastingham 70 F5
Laverton 112 D4
Lawkland 130 F5
Lawkland Green 131 A4
Layerthorpe 228 E4
Leake 65 F5
Lealholm 30 B6
Lealholm Side 30 D7
Leathley 177 D2
Leavening 147 E1
Lebberston 100 D5
Leck 102 E7
Ledsham 201 B8
Ledston 200 F7
Ledston Luck 194 F1
Leeming 63 D4
Leeming Bar 63 C5
Leighton 85 C2
Leppington 169 C8
Levisham 72 D5
Leyburn 60 D5
Leysthorpe 93 B1
Lindley 177 C4
Lingdale 9 F7
Lingerfield 162 B6
Lingfield 3 F5
Linton 180 A1
Linton 134 D1
Linton-on-Ouse 164 E7
Little Airmyn 205 E4
Little Ayton 8 B1
Little Barugh 95 C2
Little Crakehall 62 D5
Little Fencote 63 C8
Little Fenton 196 B6
Little Habton 121 A8
Little Heck 203 D1
Little Hutton 116 B7
Little Ouseburn 164 A7
Little Preston 194 B1
Little Ribston 180 A8
Little Sessay 116 C5
Little Skipwith 192 D1
Little Smeaton 23 C2
Little Smeaton 206 C3
Little Stainforth 131 D6
Little Studley 214 C7
Littlethorpe 214 F1
Litton 107 A5
Liverton 10 D6
Liverton Mines 10 C8
Lockton 72 D4
Lodge Green 36 F5
Lofthouse 110 C4
Londonderry 63 E2
Long Drax 205 A6
Long Lease 33 A7
Long Marston 182 A6

Long Preston 153 F5
Longnewton 5 A7
Longscales 160 C4
Loscoe 200 C1
Lothersdale 187 A8
Low Bentham 128 F8
Low Bradley 173 E3
Low Catton 185 C8
Low Coniscliffe 2 F4
Low Dalby 72 F2
Low Dinsdale 4 C1
Low Ellington 86 A6
Low Garth 29 F4
Low Gate 138 F6
Low Gatherley 21 D1
Low Green 160 A6
Low Grantley 112 E1
Low Hawsker 33 A6
Low Hutton 147 C6
Low Laithe 137 F2
Low Marishes 122 C8
Low Mill 48 E2
Low Row 37 C4
Low Snaygill 173 D4
Low Town 5 B1
Low Whita 37 D5
Low Worsall 24 A8
Lower Altofts 200 A3
Lower Dunsforth 142 A4
Lower Micklectown 200 D6
Lower Westhouse 103 B4
Lowgill 128 F3
Lowna 70 A6
Lumb 187 A4
Lumby 195 E1
Lund 198 D3
Lythe 12 E1

M

Malham 133 A1
Maltby 6 C4
Malton 215 C4
Manfield 2 B4
Manor Park 176 B2
Margrove Park 9 D6
Markington 139 D3
Marrick 38 F4
Marsett 57 A1
Marske 39 C7
Marton 94 F6
Marton 141 D1
Marton 7 B7
Marton-in-the-Forest ..144 E7
Marton-le-Moor 114 F1
Masham 86 B3
Masongill 103 A6
Maunby 64 D1
Meagill 159 D3
Mearbeck 153 D7
Melmerby 83 F8
Melmerby 114 C7
Melsonby 21 A7
Menethorpe 147 D6
Merrybent 2 E5
Methley 200 B5
Methley Junction 200 A4
Mewith Head 129 E6
Mickleby 12 A4
Micklefield 194 F4
Mickletown 200 B5
Mickley 112 F7
Middlecave 215 A5
Middleham 60 E2
Middlesmoor 231 B6
Middlethorpe 110 B5
Middleton 187 A6
Middleton 218 C7
Middleton 95 E8
Middleton One Row 4 D3
Middleton Quernhow 88 B1
Middleton St George 4 B4
Middleton Tyas 21 D5
Middleton-on-Leven 25 D8
Milby 141 B6
Mill Dam 129 C6
Mill Hirst 159 F7
Minskip 141 A3
Monk Fryston 202 B8
Monkhill 201 B1
Monkroyd 186 D4
Moor End 188 D6
Moor Monkton 165 A3
Moorsholm 10 A5
Morton-on-Swale 64 A6
Moss 207 D1
Moulton 21 D3
The Mount 214 D3
Mount Pleasant 7 B5
Mowden 3 A6
Moxby 144 D5
Muker 36 A5
Murton 184 D7
Muscoates 94 A3
Muston 100 F2
Myton-on-Swale 141 F5

N

Naburn 191 D8
Nappa 171 B8
Nawton 93 E7
Neasham 4 A1
Nesfield 175 B4
Nether Burrow 102 B6
Nether Poppleton 224 A2
Nether Silton 66 B7
Netherby 179 B1
New Earswick 225 D3
New Fryston 201 B6
New Houses 105 C4
New Micklefield 195 A3
New Park 219 B5
New Road Side 187 B5
New Row 8 F6
New Thirsk 211 A3
New Town 201 B2
New York 137 F1
Newall 176 F1
Newbiggin 57 F6
Newbiggin 101 A5
Newbiggin 82 D8
Newbridge 96 A8
Newby 104 A1
Newby 7 A3
Newby 75 E5
Newby 140 D6
Newby Cote 104 B1
Newby Wiske 64 D6
Newholm 13 A1
Newland 205 B3
Newsham 19 D8
Newsham 89 A8
Newsholme 171 A6
Newsholme 205 E8
Newthorpe 195 D3
Newton Kyme 189 B7
Newton Morrell 21 E8
Newton Mulgrave 11 E6
Newton under Roseberry .8 B4
Newton upon Derwent ..185 E4
Newton-le-Willows 62 B4
Newton-on-Ouse 165 B6
Newton-on-Rawcliffe ...72 A5
Nidd 161 E6
Norby 211 A4
Normanby 94 F4
Normanton 200 C1
North Cowton 22 C3
North Deighton 180 B6
North Duffield 199 A8
North Featherstone ...200 E1
North Grimston 148 E6
North Ings 119 D1
North Kilvington 89 E8
North Lees 113 E4
North Otterington 64 D4
North Rigton 178 B5
North Stainley 113 D7
Northallerton 210 D4
Norton 206 E2
Norton-le-Clay 115 C2
Norton-on-Derwent 215 D3
Norterfield 87 B3
Nun Appleton 190 F3
Nun Monkton 165 A4
Nunnington 93 E2
Nunthorpe 7 D5
Nunthorpe 231 C8
Nunwick 114 A5

O

Oak Tree 4 E4
Oakdale 161 B2
Oatlands 222 F6
Octon 151 F8
Old Byland 91 F8
Old Malton 215 E2
Old Micklefield 194 F4
Old Thirsk 211 C4
Oldstead 91 C3
Ormesby 7 C8
Osbaldwick 229 C4
Osgodby 100 C4
Osgodby 100 E7
Osgodby Common 198 C6
Osmotherley 45 C4
Oswaldkirk 93 A1
Otterburn 154 E4
Oughtershaw 80 C4
Oulston 117 E5
Outhgill 34 A8
Over Burrow 102 B7
Over Silton 66 B8
Overton 93 D5
Overtown 102 C7
Oxton 190 A6

P

Padside 159 B6
Padside Green 159 C6

Painsthorpe 170 B5
Pannal 222 E3
Pannal Ash 222 B5
Park 186 F5
Park End 7 B8
Parlington 194 E6
Pateley Bridge 137 C5
Patrick Brompton 62 C5
Pickering 95 D6
Pickhill 88 C6
Picton 24 D6
Piercebridge 2 A6
Place Newton 123 C3
Pockley 69 B1
Pollington 207 F6
Poole 201 F5
Port Mulgrave 11 F8
Potterton 188 C1
Potto 25 D2
Preston-on-Tees 5 F7
Preston-under-Scar 59 E6
Primrose Valley 101 C1

R

Rainton 114 E6
Ramsgill 110 E1
Raskelf 116 E2
Rathmell 153 C6
Ravenscar 15 C2
Ravensworth 20 A7
Raw 33 B4
Rawcliffe 205 A1
Rawcliffe 224 E2
Raydale 57 A1
Raygill 186 E8
Red Hill 201 A4
Redmire 59 C6
Reeth 38 B6
Reighton 127 D6
Riccall 198 A8
Richmond 209 C7
Rievaulx 92 B8
Rillington 122 F5
Ripley 161 C7
Ripon 214 E5
Risplith 138 E7
Robin Hood's Bay 33 D4
Roecliffe 140 F4
Romanby 210 B3
Rookwith 62 A1
Rosedale Abbey 49 E3
Rossett Green 222 D5
Roundhill Village 5 F5
Rowden 110 C4
Roxby 11 C7
Roxby 25 D5
Rufforth 182 C6
Runswick Bay 12 A7
Rushton 98 D6
Ruswarp 208 B3
Rylstone 156 B5
Ryther 190 F1
Ryton 121 F6

S

Sadberge 4 B8
St John's 194 F8
Salton 94 D3
Sand Hutton 168 B5
Sandhutton 89 A4
Sandsend 13 A3
Satron 36 D4
Sawdon 98 C7
Sawley 138 F6
Saxton 195 D8
Scackleton 119 C4
Scagglethorpe 122 D3
Scalby 75 F7
Scaling 11 A4
Scaling Dam 11 A4
Scampston 123 A6
Scarborough 213 B5
Scarthingwell 195 F7
Scawton 91 F4
Scorton 41 F7
Scotton 40 F2
Scotton 162 A6
Scrayingham 168 F7
Scriven 162 B6
Scruton 63 D7
Seamer 6 F1
Seamer 99 E6
Seave Green 47 A7
Sedbusk 36 E6
Selby 232 C6
Selly Hill 32 A8
Selside 105 A6
Sessay 116 B6
Settle 131 E3
Settrington 122 D1
Sexhow 25 D4
Sharow 214 F6
Shaw Mills 138 F1
Sherburn 124 D8
Sherburn in Elmet 195 E5

Sheriff Hutton 145 C5
Shipton 165 F5
Sicklinghall 179 E3
Silpho 74 E7
Silsden 174 C2
Simonstone 56 D6
Sinderby 88 C4
Sinnington 95 A8
Skeeby 21 A1
Skelton 224 C6
Skelton on Ure 140 E7
Skerne Park 3 C3
Skewsby 119 A1
Skipton 216 F4
Skipton-on-Swale 88 E2
Skipwith 192 E1
Skirethorns 134 C2
Skirpenbeck 169 A4
Skyreholme 157 F7
Slapewath 9 C6
Sledmere 150 B3
Sleights 32 A6
Slingsby 120 C6
Small Banks 174 F3
Smelthouses 137 F3
Snainton 98 A5
Snaith 204 C1
Snape 87 A7
Sneaton 32 D6
Sneatonthorpe 32 E5
Sockburn 23 C5
Sourby 176 D8
South Bank 228 B1
South Duffield 199 A4
South Kilvington 211 B7
South Kilvington 10 E8
South Loftus 10 E8
South Milford 195 F1
South Otterington 64 F2
South Stainley 139 E2
Sowerby 211 C1
The Spa 213 B4
Spacey Houses 223 A2
Spaunton 70 E4
Speeton 127 F5
Spennithorne 60 E8
Spofforth 179 E5
Sproxton 92 F4
Stackhouse 131 D4
Stainburn 177 F3
Stainforth 131 E6
Stainsacre 32 F4
Stainton 39 C3
Stainton 6 D5
Staintondale 54 B5
Stalling Busk 81 B8
Stamford Bridge 168 D2
Stanwick-St-John 1 E2
Stape 71 F8
Stapleton 3 A2
Starbeck 220 C4
Starbotton 107 F5
Staupes 160 C4
Staveley 140 F1
Staxton 99 E2
Stead 176 A1
Stean 110 A4
Stearsby 118 F2
Stillingfleet 191 C3
Stillington 144 C6
Stirton 216 C6
Stock 171 C3
Stockton on the Forest 167 D3
Stokesley 26 D7
Stone House 78 F8
Stonegate 30 D8
Stonegrave 119 D8
Strawnow 9 F6
Street 29 F3
Street Houses 190 C8
Streetlam 42 F5
Strensall 167 A7
Strensall Camp 167 B6
Studfold 105 D1
Studley Roger 113 D1
Studley Royal 113 C1
Stutton 189 D4
Suffield 75 A5
Summerbridge 138 A1
Summerscales 158 C1
Sutton 201 F4
Sutton Howgrave 87 F1
Sutton upon Derwent ..185 C1
Sutton-in-Craven 187 F6
Sutton-on-the-Forest .144 C3
Sutton-under-
  Whitestonecliffe 90 E5
Swainby 45 E8
Swaledale 37 C1
Swartha 174 D1
Swathgill 119 B4
Swetton 111 F4
Swillington 194 A1
Swillington Common ..194 A3
Swincliffe 160 E4
Swinden 154 C1
Swinithwaite 59 C4
Swinton 121 C4
Swinton 86 B2

T

Tadcaster ....18.
Tame Bridge ....2.
Tang ....16.
Tang Hall ....22.
Tanton ....
Temple Hirst ....20.
Terrington ....11.
Theakston ....8.
Thimbleby ....4.
Thirlby ....9.
Thirn ....8.
Thirsk ....21.
Thixendale ....17.
Tholthorpe ....14.
Thoralby ....9.
Thorganby ....19.
Thorgill ....4.
Thorlby ....21.
Thormanby ....11.
Thornaby-on-Tees ......
Thornborough ....8.
Thorns ....3.
Thornthwaite ....15.
Thornton ....
Thornton in Lonsdale 10.
Thornton Rust ....5.
Thornton Steward ......6.
Thornton Watlass .....8.
Thornton-in-Craven ..17.
Thornton-le-Beans .....6.
Thornton-le-Clay ....14.
Thornton-le-Dale .....9.
Thornton-le-Moor ......6.
Thornton-le-Street ....6.
Thorp Arch ....18.
Thorpe ....18.
Thorpe Bassett ......12.
Thorpe Underwood ....16.
Thorpe Willoughby ...19.
Thresfhield ....6.
Thrintoft ....6.
Throxenby ....21.
Thruscross ....15.
Thwaite ....3.
Thwing ....17.
Timble ....17.
Tockwith ....18.
Tollerton ....14.
Tollesby ....
Topcliffe ....13.
Tosside ....15.
Toulston ....18.
Town Head ....17.
Towthorpe ....14.
Towthorpe ....16.
Towton ....18.
Trawden ....18.
Tunstall ....4.
Tunstall ....10.

U

Uckerby ....2.
Ugglebarnby ....3.
Ugthorpe ....3.
Uleskelf ....19.
Ulshaw ....6.
Upper Dunsforth .....14.
Upper Helmsley ......16.
Upper Poppleton .....16.
Upsall ....0.
Ure Bank ....21.
Urlay Nook ....0.
Urra ....2.

V

Vicar's Green ....3.

W

Waithwith Banks ......4.
Wake Hill ....11.
Walden Stubbs ....20.
Walkerville ....2.
Walmgate Stray ......22.
Walshford ....18.
Walton ....18.
Warlaby ....6.
Warsill ....13.
Warthermarske ....8.
Warthill ....16.
Washfold ....1.
Wass ....20.
Water Fryston ....20.
Wath ....11.
Wath ....11.
Wath ....1.
Weaverthorpe ....12.
Weeton ....17.
Welburn ....9.
Welburn ....14.
Welbury ....4.

...........................87 A4
...nington 102 B1
...nsley 60 A4
...nsleydale 57 A5
...coe Hill 178 B1
...st Appleton 41 C1
...st Ayton 99 A7
...st Barnby 12 C3
...st Burton 58 F1
...t Cliff 208 B7
...st Field 227 A2
...t Garforth 194 B3
...st Haddlesey 203 A5
...st Harlsey 44 D5
...st Heslerton 123 F7
...t Knapton 123 B6
...st Layton 20 A8
...st Lilling 145 C4
...st Lutton 150 B8
...st Marton 171 F5
...st Ness 94 B1

West Rounton 24 D2
West Scrafton 83 F6
West Stonesdale 15 E1
West Tanfield 87 A1
West Witton 59 E3
Westerdale 28 E4
Westfield 232 C4
Westhouse 103 C4
Weston 176 E2
Westow 147 B4
Wetherby 180 D4
Wharfe 131 A8
Wharram le Street 149 A4
Whashton 20 A5
Whashton Green 20 A5
Whaw 17 B3
Wheldale 201 B5
Wheldrake 192 F8
Whenby 145 B8
Whinfield 3 F8
Whitby 208 C6

Whitewall Corner 215 C1
Whitley 207 A7
Whitley Thorpe 206 F7
Whittington 102 A7
Whitwell 42 B6
Whitwell-on-the-Hill ..146 E4
Whitwood 200 C3
Whixley 164 A5
Whorlton 25 E1
Wiganthorpe 119 E3
Wigginton 166 D5
Wigglesworth 153 C3
Wighill 181 D1
Wilberfoss 185 F5
Willerby 99 C2
Wilsill 137 E3
Wilton 97 A5
Winewall 186 B2
Winksley 112 F2
Winsley 160 D8
Winterburn 155 D5

Winton 44 C3
Wintringham 123 C4
Wistow 197 D6
Wold Newton 126 A3
Wombleton 93 F7
Womersley 206 C6
Wood Row 200 A6
Woodale 83 A2
Woodhall 58 B5
Woodhall 199 B2
Woodhouse 200 A1
Woodlands 220 C1
Woodthorpe 230 C7
Worton 57 F5
Wray 128 A6
Wrayton 102 B3
Wrelton 71 C1
Wressle 199 D2
Wycoller 186 C2
Wydra 160 A1
Wykeham 122 B6

Wykeham 98 E6

Y

Yafforth 43 C1
Yarm 5 D3
Yearsley 118 C5
Yedingham 97 D2
Yockenthwaite 81 A1
York 233 B3
Youlthorpe 169 C2
Youlton 142 E2

A

A W Nielson Rd DN14 ...205 F2
Abber La LS24 ...182 A2
Abbeville Ave 1 YO21 ...208 B6
Abbey Cl 12 LS29 ...175 A4
Abbey Crags Way HG5 ...221 C3
Abbey Cty Inf Sch DL3 ...3 B5
Abbey Gdns
Darlington DL3 ...3 B5
Pontefract WF8 ...201 B2
Abbey Hill BD23 ...155 C5
Abbey Jun Sch DL3 ...3 B5
Abbey La YO22 ...208 E7
Abbey Leisure Ctr YO8 ...232 C5
Abbey Mews WF8 ...201 B2
Abbey Mill Gdns HG5 ...221 C3
Abbey Mill View HG5 ...221 C3
Abbey Rd Darlington DL3 ...3 B5
Knaresborough HG5 ...221 B3
Sadberge DL2 ...4 C7
Abbey St YO30 ...228 A7
Abbey Walk Ret Pk YO8 ...232 C6
Abbey Wlk
Pontefract WF8 ...201 B2
Selby YO8 ...232 C5
Abbey Yd YO8 ...232 C5
Abbot St YO31 ...233 C4
Abbot's Garth YO12 ...99 D6
Abbot's Rd Selby YO8 ...232 E3
Whitby YO22 ...208 E5
Abbots Way HG5 ...221 C3
Abbot's Wlk YO22 ...208 E5
Abbotsford Rd YO10 ...228 F3
Abbotsway YO31 ...228 E8
Abbotts Cl LS25 ...194 F8
Abbotts Ct YO17 ...215 E4
Abelton Gr 33 YO32 ...166 E5
Aberdeen La 19 YO11 ...213 A6
Aberdeen Pl 20 YO11 ...213 A6
Aberdeen Rd DL1 ...3 E8
Aberdeen St 17 YO11 ...213 A6
Aberdeen Terr 21 YO11 ...213 A6
Aberdeen Wlk 16 YO11 ...213 A6
Aberford C of E Prim Sch LS25 ...194 F8
Aberford Rd
Barwick in Elmet & Scholes LS15 ...194 C8
Bramham cum Oglethorpe LS23 ...188 E5
Garforth LS25 ...194 D4
Abram's View YO11 ...213 B2
Acacia Ave YO32 ...225 E4
Acacia Dr WF10 ...201 B3
Academy Gdns DL2 ...1 D8
Acaster Ave YO23 ...191 A3
Acaster Dr LS25 ...194 D3
Acaster La
Acaster Malbis YO23 ...231 B1
Acaster Selby YO23 ...191 A4
Accommodation Rd YO25 ...151 D6
Acklam Grange Sec Sch TS5 ...6 D7
Acklam Rd TS17 ...6 C8
Acklam Whin Prim Sch TS5 ...6 D6
Ackton La WF7 ...200 D1
Ackton Pasture La WF7 ...200 D2
Ackton Pastures Jun & Inf Sch WF10 ...200 D3
Acomb Prim Sch YO24 ...227 E3
Acomb Rd YO24 ...227 D3
Acomb Wood Cl YO24 ...230 C7
Acomb Wood Dr YO24 ...230 B7
Acorn Cl 6 YO8 ...198 B4
Acorn Way
Gateforth YO8 ...197 B1
York YO24 ...230 D7
Acre Fold 21 LS29 ...174 F4
Acre Mdw 1 BD22 ...187 B6
Acre Rd 2 BD22 ...187 B6
Acres Cl 24 YO62 ...92 F6
Acres La Brompton YO13 ...98 C4
Helmsley YO62 ...93 A6
Scrayingham YO41 ...169 B8
Acres The
Addingham LS29 ...175 A5
Glusburn BD20 ...187 E6
Stokesley TS9 ...26 C8
Acresfield 11 BB8 ...186 A3
Acworth St 3 YO12 ...212 E4
Adam's Field La YO61 ...117 F4
Adcott Rd TS5 ...6 E7
Addingham Mid Sch LS29 ...174 F5
Addingham Prim Sch LS29 ...174 F5
Addingham Wharfedale LS29 ...174 E4
Addison Ave 18 WF6 ...200 B1
Addison Rd TS9 ...8 A1
Addison Villas HG3 ...219 A8
Addlethorpe La LS22 ...179 C3
Adelaide Rd
Middlesbrough TS7 ...7 B6
6 Norton DN6 ...206 E2
Adelaide St 3 YO23 ...228 B2
Adlington Cl 8 YO32 ...167 A7
Admirals Ct YO7 ...211 A2
Admirals' Ct YO7 ...211 A2
Agar St YO31 ...233 C3
Agnes Ing La LA2 ...128 A7
Agnesgate HG4 ...214 D5
Aikengill Rd LA2 ...129 A4
Ailcey Rd HG4 ...214 D5
Ainderby Rd DL7 ...210 B2
Ainsford Way TS7 ...7 D8
Ainstable Rd TS7 ...7 D8
Ainsty Ave YO24 ...230 F8
Ainsty Dr 2 LS22 ...180 C4
Ainsty Gr YO24 ...230 F8
Ainsty Rd
Harrogate HG1 ...219 F4
Wetherby LS22 ...180 C4
Ainsty View
Acklam YO17 ...169 E8
Whixley YO26 ...164 A4
Ainsworth Way TS7 ...7 D8
Ainthorpe La YO21 ...29 C7
Aintree Ct
9 Darlington DL1 ...3 F6
York YO24 ...230 F8
Aire Cres BD20 ...187 E7
Aire Rd LS22 ...180 B4
Aire St Castleford WF10 ...200 E4
Glusburn BD20 ...187 F7
Knottingley WF11 ...202 A3
Aire Valley Cl BD20 ...173 D3
Aire Valley Dr BD20 ...173 D3
Aire View Inf Sch BD20 ...174 C1
Airedale Ave
Gargrave BD23 ...155 D1
Skipton BD23 ...217 B4
Airedale Dr WF10 ...201 B5
Airedale High Sch WF10 ...201 B4
Airedale Mews 1 BD23 ...216 E3
Airedale Rd
Castleford WF10 ...201 A4
Scotton DL9 ...40 D4
Airedale Trading Pk BD20 ...187 F8
Airedale View 1 BD20 ...187 F8
Aireside Ave BD20 ...173 D1
Aireside Terr BD20 ...173 D2
Aireville Dr BD20 ...174 C1
Aireville Sch BD23 ...216 D4
Aireville Swimming Baths BD23 ...216 D4
Aireyholme La TS9 ...8 B2
Airmyn Park Prim Sch DN14 ...205 E4
Airmyn Rd DN14 ...205 D3
Airy Hill CP Sch YO21 ...208 D5
Airy Hill La TS12 ...9 D8
Aiskew Leeming Bar C of E Sch DL7 ...63 C4
Aislabie Cl HG4 ...214 A5
Aislabie Garth HG4 ...214 A5
Aislaby Carr La YO18 ...95 C7
Aislaby La Aislaby YO21 ...32 A8
Aislaby YO18 ...95 C6
Aislaby Rd TS16 ...5 D4
Aismunderby Cl HG4 ...214 C3
Aismunderby Rd HG4 ...214 C4
Aisne Rd DL9 ...209 C1
Aketon Rd WF10 ...200 D3
Alanbrooke Barracks Cty Prim Sch YO7 ...89 A1
Alanbrooke Ind Est YO7 ...115 B8
Alandale Cres LS25 ...194 B3
Alandale Rd LS25 ...194 B4
Albany Ave HG1 ...219 E5
Albany Rd
Harrogate HG1 ...219 E5
Middlesbrough TS7 ...7 B6
Albany St 3 YO26 ...227 F5
Albany Wlk LS29 ...218 A3
Albatross Way DL1 ...3 E5
Albemarle Back Rd 10 YO11 ...212 F6
Albemarle Cres 18 YO11 ...213 A6
Albemarle Rd YO23 ...228 B2
Albermarle Dr 3 DL9 ...40 F5
Albert Cl 1 YO32 ...228 F8
Albert Hill BD24 ...131 E2
Albert Pl
Harrogate HG1 ...220 C4
1 Whitby YO21 ...208 D7
Albert Rd
Eaglescliffe TS16 ...5 E5
12 Glusburn BD20 ...187 E7
Harrogate HG1 ...219 E5
1 Scarborough YO12 ...213 A7
Albert St 33 Earby BB18 ...172 A1
Glusburn BD20 ...187 F7
Harrogate HG1 ...219 D2
Normanton South WF6 ...200 B2
8 Scarborough YO12 ...213 A7
York YO10 ...233 C1
Albert Terr
5 Harrogate HG1 ...219 D1
Skipton BD23 ...216 F4
Albion Ave YO26 ...227 B6
Albion Cres 3 YO11 ...213 A4
Albion Pl 14 YO21 ...208 D6
Albion Rd 25 Earby BB18 ...172 A1
Scarborough YO11 ...213 A4
Albion St Boosbeck TS12 ...9 E7
Boston Spa LS23 ...188 E7
Castleford WF10 ...200 E4
Albion St *continued*
28 Earby BB18 ...172 A1
York YO1 ...233 B1
Albion Terr 9 LS23 ...188 E7
Alcelina Ct YO23 ...233 B1
Alcuin Ave YO10 ...229 A4
Aldborough Gate 13 YO51 ...141 B4
Aldborough Way YO26 ...227 F5
Aldbrough & Boroughbridge CP Sch YO51 ...141 C5
Aldenham Rd TS14 ...8 E5
Alder Ave HG5 ...221 E5
Alder Carr La YO18 ...49 E2
Alder Hill St 1 BB18 ...172 B1
Alder Rd HG1 ...219 F5
Alder Way YO32 ...225 D2
Alderley Ct YO32 ...225 E3
Alderman Leach Inf Sch DL3 ...3 B6
Alders Rd YO18 ...49 C4
Aldersley Ave BD23 ...217 B3
Alderson Cres YO12 ...99 E7
Alderson Rd HG2 ...222 E8
Alderson Sq HG2 ...222 E8
Aldersyde YO24 ...230 E7
Aldreth Gr YO23 ...228 C2
Aldridge Rd TS3 ...7 B8
Aldwark YO1 ...233 C3
Aldwych Cl TS6 ...7 E8
Alexander Ave
6 East Ayton/West Ayton YO13 ...99 B8
York YO31 ...225 E2
Alexander Cl YO7 ...211 C4
Alexander Rd DL9 ...209 C2
Alexandra Cres 10 LS29 ...218 A4
Alexandra Ct
Skipton BD23 ...216 F2
York YO10 ...228 E4
Alexandra Park Rd HG5 ...221 C7
Alexandra Pk YO12 ...212 D5
Alexandra Pl 3 HG5 ...221 B8
Alexandra Rd
Harrogate HG1 ...219 D3
Strensall YO32 ...167 A6
Alexandra Way DL10 ...209 C7
Alexandria Dr DL2 ...4 D4
Algarth Rd YO31 ...229 B7
Algarth Rise YO31 ...229 B7
All Saints Jun & Inf Sch WF7 ...200 E1
All Saints Prim Sch LS29 ...218 B4
All Saints RC Comp Sch YO24 ...233 A1
All Saints RC Prim Sch YO7 ...211 B2
All Saints Rd 1 YO12 ...212 F4
Allan St Darlington DL1 ...3 D6
2 York YO30 ...228 C7
Allen Cl YO10 ...229 A4
Allen Gr TS9 ...26 B7
Allenby Rd
20 Helmsley YO62 ...92 F6
Hipswell DL9 ...209 C1
Allendale YO24 ...230 D8
Allendale Rd TS7 ...7 D8
Allens West Sta TS16 ...5 D5
Allensway TS17 ...6 C7
Allerdale Cl YO7 ...211 C4
Allerston La YO18 ...97 C4
Allerton Balk TS15 ...5 D2
Allerton Bywater Prim Sch WF10 ...200 D7
Allerton Dr
22 Poppleton YO26 ...165 F1
Poppleton YO26 ...224 A1
Allerton La HG5 ...163 D4
Allerton Wath Rd DL6 ...65 D4
Allertonshire Sch DL6 ...210 D6
Allhallowgate HG4 ...214 C5
Allington Dr YO31 ...229 B6
Allington Way
Darlington DL1 ...3 F5
Great Burdon DL1 ...4 A5
Allison Ave TS17 ...6 B4
Allison St TS14 ...8 E6
Allotments La YO61 ...143 F3
Alma Gdns HG4 ...214 D4
Alma Par 2 YO11 ...212 F5
Alma Rd BB8 ...186 B3
Alma Sq 3 YO11 ...212 F5
Alma Terr Selby YO8 ...232 C6
3 Skipton BD23 ...217 A4
York YO10 ...228 D2
Alma Way 2 YO18 ...96 A6
Almery Terr YO30 ...233 A3
Almond Cl 7 Filey YO14 ...101 B4
Hambleton YO8 ...197 B1
Almond Gr 11 Filey YO14 ...101 B4
Northallerton DL7 ...210 D3
Scarborough YO12 ...212 D5
York YO32 ...225 D4
Almond Tree Ave
Carlton DN14 ...204 C3
Malton YO17 ...215 D6
Almond Wlk 4 DL9 ...209 B1
Almscliffe Dr LS17 ...178 B2
Almscliffe Garth LS17 ...178 B4
Almsford Ave HG2 ...222 E6
Almsford Bank HG2 ...222 E5
Almsford Cl HG2 ...222 F6
Almsford Dr
Harrogate HG2 ...222 F6
York YO26 ...227 C5
Almsford End HG2 ...222 E6
Almsford Oval HG2 ...222 F6
Almsford Pl HG2 ...222 E6
Almsford Rd
Harrogate HG2 ...222 F6
York YO26 ...227 C5
Almsford Wlk HG2 ...222 F6
Almshouse Hill 1 LS23 ...188 E5
Alne CP Sch YO61 ...142 F4
Alne Rd
Easingwold YO61 ...143 B8
Tollerton YO61 ...143 A3
Alne Terr YO10 ...228 E2
Alness Dr YO24 ...230 B7
Altofts La WF10 ...200 B3
Altofts Rd WF6 ...200 A1
Alum House La TS9 ...26 B2
Alverton Cty Inf Sch DL6 ...210 F6
Alverton Dr DL3 ...3 B8
Alverton La DL7 ...210 D4
Alvin Wlk 9 YO41 ...185 B2
Alvis Gr YO10 ...229 D4
Alwyn Rd DL3 ...3 D8
Alwyne Dr YO30 ...224 E1
Alwyne Gr YO30 ...224 E1
Amber St YO31 ...233 C4
Amberly St 4 YO26 ...227 E5
Amble Cl YO62 ...70 B2
Ambler St WF10 ...200 E4
Ambler's La YO30 ...165 F7
Ambleside Ave
10 Barnoldswick BB18 ...171 D2
York YO10 ...229 B4
Ambleside Gr TS5 ...6 E8
Ambrey Cl 16 YO14 ...126 F8
Ambrose Rd HG4 ...214 C4
Ambrose St YO10 ...228 D1
America La BD20 ...187 F4
Amesbury Cres TS8 ...6 F5
Amiens Cres DL9 ...209 D1
Amotherby CP Sch YO17 ...121 A4
Amotherby La YO17 ...121 A6
Amplecarr YO61 ...117 B5
Ampleforth Abbey & Coll YO62 ...92 D1
Ampleforth Coll Jun Sch YO62 ...118 F7
Ampleforth St Benedicts RC Prim Sch YO62 ...92 C1
Amy Johnson Way YO30 ...225 A3
Anchor Rd 2 HG1 ...220 A3
Anchorage La DL7 ...210 C5
Anchorage Way YO21 ...208 C5
Anchorite La 7 YO18 ...95 F7
Ancress Wlk YO23 ...233 B1
Ancroft Cl YO1 ...233 C1
Andersen Rd DN14 ...205 F2
Anderson Gr 6 YO24 ...227 F2
Anderson St 6 WF8 ...201 B1
Anderton St 18 BD20 ...187 E8
Andrew Dr 4 YO32 ...225 F1
Andrew La YO18 ...71 B4
Anfield Ct 8 DL1 ...3 F6
Angel Ct 8 TS9 ...26 C7
Angel Yd 1 YO21 ...208 D6
Angelica Cl 12 HG3 ...161 B3
Angram Cl YO30 ...224 F1
Angram La
Barlby with Osgodby YO19 ...198 A6
Muker DL11 ...35 E6
Tollerton YO61 ...143 B3
Angram Rd YO26 ...182 A5
Angrove Cl TS9 ...7 F1
Angrove Dr TS9 ...7 F1
Annan Cl YO24 ...230 C6
Annandale Gr 1 YO13 ...75 D5
Annas Garth DL8 ...60 F4
Anne St YO23 ...228 C2
Annumhills Rd YO8 ...199 D7
Anserdale La YO62 ...70 E5
Anson Croft 5 YO8 ...196 E1
Anson Dr YO10 ...231 D8
Anteforth View DL10 ...20 E3
Anthea Dr YO31 ...225 E1
Anthony La HG4 ...114 E1
Anvil Sq 3 DL11 ...38 B6
Anzio Rd DL9 ...209 C1
Apedale Rd
Castle Bolton with East & West Bolton DL8 ...37 F1
Redmire DL8 ...59 C8
Apley Cl HG2 ...220 A1
Apollo St 5 YO10 ...228 E3
Apple Garth
10 Easingwold YO61 ...117 D1
15 Poppleton YO26 ...165 F1
Apple Tree Gdns 2 LS29 ...175 C2
Appleby Ave HG5 ...220 D8
Appleby Cres HG5 ...220 D8
Appleby Ct HG5 ...220 D8
Appleby Gate HG5 ...220 D7
Appleby Glade YO32 ...225 D7
Appleby Gn HG5 ...220 D8
Appleby La
Aldbrough DL11 ...1 F1
Kirkby Malzeard HG4 ...112 B4
Appleby Pl 2 YO31 ...229 A5
Appleby Way HG5 ...220 D7
Appleby Wlk HG5 ...220 D8
Applecroft Rd
Selby YO8 ...232 A4
York YO31 ...229 B7
Applegarth
Barnoldswick BB18 ...171 E2
Applegarth *continued*
Coulby Newham TS8 ...
Applegarth Ct DL7 ...21
Applegarth St 15 BB18 ...17
Applegartn CP Prim Sch DL7 ...21
Appleton Ct YO23 ...23
Appleton La
Appleton-le-Street with Easthorpe YO17 ...12
Coneysthorpe YO60 ...12
Appleton Rd YO23 ...23
Appleton Roebuck CP Sch YO23 ...19
Appleton Wiske CP Sch DL6 ...2
Appletree Dr YO8 ...19
Appletree Way
Malton YO17 ...21
10 Sherburn in Elmet LS25 ...19
Appletreewick Stone Circle BD23 ...13
Appley Cl TS16 ...
Apron La HG3 ...14
Arbour The
4 Glusburn BD20 ...17
Ilkley LS29 ...21
Arbour Way YO17 ...21
Archbishop Holgates Sch YO10 ...22
Archbishop of York C of E Jun Sch YO23 ...23
Archer La HG3 ...14
Archer Rd DL2 ...
Archers Gn The DL10 ...4
Archers Mdw HG5 ...22
Archie St 3 HG1 ...21
Arden La YO62 ...9
Arena View 12 DL10 ...4
Arenhall Cl 2 YO32 ...22
Argam La YO25 ...12
Argill DL8 ...6
Argyle Rd YO21 ...20
Argyle St YO23 ...22
Arkendale La HG5 ...14
Arkendale Rd HG5 ...16
Arkengarthdale C of E Prim Sch DL11 ...1
Arkengarthdale Rd DL11 ...3
Arkle Cres DL1 ...
Arlington Rd
Middlesbrough TS5 ...
York YO30 ...22
Armoury Rd YO8 ...23
Armstrong Cl 7 WF6 ...20
Army Foundation Coll HG3 ...16
Arncliffe C of E Prim Sch BD23 ...10
Arncliffe Dr WF11 ...20
Arncliffe Rd HG2 ...22
Arndale Way 8 YO14 ...10
Arnold Rd DL1 ...
Arnside Cres WF10 ...20
Arnside Pl 2 YO10 ...22
Arran Ct LS25 ...19
Arran Dr LS25 ...19
Arran Pl YO31 ...22
Arrows Cres 10 YO51 ...14
Arrows Terr 9 YO51 ...14
Arthington Ave HG1 ...21
Arthur Pl 6 YO30 ...22
Arthur St
6 Barnoldswick BB18 ...17
Earby BB18 ...18
Great Ayton TS9 ...
York YO10 ...22
Arthurs Ave HG2 ...22
Arthurs Cl HG2 ...22
Arthurs Gr HG2 ...22
Arundel Gr YO24 ...23
Arundel Pl
12 Scarborough YO11 ...21
9 Whitby YO21 ...20
Arundel Rd 5 DN6 ...20
Ascot Rd LS25 ...19
Ascot Way YO24 ...22
Ash Bank Ave 2 HG4 ...11
Ash Bank Cl 1 HG4 ...11
Ash Bank Rd HG4 ...11
Ash Cl 1 Ilkley LS29 ...17
Newton on Derwent YO41 ...18
York YO31 ...22
Ash Croft 7 DL10 ...4
Ash Gn TS8 ...
Ash Gr
13 Barnoldswick BB18 ...17
Danby YO21 ...2
12 Filey YO14 ...10
Glusburn BD20 ...18
Ilkley LS29 ...21
7 Kirkbymoorside YO62 ...7
1 Kirklevington TS15 ...2
Northallerton DL6 ...21
1 Riccall YO19 ...19
Ripon HG4 ...214
Scarborough YO12 ...212
Whitby YO21 ...20
Ash Hill TS8 ...
Ash La
Church Fenton LS24 ...19
Garforth LS25 ...194
8 Haxby YO32 ...16
Little Fenton LS25 ...196
Ash Lea YO21 ...29
Ash Rd 13 Filey YO14 ...10

d *continued*
orough TS14 . . . . .8 F7
gate HG2 . . . . .222 E6
idge 5 DL6 . . . . . . .210 E3
11 Glusburn BD20 . .187 E7
LS29 . . . . .218 C5
den BB8 . . . . .186 B1
O26 . . . . .227 E4
ee Cl DL8 . . . . .62 F2
ee Garth LS24 . . . .195 E7
ee Rd
dale DL8 . . . . .63 A2
sborough HG5 . . . . . .221 B6
ee Wlk 22 LS29 . . .176 C1
nk La Firby DL8 . . . . .62 F1
ff Hutton YO60 . . . . . .145 F6
ourne Cl 12 YO51 . . .141 B4
ourne Rd 10 YO51 . . .141 B4
ourne Way YO24 . . . .230 C8
rn Pl LS29 . . . . .218 A3
rn Rd YO11 . . . . . . .212 E4
rn Rise 10 YO11 . . . .212 E4
rn Way LS22 . . . . . . .180 B4
rnham Cl 4 DN6 . . .206 F2
rnham Wlk 5
. . . . .206 F2
le Cl DL2 . . . . .4 E4
le La LS22 . . . . .180 B4
le Rd
nnington YO19 . . . . . .184 F7
sley YO62 . . . . .92 F6
ne Gr WF8 . . . . .201 D2
own Rise YO13 . . . . .75 C8
owne Cl DL8 . . . . .62 E5
owne Ct DL8 . . . . .62 E5
The DL10 . . . . .21 C7
ld
assington BD23 . . . . .134 E3
erby LS22 . . . . .180 C3
ld Ave YO17 . . . . . . .215 D5
ld Cl
able Burton DL8 . . . . . .61 C5
ey Bridge HG3 . . . . . .137 B4
ld Court Rd
. . . . .137 B4
ld Rd Danby YO21 . . . .29 B6
gate HG1 . . . . .219 E4
ckering YO18 . . . . .96 A6
ld St WF6 . . . . .200 A2
rd Ave TS5 . . . . .6 D8
rd Pl YO24 . . . . .227 D2
p La WF6 . . . . .200 A2
rth Ct HG2 . . . . .222 C5
rth Way HG2 . . . . . . .222 C5
ove Cres LS25 . . . . .194 D2
nds Cl DL6 . . . . .210 F4
nds Ct DL6 . . . . .210 F4
nds Dr DL7 . . . . .63 C5
nds Prim Sch
. . . . .218 C5
nds Rd
LS29 . . . . .218 C5
allerton DL6 . . . . .210 F4
a Cl YO8 . . . . .232 D4
a Rd DL7 . . . . .210 D4
y Ct 2 YO14 . . . . . . .101 B3
y Park Cres
. . . . .229 B6
y Park Rd YO31 . . . .229 B7
ead 4 LS23 . . . . . . .188 E7
eade Cl YO24 . . . . . .230 B8
n Ave YO30 . . . . .228 B8
n Rd WF10 . . . . .200 E3
ee Dr YO8 . . . . .197 D1
lle Ave
scliffe TS16 . . . . .5 E6
orough YO12 . . . . . . .212 F6
lle Cl HG2 . . . . .222 C5
lle Coll HG2 . . . . . . .222 B6
lle Dr 9 DL2 . . . . .22 E8
lle Gr HG2 . . . . .222 C5
lle St YO31 . . . . .228 D7
ood Cl 5 YO62 . . . . . .92 F7
ood Dr TS9 . . . . .26 C8
ood Glade YO32 . . .225 C6
ood Pl HG5 . . . . .221 E5
orth Rd WF8 . . . . . . .201 C2
n Ave WF8 . . . . .201 C2
m Bryan Coll TS14 . . . .8 F7
Ave DL10 . . . . .209 E8
Hall* DL10 . . . . .20 D2
rn & Campsall Sports Ctr
. . . . .206 F1
w Dale TS14 . . . . .8 D6
w Rigg La YO18 . . . . .71 A5
am Bryan Coll
am Bryan YO23 . . . . . .182 F2
le DL8 . . . . .63 A2
ring YO18 . . . . .95 F8
am Bryan Coll Harrogate
HG2 . . . . .223 A7
am Bryan La
. . . . .230 A6
am Croft 1 YO24 . . .227 B1
am Fields La
. . . . .182 F2
am Gr YO24 . . . . . . .227 B2
am La
am Bryan YO24 . . . . . .230 A8
YO24 . . . . .227 B1
igg Prim Sch DL8 . . .57 E5
ith CP Sch LS21 . . .176 D3
ith La LS21 . . . . . . .176 D3
ith Moor Rd
. . . . .176 D5
n Cl 3 YO19 . . . . . . .184 F7
n La BB18 . . . . .172 A1

Aspen Way
Slingsby YO62 . . . . .120 B5
Tadcaster LS24 . . . . .189 D6
Aspin Ave HG5 . . . . .221 B4
Aspin Dr HG5 . . . . .221 C4
Aspin Gdns HG5 . . . . . . .221 C4
Aspin Gr 4 HG5 . . . . . . .221 C4
Aspin La HG5 . . . . .221 C3
Aspin Oval HG5 . . . . . . .221 B4
Aspin Park Ave 1 HG5 . .221 C4
Aspin Park CP Sch
HG5 . . . . .221 C5
Aspin Park Cres HG5 . . .221 B4
Aspin Park Dr HG5 . . . . .221 B4
Aspin Park La HG5 . . . . .221 C4
Aspin Park Rd HG5 . . . . .221 C4
Aspin View HG5 . . . . . . .221 C4
Aspin Way HG5 . . . . .221 C4
Asquith Ave
Scarborough YO12 . . . . .212 E3
York YO31 . . . . .229 A5
Assembly St 7 WF6 . . . .200 A1
Astbury TS8 . . . . .7 C4
Asterley Dr TS5 . . . . .6 D8
Astley Ave LS26 . . . . . . .194 A1
Astley La
Great & Little Preston
LS26 . . . . .200 B8
Swillington LS26 . . . . . . .194 A1
Astley Lane Ind Pk
LS26 . . . . .200 B8
Astley Way LS26 . . . . . . .200 A8
Atcherley Cl YO10 . . . . .231 D8
Athelstan CP Sch
LS25 . . . . .195 F3
Athelstan La 7 LS21 . . . .177 A1
Athelstans Ct LS25 . . . . .195 F4
Atkinson Ave DL10 . . . . .209 D8
Atkinson Ct WF6 . . . . . . .200 A1
Atkinson La WF8 . . . . . .201 C1
Atlantis Water Pk*
YO12 . . . . .212 F8
Atlas Rd YO30 . . . . .225 A3
Atlas Wynd TS16 . . . . .5 E3
Attermire Cave*
BD24 . . . . .132 A3
Atterwith La YO26 . . . . . .182 A7
Auborough St 5 YO11 . . .213 A6
Auckland Ave DL3 . . . . . . .3 B6
Auckland Oval DL3 . . . . . .3 B7
Auckland St TS14 . . . . .8 F7
Auckland Way 7 YO21 . . .208 C6
Audax Cl YO30 . . . . .225 A3
Audax Rd YO30 . . . . .225 A3
Audby La LS22 . . . . .180 C4
Audus St 10 YO8 . . . . . . .232 C5
Augusta Cl DL1 . . . . .3 F7
Aumit La YO62 . . . . .92 E1
Aunums Cl 7 YO18 . . . . . .96 D5
Auster Bank Ave LS24 . . .189 F7
Auster Bank Cres
LS24 . . . . .189 F7
Auster Bank Rd LS24 . . .189 F7
Auster Bank View
LS24 . . . . .189 F7
Auster Rd YO30 . . . . . . .225 B3
Austfield La LS25 . . . . . .202 B8
Austin Rd WF10 . . . . . . .201 B4
Austwick C of E Prim Sch
LA2 . . . . .130 E7
Austwick Rd BD24 . . . . . .131 C8
Ava Rd DL9 . . . . .40 C4
Avens Way TS17 . . . . .6 A5
Avenue A LS23 . . . . .181 A2
Avenue B LS23 . . . . .181 A1
Avenue Bank HG4 . . . . . . .86 C4
Avenue C E LS23 . . . . . . .181 B1
Avenue C W LS23 . . . . . .181 A1
Avenue Cl HG2 . . . . .220 D4
Avenue D LS23 . . . . .181 A1
Avenue E E LS23 . . . . . . .181 B1
Avenue E W LS23 . . . . . .189 A8
Avenue F LS23 . . . . .181 B1
Avenue G LS23 . . . . .181 B1
Avenue Gr 11 HG2 . . . . . .220 C3
Avenue House Ct HG5 . .162 F3
Avenue Pl 7 HG2 . . . . . . .220 C3
Avenue Prim Sch The
TS7 . . . . .7 D6
Avenue Rd
Harrogate HG2 . . . . .220 C3
Scarborough YO12 . . . . .212 E4
York YO30 . . . . .233 A4
Avenue St 8 HG2 . . . . . . .220 C3
Avenue Terr
5 Harrogate HG2 . . . . . .220 C3
York YO30 . . . . .233 A4
Avenue The
Campsall DN6 . . . . .206 E1
Collingham LS22 . . . . . . .180 A1
Dalby-cum-Skewsby
YO60 . . . . .119 B2
Eaglescliffe TS16 . . . . .5 E6
26 Filey YO14 . . . . .101 B3
Gilling East YO62 . . . . . .118 E7
Great Ribston with Walshford
LS22 . . . . .180 C8
Guisborough TS14 . . . . . . .8 D6
Harrogate HG1 . . . . .220 C4
3 Haxby YO32 . . . . .166 E5
Haxby YO32 . . . . .225 D8
Knaresborough HG5 . . . .221 A7
Masham HG4 . . . . .86 C3
Middlesbrough TS5 . . . . . . .6 F8
Middlesbrough TS7 . . . . . . .7 D6
Norton YO17 . . . . .215 C2
Nun Monkton YO26 . . . . .165 A4
Nunnington YO62 . . . . . . .93 E1

Avenue The *continued*
8 Pateley Bridge HG3 . . . .137 C4
Richmond DL10 . . . . .209 D7
Rufforth YO23 . . . . .182 C6
Skutterskelfe TS15 . . . . . . .25 E6
1 Sleights YO22 . . . . .32 A6
Snape with Thorp DL8 . . . . .87 A7
South Milford LS25 . . . . . .195 F2
Stainton Dale YO13 . . . . . . .54 A8
Stokesley TS9 . . . . .26 C7
Thirkleby High & Low
with Osgodby YO7 . . . . . .116 D8
West Hauxwell DL8 . . . . . . .61 C8
Whitby YO21 . . . . .208 B4
Wighill LS24 . . . . .181 D2
York YO30 . . . . .228 A6
Avenue Victoria YO11 . . .213 A3
Aviation Rd LS25 . . . . . .196 A4
Aviator Ct YO30 . . . . . . .224 F3
Aviemore Ct 10 DL1 . . . . . .3 F6
Aviemore Rd TS8 . . . . .6 F5
Avocet Cres 11 YO12 . . . . .99 F6
Avon Dr
Barnoldswick BB18 . . . . . .171 E2
Guisborough TS14 . . . . .8 E6
York YO32 . . . . .225 F6
Avon Garth LS22 . . . . . . .180 B3
Avon Rd 8 DL2 . . . . .22 D8
Avondale Rd HG1 . . . . . . .219 F4
Avondale St 7 BB8 . . . . . .186 A3
Avro Cl TS18 . . . . .5 F7
Awnhams La YO42 . . . . . .169 D2
Axminster Rd TS8 . . . . .6 F5
Axton Cl TS17 . . . . .6 A6
Aylesham Ct YO32 . . . . . .225 E3
Aylton Dr TS5 . . . . .6 E6
Aynham Cl 2 BD23 . . . . .134 E2
Aynholme Cl 10 LS29 . . . .174 F4
Aynholme Dr 1 LS29 . . . .175 A4
Ayresome Way 1 DL1 . . . . .3 F6
Aysgarth Gr DL7 . . . . . . .210 B2
Aysgarth Rd DL1 . . . . .3 D4
Aysgarth Sch DL8 . . . . . . .62 A4
Ayton Castle* YO13 . . . . .99 A8
Ayton Rd YO12 . . . . .99 C7
Azerley Gr HG3 . . . . .219 A4
Azerley La HG4 . . . . .112 F3

B

Babyhouse La BD20 . . . .173 A1
Bachelor Ave HG1 . . . . . .219 D7
Bachelor Dr HG1 . . . . . . .219 D7
Bachelor Gdns HG1 . . . . .219 D6
Bachelor Hill YO24 . . . . .227 C2
Bachelor Rd HG1 . . . . . . .219 D6
Bachelor Way HG1 . . . . . .219 D6
Back Ave Victoria 2
YO11 . . . . .213 A3
Back Beck La LS29 . . . . .174 F4
Back Bridge St BD23 . . .216 F4
Back Cheltenham Mount
HG1 . . . . .219 D3
Back Colne Rd 9 BD20 . . .187 E7
Back Dragon Par HG1 . . .219 E3
Back Dragon Rd HG1 . . .219 E3
Back Elmwood St 3
HG1 . . . . .219 E4
Back Gate LA6 . . . . .103 D3
Back Gn BD23 . . . . .153 F5
Back Grove Rd LS29 . . . .218 B4
Back La
Acaster Selby YO23 . . . . .191 B3
Airton BD23 . . . . .155 A6
Aiskew DL7 . . . . .63 C5
Alne YO61 . . . . .142 F4
Ampleforth YO62 . . . . .92 C1
Appleton Roebuck YO23 . . .191 A5
Appleton-le-Moors YO62 . . .70 F2
Asselby DN14 . . . . .205 D6
Bagby YO7 . . . . .90 B3
Barkston Ash LS24 . . . . . .195 F6
Barlby with Osgodby
YO8 . . . . .198 C4
Barton DL10 . . . . .21 C7
Barton-le-Street YO17 . . . .120 E5
1 Bedale DL8 . . . . .63 A3
Bilbrough YO23 . . . . .182 D1
Birstwith HG3 . . . . .160 D5
Bolton-on-Swale DL10 . . . . .41 E5
7 Boroughbridge YO51 . . . .141 B5
Borrowby YO7 . . . . .65 E4
Bradleys Both BD20 . . . . .173 E4
10 Brafferton YO61 . . . . . .115 F1
Bramham LS23 . . . . .188 E6
Burley in Warfedale
LS29 . . . . .176 C1
Carlton Miniott YO7 . . . . . .89 B3
Carthorpe DL8 . . . . .87 E7
Cawood YO8 . . . . .197 A8
Cold Kirby YO7 . . . . .91 C8
Copmanthorpe YO23 . . . . .230 A2
Copt Hewick HG4 . . . . . . .114 B2
Cottingwith YO42 . . . . . . .193 C5
Crakehall DL8 . . . . .62 E4
Crathorne TS15 . . . . .24 F6
Dalton YO7 . . . . .115 E7
Dishforth YO7 . . . . .115 A4
Drax YO8 . . . . .204 F5
Eaglescliffe TS16 . . . . .5 E4
Easingwold YO61 . . . . . . .117 D1
East Tanfield DL8 . . . . .87 D2
Ebberston & Yedingham
YO13 . . . . .97 D5
Ellerton YO42 . . . . .193 C1
Fewston HG3 . . . . .159 F1
Flaxton YO60 . . . . .145 F1

Back La *continued*
Giggleswick BD24 . . . . .130 F2
Great & Little Broughton
TS9 . . . . .26 E5
Great Ouseburn YO26 . . . .164 A8
Great Preston WF10 . . . . .200 D6
Gristlthorp YO14 . . . . .100 E5
Guisborough TS9 . . . . .8 A4
Hambleton YO8 . . . . .196 F1
Harome YO62 . . . . .93 C5
Hawsker-cum-Stainsacre
YO22 . . . . .32 F5
11 Haxby YO32 . . . . .166 D5
Hebden BD23 . . . . .135 A2
Hellifield BD23 . . . . .154 B3
Hemingbrough YO8 . . . . . .198 F1
Hetton BD23 . . . . .155 F5
Hirst Courtney YO8 . . . . . .203 F3
Holtby YO19 . . . . .184 E8
Hunsingore LS22 . . . . .180 E8
Hutton-le-Hole YO62 . . . . . .70 C4
Huttons Ambo YO60 . . . . . .147 B7
Kirby Wiske YO7 . . . . .88 E7
Kirkby Malham BD23 . . . . .154 F8
Kirkby Malzeard HG4 . . . . .112 C5
Lockton YO18 . . . . .72 E4
Long Preston BD23 . . . . . .153 F5
Longnewton TS21 . . . . .4 F8
Low Coniscliffe & Merrybent
DL2 . . . . .2 E4
Low Worsall TS15 . . . . .24 C7
Luttons YO17 . . . . .150 B8
Malham BD23 . . . . .132 F2
Markington with Wallerthwaite
HG3 . . . . .139 C3
Marton YO62 . . . . .94 F5
Marton cum Grafton
YO51 . . . . .141 D1
Melmerby HG4 . . . . .114 B7
8 Middleham DL8 . . . . .60 E2
Morton-on-Swale DL7 . . . . . .64 A6
Moulton DL10 . . . . .21 E3
Newby Wiske DL7 . . . . .64 D3
Newholm-cum-Dunsley
YO21 . . . . .13 A1
Newton-on-Ouse YO30 . . . .165 B6
North Cowton DL7 . . . . .22 B3
North Duffield YO8 . . . . . .199 A7
Norton DN6 . . . . .206 E2
Osmotherley DL6 . . . . .45 B4
Raskelf YO61 . . . . .116 F2
Rathmell BD24 . . . . .153 C6
Reeth, Fremington & Healaugh
DL11 . . . . .38 B6
2 Riccall YO19 . . . . .198 A8
Rookwith HG4 . . . . .86 A8
Scorton DL10 . . . . .41 E6
Settrington YO17 . . . . . . .148 D8
Sicklinghall LS22 . . . . . . .179 E3
Sinnington YO62 . . . . .95 A8
Skelton HG4 . . . . .140 E7
Stillington YO61 . . . . .144 C6
Sutton-under-Whitestonecliffe
YO7 . . . . .90 E5
Thirkleby High & Low
with Osgodby YO7 . . . . . . .116 D8
Thirsk YO7 . . . . .211 B1
Tholthorpe YO61 . . . . .142 D5
Thormanby YO61 . . . . .116 F6
Thornton Steward DL8 . . . . .61 C2
Topcliffe YO7 . . . . .115 C7
Trawden BB8 . . . . .186 A1
Tunstall DL10 . . . . .41 B3
Tunstall LA6 . . . . .102 A4
Weaverthorpe YO17 . . . . . .124 E1
Weeton LS17 . . . . .178 C2
Wennington LA2 . . . . .102 C2
West Tanfield HG4 . . . . .87 A1
West Witton DL8 . . . . .59 C4
Westerdale YO21 . . . . .28 E5
Whixley YO26 . . . . .164 A3
Whorlton DL6 . . . . .45 D8
Wilberfoss YO41 . . . . .185 F5
Wold Newton YO25 . . . . . .126 A4
Wombleton YO62 . . . . .93 E7
Wray-with-Botton LA2 . . . .128 A6
York YO26 . . . . .227 A5
Back La S
Middleton YO18 . . . . .95 E8
Wheldrake YO19 . . . . .192 F7
Back Middleton Rd 9
LS29 . . . . .218 A4
Back Newton La
WF10 . . . . .201 A7
Back Nook 1 DL8 . . . . .58 F1
Back Northgate WF8 . . . .201 B1
Back O' Newton YO41 . . .185 E3
Back of Parks Rd YO62 . . .70 C2
Back of the Beck 6
BD23 . . . . .216 F4
Back Parish Ghyll Rd 8
LS29 . . . . .218 B4
Back Park St YO8 . . . . . .232 D5
Back Rd Birstwith HG3 . . .160 B5
Thormanby YO61 . . . . .116 F5
Back Regent Pl 4 HG1 . .220 C4
Back Royal Par 5 HG1 . .219 C2
Back Sea View YO14 . . . .101 C1
Back Side YO17 . . . . .149 B5
Back St
Boroughbridge YO51 . . . . .141 C5
Bramham LS23 . . . . .188 E6
Burton Fleming YO25 . . . . .126 E3
Langtoft YO25 . . . . .151 D5
10 Middleham DL8 . . . . . . .60 E2
Wold Newton YO25 . . . . . .126 A4
Back St Hilda's Terr
YO21 . . . . .208 D7

Back Station Rd 17
BD20 . . . . .187 E8
Back Syke DL8 . . . . .57 D5
Back West View 2
YO30 . . . . .228 B7
Back Weston Rd 5
LS29 . . . . .218 B4
Back York Pl 6 HG1 . . . .219 D1
Backhouse St YO31 . . . . .233 B4
Backside La YO62 . . . . . . .93 E6
Backstone La LS29 . . . . .218 C3
Backstone Way LS29 . . . .218 C4
Bacon Ave WF6 . . . . .200 B2
Bad Bargain La YO31 . . .229 A5
Baden St HG1 . . . . .219 F4
Bader Ave TS17 . . . . .6 B6
Bader Prim Sch TS17 . . . . .6 B6
Badger Butt La BD23 . . . .155 B5
Badger Gate BD23 . . . . . .134 D3
Badger Hill Dr 14 DL8 . . . .63 B3
Badger Hill Prim Sch
YO10 . . . . .229 B2
Badger La DN6 . . . . .207 A3
Badger Paddock 5
YO31 . . . . .225 E2
Badger Wood Glade
LS22 . . . . .180 C4
Badger Wood Wlk
YO10 . . . . .229 D3
Badgerbeck Rd 2 DL9 . . .209 B1
Badgers Gate LS29 . . . . .175 C6
Badminton Ct 18 DL1 . . . . .3 F6
Baffam Gdns YO8 . . . . . . .232 B2
Baffam La YO8 . . . . .232 B2
Bagby La YO7 . . . . .90 B2
Bagdale YO21 . . . . .208 C6
Baghill La WF8 . . . . .201 C1
Baildon Ave LS25 . . . . . .194 D2
Baildon Cl 3 YO26 . . . . . .227 D4
Baile Hill Terr YO1 . . . . .233 B1
Bailey Ct DL7 . . . . .210 C4
Bailey La BD23 . . . . .152 E3
Bailey St BB18 . . . . .172 B1
Bailey The BD23 . . . . . . .217 A4
Bainbridge C of E Prim Sch
DL8 . . . . .57 D5
Bainbridge Dr YO8 . . . . .232 C4
Bairnswood Sch YO12 . . .212 B6
Baker St
Appleton Wiske DL6 . . . . . . .24 A3
York YO30 . . . . .228 C7
Bakersfield Dr DN14 . . . .202 F3
Baldersby Garth YO7 . . . . .88 D1
Baldersby St James C of E
Prim Sch YO7 . . . . .114 E7
Baldersdale Ave 1
HG5 . . . . .221 D5
Baldoon Sands TS5 . . . . . . .6 D6
Baldwin St 4 HG1 . . . . . .219 C5
Balfour St YO26 . . . . . . .227 F5
Balfour Terr TS5 . . . . .6 D8
Balfour Way YO32 . . . . . .167 A6
Balk La DN14 . . . . .207 F7
Balk The
Bishop Wilton YO41 . . . . . .169 C2
Marton-le-Moor HG4 . . . . .114 E1
Slingsby YO62 . . . . .120 B5
Balk Top YO7 . . . . .115 B1
Balksyde YO62 . . . . .120 B5
Ball Grove Dr BB8 . . . . . .186 A3
Ballhall La YO42 . . . . . . .193 E6
Balmer Hill DL2 . . . . .1 C8
Balmoral Ave TS17 . . . . . . .6 C8
Balmoral Rd
Barmpton DL1 . . . . .3 E8
Lingdale TS12 . . . . .9 F6
Middlesbrough TS3 . . . . .7 C8
Ripon HG4 . . . . .214 C3
Balmoral Terr 5 YO23 . . .228 B1
Balne Hall Rd DN14 . . . . .207 F5
Balne Moor Rd DN14 . . . .207 B6
Balshaw Rd LA2 . . . . .129 B3
Baltimore Way DL1 . . . . . . .3 D7
Banbury Rd WF8 . . . . . . .201 C2
Bancroft Fold 18 BB18 . . .171 D1
Bancroft Steam Mus*
BB18 . . . . .171 D1
Bands La DL8 . . . . .56 C4
Bank Bottom LA6 . . . . . . .103 D3
Bank Cl 2 YO22 . . . . .32 A6
Bank Dike Hill HG3 . . . . .159 A4
Bank Hall Cl LA6 . . . . . . .103 D4
Bank House La LA6 . . . . .103 B5
Bank La Egton YO21 . . . . . .30 E5
Faceby TS9 . . . . .25 F1
Grassington BD23 . . . . . . .134 E3
Great & Little Broughton
TS9 . . . . .26 F3
Silsden BD20 . . . . .174 C4
Bank Rd Glusburn BD20 . .187 E8
Selby YO8 . . . . .232 D6
Bank Side
2 Eastfield YO11 . . . . .100 A7
Rawcliffe DN14 . . . . .205 A2
Bank St
Barnoldswick BB18 . . . . . .171 D1
Castleford WF10 . . . . .200 E4
11 Wetherby LS22 . . . . . . .180 C3
Bank The DL10 . . . . .41 D4
Bank Top LA6 . . . . .103 D3
Bank Top La 4 TS13 . . . . . .12 A7
Bank Wood Rd WF8 . . . . .206 A6
Bankfield La DN14 . . . . . .205 A7
Bankfield St BB8 . . . . . . .186 A2
Bankhead Cl DL6 . . . . . . .210 F4

Bankhead Rd DL6 ....210 F4
Banklands Ave BD20 ...174 C1
Banklands La BD20 .....174 C1
Banks Bridge Cl BB18 ..171 E2
Banks Hill 1 BB18 ......171 D2
Banks La DL10 ....41 E7
Banks Rd Brompton DL6 ..44 A2
  Darlington DL1 ....3 E6
Bankside Cl 5 YO26 ...165 F1
Bankwell Rd BD24 .....174 B1
Bannisdale 6 YO24 ....230 C7
Bannister Cl BB18 .....186 B2
Bannister Wlk BD22 ...187 B6
Banqueting House*
  LS21 ....176 D1

Bar La
Bramham cum Oglethorpe
  LS23 ....188 F7
  Garforth LS25 ....194 D4
  Hambleton YO8 ....196 E1
  Knaresborough HG5 .....162 D5
  Roecliffe YO51 ....141 A5
  York YO1 ....233 A2
Bar Pl HG1 ....219 D5
Bar St YO11 ....213 A6
Bar The 6 DL10 ....209 C6
Barbara Gr 4 YO24 .....227 F3
Barbeck YO7 ....211 C3
Barbeck Cl YO7 ....211 D3
Barberry TS8 ....7 B4
Barberry Cl Ingleby TS17 ..6 B5
  20 Killinghall HG3 .....161 B3
Barbers Dr YO23 ....230 B4
Barbican Ctr YO10 .....233 C1
Barbican Leisure Ctr
  YO10 ....233 C1
Barbican Mews YO10 ...228 E3
Barbican Rd YO10 ......233 C1
Barbondale Gr HG5 .....221 C5
Barbondale Rd LA10 ....77 A7
Bardale Cl 2 HG5 ....221 D6
Barden Ct 6 YO30 ......224 F1
Barden Fell View 3
  BD23 ....134 E2
Barden La DL8 ....40 B1
Barden Moor Rd DL1 ....3 E4
Barden Pl 9 YO14 ......101 A3
Barden Rd BD23 ....157 A1
Barden Terr* BD23 ....157 C4
Bardney Rd 11 YO14 ...126 F8
Bardsley Cl TS16 ....5 E7
Barefoot St HG4 ....214 C4
Barf Bank DL8 ....61 A2
Barf La YO41 ....169 D4
Barff Cl 10 YO8 ....197 D1
Barff Gr 6 YO8 ....197 B2
Barff La YO8 ....197 C1
Barff View YO8 ....203 D7
Barfield Rd YO31 ....228 F8
Bargate DL10 ....209 B6
Bark House La LA2 .....131 B8
Bark La
  Addingham LS29 ....175 A5
  Embsay with Eastby
  BD23 ....157 A1
Barker La YO1 ....233 A2
Barker's La
  Newholm-cum-Dunsley
  YO21 ....13 A1
  Snainton YO13 ....98 A4
Barkery The TS8 ....7 B3
Barkhouse Bank HG3 ...138 F4
Barkhouse Wood La
  WF11 ....202 D6
Barknotts Terr YO17 ...215 C3
Barkston Ash RC Prim Sch
  LS24 ....195 E7
Barkston Ave YO26 ....227 A3
Barkston Cl 3 YO26 ...227 A3
Barkston Gr YO26 ......227 A3
Barkston Rd YO26 .....227 A3
Barlby Bridge CP Sch
  YO8 ....232 D5
Barlby By Pass 2 YO8 .198 B4
Barlby CP Sch YO8 .....198 B4
Barlby Cres YO8 ....232 F7
Barlby High Sch YO8 ...198 B5
Barlby Rd YO8 ....232 E6
Barley Cl YO17 ....215 D2
Barley Horn Rd LS24 ...190 B2
Barley Rise YO32 ......167 A6
Barley View YO23 ......225 C8
Barleycroft YO11 ......213 C1
Barleyfields La 5 LS22 .180 C3
Barleyfields Rd
  4 Wetherby LS22 ....180 C3
  4 Wetherby LS22 ....180 C4
Barleyhill Rd LS25 .....194 B4
Barley's Yd YO7 ....211 B3
Barlow C of E Prim Sch
  YO8 ....204 C7
Barlow Cl TS14 ....8 F6
**Barlow Common Nature
  Reserve*** YO8 ....204 B7
Barlow Common Rd
  YO8 ....204 B8
Barlow Rd YO8 ....204 B6
Barlow St YO26 ....227 D4
Barmby Ave YO10 ......231 E8
Barmby Cl 4 YO30 .....224 F1
Barmby Ferry Rd 1
  YO8 ....198 F1
**Barmby on the Marsh City
  Prim Sch** DN14 ....205 B7
Barmoor Cl YO13 ......75 D6

Barmoor Gn YO13 ....75 D6
Barmoor La YO13 ....75 C6
Brampton La YO13 ......75 D6
Barn Field Cl BB8 ......186 A3
Barnaby Pl TS14 ....8 E7
Barnard La YO13 ....98 C4
Barnard's Rd YO21 ......31 A4
Barnbow La LS15 ....194 A6
Barnes Rd
  Castleford WF10 ....200 E3
  Darlington DL3 ....3 A6
Barney La YO60 ....146 A1
Barnfield Way YO23 ....230 A2
Barnhill La DN14 ......205 F7
Barningham Rd DL11 ...18 G7
Barnoldswick CE Sch
  BB18 ....171 D1
Barnoldswick La LA6 ...103 A2
Barns Wray 2 YO61 ...117 D1
Barnsdale Est WF10 ...200 D3
Barnsdale Rd
  Ledston WF10 ....200 E7
  Micklefield WF10 ......200 B5
Barnsdale View DN6 ...206 E2
Barnwell Cres HG2 .....222 B5
Barnwood Cres BB18 ..172 B1
Barnwood Rd BB18 ....172 A1
Barnygate La YO60 ....147 A7
Barons Cres YO23 .....230 B2
Barr La YO32 ....167 D4
Barrack View DL10 ....209 C8
Barracks Bank DL10 ....21 A2
Barret St 6 BB18 ......172 A1
Barret Ave 3 YO24 ....227 F3
Barret Rd DL3 ....3 A5
Barrington Garth
  DN14 ....202 F3
Barrowby La
  Austhorpe LS15 ....194 A4
  Kirkby Overblow HG3 ...179 A3
Barrowcliff Cty Jun Sch
  YO12 ....212 C7
Barrowcliff Rd YO12 ...212 D7
Barry Bank YO21 ....11 F1
Barry's La YO12 ....212 E2
Barse Beck La HG3 ....160 D5
Barstow Ave YO10 .....228 F3
Barstow Fall 2 WF8 ...201 C2
Bartindale Rd YO14 ....127 A5
Bartle Garth YO1 ......233 C3
Barton C of E Sch DL10 .21 D7
Barton Pl DL3 ....3 E6
Bartons Garth YO8 ....232 B2
Barugh La
  Barugh (Great & Little)
  YO17 ....95 B2
Barwic Par YO8 ....94 F4
Barwick Fields TS17 .....6 A6
Barwick Inf Sch LS15 .194 C8
Barwick La Ingleby TS17 ..6 A4
  Ingleby Barwick TS17 ....5 F5
Barwick Parade CP Sch
  YO8 ....232 E4
Barwick Rd LS25 ......194 C5
Barwick Terr 9 YO12 ..212 F5
Barwick View TS17 ......6 A5
Barwick Way TS17 ....6 A4
Bassett Cl YO8 ....232 C3
Bassleton La TS17 ......6 A6
Bates Ave DL3 ....3 B7
Bateson Cl YO10 ....229 C1
Bath St LS29 ....218 C5
Battersby Ave TS9 .....27 C7
Battersby Junc TS9 ....27 C6
Battersby Sta TS9 .....27 C6
**Battle of Bramham Moor
  (site of)*** LS24 ....188 F4
**Battle of Marston Moor (site
  of)*** YO26 ....181 E7
**Battle of Standard Hill (site
  of)*** DL6 ....43 E4
Battle of Towton (site of)*
  LS24 ....195 D8
Battleflats Way YO41 ..168 D2
Battling Hills La YO18 ...49 B5
Bawhead Rd 24 BB18 ...172 A1
Bawtry Cl YO8 ....232 D3
Baxby Manor* YO61 ...117 B6
Baxby Terr 2 DL2 ......22 D8
Baxter Wood BD20 ....187 E8
Baxtergate YO21 ......208 D6
Baxton's Sprunt 1 YO62 .92 F7
Bay Bolton Ave DL8 ....59 F3
Bay Horse Yd 8 BD23 ..216 F4
Bay Cl DL3 ....3 A4
Baysdale Ave YO10 ....229 D3
Baysdale Cl TS14 ....8 F6
Baysdale Rd TS17 ....6 B7
Bazeley's La YO17 .....215 E1
Beach Rd The YO14 ...101 B3
Beach The YO14 ....101 B3
Beacon Bank YO62 .....92 D1
Beacon Brow Rd YO13 ..75 A7
Beacon Grange Pk DL2 ..4 C7
Beacon Hill DL2 ....4 B7
Beacon Rd
  Millington YO42 ....170 B1
  Seamer YO12 ....99 D7
Beacon Rise 4 LS29 ...175 C2
Beacon St 5 LS29 .....175 A4
Beacon View 3 BD23 ..217 E8
Beacon Way YO22 ......32 A6
Beaconsfield St
  Northallerton DL7 ......210 D4

Beaconsfield St continued
  3 Scarborough YO12 ...212 E3
  York YO24 ....227 D3
Beadlam Ave TS7 ....7 D6
Beagle Garth YO23 .....230 B2
Beagle Croft YO41 .....168 C1
Beagle Ridge Dr YO24 ..227 C1
Beagle Spinney YO41 ..168 C1
Beal La Beal DN14 .....202 D4
  Cridling Stubbs WF11 ..202 C1
Beale Cl TS17 ....6 B5
Beamsley Ct BD23 .....217 A2
Beamsley La BD23 .....174 F7
Beamsley View 18 LS29 .175 C2
Bean Sheaf La YO17 ....96 A3
Beancroft Rd WF10 ...200 E3
Beancroft St WF10 ....200 E3
Beanland La YO32 .....167 D2
Beanlands Dr 7 BD20 .187 E7
Beanlands Par LS29 ...218 C5
Beanlands Pl
  8 Glusburn BD20 ....187 E7
  8 Glusburn BD20 ....187 E8
Bean's Way YO31 ....229 B8
Beatswell Lawn HG4 ..113 C8
Beaufighter Cl DL10 ....41 F6
Beaufort Cl YO10 ......229 B3
Beaulieu Cl 11 YO32 ...225 F5
Beaumont Hill Sch DL1 ..3 D8
Beaumont Hill Rd WF8 ..232 A2
Beaverdyke YO30 ......224 F1
Becca La LS25 ....194 F8
Beck Cl 6 YO41 ....185 B2
Beck Closes Rd YO26 .142 A3
Beck Hole YO11 ....100 B6
Beck Hole Rd YO22 .....31 C1
Beck Isle Mus of Rural Life*
  YO18 ....95 F7
Beck La Cloughton YO13 ..54 C1
  Collingham LS22 ....180 A1
  Farndale East YO62 .....48 F2
  Leborston YO11 ....100 D5
  South Kilvington YO7 ..211 B6
  Wheldrake YO19 ....193 A8
Beck Mdw LS15 ....194 C7
Beck Mill Cl YO17 .....215 D3
Beck Row YO41 ....169 D5
Beck Side BD23 ....173 B4
Beck Side Cl BD20 ....173 D1
Beckbridge La 2 WF6 .200 B1
Beckbridge Rd WF6 ...200 B2
Beckbridge Way WF6 ..200 B1
Beckclose La YO8 ....87 F6
Beckdale Rd YO62 ......92 E7
Beckett Cl 8 YO62 .....93 D7
Beckfield La
  Fairburn WF11 ....201 C7
  York YO26 ....227 B5
Beckfield Pl YO26 ......227 B4
Beckfields Ave TS17 .....6 A4
Becklands Cl YO51 ....141 A5
Becklands La YO51 ....141 A4
Becks Brow BD23 .....153 C3
Becks Cl 5 YO32 ......225 C8
Beckside Catterick DL10 ..41 A4
  7 Elvington YO41 ......185 B2
  Northallerton DL7 ......210 B4
  4 Staithes TS13 ....13 K2
  Trawden Forest BB8 ...186 B2
  Wilberfoss YO41 ....185 F6

Beckside Cl
  18 Addingham LS29 ....174 F4
  22 Burley in Warfedale
  LS29 ....176 C1
Beckwith Ave HG2 .....222 B7
Beckwith Cl
  Harrogate HG2 ....222 A7
  Harrogate HG2 ....229 C7
Beckwith Cres HG2 ....222 B7
Beckwith Dr HG2 ......222 B6
Beckwith Head Rd
  HG3 ....178 C8
Beckwith Rd HG2 ......222 A7
Beckwith Wlk HG2 ....222 A7
Beckwithshaw CP Sch
  HG3 ....178 A8
Bedale Ave
  Scarborough YO12 .....212 E8
  York YO10 ....229 D4
Bedale C of E Prim Sch
  DL8 ....63 A2
Bedale High Sch DL8 ...63 A2
Bedale La HG4 ....114 A8
Bedale Mus* DL8 ......63 A3
Bedale Rd Aiskew DL7 ..63 C4
  Scotton DL9 ....40 F2
  Well DL8 ....87 A4
Bedburn Dr DL3 ....2 F5
Bedern Bank DL8 ....62 A2
Bedern Bank 8 HG4 ...214 C5
Bedern Ct 16 HG4 .....214 C5
Bedford St DL1 ....3 D4
Bedfords Fold 6 LS25 .202 A7
Bedlam Hill YO7 ....65 E4
Bedlam La
  Fewston HG3 ....159 F2
  Staveley HG5 ....140 E1

Beech Cl continued
  Farnham HG5 ....162 D7
  Great Ayton TS9 ....77 F1
  Hunton DL9 ....40 E2
  Scruton DL7 ....63 F7
  7 Sherburn in Elmet LS25 .195 F4
  Snape with Thorp DL8 ...87 A7
  3 South Milford LS25 ...195 F2
  Tadcaster LS24 ....189 F6
Beech Cres
  Castleford WF10 ....201 B3
  Whitwell-on-the-Hill
  YO60 ....146 E4
Beech Croft
  Barlby with Osgodby
  YO8 ....198 B6
  Pontefract WF8 ....201 C2
Beech Ct YO23 ....231 A3
Beech Dr
  6 Kirkbymoorside YO62 ..70 B1
  19 Scalby YO13 ....75 D5
  South Milford LS25 .....195 F2
Beech Glade YO31 .....225 F2
Beech Gr
  1 Airmyn DN14 ....205 E4
  Burton Salmon LS25 ...200 F1
  Camblesforth YO8 .....204 C5
  Harrogate HG2 ....219 C1
  Knaresborough HG5 ...221 B8
  Maltby TS8 ....6 C4
  Northallerton DL6 .....210 E5
  Sowerby YO7 ....211 C1
  Sherburn in Elmet LS25 .195 F4
  Whitby YO21 ....208 B6
  York YO26 ....227 C4
Beech Hill
  Carleton BD23 ....173 A4
  6 Knaresborough HG5 ..221 A6
  5 Pontefract WF8 ......201 C1
Beech Hill Rd BD23 ....173 A4
Beech La
  18 East Ayton/West Ayton
  YO13 ....99 A7
  3 Spofforth HG3 ....179 E6
Beech Pk YO19 ....198 A8
Beech Rd 2 YO32 ......167 A6
Beech Rd
  Boston Spa LS23 ......188 E8
  Campsall DN6 ....206 E1
  Darlington DL1 ....3 F7
  Harrogate HG2 ....222 E6
  Ripon HG4 ....214 B3
Beech St
  22 Barnoldswick BB18 ..171 D1
  10 Glusburn BD20 .....187 E8
  York YO31 ....228 D7
Beech Tree Cl 2 YO30 .164 F7
Beech Tree La YO8 ...204 C5
Beech View LS25 ......194 E8
Beech Wlk
  6 Eastfield YO11 ......100 A7
  Tadcaster LS24 ....189 D6
Beeches End LS23 .....188 F8
Beeches The
  Skelton YO30 ....224 C4
  11 Stokesley TS9 ....26 C7
Beechfield
  Coulby Newham TS8 .....7 A5
  Hawsker-cum-Stainsacre
  YO22 ....33 A6
  Newby Wiske DL7 ....64 F1
  Newton-on-Ouse YO30 .165 B6
Beechfield Cl YO8 .....197 B1
Beechnut La WF8 ......201 B1
Beechtree Rd LS24 ...189 D5
Beechville Ave YO12 ...212 C6
Beechwood Ave 2 TS9 ..26 C8
Beechwood Cl
  11 Bedale DL8 ....63 A2
  Markington with Wallerthwaite
  HG3 ....139 C4
Beechwood Cres 6
  HG2 ....219 C1
Beechwood Croft
  LS25 ....195 F3
Beechwood Dr BD23 ..216 D5
Beechwood Glade
  Sherburn in Elmet LS25 .195 F3
  7 York YO24 ....227 B1
Beechwood Rise 1
  LS22 ....180 C4
Beeforth Cl YO32 .....225 D3
Beeston's La LS17 .....178 C4
Beggarmans Rd DL8 ....80 C8
Beilby St 13 YO10 ......228 D1
Belcombe Way 8 YO30 .228 A7
Belford La HG4 ....112 A3
Belford Pl 3 HG1 ......219 D2
Belford Rd 2 HG1 .....219 D2
Belford Sq 9 HG1 .....219 D1
Belgrave Cres
  Harrogate HG2 ....222 F7
  14 Ilkley LS29 ....175 C2
Belgrave Rd YO11 .....212 F5
Belgrave St
  8 Skipton BD23 ....216 F4
  York YO31 ....228 C7
Belgrave Terr
  3 Hurworth-on-Tees DL2 .22 D8
  14 Scarborough YO11 ..212 F5

Bell Cl Haxby YO32 2
  5 Seamer YO12 2
Bell End Gn YO18 4
Bell La Cawood YO8 1
  Huby YO61 1
  Husthwaite YO61 1
  Rawcliffe DN14 2
  Ulleskelf LS24 1
Bellaby Pk 7 YO62 .....
Bellburn La DL3 ....
Belle Hill BD24 1
Belle Vue LS29 2
Belle Vue Par 10 YO11 .2
Belle Vue Pl 11 YO11 ..2
Belle Vue St
  44 Filey YO14 1
  Scarborough YO12 2
  York YO10 2
Belle Vue Terr
  Whitby YO21 2
  York YO10 2
Bellerby Camp DL8 ....
Bellerby Rd HG2 2
Bellerbyhurn Rd YO17 ..
Bellevue Terr
  Ripon HG4 2
  2 Skipton BD23 2
Bellfarm Ave YO31 2
Bellground La YO30 ... 1
Bellhouse La YO21 ....
Bellhouse Way YO24 ..2
Bellingham Cl YO7 2
Bellman Wlk 3 HG4 ... 2
Bellmans Croft YO23 .. 2
Bell's St 15 YO22 2
Bellwood Ave
  Boston Spa LS23 1
  Lockwood TS12 ....
Bellwood Dr YO24 2
Belmangate TS14 ......
Belmont Cl
  Harrogate WF11 2
  Newport ....
Belmont Ave
  Harrogate HG2 2
  11 Otley LS21 ....
Belmont Cl 3 YO30 ... 2
Belmont Gr 1 HG2 2
Belmont Prim Sch TS14 .
Belmont Rd
  Harrogate HG2 2
  Ilkley LS29 1
  Scarborough YO11 2
Belmont Terr 2 HG2 ...2
Belmont Wharf BD23 .. 2
Belthorpe La YO42 ....
Belton Park Dr 7 DL9 .
Belvedere Pl YO11 2
Belvedere Rd YO11 2
Belvoir Ave YO14 1
Belvoir Dr WF11 ......
Ben La BB18 1
Ben Rhydding Dr LS29 .
Ben Rhydding Prim Sch
  LS29 1
Ben Rhydding Rd
  LS29 2
Ben Rhydding Sta
  LS29 2
Bence The YO42 1
Benedict Ave YO8 2
Beningbrough Dr HG3 ..
Beningbrough La
  YO30 1
Benjy La YO19 1
Benkhill Dr 18 DL8 ...
Bennett St 13 BD23 .. 2
Bennions Way 5 DL10 .
Bennison La YO21 ....
Bensham Rd DL1 .....
Benson La WF6 2
Bent La Colne BB8 ... 1
  Sutton BD20 1
Bent Rigg La YO13 ...
Bentham Moor Rd
  LA6 1
Bentham Rd LA6 1
Bentham St LA6 1
Bentinck Ave TS5 ....
Bentley Wynd TS16 ...
Benton Cap La BD22 ..1
Bents La YO18 ....
Beresford Cl 8 DL8 ...
Beresford Terr YO23 .. 2
Berghill La YO7 ......
Berkeley Terr YO26 ... 2
Berkley Dr TS14 .....
Bernard La YO26 1
Bernica Gr TS17 .....
Berry Bank DL11 ....
Berry La LS26 2
Berrygate La HG3 ....
Berry's Ave 5 HG5 ... 2
Berwick Rd
  Achdeacon Newton DL3 .
  18 Scotton DL9 ......
Bestmire La DL6 .....
Betteras Hill Rd LS25 ..2
Betton Rise YO13 ....
Between Dikes Rd
  YO8 2
Beulah St 1 HG1 2
Beverley Balk YO41 .. 1
Beverley Cl 12 YO11 .. 2
Beverley Gate YO12 .. 2
Beverley Rd
  11 Eastfield YO11 ... 1

ley Rd *continued*
esbrough TS7 . . . . 7 D6
YO17 . . . . .215 E3
ley Rise LS29 . . . . . .175 C2
ley Sch TS4 . . . . 6 F8
ley Rd HG1 . . . . .219 B5
ley St YO23 . . . . .228 C2
ey Gr TS5 . . . . .6 C1
l Cl WF8 . . . . .201 C1
y Dr TS6 . . . . 7 A8
rton Way LS21 . . . . . .176 F1
ey Gate YO13 . . . . .73 F6
ey Howe YO12 . . . . . .212 B4
ey Way TS8 . . . . 7 A5
ale Cl YO8 . . . . E Bedale DL8 . . .63 B3
cally YO12 . . . . .75 D5
eadow Dr S Gore YO14 .174 E4
nton La LS25 . . . . .196 C6
ale Cl
rlletton DL7 . . . . .210 C2
YO30 . . . . .224 E2
ale Rd HG1 . . . . .221 D6
E Prim Sch TS9 . . . .46 F6
n Cl HG1 . . . . .219 E6
n Gr HG1 . . . . .219 D4
n Grange CI HG1 . . . .219 D5
n Grove Ave HG1 . . .219 E5
n Gr La HG1 . . . . .219 E6
La HG1 . . . . .220 D6
n Sch La HG1 . . . . .210 B7
ngton Carr La
. . . . .99 B1
La BD20 . . . . .187 D7
cy La YO61 . . . . .117 E2
se La HG4 . . . . .86 F3
Ave Malton YO17 . . . .215 D6
hts YO22 . . . . .32 A6
Cl E Filey YO14 . . .101 B3
hton DL10 . . . . .40 F2
rklevington TS15 . . . . . . .24 E8
horpe Willoughby YO8 .197 B1
Cres 10 YO22 . . . . . . .32 A6
Dr 2 Eazeby TS9 . . . . .25 F1
La LS25 . . . . .194 D2
Gr
leford WF10 . . . . .201 B3
pgate HG1 . . . . .219 E6
La LS25 . . . . .194 D1
Hall La BB18 . . . . . . .172 B1
La E YO32 . . . . .166 E5
Rd DL1 . . . . .3 D8
View 7 YO18 . . . . . . .96 A6
es The TS8 . . . . 7 A5
ewood Cl S DL4 . . . . . .5 D5
wood Cl 6 LS24 . .131 D2
wood Cl 6 LS29 . .218 A4
wood Mews HG2 . . . . .222 F7
wood Rd TS7 . . . . .7 C6
Gdn* LS25 . . . . .195 B7
La Hensall DN14 . . . .203 D2
pgton DN14 . . . . .202 F4
Ridding La DL8 . . . . . .60 B1
ale Field La LS22 . . . .188 B8
orth Way 1 YO42 . . . .92 C1
Cl YO30 . . . . .209 C2
Brow Rd TS12 . . . . .9 D5
Field Bank YO21 . . . .28 F6
Head La YO62 . . . . .70 F4
La YO42 . . . . .199 D8
ey La DL2 . . . . .23 B1
Crag Cl 2 HG3 . . . . .161 B2
ale Ave HG5 . . . . .221 D5
ale Gr 4 YO30 . . . . .227 B5
r La
rton on Derwent
. . . . .185 D4
rerfoss YO41 . . . . .185 F6
tt La CA17 . . . . .14 B7
ills HG3 . . . . .140 A3
s La WF11 . . . . .202 B4
Rd YO8 . . . . .202 F5
ands 1 YO62 . . . . .93 D7
with La LA2 . . . . .128 F7
with Cl E Prim Sch
. . . . .160 B1
with Dr YO26 . . . . .227 E4
with Grange HG3 . . .160 C6
with Rd HG1 . . . . .220 A3
eyley Ave TS5 . . . . .6 E7
p Cl 11 HG3 . . . . .137 C4
p Ct YO9 . . . . .232 B6
p Garth 2 HG3 . . . .137 C4
p Monkton C of E Prim
Sch HG3 . . . . .140 B5
p Thornton C of E Prim
HG3 . . . . .139 A2
p Thornton RC Prim
HG3 . . . . .139 A2
p Way 1 HG3 . . . . . .137 C4
p Witton Sch
. . . . .169 F2
pdale Cl HG5 . . . . . . .221 D6
pdale Dr
ollingham LS22 . . . . . . .180 A1
llingham LS22 . . . . . . .188 A8
pdike Rd
ood YO8 . . . . .197 A6
burn in Elmet LS25 . .196 A4
pgate St YO23 . . . . . .233 B1
phill Jun YO13 . . . . . .233 B1
phill Senior YO1 . . . .233 B1
ppsgarth DL7 . . . . .210 C4
ppsway YO10 . . . . . . .229 C3

Bishopthorpe Inf Sch
YO23 . . . . .231 A4
Bishopthorpe Pal*
. . . . .231 84
Bishopthorpe Rd
YO23 . . . . .231 B5
Bishopton HG4 . . . . . . .214 A5
Bishopton La
Great Burdon DL1 . . . . .4 A7
Ripon HG4 . . . . .113 D2
Bisley Ct 1 DL1 . . . . .3 F6
Bismarck St YO26 . . . . .227 F5
Bitterdale La YO62 . . . . . .70 A3
Black Abbey La 11 BD20 .187 E8
Black Bank Rd LA2 . . . .130 E3
Black Diamond St 2
WF6 . . . . .200 A1
Black Dike La YO26 . . . .182 F8
Black Fen La YO8 . . . . . .203 C7
Black Gill La
Airton BD23 . . . . .154 B8
Settle BD23 . . . . .132 A1
Black Hill YO62 . . . . . . .118 E5
Black Hill Rd HG3 . . . . . .137 F8
Black Horse La TS15 . . . .25 C3
Black Sike La YO13 . . . . .98 B4
Black Wlk WF8 . . . . . . .201 B1
Blackbird Way 8 HG2 . . .99 F6
Blackburn La WF11 . . . .202 B2
Blacklee Cl 3 YO32 . . . .167 B8
Blacksmith Bank DL8 . . .62 E5
Blacksmith Hill YO22 . . . .53 A7
Blackthorn TS8 . . . . .7 B6
Blackthorn Dr YO31 . . . .225 E2
Blackthorn La HG3 . . . . .222 C3
Blackwell DL3 . . . . .3 B3
Blackwell La DL3 . . . . .3 C4
Blackwood La YO8 . . . . .198 F7
Blackwood Rd YO8 . . . . .198 E8
Blair Ave TS17 . . . . .5 F4
Blair Pk HG3 . . . . .221 C5
Blake Ct YO19 . . . . .193 A8
Blake Gate HG3 . . . . . . .136 C1
Blake St YO1 . . . . .233 B3
Blakeley Cres 3 BB18 . .171 D2
Blakelow La YO30 . . . . . .224 F3
Blakeney Pl YO10 . . . . . .228 F3
Blakey Bank YO62 . . . . . .49 A5
Blakey Cl YO7 . . . . .211 C1
Blakey La YO7 . . . . .211 C1
Blakey Rd YO62 . . . . .70 B6
Bland La YO26 . . . . .227 A4
Blandford St DL1 . . . . .3 D6
Blands Ave WF10 . . . . . .200 D7
Bland's Cliff 12 YO11 . . .213 A6
Blands Cres 3 WF10 . . .200 D7
Blands Gr 4 WF10 . . . . .200 D7
Blands Hill HG5 . . . . . . .221 A4
Blansby Park La YO18 . . .96 A8
Blansby Park La YO18 . . .96 A8
Blatchford YO30 . . . . . . .228 B8
Blawath Rd YO18 . . . . . . .51 A2
Blayshaw La HG3 . . . . . .130 E4
Blazefield Bank HG3 . . .137 D3
Blea Moor Rd LA6 . . . . . .78 E2
Blea Pit La HG4 . . . . . . .140 E8
Bleaberry La YO41 . . . . .169 B5
Bleach La DL3 . . . . .2 E4
Bleara Rd BD23 . . . . . . .186 B8
Blenheim Ave 4 YO21 . .208 B7
Blenheim Ct DL10 . . . . . . .41 F6
Blenheim Ct
Harrogate HG2 . . . . .220 C2
Rawcliffe YO30 . . . . .224 D3
Blenheim St 12 YO12 . . .213 A7
Blenheim Way 6 YO32 . .222 C7
Bleriot Way YO30 . . . . . .225 A3
Blind La Aiskew DL8 . . . . .63 B3
Barton DL10 . . . . .21 D7
Burton in Lonsdale LA6 . .102 F3
Guisborough TS14 . . . . .8 C6
Hurworth DL2 . . . . .22 E8
Knaresborough HG5 . . . . .221 D2
Scorton DL10 . . . . .42 B8
Scruton YO26 . . . . .181 B8
Blind Piece La YO7 . . . . .116 A6
Bloe Beck La LA2 . . . . . .129 E6
Bloody Beck Hill YO13 . . .54 A7
Blossom St YO24 . . . . . .233 A1
Blossomgate HG4 . . . . . .214 B5
Blue Bank YO22 . . . . .32 A4
Blue Barn La TS15 . . . . . .25 C6
Blue Bell Gr TS5 . . . . .6 F6
Blue Bridge La YO10 . . . .228 F4
Blue Hill Way HG3 . . . . . .41 A5
Blue Slates Cl YO19 . . . .193 A8
Bluebeck Dr YO30 . . . . .227 E8
Bluebell Mdw 18 HG3 . .161 B3
Bluebell Wlk 8 HG3 . . .161 B3
Blyth Cl YO8 . . . . .232 A5
Boar La TS17 . . . . .6 B5
Boat La Barford DL11 . . . . . .1 C7
Great Ouseburn YO26 . . .164 C8
Kirby Hall YO26 . . . . .142 C1
Micklefield Green LS26 . . .200 D5
Boatcliffe Rd YO14 . . . . .127 D7
Boathouse La DL2 . . . . . . .4 F4
Bob La YO7 . . . . .65 E3
Bodmin Ave YO8 . . . . . . .200 A2
Bodner Hill YO61 . . . . . .118 F1
Boeing Way TS18 . . . . . . .5 F7
Bog La
Askham Bryan YO24 . . . .230 B6
Barwick in Elmet & Scholes
LS15 . . . . .194 A7
Stirton with Thorlby
BD23 . . . . .216 D7
Boggart La LS24 . . . . . . .190 C2

Boggy La DL10 . . . . .209 B5
Boghole Bank DL6 . . . . . .45 B3
Boghouse La TS13 . . . . . .10 F3
Bogs La
Bridge Hewick HG4 . . . . .114 C1
Harrogate HG1,HG2 . . . .220 C5
Bolckow St TS14 . . . . .8 F7
Bold Venture St BD23 . . .216 F2
Boldron Cl 8 TS18 . . . . . .5 D8
Bolland St 18 BB18 . . . .171 D2
Bolling Rd LS29 . . . . . . .218 D4
Boltby Rd YO30 . . . . . . .224 F2
Bolton Abbey Sta
. . . . .174 D8
Bolton Abbey
BD23 . . . . .174 D8
Bolton Castle* DL8 . . . . . .59 B6
Bolton Cross DL10 . . . . . .41 F5
Bolton Ct 14 DL8 . . . . . . .60 D5
Bolton La YO42 . . . . .169 E8
Bolton on Swale C of E Prim
Sch DL10 . . . . .41 F6
Bolton Priory (rems of)*
. . . . .157 F1
Bolton Rd
Draughton BD23 . . . . . . .174 F7
Silsden BD20 . . . . .174 D3
Bolton Way
18 Leyburn DL8 . . . . .60 D5
Richmond DL10 . . . . .209 C8
Bolton-on-Swale Nature
Reserve* DL10 . . . . .41 F5
Bonby La YO9 . . . . .192 E2
Bond End HG5 . . . . .221 B6
Bond La
Appleton Roebuck YO23 . .190 F5
Settle BD23 . . . . .131 D2
Bond St YO8 . . . . .232 A5
Bondgate Helmsley YO62 . .92 F6
Pontefract WF8 . . . . . . .201 C1
Ripon HG4 . . . . .214 C4
Selby YO8 . . . . .232 B7
Bondgate Gn HG4 . . . . .214 D4
Bondgate Green Cl 6
HG4 . . . . .214 C4
Bondgate Green La
HG4 . . . . .214 C4
Bondings Rise 5 LS25 . .196 A4
Bonington Ct 7 TS9 . . . .227 E4
Bonny Gr TS8 . . . . .7 C5
Bonnygate La YO61 . . . .118 F5
Bonnygrove Way TS8 . . . .7 B5
Boonhill Rd YO62 . . . . . . .69 F4
Boosbeck Rd TS12 . . . . . .9 D8
Boot In 28 BB18 . . . . . . .172 A1
Booth Ferry Rd DN14 . . .205 F4
Booth Sq 27 LS29 . . . . .176 C1
Bootham YO30 . . . . .233 A3
Bootham Cres YO30 . . . .233 A4
Bootham Park Hospl
YO31 . . . . .233 B4
Bootham Row YO31 . . . .233 B3
Bootham Sch YO31 . . . . .233 A3
Bootham Terr YO30 . . . .233 A3
Boothferry Prim Sch
DN14 . . . . .205 F2
Boothferry Rd DN14 . . . .205 F2
Boothwood Rd YO30 . . . .224 E1
Booty La DN14 . . . . .206 F7
Borage Rd 8 HG3 . . . . .161 B3
Bore Tree Baulk YO9 . . .184 D6
Borage 9 YO62 . . . . .92 F6
Borough Mere La
YO7 . . . . .215 D8
Borough Rd
Darlington DL1 . . . . .3 D5
Richmond DL10 . . . . .209 B8
Boroughbridge High Sch
HG5 . . . . .141 B5
Boroughbridge Rd
Bishop Monkton HG3 . . . .140 B5
Bridge Hewick HG4 . . . . .114 B1
Dishforth YO7 . . . . .115 A2
Knaresborough HG5 . . . . .220 F4
North Otterington DL7 . . . .64 E6
Northallerton DL7 . . . . . . .210 C1
Ripon HG4 . . . . .214 D3
Scriven HG5 . . . . .162 A6
Westwick YO51 . . . . .140 D4
York YO26 . . . . .164 B4
York YO26 . . . . .227 D5
Borras Green La
HG4 . . . . .214 B4
Borrage La DL6 . . . . .210 F7
Borrowby La TS13 . . . . . .11 D7
Staithes TS13 . . . . .13 A1
Borrowbydale Ave
HG5 . . . . .221 D6
Borrowdale Dr
Castleford WF10 . . . . . . .201 B5
York YO30 . . . . .224 F1
Boss Moor La BD23 . . . .155 F8
Boston Dr TS7 . . . . .7 B6
Boston Rd Clifford LS23 .188 E7
Wetherby LS22 . . . . .180 C2
Boston Spa C of E Sch
LS23 . . . . .188 E8
Boston Spa Comp Sch
LS23 . . . . .188 D8
Boston Spa Primrose Lane
Jun & Infants Sch
LS23 . . . . .188 E8

Botheby Wood BD23 . . .216 E5
Bottom House La YO22 . .33 B5
Bottoms La YO22 . . . . . . .33 B6
Bottoms Rd LA2 . . . . . . .128 E2
Boulderdshaw La DL11 . .17 D1
Boulsworth Dr BB8 . . . . .186 B1
Boulsworth Gr 9 BB8 . .186 A3
Boundary Ave BD20 . . . .187 E7
Boundary Way DL10 . . . .209 F8
Bourlon Rd DL9 . . . . .40 E3
Bournemouth Rd TS3 . . . .7 C8
Bouthwaite Dr 15 YO26 . .227 E4
Bow Bridge Dr BD23 . . .217 D7
Bow Bridge La YO21 . . . .29 A7
Bow Bridge View
BD23 . . . . .217 D7
Bow La LS29 . . . . .189 F7
Bow St TS14 . . . . .8 F7
Bowcar La DL7 . . . . .63 A8
Bowcarr La YO26 . . . . . .163 D8
Bowcliffe Rd LS23 . . . . .188 E5
Bower Cres 8 DL8 . . . . . .63 B2
Bower Rd HG1 . . . . .219 D3
Bower Wlk YO17 . . . . . . .215 E4
Bowes Ave YO31 . . . . . .228 E5
Bowes La YO14 . . . . .100 F5
Bowesfield Cres TS18 . . .6 A8
Bowesfield Ind Est TS18 . .6 A8
Bowesfield La TS18 . . . . . .6 A7
Bowland Cl HG2 . . . . . . .220 D1
Bowland Ct HG2 . . . . . . .220 D1
Bowland Ave YO42 . . . . .193 E2
Bowland View HG3 . . . . .203 E3
Bowling Gn YO30 . . . . . .225 A1
Bowling Green Ct
YO31 . . . . .228 D3
Bowling Green La
9 Hunmanby YO14 . . . .126 F8
Manfield DL2 . . . . .2 B4
Bowling La YO17 . . . . . . .215 E4
Bowling Rd BD23 . . . . . .216 D3
Bowman St DL3 . . . . .3 D7
Bowness Dr YO30 . . . . . .224 E1
Bowthorpe La YO8 . . . . .199 B5
Bowyers Cl YO23 . . . . . .230 C4
Box Hill YO12 . . . . .212 C3
Box La WF8 . . . . .201 C1
Boyle & Petyts Sch
BD23 . . . . .174 F8
Boythe The LS15 . . . . . . .194 B8
Boynton La
Barlow-le-Street YO17 . . .147 E4
Rawcliffe DN14 . . . . .205 A1
Boynton Rd DL2 . . . . .22 E2
Bracewell La BD23 . . . . .171 B4
Bracewell St 18 BB18 . .171 D2
Bracken Cl
Whitby YO22 . . . . .208 E4
York YO32 . . . . .225 F4
Bracken Cres TS14 . . . . . .8 D6
Bracken Field BD23 . . . .134 B3
Bracken Hill
Scarborough YO12 . . . . .212 C7
2 York YO10 . . . . .229 C3
Brackenber Cl YO24 . . . .227 A2
Brackenber Rd YO24 . . .227 A2
Brackenber La DL8 . . . . .60 C3
Brackenber St 3 DL9 . . .40 E4
Brackenber YO24 . . . . . .227 A2
Brackenfield Sch HG1 . .219 A2
Brackenhill Ave YO8 . . . .232 A4
Brackenhill La
Brayton YO8 . . . . .232 A3
Church Fenton LS24 . . . .196 C8
Sleights YO22 . . . . .32 A5
Brackenhills YO26 . . . . .165 F1
Brackenhoe Sec Sch
TS4 . . . . .7 B8
Brackenley Ave 2
BD23 . . . . .217 C7
Brackenley Cl BD23 . . . .217 C7
Brackenley Cres BD23 . .217 C7
Brackenley Dr BD23 . . . .217 C7
Brackenley La BD23 . . . .217 C7
Brackenley La BD23 . . . .217 A7
Brackenthwaite La
HG3 . . . . .222 A1
Brackenwell La LS17 . . . .178 B4
Brackenwood Cl 2
LS29 . . . . .218 E4
Brackit La YO61 . . . . .91 B2
Bracknell Rd TS17 . . . . . . .6 E5
Bradforts Cl 8 LS23 . . . .188 E6
Bradley Ave
Castleford WF10 . . . . . . .200 E4
Northallerton DL6 . . . . . . .210 F2
Bradley Cres YO23 . . . . .182 D6
Bradley Dr YO24 . . . . . . .230 D8
Bradley Gr BD20 . . . . . . .174 B1
Bradley La YO23 . . . . . . .182 C5
Bradley Rd
Pickering YO18 . . . . .71 F4
Silsden BD20 . . . . .174 B2
Bradleys Both CP Sch
BD20 . . . . .173 E3
Bradleys Terr 2 TS9 . . . . .8 A2
Bradworth Dr 3 YO11 . .100 A6
Bradworth Dr 2 YO11 . .100 A6
Braeburn Cty La YO11 . .100 A6
Braegate La LS24 . . . . . .190 E7
Braemar Dr YO24 . . . . . .194 D4
Braeside TS11 . . . . .24 E8
Braeside Gdns YO24 . . .227 A2
Brafferton C of E Prim Sch
YO61 . . . . .115 F1

Brafferton Hall Garde 3
. . . . .115 F1
Braham La HG5 . . . . . . .179 F7
Brailsford Cres YO30 . . .228 A8
Braimber La YO51 . . . . .141 C1
Braithegayte YO19 . . . . .192 F8
Braithwaite Endowed C of E
Prim Sch HG3 . . . . . . .159 B7
Braithwaite Hall* DL8 . . .84 D8
Braithwaite La
Dacre HG3 . . . . .159 A7
East Witton Town DL8 . . . .84 E8
Braker La YO26 . . . . . . .163 F4
Bramall La HG4 . . . . .3 F6
Bramble Cl DL11 . . . . . .161 B3
Bramble Dene YO24 . . . .230 D7
Bramble Cl 11 HG5 . . . .221 B4
Brambles 8 YO8 . . . . . . .197 B1
Brambles The 6 LS29 . .175 C2
Bramcote Prep Sch for Boys
YO11 . . . . .213 A3
Brame La HG3 . . . . .177 A8
Bramham Ave YO26 . . . .227 A3
Bramham CP Sch
LS23 . . . . .188 E6
Bramham Dr HG3 . . . . . .219 A8
Bramham Gr YO26 . . . . .227 A3
Bramham La LS23 . . . . . .188 A6
Bramham Park Gdns*
LS23 . . . . .188 C4
Bramham Pk* LS23 . . . .188 C4
Bramham Rd
Boston Spa LS23 . . . . . . .188 E7
Thorner LS14 . . . . .188 A3
York YO26 . . . . .227 A2
Bramley Ave YO8 . . . . . .198 B5
Bramley Garth YO31 . . . .229 B6
Bramper La DL7 . . . . .42 E1
Branch Rd BD23 . . . . . . .216 E3
Brandon Gr YO32 . . . . . .226 E3
Brandsby Bank YO61 . . .118 D3
Brandsby Gr YO31 . . . . .225 E2
Brandsby Rd YO61 . . . . .118 A1
Brandsby St YO61 . . . . .118 A1
YO10 . . . . .229 D3
Brankin Dr DL1 . . . . .3 E4
Brankin Rd DL1 . . . . .3 E3
Branklyn Gdns TS17 . . . . .6 A4
Branksome Comp Sch
DL3 . . . . .3 A6
Branksome Gr 1 TS18 . . .5 E8
Bransdale TS14 . . . . .8 D6
Bransdale Ave
Northallerton DL7 . . . . . .210 C2
11 Pontefract WF6 . . . . .200 A2
Bransdale Cl 8 HG5 . . . .221 D6
Bransdale Mews 10
WF6 . . . . .200 A2
Bransdale Rd YO62 . . . . .48 B1
Bransholme Dr YO30 . . .225 A2
Brant Bank La LS29 . . . .175 B3
Brant La LS24 . . . . .189 D4
Branton Cl YO26 . . . . . . .142 A1
Branton Ct YO26 . . . . . . .142 A1
Branton La YO26 . . . . . . .142 A1
Brass Castle La TS8 . . . . .7 C3
Brat La LS21 . . . . .177 A7
Bravener Ct YO30 . . . . . .165 B6
Brawby La YO62 . . . . .94 E1
Bray Gate YO42 . . . . . . .169 F2
Bray Rd YO10 . . . . .231 F8
Braygate Balk YO12 . . . . .72 C5
Braygate La YO12 . . . . . .72 D5
Braygate St YO17 . . . . . .121 C2
Braythorne La LS21 . . . .177 E4
Brayton C of E Prim Sch
YO8 . . . . .232 A2
Brayton Cty Inf Sch
YO8 . . . . .232 A2
Brayton Cty Jun Sch
YO8 . . . . .232 A2
Brayton High Sch
YO8 . . . . .232 A2
Brayton La YO8 . . . . .232 B1
Breakmoor Ave BD20 . . .174 C2
Brearlands BD23 . . . . . . .172 A3
Brearton La HG3 . . . . . . .162 C6
Breary Cl YO24 . . . . .227 F1
Breary Flat La HG5 . . . . .221 C7
Brechin Dr TS17 . . . . .6 B6
Breckenbrough La
YO7 . . . . .41 A3
Breckenborough Sch
YO7 . . . . .89 A6
Breckney La YO17 . . . . .122 D5
Brecks La Kippax LS25 . .194 C2
Pockley YO62 . . . . .93 B8
Strensall YO32 . . . . .167 B7
Swillington LS26 . . . . . . .194 B2
York YO32 . . . . .225 F4
Brecksfield YO30 . . . . . .224 C5
Brecon Cres TS17 . . . . . . .5 F4
Breedycroft La YO17 . . . .121 C4
Breighton Rd
Bubwith YO8 . . . . .199 D6
Wressle YO8 . . . . .199 C3
Brendon Gr TS17 . . . . . . .6 A5
Brentwood Cl 3 DL8 . . . .60 D5
Brentwood Cres YO30 . .229 C2
Brewers Ct YO7 . . . . . . .211 B3
Brewerton St HG5 . . . . .221 A5

Brewery La
5 Bispn HG4 ....214 C4
Skipton BD23 ....216 F4
Brewery Rd LS29 ......218 C4
Brewster Terr HG4 ....214 C6
Briar Ave YO26 ....227 B4
Briar Cliffe YO8 ....238 A3
Briar Dr YO31 ....225 F2
Briar Pk **5** YO62 ......93 D7
Briar Rd TS17 ....6 B7
Briar Wlk DL3 ....3 B3
Briardene Ave 9 YO12 ..75 E5
Briarfield Cl LS29 ......218 D3
Briars Ct YO10 ....190 E5
Briars Dr YO23 ....190 E5
Briars The HG5 ....221 B7
Briaround Cl YO08 ......202 F7
Brick Kiln La YO8 ......203 D6
Brick Lands La YO6 ....203 F4
Brickfield La YO51 ......141 D4
Brickhill La YO8 ....204 F4
Brickkiln La
Aldbrough DL11 ....2 A3
Forcett & Carkin DL11 ..20 C8
Brickyard La YO7 ......89 C6
Brickyard Rd YO51 ......141 A4
Bridge Beck La YO7 ....66 C7
Bridge Cl
Burniston YO13 ....75 D7
3 Colburn DL9 ....41 A5
Haxby YO32 ....225 C7
5 Knaresborough HG5 ..221 A5
Bridge Cres DN14 ......205 C8
Bridge End DL6 ....65 B5
Bridge Foot LS23 ......188 F8
Bridge Garth
2 Boston Spa LS23 ....188 E7
South Milford LS25 ....195 F2
Bridge Gn YO7 ....29 C7
Bridge Hill LS21 ....176 C7
Bridge Holm La YO22 ..33 C2
Bridge La Ilkley LS29 ..218 A5
Pollington DN14 ....207 F6
York YO10 ....233 B4
Bridge Rd Airmyn DN14 ..205 E4
Bishopthorpe YO23 ......230 F3
Boston Spa LS23 ....188 F8
Brompton-on-Swale DL10 ..41 B6
Glusburn BD20 ....187 E7
Hurworth DL2 ....3 B3
Malton YO17 ....215 C5
Old Byland & Scawton
YO7 ....91 F7
10 Stokesley TS9 ....26 C7
Bridge St 5 Bedale DL8 ..63 A3
9 Brafferton YO61 ......115 F3
Castleford WF10 ....200 F4
Egglescliffe TS16 ....5 D4
13 Helmsley YO62 ....92 F6
16 Normanton South WF6 ..200 B2
16 Pickering YO18 ....95 F7
Richmond DL10 ....209 B6
Skipton BD23 ....216 F4
Tadcaster LS24 ....189 E6
Thirsk YO7 ....211 B3
Whitby YO22 ....208 D7
York YO1 ....233 B2
Bridge Terr DL10 ......209 B6
Bridge View Rd HG4 ..214 C7
Bridges Ct YO8 ....232 D6
Bridges La YO42 ....193 E4
Bridle Way **1** YO26 ....227 A3
Bridle Wlk YO8 ....232 C4
Bridlington Rd
Hunmanby YO14 ....127 A7
Sledmere YO25 ....150 C4
1 Stamford Bridge YO41 ..168 D2
Wold Newton YO25 ....126 A4
Bridlington St YO14 ..126 F8
Brier Hill YO23 ....209 C7
Brier La YO8 ....29 C4
Briercliffe YO12 ....212 D7
Briergate YO32 ....225 C7
Brierlands Cl LS25 ....194 D4
Brierlands La LS25 ....194 F4
Brierley Rd YO12 ....99 E7
Briery Cl **11** LS29 ....175 C2
Brigg La YO8 ....204 D5
Briggate HG5 ....221 B5
Brigg's Ave WF10 ......200 E3
Briggs St YO31 ....233 C4
Bright St 11 Colne BB8 ..186 A3
Darlington DL1 ....3 E5
1 Glusburn BD20 ....173 E1
Skipton BD23 ....216 F4
York YO26 ....227 F5
Bright Terr BB8 ....186 A1
Brighton Rd LS29 ......218 E3
Brigshaw Dr WF10 ....200 C8
Brigshaw High Sch
WF10 ....200 C8
Brigshaw La WF10 ....200 D8
Brind La DN14 ....199 F2
Brindle Park Dr WF10 ..201 A3
Brindleys La YO23 ......199 F3
Brinkburn Ave DL3 ......3 B7
Brinkburn Dr DL3 ....3 B6
Brinkburn Rd
Darlington DL1 ....3 B6
4 Scarborough YO12 ..212 E5
Brinkworth Terr **11**
YO10 ....228 E3
Briscoe Ridge La YO13 ..177 F6
Briscoe Way TS8 ....6 E5

Britannia Rd DN14 ....205 F1
Britannia St 2 YO12 ..212 E5
Britannia Way DN14 ..205 F2
Broach La Heck DN14 ..203 D1
Kellington DN14 ....203 C1
Broach Rd Heck DN14 ..207 D8
Hensall DN14 ....203 C1
Broad Acres YO32 ....225 C7
Broad Balk YO17 ......149 A5
Broad Balk La YO7 ....115 B1
Broad Carr Rd HG3 ....110 D2
Broad Cl TS8 ....6 D5
Broad Dubb Rd HG3 ..177 C8
Broad Gate
Brompton YO13 ....98 B7
Hunsingore LS22 ......180 F8
Marton cum Grafton
YO26 ....141 F1
Broad Gate Rd YO21 ..28 E4
Broad Head La BD22 ..187 E2
Broad Highway YO10 ..192 F8
Broad La
Appleton Roebuck YO23 ..191 A6
6 Beal DN14 ....202 D4
Catton YO41 ....185 C7
Cawood YO8 ....197 A6
Church Fenton LS24 ..196 D6
Rufforth YO23 ....182 A7
Wistow YO8 ....197 A5
Broad Oak **11** YO11 ..100 A6
Broad Oak La **2** YO32 ..166 D8
Broadacres DN14 ......204 D3
Broadacres Garth
DN14 ....204 D3
Broadfield La HG4 ....138 B8
Broadfield Way **11** LS29 ..174 E4
Broadgate Rd TS5 ......6 EB
Broadlands YO19 ......193 A8
Broadlands Dr **5** YO13 ..99 B8
Broadmanor YO8 ......199 A7
Broadmires La YO18 ....96 C5
Broadrum La YO18 ......96 B5
Broadstone Way YO30 ..224 E3
Broadway
Scarborough YO12 ......212 D7
York YO10 ....231 E8
Broadway Gr **3** YO10 ..231 E8
Broadway The DL1 ......3 E5
Broadway W YO10 ....231 D8
Broadwell Rd TS4 ......7 A8
Brockfield Pk Dr YO31 ..225 F2
Brockfield Rd YO31 ..225 E2
Brockholme La DL6 ....65 A4
Brocklesby Rd TS14 ....8 F5
Brockley Cl LS24 ......196 B7
Broc-o-Bank **11** DN6 ..206 E2
Brogden La BB18 ......171 B1
Brokes La DL11 ....40 B6
Bromley La TS8 ....7 B3
Bromley St **2** YO26 ..227 F5
Brompton Carr La
YO13 ....98 B4
Brompton Com Prim Sch DL6 ..43 F3
Brompton Hall Sch
YO13 ....98 C5
Brompton Ings Rd
YO13 ....98 D3
Brompton La DL6 ......43 E4
Brompton on Swale C of E
Prim Sch DL10 ....41 B7
Brompton Rd
Newton-le-Willows DL8 ..62 B4
Northallerton DL6 ......210 D5
Brompton YO23 ....228 A7
Brompton-by-Sawdon Cofe
Sch YO13 ....98 C5
Bronte Cl YO12 ....212 D5
Bronte Ct WF8 ....201 B1
Bronte Dr DL9 ....41 A5

Brooksbank Rd TS7 ....7 D7
Brookside
Collingham LS22 ......188 A8
Hovingham YO62 ......119 E6
Skelton & Brotton TS12 ..9 D8
Sleights YO22 ....32 B6
Brookside Ave 11 DL8 ..63 B2
Brookside Cl 11 DL8 ..63 B2
Brookwood Way TS16 ..5 E4
Broom House La
Egton YO21 ....30 F4
Ugthorpe YO21 ....12 B2
Broom Rd LS24 ....189 D5
Broom Wlk YO10 ......212 F7
Broome Cl
10 Pontefract WF6 ......200 A2
Skelton YO30 ....225 F5
Broome Way YO32 ....226 A5
Broomfield HG3 ....160 E6
Broomfield Gr **11** WF11 ..202 A3
Broomfield CP Sch
DL7 ....210 D2
Broomhill WF10 ....201 A3
Broomhill Gr **10** WF11 ..202 A2
Broomhill Gr **11** WF11 ..202 A2
Broomhill Mdw WF11 ..202 A2
Broomhill Sq **4** WF11 ..202 A2
Broomhill Wlk **8** WF11 ..202 A2
Brootes La BD23 ....107 C2
Brotes La YO26 ....164 B5
Brotherton Cty Prim Sch
WF11 ....201 E4
Brough Ave **5** DL9 ......41 A5
Brough Hall * DL10 ....41 B4
Brough Mdws DL10 ....41 D5
Brough Rd **28** DL10 ....40 E4
Brougham Cl YO30 ....227 F8
Brougham St
Darlington DL1 ....3 C7
Skipton BD23 ....217 A3
Broughton Ave BD23 ..216 D3
Broughton Gr BD23 ..216 D3
Broughton Rd
Brompton YO17 ....121 C3
11 East Ayton/West Ayton
YO13 ....99 A7
Malton YO17 ....215 A5
Skipton BD23 ....216 D3
Broughton Way
11 Harrogate HG2 ......220 C3
4 York YO10 ....229 B4
Brow La LA2 ....129 D6
Browcliff BD20 ....174 C2
Brown Bank Rd
Kirkby Malzeard HG4 ..111 F5
Norwood HG3 ....177 B8
Brown Cow Rd YO8 ..202 A8
Brown Howe Rd YO18 ..51 A1
Brown La YO13 ....141 F1
Brown Moor **22** YO41 ..168 D2
Brown Rigg Rd YO13 ..53 F5
Browney Croft YO10 ..233 C1
Browning Cl **3** DL9 ....40 E4
Brownmoor La YO61 ..142 F7
Brownmoor La
Huby YO61 ....144 A2
Sutton-on-the-Forest
YO61 ....166 B8
Brownroyd **14** BB18 ..172 B1
Browns Ct **4** BD20 ..173 E3
Browns Fold BD23 ....134 E3
Brown's Terr 4 TS13 ..11 F7
Brownsfield Rd BD23 ..216 F4
Broxa La YO13 ....74 C6
Broxa Moor La YO13 ..74 C7
Bruce Way **5** YO18 ....95 F6
Brunel Way DL1 ....3 D5
Brunswick Cl **2** YO23 ..167 C8
Brunswick Dr HG1 ....219 A2
Brunswick Pl **11** HG1 ..219 D1
Brunswick St
York YO1 ....233 A1
Brunswick Sh Ctr
Whitby YO21 ....208 D6
York YO23 ....228 B1
Brunt Acres Rd DL8 ..56 D4
Bruntwaite La BD20 ..174 E1
Brunton Bank DL8 ......59 A7
Brunton La HG5 ....163 B6
Brunton Rd La2 ....131 A6
Bry Hills YO12 ....99 D6
Bryan Cl **8** DL6 ....210 E2
Bryden Cl DL6 ....210 E2
Bryony Ct YO8 ....232 B2
Bryony Rd **4** HG3 ....161 B3
Bryony Way **5** HG3 ..161 B3
Bubwith Cty Prim Sch
YO8 ....199 D7
Buck Haw Brow BD24 ..131 B4
Buck La YO8 ....147 B6
Buck Stone La BD22 ..187 C8
Buckden Cl **11** YO26 ..143 D8
Buckden Wood La
BD23 ....107 D8
Buckingham Sq
8 Helmsley YO62 ......92 F6
Helmsley YO62 ....92 F6
Buckingham St 11 YO11 ..233 B1
Buckingham Way
WF11 ....201 E4

Buckle Ct YO8 ....232 B7
Buckle La WF6 ....200 A1
Bucks La **11** BD24 ....131 D2
Buess La DL1 ....4 A7
Buffet Hill La LA2 ......129 C7
Bugthorpe La YO41 ..169 D5
Bugthorpe La Town E
YO41 ....169 E5
Bull Alley La DN14 ....204 B3
Bull Balk **14** YO41 ....185 E4
Bull Hill DL8 ....61 E8
Bull Ing La BD23 ......134 D3
Bull La Huby YO61 ....166 B2
Bull YO10 ....228 F3
Bull Moor La YO60 ..168 A8
Bull Piece La YO17 ....122 D3
Bullamoor Cl DL6 ....210 F5
Bullamoor Cty Jun Sch
DL6 ....210 F5
Bullamoor Rd DL6 ....210 E5
Buller St YO8 ....232 B6
Bullock La YO7 ....89 A5
Bullytree La LS25 ....195 F2
Burdale Cl YO17 ......215 F2
Burdike Ave YO30 ....228 A8
Burdock La YO23 ......161 B3
Burdyke Inf Sch YO30 ..228 B8
Burgate YO18 ....95 F7
Burgoyne Cl HG4 ....113 D3
Burke Rd YO17 ....215 C5
Burke St HG1 ....219 E5
Burlands La YO26 ....182 F7
Burley Ave HG1 ....161 A3
Burley Bank Cl HG3 ..161 A3
Burley Bank Rd HG3 ..161 A3
Burley La YO7 ....115 C1
Burley La HG3 ....195 F2
Burley in Wharfedale Sta
LS29 ....176 C1
Burley La3 ....161 A3
Burley Mid Sch LS29 ..176 C1
Burlington Ave YO10 ..229 C4
Burlyn Rd **3** YO14 ..127 A8
Burma Rd DL2 ....3 F2
Burn Bridge La HG3 ..222 C2
Burn Bridge Oval HG3 ..222 C2
Burn Bridge Rd HG3 ..222 C2
Burn Hall Cl YO30 ....203 D7
Burn St HG1 ....203 B6
Burn Wood Ct TS21 ....5 A7
Burnby Cl HG3 ....219 B5
Burneston C of E Prim Sch
DL8 ....87 E8
Burneston Hargill DL8 ..87 F8
Burnett Cl HG2 ....140 A2
Burnham Rd DL6 ......210 D3
Burnholme Ave YO31 ..229 B6
Burnholme Com Coll
YO31 ....229 A6
Burnholme Dr YO31 ..229 A5
Burnholme Gr YO31 ..229 A5
Burniston Gdns YO13 ..75 D7
Burniston Rd YO12 ..212 E8
Burnleys Ct LS26 ....200 B4
Burnleys Dr LS26 ....200 B4
Burnleys Mews LS26 ..200 B4
Burnleys View LS26 ..200 B4
Burnmoor Cres LA6 ..103 D3
Burnmoor Dr TS16 ....5 D5
Burnroyd Ave **8** LS25 ..194 C3
Burns Ct YO24 ....230 B7
Burns Hill **11** LS29 ..174 F4
Burns Way
Boston Spa LS23 ......188 E2
Harrogate HG1 ....219 F7
Burnsall Cl **2** YO14 ..101 A3
Burnsall Dr YO26 ......227 E4
Burnsall La BD23 ......135 A1
Burnsall Mews BD23 ..216 E5
Burnsall Prim Sch
BD23 ....157 B8
Burnside Ave **4** YO11 ..100 A6
Burnside Cl YO11 ....219 B5
Burnside Cres YO11 ..216 E5
Burnside Cl HG1 ......219 B5
Burnside Rd HG1 ......219 B5
Burnside Wlk HG1 ....219 B5
Burnt Yates C of E Endowed
Prim Sch HG3 ......160 F8
Burnthouse Bank DL6 ..45 B3
Burr Bank **11** YO11 ..213 B6
Burrard Ave DL10 ....209 B7
Burrill Ave YO30 ......228 B7
Burrill Rd DL8 ....62 D5
Burrill Rd **18** YO32 ..166 D5
Burrow Rd LA6 ....102 B7
Burstall Dr **21** YO8 ..232 B7
Bursett Rd DL8 ....56 C4
Burton Ave YO30 ......228 A7
Burton Comm La
LS25 ....202 A6
Burton Fields Cl **2**
YO41 ....168 D2
Burton Fields Rd **4**
YO41 ....168 D2

Burton Fleming Rd
YO25 ....126 ...
Burton Gn HG3 ....219 ...
Burton Hill 3 LA6 ......10...
Burton In Lonsdale C of E Pr
Sch HG3 ....10...
Burton Rd LA2 ....10...
Burton Salmon CP Sch
LS25 ....200...
Burton Stone La YO30 ..2...
Burtondale Rd **11** YO12 ..2...
Burtree Ave YO30 ......2...
Burtree La YO21 ....2...
Burwains La BD22 ....1...
**Burwen Castle (Roman
Fort)* BD23 ....1...
Burwen Castle Rd
BD23 ....1...
Busby La TS9 ....2...
Busk La LS24 ....1...
Busky Dike La LS21 ......1...
Butcher La Potto DL6 ....6...
Whitley DN14 ....2...
Butcher Terr YO23 ......2...
Butcher's La YO25 ......1...
Butler Rd HG1 ....2...
Butt Fields La DN14 ....2...
Butt Hedge YO26 ......1...
Butt La 22 Haxby YO32 ..1...
Kippax LS25 ....1...
Butt La
Carlton Husthwaite YO7 ..1...
Guisborough TS14 ......
Wold Newton YO25 ....
Buttacre La YO23 ......1...
Butter Mkt **8** DN14 ....2...
Buttercup Cl **6** HG3 ..1...
Butterfield Cl HG3 ....1...
Butterfield Dr TS16 ....
**Butterfly World* TS18
Buttermere Ave
Middlesbrough TS5 ......
4 Wetherby LS22 ......1...
Buttermere Ct **9** YO30 ..2...
Buttermere Dr YO30 ..2...
Butters Cl **30** YO22 ......
Butterwick La YO17 ....1...
Buttery La YO17 ....1...
Butterwick Rd YO17 ..1...
Foxholes YO17 ....1...
Langtoft YO25 ....1...
Butthouse Rigg DL11 ....
Buttle Bank DL8 ....
Butts BB18 ....1...
Butts Cl **10** YO41 ......1...
Butts Hill YO14 ....1...
Butts La Bainbridge DL8 ..
Barton-le-Willows YO60 ..
Bentham LA2 ....
Egglescliffe TS16 ......
Monk Fryston LS25 ......1...
South Milford LS25 ....1...
Butts The **12** WF8 ......
Buxton Ave TS7 ....
Byards Pk **11** HG5 ......2...
Byefield Gr YO13 ....
Byemoor Ave TS9 ......
Byemoor Cl TS9 ....
Byland Abbey (rems of)*
YO6 ....
Byland Ave
Northallerton DL6 ......2...
Thirsk YO7 ....2...
Byland Ct **5** YO21 ......
Byland Gr HG1 ....2...
Byland Mews HG1 ......2...
Byland Pl
Harrogate HG1 ....2...
Whitby YO21 ....2...
Byland Rd
Harrogate HG1 ....2...
Whitby YO21 ....2...
Bylands Way DL3 ....
Byng Rd DL9 ....
Byram Cl **3** DL6 ......2...
Byram Ct **3** DL6 ......2...
Byram Park Ave WF11 ..2...
Byram Park Rd WF11 ..2...
Byron Ave **8** DN6 ......2...
Byron Ct DL2 ....
Byron Dr YO30 ....2...
Byron Rd **21** BD23 ....2...
Byron St **2** BD23 ......2...
Byron Wlk Mews HG2 ..2...
Byward Dr YO12 ....2...
Byway The DL1 ....
By-Ways HG2 ....2...

C

Cabin La **2** HG3 ......1...
Caburn Cl **2** YO12 ....2...
Caedmon Ave YO21 ....2...
Caedmon Cl YO31 ......2...
Caedmon Sch YO21 ....2...
Cairnborrow **2** YO24 ..2...
Caithness Cl **3** YO30 ..2...
Calcaria Cres LS24 ....1...
Calcaria Rd LS24 ......1...
Calcutt HG5 ....2...
Caldbeck Cl **11** YO30 ....
Calder Ave YO26 ......2...

r Cres DN14 .....207 F6
onia St YO12 ....212 E5
onian Way DL1 ....3 F8
l YO32 ....225 D8
all La BB18 ....171 D1
Vood La B20 ....172 E1
rnia Dr WF10 ....200 B3
rnia Gr **7** TS9 ....8 A2
rnia Rd YO22 ....208 E5
s La B023 ....155 A6
t Cl YO32 ....225 C7
st Hos DL11 ....36 C4
hool Rd N060 ....145 D5
ill Rd B023 ....108 B4
igh Rd B023 ....79 D5
a B023 ....172 A3
lesforth CP Sch
....204 C4
rian Cl **2** YO32 ....225 F3
ridge Ave TS7 ....7 B5
ridge Cres **1**
....219 D2
idge Pl
arrogate HG1 ....219 D2
orough YO12 ....212 E4
ridge Rd
rate HG1 ....219 D2
esbrough TS5 ....6 E8
idge St
dale HG1 ....219 D2
anton South Wf6 ....200 A1
orough YO12 ....212 F6
ork YO24 ....228 A3
idge Terr
rogate HG1 ....219 D2
arborough YO11 ....213 A4
en Rd WF10 ....201 B4
idge La 204 B6
ron Gr YO23 ....228 C1
La DN14 ....204 C3
ock La B024 ....111 D2
Hill Cl HG4 ....214 D3
bell Ave
....113 D3
B024 ....227 E2
bell St **1** B020 ....187 E8
ton Cl YO13 ....75 D5
ion Dr TS14 ....8 D6
ion Gr
ry Newham TS7 ....7 B6
rrogate HG3 ....161 B3
La TS15 ....25 B4
ion Rd DL1 ....3 D7
leshon Rd YO23 ....228 B1
sall Balk DN6 ....206 E1
sall Hall Rd **11**
....206 E1
smount Sch
....206 D1
al Rd HG1 ....220 C4
al Terr **5** HG1 ....220 C4
La HG4 ....114 E2
an La DL8 ....60 E2
Garth DN14 ....207 F6
Rd
gwith YO42 ....193 C5
YO8 ....214 D4
View YO8 ....232 D4
YO23 B023 ....216 F4
erra Rd TS7 ....7 B6
r La HG3 ....179 E6
er Ave **2** YO13 ....99 A7
er St YO12 ....212 E5
am Gr YO10 ....229 D3
on Hall La DN14 ....202 F1
on St WF10 ....200 F3
n Gr TS15 ....5 E2
Lee Ave TS17 ....6 C5
s Garth La **2** YO62 ....92 F6
rbury Cl
xby YO21 ....166 D5
rbury Ct **8** WF8 ....201 C2
n Gdns TS5 ....6 E6
Hill YO21 ....229 F1
in Cook & Staithes
tage Ctr* TS13 ....13 K2
in Cook Birthplace
e* TS7 ....7 B7
in Cook Cres
....208 E6
in Cook Meml Mus*
....208 D7
in Cook's Cl
rwell TS13 ....11 D8
es TS13 ....13 K1
in Cook's Cres TS7 ....7 C6
in Cook's 'Mon'*
....8 D1
in Cook's Schoolroom
e* TS9 ....8 A1
in Cook's Way TS9 ....8 A1
am Dr LS29 ....218 E4
nal Cl **15** LS25 ....195 F4
nals Cl **3** YO8 ....197 B8
ess House La
....138 E4
La Cl YO8 ....232 B6
St YO10 ....228 D1
te Hill **12** YO14 ....101 B3
Fleet La TS3 ....7 C8

Carl St YO23 ....228 C2
Carla Beck La B023 ....173 B4
Carlbury Ave TS5 ....6 D6
Carlbury Cres DL3 ....3 A5
Carless La YO14 ....100 F4
Carleton Ave B023 ....216 E3
Carleton Dr DL3 ....3 A5
Carleton Endowed Prim Sch
....173 B4
Carleton La B023 ....173 C4
Carleton New Rd
B023 ....216 E1
Carleton Rd B023 ....216 E1
Carleton St
1 Skipton B023 ....216 F3
17 York YO26 ....227 F5
Carlile Hill TS8 ....6 E5
Carline Mead **2E** HG3 ....161 B3
Carline St **1B** YO26 ....227 F5
Carlton & Faceby C of E Prim
Sch TS9 ....26 A3
Carlton App **1** LS22 ....180 B3
Carlton Ave Thirsk YO7 ....211 B1
York YO10 ....229 B3
Carlton Cl
4 Carlton Miniott YO7 ....89 C4
Eggborough DN14 ....202 F1
19 Normanton South WF6 ....200 A1
Carlton Dr TS17 ....6 A6
Carlton Gdns **8** WF6 ....200 B1
Carlton La YO62 ....92 F7
Carlton Miniott CP Sch
YO7 ....89 A4
Carlton Moor Cres DL1 ....3 E4
Carlton Rd
Carlton Miniott YO7 ....89 A3
4 Filey YO14 ....101 B3
Harrogate HG2 ....222 D7
Helmsley YO62 ....92 F7
Sutton upon Derwent
....185 C1
Carlton St WF6 ....200 B1
Carlton Terr **6** YO11 ....213 A4
Carlton Twrs* DN14 ....204 D2
Carlton-in-Snaith CP Sch
....204 C3
Carlyle Cres WF10 ....201 A4
Carlyle Rd WF10 ....201 A4
Carmel Gr DL3 ....3 B4
Carmel RC Aided Comp Sch
DL3 ....3 A5
Carmel Rd N DL3 ....3 B5
Carmel Rd S DL3 ....3 B4
Carmelite St YO1 ....233 C2
Carmires Ave
Haxby YO32 ....166 F5
Knaresborough HG5 ....221 A4
Carnagil Rd DL9 ....209 B1
Carnagil CP Sch DL9 ....40 D4
Carney St TS12 ....9 F7
Carnot St YO26 ....227 F5
Carnoustie Cl **1** YO26 ....227 B4
Carnoustie Dr TS16 ....5 E5
Carnoustie Gdns **2**
WF6 ....200 B1
Caroline Cl **5** YO24 ....227 F3
Carousel Wlk LS25 ....195 F4
Carpenters Yd YO17 ....215 C4
Carpley Green Rd DL8 ....57 D3
Carr Ave LS25 ....195 F4
Carr Bridge La B024 ....24 D3
Carr Cl
13 Hemingbrough YO8 ....198 F1
Rainton with Newby YO7 ....114 F6
Ripon HG4 ....214 B3
Carr Field La YO26 ....141 F1
Carr Fields La YO12 ....99 B5
Carr Head La B020 ....187 C8
Carr Hill La YO21 ....32 B7
Carr Hill Ridge YO21 ....32 B7
Carr House La
Cayton YO11 ....100 A5
Heslerton YO17 ....98 A1
Carr Inf Sch YO26 ....227 C5
Carr Jun Sch YO26 ....227 C5
Carr La Ampleforth YO62 ....92 B1
Azerley HG4 ....113 A4
Barlow YO8 ....204 C7
Castleford WF10 ....200 F3
Cawton YO62 ....119 C8
Cayton YO11 ....100 A5
Cayton YO11 ....99 B7
Escrick YO19 ....192 B5
Glaisdale YO21 ....30 D4
Gristhorpe YO11 ....100 E4
Heslerton YO17 ....124 A8
Kilburn High & Low YO61 ....91 B3
Little Ouseburn YO26 ....164 A7
Long Drax YO8 ....204 F6
Muston YO14 ....100 F3
Newby & Scalby YO13 ....75 C5
Newton on Derwent
YO41 ....185 F4
Rainton with Newby YO7 ....114 F6
Roecliffe YO51 ....140 E3
Sheriff Hutton YO60 ....145 E6
Stillington YO61 ....144 C6
Sutton-on-the-Forest
YO61 ....144 D2
Thirlby YO7 ....90 F6
Thornamby YO16 ....116 E4
Wetherby LS22 ....180 D4

Carr La continued
Wistow YO8 ....197 A3
York YO26 ....227 D5
Carr Leys La YO7 ....66 A4
Carr Mill Mews BD22 ....187 B5
Carr Rd **7** BB18 ....171 D2
Carr Side Rd YO26 ....163 F8
Carr View TS8 ....232 F4
Carr The HG3 ....222 C7
Carr Wood Rd WF10 ....200 F3
Carrbank La YO32 ....167 E3
Carrfield YO24 ....230 C8
Carrfield Dr LS15 ....194 B8
Carrfield La LS15 ....194 B8
Carrfield Rd LS15 ....194 B8
Carriage Dr The YO11 ....213 B7
Carriers Croft B023 ....227 E3
Carriers Row B88 ....186 B2
Carrington Ave **1** YO12 ....212 E5
Carronck St **3** YO32 ....225 F1
Carter Ave YO31 ....228 F5
Carter La YO31 ....228 F5
Carter La **22** YO62 ....70 B1
Carter St **1** Ilkley LS29 ....218 E6
Longewinton TS16 ....5 A4
Cartmell Terr DL3 ....3 C6
Cass House Rd TS8 ....6 E4
Cass La
Knaresborough HG5 ....221 A4
South Milford LS25 ....195 E1
Castelo Gr **1** YO18 ....96 A6
Castle Bank DL6 ....25 E1
Castle C of E Jun Sch
HG5 ....221 B6
Castle Cl Cawood YO8 ....197 A8
11 Haxby YO32 ....166 D5
Killinghall HG3 ....161 C5
Middleton St George DL2 ....4 C3
Northallerton DL7 ....210 D5
2 Spofforth HG3 ....179 E6
11 Thornton Dale YO18 ....96 D5
Castle Dyke Wynd TS16 ....5 E3
Castle End DL8 ....59 B6
Castle Garth
Pontefract WF8 ....201 C1
4 Thornton Dale YO18 ....96 D5
Castle Gate **4** LS29 ....218 B4
Castle Gdns **2** LS29 ....218 B4
Castle Hill
6 Hunmanby YO14 ....126 F8
5 Ilkley LS29 ....218 B4
Richmond DL10 ....209 C6
4 Settle B024 ....131 E3
Castle Hill Cl HG2 ....222 B6
Castle Hill Dr HG2 ....222 B6
Castle Hill Glade HG2 ....222 B6
Castle Hill Gr HG2 ....222 B6
Castle Hill La YO8 ....204 F5
Castle Howard*
....120 D3
Castle Howard Rd
YO17 ....215 A4
Castle Ings **1** HG3 ....179 E5
Castle Ings Cl **1** HG3 ....221 A5
Castle Ings Rd **3** HG3 ....221 A5
Castle La Danby YO21 ....29 D6
11 East Ayton/West Ayton
YO13 ....99 B8
Castle Mdws DL8 ....82 A7
Castle Rd Colne B88 ....186 A4
5 Ilkley LS29 ....218 B4
Killinghall HG3 ....161 C5
18 Pickering YO18 ....95 F7
Scarborough YO11 ....213 A6
Thornton Dale YO18 ....96 D5
Whitby YO21 ....208 A6
Castle Rise **1** YO13 ....99 A7
Castle St WF10 ....201 B4
Castle Side YO60 ....145 C5
Castle Yd **1** LS29 ....218 B4
Spofforth HG3 ....179 E6
Castle Steads (Fort)*
DL8 ....84 C8
Castle Steads* DL11 ....19 D6
Castle Terr
Richmond DL10 ....209 C6
2 Scarborough YO11 ....213 B6
Castle View
2 Newby & Scalby YO13 ....75 D5
Sheriff Hutton YO60 ....145 C5
Castle View Terr BD23 ....134 E3
Castlebergh Hospl
BD24 ....131 C2
Castleberg La **8** BD24 ....131 E2
Castleford High Sch
WF10 ....200 F4
Castleford La
Featherstone WF7 ....200 D2
Knottingley WF11 ....201 D3
Castleford Mus Room*
....200 E4
Castleford Normanton &
District Hospl WF10 ....200 D3
Castleford Park Sch
....200 C4
Castleford Rd WF6 ....200 B2
Castleford Redhill Mid Sch
WF10 ....201 B4

Castleford RUFC
WF10 ....200 C3
Castleford Three Lane Ends
WF10 ....200 D4
Castleford Tigers RLFC
....200 F5
Castlegate
East Ayton/West Ayton
YO13 ....99 A7
6 Helmsley YO62 ....92 F6
Kirkbymoorside YO62 ....70 B1
3 Knaresborough HG5 ....221 B5
Malton YO17 ....215 C4
10 Pickering YO18 ....95 F7
Scarborough YO11 ....213 B7
Thirsk YO7 ....211 B2
York YO1 ....233 B2
Castlegate Bar* DL10 ....209 C6
Castlekeep Cl DL10 ....209 C8
Castleton Ave
Middlesbrough TS5 ....6 D8
Northallerton DL7 ....210 C1
Castleton Moor Sta
YO21 ....29 A7
Castleton Prim Sch
YO21 ....29 A7
Castleton Rd DL9 ....40 F4
Cat Bank DL11 ....39 C6
Cat La Balne DN14 ....207 A5
Bilbrough YO23 ....182 D5
Upper Poppleton YO26 ....182 D8
Catharic Cl DN14 ....206 F7
Cathedral C of E Prim Sch
HG4 ....214 D5
Cathedral Cl HG4 ....214 D5
Catherine Love Dr **15**
YO8 ....232 B7
Catherine St **2** TS12 ....9 F7
Cattal Moor La YO26 ....181 B8
Cattal St YO26 ....164 A2
Cattal Sta YO26 ....164 A3
Catterick Bridge*
....41 C6
Catterick La DL10 ....41 C4
Catterick Race Course
DL10 ....41 C5
Catterton La LS24 ....190 A6
Cattle La LS25 ....194 F8
Cattlelaith La WF11 ....201 E2
Catton La YO7 ....115 A7
Catton Moor La YO7 ....114 F8
Caudle Hill WF11 ....201 C6
Causeway Dr TS5 ....6 E6
Causeway The DL1 ....3 E5
Cautley Dr HG3 ....161 C5
Cautley Gr HG3 ....161 C5
Cavalry Ct **9** YO12 ....75 F5
Cavendish Ave
Harrogate HG2 ....219 E1
8 Pontefract WF8 ....201 C2
Cavendish Ct HG2 ....222 F8
Cavendish Gr YO10 ....229 D3
Cavendish Rd TS4 ....7 A8
Cawcliff La YO18 ....97 A5
Cawdel Cl **4** LS25 ....195 F2
Cawdel Way LS25 ....195 F2
Cawder Ghyll B023 ....217 A1
Cawder La B023 ....217 A1
Cawder Rd B023 ....217 A1
Cawood C of E Prim Sch
....197 B8
Cawood Cres LS24 ....190 C1
Cawood Dr TS5 ....6 E7
Cawood Rd YO8 ....197 D6
Cawood Way
Coulby Newham TS8 ....6 D4
Tadcaster LS24 ....189 D6
Cedar Glade YO19 ....184 E7
Cedar Gr **2** Barton DL10 ....21 C7
3 Filey YO14 ....101 B4
Sutton BD20 ....187 E7
York YO31 ....229 B7

Cedar Grange HG2 ....222 D7
Cedar Mews **4** DL2 ....22 D8
Cedar Rd DL3 ....3 B6
Cedar Ridge LS25 ....194 E5
Cedar Vale **6** YO62 ....70 B1
Cedarhurst Dr TS12 ....9 F7
Cedarwood **8** DL2 ....4 C4
Cedarwood Ave **1** TS9 ....26 C8
Cedarwood Cl **8** YO24 ....227 B1
Cedarwood Glade TS8 ....6 E4
Celtic Cl WF6 ....227 B5
Cemetery La DL3 ....3 A5
Cemetery Rd
40 Earby BB18 ....172 A1
Normanton South WF6 ....200 B1
Thirsk YO7 ....211 A3
York YO31 ....233 C1
Centenary Rd DN14 ....205 F3
Central Av **6** YO61 ....143 D8
Central Dr
Castleford WF10 ....200 C4
Ripon HG4 ....214 B6
Central St **1** TS16 ....5 E3
Central Way **6** TS9 ....8 A2
Centre La LS24 ....189 E6
Centre Rd BD20 ....186 D7
Century Rd YO7 ....211 A1
Centurion La LS24 ....178 A1
Centurion Way YO30 ....225 B3
Century Wlk **1** HG2 ....220 B3
Ceres Rd LS22 ....180 C3
Chacksfield Rd DL10 ....41 E4
Chadderton Cl TS12 ....9 E8
Chadderton Dr TS17 ....6 C7
Chain Bar La HG3 ....161 A4
Chain La HG5 ....221 C6
Chair Wlk HG3 ....139 B8
Chaldon Cl **3** YO32 ....167 A6
Chaldron Way TS16 ....5 D6
Chalfield Cl TS17 ....6 B4
Chalfonts YO24 ....227 F1
Chalford Oaks TS5 ....6 D8
Challacombe Cres TS17 ....6 A3
Challoner Rd TS15 ....24 E7
Chaloner St TS14 ....8 F6
Chaloner's Cres YO24 ....230 D7
Chaloner's Rd YO24 ....230 D7
Chamber End Fold **5**
....234 E3
Chancery Ct YO24 ....227 C3
Chancery Rise TS18 ....6 A6
Chandler Cl DL10 ....209 F8
Chandlers Ct YO11 ....213 B2
Chandlers Ridge Prim Sch
TS7 ....7 D5
Chandlers Wharf
YO17 ....215 C3
Chanting Hill Cl YO60 ....146 E6
Chantry Ave TS5 ....169 F1
Chantry Bank DL8 ....59 D3
Chantry Cl YO24 ....230 C8
Chantry Ct HG3 ....161 C7
Chantry Dr
East Ayton/West Ayton
YO13 ....99 B8
2 Ilkley LS29 ....218 B3
Chantry Gap YO13 ....165 F1
Chantry Garth DL8 ....59 D3
Chantry Gr YO13 ....165 F1
Chantry La
Bishopthorpe YO23 ....231 B4
Scotton HG5 ....162 A6
Stutton with Hazlewood
LS24 ....189 B3
Chantry Rd
East Ayton/West Ayton
YO13 ....99 B8
Northallerton DL7 ....210 B3
Chapel Balk Rd YO8 ....198 F1
Chapel Bridge* DL11 ....1 C7
Chapel Cl
Bilton-in-Ainsty with Bickerton
LS22 ....181 B5
21 Helmsley YO62 ....92 F6
Rawcliffe DN14 ....205 A1
Chapel Croft **2** B023 ....134 E2
Chapel Ct
Gargrave B023 ....155 D1
Huby YO61 ....144 A4
Chapel Fields Rd
YO26 ....227 A3
Chapel Fold **2** B023 ....134 E3
Chapel Garth
Dalton YO7 ....115 E7
Markington with Wallerthwaite
HG3 ....139 C3
Thirkleby DL7 ....43 F3
Chapel Gate
Kirkby Malham B023 ....154 F8
Malham B023 ....132 F1
Sherburn YO17 ....124 D6
Chapel Haddlesey C of E
Prim Sch YO8 ....203 B5
Chapel Hill
Boroughbridge YO51 ....141 C5
Kearby with Netherby
LS22 ....179 B1
Skipton B023 ....217 A5
Chapel Hill La LS21 ....178 A1
Chapel La
Askham Bryan YO23 ....182 F3
Barwick in Elmet LS15 ....194 C8
Boston Spa LS23 ....188 E7
Brayton YO8 ....232 B1
Brompton YO13 ....98 B7
5 Burton in Lonsdale LA6 ....102 F3

Chapel La continued
15 Easingwold YO61 ....143 C8
13 Eastfield YO11 ....100 B6
Finghall DL8 ....61 E4
Halton East BD23 ......174 C8
Harome YO62 ....93 C4
Hebden BD23 ....135 A2
Horton in Ribblesdale
  BD24 ....105 C3
Ilkley LS29 ....218 A4
Langtoft YO25 ....151 D5
Little Smeaton WF8 .....206 B3
Marton-le-Moor HG4 ....114 F1
Rawcliffe DN14 ....205 A2
Reighton YO14 ....127 E5
3 Riccall YO19 ....192 A1
2 Spofforth HG3 ....179 E5
3 Thornton Dale YO18 ...96 D5
Tollerton YO61 ....143 A3
Westow YO60 ....147 B7
Chapel of Our Lady*
  YO11 ....213 C7
Chapel Rd
29 Scarborough YO11 ...213 A6
Settrington YO17 ....122 D1
Chapel Riggs 4 DL10 ...41 E4
Chapel Row YO10 .....233 C1
Chapel Sq 8 BD24 ....131 E2
Chapel St
5 Addingham LS29 ......174 F4
6 Beadlam YO62 ....93 D7
4 Cawton YO62 ....173 B4
Cattal YO26 ....164 A1
22 Earby BB18 ....172 A1
27 Filey YO14 ....101 B3
Grassington BD23 ......134 E3
Hambleton YO8 ....196 F1
Hillam LS25 ....202 B7
Kirk Hammerton YO26 ..164 C1
Knaresborough HG5 .....221 B5
Middleton St George DL2 ..4 C4
Nunnington YO62 ....93 E2
17 Settle BD24 ....131 D2
Tadcaster LS24 ....189 E6
Thirsk YO7 ....211 B2
Chapel Wlk
Long Preston BD23 .....153 F5
4 Riccall YO19 ....192 A1
Chapman La 1 YO32 ...167 C8
Chapman La 6 HG4 ....86 C3
Chapman Sq HG1 .....219 B2
Chapmans Ct YO24 ...230 D6
Chapman's La YO30 ...165 E7
Chapter House St YO1 ..233 B3
Charles Ave HG1 ......219 D7
Charles Ct DL10 ......209 F7
Charles Moor YO31 ...228 F7
Charles The YO8 ......232 B6
Charles Wesley Dr
  YO8 ....232 B2
Charlock TS8 ....7 B4
Charlton Ave
Knaresborough HG5 .....221 B6
4 Whitby YO21 ....208 B7
Charlton Ct 8 HG5 ....221 B6
Charlton Dr HG5 ......221 B6
Charlton Gr 5 HG5 ....221 B6
Charlton Manor Dr 10
  HG5 ....221 B6
Charlton St YO23 .....228 C2
Charnwood Dr TS7 ......7 D6
Charrington Ave TS17 ...6 A6
Charter Ave DN14 ....205 A1
Charters The YO8 .....198 B5
Chartwell Cl TS17 ....6 B4
Chase Garth Rd 16
  YO61 ....143 C8
Chase Side Ct YO24 ...230 E8
Chase The
8 Boroughbridge YO51 ..141 B4
Garforth LS25 ....194 D4
Hurworth-on-Tees DL2 ....3 E1
Knaresborough HG5 .....221 D5
Norton YO17 ....215 E2
Chatsworth Ct HG1 ....219 D4
Chatham Rd HG4 ......113 D2
Chatsworth Ave 7 WF8 .201 C2
Chatsworth Dr
10 Haxby YO32 ....166 F5
3 Wetherby LS22 ....180 B3
Chatsworth Gdns
YO12 ....212 E7
Chatsworth Gr
4 Boroughbridge YO51 ..141 B4
Harrogate HG1 ....219 C4
Chatsworth Pl HG1 ....219 D4
Chatsworth Rd HG1 ....219 D4
Chatsworth Terr
2 Harrogate HG1 ....219 E4
4 York YO26 ....227 E4
Chaucer Gn HG1 ......219 F7
Chaucer St 9 YO10 ...228 E3
Chaumont Way 1 YO32 .167 D2
Chauvel Cl DL9 ....209 C2
Cheapside
2 Knaresborough HG5 ..221 B5
17 Normanton South WF6 .200 A1
11 Settle BD24 ....131 D2
Cheapsides Rd YO17 ..215 B8
Checker La YO19 ....96 F6
Chelkar Way YO30 ....224 F1
Chelmsford Rd HG1 ...219 E2
Cheltenham Ave
Ilkley LS29 ....218 E4
Middlesbrough TS7 ....7 B5

Cheltenham Cres
6 Harrogate HG1 ....219 D2
7 Harrogate HG1 ....219 D2
Cheltenham Mount
HG1 ....219 D3
Cheltenham Par HG1 ..219 D3
Cheltenham Rd 8 HG1 .219 D3
Chelwood Wlk 12 YO24 .227 E4
Chepstow Ct 10 DL1 .....3 F6
Cherry Ave
Malton YO17 ....215 D6
Swinton YO17 ....121 B4
Cherry Cl YO21 ....208 B6
Cherry Garth YO31 ....229 B5
Cherry Garth Rd DL7 ...210 C3
Cherry Gr 7 Bedale DL8 ..63 B3
2 Ilkley LS29 ....175 C2
10 Poppleton YO26 ......165 F1
Cherry Hill La YO23 ...233 B1
Cherry La YO24 ....230 F8
Cherry Orch 2 YO32 ...225 D8
Cherry Paddock
4 Haxby YO32 ....225 D8
Kexby YO41 ....168 C2
Cherry Rd 4 YO14 ....127 A8
Cherry St YO23 ....233 B1
Cherry Tree Ave
Newton-on-Ouse YO30 ..165 B6
1 Scarborough YO12 ...212 B5
York YO32 ....225 C7
Cherry Tree Cl 15 YO8 .197 D1
Cherry Tree Dr YO11 ..101 A4
Cherry Tree Gdns 7
  DL9 ....209 B1
Cherry Tree Way 14 DL9 ..41 A5
Cherry Tree Wlk
Amotherby YO17 ....121 A4
7 Barlby YO8 ....198 B4
Cherry Wood Cres
YO19 ....231 C5
Cherrytree Cl HG4 ....140 E7
Cherrywood Ave 4 TS9 .26 C8
Cherwell Croft YO8 ....196 F1
Cherwell Ct YO8 ......196 F1
Cheshire Ave YO32 ....167 A6
Cheshire Sq 8 YO7 .....89 B1
Chester-Pit La YO61 ..117 F2
Chesney Fields 4 YO24 .227 D1
Chessingham Gdns
YO24 ....230 C6
Chessingham Pk YO19 .184 F6
Chester Court Rd YO8 .204 A6
Chester La DL6 ....65 D8
Chesterton Ave TS17 ....6 A6
Chestnut Ave
2 Airmyn DN14 ....205 E4
Harrogate HG1 ....219 F3
11 Hemingbrough YO8 ..198 F1
Malton YO17 ....215 D5
Thornton Dale YO18 ....96 D6
2 Topcliffe YO7 ....89 A1
11 Topcliffe YO7 ....89 B1
Welburn YO60 ....146 E6
York YO31 ....228 F6
Chestnut Bank YO12 ..212 D6
Chestnut Cl
3 Catterick DL10 ....41 D5
3 Ilkley LS29 ....218 E3
Richmond DL10 ....209 C8
Scarborough YO12 ....212 D6
Chestnut Cres
6 Catterick Garrison DL9 .40 F5
5 Catton YO7 ....89 A1
Chestnut Croft 7 YO8 .198 F1
Chestnut Ct 9 YO8 ....198 F1
Chestnut Dr
11 Barnoldswick BB18 ..171 D1
8 Hemingbrough YO8 ..198 F1
Middlesbrough TS7 ......7 C6
Chestnut Garth 4 YO8 .198 F1
Chestnut Gr
Harrogate HG1 ....219 E6
Norton YO17 ....215 F2
York YO26 ....227 C4
Chestnut Mews 6 YO8 .197 A8
Chestnut Rd
Cawood YO8 ....197 A8
Eaglescliffe TS16 ....5 E6
Chestnut Rise 6 YO8 .198 F1
Chestnuts The
6 Haxby YO32 ....225 D8
Hensall DN14 ....203 D2
Pontefract WF8 ....201 C2
Chevin Dr YO14 ....101 A3
Cheviot Cl 1 YO32 ....225 F3
Chew La
Gargrave BD23 ....155 C1
Skipton YO12 ....99 D6
Chichester Cl 15 YO13 ..75 D5
Chieftain Rd DL10 ......40 C4
Chiltern Ave WF10 ....200 C3
Chiltern Way YO32 ...225 F5
Chilvers Ct 4 YO18 ...232 A1
Chimes Rd YO8 ....232 C6
China St DL3 ....3 D7
Chippendale Jun Sch
LS21 ....176 F1
Chippendale Rise 8
  LS21 ....177 A1
Chippenham Rd TS4 .....7 A7
Cholmley Way YO22 ..208 F3
Christ Church C of E
  BB18 ....186 A3
Christ Church Oval
HG1 ....219 C3
Christchurch C of E Prim Sch
BD23 ....216 F3
Christina St 5 HG1 ....219 C5

Christ's Hospl DL8 ......63 A1
Christy Gate Rd YO21 ...28 E4
Chubb Hill Rd YO21 ...208 D6
Chudleigh Rd
Harrogate HG1 ....219 E3
1 York YO26 ....227 F5
Church Ave
Clapham LA2 ....130 C8
Harrogate HG1 ....219 F3
3 Harrogate HG1 ......219 D5
Swillington LS26 ......194 A1
Church Balk YO19 .....184 E7
Church Bank
Aysgarth DL8 ....58 F3
Hunton DL8 ....61 F7
Kirkby Malzeard HG4 ...112 D5
Church Cl
Askham Bryan YO23 ....182 F3
Bagby YO7 ....90 C3
4 Bubwith YO8 ....199 D7
Carleton BD23 ....173 B4
10 Filey YO14 ....101 B4
1 Hambleton YO8 .....196 F1
Killinghall HG3 ....219 A8
Kirby Hill YO51 ....141 B7
Middleton St George DL2 ..4 C3
Newby & Scalby YO13 ...75 C5
Sawley HG4 ....138 E6
Sharow HG4 ....214 F7
4 Swillington LS26 ....194 A1
4 Tollerton YO61 ......143 B3
Wheldrake YO19 ......193 A7
Church Cliff Dr 9 YO14 .101 B4
Church Cres
Stutton with Hazlewood
  LS24 ....189 D4
Swillington LS26 ......194 A1
Church Croft
Barkston Ash LS24 .....195 F7
2 Brayton YO8 ....172 C8
Church Cswy LS23 ....188 F8
Church Ct 16 WF6 .....200 A1
Church Dike La YO8 ...204 F5
Church Dr
Great Ayton TS9 ....7 F1
Lockwood TS12 ....9 E7
Church End
Cawood YO8 ....197 B8
Sheriff Hutton YO60 ...145 D5
Church Farm YO7 .....211 A6
Church Farm Cl YO23 .182 C6
Church Farm View
LS15 ....194 C8
Church Fenton La
LS24 ....190 B3
Church Fenton Sta
LS24 ....196 A8
Church Field La 2
  YO26 ....164 A8
Church Field Rd YO6 ..206 E1
Church Fields 9 WF6 ..200 A1
Church Garth DL6 ....23 C3
Church Gdns LS25 ....194 C3
Church Gn 3 YO41 ....185 C2
Church Hill
4 Bramham LS23 ......188 E5
Crayke YO61 ....118 A1
10 Hunmanby YO14 ...126 F8
Hunsingore LS22 ......180 E8
Malton YO17 ....215 C4
North Rigton LS17 .....178 B3
Reighton YO14 ....127 C6
3 Selby YO8 ....232 D5
Sherburn in Elmet LS25 .195 E4
Stillingfleet YO19 ......191 D3
Thorner LS14 ....188 A3
Thornton Dale YO18 ....96 D6
8 Wistow YO8 ....197 D6
Church La
Allerston YO18 ....97 B5
Appleton Roebuck YO23 .190 F4
Aysgarth DL8 ....58 F3
Bagby YO7 ....90 C3
Barton DL10 ....21 C8
Bishopthorpe YO23 ....231 A4
Bolton Percy YO23 .....190 D4
Boroughbridge YO51 ..141 B5
Brompton YO13 ....98 C5
Broughton BD23 ....157 A8
Carlton DN14 ....204 C3
Catton YO41 ....185 D8
Cayton YO11 ....100 B6
Collingham LS22 ......180 A1
Cropton YO18 ....71 B4
Cundall with Leckby
  YO61 ....115 C3
Dunnington YO19 .....184 E7
Eislack BD23 ....172 D4
Escrick YO19 ....192 A5
Faceby TS9 ....25 F1
Fylingdales YO22 ....33 C4
Gargrave LS25 ....194 C4
Gargrave BD23 ....172 D8
Gateforth YO8 ....202 F8
Giling East YO62 ......118 F7
Guisborough TS7 ....7 E5
Guisborough TS9 ....8 A4
Guisborough TS14 ......8 F7
Hampsthwaite HG3 ....161 A6
Hebden BD23 ....135 A1
Hensall DN14 ....203 C1
Hutton Buscel YO13 ....98 F7
Ingleby Greenhow TS9 ..27 B5
Kelbrook & Sough BB18 .186 A8

Church La continued
Kellington DN14 ......202 E3
Kirby Hall YO51 ......141 A4
Kirby Hill YO51 ....141 B7
Knaresborough HG5 ...221 A6
Langtoft YO25 ....151 C5
Low Worsall TS15 ......24 A8
Marton cum Grafton
  YO51 ....138 C1
Martons Both BD23 ...172 A5
Mickklefield LS25 ......194 F4
Micklletown LS26 ......200 B5
Middlesbrough TS5 .....6 E7
Middlesbrough TS7 .....7 D7
Middleton YO18 ....95 E8
Milby YO51 ....141 B7
4 Monk Fryston LS25 ..202 A8
Moor Monkton YO26 ..165 B2
Nether Poppleton YO26 .224 B3
New Earswick YO32 ...225 D6
1 Normanton South WF6 .200 A1
North Featherstone
  WF7 ....200 E1
Pannal HG3 ....222 D4
Poppleton YO26 ......224 A3
Redmire DL8 ....59 C5
Ripon HG4 ....214 B5
Sadberge DL2 ....4 C7
Scarborough YO11 ....213 B7
6 Selby YO8 ....232 D5
Sessay YO7 ....116 C6
Settrington YO17 .....122 D1
Sinnington YO62 ....71 A1
Skelton YO30 ....224 B5
Slingsby YO62 ....120 B6
South Stainley with Cayton
  HG3 ....159 E2
9 Spofforth HG3 ....179 E6
Stainburn LS21 ....177 E3
Stainforth BD24 ......131 E6
10 Stamford Bridge YO41 .168 D2
Strensall YO32 ....167 A7
Stutton with Hazlewood
  LS24 ....189 E4
Swillington LS26 ......194 A1
Terrington YO60 ......119 F1
Thormanby YO61 .....116 F5
Thorton Dale YO18 ....96 D6
Thwing YO25 ....126 A1
Tunstall LA6 ....102 B4
Welburn YO60 ....146 E6
Weston LS21 ....176 D1
Westow YO60 ....147 B4
Wheldrake YO19 ......193 A7
Whitby YO22 ....208 E7
Whorlton DL6 ....25 D1
Wigglesworth BD23 ...153 D3
Wighill LS24 ....181 D1
Wilberfoss YO41 ......123 C4
York YO1 ....233 B2
Church Mdw 4 DL10 ....41 D5
Church Mdws 9 LS23 .188 E6
Church Mews
6 Boroughbridge YO51 ..141 B5
Sherburn in Elmet LS25 .195 F4
6 York YO26 ....227 C3
Church Rd
20 Glusburn BD20 .....187 E7
Great Preston LS26 ...200 C8
Linton BD23 ....134 E2
Pontefract WF6 ....200 A3
Scotton DL9 ....40 E4
Stainton Dale YO13 ....54 A7
Stamford Bridge YO41 .168 D2
Thornton in Craven
  BD23 ....171 F3
York YO10 ....229 D4
Church Rise YO19 ......167 F1
Church Row
Hurworth-on-Tees DL2 ...3 E1
Melsonby DL10 ....20 F7
Church Side LS26 .....200 B5
Church Sq YO21 ......208 C7
Church St
Addingham LS29 ......175 A4
Amotherby YO17 .....121 B4
Asenby YO7 ....115 B7
Barkston Ash LS24 ....195 F7
Bellerby DL8 ....60 D7
Bilton-in-Ainsty with Bickerton
  YO26 ....181 D5
Boston Spa LS23 .....188 E8
Broughton BD23 ......172 D7
Bubwith YO8 ....199 D7
Carleton BD23 ....173 B4
Copmanthorpe YO23 ..230 B2
Danby YO21 ....29 B7
Dunnington YO19 ....184 E7
6 Easingwold YO61 ..143 C8
3 Filey YO14 ....101 B3
Gargrave BD23 ......155 D1
6 Glusburn BD20 ....187 E8
Goldsborough HG5 ...163 A3
Guisborough TS14 .....8 F7
6 Helmsley YO62 .....92 F6
Heslerton YO17 ......123 E7
Ingleton LA6 ....103 D3
Kirk Hammerton YO26 .164 C2
Kirkby Malzeard HG4 ..112 D5
Knottingley WF11 ....201 E4
Long Preston BD23 ...153 F5
6 Masham HG4 ....86 C3

Church St continued
6 Middleham DL8 ......60 E2
Norton YO17 2
2 Scarborough YO11 2
Settle BD24 2
4 Skipton BD23 2
5 Staithes TS13 2
Trawden BB8 1
Ulleskelf LS24 4
Well DL8 4
West Tanfield HG4 4
Whitby YO22 2
Whixley YO26 1
York YO1 2
Church Stairs St 3 2
YO11 2
Church View
1 Brompton DL6 2
3 Brompton DL6 2
11 Hurworth DL2 3
Kirby Hill YO51 1
Ledston LS25 2
Norton DN6 2
Sherburn in Elmet LS25 ..1
South Milford LS25 2
Thirsk YO7 2
Church View Mews 7
LS23 1
Church Wind
Alne YO61 1
Burneston DL8 8
Church Wlk
Lindrick with Studley
  Royal & Fountains HG4 ..1
1 Willerby YO12 4
York YO31 2
Church Wynd DL10 2
Churchfield Dr 22 YO32 .1
Churchfield La
Castleford WF10 2
Little Smeaton DN6 2
Churchill Cl 3 TS9 ......
Churchill Way 4 BD20 ..1
Churchside Villas
LS26 1
Churchville LS25 1
Churchville Ave LS25 1
Churchville Dr LS25 1
Churchville Terr LS25 ...1
Churwell Cl WF10 2
Cinder La
Castleford WF10 2
Clifford LS23 1
Lindley LS21 1
Upper Poppleton YO26 ..1
Upper Poppleton YO26 ..2
York YO1 2
Citadilla Cl 5 DL10 ......
Clack La DL6 ....
Clapdale Dr LA2 2
Clapdale Way 5 LA2 1
Clapgate Bank DL11 ....
Clapham C E Prim Sch
LA2 1
Clapham Sta LA2 1
Clare Ave DL3 ....
Claremont 28 YO13 7
Claremont Dr TS7 ....
Claremont Gr HG3 1
Claremont La HG3 1
Claremont St 5 HG1 2
Claremont Terr YO31 ...2
Clarence Ave YO14 1
Clarence Dr Filey YO14 ..1
  Harrogate HG1 2
Clarence Pl
7 Scarborough YO11 ...2
3 Whitby YO21 2
Clarence Rd
Middlesbrough TS7 .....
Scorton DL10 ....
3 York YO7 ....
Clarence St
2 Barnoldswick BB18 ...1
6 Colne BB8 1
4 Trawden Forest BB8 ..1
York YO31 2
Clarendon Rd
Boston Spa LS23 1
Great Burdon DL1 .....
Thornaby TS17 ....
Clarendon St 16 BB8 ...1
Clareton La HG5 1
Clark Ct WF7 2
Clark St 1 YO12 2
Clarkson Cl 4 HG5 2
Clarkson Ct LS25 2
Clarkson St 7 YO21 2
Claro Ave HG1 2
Claro Mews 4 HG5 2
Claro Pk HG1 2
Claro Rd
Harrogate HG1 2
Ripon HG4 2
Claro Way HG1 2
Claude Ave TS5 ....
Claver Cl DL6 ....
Clavery Ley La YO62 ...
Claxton Ave DL3 ....
Clay Hill YO41 1
Clay La Bubwith YO8 ...1
Ragdale BD23 1
Camblesforth YO8 2
Cliffe YO8 1
Clay Pit La YO51 1
Clay Pl 3 YO24 2

gate YO31 .....229 B6
rpenny Hospl 117 D1
rpit La
ston DN14 .....204 C3
ston WF10 .....201 A8
East Ayton/West Ayton
YO13 .....99 B8
rton Hall Rd BD20 .....187 F7
rton Mews 8 WF6 .....200 A2
rton Pl 9 WF6 .....200 A2
rton Rd 7 BB18 .....171 E1
asby La DL2 .....2 F1
asby Way TS16 .....5 D6
ment St 4 YO23 .....233 B1
menthorpe YO23 .....233 B1
wedon House Sch 176 A1
regate TS7 .....7 C5
reland Ave
rlington DL3 .....3 C5
ttingley WF11 .....201 F2
bley YO12 .....212 D8
kesley TS9 .....26 C8
reland Coll of Art &
.sign TS5 .....6 E8
reland Dr DL7 .....210 D2
reland Rd Boltby YO7 .....91 B8
terick Garrison DL9 .....40 F4
rborough YO12 .....212 E6
rton DL10 .....41 F7
reland Rein
port YO7 .....66 A3
reland Terr DL3 .....3 B5
reland Trad Est DL3 .....3 B6
reland Way 1 TS9 .....25 F1
reland Way
Carlton Miniott YO7 .....89 C4
k YO32 .....225 F3
6 Bridge Pl 6 YO11 .....213 A5
7 Bridge Terr 8 .....213 A5
Brow TS13 .....11 C7
Cres LS25 .....194 E1
Dr 24 DL8 .....60 D5
Gate Rd DL11 .....35 E4
Hill Rd DN6 .....206 D2
La
vholm-cum-Dunsley 13 B2
YO13 .....97 F5
twell-on-the-Hill 146 E4
ton YO18 .....97 A5
relton YO18 .....95 B8
ord 188 D8
ord Rd
boss La LS23 .....188 F8
ey LS29 .....218 A6
ord St
Barnoldswick BB18 .....171 E1
Skipton BD23 .....216 F3
k YO1 .....233 B2
ord's Terr 9 YO14 .....101 B3
prds Twr* YO1 .....233 B1
on Ave TS18 .....5 E6
on Dale YO18 .....228 A6
on La LS21 .....176 F3
on Moor Gate 225 A2
on Moor Ret Pk 224 E3
on Moorgate 225 B3
on Pl 3 YO30 .....228 A7
on Prep Sch 233 A4
on Rd Darlington DL1 .....3 D4
ey LS29 .....218 D3
k YO30 .....233 A4
on St Earby BB18 .....186 A8
Scarborough YO12 .....212 F6
wden Forest BB8 .....186 A1
on Without Jun Sch 227 F8
t Bank HG3 .....160 E6
t Bank La HG3 .....160 F6
t Garth HG2 .....160 F8
t La
heroe St 8 BD23 .....216 D3
e Gr YO24 .....227 F2
e Rd 1 HG3 .....179 E6
t Twr* HG4 .....214 C6
hill Field La 163 F3
kwood Gdns TS16 .....5 E5
e Garth La BD23 .....172 D3
ggerby Rigg DL11 .....35 F5
sters The
Hemingbrough YO8 .....198 F1
aerfoss YO41 .....185 F6
k YO31 .....233 C3
sters Wlk YO31 .....233 C3
e Rd BD22 .....187 B5
e Rd WF10 .....200 F4
e The
wick in Elmet LS15 .....194 B7

Close The continued
Boroughbridge YO51 .....141 A3
Boston Spa LS23 .....188 E8
Cawood YO8 .....197 A7
6 Collingham LS22 .....188 A8
East Ayton/West Ayton
YO13 .....99 B8
4 Fylingdales YO22 .....33 D4
Hunmanby Sands YO14 .....101 C1
Longnewton TS21 .....4 F7
Neasham DL2 .....4 A1
Northallerton DL7 .....210 B2
Norton DN6 .....206 E2
Riccall YO19 .....198 A8
Scalby YO12 .....212 B8
Skipton BD23 .....216 E4
Studley Roger HG4 .....113 D1
Thirsk YO7 .....211 C1
Thorner LS14 .....188 A3
Thornton Dale YO18 .....96 D5
Towton LS24 .....189 E2
York YO30 .....227 F8
Clotherholme Rd HG4 .....214 A5
Clough La DN6 .....207 B2
Clover Hill BD23 .....217 B5
Clover Way 1 HG3 .....161 B3
Cloverley Cl YO41 .....168 C2
Clowbeck St DL3 .....3 B8
Coach La
10 Hurworth-on-Tees DL2 .....3 E1
Lindley LS21 .....177 D3
Coach Rd
Harrogate HG1 .....219 F2
Sheriff Hutton YO60 .....145 D4
Sleights YO22 .....32 A6
Coach St BD23 .....216 F4
Coach Street Yd 10
BD23 .....216 F4
Coachman's Ct 6 HG2 .....220 B1
Coal Pit La
Kirk Smeaton WF8 .....206 A2
Rimington BB7 .....171 A1
Coalmine La DL6 .....66 C2
Coarse La HG3 .....159 A4
Coastal Rd YO13 .....75 D7
Coastguard Hill YO14 .....127 E5
Coates Ave BB18 .....171 E2
Coates Fields BB18 .....171 E2
Coates La
Barnoldswick BB18 .....171 E2
Kettlewell with Starbotton
BD23 .....107 F5
Coates Lane Inf Sch
BB18 .....171 E2
Coates Marsh La
DN14 .....204 B2
Coatham Ave DL2 .....4 D3
Coatham La TS21 .....5 B7
Cob Castle* DL8 .....63 B1
Cob La BB18 .....186 A6
Cobble Carr TS14 .....8 E6
Cobble La WF8 .....201 C1
Cobbler's La WF8 .....201 C1
Cobblers Lane Inf Sch
WF8 .....201 D1
Cobby Syke Rd HG3 .....159 F1
Cobcroft La WF11 .....206 B8
Cobden St
Barnoldswick BB18 .....171 D1
Darlington DL1 .....3 E5
Thornaby TS17 .....6 B8
Coble La YO60 .....145 D5
Cobshaw La DL8 .....62 F6
Cochrane St YO8 .....232 D3
Cock Garth YO17 .....122 D1
Cock La Gainford DL2 .....1 E8
Piercebridge DL2 .....2 A7
Cock Lodge (site of)*
YO7 .....115 C6
Cockburn St 5 TS12 .....9 F7
Cocked Hat YO14 .....139 C8
Cockerhill La YO62 .....93 E7
Cockerton C of E Prim Sch
DL3 .....3 A6
Cockerton Gn DL3 .....3 B6
Cockhill La BB8 .....186 A4
Cocking La LS29 .....174 E3
Cocklakes La YO7 .....114 F1
Cockmoor Rd YO13 .....74 A1
Cockpit Cl HG4 .....113 C7
Cockrah Rd YO13 .....74 F2
Cockret Cl 8 YO8 .....232 B6
Cockret Ct YO8 .....232 B7
Cockret Rd YO8 .....232 B7
Cockshaw Bank La
HG4 .....113 B4
Cockshott Pl 5 LS29 .....174 F4
Coda Ave YO23 .....231 B3
Codlin Rd 1 TS15 .....25 C5
Coeside YO24 .....230 B7
Coggan Way YO23 .....230 F4
Colber La YO23 .....138 F2
Colbert Ave LS29 .....218 E5
Colburn CP Sch YO7 .....41 A5
Colburn Dr DL9 .....40 F5
Colburn La DL9 .....40 F6
Colburn Sidings DL9 .....40 F4
Cold Bath Pl HG2 .....219 C1
Cold Bath Rd HG2 .....222 C8
Cold Cotes Rd HG3 .....160 B4
Cold Kirby Rd YO7 .....91 C8
Coldhill La LS25 .....195 C6
Coldie Hill 11 TS15 .....25 C5
Coldstone La YO7 .....88 B2
Coldyhill La YO12 .....212 B8
Cole St YO21 .....233 B4
Coledale Cl 2 YO30 .....224 F1

Colenso St YO23 .....233 B1
Coleridge Dr HG1 .....219 E7
Coleridge Gdns DL1 .....3 D3
Coleridge Way 1 WF8 .....201 B1
Colescliffe Cres YO13 .....212 C8
Colescliffe Rd YO12 .....212 C8
Colin St BB18 .....171 D2
Coll of St John The
YO31 .....233 B3
College Ave YO11 .....213 A2
College Ct
1 Low Bradley BD20 .....173 E3
4 Scarborough YO11 .....212 F4
College Farm Cl YO14 .....207 A8
College Farm La S LS22 .....180 A2
College Gr WF10 .....200 D3
College La
Bradleys Both BD20 .....173 E3
5 Masham HG4 .....86 C3
Scarborough YO11 .....213 A1
College of Law YO23 .....231 B7
College of Ripon & York St
Johns
York YO30 .....229 B3
York YO31 .....233 B3
College Rd
Bradleys Both BD20 .....173 E3
Copmanthorpe YO23 .....230 A3
Harrogate HG2 .....222 B8
Ripon HG4 .....214 B6
College St
Harrogate HG2 .....222 B8
York YO1 .....233 B3
Colley Broach Rd
YO61 .....117 F7
Collier Hag La YO23 .....182 B3
Collier La
Lotherton cum Aberford
LS25 .....195 A6
West Layton DL11 .....20 A8
Colliergate YO1 .....233 B2
Collin Bank YO13 .....75 A7
Collin Bank HG3 .....160 E6
Collinge Rd 8 BD22 .....187 B6
Collingham Way 12
YO14 .....101 A3
Collingwood Ave
YO24 .....227 F2
Collingwood Gdns
YO17 .....215 A3
Collin's Hill HG3 .....223 D7
Collinson La YO12 .....122 F5
Colliwath La DL8 .....60 F4
Colne & Broughton Rd
BD23 .....172 C4
Colne Rd
Cowling BD22 .....187 A5
Earby BB18 .....172 A1
Kelbrook & Sough BB18 .....186 A8
Sutton BD20 .....187 C7
Trawden Forest BB8 .....186 A1
Colonel's Wlk 8 WF8 .....201 B1
Colorado Way 11 WF10 .....200 F2
Colstan Rd DL6 .....210 E3
Colton Junc LS24 .....190 E7
Colton La LS24 .....190 E6
Columbine Gr 26 HG2 .....161 B3
Columbus Ravine
YO12 .....212 F7
Colville Cres 8 DL9 .....41 A5
Colville Rd 7 DL9 .....41 A5
Comfort La DL10 .....20 C5
Comfrey Cl 22 HG3 .....161 B3
Comfrey Manor TS8 .....7 B4
Commercial St
9 Barnoldswick BB18 .....171 D1
Harrogate HG1 .....219 D3
Norton YO17 .....215 D3
Scarborough YO12 .....212 E5
12 Settle BD24 .....131 E2
Tadcaster LS24 .....189 E6
Commercial Yd 1 HG5 .....221 B5
Common Balk La YO7 .....140 A3
Common Croft La
YO26 .....165 C1
Common Holme La
LS29 .....175 C3
Common La Bean DN14 .....202 D3
Burn YO8 .....203 E7
Carlton Husthwaite YO7 .....116 F8
Catton YO41 .....185 E8
Coverham with Agglethorpe
DL8 .....60 A2
Dunnington YO19 .....184 F5
Fangfoss YO41 .....169 B1
Glaisdale YO21 .....29 F1
Hambleton YO8 .....196 F1
Harome YO62 .....93 E5
Hartley CA17 .....14 A8
Knottingley WF11 .....202 B1
Norton DN6 .....206 E2
Scruton DL7 .....63 F7
South Milford LS25 .....195 C8
Sutton upon Derwent
YO41 .....193 C8
Temple Hirst YO8 .....203 F4
Thorganby YO19 .....192 F5
Ulleskelf LS24 .....190 C2
Walden Stubbs DN6 .....206 F4
Warthill YO19 .....167 F2
West Morton DL8 .....59 F2
York YO10 .....229 B1
Common Rd
Barkston Ash LS24 .....195 F7
Church Fenton LS24 .....196 A7

Common Rd continued
Dunnington YO19 .....184 F7
Skipwith YO8 .....192 E1
Strensall YO60 .....145 D1
Commondale Sta YO21 .....9 E1
Compton La LS23 .....188 A7
Compton St YO30 .....228 A6
Conan Dr DL10 .....209 D8
Conan Gdns DL10 .....209 D8
Concorde Pk YO30 .....225 A3
Concorde Way TS18 .....5 F7
Coney Moor Gr LS26 .....200 C6
Coney St YO1 .....233 B2
Coneycroft 1 YO19 .....184 F7
Coneygarth La
Dunnington YO19 .....184 E5
Tunstall LA6 .....102 A4
Conference Cl YO17 .....215 B4
Conifer Cl 6 YO32 .....225 D3
Conifers Cl 2 YO8 .....197 D1
Coniscliffe Mews DL3 .....3 A4
Coniscliffe Rd DL3 .....3 A4
Coniston Ave BB18 .....171 D2
Coniston Cl 7 YO30 .....224 E1
Coniston Dr
Castleford WF10 .....201 C4
York YO10 .....229 B4
Coniston Gdns 6 YO12 .....99 F7
Coniston Gr
1 Colne BB8 .....186 A3
Middlesbrough TS5 .....6 E7
York HG1 .....220 B4
Coniston Way
8 Eastfield YO11 .....99 F7
Thirsk YO7 .....89 C4
Conistone La BD23 .....108 B3
Connaught Rd
Ilkley LS29 .....218 D3
Middlesbrough TS7 .....7 D6
Connaught Way YO32 .....225 F6
Cononley La BD20 .....173 D1
Cononley Prim Sch
BD20 .....173 D2
Cononley Rd BD20 .....187 D8
Cononley Sta BD20 .....173 D1
Conowl Cl 2 YO62 .....92 F6
Conroy Cl 11 YO61 .....143 D8
Consort St BD23 .....217 B4
Constable Burton Hall*
DL8 .....61 C6
Constable Rd
Hunmanby YO14 .....127 A8
Ilkley LS29 .....218 D3
Constable Ridge Rd
HG3 .....160 B2
Constantine Ave
10 Copmanthorpe YO23 .....41 A5
York YO10 .....229 A4
Constantine Gr 11 DL9 .....41 A5
Constitution Hill 3
BD24 .....131 E2
Conway Cl YO30 .....224 E3
Conway Cres BB18 .....171 E1
Conyers Ave DL3 .....3 A6
Conyers Cl DL10 .....209 D8
Conyers Ings YO11 .....99 A7
Conyers La DL7 .....22 E2
Conyers Rd DL7 .....22 E2
Conyers St TS15 .....5 E2
Cookgate TS7 .....7 C5
Cooks Cl 2 DL6 .....45 A7
Cooks Gdns 3 YO13 .....75 D5
Cook's Row 5 YO11 .....213 B6
Coolham La BB18 .....186 B6
Coombe Dr DL1 .....3 F6
Coombes Cl YO61 .....144 C3
Coomboots Brow YO13 .....75 A6
Cooper Cl DL6 .....25 D2
Cooper La
Blubberhouses LS21 .....159 C1
Potto DL6 .....25 D2
Cooper Lane Shepherd
LS21 .....159 C2
3 Cooper Rd 12 YO14 .....101 B3
Coopers Dr YO23 .....230 B3
Cosgrove La HG5 .....162 D8
Cosgrove Rd HG1 .....140 A2
Cophill La YO7 .....66 A4
Copley La LS25 .....195 B7
Copmanroyd LS21 .....177 A2
Copmanthorpe Jun Sch
YO23 .....230 B3
Copmanthorpe La
YO23 .....230 B3
Copmanthorpe Prim Sch
YO23 .....230 B3
Copmanthorpe Recn Ctr &
Sports Club YO23 .....230 B2
Copper Beeches The 2
YO19 .....184 E7
Coppergate Wlk HG1 .....117 D1
Copperfield Cl YO17 .....215 C5
Coppergate
1 Riccall YO19 .....191 F1
York YO1 .....233 B2
Coppergate Wlk YO1 .....233 B2
Coppertop Mews 4
WF8 .....201 C2
Coppice Ave HG1 .....219 C4
10 Haxby YO32 .....166 E5
Coppice Cl
Harrogate HG1 .....219 C4
Coppice Dr HG1 .....219 C3
Coppice Gate HG1 .....219 C4
Coppice La HG1 .....71 B1
Coppice Rise HG1 .....219 C5

Coppice The
Barwick in Elmet LS15 .....194 B7
Bishopthorpe YO23 .....230 F4
Brayton YO8 .....197 C1
Ilkley LS29 .....218 A6
Leeming DL7 .....63 F3
14 Sherburn in Elmet LS25 .....195 F4
5 Sutton BD20 .....187 E7
Coppice Valley CP Sch
HG1 .....219 C5
Coppice Valley Pool
HG1 .....219 D4
Coppice View HG1 .....219 D4
Coppice Way HG1 .....219 C5
Copsy La
Cononley BD20 .....173 C2
Sutton BD20 .....187 E4
Copsy Rd LS29 .....174 F4
Copsy Wood Dr LS29 .....218 B2
Copse Hill 1 YO14 .....101 A4
Copse The
3 North Featherstone
WF7 .....200 E1
4 Scarborough YO12 .....212 B5
Copsewood Wlk BD19 .....26 C8
Copwood Gr 7 YO32 .....225 C8
Corban La YO32 .....166 B6
Corban Way 21 YO32 .....166 D5
Corber Hill 7 DL6 .....43 F3
Corbie Way YO18 .....96 A7
Corby Ave TS5 .....6 E7
Cordike La
Birdsall YO17 .....148 D6
Langton YO17 .....147 F6
Cordilleras La DL11 .....39 C8
Corn Mill Gdns YO12 .....212 D7
Corn Mill La 30 LS29 .....176 D1
Cornbell Gate 4 HG4 .....113 D2
Cornborough Av YO31 .....228 F6
Cornborough Rd
YO60 .....145 C3
Cornel Rise 28 HG3 .....161 B3
Cornelian Ave YO11 .....100 B8
Cornelian Cl
1 Scarborough YO11 .....100 B8
Scarborough YO11 .....213 C1
Cornelian Dr
2 Scarborough YO11 .....100 B8
Scarborough YO11 .....213 C1
Cornelius Cswy YO8 .....198 E8
Corner Cl 2 YO62 .....166 D5
Cornfield Rd TS17 .....6 A8
Cornflower Way 1 HG3 .....161 B3
Cornforth Hill DL10 .....209 B6
Cornlands YO17 .....215 D2
Cornlands Rd YO24 .....227 B1
Cornmill Cl YO8 .....197 B8
Cornwall Ave
Darlington DL1 .....3 E6
Silsden BD20 .....174 B1
Cornwall Dr YO10 .....231 E8
Cornwall Rd HG1 .....219 B2
Cornwood Way 11 YO32 .....225 C8
Coronation Ave
6 Colburn DL9 .....41 A5
Harrogate HG2 .....222 F7
3 Hinderwell TS13 .....11 F7
Coronation Gr HG2 .....222 F7
Coronation Hospl
LS29 .....218 C3
Coronation Pl DL10 .....209 A7
Coronation Rd
Crakehall DL8 .....62 E5
Harrogate HG2 .....222 F7
Coronation St 8 BB18 .....171 E1
Corporation Rd DL3 .....3 C6
Corpse Rd
North Otterington DL7 .....64 E5
Thornton-le-Moor DL6 .....65 A4
Cosmo Ave YO31 .....229 A5
Costa La YO18 .....95 D6
Costa Way YO18 .....95 F7
Cotchers La LS24 .....195 D8
Cotcliffe Bank DL6 .....65 C5
Cote Hill Rd HG3 .....160 B4
Cote La Healey HG4 .....85 D5
Sproxton YO62 .....92 C4
Cotescue Bank DL8 .....60 C1
Cotswold Dr LS25 .....194 C3
Cotswold Way YO23 .....226 A5
Cottage Cl DL6 .....210 E5
Cottage La YO60 .....145 C4
Cottagers La DL2 .....2 C3
Cottam La LS25 .....151 C5
Cotterdale Cl HG5 .....221 C6
Cotterdale Holt 9 LS22 .....180 A1
Cottom La YO8 .....204 D4
Cotton Tree La BB8 .....186 A3
Coulby Farm Way TS8 .....7 A5
Coulby La YO18 .....97 A6
Coulby Manor Way TS8 .....6 F5
Coulby Newham Sec Sch
TS8 .....7 A5
Coulson Cl 6 YO32 .....167 C8
Coulter Beck La LA6 .....102 D7
Coulthurst Craven Sports Ctr
The BD23 .....216 F3
Coulton La YO62 .....119 A6
Count Be Durgh Terr 4
YO23 .....228 B1

Coupland Rd
Garforth LS25 ....194 C4
1 Selby YO8 ....232 C6
Courby Hill HG4 ....86 F7
Courcey Gr YO26 ....227 C4
Court Dr YO8 ....232 A4
Court Green Cl YO13 ....54 D1
Court La BD23 ....217 A4
Court Moor La YO62 ....70 A4
Court The 6 DL8 ....63 A2
Courtneys Selby YO8 ....232 B4
Wheldrake YO19 ....193 A8
Courts Cl 7 DN14 ....205 E4
Courtyard The
Bishopthorpe YO23 ....231 B4
11 Pontefract WF8 ....201 C2
Coutances Way LS29 ....218 F5
Cove Rd BD23 ....132 F2
Cover La
Carlton Town DL8 ....83 E7
Marton-le-Moor HG4 ....114 E1
Coverdale Dr
1 Knaresborough HG5 ....221 A7
Scarborough YO12 ....212 B4
Coverdale Garth 2
LS22 ....188 A8
Coverdale La TS13 ....12 A4
Coverham Abbey (rems of) *
DL8 ....60 C2
Coverham La DL7 ....210 C2
Coverham La DL8 ....60 C1
Covert The
9 Topcliffe YO7 ....89 B1
York YO24 ....230 F7
Cow & Calf Rocks*
LS29 ....218 D2
Cow Close La
Kirkby Malham BD23 ....154 E8
Lockwood TS12 ....10 B8
Cow Gate La BD23 ....171 B7
Cow La Cowling BD22 ....187 B6
Knottingley WF11 ....202 A2
Lothersdale BD20 ....172 F1
Middleton Tyas DL10 ....21 E5
Womersley DN6 ....206 D6
Cow Pasture La YO42 ....193 C3
Cow Wath Bank YO22 ....51 E8
Cow Wath Cl 30 YO12 ....75 D5
Cowbar Bank 1 TS13 ....13 K2
Cowbar La TS13 ....13 J2
Cowcliff Hill YO17 ....148 F6
Cowgarth La 1 BB18 ....172 B1
Cowgill St 7 BB18 ....172 A1
Cowhouse Bank YO62 ....68 F3
Cowie Dr YO8 ....232 D5
Cowland La YO7 ....88 D3
Cowley Cl TS16 ....5 E7
Cowley Rd TS5 ....6 E7
Cowling Hill La BD22 ....186 F7
Cowling La DL8 ....62 D3
Cowling Prim Sch
BD22 ....187 A6
Cowling Rd DL8 ....62 D2
Cowlings Cl 16 YO14 ....127 A8
Cowpasture Rd LS29 ....218 C3
Cowper La YO23 ....191 C8
Cowper St 8 BD23 ....217 A3
Cowton Castle* DL7 ....22 C1
Cowton La YO14 ....127 C6
Cowton Way TS16 ....5 D6
Coxlea Gr YO13 ....54 D1
Coxwold Dr DL1 ....3 D4
Coxwold Hill 8 LS22 ....180 C4
Coxwold Pottery*
YO61 ....117 D8
Coxwold View 1 LS22 ....180 C3
Crab La Harrogate HG1 ....219 D6
Seamer YO12 ....99 E6
Crab Tree La WF8 ....206 A1
Crabmill La YO61 ....143 D8
Crabtree Gn LS22 ....188 A8
Crabtree Gr 1 YO32 ....225 D3
Crabtree Hill LS22 ....188 A8
Cracoe Prim Sch
BD23 ....156 B6
Cradley Dr TS5 ....6 E6
Crag Bank YO20 ....28 B8
Crag Cl 6 BD20 ....187 E7
Crag Gdns LS23 ....188 E5
Crag Hill La HG3 ....161 B6
Crag Hill Rd YO13 ....53 F8
Crag La
Bradleys Both BD20 ....173 E2
Felliscliffe HG3 ....160 D4
Huby LS17 ....178 B2
Killinghall HG3 ....161 B1
Killinghall HG3 ....161 C1
Knaresborough HG5 ....221 B5
North Rigton LS17 ....178 B3
Pannal HG3 ....178 C8
Sutton BD20 ....187 D6
Crag Side Rd DL8 ....57 B2
Crag The 8 LS22 ....188 E5
Crag View
Cononley BD20 ....173 D1
Threshfield BD23 ....134 B3
Weeton LS17 ....178 B2
Crag View Rd BD20 ....217 B3
Cragdale 18 BD24 ....131 D2
Cragdale Rise 1 HG5 ....221 D6
Cragg Bottom Rd
BD22 ....187 C1
Cragg Dr LS29 ....218 C3
Cragg Hill Rd BD24 ....105 C3
Cragg La LA2 ....130 C4

Craggs La
Arrathorne DL10 ....41 A1
Tatham LA2 ....129 A3
Craig St DL3 ....3 C6
Craiglands Pk LS29 ....218 C5
Craiglands Rd LS29 ....218 C3
Craigmore Dr LS29 ....218 E4
Craigs Way YO7 ....211 C4
Crake La HG3 ....159 F6
Crakehall C of E Prim Sch
DL8 ....62 E4
Cranberry TS8 ....7 B5
Cranbrook Ave YO26 ....227 C5
Cranbrook Rd YO26 ....227 C5
Cranbrooks The YO19 ....192 F8
Cranfield Pl 4 YO24 ....230 C8
Cranford Gdns TS5 ....6 D8
Crank La DL7 ....63 B7
Crankley La YO61 ....143 B7
Cranwell Gr TS17 ....6 B6
Craven Bank La BD24 ....131 B3
Craven Coll BD23 ....131 D2
Craven Cres 3 LS29 ....174 F4
Craven Ct
Cowling BD22 ....187 C6
Northallerton DL7 ....210 B3
Richmond DL10 ....209 B6
Silsden BD20 ....174 C1
Craven Dr BD20 ....174 C1
Craven Garth 3 DN14 ....202 D4
Craven Mus* BD23 ....217 A4
Craven Ridge La BD24 ....131 B3
Craven Ridge La Ends
BD24 ....131 B3
Craven St 8 Colne BB8 ....186 A3
Harrogate HG1 ....219 D4
Scarborough YO11 ....213 A4
Skipton BD23 ....216 F3
Craven Way
6 Boroughbridge YO51 ....141 B4
Dent LA10 ....78 B8
Cravendale Rd 8 DL9 ....40 F5
Cravengate DL10 ....209 B6
Craven's Hill YO13 ....54 C3
Crawford Cl YO26 ....181 C7
Crawley Way YO31 ....229 B6
Cray Thorns Cres YO7 ....115 A4
Crayke C of E Prim Sch
YO61 ....117 F1
Crayke Castle* YO61 ....117 F1
Crayke La YO61 ....117 F2
Crayke Manor* YO61 ....117 F2
Crescent Ave YO21 ....208 C7
Crescent Back Rd 8
YO11 ....213 A5
Crescent Ct LS29 ....218 B4
Crescent Gdns HG1 ....219 C2
Crescent Hill 2 YO14 ....101 B3
Crescent Par 4 LS29 ....214 C6
Crescent Rd
Harrogate HG1 ....219 C2
Ripon HG4 ....214 B6
Crescent The
18 Bedale DL8 ....63 B3
Burton Fleming YO25 ....126 E3
Carlton TS9 ....26 A2
Eaglescliffe TS16 ....5 D4
Filey YO14 ....101 B3
Garforth LS25 ....194 D4
2 Hartwith cum Winsley
HG3 ....138 A1
17 Helmsley YO62 ....92 F6
Ilkley LS29 ....218 A4
Kelfield YO19 ....191 D1
Kexby YO41 ....185 C5
Kippax LS25 ....194 D1
Micklefield LS25 ....195 A3
Middlesbrough TS7 ....7 D6
Middleton St George DL2 ....4 C4
North Rigton LS17 ....178 B3
Northallerton DL6 ....210 E4
Otley LS21 ....177 A1
6 Riccall YO19 ....197 F8
Richmond DL10 ....209 D7
Ripon HG4 ....214 B6
Scalby YO12 ....212 B7
Scarborough YO11 ....213 A5
Sicklinghall LS22 ....179 E3
Stainton Dale YO13 ....54 A8
Stamford Bridge YO41 ....168 D2
Thornaby TS17 ....6 B8
Thornton Dale YO18 ....96 D5
York YO24 ....233 A1
Crest Hill LS26 ....194 A1
Crest The LS26 ....194 A1
Crestbrooke DL7 ....210 D3
Crestholme Cl 6 HG5 ....221 D5
Crewe Rd WF10 ....201 B4
Creyke View DN14 ....205 A1
Crichton Ave YO30 ....228 B8
Cricket La TS6 ....7 F8
Cricketers Way 8 LS25 ....195 F4
Cridling Gdns DN6 ....206 F2
Crimple Ave LS22 ....180 A8
Crimple La HG3 ....223 D7
Crimple Mdws HG3 ....222 D3
Crinan Ct
Pontefract WF6 ....200 A2
3 York YO32 ....225 F6
Cringle Carr La DL7 ....65 B3
Cringle Moor Chase
TS9 ....26 F4
Cringles La DL8 ....174 C4
Cringley La DL8 ....57 E5
Crocus Ct 5 DL9 ....41 A5
Croft Ave
8 Knottingley WF11 ....202 A3

Croft Ave continued
Middlesbrough TS5 ....6 D8
4 Normanton South WF6 ....200 B2
Otley LS21 ....176 F1
Croft C of E Prim Sch
DL2 ....22 C8
Croft Cl
Carlton Husthwaite YO7 ....116 F7
14 Easingwold YO61 ....143 C8
Ingleton LA6 ....103 D3
Croft Ct YO23 ....231 A4
Croft Dr LS23 ....188 E6
Croft Farm Cl YO23 ....230 B3
Croft Gdns YO21 ....211 B1
Croft Head Terr 2
BD20 ....187 E7
Croft Heads YO7 ....211 B1
Croft Hill Carthorpe DL8 ....87 E2
22 Glusburn BD20 ....187 E7
Croft Hills TS9 ....26 A2
Croft House Dr 8 LS21 ....176 F1
Croft House Fold 10
LS29 ....175 A4
Croft House La YO23 ....135 A1
Croft La
Carlton Husthwaite YO7 ....116 F8
Newton kyme cum Toulston
LS24 ....189 B7
Snainton YO13 ....97 F5
Walton LS23 ....181 A2
Croft Motor Racing Circuit*
DL2 ....22 C5
Croft Rd
Bramham cum Oglethorpe
LS23 ....188 E6
Camblesforth YO8 ....204 D4
Catterick Garrison DL9 ....209 C1
Eaglescliffe TS16 ....5 D4
Hurworth DL2 ....3 B2
Ingleton LA6 ....103 D3
Croft St 12 Earby BB18 ....172 B1
6 Glusburn BD20 ....187 E7
Crofters Gn HG3 ....219 A8
Croftlands YO7 ....211 B1
Crofts Ave
4 Pickering YO18 ....96 A6
Richmond DL10 ....209 B7
Crofts The
1 Glusburn BD20 ....173 F1
1 Sutton BD20 ....187 E6
Croftside 1 YO26 ....227 B3
Croftway
Barwick in Elmet LS15 ....194 C8
Camblesforth YO8 ....204 C5
Selby YO8 ....232 C4
Sherburn in Elmet LS25 ....195 F4
2 York YO26 ....227 B3
Crombie Ave YO30 ....228 B7
Cromer St YO30 ....228 B7
Cromwell Ave 22 YO14 ....101 B3
Cromwell Cl 5 WF11 ....201 E4
Cromwell Cres 6 WF8 ....201 C1
Cromwell Dr DL7 ....64 A6
Cromwell Gdns 6 YO11 ....212 F4
Cromwell Par 5 YO11 ....212 F4
Cromwell Rd
Harrogate HG2 ....222 E7
Scarborough YO11 ....212 F4
Cromwell Rise LS25 ....200 D8
Cromwell St 8 BD23 ....217 A3
Cromwell Terr 7 YO11 ....212 F4
Crook Bank La DL11 ....38 F6
Crook La HG4 ....85 E5
Crooked La YO26 ....164 C2
Crookland La YO32 ....166 F5
Croom Medieval Village*
YO25 ....150 A4
Croome Dale La YO17 ....150 C6
Croome Rd YO25 ....150 B4
Cropstones LS23 ....188 F5
Cropton La YO18 ....71 B2
Cropton Rise YO12 ....212 B4
Cropton Way TS8 ....7 B5
Crosby Rd DL6 ....210 E4
Crosby St DL3 ....3 C7
Crosland Cl 22 YO62 ....92 F6
Cross Bank BD23 ....217 F6
Cross End Fold 3 LS29 ....175 A4
Cross Gate YO13 ....75 D5
Cross Haw La 8 LA2 ....130 C8
Cross Head Bank DL8 ....60 D7
Cross Hill
Fairburn WF11 ....201 D6
Sutton-under-Whitestonecliffe
YO7 ....90 D5
Cross Hills La YO8 ....232 A5
Cross La Bentham LA2 ....128 E8
Brompton YO13 ....98 C5
Burneston DL8 ....87 D3
Burniston YO13 ....75 D7
Farndale East YO62 ....48 E4
Flaxton YO60 ....167 E8

Cross continued
Fulford YO19 ....231 F5
Giggleswick BD24 ....130 F2
Great Ouseburn YO26 ....164 B8
Little Ayton TS9 ....26 A2
Pickhill with Roxby YO7 ....88 C6
Scalby YO12 ....212 C8
Sinnington YO62 ....95 A8
Snainton YO13 ....97 F3
Stonebeck Up HG3 ....110 B5
Cross Lane Hospl
YO12 ....212 D8
Cross Lanes DL10 ....209 E7
Cross Queen St 9 WF6 ....200 A1
Cross Rd LA2 ....128 E7
Cross Rein Bank DL7 ....23 A1
Cross Row Boosbeck TS12 ....9 E7
Swillington LS15 ....194 A3
Cross St 6 Cowling BD22 ....187 B6
14 Earby BB18 ....172 A1
Scarborough YO11 ....213 A4
Skipton BD23 ....216 F3
5 York YO24 ....227 C3
Cross The LS15 ....194 B8
Cross Top DL8 ....57 E7
Crossbeck Cl 2 LS21 ....218 B3
Crossbeck Rd
Ilkley LS29 ....218 B3
Northallerton DL6 ....210 F5
Crossbeck Way TS7 ....7 D8
Crosscliff TS8 ....6 F5
Crossdale Rd YO18 ....72 E3
Crossfield Cl HG3 ....223 F1
Crossfield Cres YO19 ....231 E6
Crossfields TS8 ....7 A4
Crossgate La
22 Pickering YO18 ....95 F6
18 Pickering YO18 ....96 A6
Crossgates HG3 ....138 B5
Crosshill La DN14 ....207 E6
Crosshills Rd BD20 ....173 D1
Crossings The 8 DN14 ....205 E4
Crosslands Rd 2 YO10 ....231 E8
Crossley Pl BD23 ....216 F4
Crossley St 8 LS22 ....180 C3
Crossman Dr 2 WF6 ....200 B2
Crossmoor La YO32 ....166 E6
Crossway The
Darlington DL1 ....3 F7
2 York YO31 ....228 E8
Crossways YO10 ....229 C2
Crossways Cres HG2 ....220 D3
Crossways Dr HG2 ....220 D2
Crossways The LS17 ....177 A1
Crow Hill La HG3 ....160 D4
Crow Nest Rd LA2 ....130 F6
Crowberry Dr HG3 ....161 B3
Crowdy Cl YO22 ....208 E4
Crowfoot La DL6 ....43 D5
Crowgarth HG4 ....140 D7
Crown Cres YO11 ....213 A4
Crown Gr YO17 ....215 E3
Crown Sq 24 YO62 ....70 B1
Crown St
34 Burley in Warfedale
LS29 ....176 C1
Darlington DL1 ....3 D3
Crown Terr YO11 ....213 A4
Crowood Ave TS9 ....26 C8
Crowtrees LA2 ....128 E6
Crummack La LA2 ....130 E8
Crummock 3 YO24 ....230 C7
Cuddy Brown Cl 7 YO18 ....96 A6
Cuddy La DL6 ....45 B4
Culvert La BD23 ....216 A4
Cumberland Cl 8 YO32 ....167 B6
Cumberland Gdns
DL10 ....21 C4
Cumberland Rd WF10 ....201 C5
Cumberland St
6 Skipton BD23 ....216 F3
York YO1 ....233 B2
Cumbernauld Rd TS17 ....6 C7
Cumbrian Ave 4 YO32 ....167 B6
Cundall Ave YO7 ....115 B6
Cundall Cl 6 YO32 ....167 C8
Cundall Manor Sch
YO61 ....115 C3
Cunliffe Rd LS29 ....218 B4
Cunningham Ave TS17 ....6 B6
Cunningham Rd DL9 ....40 F4
Cupid's Alley YO17 ....149 B6
Curfew Rd HG4 ....214 C3
Curlew Cl 18 Ilkley LS29 ....175 C2
Leyburn DL8 ....60 E4
Curlew Cres 2 DL7 ....60 C7
Curlew Glebe 8 YO19 ....184 E7
Curly Hill LS29 ....218 A7
Currer La LS29 ....175 B6
Currie Cl DL9 ....209 C2
Curson Terr YO8 ....198 E3
Curtain La DL11 ....1 D5
Curtain The DL11 ....1 C4
Curteis Dr DL10 ....41 E4
Curzon Terr YO23 ....228 B1
Custance Wlk YO23 ....233 A1
Cut Rd WF11 ....202 D5
Cut Throat La HG3 ....138 F1
Cutler La LS26 ....200 A6
Cutpurse La DL10 ....209 C8
Cutsyke Ave WF10 ....200 D3
Cutsyke Crest WF10 ....200 D3
Cutsyke Rd WF10 ....200 D2
Cycle St 4 YO10 ....229 A3
Cygnet Cl 7 YO14 ....101 A4

Cygnet St YO23 23
Cypress Cl DL3 ....
Cypress Gdns HG4 21
Cypress Rd TS7 ....

D

Dacre Ct LS24 19
Dacre Hall Pk HG3 15
Dacre La HG3 15
Dacre Pasture La
HG3 15
Daffy La YO61 11
Dairy La HG3 15
Daisy Cl 8 DL9 4
Daisy Hill BD20 17
Dakyn Cl DL7 2
Dalacres Cres BD23 17
Dalacres Dr BD23 17
Dalby Ave HG2 22
Dalby Bank YO60 16
Dalby Cl YO12 23
Dalby Ct YO24 23
Dalby Forest Dr YO18 9
Dalby Mead YO32 22
Dale Ave YO13 7
Dale Bank HG1 2
Dale Cl Burniston YO13 7
Hampsthwaite HG3 16
7 Hurworth-on-Tees DL2 ....
Selby YO8 23
Thornton Watlass HG4 8
Dale Cres BD23 17
Dale Croft 20 LS29 17
Dale Dike Gr YO30 22
Dale Edge 11 YO11 2
Dale End Danby YO21 2
Kirkbymoorside YO62 7
Dale Garth YO12 21
Dale Gr DL8 6
Dale Rd Carleton BD23 17
Darlington DL3 ....
Sadberge DL2 ....
Dale Rise YO13 7
Dale St 1 Earby BB18 17
York YO23 23
Dale Stone Cl WF11 20
Dale The LS25 19
Dale View 8 Earby BB18 17
Ilkley LS29 21
Dale Way 2 DL8 6
Dalefield Ave WF6 20
Dalefield Rd WF6 20
Dalehouse Bank TS13 ....
Dales Countryside Mus* ....
Dale's La YO31 22
Dales Park Rd TS8 ....
Dalesbridge Outdoor Ctr*
 ....
Daleside Ave HG2 22
Daleside Gdns HG2 22
Daleside Pk HG3 15
Daleside Rd
Farndale East YO62 4
Farndale West YO62 4
Harrogate HG2 22
Rosedale East Side YO18 4
Rosedale West Side YO18 4
Dalewood Wlk 3 TS9 2
Dalguise Gr YO31 23
Dallamires Cl HG4 21
Dallamires La HG4 21
Dallamires Way N
HG4 ....
Dallamires Way S
HG4 ....
Dalmally Cl YO24 22
Dalton Hill YO19 15
Dalton La Dalton YO7 11
Wothersome LS23 18
Dalton Terr YO24 22
Dam Bank Rd LA2 ....
Dam Head 14 BB18 17
Dam Hill YO23 18
Dam La
Appleton Roebuck YO23 19
Leavening YO17 14
Markington with Wallerthwaite
HG3 ....
Saxton with Scarthingwell
LS24 19
Selby YO8 23
Dame La DL8 ....
Danby C of E Prim Sch
YO21 ....
Danby La DL7 ....
Danby St DL9 4
Danby Sta YO21 2
Dandy Mill Ave WF8 20
Dandy Mill Croft 8
WF8 20
Dandy Mill View WF8 20
Dane Ave
Thorpe Willoughby YO8 19
York YO26 22
Dane Rd DL9 4
Danebury Cres YO26 22
Danebury Dr YO26 22
Danelaw Fields 1 DL6 4
Danelaw Rd DL6 4

s Croft 2 YO10 .....231 D8
s Ct 5 YO19 .....198 A8
s Dyke 34 YO12 .....75 D5
scroft YO8 .....232 C2
near Rd YO24 .....227 D2
sgate YO26 .....227 D2
smead YO10 .....231 D8
smoor Cres DL3 .....3 B5
sswell Cl 3 YO41 .....168 D2
erous Cnr HG1 .....160 A2
k Way LS29 .....218 D5
m Ave YO7 .....211 A1
m Dr YO10 .....231 E8
m Rd YO10 .....231 E8
le Cl YO32 .....225 D4
y Ct DL6 .....40 F4
y Rd YO8 .....232 E4

Deepdale Ave
Eastfield YO11 .....100 A8
Middlesbrough TS4 .....7 A8
Scarborough YO12 .....213 A1

Deepdale La
Boston Spa LS23 .....180 D1
Dent LA10 .....77 F8
Deepdale Way 7 DL1 .....3 E6
Deepfurrows La YO41 .....185 D3
Deeping Way YO8 .....232 A6
Deer Hill Gr YO30 .....224 F3
Deighton Ave 16 LS25 .....195 F4
Deighton La
Brompton DL6 .....43 E5
Little Smeaton DL6 .....23 E1
Deighton Rd
Coulby Newham TS4 .....7 A7
Spofforth with Stockeld HG3 .....179 F6
Wetherby LS22 .....180 C4
Deigton Gate Jun & Inf Sch
LS22 .....180 C4
Del Pyke YO31 .....233 C4
Delamere Cl 6 YO32 .....166 D5
Delamere Cres HG2 .....220 D1
Delamere Rd TS3 .....7 B8
Delaney Cl 8 YO24 .....131 D2
Delf La YO7 .....64 A4
Dell The 3 YO30 .....224 B5
Delves La YO22 .....30 F3
Delwood YO10 .....231 D7
Dene Cl DN14 .....203 C2
Dene Gr DL3 .....3 C6
Dene Mdw 3 YO13 .....99 B8
Dene Park Cl HG1 .....219 F6
Dene Rd DL6 .....45 A7
Dene The YO12 .....212 E7
Deneside Rd DL3 .....3 B6
Denesway LS25 .....194 D3
Denevale TS15 .....5 E3
Denison Ave 8 YO12 .....99 D6
Denison Rd YO8 .....232 E4
Dennis La BD20 .....174 A2
Dennis St YO1 .....233 C2
Dennison St
1 York YO31 .....228 E6
Malton YO17 .....233 C4
Dentdale Dr HG5 .....221 C6
Denton Rd LS29 .....218 A5
Denton Terr WF10 .....200 F4
Denver Dr DL2 .....4 D4
Denver Rd 4 DN6 .....206 F2
Denwell Terr WF8 .....201 B1
Depot La 11 YO12 .....212 E4
Deramore Cl YO10 .....229 C3
Deramore Dr W YO10 .....229 C3
Derby Rd TS7 .....8 E6
Derby The TS7 .....7 A8
Dere Street Roman Rd*
DL11 .....22 B2
Derrings La YO61 .....142 D6
Derventio Roman Fort*
WF11 .....215 D4
Derwent Ave
Garforth LS25 .....194 C3
9 Scarborough YO12 .....212 E4
York YO31 .....228 F4
Derwent Cl 2 Colne BB8 .....186 A3
Elvington YO41 .....185 B3
2 Stamford Bridge YO41 .....168 D2
Derwent Ct YO41 .....185 C2
Derwent Dr
4 Barlby YO8 .....198 B5
Castleford WF10 .....201 C5
Wheldrake YO19 .....192 F7
Derwent Est YO19 .....184 E7
Derwent Inf Sch YO10 .....229 B4
Derwent Jun Sch
YO10 .....229 B4
Derwent Pk YO19 .....193 A8
Derwent Rd
Harrogate HG1 .....220 B3
Huttons Ambo YO17 .....215 A2
Whitby YO21 .....208 A7
York YO10 .....231 D8
Derwent St 7 YO12 .....212 E4
Derwent Swimming Pool &
Fitness Ctr YO17 .....215 D4
Desmond Rd DL2 .....4 C3
Deveron Way YO24 .....230 B7
**Devil's Arrows Standing
Stones***.....141 B5
Devon Pl YO10 .....228 F3
Devonshire Dr YO12 .....212 E7
Devonshire Gn HG4 .....114 F1
Devonshire Pl
Harrogate HG1 .....219 E3
12 Skipton BD23 .....216 F4
Devonshire Rd DL1 .....3 E6
Devonshire St 8 BD23 .....217 A3
Devonshire Way HG1 .....219 F4
Dew La TS7 .....7 D7
Dewberry TS8 .....7 B4
Dewsbury Terr YO1 .....233 A1
Dexta Way DL7 .....210 C3
Diamond Gr HG1 .....220 C4
Diamond Pl HG1 .....220 C4
Diamond Rd TS17 .....6 B8
Diamond St YO31 .....233 C4
Dibble Bridge Bank
YO21 .....28 F6
Dibdale Rd DL2 .....4 A1

Deepdale continued
7 Hutton Rudby TS15 .....25 C5
5 York YO24 .....230 D8
Dick La BD22 .....187 B6
Dick Scot La DL11 .....19 D7
Dickens Cl 1 YO32 .....225 F1
Dickens Rd YO17 .....215 C6
Dickey La YO8 .....197 D5
Dickson Rd 4 YO24 .....227 B1
Dicky Grounds La
YO7 .....121 D8
Dijon Ave YO24 .....227 C2
Dike La HG3 .....159 C8
Dikehollin La DL8 .....58 E2
Dikelands Cl 10 YO26 .....165 F1
Dikelands La YO26 .....165 F1
Dikes La TS9 .....8 C2
Dilys Gr 5 YO26 .....227 E4
Dimmingdale Rd TS12 .....10 A3
Dinghorpe Rd YO24 .....230 F7
Dinsdale Cl DL2 .....4 C4
Dinsdale Ct 5 DL2 .....4 C4
Dinsdale Dr TS16 .....5 E5
Dinsdale Sta DL2 .....4 C4
Diomed Ct TS7 .....7 B7
Dishforth Airfield
YO7 .....115 A2
Dishforth Airfield CP Sch
YO7 .....115 B2
Dishforth C of E Prim Sch
YO7 .....114 F4
Dishforth Rd
Copt Hewick HG4 .....114 B2
Sharow HG4 .....214 F6
Disraeli Cl YO22 .....225 E5
Dixon La YO1 .....233 C1
Dixon Rd HG1 .....219 D4
Dixon Terr HG1 .....219 D4
Dixons Bank TS8 .....7 C5
Dixsons Yd YO1 .....233 C2
Dob Park Rd LS21 .....176 F4
Dobella Ave DN14 .....205 A1
Dobella La DN14 .....205 B1
Doctor Laithe 8 BD23 .....134 D2
Doctor's Hill LA2 .....128 E8
Doctors La WF10 .....200 D7
Doctor's La TS15 .....25 C5
Dodder Carr Rd TS13 .....10 F3
Dodford Rd TS14 .....8 E6
Dodgson La
Lothersdale BD20 .....186 D8
Thornton in Craven
BB18 .....172 C1
Dodgson Terr 2 YO26 .....227 D4
Dodmire Jun & Inf Sch
DL1 .....3 E4
Dodsworth Ave YO31 .....228 E7
Doe Park La YO41 .....169 B4
Doe Pk YO30 .....224 F2
Dog Hill DL8 .....60 D2
Dog Hill Brow BD24 .....131 D6
Dog Kennel La YO18 .....96 E5
Dolegate YO41 .....168 F4
Dolly La DL7 .....64 C8
Dolphin Ctr The DL1 .....3 C5
Dolphin Way YO14 .....100 F5
Don Ave YO24 .....230 E8
Don Pedro Ave WF6 .....200 B1
Don Pedro La WF6 .....200 B1
Donald Smith Ct DL8 .....61 C5
Doncaster Rd
Brayton YO8 .....232 B3
Knottingley WF11 .....201 E2
North Elmsall WF9 .....206 A1
Doran Ct 15 YO14 .....101 B3
Dorchester Rd LS24 .....189 D5
Doriam Ave YO31 .....225 F2
Doriam Dr YO31 .....225 F2
Dorkings The TS9 .....26 E5
Dorset Cl HG1 .....219 A3
Dorset Cres HG1 .....219 A3
Dorset Rd TS14 .....8 E5
Dorset St BD23 .....217 A3
Dorts Cres YO41 .....185 C6
Dotcliffe Rd BB18 .....186 A7
Doubtlegates Ave 8
HG4 .....113 D2
Doublegates Cl 8 HG4 .....113 D2
Doublegates Ct 10 HG4 .....113 D2
Doublegates Gn 9 HG4 .....113 D2
Doublegates Wlk 7
HG4 .....113 D2
Doubting Castle*.....10 D1
Douglas Cl TS18 .....5 F7
Douglas St 3 YO8 .....232 C5
Douky Bottom Cave*.....133 F7
Dove Cl LS22 .....180 B4
Dove Cote Gdns DN14 .....203 D2
Dove St YO23 .....233 A1
Dovecot Cl YO14 .....100 C4
Dovecote Dr WF10 .....200 F7
Dovecote Garth 5
YO41 .....185 B2
Dovecote Mews YO7 .....115 D1
Dovedale Ave YO12 .....212 D8
Dovelands HG2 .....186 E6
Dowber Way YO7 .....211 D4
Dower Chase YO19 .....192 A6
Dower Rd YO19 .....192 B6
Dowell La LS23 .....188 E8
Downdale Rd YO13 .....54 B4
Downdinner Hill YO21 .....208 C6
Downholme Rd DL9 .....209 B1
Downland Cres WF11 .....202 A1
Downside Rd TS5 .....6 D8
Downstead DL6 .....23 C6
Dragon Par HG1 .....219 E3

Dragon Rd HG1 .....219 E3
Dragon Terr HG1 .....219 E3
Drake Cl YO21 .....208 B5
Drake Rd YO21 .....233 B1
Drakes Cl YO23 .....225 F5
Drapers Croft YO23 .....230 B4
Drax CP Sch YO8 .....204 F5
Dreaken Fold 4 YO13 .....99 A7
Drebley La BD23 .....157 D6
Dresser Cl DL10 .....209 C8
Driffield Rd YO25 .....151 F7
Driffield Terr YO24 .....228 A2
Drift La HG4 .....138 B8
Dringfield Cl 2 YO24 .....230 D8
Dringhouses Prim Sch
YO24 .....230 F8
Dringthorpe Rd YO24 .....230 F7
Drive The
Harrogate HG1 .....220 C5
Harrogate HG2 .....222 B5
7 High & Low Bishopside
HG3 .....137 C4
Kippax LS25 .....194 D1
12 Swillington LS26 .....194 A1
Threshfield BD23 .....134 B3
Drome Rd YO23 .....230 C2
Dromonby Bank TS9 .....26 C8
Drovers Way YO7 .....211 D4
Drovers Wlk BD23 .....154 B3
Druggist La YO7 .....129 C4
Druggon Rd DL9 .....40 E3
Druids Mdw 8 YO51 .....141 B5
Drummond View
YO23 .....231 B4
Drury Cl HG3 .....222 F2
Drury La HG3 .....222 F2
Dryden Cl HG1 .....219 E7
Dryhurst Cl 2 DN6 .....206 F2
Dubbing Garth La DL11 .....37 B4
Dubb's La DL11 .....81 C1
Duchess of Kents Military
Hospl 40 F4
Duck La
5 Burton in Lonsdale LA6 .....102 F3
High Bentham LA2 .....129 A8
Settle BD24 .....131 D2
Skipton BD23 .....217 A4
20 Trawden Forest BB8 .....186 A3
Duke's La YO25 .....151 F7
Dukes Wharf YO23 .....233 B1
Dukesway TS17 .....6 B5
Dulverton Cl 8 HG4 .....201 C2
Dulverton Rise WF8 .....201 C2
Dulverton Way HG4 .....201 C2
Dumb Tom's La LA6 .....103 B1
Dumfries Sq 8 YO7 .....40 E4
Duna Way YO62 .....70 C1
Duncan Cl 6 HG1 .....219 C5
Duncan St 8 YO1 .....233 B2
Duncombe La YO25 .....202 A8
Duncombe Cl
2 Eastfield YO12 .....99 F7
Malton YO17 .....215 A3
Duncombe La YO32 .....167 B8
Duncombe Pk*.....92 E6
Duncombe Pl YO1 .....233 B3
Dundas Gdns YO21 .....208 B6
Dundas St
Richmond DL10 .....209 C7
York YO1 .....233 C2
Dunderdale Cres
WF10 .....201 B5
Dunelm Wlk DL1 .....3 E7
Dunhill Rd DN14 .....205 F2
Dunkeswick La LS17 .....178 D4
Dunnington C of E Prim Sch
YO19 .....184 E7
Dunnington Dr YO8 .....196 E1
Dunnock La YO7 .....141 F8
Dunroyal Cl YO61 .....141 F8
Dunsley Cres YO21 .....208 A8
Dunsley La YO21 .....32 A8
Dunslow Cl YO11 .....99 F6
Dunslow Rd YO11 .....99 F6
Dunsmore Cl TS8 .....6 C4
Dunwell Ave 2 YO12 .....212 B7
Durham La TS16 .....5 D5
Durham Lane Ind Pk
TS16 .....5 D6
Durham Lane Prim Sch
TS16 .....5 D6
Durham Pl 5 YO12 .....213 A7
Durham St
8 Scarborough YO12 .....212 F7
6 York YO10 .....228 E3
Durham Way HG3 .....219 A5
Durlston Dr YO32 .....167 A3

Duxbury St 11 BB18 .....172 B1
Dyke Hall La LA10 .....78 A8
Dykelands Cl YO19 .....192 F7
Dykes La YO23 .....230 A1
Dyon La YO8 .....199 B3
Dyon Rd YO8 .....199 D3
Dyson la DL11 .....18 G7

E

Eagle Pk TS8 .....7 C5
Eaglescliffe Sta TS16 .....5 E6
Earby Springfield Prim Sch
BB18 .....172 B1
Earfit La YO23 .....191 A8
Earl Edwin Dr DL10 .....209 D8
Earle St YO31 .....233 C4
Eartham St 11 BB18 .....172 B1
Earls Court Rd TS8 .....6 E5
Earls View 3 BD20 .....187 E6
Earlsdon Ave TS5 .....6 D7
Earlsway TS17 .....6 C5
Earswick Chase YO32 .....225 F7
Earswick Village YO32 .....225 F7
Easby Abbey (rems of)*
DL10 .....209 E5
Easby Cl 11 Bedale DL8 .....63 B2
8 Ilkley LS29 .....175 C2
Easby Dr LS29 .....175 C2
Easby La Easby TS9 .....27 A8
Great Ayton TS9 .....7 F1
Easby Low Rd DL10 .....209 D7
Easingwold CP Sch
YO61 .....117 C1
Easingwold Sch YO61 .....143 C8
Eason Ave YO24 .....230 E8
Eason View YO24 .....230 E8
East Acres DL3 .....3 C5
East Ave
1 Easingwold YO61 .....143 D8
16 Glusburn BD20 .....187 E7
2 Scalby YO13 .....75 D5
East Ayton CP Sch
YO13 .....99 A8
East Bank 2 LS25 .....195 F4
East Barnby La YO21 .....12 C3
East Beck Ct LS21 .....176 F4
East Brow Rd HG3 .....72 C4
East Carr 3 WF11 .....100 B6
East Castle St 6 BD23 .....217 A3
East Cl DL2 .....4 C4
East Comm La YO8 .....232 F4
East Cowton C of E Prim Sch
DL7 .....22 E1
East Cres YO21 .....208 D7
East End YO60 .....145 D5
East Garforth CP Prim Sch
LS25 .....194 D4
East Gate YO13 .....98 D6
East Heslerton La
YO17 .....124 A8
East Ings La YO18 .....95 F4
East La Ampleforth YO62 .....92 D1
Castle Bolton with East &
West Bolton DL8 .....59 B6
Embsay BD23 .....217 D7
Yafforth DL7 .....43 C1
East Lea View 21 YO11 .....100 B6
East Moor Gdns YO19 .....231 F5
East Mount Rd
Darlington DL1 .....3 D6
York YO24 .....233 A1
East Neville St 1 BD23 .....217 A3
East Par Harrogate HG1 .....219 E2
East Parade
Ilkley LS29 .....218 C4
York YO31 .....228 F6
East Park Rd
Harrogate HG1 .....219 E2
3 Scalby YO13 .....75 D5
6 Spofforth HG3 .....179 E5
East Mt Melsonby DL10 .....20 F7
Northallerton DL6 .....210 E4
Norton YO17 .....215 E3
East Sandgate 12 YO11 .....213 B6
East Side 8 TS15 .....25 D5
East Side Sq 3 LS25 .....155 D1
Gayles DL11 .....19 E6
Swinton YO17 .....121 B4
East Terr YO21 .....208 D7
East View Barton DL10 .....21 D8
3 Campsall DN6 .....206 E1
Kippax LS25 .....194 D1
16 Knottingley WF11 .....202 A2
Middleton St George DL2 .....4 D3
Sherburn in Elmet LS25 .....195 F3
Thornton BB8 .....186 A3
East View Cs HG5 .....162 F3
East Way Whitby YO21 .....208 B7
York YO31 .....228 F6
East Whitby CP Sch
YO22 .....208 F4
East Witton Rd DL8 .....60 E2
Eastborough YO11 .....213 B6
Eastbourne Comp Sch
DL1 .....3 E5
Eastbourne Gdns 3 TS3 .....7 C8
Eastbourne Gr YO31 .....228 F5
Eastbourne Rd DL1 .....3 D5

248 Eas - Fer

Eastburn Jun & Inf Sch
BD20 ....187 F7
Eastbury CI TS17 ....6 B4
Eastby Rd HG1 ....219 F6
Eastern Terr YO31 ....228 E6
Easterside La YO62 ....67 F4
Easterside Prim Sch
TS4 ....7 A7
Easterside Rd TS4 ....7 A7
Eastfield
Amotherby YO17 ....121 B4
Knaresborough HG5 ....221 D6
Eastfield Ave
Haxby YO32 ....225 C2
Norton YO17 ....215 E3
Richmond DL10 ....209 D8
Eastfield CI LS24 ....189 F7
Eastfield Cres YO10 ..229 C2
Eastfield Ct YO32 ....29 C7
Eastfield Dr YO26 .....224 A1
Eastfield Gr WF6 ....200 B2
Eastfield La
Dunnington YO19 ....184 F8
Kellington DN14 ....202 F4
Spennithorne DL8 ....61 A3
Thoralby DL8 ....58 E2
Eastfield Rd
Norton YO17 ....215 E3
Pickering YO18 ....96 A6
Eastfields TS9 ....26 C7
Eastgate Helmsley YO62 .92 F6
Pickering YO18 ....96 A6
3 Seamer YO12 ....99 D6
Easthollme Dr YO30 ...224 E1
Easthorpe Dr YO26 ....224 A1
Easton La YO21 ....29 D6
Eastward Ave YO10 ....231 E7
Eastway YO11 ....100 A7
Eaton Ct YO62 ....29 C1
Eaton Ct YO42 ....230 B8
Eaton Rd LS29 ....218 A3
Eavestone Gr HG3 .....219 A4
Ebenezer Terr HG1 ....219 D2
Ebor CI DL10 ....21 A1
Ebor Ct
Northallerton DL7 ....210 D3
7 Selby YO8 ....232 C6
Ebor Mount LS25 ......194 D1
Ebor Prep Sch YO30 ..228 A7
Ebor Rise HG1 ....219 B2
Ebor St Selby YO8 .....232 C5
York YO23 ....233 B1
Ebor Way
Poppleton YO26 ....165 F1
Poppleton YO26 ....224 A2
Ebsay Dr YO30 ....225 A1
Eden Ave YO8 ....232 D3
Eden Camp Modern History
Mus★ YO17 ....215 E8
Eden CI
3 Hurworth-on-Tees DL2 ..3 D1
1 Hutton Rudby TS15 .....25 C4
York YO24 ....230 C7
Eden Cres DL1 ....3 C4
Eden Crest DL2 ....1 D7
Eden La DL2 ....1 D8
Eden Park Rd 2 TS15 ..25 C4
Eden Pk DL2 ....1 D7
Eden Rd DL7 ....210 B2
Edendale WF10 ....200 F4
Edenhouse Rd YO17 ...215 E8
Edens Way HG4 ....214 C2
Edge Dell YO9 ....99 E8
Edge La
Grassington BD23 ....134 E3
Long Preston BD23 ....153 E6
Edgecombe Dr DL3 .....3 A6
Edgehill Rd YO12 ....212 E2
Edgemoor Rd DL1 ....3 E3
Eden La DL2 ....3 A6
Edgeshall La LA2 ....130 C8
Eglington Ave TS14 .....8 F6
Egremont CI 1 YO41 ..168 D2
Egton Ave TS7 ....7 C5
Egton C of E Prim Sch
YO21 ....31 B5
Egton Cliff YO21 ....31 A5
Egton La YO21 ....30 F5
Egton Sta YO21 ....31 A5
Eight Acre La HG4 ......113 A5
Eighth Ave YO31 ....228 E5
El Alamein Rd 8 DL9 ..209 C1
Elbolton Cave★ BD23 ..156 E8
Elder Rd DL10 ....210 D4
Elder's St YO11 ....213 A6
Eldmire La YO7 ....115 D6
Eldon St YO31 ....233 C4
Eldon Terr YO31 ....233 C4
Eldroth Rd LA2 ....130 C5

Eldwick CI YO30 ....224 F2
Eleanor Dr HG2 ....220 C1
Eleanor Rd HG2 ....220 C1
Electric Ave HG1 ....219 B5
Elgin Rd TS17 ....6 B6
Elgin St 8 YO21 ....208 D6
Elizabeth Ct
7 Selby YO8 ....232 B6
Sherburn in Elmet LS25 ..195 E4
Elizabeth Dr WF10 .....201 B4
Elizabetham Ct 8 WF8 ..201 C1
Eland Ct 16 DL1 ....3 F6
Ellarfield La LS25 ....195 F5
Ellen Gr HG1 ....220 C4
Ellenthorpe La YO51 ..141 D6
Eller Gates YO21 ....30 C6
Eller Gill La BD23 ....172 D4
Eller Mews 8 BD23 .....216 E3
Ellerbeck Ct TS9 ....26 D6
Ellerbeck Way
Great & Little Broughton
TS9 ....26 D6
Middlesbrough TS7 ....7 D8
Whitby YO22 ....208 E4
Ellerby Bank TS13 ......11 F4
Ellerby La TS13 ....11 F5
Ellerclose Rd 22 DL8 ...60 D5
Ellerholme La DL11 .....38 F5
Ellerington CI LA6 ......103 D3
Ellerker La LS14 ....188 A3
Ellerker Rd LS14 ....188 A3
Ellers La BD24 ....59 A2
Ellers Rd BD20 ....187 E6
Ellerton Priory (rems of)★
DL11 ....39 A4
Ellerton Rd TS18 ....5 D8
Elliot Ct YO10 ....231 D7
Elliot St BD23 ....216 F4
Elliott St BD20 ....174 B1
Ellis Ct HG1 ....219 B2
Ellis La LS25 ....194 C5
Ellison Ave 8 YO12 ......75 D5
Ellwood Cotts BD24 ...131 D4
Elm Ave Kippax LS25 ..194 C2
Northallerton DL6 ....210 F5
Elm CI DL11 ....38 B4
Elma Gr YO30 ....224 E2
Elmer Dr LS15 ....194 C8
Elmet Rd LS15 ....194 C7
Elmete Ave LS25 ....195 F4
Elmete Rd WF10 ....201 B5
Elmfield Ave YO31 .....228 F8
Elmfield CI
8 Glusburn BD20 ....187 F8
Hurworth DL2 ....3 D1
Hurworth-on-Tees DL2 ....22 D8
Elmfield Terr YO31 ....228 F7
Elmlands Gr YO31 ....228 F8
Elmpark Vale YO31 ....229 A8
Elmpark View YO31 ...229 A8
Elmpark Way YO31 .....229 A8
Elms CI 2 YO19 ....191 F1
Elms La
6 Helmsley YO62 ....92 F6
3 Helmsley YO62 ....92 F6
Elmslac Rd 7 YO62 ......92 F7
Elmtree Gdns 3 YO26 .227 C3
Elmville Ave YO12 ......212 E6
Elmwood Ave LS15 .....194 B8
Elmwood Chase LS15 .194 B8
Elmwood CI 6 TS9 ......26 C8
Elmwood La LS15 ....194 B8
Elmwood St 4 HG1 .....219 E4
Elphin Bridge La
YO61 ....117 B6
Elslack La BD23 ....172 C4
Elston CI YO30 ....228 A8
Elston PI YO8 ....232 C6
Eltham Cres TS17 ....6 B7
Elton La HG3 ....160 E6
Elton Par DL1 ....3 B5
Elvington C of E Prim Sch
YO41 ....185 B3
Elvington Ind Est
YO41 ....185 A3
Elvington La YO19 .....184 E3
Elvington Pk YO41 .....185 A3
Elvington Terr YO10 ..228 E4
Elwick Ave TS5 ....6 E8
Elwick Gr YO10 ....229 C4

Elwick La YO26 ....164 B7
Ely CI HG3 ....219 A5
Embleton Dr 1 HG2 ...220 C1
Embleton Rd LS26 ......200 B4
Embsay C of E Prim Sch
BD23 ....217 D8
Embsay Junc BD23 ....217 C6
Embsay Sta BD23 ....217 D7
Embsay Steam Rly★
BD23 ....217 E7
Emerald St YO31 ....233 C4
Emerson Ave TS5 ....6 E8
Emerson CI 2 DL6 ......25 D1
Emerson Rd DL2 ....3 A3
Emery CI DL2 ....3 A3
Emgate 2 DL8 ....63 A3
Emley Moor Rd DL1 ......3 E4
Emmerson St 8 YO31 .228 E5
Emmet La HG3 ....160 C5
Emmott CI BB8 ....186 B3
Emmott La BB8 ....186 B4
Emsworth Dr TS16 ....5 D5
Enclosure Gdns 1
YO10 ....229 B1
Endcliff Cres YO12 .....212 D8
Endeavour Wharf★
YO21 ....208 D6
Endfields Rd 1 YO10 ..231 E8
Endsleigh Dr TS5 ....6 D8
Enfield Chase TS14 ......8 F5
Enfield CI 4 DL9 ....40 E4
Enfield Cres
6 York YO24 ....227 F3
7 York YO24 ....228 A3
Engine Shed La BD23 .216 D3
England La WF11 ....201 F2
English Martyrs RC Prim Sch
YO24 ....227 F3
Ennerdale Ave YO31 ..229 B5
Enter La LA6 ....103 D3
Enterpen TS15 ....25 C4
Enterprise Way
Bradleys Both BD20 ......173 D4
Sherburn in Elmet LS25 ..196 B4
Whitby YO22 ....232 F8
Eppleby Forcett C of E Prim
Sch DL11 ....1 A4
Epsom Ct 11 DL1 ....3 F6
Eridge Rd TS14 ....8 F6
Ermysted St 4 BD23 ...216 F4
Ermysteds Gram Sch
BD23 ....216 F4
Eryholme La DL2 ....22 F7
Escrick C of E Prim Sch
YO19 ....192 A5
Escrick Dr YO19 ....192 B5
Escrick Park Gdns
YO19 ....192 B5
Escrick St YO10 ....233 C1
Esher Ave TS6 ....7 F8
Eshington La DL8 ....58 F2
Eshton Rd BD23 ....155 D2
Esk Dr YO26 ....227 B8
Esk Leisure Ctr YO21 ..208 C7
Esk Rd DL1 ....3 D3
Eskdale Ave
Normanton WF6 ....200 A2
York YO10 ....229 C3
Eskdale CI
8 Pontefract WF6 ....200 A2
Sleights YO22 ....32 A5
Eskdale Croft WF6 ......200 A2
Eskdale Ct 12 WF6 .....200 A2
Eskdale Rd YO22 ....208 F3
Eskdaleside YO22 ....31 F5
Eskew La LA2 ....128 E7
Eslington Rd YO11 .....212 D4
Esp La BB18 ....171 C1
Esplanade
Harrogate HG2 ....219 C2
Scarborough YO11 ....213 A4
Whitby YO21 ....208 D7
York YO26 ....233 A2
Esplanade Cres YO11 ..213 B2
Esplanade Gdns YO11 .213 A3
Esplanade Rd YO11 ....213 A3
Estell La YO13 ....74 C5
Estill CI 2 YO11 ....100 B6
Estoril Rd S DL1 ....3 F4
Ethel Cres HG5 ....221 C6
Ethel St 12 BB18 ....171 E1
Etive PI YO24 ....230 B7
Eton Dr 17 YO32 ....166 D5
Eton Rd Goole DN14 ...205 F3
Middlesbrough TS5 ....6 E8
Ettersgill Dr DL3 ....3 A5
Ettington Ave TS3 ....7 B8
Etty Ave YO10 ....229 B4
Euclid Ave HG1 ....219 B5
Eva Ave YO30 ....224 D2
Evelyn Cres YO30 ....228 B7
Evelyn Ct 5 HG3 ....161 B2
Evelyn Dr YO12 ....212 D4
Evergreen Way 1 YO8 .197 D1
Everingham Rd TS15 ....5 D2
Eversley Ave LS25 ......195 F3
Eversley Ct LS25 ....195 F3
Eversley Garth Cres
LS25 ....195 F4
Eversley Mount LS25 ..195 F3
Evesham Rd TS5 ....7 B8
Ewart St YO12 ....212 E3
Ewden CI 8 YO14 ....126 F8
Ewe Leys La YO7 ....66 A5
Ewelands Hill YO7 ....90 C7
Exchange St 8 WF6 .....200 A1

Exelby CI DL8 ....63 D1
Exelby La DL7 ....63 D3
Exeter Cres 10 HG3 ....161 B3
Exeter Dr DL1 ....3 F7
Express Way WF6 ....200 A3

F

Faber CI YO23 ....230 B3
Faber St YO31 ....228 E5
Faceby Rd TS9 ....26 A2
Fadmoor Bank YO62 ...69 A9
Fadmoor La YO62 ....69 F4
Fairburn Cty Prim Sch
WF11 ....201 D6
Fairburn Dr LS25 ....194 D3
Fairburn Sports & Recn Ctr
WF11 ....201 D6
Fairburn Rd 11 YO41 ..168 D2
Fairfax Ave
Harrogate HG2 ....220 B2
North Featherstone
WF7 ....200 E1
Selby YO8 ....232 B4
Fairfax CI
11 Ampleforth YO62 ....92 C1
Bolton Percy YO23 ....190 D4
Fairfax Cres YO26 ......181 C7
Fairfax Croft YO23 .....230 B2
Fairfax House★ YO1 ...233 C2
Fairfax Rd DL2 ....189 A1
Fairfax St
1 Scarborough YO12 ...212 E5
10 Skipton BD23 ....217 A3
York YO1 ....233 B1
Fairfax Wlk 3 HG2 .....220 B3
Fairfield
Fairburn WF11 ....201 D7
Thirsk YO7 ....211 C4
Fairfield Ave TS7 ....7 D7
Fairfield CI 21 LS25 ...195 F4
Fairfield Cres YO12 ....212 B8
Fairfield Dr BD23 ....216 F8
Fairfield Link LS25 .....195 F4
Fairfield Rd DL3 ....3 C6
Fairfield St DL3 ....3 C6
Fairfield Way
8 Tadcaster LS24 ....189 E6
Whitby YO22 ....208 F3
Fairfields Dr YO30 .....224 B5
Fairheath Rd LA2 ....128 E5
Fairholme La DL7 ....64 A4
Fairmead CI YO22 ......208 E4
Fairmead Way YO22 ...208 E4
Fairview TS21 ....5 A7
Fairview Gdns DL10 ...209 C8
Fairway
Normanton South WF6 ..200 B1
4 Scalby YO12 ....75 E5
York YO30 ....228 A8
Fairway App WF6 ....200 B1
Fairway CI
8 Normanton South WF6 ..200 B1
8 Sherburn in Elmet LS25 ..195 F4
Fairway Dr
Normanton South WF6 ..200 B1
10 Poppleton YO26 ....165 F1
Fairway Mdws 8 WF6 .200 B1
Fairway The
Darlington DL1 ....3 C5
Middlesbrough TS8 ....7 C5
8 North Featherstone
WF7 ....200 E1
Northallerton DL7 ....210 C3
Sherburn in Elmet LS25 ..195 F4
Tadcaster LS24 ....189 E5
Fairweather Mews 8
YO12 ....212 B5
Falcon CI 6 Haxby YO32 .166 F5
1 Scotton DL9 ....40 F2
17 Settle BD24 ....131 D2
Falcon Dr WF2 ....200 C6
Falcon Gdns 8 BD24 ..131 D2
Falcon Terr 8 YO21 ....208 D6
Falcon Way TS14 ....8 D6
Falconberg Way TS15 ...5 D2
Falconer St 1 YO24 ....227 F3
Falconers Rd YO11 .....213 A5
Falkland Rd 2 DL9 .....40 F5
Falkland St YO1 ....233 B1
Fall La Pannal HG3 ......222 B2
Thornthwaite with Padside
HG3 ....159 A6
Fallow Field 1 BD23 ...217 B5
Falmer Rd DL1 ....3 E4
Falmouth Ave WF6 .....200 A2
Falmouth Cres 20 WF6 .200 A2
Falmouth Dr DL3 ....3 C8
Falmouth Rd WF6 ....200 A2
Falsgrave Cres YO30 ..228 B7
Falsgrave Mews 6
YO12 ....212 E5
Falsgrave Rd YO12 .....212 F5

Fanacurt Rd TS14 ....8 D6
Fancy Bank TS14 ....
Far La Knayton YO7 ....
Stutton with Hazlewood
LS24 ....
Far Le
Hutton Buscel YO13 ....
Kettlewell with Starbotton
BD23 ....
Far Mead Croft 3 LS29 ..12
Farfield YO26 22
Farfield Ave HG2 12
Farfield La YO19 18
Farfield Mount 2 HG5 ..2?
Farfields CI TS21 ....
Farm CI YO21 2
Farm Croft BD23 2
Farm Garth TS9 ....
Farm La TS17 ....
Farm Way YO8 2
Farmanby CI 12 YO18 ..
Farmbank Rd TS7 ....
Farmers Way YO23 2
Farmlands Rd 1 YO24 ..2
Farmstead Rise YO32 ..2
Farnborough Ct 10 DL2 ..
Farndale Ave
Northallerton DL7 2
York YO10 2
Farndale CI 1 YO13 .....
Farndale Cres DL3 ....
Farndale Dr TS14 ....
Farndale Rd HG5 2
Farndale St YO10 2
Farnham La HG5 ....
Farnley C of E Prim Sch
LS21 ....
Farnley Hall★ LS21 1
Farnley La LS21 2
Farnley Pk LS21 ....
Farrar St YO10 2
Farside Garth YO13 .....
Farside Rd YO13 ....
Farthingale Way TS8 ....
Favell Ave WF6 2
Faven Field Rd YO7 2
Faverdale DL3 ....
Faverdale N DL3 ....
Faverdale Rd DL3 ....
Faverdale W DL3 ....
Faverdale Rd BB8 1
Fawcett Ave TS8 ....
Fawcett St YO12 ....
Fawdington Rd YO61 ...
Fawkes Dr YO26 2
Fearby Rd Fearby HG4 ..
Masham HG4 ....
32 Stockton-on-Tees TS18 ..
Fearnhead TS8 ....
Feasegate YO1 ....
Feathercote CI LA6 1
Featherbed La
Bilton-in-Ainsty with Bickerton
LS24 ....
Ellerbeck DL6 ....
Federation St 12 BB18 ..1
Feeding Pasture La
YO60 ....
Feetham Ave DL1 ....
Feethams Sports Gd
DL1 ....
Felbrigg La TS17 ....
Feldom La DL11 ....
Felixstowe Dr 10 DL9 ...
Fell La Cracoe BD23 .....
Winton CA17 ....
Fell Rd LA6 ....
Fell View BD23 ....
Fell View Sq 8 BD23 ....
Fellbrook Ave YO26 ....
Felliscliffe Cty Prim Sch
HG3 1
Fenby Ave DL1 ....
Fence Dike La DL7 ....
Fenton Ave BB18 1
Fenton CI 10 YO11 1
Fenton La Malton YO17 ..2
Sherburn in Elmet LS25 ..1
Fenton St Boosbeck TS12 ..
38 Burley in Warfedale
LS29 ....
Fenwick CI 1 YO11 1
Fenwick Comm La
DN6 ....
Fenwick La DN6 ....
Fenwick St YO23 2
Fenwick's La YO10 2
Ferguson CI DL7 ....
Ferguson Way YO12 ....
Fern Bank Ave BB18 1
Fern CI YO32 2
Fern Gdns 11 LS29 ......
Fern St YO31 2
Ferndale Rd YO8 ....
Ferniee Rd TS4 ....
Ferniea CI YO8 ....
Fernley Green CI 6
WF11 2
Fernway YO10 2
Fernwood TS8 ....
Fernwood CI 9 Goole ...
Ferry CI 11 YO8 ....
Ferry Farm CI 2 YO19 ..
Ferry La Airmyn DN14 ...
Bishopthorpe YO23 ....
Bubwith YO8 ....
Snaith & Cowick DN14 ...

y La continued
nganby YO19 . . . . .193 B5
ybridge By-Pass
.1 . . . . .201 E3
ybridge Inf Sch
. . . . .201 E3
ybridge Rd
leford WF10 . . . . .200 F4
tefract WF8 . . . . .201 C1
bridge Service Area
e La YO1 . . . . .233 B2
rsham Cres 4
. . . . .228 C7
rsham Dr 10 YO62 . . . . .70 B1
rsham Rd YO4 . . . . .92 F7
ster Way YO31 . . . . .233 C1
ston Cl 9 YO14 . . . . .101 A3
ston Cres HG1 . . . . .219 B4
ston Gr 9 YO30 . . . . .224 F1
Ave YO8 . . . . .197 B1
Cl YO21 . . . . .208 A7
Cl Rd 10 YO13 . . . . .75 D5
Dr 1 Pickering YO18 .95 F6
aster LS24 . . . . .189 F7
Gr Gr 7 D6 9 . . . . .40 E3
Head WO1 . . . . .185 F6
House Rd 2 YO21 . .208 C7
La Aberford LS25 . .194 F8
bston YO13 . . . . .75 D8
dall DN14 . . . . .207 F8
bleton YO8 . . . . .196 F1
sall DN14 . . . . .203 D2
ington YO10 . . . . .229 C2
by & Scalby YO13 . . . . . . .75 E5
cliffe DN14 . . . . .205 A1
on YO8 . . . . .197 C7
Lane Sports Ctr
. . . . .197 B1
Rd YO8 . . . . .203 A5
View
n YO17 . . . . .215 E2
YO31 . . . . .228 C7
head Cl 12 WF8 . . . . . . .201 C1
head Dr
wick in Elmet LS15 . . . .194 C8
husburn BD20 . . . . .187 E7
head Paddock
. . . . .188 E8
ing's Yd DL10 . . . . .209 A7
lside YO12 . . . . .212 D7
stead Cres YO12 . .212 B8
way
ygate HG1 . . . . .219 F7
ey LS29 . . . . .218 E4
way Cl HG1 . . . . .219 F7
Ave 24 Colburn DL9 . . .41 A5
v YO31 . . . . .228 F4
Ave HG4 . . . . .214 A6
Brigg Nature Reserve*
. . . . .101 D4
C of E Inf Sch
.4 . . . . .101 B3
ard Cl 5 DL9 . . . . .40 E4
CP Sch YO14 . . . . .101 B3
Folk Mus* YO14 . .101 B3
ead Dr Folkton YO11 . .100 A2
manby YO14 . . . . .127 A8
borough YO11 . . . . .213 A2
r Sch YO14 . . . . .101 A3
r Sta YO14 . . . . .101 B3
Terr YO30 . . . . .228 C7
een Gdns HG3 . . . . . . .160 F5
Garth Cl LS23 . . . . .188 E6
ls Way DL7 . . . . .210 C6
le Cl 4 HG4 . . . . .214 C5
le Hill LS25 . . . . .195 F5
le St Hensall DN14 . .203 D2
Knaresborough HG5 . . . .221 A6
ham BD23 . . . . .133 A1
Malton YO17 . . . . .215 C4
mond DL10 . . . . .209 C6
tipon HG4 . . . . .214 C5
v YO8 . . . . .232 C5
off Hutton YO60 . . . . . . .145 C5
lsky YO7 . . . . .211 C3
oury Ave YO23 . . . . . . .228 C1
oury St YO23 . . . . .228 C1
rt TS17 . . . . .6 B8
heath Cl 5 YO24 . . .227 C1
ree Cl Hilton TS15 . . . .6 C2
rpe Willoughby YO8 .197 B2
ree Dr Filey YO14 . .101 B4
ree Dr YO30 . . . . .206 E2
ree La YO8 . . . . .197 B2
ree View LS26 . . . . .200 C6
ree Way YO8 . . . . .197 B2
rees The YO8 . . . . .197 B2
ank Cl 13 YO32 . . . . . . .167 A7
eck Rd LS23 . . . . .188 E6
La 8 HG4 . . . . .214 B5
y Rd Bedale DL8 . . . .63 A2
mond DL10 . . . . .209 B8
Ave Harrogate HG2 .222 E6
on HG4 . . . . .214 D4
Cl 22 YO14 . . . . .101 B3
Cres HG2 . . . . .222 E6
Dr HG2 . . . . .222 E6
Gate HG2 . . . . .222 E6
Gr HG2 . . . . .222 E6
Rd HG2 . . . . .222 E6
Ave 26 Colburn DL9 . .41 A5
rogate HG2 . . . . .220 C3
with with Darley
. . . . .160 A4
ickering YO18 . . . . .95 F7
Wetherby LS22 . . . . .180 C3

First Ave continued
York YO31 . . . . .228 F6
First Comm La YO8 . . .197 D4
First Moor Jun Sch DL1 . .3 F4
Firth St BD23 . . . . .217 A2
Firthfields LS25 . . . . .194 D4
Firthland Rd YO18 . . . . .95 F7
Firthmoor Cres DL1 . . . .3 E4
Firtree Ave TS6 . . . . .7 E8
Firtree Cl
4 Earswick YO32 . . . . . . .225 F7
York YO24 . . . . .227 E3
Firtree Cres LS24 . . . . . .189 D5
Firville Ave WF6 . . . . . . .200 A1
Firwood Whin 5 YO32 .225 F3
Fishbeck La BD20 . . . . . .174 D2
Fishburn Rd 4 YO21 . . .208 D5
Fisher Green La HG4 . .214 F4
Fisher Row 3 HG4 . . . . .86 C3
Fisher St 6 HG5 . . . . . . .221 B5
Fishergate
3 Boroughbridge YO51 .141 B5
Knottingley WF11 . . . . . .201 E3
11 Ripon HG4 . . . . .214 C5
York YO10 . . . . .233 C1
Fishergate Prim Sch
YO10 . . . . .233 C1
Fishergreen HG4 . . . . . .214 D4
Fishers Garth 10 YO18 .95 F6
Fitzalan Rd 18 DL8 . . . . .63 A2
Fitzjohn Cl YO17 . . . . . .215 C6
Fitzwilliam Dr
Darlington DL1 . . . . .3 D7
Malton YO17 . . . . .215 A4
Five Hills La DL10 . . . . . .21 D5
Five Lane Ends HG4 . . .86 D5
Flake La TS13 . . . . .12 A3
Flamingo Land Zoo & Family
Funpark* 95 C2
Flashley Carr La DN6 . .207 F1
Flask La DL8 . . . . .87 C3
Flass La WF10 . . . . .200 E3
Flat Cliffs YO14 . . . . .101 C1
Flat La
Bolton-on-Swale DL10 . . . .41 E6
Hellifield BD23 . . . . .153 F3
Flats Bank DL11 . . . . .19 F6
Flats La
Barwick in Elmet LS15 . .194 B7
Thirkleby High & Low
with Osgodby YO7 . . . . . . .90 D1
West Witton DL8 . . . . .59 D4
Flatts La
Eston & South Bank TS6 . . .7 F7
Welburn YO62 . . . . .94 A7
Wombleton YO62 . . . . . . .93 F6
Flavian Gr YO10 . . . . . . .227 F8
Flaxdale Cl 21 HG5 . . . .221 D6
Flaxley Ct YO4 . . . . .232 B5
Flaxley Rd YO8 . . . . .232 A7
Flaxman Ave YO10 . . . .229 A4
Flaxman Croft YO23 . . .230 B3
Flaxton Cl DL11 . . . . .18 E7
Flaxton Rd YO32 . . . . . .167 B7
Fleck Way TS17 . . . . .6 B5
Fleet Bank La YO61 . . . .143 C1
Fleet La
Barmby on the Marsh
DN14 . . . . .205 A7
Mickletown LS26 . . . . . . .200 A6
Tockwith YO26 . . . . .181 C7
Fleetham La
Cundall with Leckby YO7 . .115 C4
Kirkby Fleetham with Fencote
DL7 . . . . .63 C8
Fleets La BD23 . . . . .156 A6
Fleming Ave 3 YO31 . . .228 E5
Fletcher Ct 3 HG2 . . . . .166 C5
Fletcher's Croft YO23 . .230 C3
Flimthill La LS23 . . . . . . .180 E2
Flints Terr DL10 . . . . . . .209 C7
Flixton Carr La YO11 . . .99 F4
Flock Leys 12 YO13 . . . .75 D5
Flora Ave DL3 . . . . .3 B5
Florence Ct 12 YO11 . . .141 B5
Florence Gr YO30 . . . . .224 D2
Florence Rd HG2 . . . . . .219 B1
Flotmanby La YO14 . . .100 D2
Flow Edge DL8 . . . . .57 F7
Flower Ct 1 YO11 . . . . . .100 B6
Flower Garth
46 Filey YO14 . . . . .101 B3
Scarborough YO12 . . . . .212 C6
Flowergate 47 YO21 . . .208 D7
Fog La YO42 . . . . .193 E4
Fold La BD22 . . . . .187 B6
Fold The Filey YO14 . . .101 B3
Thornton in Craven
BD23 . . . . .172 A3
Folks Cl 15 YO32 . . . . . .159 C8
Folks Ct 8 YO32 . . . . . . .166 F5
Follifoot C of E Prim Sch
HG3 . . . . .223 F4
Follifoot La HG3 . . . . . . .223 B2
Follifoot Rd HG3 . . . . . .222 F3
Folliott Ward Cl YO17 . .215 B5
Folly La
Barnoldswick BB18 . . . . .171 D1
Bramham cum Oglethorpe
LS23 . . . . .188 E5
Folly View 2 LS23 . . . . .188 E5
Fontenay Rd DL10 . . . . .209 D8
Fonteyn Ct TS8 . . . . .6 F5
Forcett Cl
East Layton DL11 . . . . . . .20 C8
Middlesbrough TS5 . . . . . . .6 E7
Forcett Gdns DL11 . . . . . .1 D3

Forcett La DL10 . . . . .20 D5
Fordlands YO8 . . . . .197 B2
Fordlands Cres YO19 . .231 E5
Fordlands Rd YO19 . . . .231 E6
Fordon La
Willerby YO12 . . . . .125 E7
Wold Newton YO25 . . . .126 A6
Fordon Pl TS4 . . . . .7 A8
Fordyce Rd TS8 . . . . .6 E4
Fore La Cowesby YO7 . .66 B4
West Tanfield DL8 . . . . . . .87 D3
Whorlton DL6 . . . . .25 F1
Foreshore Rd YO11 . . . .213 A5
Forest Ave HG2 . . . . .220 D3
Forest Cl
3 Harrogate HG2 . . . . . .220 D3
27 Haxby YO32 . . . . .166 E5
Forest Cres HG2 . . . . . . .220 D4
Forest Dr Colburn DL9 . .41 A5
Dishforth YO7 . . . . .115 A4
Middlesbrough TS7 . . . . . . .7 D7
Forest Gdns HG2 . . . . . .220 D3
Forest Gr
27 Harrogate HG2 . . . . . .220 D3
York YO31 . . . . .228 F6
Forest Grange Cl 2
HG2 . . . . .220 D4
Forest La Aine YO61 . . .143 B5
Fulford YO19 . . . . .184 A2
Harrogate HG2 . . . . .220 D3
Kirklevington TS15 . . . . . .24 D8
Strensall YO32 . . . . .167 A8
Forest Lane Head
HG2 . . . . .220 D5
Forest Moor Rd HG5 . .220 F3
Forest Moor Rd HG5 . .220 E3
Forest Mount 8 HG2 . .220 D4
Forest of Galtres Prim Sch
YO30 . . . . .165 F5
Forest Rd
Appletreewick HG3 . . . . .157 F8
Northallerton DL6 . . . . . .210 E5
Pickering YO18 . . . . .96 A6
Forest Rise HG2 . . . . . . .220 D3
Forest Sch The HG5 . . .221 C6
Forest Way
Harrogate HG2 . . . . .220 D3
York YO31 . . . . .228 F6
Foresters Ct 5 YO12 . . . .75 F5
Foresters Wlk YO41 . . .168 C1
Forester's Wlk YO41 . .227 B1
Forestgate YO32 . . . . . .225 C7
Forge Cl YO32 . . . . .226 A2
Forge Gn HG2 . . . . .223 F4
Forge Hill La WF11 . . . .201 F3
Forge La
Deighton YO19 . . . . .192 A7
Kirkby Fleetham with Fencote
DL7 . . . . .42 C1
Tollerton YO61 . . . . .143 A3
Forge Valley Wood Reserve*
YO13 . . . . .75 A1
Forge Way DL1 . . . . .3 D6
Forkers La YO17 . . . . . . .122 D2
Forth St YO26 . . . . .227 F6
Fortune Cl HG5 . . . . . . .220 E7
Fortune Hill HG5 . . . . . .220 E8
Foss Ave LS22 . . . . .180 B4
Foss Bank YO31 . . . . . . .233 C3
Foss Ct YO31 . . . . .225 E1
Foss Field La YO23 . . . .191 B8
Foss Garth YO41 . . . . . .185 F5
Foss Islands Rd YO31 . .233 C3
Foss La YO22 . . . . .32 C2
Foss Wlk YO26 . . . . .227 B8
Fossdale Cl 5 HG5 . . . . .221 D6
Fosse Way LS25 . . . . . . .194 D4
Fossgate YO1 . . . . .233 C2
Fossland View 4 YO32 .167 A7
Fossway
Stamford Bridge YO41 . .168 D1
York YO31 . . . . .228 D7
Foster Ave
Normanton South WF6 . .200 A1
Silsden BD20 . . . . .174 B1
Foster Gate YO8 . . . . . . .232 D4
Foster Rd 41 BB18 . . . .171 D2
Foster Wlk LS25 . . . . . . .195 F4
Fostergate YO8 . . . . .197 A8
Foston C of E Prim Sch
YO60 . . . . .146 A3
Foston Gr 4 YO31 . . . . .228 F8
Foston La YO60 . . . . .146 B2
Fother Ingay Dr DL1 . . . .3 F8
Fothergill Way 3 YO51 .141 B4
Fothill La YO13 . . . . .98 E6
Foulbridge La YO13 . . . .97 F3
Foulds Rd BB8 . . . . .186 A1
Foulgate Nook La
YO13 . . . . .112 B6
Foundry La 5 WF11 . . . .202 A2
Fountain St TS14 . . . . .8 F6
Fountains Abbey*
. . . . .139 B7
Fountains Ave
Boston Spa LS23 . . . . . . .188 E8
Ingleby TS17 . . . . .6 B5
Fountains C of E Prim Sch
HG4 . . . . .138 D8
Fountains Cl
Guisborough TS14 . . . . . . .8 F6
18 Whitby YO21 . . . . . . .208 C6
Fountains Dr TS5 . . . . . . .6 E8
Fountains Gate HG4 . . .112 F1
Fountains La HG4 . . . . . .139 B7

Fountains Mill* HG4 . .139 B7
Fountains Pl DL6 . . . . . .210 E6
Fountains Rd DL6 . . . . .210 E6
Fountains View DL3 . . . . .3 A6
Fountayne Rd
Knaresborough HG5 . . . .221 C4
Morton-on-Swale DL7 . . .64 A7
Fountayne Rd
18 Hunmanby YO14 . . .126 F8
18 Hunmanby YO14 . . .126 F8
Fountayne St YO31 . . . .228 C7
Four La Ends
Burythorpe YO17 . . . . . .147 D4
Lawkland BD24 . . . . .130 F3
Four Lanes Ends BB7 . .152 C1
Four Riggs DL3 . . . . .3 C5
Fourscore Dr 11 YO22 . . .32 A6
Fourth Ave
26 Colburn DL9 . . . . .41 A5
York YO31 . . . . .228 E5
Fox Cl 8 DL2 . . . . .22 D8
Fox Covert YO31 . . . . . .225 F2
Fox Covert Cl 15 DL8 . .63 B3
Fox Covert Rd WF8 . . . .206 C1
Fox Ct HG1 . . . . .219 E4
Fox Garth
6 Brafferton YO61 . . . . .115 F1
Poppleton YO26 . . . . .224 A3
Fox Glade YO41 . . . . . . .168 C2
Fox Heads La LS22 . . . .179 D4
Fox Hill La YO8 . . . . .232 A3
Fox La
Chapel Haddlesey YO8 . .203 C5
Hambleton LS25 . . . . . . .196 D1
Thornton-le-Dale YO18 . . .96 C3
Thorpe Willoughby YO8 . .197 B1
Thorpe Willoughby YO8 . .197 B1
Foxberry Ave TS5 . . . . . . .6 D6
Foxbridge Way WF6 . . .200 C2
Foxcliff WF11 . . . . .201 E5
Foxcroft 3 YO32 . . . . . . .225 C7
Foxdale Ave YO8 . . . . . .197 B1
Foxglove Cl
2 Killinghall HG3 . . . . . .161 B3
Northallerton DL7 . . . . . .210 C1
Foxglove Ct 10 DL9 . . . .41 A5
Foxhill La YO8 . . . . .232 A3
Foxholme La HG4 . . . . . .86 B3
Foxthorn Paddock
YO10 . . . . .229 D3
Foxton Cl YO24 . . . . .230 C8
Foxton La DL6 . . . . .44 E2
Foxwood La
3 York YO24 . . . . .227 C1
York YO24 . . . . .230 D8
Foxwood Sch BD24 . . . .105 C4
Frances Rd DL10 . . . . . . .209 C7
Frances St YO10 . . . . . . .228 D1
Francis Ct 2 YO8 . . . . . .197 B2
Frances La HG2 . . . . .164 F4
Frank St
24 Barnoldswick BB18 . .171 D1
3 Barnoldswick BB18 . .171 D1
8 Barnoldswick BB18 . .171 E1
Franklin Mount HG1 . . .219 D4
Franklin Rd HG1 . . . . . . .219 D3
Franklin Sq HG1 . . . . . . .219 D4
Franklin St 19 YO12 . . .212 F6
Frank's La YO26 . . . . . . .164 A5
Fraser Rd 3 TS18 . . . . . . .5 E8
Frazer Ct YO30 . . . . .227 E8
Frederic St YO30 . . . . . .233 A3
Freebrough Rd TS12 . . .10 A4
Freehold La YO17 . . . . . .215 D8
Freely La LS23 . . . . .188 E6
Freeman's Way HG3 . . .223 D8
Freemans Way
Leeming DL7 . . . . .63 C4
Wetherby LS22 . . . . .180 D3
Freeston Ct 18 WF6 . . . .200 A2
Freeston Dr 18 WF6 . . . .200 A2
French Rd DL9 . . . . .209 C2
French St HG1 . . . . .219 F4
Frenchgate DL10 . . . . . .209 C6
Friarage CP Sch YO11 . .213 B6
Friarage Gdns DL6 . . . .210 D5
Friarage Hospl DL6 . . . .210 E5
Friarage Mount DL6 . . .210 D5
Friarage St DL6 . . . . .210 D5
Friargate
Scarborough YO11 . . . . .213 A6
York YO1 . . . . .233 B2
Friars Cl YO31 . . . . .184 D7
Friars' Gdns 10 YO11 . .213 A6
Friars Hill YO62 . . . . .95 A8
Friars Mdw YO8 . . . . . . .232 C8
Friars Pardon DL2 . . . . . . .3 E1
Friars' Way YO11 . . . . . .213 A6
Friars Wlk YO31 . . . . . . .228 E8
Friary Com Hospl
DL10 . . . . .209 B7
Friendship Ct 2 YO8 . .232 C6
Frith Mews 4 YO8 . . . . .232 C6
Frobisher Dr 8 YO21 . . .208 D5
Frogmire Cl HG5 . . . . . .221 B7
Frogmire Dr HG5 . . . . . .221 B7
Frogmire Rd HG5 . . . . . .221 B7
Front Nook 2 DL8 . . . . . .58 F1
Front St
Appleton Wiske DL6 . . . . .24 B3
6 Bramham LS23 . . . . . .188 E5
Burton Fleming YO25 . . .126 E3
Burton Leonard HG3 . . .140 A2
Castleford WF10 . . . . . . .200 F3
Grosmont YO22 . . . . .31 C4
Langtoft YO25 . . . . .151 C5
Lastingham YO62 . . . . . . .70 E5
Naburn YO19 . . . . .191 D8

Front St continued
Thirsk YO7 . . . . .211 C1
Topcliffe YO7 . . . . .115 C7
Wold Newton YO25 . . . .126 A4
York YO24 . . . . .227 C3
Front The DL2 . . . . .4 D3
Fryer Cres DL1 . . . . .3 E6
Fryston Comm La
LS25 . . . . .202 A8
Fryston La WF11 . . . . . . .201 C3
Fryston Rd WF10 . . . . . .201 B5
Fryton La YO62 . . . . .120 A7
Fryup Cres TS14 . . . . .8 E5
Fulbeck Rd TS3 . . . . .7 D8
Fulford Cross YO10 . . . .228 D1
Fulford Cross Specl Sch
YO10 . . . . .228 D1
Fulford Pk YO10 . . . . . . .231 D7
Fulford Rd
Scarborough YO11 . . . . .212 F3
York YO10 . . . . .231 D8
Fulford Sch YO10 . . . . . .231 E7
Fulfordgate YO10 . . . . . .231 E7
Fulham La DN14 . . . . . . .206 F7
Fuller-Good Rd 14 DL10 . .41 E4
Fullicar La DL6 . . . . .43 F3
Fulmar Head TS14 . . . . . . .8 D6
Fulthorpe Ave TS13 . . . .3 A5
Fulthorpe Gr DL3 . . . . . . .3 A5
Fulwith Ave HG2 . . . . . .222 F5
Fulwith Cl HG2 . . . . .222 F5
Fulwith Dr HG2 . . . . .222 F5
Fulwith Gate HG2 . . . . .222 F5
Fulwith Gr HG2 . . . . .222 F5
Fulwith Mill La HG2 . . .222 F5
Fulwith Rd HG2 . . . . . . .222 F5
Fummerlea La LA2 . . . .130 C5
Furlong Rd 22 YO41 . . .168 D2
Furlongs Ave YO17 . . . .215 F3
Furnace La HG4 . . . . .87 A1
Furness Dr
Bentham LA2 . . . . .129 A8
York YO30 . . . . .224 E1
Furnessford Rd LA2 . . .128 D6
Furnwood 2 YO32 . . . . .225 D7
Furrows The 16 YO11 . .100 B7
Fushetts La LA2 . . . . . . .129 A8
Fyling Rd YO21 . . . . .208 A6
Fylingdales Ave 6
YO30 . . . . .224 E1
Fylingdales C of E Prim Sch
YO22 . . . . .33 C4

G

Gable Ct YO7 . . . . .115 A4
Gable Pk YO23 . . . . .182 C6
Gables Cl 8 DN14 . . . . .202 D4
Gables The
18 Hurworth-on-Tees DL2 . .3 E1
Knaresborough HG5 . . . .221 A8
Middlesbrough TS7 . . . . . .7 B6
Scriven HG5 . . . . .162 C5
Gainford C of E Prim Sch
DL2 .1 C7
Gainforth Wath Rd
YO13 . . . . .53 F5
Gainsborough Ct
BD23 . . . . .216 E4
Gaits DL8 . . . . .56 C4
Gale Bank DL8 . . . . .60 B3
Gale Farm Ct 8 YO24 . .227 C3
Gale Garth YO61 . . . . . .142 F4
Gale Gate YO26 . . . . . . .142 A1
Gale La Beadlam YO62 . .93 D6
Stainburn LS21 . . . . .177 E3
Thorganby YO19 . . . . . . .192 F4
York YO24 . . . . .227 C2
Gale Rd YO61 . . . . .142 F4
Gale The YO60 . . . . .146 E1
Gallabar La YO51 . . . . . .141 E1
Galley Hill Prim Sch
TS14 . . . . .8 D6
Galligap La YO10 . . . . . .229 C4
Gallogate La LS17 . . . . .178 C1
Gallops The
Norton YO17 . . . . .215 E2
York YO24 . . . . .230 B8
Gallowfields Rd DL10 . .209 B7
Gallowfields Trad Est The
DL10 . . . . .209 B8
Gallowgate DL10 . . . . . .209 C7
Gallowheads La YO62 . .95 A6
Gallows Hill
Castleford WF10 . . . . . . .201 B4
Ripon HG4 . . . . .214 C2
Gallows Hill Dr HG4 . . .214 C2
Gallows Hill La YO13 . . .98 D5
Gallows Hill Pk HG4 . . .214 D2
Gallruanhoe La YO30 . .233 A3
Galphay La HG4 . . . . . . .113 A3
Galtres Ave YO31 . . . . . .229 B7
Galtres Dr 7 YO61 . . . . .143 D8
Galtres Gr YO30 . . . . . . .227 F7
Galtres Rd
Northallerton DL6 . . . . . .210 E6
York YO31 . . . . .229 B7
Galtres Sch YO31 . . . . . .229 B5
Ganton Cl YO21 . . . . . . .208 C5
Ganton Hill YO12 . . . . . .125 B7
Ganton Pl YO24 . . . . . . .230 E7
Ganton Rd YO25 . . . . . .125 C4
Gaol The YO61 . . . . .144 E7
Gap Rd YO14 . . . . .127 D8

Garbett Way **1** YO23 . . . . .231 B3
Garburn Gr **3** YO30 . . . . .224 E1
Garbutt Gr YO26 . . . . . .227 D5
Garbutt La
. . **4** Whorlton DL6 . . . . .25 D1
. . **1** Whorlton DL6 . . . . .25 D1
Garbutts La TS15 . . . . . .25 B5
Garden Cl
. . **3** Glusburn BD20 . . . . . .187 D7
. . Sherburn in Elmet LS25 . .195 E4
Garden Flats La YO19 . .184 E7
Garden House Cl LS26 . .200 B6
Garden La
. . **11** Knottingley WF11 . . . .202 A3
. . Sherburn in Elmet LS25 . .195 E4
Garden Pl YO1 . . . . .233 C2
Garden St
. . Castleford WF10 . . . . . .200 E3
. . **8** Normanton South WF6 .200 A1
. . York YO31 . . . . .233 B4
Garden Village LS25 . . .195 A3
Garden Way **3** YO18 . . . .95 F6
Gardeners Cl **3** YO23 . . .230 B3
Gardeners Row WY025 . .150 B3
Gardens Rd BD23 . . . . . .155 D2
Gardens The **10** YO14 . . .101 B4
Garfield Rd YO12 . . . . . .212 E6
Garfield Terr YO26 . . . . .227 F5
Garforth Barleyhill Infants
. . Sch LS25 . . . . .194 C3
Garforth Green Lane Prim
. . Sch LS25 . . . . .194 C4
Garforth Leisure Ctr
. . LS25 . . . . .194 D3
Garforth St Benedicts RC
. . Prim Sch LS25 . . . . . . .194 C4
Garforth Sta LS25 . . . . .194 C4
Gargrave C of E Prim Sch
. . BD23 . . . . .155 C1
Gargrave House Gdn
. . BD23 . . . . .155 C1
Gargrave Rd
. . Broughton BD23 . . . . . .172 D6
. . Skipton BD23 . . . . .216 D4
Gargrave Sta BD23 . . . . .172 C8
Garibaldi St **4** YO11 . . .213 B6
Garland St **3** YO26 . . . .227 E4
Garlands Hill **3** YO1 . . .212 F3
Garlands The
. . Scarborough YO11 . . . . .212 F3
. . York YO30 . . . . .228 A8
Garman Carr La YO8 . . .197 D6
Garnet Brow La LA2 . . . .130 D2
Garnet La **1** LS24 . . . . .189 D5
Garnet Rd TS17 . . . . .6 B8
Garnet Terr YO26 . . . . . .227 E5
Garrick Cl YO8 . . . . .232 B1
Garrow Hill YO10 . . . . . .228 F2
Garrow Hill Ave YO10 . .229 A3
Garrowby Rd YO41 . . . .169 F3
Garrowby St YO42 . . . . .169 F3
Garrowby St YO41 . . . . .169 E3
Garrowby View **5** YO41 .168 D2
Garrs End La BD23 . . . . .134 E3
Garrs La **16** BD23 . . . . .134 E3
Garsbeck Way TS7 . . . . .7 D8
Garsdale Fold **8** LS22 .180 A1
Garsdale Rd HG5 . . . . . .221 D6
Garsdale Sta LA10 . . . . . .55 A6
Garth Ave
. . Collingham LS22 . . . . . .188 A2
. . **4** North Duffield YO8 . . .199 A7
Garth Cl **11** Catterick DL10 .41 D5
. . Hambleton YO8 . . . . . . .196 E1
. . **6** Wistow YO8 . . . . . . .197 D6
. . Dar YO8 . . . . .196 E1
Garth End
. . Collingham LS22 . . . . . .188 A8
. . Kirk Deighton LS22 . . . .180 B5
Garth End Rd YO13 . . . . . .99 A7
Garth Grange **5** YO30 . .164 F7
Garth La
. . Hambleton YO8 . . . . . . .196 E1
. . Snainton YO13 . . . . .98 A5
Garth Mdws **10** DL10 . . .41 D5
Garth Mill **11** YO24 . . . .202 D4
Garth Morrell YO8 . . . . .232 C2
Garth Rd
. . **4** Hambleton YO8 . . . . .196 E1
. . York YO32 . . . . .225 F4
Garth Terr YO30 . . . . . . .228 B7
Garth The
. . **8** Collingham LS22 . . . .188 A8
. . Sinnington YO62 . . . . .71 A6
. . **4** Stokesley TS9 . . . . . . .26 C7
. . Tunstall DL10 . . . . .41 B2
. . Whitby YO21 . . . . .208 B7
Garth View YO8 . . . . . . .198 F1
Garthends La **3** YO8 . . .198 F1
Garths End YO10 . . . . . .231 E8
Garth's End YO10 . . . . . .231 E8
Garthway **4** YO32 . . . . .225 D3
Gas House La LA2 . . . . . .129 A8
Gas St BD23 . . . . .216 F3
Gas Works La LS23 . . . . .188 F8
Gascoigne Ave LS15 . . . .194 B7
Gascoigne Cres HG1 . . . .219 F4
Gascoigne Ct LS15 . . . . .194 B7
Gascoigne Rd LS15 . . . . .194 B7

Gascoigne View LS15 . . .194 B7
Gascoigne Wood Mine
. . LS25 . . . . .196 C2
Gate Bridge Rd HG4 . . . .112 D2
Gate La Borrowby YO7 . . . .65 E4
. . Low Coniscliffe & Merrybent
. . DL2 . . . . .2 A2
Gate Way YO21 . . . . .29 B4
Gatecliff Brow BD23 . . . .155 F4
Gateforth La YO8 . . . . . .197 B6
Gateforth La YO8 . . . . . .196 F1
Gateforth New Rd
. . YO8 . . . . .203 A8
Gatehead La YO42 . . . . .193 D7
Gatehowe Rd YO17 . . . . .170 A7
Gatela Rd YO13 . . . . .53 D2
Gateland Cl YO32 . . . . . .225 D3
Gateland Field La
. . DN14 . . . . .205 B6
Gateley Garth YO61 . . . .143 B8
Gatesgarth Cl YO12 . . . .212 B8
Gatherley Rd DL10 . . . . . .41 C7
Gauber Rd LA6 . . . . .78 F1
Gaudy La DL8 . . . . .56 C3
Gay Mdws YO32 . . . . . . .167 D2
Gaylands La BB18 . . . . . .172 B1
Gayle La DL8 . . . . .56 C4
Gayton Sands TS5 . . . . . . .6 D6
Gazelle Way YO7 . . . . . .115 B1
Geecroft La LS22 . . . . . .179 D3
Geldof Rd YO32 . . . . . . .225 F1
General La YO42 . . . . . . .193 E6
Geneva Cres DL1 . . . . .3 D4
Geneva La DL1 . . . . .3 D4
Geneva Rd DL1 . . . . .3 E4
Gennell La YO60 . . . . . . .145 E1
Gennwhaton Fst Sch
. . WF10 . . . . .200 F4
Gentian Glade HG3 . . . . .219 A4
George Cayley Dr
. . YO30 . . . . .225 A3
George Ct YO31 . . . . . . .233 C3
George Hudson St
. . YO1 . . . . .233 B2
George St
. . **18** Addingham LS29 . . . .174 F4
. . Carleton BD23 . . . . .173 B4
. . **10** Earby BB18 . . . . . . .172 A1
. . **3** Scarborough YO12 . . . .213 A6
. . **3** Selby YO8 . . . . .232 D6
. . **11** Skipton BD23 . . . . . .217 A3
. . Snaith DN14 . . . . .204 C1
. . **12** Whitby YO21 . . . . . .208 D6
. . **7** Wistow YO8 . . . . .197 D6
. . York YO1 . . . . .233 B2
George Terr **1** YO8 . . . .198 B4
Gerard Ave YO31 . . . . . .229 A5
Germain Rd YO8 . . . . . . .232 E4
Germain St YO8 . . . . .232 E5
Gerrick La TS12 . . . . .10 C3
Gerrie St TS12 . . . . .9 D7
Ghyll Brow YO21 . . . . . . .30 D4
Ghyll La BB18 . . . . .171 E2
Ghyll Mdws BB18 . . . . . .171 E2
Ghyll Mews LS29 . . . . . .218 A3
Ghyll The DL10 . . . . .209 D8
Ghyll Royd LS29 . . . . . . .218 A3
Ghyll Wood **28** LS29 . . .175 C2
Gibb St BD22 . . . . .187 B6
Gibbet Hill YO61 . . . . . . .117 C5
Gibson La **2** LS25 . . . . .194 D1
Gibson Lane Jun Sch
. . LS25 . . . . .194 D1
Giggleswick CP Sch
. . BD24 . . . . .131 D3
Giggleswick Sch
. . BD24 . . . . .131 C2
Giggleswick Sta BD24 . .131 C1
Gilcar St WF6 . . . . .200 B2
Gilcar Way WF6 . . . . . . .200 B3
Gildercliffe YO12 . . . . . .212 C7
Giles Ave YO31 . . . . .229 A5
Gill Bank Rd LS29 . . . . . .218 A6
Gill Cl **6** LS29 . . . . .174 E4
Gill Croft YO61 . . . . .117 C1
Gill La Cowling BD22 . . . .187 A6
. . Kearby with Netherby
. . LS22 . . . . .179 C1
. . Nesfield with Langbar
. . LS29 . . . . .175 A4
. . Rosedale West Side YO18 . .49 E2
Gillamoor Ave YO31 . . . .229 B5
Gillamoor Bank YO62 . . . .70 A5
Gillamoor C of E Prim Sch
. . YO62 . . . . .70 A4
Gillamoor Rd YO62 . . . . . .70 A2
Gillann St **12** WF11 . . . .202 A2
Gillgate Rd HG4 . . . . . . .112 B4
Gilling Castle* YO62 . . .118 F7
Gilling Cres DL1 . . . . .3 E4
Gilling Rd Aske DL10 . . . .20 E1
. . Richmond DL10 . . . . . . .209 D7
Gilling Way YO17 . . . . . .215 C5
Gillings Ct YO7 . . . . .211 A3
Gilling's End YO10 . . . . .209 C8
Gillingwood Rd YO30 . . .224 F3
Gills Fold BD23 . . . . .134 E3
Gills The LS21 . . . . .177 A1
Gillygate YO31 . . . . .233 B3
Gillylees YO12 . . . . .212 C5
Gilmonby Rd TS3 . . . . .7 B6
Gilsforth Hill YO26 . . . . .164 A3
Gilsforth La YO26 . . . . . .164 A3

Gilstead Way LS29 . . . . .218 B5
Gilsthwaite La YO26 . . . .164 A3
Gindhill La LS21 . . . . . . .178 A4
Ginnel The **1** HG1 . . . . .219 D2
Gipsey Cnr YO19 . . . . . .184 E3
Girls High Sch BD23 . . . .216 E4
Girton Wlk DL1 . . . . .3 D7
Girvan Cl YO24 . . . . .230 B7
Gisburn Rd
. . Barnoldswick BB18 . . . . .171 D2
. . Hellifield BD23 . . . . .154 B3
Gisburn Road CP Sch
. . BB18 . . . . .171 D1
Gisburn St
. . Barnoldswick BB18 . . . . .171 D2
. . Skipton BD23 . . . . .216 D3
Givendale Gr **3** YO10 . .229 C4
Givendale Rd YO12 . . . . .212 D8
Glade Rd YO19 . . . . .192 B2
Glade The
. . Escrick YO19 . . . . .192 A6
. . Scarborough YO11 . . . . .212 F3
. . Normanton South WF6 . .200 B2
. . Scarborough YO12 . . . . .212 E6
. . **14** Skipton BD23 . . . . . .216 F4
. . York YO31 . . . . .233 C4
Glaisby Ct YO31 . . . . . . .229 A6
Glaisdale Ave TS5 . . . . . . .6 F8
Glaisdale CP Sch YO21 . .30 D4
Glaisdale Hall La YO21 . .30 C4
Glaisdale Rd TS15 . . . . . . .5 F3
Glaisdale Sta YO21 . . . . . .30 D3
Glasgow Dr **3** DL9 . . . .209 C1
Glasshoughton Fst Sch
. . WF10 . . . . .200 F4
Glasshouses CP Sch
. . HG3 . . . . .137 D3
Glaves Cl YO13 . . . . .99 B7
Glebe Ave
. . Full Sutton YO41 . . . . . .169 A2
. . Harrogate HG2 . . . . . . .219 C2
. . Norton YO26 . . . . .227 D5
Glebe Cl Barton DL10 . . .21 C7
. . Bolton DL10 . . . . .63 A2
. . Kirkby Hill YO51 . . . . . .190 D4
. . Manfield DL2 . . . . .2 C4
. . **3** Strensall YO32 . . . . . .167 B7
Glebe Ct DL10 . . . . .21 A7
Glebe Field Dr **11** LS22 .180 B3
Glebe Gdns TS13 . . . . . . .11 A8
Glebe La DL2 . . . . .4 C5
Glebe Mdw HG4 . . . . . . .214 F6
Glebe Rd Campsall DN6 . .206 F1
. . Darlington DL1 . . . . .3 D8
. . Harrogate HG2 . . . . . . .219 C1
. . Stokesley TS9 . . . . .26 C7
Glebe Sq DL7 . . . . .64 C5
Glebe St WF10 . . . . .200 E4
Glebe Way **3** YO32 . . . .166 E5
Gledstone Rd BD23 . . . . .171 E5
Gledstone View **8**
. . BB18 . . . . .171 D2
Glen Ave YO31 . . . . .228 E5
Glen Cl
. . Newby & Scalby YO13 . . .75 C5
. . York YO10 . . . . .231 E6
Glen Esk Rd YO22 . . . . .208 C3
Glen Rd YO31 . . . . .228 E5
Glencoe Cl LS25 . . . . . . .200 C8
Glencoe Croft LS25 . . . . .200 C8
Glencoe Gdns LS25 . . . . .200 C8
Glencoe St **1** YO30 . . . .228 B7
Glencoe Terr LS25 . . . . . .200 C8
Glendale
. . Guisborough TS14 . . . . . . .8 D5
. . **9** Hutton Rudby TS15 . . .25 C5
Glendale Rd TS7 . . . . .7 B6
Gleneagles Rd
. . Darlington DL1 . . . . .3 F8
. . Middlesbrough TS4 . . . . . .7 A8
. . North Featherstone
. . WF7 . . . . .200 E1
Glenfield Ave LS22 . . . . .180 C2
Glenmore Dr YO17 . . . . .215 E2
Glenn Cres TS7 . . . . .7 B5
Glenridding YO24 . . . . . .230 D7
Glenside YO12 . . . . .212 E7
Globe St
. . **10** Harrogate HG2 . . . . .220 C3
. . Scarborough YO12 . . . . .212 E4
. . Tadcaster LS24 . . . . . . .189 F6
. . Thorp Arch LS23 . . . . . .181 A2
. . **3** Willerby YO12 . . . . . .99 D7
Glusburn CP Sch
. . BD20 . . . . .187 E7
Glynndale Dr YO12 . . . . .212 A8
Glynwed Ct **2** BD23 . . .216 E3
Goat La BD24 . . . . .131 F7
Goathland CP Sch
. . YO22 . . . . .51 C8
Goathland Gr TS14 . . . . . . .8 E5
Goats Rd DL11 . . . . .18 H5
Godfrey Rd **2** DL10 . . . .41 E4
Godley Cl YO30 . . . . .224 C3
Godwinsway **10** YO41 . .168 D2
Goker La YO51 . . . . .141 E1
Gold Thread La **3** YO8 . .197 B8
Golden Acres DL7 . . . . . . .22 E2
Golden Butts Rd LS29 . . .218 C4
Goldhill La YO7 . . . . .90 D6

Goldsborough C of E Prim
. . Sch HG5 . . . . .162 F3
Goldsborough Ct HG5 . .163 A3
Goldsborough La YO21 . .12 C4
Golf Links Ave **6** LS24 . .189 E5
Golf Links Cres **4** LS24 .189 E5
Golf Links Cres **4** LS24 .189 E5
Golf Links Ct LS24 . . . . .189 E5
Good Hope Cl WF6 . . . . .200 B2
Goodall Cl **11** BB18 . . . .172 A1
Goodenber Rd LA2 . . . . .129 A8
Goodramgate YO1 . . . . . .233 B2
Goodrick Cl HG2 . . . . . . .222 B5
Goodsyard The YO8 . . . .232 D5
Goodwood Ave LS25 . . . .194 C1
Goodwood Cl YO12 . . . . .212 B6
Goodwood Gr YO26 . . . . .227 F1
Goodwood Rd **3** DL9 . . .40 E3
Goody Cross LS26 . . . . . .194 A1
Goody Cross La LS26 . . . .194 A1
Goole Coll DN14 . . . . . . .205 F2
Goole Gram Sch DN14 . . .205 F3
Goose Green Cl **8** DL9 . .40 E3
Goose La YO61 . . . . .144 C1
Goose Mire La YO12 . . . . .99 C6
Goose Track La YO60 . . .145 D6
Goosecroft Gdns DL6 . . .210 D5
Goosecroft La
. . East Harlsey DL6 . . . . . . .44 D6
. . Northallerton DL6 . . . . . .210 D5
Gooselands BD24 . . . . . .153 C6
Gooselands Hill BD23 . . .107 D2
Goosepastures TS16 . . . . . .5 E3
Gordale Cl **3** BB18 . . . . .171 D1
Gordale La BD23 . . . . . . .133 A2
Gordale Mount HG5 . . . .221 C6
Gordon Ave HG1 . . . . . . .219 E6
Gordon Cres DL10 . . . . . .209 D8
Gordon St
. . **23** Glusburn BD20 . . . . .187 E7
. . Ilkley LS29 . . . . .218 C4
. . Scarborough YO12 . . . . .212 E5
. . York YO10 . . . . .228 E3
Gordon Terr BD20 . . . . . .173 C1
Gore La DN14 . . . . .207 B5
Gore Sands TS5 . . . . .6 D6
Gormire Ave **2** YO31 . . .225 D3
Gormire Cl YO7 . . . . .211 D3
Gorse Cl YO8 . . . . .232 C2
Gorse Hill **1** YO19 . . . . .184 F7
Gorse La LS25 . . . . .195 D3
Gorse Paddock YO32 . . .225 F2
Gosden St **8** BD23 . . . . .217 A3
Goslipgate **11** YO18 . . . . .95 F6
Gough Rd DL9 . . . . .40 D4
Gouldings Cl YO11 . . . . .100 A7
Goulton La TS9 . . . . .25 E3
Southwaith Cl YO30 . . . .224 A6
Government House Rd
. . YO30 . . . . .228 A6
Gowans The YO61 . . . . . .144 C3
Gowdall Broach DN14 . . .207 E8
Gowdall La
. . Pollington DN14 . . . . . . .207 F7
. . Snaith & Cowick DN14 . .204 B1
Gowdall Rd DN14 . . . . . .203 E2
Gower Rd Aske DL10 . . . .20 D1
. . Richmond DL10 . . . . . . .209 C8
. . York YO24 . . . . .230 E8
Gowland La YO13 . . . . . . .54 B2
Gowthorpe YO8 . . . . .232 C5
Gracious St Huby YO61 . .144 A4
. . **7** Knaresborough HG5 . .221 B5
Grafton Cl TS14 . . . . .8 F6
Grafton La YO51 . . . . . . .141 C3
Grafton St WF10 . . . . . . .200 F3
Graham Cl YO11 . . . . . . .213 B7
Graham Cres YO12 . . . . .212 C5
Graham Dr WF10 . . . . . .201 A4
Graham Rd HG4 . . . . . . .113 D3
Graham Sch YO12 . . . . . .212 B8
Grainbeck La HG3 . . . . . .219 A7
Grainger Row HG4 . . . . .214 C5
Grainger St DL3 . . . . .3 D4
Grains La BD23 . . . . .154 E8
Grammar Sch La DL6 . . .210 D3
Grampian Cl **4** YO32 . . .225 F5
Granary Ct YO1 . . . . .233 B3
Granby Pk HG1 . . . . .219 F3
Granby Rd HG1 . . . . .219 F3
Grandage La BD22 . . . . .187 A7
Grange Ave Aiskew DL7 . .63 C4
. . Filey YO14 . . . . .101 B3
. . Garforth LS25 . . . . .194 C3
. . Harrogate HG1 . . . . . . .219 D5
. . **5** Hurworth-on-Tees DL2 . . .3 D1
. . Hurworth-on-Tees DL2 . . . .22 D8
. . Ilkley LS29 . . . . .218 D4
. . Scarborough YO12 . . . . .212 E4
. . Scarborough YO12 . . . . .212 A8
. . Tadcaster LS24 . . . . . . .189 F6
. . York YO10 . . . . .231 E8
Grange Cres
. . Middlesbrough TS7 . . . . . . .7 B6
. . **10** Tadcaster LS24 . . . .189 E6
Grange Ct YO12 . . . . .99 D7
Grange Dr TS9 . . . . .26 C7
Grange Est LS29 . . . . . . .218 D4
Grange Garth YO10 . . . . .228 D2

Grange La **1** Dacre HG3 . . .1
. . Rufforth YO26 2
. . Scackleton YO62 1
. . Stonebeck Down HG3 1
. . York YO26 2
Grange Park Cl WF10 . . .20
Grange Park Rd HG4 2
Grange Rd **19** Bedale DL8 . . .
. . Brompton-on-Swale DL10 . .
. . Burley in Wharfedale
. . LS29 1
. . **8** Campsall DN6 2
. . Castleford WF10 2
. . Colburn DL9 . . . .
. . Darlington DL1 . . . .
. . Farnhill BD20 1
. . Goole DN14 2
. . Tadcaster LS24 1
. . Thornaby TS17 . . . .
Grange St **4** YO10 22
Grange Terr HG4 2
Grange The
. . Kirby Hill YO51 1
. . Thirsk YO7 2
Grange View
. . **1** Otley LS21 1
. . Towton LS24 . . . .
Grangefield Ave **32**
. . LS29 2
Granger Ave YO26 22
Grangeside DL3 . . . .
Grant Cl DL6 . . . .
Grantham Dr YO26 2
Grantley Cl HG3 . . . .
Grantley Dr HG3 . . . .
Grantley Hall Coll
. . HG4 1
Grantley Pl **4** HG3 2
Grants Ave YO10 2
Granville Rd
. . **2** Filey YO14 10
. . **4** Harrogate HG1 2
. . Scarborough YO11 2
Granville Sq **3** YO11 . . .2
Granville St
. . **20** Normanton South WF6 .20
. . Skipton BD23 2
Granville Terr **4** YO10 . . .2
Grape La Whitby YO22 2
. . York YO1 2
Grasmere Ave **3** LS22 . .18
Grasmere Cl **11** BB18 . .1
Grasmere Cres HG2 2
Grasmere Dr YO10 2
Grasmere Gr **5** YO30 . . .2
Grass Croft TS21 . . . .
Grass Wood La BD23 1
Grassfield Cl HG3 1
Grassgill La DL8 . . . .
Grassholme YO24 2
Grassington Ave TS7 . . . .
Grassington C of E Prim Sc
. . BD23 1
Grassington Rd
. . Middlesbrough TS4 . . . .
. . Skipton BD23 2
Gravel Hole La
. . Sowerby YO7 . . . .
. . Thirsk YO7 . . . .
Gravelhill La DN14 2
Gravelly Hill La LS17 1
Gray La YO62 . . . .
Gray St **28** Whitby YO21 . .2
. . York YO23 2
Grays Rd YO62 . . . .
Grayson Dr YO26 2
Grayston Plain La
. . HG3 . . . .
Great & Little Preston C of
. . Inf Sch LS26 2
Great & Little Preston Prim
. . Sch LS26 2
Great Auk TS14 . . . .
Great Ave DL14 2
Great Ayton Sta TS9 . . . .
Great Cl YO8 1
Great Close La BD24 1
Great Croft Cl **4** YO13 . . .
Great Moor Rd YO13 . . . . .
Great North Rd
. . Ledsham LS25 2
. . Micklefield LS25 2
Great North Way
. . YO26 2
Great Ouseburn Cty Prim S
. . YO26 1
Great Pasture LS29 2
Great Side Rd YO17 . . . .
Great Smeaton Cty Prim Sc
. . DL6 . . . .
Greatwood Ave BD23 2
Greatwood Prim Sch
. . BD23 2
Greavefield La WF8 20
Greaves Smithy LS29 1
Grebe Ave DL9 . . . .
Green Ave LS25 1
Green Balk
. . Great & Little Broughton
. . TS9 . . . .
. . Millington YO42 1
Green Bank La HG4 1
Green Cl
. . Bradleys Both BD20 1
. . **2** Linton-on-Ouse YO30 . .1

Green Cl continued
ddlesbrough TS7 ....7 D5
eeton with Eastburn
20 ....187 F7
en Cres The Y062 ....120 B5
een Croft Gdns 24
911 ....100 B6
een Dike Y032 ....225 C8
een Dikes La Y025 ...151 F1
en Dyke La Y062 .....120 C5
een Dykes 215 A3
een Dykes La Y010 ..228 E7
een End Ave 32 BB18 ..172 A1
een End Rd 34 BB18 ..172 A1
en Gate La
akehall DL8 ....62 E5
ddale Y021 ....27 F8
ng Preston B023 ....153 F5
en Haggs La HG3 ....223 F1
en Hammerton C of E
Sch Y026 ....164 B3
een Head La B024 ...131 E2
een Hill La HG3 ......118 E6
een Hill La BD22 .....187 A5
een Hills Y060 ....168 B7
een Hills La DL7 ....64 B6
een Howard's Regimental
Mus 209 C6
en Howard's Dr 8
012 ....75 F5
en Howards Rd
ckering Y018 ....96 A6
chmond DL10 ....209 B8
en Island Y012 ....99 D7
en La
Idingham LS29 ....174 F4
plleton Roebuck Y023 ..191 B6
armby on the Marsh
N14 ....205 A6
arton-le-Street Y017 ....120 E8
dale DL8 ....62 F3
shopthorpe Y024 ....231 A6
tton Spa LS23 ....188 F7
atterick Y062 ....224 E4
tton Leonard HG3 ....140 B2
rton-on-Forse HG4 ....86 D6
stleford WF10 ....200 E3
tlewton Y062 ....119 B6
lllingham LS22 ....188 A8
meythorpe & Clareton
55 ....163 B5
nstable Burton DL8 ....61 A6
atnall Y062 ....47 C4
ndall with Leckby
61 ....115 D4
arlington DL1 ....3 D8
shforth Y07 ....115 A2
ast Rounton TS15 ....24 F4
adnor Y062 ....69 G3
erndale West Y062 ....48 E1
alkton Y012 ....99 F1
arforth LS25 ....194 D4
usburn BD20 ....187 D7
eat Ouseburn Y026 ....142 A1
atland B023 ....157 C1
arnow Y062 ....93 C5
arrogate HG2 ....222 C6
eck DN14 ....207 D8
arton BD23 ....171 B5
utton Rudby TS15 ....25 B4
dley LS26 ....176 C2
ggleton LA6 ....103 E2
ppax LS25 ....194 C2
rby Wiske DL7 ....178 D2
orth Cowton DL7 ....22 B2
orth Duffield Y08 ....198 F8
dley LS21 ....176 F1
ngtoft Y025 ....151 D5
obberston Y011 ....100 D5
eston WF10 ....200 D2
ttle Ayton TS9 ....27 A8
atlethorpe HG4 ....140 A2
ckland DL11 ....38 E7
aunby Y07 ....64 D1
lanwith with Hazlewood
24 ....189 D4
tton BD22 ....187 F2
061 ....144 E4
ickletown LS26 ....200 C5
iddlesbrough TS5 ....6 E8
oor Monkton Y026 ....164 F1
wsby TS7 ....7 C3
orth Cowton DL7 ....22 B2
orth Duffield Y08 ....198 F8
dley LS21 ....176 F1
ngtoft Y025 ....151 D5

Green La continued
Whorlton DL6 ....45 F7
Wigginton Y032 ....166 D5
Winksley HG4 ....112 F2
Wressle DN14 ....205 D8
York Y030 ....225 A1
York Y024 ....227 D8
Green La E Y07 ....211 B1
Green La W Y07 ....211 A1
Green Lane Prim Sch
TS5 ....6 E8
Green Mdw BB8 ....186 A1
Green Mdws Y031 ....229 A7
Green Park Ave 15
Y011 ....100 B6
Green Park Rd 14 Y011 ..100 B6
Green Pastures B23 .....62 C5
Green Row LS26 ....200 B5
Green St
7 Cowling BD22 ....187 B6
Darlington DL1 ....3 D5
Green Sward Y031 ....229 A8
Green Sykes Rd BD22 ..187 A6
Green The Brompton DL6 ..43 F3
Castleford WF10 ....201 B4
1 Clapham LA2 ....130 C8
Cleasby DL2 ....2 F1
Conistone with Kilnsey
BD23 ....134 B6
20 Dunnington Y019 ......184 F7
Garforth LS25 ....194 C3
Hellifield BD23 ....154 B3
High Coniscliffe DL2 ....2 C6
Kettlewell with Starbotton
BD23 ....108 B3
Kirkby Malzeard HG4 ......112 A6
8 Kirklevington TS15 ....24 E8
Linton-on-Ouse Y030 .....164 F8
Longnewton TS21 ....5 A7
1 Otley LS21 ....176 F1
Rawcliffe DN14 ....205 A1
Scalby Y012 ....212 B7
Seamer TS9 ....6 F1
5 Seamer Y012 ....99 D6
1 Skelton Y030 ....224 B5
Slingsby Y062 ....120 E3
11 Thirsk Y07 ....211 C3
Tockwith Y026 ....181 C7
2 Tollerton Y061 ....143 B3
7 Topcliffe Y07 ....89 B1
Wistow Y08 ....197 D6
York Y026 ....227 C3
Green Village Y07 ....88 C5
Green Wlk BB18 ....172 A1
Green Way
Glusburn BD20 ....187 E8
Harrogate HG2 ....222 C6
Middlesbrough TS7 ....7 D7
York Y032 ....225 F4
Green Ways 2 Y08 ....197 D6
Green Wlk BB18 ....172 A1
Greenacre Cl TS9 ....7 F1
Greenacres
Morton-on-Swale DL7 ......64 A6
Skipton BD23 ....217 B5
Stainton & Thornton TS8 ...6 D4
York Y032 ....225 F4
Greenacres Cl 3 Y08 ...197 D1
Greenacres Cres 7
Y08 ....197 D1
Greenacres Gr 4 Y08 ...197 D1
Greenacres Gr 5 Y08 ...197 D1
Greenbank 3 BB18 ....172 B1
Greenbank Cl WF10 .....200 D3
Greenbank Rd DL3 ....3 B5
Greenberfield La
BB18 ....171 E2
Greencliffe Dr Y030 .....228 A6
Greencroft Cl 2 Y019 ..184 F7
Greencroft Ct 1 Y019 ...184 F7
Greendown Cl LS29 .....218 D4
Greenfield Ave LS25 ....194 D1
Greenfield Cl DL2 ....3 E1
Greenfield Dr
1 Brayton Y08 ....197 D1
Eaglescliffe TS16 ....5 D8
Greenfield Gdns BD20 ..187 E7
Greenfield Park Dr
Y031 ....229 A7
Greenfield Rd 8 Y08 ....213 A4
Greenfield St 5 BD23 ...216 D3
Greenfields DN14 ....207 F6
Greenfields Ave HG2 ...220 C2
Greenfields Dr HG2 ......220 C2
Greenfields Rd HG2 ......220 C2
Greenfinch Cl 8 Y07 ....211 B2
Greenfoot La LA2 ....128 E8
Greengales Ct Y019 ......193 A8
Greengales La Y019 ......193 A8
Greengate
Malton Y017 ....215 C4
Scarborough Y012 ....212 D4
Greengate Dr HG5 ....221 B8
Greengate La
Collingham LS22 ....188 F6
Kirkby Fleetham with Fencote
DL7 ....42 B1
Knaresborough HG5 ....221 B8
Thornton-le-Dale Y018 ......96 C6
Greengate View HG5 ....221 B8
Greengates La 142 E3
Greenhill Cres HG5 ......210 E3
Greenhill La Y07 ....66 B4
Greenholme Cl
12 Boroughbridge Y051 ..141 B6
7 Burley in Warfedale
LS29 ....176 C1
Greenhow Hill HG3 ......136 C2

Greenhow Hill Rd
HG3 ....159 B6
Greenhow Pk LS29 ......176 B1
Greenhowsyke La DL6 ..210 E4
Greenland La Y07 ....3 C2
Greenlands TS15 ....25 C6
Greenlands La Y08 ....197 C3
Greenlands Rd Y018 ......95 F6
Greenless La LS21 ....177 E4
Greenroyd Gr BD20 .....187 E6
Greens Yd Y022 ....208 E7
Greensborough Ave 3
Y026 ....227 B5
Greenshaw Dr Y032 .....225 C8
Greenside 18 Y019 ......184 F7
Greenside Cl 24 Y019 ..184 F7
Greenside Ct 5 DL2 ....3 E1
Greenside Wlk 25 Y019 ..184 F7
Greenstead Rd Y012 ....212 B8
Greenway The
2 Haxby Y032 ....225 C7
2 Middleton St George DL2 ..4 C4
Greenways Dr 9 Y08 ...197 D6
Greenways The DL7 ......63 C8
Greenwood Pk HG3 .....137 B4
Greenwood Ave HG3 ....137 B4
Greenwood Gr Y024 ....230 C8
Greet's Hill Y017 ....169 E7
Gregory Cl Y030 ....224 C5
Grenadier Dr DL6 ....210 F3
Grendon Gdns 8 DL2 .....4 C4
Grenley St 8 WF11 ......202 A2
Grenville Rd TS17 ....6 B6
Grenwich Cl 6 Y030 .....224 E3
Gresham Cl DL1 ....3 D7
Gresley Ct 3 Y026 ....227 B4
Greta Heath 2 LA6 ......102 F2

Grewelthorpe C of E Prim
Sch HG4 ....112 C7
Grey Ct Y061 ....142 B4
Grey St HG2 ....222 E7
Grey Thorn La HG5 ......163 D3
Grey Towers Dr TS7 ....7 D5
Greyfriars Cl DL3 ....3 A5
Greylands Park Ave
Y012 ....212 C8
Greylands Park Dr
Y012 ....212 C8
Greylands Park Gr 3
Y012 ....212 C8
Greylands Park Rd
Y012 ....212 C8
Greystoke Rd Y030 ....224 E1
Greystoke Cl 2 LS26 ....176 C1
Greystoke Rd Y032 ......225 C7
Greystone Head HG4 ....112 A4
Greystone
Aldbrough DL2 ....2 A4
Stanwick St John DL11 ......1 A4
Greystone Pk LS25 ....188 F1
Greystonegill La LA2 ....129 D7
Greystones Ave HG3 ...161 B4
Greystones Cl LS25 ......188 F1
Greystones La BB8 ....186 A3

H

Habton Rd Y017 ....121 B7
Hackforth & Hornby C of E
Prim Sch DL8 ....62 E8
Hackforth Rd 2 TS18 .....5 D8
Hackness C of E Prim Sch
Y013 ....74 E5
Hackness Dr Y012 ....212 A8
Hackness Rd Y012 ....212 A8
Haddlesey Rd WF11 ....202 D5
Haddocks La Y07 ....142 B4
Hadrian Ave Y010 ....229 B3

Hag La
Cottingwith Y042 ....193 C4
Raskelf Y061 ....142 E8
South Kilvington Y07 ....211 D6
Sproxton Y062 ....92 D4
Hag La Colton LS24 ......190 E8
Cottingwith Y042 ....193 C4
Cowesby Y07 ....66 C4
Dunnington Y019 ....184 F6
Hemingbrough Y08 ....199 A1
South Milford LS25 ....196 C2
Hagg Rd Y062 ....69 F2
Haggersgate 10 Y021 ..208 D7
Haggitt Hill La DL6 ....23 C3
Hags La DN6 ....207 D2
Hags Rd HG3 ....223 C4
Hague St 31 Y012 ....75 D5
Hagworm Hill * Y07 ....75 C2
Haig Rd DL9 ....209 G8
Haig St Y08 ....232 B6
Haigh La DN14 ....207 A6
Hailsham Ave TS17 ....6 B5
Hailstone Dr DL6 ....210 F5
Hales La Y08 ....204 E5
Haley's Terr Y031 ....228 E8
Half Acres Jun & Inf Sch
WF10 ....200 E4
Half Moon St 1 Y030 ...164 F7
Halfpenny Cl HG5 ....221 C7
Halfpenny La HG5 ....221 C7
Halifax Ct 7 Y030 ....225 A1
Halifax Way Y041 ....185 A3
Hall Arm La Y051 ....141 D5
Hall Ave 10 BD20 ....187 E6
Hall Brow BD23 ....155 A5
Hall Cl 11 Airmyn DN14 ...205 E4
Austwick LA2 ....130 C2
Burley in Warfedale
LS29 ....176 B1

Grove Rd continued
Ilkley LS29 ....218 A3
Grove Road CP Sch
HG1 ....219 D4
Grove St 33 Earby BB18 ..172 A1
9 Harrogate HG2 ....220 C3
Norton Y017 ....215 E3
15 Whitby Y021 ....208 D6
Grove Terr 11 DL8 ....60 E2
Grove Terrace La
Y031 ....233 C4
Grove The
Eaglescliffe TS16 ....5 E2
Guisborough TS14 ....8 D5
Harrogate HG1 ....219 E4
5 Hutton Rudby TS15 ......25 D5
Ilkley LS29 ....218 A4
Kellington DN14 ....203 A3
Kippax LS25 ....194 D1
Middlesbrough TS5 ....6 E8
Middlesbrough TS7 ....7 B7
Normanton South WF6 ....200 A1
Norton Y017 ....215 E2
1 Seamer Y012 ....99 D6
Skipton BD23 ....217 C3
Swillington LS26 ....194 A1
York Y024 ....230 E6
Grove View Y031 ....228 A6
Grundy Way 11 DL10 .....41 E4
Grunton La DL2 ....2 D7
Grysedale La BD23 ....134 B2
Guadaloupe Rd DL9 ......40 C4
Guards Ct 7 Y012 ....75 F5
Guildford Rd TS6 ....7 E8
Guisborough Mus *
TS14 ....8 F7
Guisborough Rd
Aislaby Y021 ....31 F8
Great Ayton TS9 ....7 F1
Lockwood TS12 ....10 A5
Middlesbrough TS7 ....7 C6
Thornaby TS17 ....6 B8
Whitby Y021 ....208 A5
Guisborough RUFC TS14 ..8 F6
Guisborough Swimming Pool
TS14 ....8 E7
Gunby Rd Y08 ....199 D5
Gunbywood Rd Y08 ......199 D6
Guncroft La Y062 ....69 D1
Guning La DL11 ....36 B4
Gurnard La TS8 ....7 D5
Gurney Pease Prim Sch
DL1 ....3 D6
Gurney St DL1 ....3 D6
Guy La Y07 ....114 F2
Gypsy La
Castleford WF10 ....201 B3
Middlesbrough TS7 ....7 D6
Gypsy Lane Sta TS7 ....7 D6

Hall Cl continued
Cawood Y08 ....191 D3
11 Glusburn BD20 ....187 E6
Hall Croft BD23 ....216 E4
Hall Ct WF11 ....201 E4
Hall Dr
Burley in Warfedale
LS29 ....176 B1
Glusburn BD20 ....187 E6
Middlesbrough TS5 ....6 F7
Hall Farm Cl 11 Y019 ...197 F8
Hall Farm Pk LS25 ....194 A1
Hall Garth 2 Y018 ....95 F7
Hall Garth Cl LS24 ....190 C3
Hall Garth La Y062 ....70 E4
Hall Gdns B023 ....173 F1
Hall Green La LS17 ....178 C4
Hall Ings La Y062 ....70 E4
Hall La Askwith LS21 ....176 C4
Blubberhouses LS21 ....159 C2
Caldwell DL11 ....1 C4
Church Fenton LS24 ....196 C7
Harome Y062 ....93 C4
Harrogate HG1 ....219 E6
Hawnby DL6 ....46 B1
Huddleston with Newthorpe
LS25 ....195 C3
Leathley LS21 ....177 D1
Ledston WF10 ....200 F7
Myton-on-Swale Y061 .....142 A6
Norton DN6 ....206 E2
Sheriff Hutton Y060 ....186 A2
Hall Moor Cl TS15 ....24 E8
Hall Orchards Ave
LS22 ....180 D3
Hall Park Cl 2 Y013 ....75 D5
Hall Park Croft LS25 .....200 D8
Hall Park Gr 9 Y013 ......75 D5
Hall Park Mdws LS25 ...200 D8
Hall Park Orch LS25 .....200 D8
Hall Park Rd
Hunmanby Y014 ....126 F8
Walton LS23 ....181 A2
Hall Pasture 9 Y022 ......32 A6
Hall Pk Wistow Y08 ....198 A5
York Y010 ....229 B1
Hall Rd
Swillington LS26 ....194 A1
Trawden Forest BB8 ....186 A2
Hall Rise
Burley in Warfedale
LS29 ....176 B1
2 Haxby Y032 ....166 F5
Hall Sq 5 Y051 ....141 B5
Hall Tower Hill * LS15 ..194 B8
Hall View Dr DL3 ....3 A6
Hall Way 9 BD20 ....187 E6
Halladale Cl 11 Y024 ...230 B7
Hallam Cl 2 LS24 ....189 E6
Hallam La LS21 ....176 D3
Hallam's Yd 4 BD23 .....216 F4
Hallard Way 17 Y032 ....167 B7
Hallcroft Dr 18 LS29 .....175 A4
Hallcroft La Y023 ....230 A3
Hallfield Ave LS25 ....194 F4
Hallfield La
Nawton Y062 ....69 C3
Wetherby LS22 ....180 C3
Hallfield Rd Y031 ....228 E5
Hallfield Terr LS25 ....194 F4
Hallgarth Alne Y061 ....142 F4
Great & Little Broughton
TS9 ....26 E5
Hallgarth Comp Sch TS5 ..6 F7
Hallwith Rd DL8 ....63 A3
Halnaby Ave DL3 ....2 F5
Halstead Rd HG2 ....222 E7
Hambleton Ave
Northallerton DL7 ....210 C2
Thirsk Y07 ....211 D3
York Y010 ....229 C4
Hambleton C of E Prim Sch
Y08 ....196 F1
Hambleton Cl
13 Easingwold Y061 ....143 D8
9 Thirsk Y07 ....211 C3
Hambleton Ct 3
Y061 ....143 C8
Hambleton Gate TS9 ......26 C7
Hambleton Gr HG5 ....221 B6
Hambleton La Y062 ....91 F2
Hambleton Leisure Ctr
DL6 ....210 C3
Hambleton Pl 2 Y07 .....211 C3
Hambleton Rd
6 Catterick Garrison DL9 ..40 E3
Harrogate HG2 ....222 E7
Norton Y017 ....215 E2
Hambleton Terr Y031 ....228 C7
Hambleton View
14 Haxby Y032 ....166 D5
Thirsk Y07 ....211 D3
3 Tollerton Y061 ....143 B3
Hambleton Way
Easingwold Y061 ....143 D8
York Y032 ....225 F3
Hamer Bank Y018 ....49 A4
Hamerton Cl 10 Y014 ...127 A8
Hamerton Rd 10 Y014 ...127 A8
Hamhall La DL7 ....63 D6
Hamilton Ave HG5 ....222 E8

Hamilton Cl YO13 ....75 C5
Hamilton Ct WF6 ....200 A2
Hamilton Dr
  Darlington DL1 ....3 D8
  York YO24 ....227 E2
Hamilton Dr E YO24 .....227 F2
Hamilton Dr W YO24 ....227 D2
Hamilton Gn YO17 ....215 B3
Hamilton Way YO24 .....227 E2
Hamlet The ⑧ DL4 ......202 F2
Hamley La YO62 ....70 F3
Hammer Rd HG4 ....85 B7
Hammersike Rd
  Cawood YO8 ....196 F5
  Wistow YO8 ....197 A4
Hammerton Cl
  Green Hammerton YO26 .164 D3
  ⑤ York YO26 ....227 B3
Hammerton Dr
  Garforth LS25 ....194 D3
  Hellifield BD23 ....154 B3
Hammerton Sta YO26 ...164 C3
Hammond Dr DL1 ....3 C4
Hammond Rd YO13 ....54 A8
Hampden St YO1 ....233 B1
Hampden Way LS17 ......6 B6
Hampshire Cl
  Ilkley LS29 ....218 D4
  ⑤ Pontefract WF8 .....201 C2
Hampsthwaite C of E Prim
  Sch HG3 ....161 A5
Hampsthwaite Rd
  HG1 ....219 C4
Hampton Rd YO12 ......212 E5
Hancow Rd
  Hartoft YO18 ....50 A1
  Rosedale East Side YO18 .49 F3
Handal Cl TS14 ....9 A6
Handley Cl
  Stockton-on-Tees TS18 .....5 F7
  York YO30 ....225 A2
Hang Bank DL10 ....21 B8
Hanger La DN14 ....204 B3
Hanghow La DL8 ....84 C8
Hanging Stone La YO18 .49 E4
Hangingstone Rd
  LS29 ....218 D2
Hankins La YO42 ....193 D3
Hanover Pl WF11 ....201 D4
Hanover Rd ⑥ YO11 ....212 F5
Hanover St E ⑤ YO26 ..227 A2
Hanover St W ⑦ YO26 .227 F5
Hansom Pl YO31 ....225 C7
Hanson Ave WF6 ....200 A1
Harborough Cl ⑳ YO14 .126 F8
Harbour Rise ⑤ DL8 ....63 A2
Harbour View ⑦ DL8 ...63 A3
Harcourt Ave YO12 ....212 E3
Harcourt Cl
  Bishopthorpe YO23 ....231 A4
  Wheldrake YO19 ....192 F7
Harcourt Dr
  Addingham LS29 ....174 F5
  Harrogate HG1 ....219 E2
Harcourt Pl ⑷ YO11 ...213 A5
Harcourt Rd ⑷ HG1 ....219 E3
Harcourt St YO31 ......228 E5
Hard Gate BD23 ....134 A3
Hard Stiles DL11 ....39 B7
Hardcastle Ave ⑧ WF8 .201 B1
Harden Cl YO30 ....224 F2
Harden Rd BB18 ....186 A7
Hardenshaw La YO8 ...204 B4
Hardigate Rd YO18 ....72 B7
Hardings La
  Glusburn BD20 ....187 F8
  Middleton LS29 ....218 A8
Hardisty Hill HG3 ......159 C3
Hardrada Way ⑧ YO41 .168 D1
Hardy Mdws ⑾ BD23 ..134 E2
Hardy St YO8 ....232 E4
Harebell Cl
  ⒄ Harrogate HG3 ....161 B3
  Northallerton DL7 .....210 C1
Harecroft Rd ⑫ LS21 ...177 A1
Haregill Bank HG4 ......85 E6
Harehills La BD22 ......187 E1
Haresfield Way TS17 .....6 A5
Harewell Cl HG3 ....137 D3
Harewell La ⑷ HG3 ....137 D3
Harewood Ave
  ⑤ Normanton South WF6 .200 B2
  ⑾ Scalby YO12 ....75 C5
  ⑾ Scalby YO12 ....212 D8
Harewood Chase DL7 ...210 D2
Harewood Cl
  Morton-on-Swale DL7 ..64 A6
  Rawcliffe YO30 ....224 D2
  ⑤ Wigginton YO32 ....166 D5
Harewood La ⑷ YO14 ..101 A1
Harewood La DL7 ......210 C3
Harewood Rd
  Collingham LS22 ......188 A8
  Harrogate HG3 ....219 A5
  Ripon HG4 ....214 A3
  Skipton BD23 ....216 E4
Harford Rd YO11 ......100 B6
Hargill
  Gilling with Hartforth & Sedbury
    DL10 ....20 E4
  Harmby DL8 ....60 E4
  West Witton DL8 ....59 C3
Hargill Cl DL8 ....60 E4
Hargill Dr DL8 ....59 C6

Hargill La Finghall DL8 ...61 E4
  ⑥ Leeming DL7 ....63 D4
  Redmire DL8 ....59 C7
Hargill Rd DL8 ....61 A3
Hargrove Rd HG2 ......220 B2
Harington Ave YO10 ..228 F4
Harker Hill DL8 ....56 C4
Harker St ⑫ WF11 ....202 A2
Harkness Cl DL7 ....63 C4
Harkness Dr DL7 ....63 C4
Harland Cl YO61 ....144 C3
Harlech Way HG2 ......222 B5
Harley Cl YO12 ....212 E5
Harley Cres DL9 ....40 F4
Harley La ⑤ YO12 .....212 E5
Harlow Ave ⑷ HG2 ....222 B7
Harlow La ⑴ YO24 ....227 F2
Harlow Cres HG2 ......222 B7
Harlow Grange Pk
  HG3 ....178 C8
Harlow Manor Pk
  HG2 ....222 B6
Harlow Moor Dr HG2 ..219 B1
Harlow Moor Rd HG2 .219 A1
Harlow Oval HG2 ......222 B8
Harlow Park Cres
  HG2 ....222 B7
Harlow Park Dr HG2 ..222 B7
Harlow Park Rd HG2 ..222 B7
Harlow Pines HG2 .....222 A7
Harlow Rd YO24 ......227 F2
Harlow Terr HG2 ......222 B7
Harlsey Castle* DL6 .....44 D5
Harlsey Cres TS18 ....5 E8
Harlsey Rd TS18 ....5 D8
Harmby Rd DL8 ....60 C5
Harness La ⑤ YO51 ...141 B4
Harold Ct YO24 ....227 D3
Harold St YO8 ....232 F4
Harolds Way ⑴ YO41 .168 D1
Harome Heads La YO62 .93 B6
Harome Heads Rd
  YO62 ....93 C6
Harper Gr BD20 ....187 E6
Harper La HG3 ....159 C6
Harper St
  Barnoldswick BB18 ...171 D1
  ⑵ Selby YO8 ....232 C5
Harper Terr TS18 ....5 D8
Harpers Sq ⑺ BD20 ..187 E6
Harpers Terr DL2 ....4 B5
Harr Gill DL8 ....58 A6
Harris Dr ⑨ DL10 ....41 E4
Harris St DL1 ....3 E4
Harrison Gr HG1 ......220 C4
Harrison St
  Barnoldswick BB18 ...171 E1
  York YO31 ....228 F6
Harrogate Coll HG1 ...219 D2
Harrogate District Hospl
  HG2 ....220 A2
Harrogate Gram Sch
  HG2 ....222 C8
Harrogate Granby High Sch
  HG1 ....220 A4
Harrogate Hill Jun Sch
  DL3 ....7 D7
Harrogate Ladies Coll
  HG1 ....219 C3
Harrogate Leisure Ctr
  HG2 ....222 E7
Harrogate Rd
  Bishop Monkton HG3 ..139 E5
  Boroughbridge HG5 ...141 A2
  Ferrensby HG5 ....162 E7
  Green Hammerton YO26 .164 B3
  Kirkby Overblow HG3 ..222 D1
  Knaresborough HG5 ...220 F5
  Littlethorpe HG4 ......214 C1
  Spofforth with Stockeld
    LS22 ....180 A4
  Weeton LS17 ....178 B2
Harrogate Rossett Acre CP
  Sch HG2 ....222 C7
Harrogate RUFC HG1 ..219 F3
Harrogate Sta HG1 ....219 D2
Harrogate Town AFC
  HG2 ....220 A2
Harrow Cliff La YO8 ....18 B3
Harrow Glade ⑤ YO30 .225 A1
Harrow Rd TS5 ....6 E8
Harrowing Dr ⑵ YO21 .208 C6
Harry Moor La YO8 ....197 B2
Harryfield La YO61 ....144 C7
Hart Hill Cres YO41 ...169 A2
Hartburn Village TS18 ...5 E8
Hartforth La DL10 .....20 E4
Hartington St ⑲ BB8 ..186 A3
Hartley La CA17 ....14 A7
Hartley Pl BD22 ....187 B6
Hartley Rd HG1 ....219 D4
Hartley St ⑫ BB8 .....172 A1
Hartlington Raikes
  BD23 ....157 B8
Hartoft St YO10 ....228 D2
Hartwith Ave ⑶ HG3 ..138 A1
Hartwith Bank HG3 ...138 A1
Hartwith Cl ⑷ HG3 ....219 A4
Hartwith Dr HG3 ......219 A4
Hartwith Way HG1 ....219 A4
Hartwith La ⑷ YO12 ..212 A8
Harvest Ct ⑶ WF8 ....201 C2
Harvest Croft LS29 ....176 B1
Harvest Way YO11 ....100 B7

Harwood Dale Rd YO13 ..54 A1
Hassacarr La YO19 ....184 F6
Hastings Cl ⑷ YO30 ..225 A1
Hastings Cres WF10 ...201 A4
Hatcase La ⑹ DL8 .....95 F7
Hatfield Ave TS5 ....6 E8
Hatfield Cl ⑶ YO30 ...224 E3
Hatfield Rd DL7 ....210 D3
Hatkill La YO41 ....169 B1
Hatterboard Dr YO12 ..212 C8
Hatters Cl YO23 ....230 B3
Haugh La YO8 ....202 F8
Haughton Comp Sch
  ....3 E7
Haughton Rd
  Darlington DL1 ....3 D6
  York YO30 ....228 C7
Hauling La YO23 ......191 C8
Hauxley Ct LS29 ......218 D5
Havelock St TS17 ....7 A6
Haven The ⑤ LS25 ...195 F2
Havercroft Rd ⑿ YO14 .127 A8
Havernook La HG4 ....86 A3
Havers Hill YO11 ......100 A6
Haverthwaites Dr
  LS25 ....188 F1
Havertop La WF6 .....200 C1
Havikil La HG5 ....162 A5
Havikil Pk HG5 ....162 A6
Havilland Rd TS17 ......6 B6
Havre Pk ⑴⑾ BB18 ...171 E1
Haw Gr BD23 ....154 B3
Haw Hill View WF6 ...200 A2
Haw La BD23 ....154 B3
Haw Pk ⑴ BD23 ......217 E8
Hawber Cote Dr BD20 .174 C1
Hawber La BD20 ......174 C1
Hawdon Ave YO8 .....232 D5
Hawes CP Sch DL8 .....56 D4
Hawes Rd HG1 ....220 B4
Hawes Visitor Ctr*
  DL8 ....56 D4
Hawke Garth ⑤ YO14 .127 A8
Hawkridge Cl TS17 .....6 A3
Hawkshead Cl ⑶ YO24 .230 B8
Hawkstone TS14 ....7 C4
Hawkswell La DL8 .....40 E1
Hawkswood ⑴ DL8 .....3 D1
Hawley St BB8 ....186 B3
Hawnby Rd YO8 ......204 E8
Hawshaw Rd BD22 ...186 C7
Hawsker C of E Prim Sch
  YO22 ....33 A7
Hawsker Intake Rd
  YO22 ....32 F5
Hawsker La
  Hawsker-cum-Stainsacre
    YO22 ....13 F1
  Whitby YO22 ....208 F6
Hawson Cl ⑼ YO11 ...100 B7
Hawthorn Ave
  ⑿ Knaresborough HG5 .221 B7
  Knottingley WF11 ....201 E2
  Malton YO17 ....215 D5
  Tadcaster LS24 ....189 D5
Hawthorn Cl
  ⑴ Addingham LS29 ...174 E4
  ⑶ Pickering YO18 .....96 A6
  Stutton with Hazlewood
    LS24 ....189 E5
Hawthorn Cres ⑥ LS24 .189 D5
Hawthorn Croft ⑴ LS24 .189 D5
Hawthorn Dr
  ⑺ Topcliffe YO7 ....89 B1
  Wilberfoss YO41 ......185 E5
  Wistow YO8 ....198 A5
Hawthorn Garth DN14 .202 F4
Hawthorn Gr YO31 ....225 E5
Hawthorn La YO10 .....96 A6
Hawthorn Spinney
  YO31 ....225 E5
Hawthorn Terr ⑸ LS24 .189 D5
Hawthorn Terr Ctr ⑵
  YO32 ....225 D3
Hawthorn Terr N
  YO32 ....225 D3
Hawthorn Terr S
  YO32 ....225 D3
Hawthorn Way YO14 ..101 C1
Hawthorn WlK ⑴ YO11 .100 A7
Hawthorne Ave
  ⑿ Haxby YO32 ....166 E5
  ⑴ Scotton DL9 ....40 F2
Hawthorne Cl YO13 ....75 D7
Hawthorne Dr
  Barnoldswick BB18 ...171 E2
  Guisborough TS14 ......8 E6
Hawthorns
  ⑶ Riccall YO19 ....197 F8
  ⑵ Riccall YO19 ....197 F8
Hawthorns La BD23 ...133 B2
Hawthorns The
  ⑶ Addington BD20 ...187 E7
  ⑾ Great Ayton TS9 .....8 A2
Haxby Moor Rd YO32 .166 F7
Haxby Rd Clifton YO31 .225 D1
  Middleton St George DL2 ...4 C4
  New Earswick YO32 ...225 D6
  York YO31 ....233 B4
Haxby Road Prim Sch
  YO31 ....225 D2
Hay Brow Cl YO13 .....75 C5
Hay Brow Cres YO13 ...75 C5
Hay La YO13 ....75 C5
Hay-a-Park La HG5 ...221 D7
Hayfield Ave LS23 ....188 E5
Hayforth Cl YO30 .....225 A2

Haygate La YO18 ......95 F5
Haygill Nook BD23 ...174 B5
Hayhills La BD20 .....174 B2
Hayton Wood View
  LS25 ....194 F8
Haywain The LS29 ...218 D3
Haywra Cres ⑥ HG1 ..219 E3
Haywra St HG1 ....219 D3
Hazel Bank HG5 ......162 D6
Hazel Cl Pannal HG3 ..222 E2
  York YO22 ....225 D2
Hazel Ct ⑾ DL8 ....63 B3
Hazel Dr HG3 ....222 C3
Hazel Garth YO31 ....229 B7
Hazel Gr
  Middlesbrough TS7 .....7 C6
  Pontefract WF8 ......201 C1
  Sutton BD20 ....187 E7
Hazel Grove Rd BD20 .187 E7
Hazel Hill ⑷ YO12 .....75 A2
Hazel Old La DN14 ...203 C2
Hazel Rd
  ⑵ Boroughbridge YO51 .141 B4
  ⑶ Filey YO14 ....101 A4
  Knottingley WF11 ....201 F1
Hazel Rise LS25 ......200 B5
Hazelheads La HG5 ...221 C8
Hazelmere Ct YO32 ...225 E3
Hazelnut Gr YO30 ....225 B2
Hazelwood Ave
  Garforth LS25 ....194 D3
  York YO10 ....229 D4
Hazing La DN14 ......207 B6
Hazler La BD23 ....157 D7
Headingley Cres ⑶ DL1 ..3 F6
Headingley Rd ⑴ DN6 .206 E2
Headland Cl ⑶ YO32 .166 E5
Headland La YO18 ....72 B4
Headlands La
  Howgrave DL8 ....87 F2
  Knottingley WF11 ....201 F2
  Pontefract WF8 ......201 B1
Headlands Prim Sch
  YO32 ....225 D8
Headlands Rd YO62 ...70 E2
Headlands The DL3 .....3 B6
Headley Cl ⑶ YO30 ..225 B1
Headley La LS23 .....188 F5
Heads Bank DL8 ....58 F3
Heads La BB18 ....186 A7
Heads Rd Newton YO13 .75 F8
  Pickering YO18 ....71 F8
Headwell La LS24 .....195 E7
Healaugh La YO26 ...181 F4
Healaugh Priory*
  LS24 ....181 E1
Heald Brow BB18 ....171 D2
Heald St WF10 ....200 F4
Healdfield Rd WF10 ..201 A4
Healdwood Rd WF10 ..201 A4
Healey Gr YO31 ......228 F8
Heathfield Prim Sch
  DL1 ....3 E5
Heath Cl ⑵ YO24 ....227 F2
Heath Cres BD20 ....173 E3
Heath Croft YO10 ....231 F7
Heath Dr
  Boston Spa LS23 ......188 D8
  ⑺ Low Bradley BD20 .173 E3
Heath Gr HG2 ....219 B1
Heath Moor Dr YO10 .231 F8
Heath Pk ⑷ LS29 .....175 C2
Heath Ride YO32 .....167 B8
Heathcliff Gdns ⑤
  YO12 ....212 C8
Heather Bank
  ⑧ Stamford Bridge YO41 .168 D2
  ⑴ Tadcaster LS24 ....189 D6
Heather Brow ⑽ BB18 .172 B1
Heather Cl ⑹ Selby YO8 .232 C3
  ⑶ Whorlton DL6 ......25 D1
  York YO32 ....226 A4
Heather Croft ⑷ YO10 .231 F8
Heather Dr YO22 .....208 E3
Heather View BD23 ..217 B3
Heather Way ⑴⑻ HG3 .161 B3
Heatherdene LS24 ....189 E6
Heatherdene Rd ⑧ DL7 .40 E4
Heathfield Dr HG5 ....221 C6
Heathfield Pk DL2 .....4 C4
Heathfield Rd ⑴ YO10 .229 A3
Heathness Rd LS29 ...174 E5
Heathrow TS17 ....6 C7
Heathrow Cl ⑶ DL2 .....4 C4
Hebden Bank HG3 ....138 F4
Hebden Bdge BD23 ..134 E2
Hebdon Rise ⑵ YO26 .227 D4
Heber Dr BD23 ....172 A5
Heber's Ghyll Dr ⑶
  LS29 ....175 C2
Heber's Gr LS29 .....175 C2
Hebron Rd TS9 ....26 B7
Heck & Pollington Lake
  DN14 ....207 E7
Heck Gill La HG3 .....160 A5
Heck La DN14 ....207 C7
Heckler Cl ⑶ HG4 ....214 C4
Heckler La HG4 ......214 C4
Heddon Gr TS17 ....6 A3
Hedley St TS14 ....8 F7
Height La BD23 ......174 C6
Height Lands La YO23 .230 B6
Heights La BD20 .....174 A2
Helena St LS25 ....200 C8
Helks Brow LA2 ......128 E2
Hell Wath Gr HG4 .....214 A2
Hell Wath La
  Littlethorpe HG4 .....214 A2

Hell Wath La continued
  Markingfield Hall HG4 ...138 ...
Hellifield CP Sch
  BD23 ....154 ...
Hellifield Rd BD23 ....155 ...
Hellifield Sta BD23 ...154 ...
Helmsdale YO24 ....230 ...
Helmsley Castle*
  ....92 ...
Helmsley Cty Prim Sch
  YO62 ....92 ...
Helmsley Dr TS14 ....8 ...
Helmsley Gr ⑿ YO32 .166 ...
Helmsley Rd TS9 ....26 ...
Helmsley Way DL7 ...210 ...
Helperby & Myton La
  YO61 ....142 ...
Helperby La YO51 ....141 ...
Helredale Gdns YO22 .208 ...
Helredale Rd YO22 ...208 ...
Helston Rd WF6 ......200 ...
Helwath Rd YO13 ......53 ...
Helwith Rd DL11 ....38 ...
Hemingbrough CP Sch
  YO8 ....198 ...
Hemingford Gdns TS15 ..5 ...
Hemishor Dr LS26 ....200 ...
Hemlington Hall Rd TS8 ..6 ...
Hemlington Hall Sch
  TS8 ....6 ...
Hemlington Lake & Recn Ctr
  TS8 ....6 ...
Hemlington Rd TS8 .....6 ...
Hemlock Ave YO31 ...225 ...
Hempbridge Cl YO8 ..232 ...
Hempbridge Rd YO8 ..232 ...
Hempland Ave YO31 ..228 ...
Hempland La YO31 ...228 ...
Hempland Inf Sch
  YO31 ....229 ...
Hempland Jun Sch
  YO31 ....229 ...
Hemsby Rd WF10 ....200 ...
Henbusk La LA2 ......130 ...
Hendon Garth YO30 ..224 ...
Henlow La YO60 .....142 ...
Henrietta Cl DL10 ....209 ...
Henrietta St YO22 ...208 ...
Henry Moore Jun Sch
  WF10 ....201 ...
Henry St BD23 ....216 ...
Hensall CP Sch DN14 .203 ...
Hensall Sta DN14 ....203 ...
Henshaws Coll HG1 ..220 ...
Henside La BD24 .....132 ...
Henside Rd BD24 ....132 ...
Henson Gr WF10 .....200 ...
Henwick Hall La YO8 .232 ...
Hepton Hill YO17 ....120 ...
Hepworth's La DN14 .204 ...
Herberts Way YO31 ..228 ...
Herbert St YO10 .....228 ...
Hercules St DL1 ....3 ...
Herdborough Rd
  YO11 ....100 ...
Herdman Dr YO23 ...230 ...
Herdsman Rd ⑶ YO24 .230 ...
Herdwick Cl ⑴ YO24 .230 ...
Hereford Rd HG1 .....219 ...
Hergill La Baldersby HG4 ..88 ...
  Kirby Hill DL11 ....19 ...
Kirkby Fleetham with Fencote
  DL7 ....63 ...
Herisson Cl ⑳ YO19 .....95 ...
Heritage Ctr The* TS12 ...9 ...
Herman Wlk YO24 ....230 ...
Hermitage The* HG4 ...87 ...
Hermitage Way YO22 .32 ...
Heron Ave YO24 ......230 ...
Heron Cl ⑴ Bedale DL8 ..63 ...
  ⑾ Thornton Dale YO18 ..96 ...
Heron Cl ⑻ Filey YO14 .101 ...
  ⑷ Hunton DL9 ....40 ...
Heron Dr DL1 ....3 ...
Heron Gate TS14 ....8 ...
Heron La YO12 ....99 ...
Heron Rise YO32 .....225 ...
Heron Tree Cl DL8 .....60 ...
Heron Way YO17 .....215 ...
Herriot Way YO7 .....211 ...
Hertford Cl ⒂ YO11 ..100 ...
Hertford Vale C of E Prim
  Sch YO12 ....99 ...
Hesketh Ave TS4 ....7 ...
Hesketh Bank YO8 ...204 ...
Heslaker La BD23 ....216 ...
Hesledene Ave TS5 .....6 ...
Heslin Cl ⑴⑶ YO32 ..225 ...
Heslin Cl ⑵ YO32 ....223 ...
Heslington Croft YO10 .231 ...
Heslington Ct ⑵ YO10 .229 ...
Heslington La
  Heslington YO10 ......231 ...
  York YO10 ....228 ...
Heslington Prim Sch
  YO10 ....231 ...
Heslington Rd YO10 ..228 ...
Hessay Pl ⑴⑸ YO26 ..227 ...
Hetherton St YO30 ...233 ...
Hetton Garth ⒀ DL8 ...60 ...
Hewitson Rd DL1 ......3 ...
Hewitts La BD20 .....173 ...
Hewley Ave YO10 ....229 ...
Hewley Dr ⑹ YO13 .....75 ...
Heworth YO31 ....229 ...
Heworth ARLFC YO31 .229 ...

rth C of E Prim Sch ...228 F6
arth Dr Y021 ...208 B6
arth Gn Y031 ...233 C4
arth Rd Y031 ...228 F6
arth Pl Y031 ...228 F6
arth Rd Y031 ...228 F6
ord Rd Y07 ...115 B1
ate Bank Y018 ...49 F3
ate La LS23 ...188 F6
aw Rd HG3 ...159 C8
rop Dr
 orough TS14 ...8 F6
 lesbrough TS5 ...6 D7
ood Rd HG2 ...219 C3
nia St Y012 ...212 E5
 La LS26 ...200 B6
stead Ct DL1 ...3 A6
te Gdns TS17 ...6 A4
Back Side Y018 ...95 E8
brdfrth Y08 ...92 B2
leys Both BD20 ...173 E3
reshfield BD23 ...134 D2
Barmer Y013 ...75 B7
Bentham CP Sch ...129 B8
Bond End HG5 ...221 A7
Bondgate BD20 ...173 E4
Catton Rd Y041 ...185 D8
Church Wynd TS15 ...5 D3
Cleugh HG4 ...214 A4
Coniscliffe C of E Sch ...2 C6
Cragwell Y021 ...31 F7
Crest BD HG3 ...137 C4
Croft Y014 ...126 F8
Croft Way BD20 ...173 E1
Eggborough La ...203 A1
Fell Cl BD24 ...131 D1
Field Y010 ...229 D4
Fold BB18 ...186 A7
Garth
 ield Y011 ...100 A7
 mond DL10 ...209 B8
Gill Rd TS7 ...7 D6
Gn Catterick DL10 ...41 D4
 len BD23 ...135 A2
Green Dr BD20 ...174 B1
Hill Gr St BD24 ...131 D2
Hill La Beadlam Y062 ...93 C8
 with HG3 ...160 C5
 ing BD22 ...187 A4
 ton Y018 ...71 C4
 n-cum-Skewsby ...119 A2
 ton DL11 ...19 D7
 gdales Y022 ...33 C5
 ton Y010 ...229 C4
 ion DL11 ...37 D4
 La DL8 ...56 F4
 sham Y060 ...147 B1
 Sigston DL6 ...44 E1
 La Y025 ...6 C4
 n Y014 ...100 F1
 n-on-Swale Y061 ...142 B6
 sham DL11 ...19 D7
 h, Fremington & Healaugh ...37 F5
 forth with Stockeld ...179 C4
 ton upon Derwent ...185 D3
 ny Y07 ...90 D6
 nton Watlass DL8 ...62 C2
 Scrafton DL8 ...83 F6
 Witton DL8 ...59 D2
Leir La Y07 ...67 D1
Market Pl Y062 ...70 B1
Mdw
 dall DN14 ...204 A1
 ny Y08 ...232 B6
Mill Dr Y012 ...75 E5
Mill La LS29 ...175 A5
Moor Edge Y012 ...212 A7
Moor La
 ughbridge HG5 ...141 A2
 rton HG3 ...161 F8
 ton-on-Ouse Y030 ...165 C8
 ns HG6 ...162 A5
Moor Rd
 n Rigton HG3 ...178 A5
 n Y051 ...140 F7
 ...100 A6
Newbiggin St ...233 B3
Oaks Y031 ...229 B7
Ousegate Y017 ...233 B2
Peak TS14 ...8 F5
Peter La HG3 ...140 A3
Petergate Y01 ...233 B3
Rd LA2 ...128 F5
Riding Aske DL10 ...20 D5
 mond DL10 ...209 C8
Rifts TS8 ...6 E1
Riggs La Y018 ...96 C3
Row
 horpe Y041 ...169 D4
 well DL11 ...1 C4
 ston DL11 ...3 C5
 sonby DL10 ...20 F7
Skellgate HG4 ...214 C5

High St Airmyn DN14 ...205 E3
Ampleforth Y062 ...92 C3
Aske DL10 ...20 E2
Austwick LA2 ...130 C7
Barmby on the Marsh DN14 ...205 A7
Barnby Y021 ...12 C4
Barton-le-Street Y017 ...120 E5
Beadlam Y062 ...93 D7
Boosbeck TS12 ...9 D8
6 Boroughbridge Y051 ...141 B5
Boston Spa LS23 ...188 E8
Boston Spa LS23 ...188 F7
Bramham LS23 ...188 E5
Buckton/Bempton Y013 ...96 D6
Burniston Y013 ...75 C8
Burton in Lonsdale LA6 ...102 F3
Carlton DN14 ...204 C2
Castleford WF10 ...200 E4
Catterick DL10 ...41 A5
Cawood Y08 ...197 B8
Cottam Y025 ...150 E5
Cropton Y018 ...71 B4
Danby Y021 ...29 A6
Malton Y017 ...215 C5
5 Eastfield Y011 ...100 A6
Gargrave BD23 ...155 D1
Glaisdale Y021 ...30 D4
Glusburn BD20 ...187 E6
Great Ayton TS9 ...7 F1
Great Broughton TS9 ...26 E4
Hampsthwaite HG3 ...160 F5
Harrogate HG2 ...220 C4
4 Helmsley Y062 ...92 F6
Heslerton Y017 ...123 F6
Hinderwell TS13 ...11 F7
Hovingham Y062 ...119 E6
Husthwaite Y061 ...117 B6
Ingleton LA6 ...103 D4
Kippax LS25 ...194 D1
Kirby Grindalythe Y017 ...149 D8
8 Knaresborough HG5 ...221 B5
Knottingley WF11 ...201 E5
Langtoft Y025 ...151 C8
Lastingham Y062 ...70 E5
6 Leyburn DL8 ...60 D5
Lingdale TS12 ...9 F7
Lockwood TS12 ...10 A5
Markington with Wallerthwaite HG3 ...139 C4
Mickleby TS13 ...12 A4
Middlesbrough TS7 ...7 C8
Newton Mulgrave TS13 ...11 E4
Normanton South WF6 ...200 A1
Northallerton DL7 ...210 D6
Norton DN6 ...206 E2
Old Byland & Scawton Y062 ...92 A4
Oldstead Y07 ...91 E5
Pateley Bridge HG3 ...137 B4
Rawcliffe DN14 ...205 A1
Rillington Y017 ...122 F5
Scalby Y013 ...75 D5
8 Settle BD24 ...131 E2
Settrington Y017 ...122 F1
Sherburn Y017 ...124 D7
Skipton BD23 ...217 A4
Slingsby Y062 ...120 B5
Snainton Y013 ...98 A5
Snaith DN14 ...204 B1
South Milford LS25 ...195 E2
Spofforth HG3 ...179 E5
3 Staithes TS13 ...13 K2
Stillington Y061 ...144 B6
Stokesley TS9 ...26 C7
Swinton Y017 ...121 B4
Tadcaster LS24 ...189 E6
Thornton Dale Y060 ...146 A4 (Thornton-le-Clay)
Wharram Y017 ...149 A6
Whitby Y021 ...208 B3
Whixley Y026 ...164 A4
Wombleton Y062 ...93 E7
Wrelton Y018 ...71 C1
High St Agnesgate HG4 ...214 C5
High Stakesby Rd Y021 ...208 A6
High Stell DL2 ...4 C4
High Town Bank Rd Y07 ...91 C5
High Trace DL6 ...210 E2
High Trees Ct LS25 ...195 F4
High Trees Sch LS23 ...188 F7
High View HG3 ...160 F8
High Wheatley LS29 ...218 E3
High Wood LS29 ...218 D3
Highbank Gr HG2 ...220 D4
Highbury Ave TS5 ...6 F8
Highcliff Rd TS14 ...8 E4
Highcliffe Ct Y030 ...228 A6
Highcroft
 Collingham LS22 ...188 A8
 6 Grassington BD23 ...134 E3
Highdale Ave 5 Y012 ...212 D8
Highdale Rd Y012 ...212 E7
Higher Hartley St 1 BD20 ...187 D7
Higher Lodge St 1 ...187 D7
Higher Rd BD23 ...152 F4
Higherlands Cl BD23 ...155 D1
Highfield
 Pollington DN14 ...207 F7
 Scarborough Y012 ...212 E4
Highfield Ave WF8 ...201 D2

Highfield Cl Y025 ...126 A4
Highfield Cres Y08 ...198 B5
Highfield Ct Y08 ...232 B1
Highfield Dr
 Allerton Bywater WF10 ...200 C7
 Garforth LS25 ...194 C3
Highfield Gn
 Allerton Bywater WF10 ...200 C7
 Sherburn in Elmet LS25 ...195 F3
Highfield Gr WF10 ...200 C7
Highfield La
 Barwick in Elmet & Scholes LS15 ...194 B7
 Fangfoss Y041 ...169 B1
 Gillamoor Y062 ...69 F5
 Huddleston with Newthorpe LS25 ...195 B2
 Nawton Y062 ...69 C2
 Scagglethorpe Y017 ...122 C2
 Womersley DN6 ...206 D5
Highfield Pl 1 WF10 ...200 D7
Highfield Rd
 Aberford LS25 ...194 F8
 2 Earby BB18 ...172 A1
 Malton Y017 ...215 C5
 Ripon HG4 ...214 B3
 Whitby Y021 ...208 A7
Highfield View 3 Y08 ...198 B4
Highfield Villas LS25 ...195 F3
Highfields La Y07 ...115 A1
Highgate Baine DN14 ...207 D6
 Glusburn BD20 ...187 D8
Highgate Pl HG1 ...219 F3
Highgrove Cl 7 Y030 ...224 E3
Highland Cl 8 WF8 ...201 C1
Highlands Ave 8 Y012 ...212 B7
Highlands Cl Y014 ...101 B1
Highmoor Cl Y024 ...230 D8
Highmoor Rd
 Darlington DL1 ...3 F4
 York Y024 ...230 D8
Highthorn Rd Y031 ...225 E2
Highthorne La Y061 ...117 B5
Highway BD24 ...131 E3
Hilbeck Gr Y031 ...229 B6
Hilbra Ave Y032 ...225 D6
Hilda St 5 Selby Y08 ...232 C5
 3 York Y010 ...228 E3
Hildenley Cl 6 Y012 ...212 B5
Hilderthorpe TS7 ...7 C6
Hildewell 3 TS13 ...13 K2
Hill Bank HG3 ...163 B7
Hill Cl DL11 ...38 B6
Hill Crest Y019 ...167 F1
Hill Crest Gdns LS25 ...222 F1
Hill End La BD22 ...186 F5
Hill Field Y08 ...232 B8
Hill Foot La DL2 ...222 B2
Hill House La DL2 ...4 A7
Hill La BB8 ...186 A4
Hill Rd WF10 ...200 F3
Hill Rise
 Middleton St George DL2 ...4 D3
 Skipton BD23 ...216 E5
Hill Rise Ave HG2 ...222 B8
Hill Rise Cl HG2 ...222 B8
Hill St
 5 Barnoldswick BB18 ...171 E1
 York Y024 ...227 F2
Hill The DL8 ...56 D4
Hill Top
 10 Burley in Warfedale LS29 ...176 C1
 Castleford WF10 ...200 C4
 Ilkley LS29 ...218 A2
 Knottingley WF11 ...201 F2
Hill Top Ave HG1 ...219 D6
Hill Top Cl
 Embsay BD23 ...217 C8
 Harrogate HG1 ...219 D6
 Sutton with Hazlewood LS29 ...189 D4
Hill Top Cres HG1 ...219 D6
 4 Wistow Y08 ...197 D6
Hill Top La Earby BB18 ...172 A1
 Pannal HG3 ...222 A4
Hill Top Mount HG1 ...219 D6
Hill Top Rd
 Harrogate HG1 ...219 D6
 4 Wistow Y08 ...197 D6
Hill Top Rise HG1 ...219 D6
Hill Top View HG1 ...219 D6
Hill Top Wlk HG1 ...219 D6
Hill View
 Langthorpe Y051 ...141 A6
 Stillington Y061 ...144 C6
 York Y031 ...229 C7
Hillam Cl LS25 ...202 B7
Hillam Hall La 4 LS25 ...202 A7
Hillam Hall View 3 LS25 ...202 A7
Hillam La
 Burton Salmon LS25 ...201 F7
 Hillam LS25 ...202 A7
Hillam Rd Y026 ...227 B8
Hillary Garth 9 Y026 ...227 E4
Hillbank Gr HG1 ...220 D4
Hillbank Rd HG1 ...220 D4
Hillbank View HG1 ...220 D4
Hillcrest
 Monk Fryston LS25 ...202 A8
 Tadcaster LS24 ...189 D5
Hillcrest Ave
 Newby & Scalby Y012 ...75 E5

Hillcrest Ave continued
 Poppleton Y026 ...224 A2
 Silsden BD20 ...174 C1
Hillcrest Cl WF10 ...201 B3
Hillcrest Ct 2 LS24 ...189 D5
Hillcrest Dr
 Castleford WF10 ...200 C7
 Loftus TS13 ...10 D8
Hillcrest Gdns Y051 ...141 A7
Hillcrest Gr 2 Y07 ...75 E5
Hillcrest Mount WF10 ...201 B3
Hillgarth WF11 ...201 F2
Hillgarth Ct 4 Y041 ...185 B2
Hillhouse DL2 ...4 C7
Hillham Hall Cl 8 LS25 ...202 A7
Hillingdon Rd TS4 ...7 B8
Hillocks La TS12 ...10 A5
Hills Rd BD23 ...155 E5
Hillsborough Terr 5 Y030 ...228 C7
Hillshaw Parkway HG4 ...214 D5
Hillside Byram WF11 ...201 E4
 Follifoot HG3 ...223 F4
 8 Ingleby Arncliffe DL6 ...45 A7
Hillside Cl
 8 Addingham LS29 ...174 F4
 9 Monk Fryston LS25 ...202 A8
 Threshfield BD23 ...134 B3
Hillside Cres BD23 ...217 C3
Hillside Dr BD23 ...134 B3
Hillside Gdns
 Langtoft Y025 ...151 D5
 Scarborough Y012 ...212 E1
Hillside Rd HG3 ...222 E3
Hillside Way Y017 ...150 B8
Hilltop Cres Y024 ...40 E4
Hilton Cl DL6 ...210 E8
Hilton Dr DL6 ...210 E8
Hilton Grange DL6 ...210 E8
Hilton La 2 HG5 ...222 A1
Hilton Rd TS9 ...6 F1
Hilton St DL6 ...210 E8
Hincks Hall La HG3 ...139 C3
Hinderwell CP Sch Y012 ...212 D2
Hinderwell La
 Hinderwell TS13 ...11 E8
 Staithes TS13 ...13 K1
Hinderwell Pl Y012 ...212 E2
Hinderwell Rd Y012 ...212 E2
Hindle Dr 2 Y014 ...101 B3
Hinsley La DN14 ...204 C2
Hinton Ave 1 Y024 ...230 C8
Hinton Cl 9 WF8 ...201 C2
Hinton La WF11 ...201 D3
Hipswell C of E Prim Sch DL9 ...209 F1
Hipswell Rd DL9 ...209 E1
Hipswell Rd W DL9 ...209 D1
Hird Ave 2 DL8 ...63 A2
Hird La TS9 ...26 F5
Hirds Yd 2 BD23 ...216 F3
Hirst Courtney & Temple
Hirst Cl 9 Y08 ...204 C1
Hirst La HG3 ...160 E5
Hirst Rd Y08 ...204 A3
Hirst St WF10 ...200 C8
Hirstfields Gdns Y012 ...212 B8
Hirstead Rd Y012 ...212 B8
Hob Cote La BD22 ...187 F1
Hob Moor Dr Y024 ...227 D2
Hob Moor Inf Sch Y024 ...227 D2
Hob Moor Jun Sch Y024 ...227 D2
Hobart Rd WF10 ...201 B3
Hob Nook La LS21 ...176 D4
Hob Stone Ct 4 Y024 ...230 C8
Hobgate Y024 ...227 D3
Hobmoor Terr Y024 ...227 F1
Hobson Cl Y023 ...230 B1
Hodge La DN6 ...206 B3
Hodgson Fold LS29 ...174 E5
Hodgson Hill Y013 ...54 B4
Hodgson La Y026 ...182 F8
Hodgson's La LS25 ...196 A5
Holbeck Ave
 Middlesbrough TS5 ...6 E6
 Scarborough Y011 ...213 B2
Holbeck Cl Y011 ...213 B2
Holbeck Hill Y011 ...213 A2
Holbeck Rd Y011 ...213 A2
Holbeck La Y051 ...141 F3
Holborn Rd HG2 ...222 D7
Holburns Croft 3 Y011 ...229 B1
Holden Gdns Y08 ...197 D2
Hole House La BB7 ...152 B2
Hole La BD20 ...174 B2
Holes La WF11 ...201 E2
Holgate DL6 ...45 E8
Holgate Bank HG5 ...163 A8
Holgate Bridge Gdn 7 Y024 ...228 A3
Holgate Cl Y017 ...215 C5
Holgate Lodge Dr Y026 ...227 E4
Holgate Rd Y024 ...233 A1

Hollingwood Gate 31 LS29 ...175 C2
Hollingwood Rise 32 LS29 ...175 C2
Hollinhurst Brow LA2 ...128 F2
Hollins DL6 ...60 B3
Hollins Beck Cl LS25 ...201 D8
Hollins Cl HG3 ...161 A5
Hollins Cres HG1 ...219 C4
Hollins Gr WF10 ...200 C7
Hollins Hall HG3 ...161 A4
Hollins La Firby DL8 ...63 B1
 Hampsthwaite HG3 ...161 A4
 Melmerby HG4 ...114 B8
 Middleton Quernhow HG4 ...88 C1
 Rosedale East Side Y018 ...49 D4
Hollins Mews HG1 ...219 C4
Hollins Rd
 10 Barnoldswick BB18 ...171 D1
 Harrogate HG1 ...219 C4
Hollow Gate HG4 ...153 C5
Hollow Moor La DL8 ...62 E7
Holly Bank Gr 3 Y024 ...227 F2
Holly Bank Rd Y024 ...227 F2
Holly Cl
 Acaster Malbis Y023 ...191 C8
 Full Sutton Y041 ...169 A2
 Thirsk Y07 ...211 B2
 Wrelton Y018 ...71 C1
Holly Ct 11 HG5 ...221 B6
Holly Garth 4 Y061 ...115 F1
Holly Garth Cl TS9 ...7 F1
Holly Gr Selby Y08 ...232 B3
 8 Thorpe Willoughby Y08 ...197 B2
Holly Rd 8 Bedale DL8 ...63 B3
 Boston Spa LS23 ...188 D8
Holly Tree Croft 2 Y019 ...184 F7
Holly Tree Ct 2 Y021 ...208 B6
Holly Tree Garth Y032 ...167 E3
Holly Tree La
 Dunnington Y019 ...184 F7
 Haxby Y032 ...225 D3
Holly Wlk Y012 ...212 D7
Hollybush Ave TS17 ...6 B5
Hollygarth La LS22 ...188 B8
Hollygate La DN14 ...202 D4
Hollyhurst Rd DL3 ...3 C6
Hollyrood Rd Y030 ...224 E3
Hollywalk Ave TS6 ...7 E8
Hollywood Y08 ...232 B7
Holm Hill Y013 ...54 C2
Holm La LA2 ...130 E6
Holme Cl Earby BB18 ...186 A8
 3 Sutton BD20 ...187 E7
Holme Cres BD20 ...187 E7
Holme Croft 1 BD23 ...134 D2
Holme Farm La LS23 ...188 A5
Holme Ghyll Y023 ...190 F4
Holme Hill 2 Y011 ...100 A6
Holme La 8 Y010 ...184 F7
Holme Ings LS29 ...175 B4
Holme La
 Glusburn BD20 ...187 E7
 Halton East BD23 ...174 B8
 Newbiggin DL8 ...58 E1
 Rudby TS9 ...25 E7
 Selby Y08 ...232 D6
Holme St 17 BB8 ...186 A3
Holme The TS9 ...26 E4
Holmebeck La HG4 ...88 B1
Holmefield Cl 3 Y08 ...232 A1
Holmefield Ct 2 Y08 ...232 A1
Holmefield La WF8 ...201 C2
Holmestead Ave Y026 ...208 A5
Holmtree La HG4 ...113 B8
Holmwood Ave TS5 ...6 F8
Holray Pk DN14 ...206 C8
Holroyd Ave Y031 ...229 A5
Holtby Gr Y012 ...212 D5
Holtby La Holtby Y019 ...167 D1
 Stockton on the Forest Y032 ...226 F2
Holy Family RC High Sch DN14 ...204 C3
Holy Family RC Prim Sch DL3 ...3 B6
Holy Rood La LS25 ...201 C1
Holy Trinity C of E Inf Sch HG4 ...214 B6
Holy Trinity Prim Sch HG4 ...214 B5
Holyoake Ave DL3 ...3 A5
Holystone Dr TS17 ...6 A4
Holywell St TS16 ...5 E5
Holywell La
 Castleford WF10 ...201 A3
 North Cowton DL7 ...22 C2
Home Farm Cl LA2 ...128 C3

Home Office Emergency
Planning Coll YO61 ....143 D6
Homefield Cl YO23 ....230 A2
Homestead Cl
  Eggborough DN14 ....203 A2
  2 York YO32 ....225 F1
Homestead Rd HG1 ....219 E2
Honey Pot 5 YO8 ....199 D7
Honey Pot Rd 2 DL10 ....41 C6
Honeypot La DL3 ....3 C7
Honeysuckle Cl
  Romanby DL7 ....210 C1
  Selby YO8 ....232 C2
Honister Gr TS5 ....6 D7
Hood La YO13 ....54 D2
Hoodstorth La HG3 ....158 F6
Hook La DN14 ....205 F4
Hook Pasture La
  DN14 ....205 F1
Hookstone Ave HG2 ....222 E7
Hookstone Chase
  HG2 ....220 D2
Hookstone Chase CP Sch
  HG2 ....220 D2
Hookstone Cl HG2 ....222 D8
Hookstone Dr HG2 ....223 A8
Hookstone Garth HG3 ....159 E5
Hookstone Grange Ct 8
  HG2 ....220 C2
Hookstone Grange Way 2
  HG2 ....220 C2
Hookstone Oval HG2 ....222 D7
Hookstone Pk HG2 ....220 D2
Hookstone Rd HG2 ....222 E7
Hookstone Way HG2 ....220 D2
Hookstone Wood Rd
  HG2 ....220 B1
  8 Harrogate HG2 ....223 B8
Hope St 5 Filey YO14 ....101 B3
  Knaresborough HG5 ....221 B5
  Scarborough YO12 ....213 A6
  York YO10 ....233 C1
Hopetown La DL3 ....3 C6
Hopgrove La N YO32 ....226 C3
Hopgrove La S YO32 ....226 E3
Hopper Hill Rd YO11 ....99 F6
Hopper La LS21 ....159 C2
Hopperton St HG5 ....163 E4
Hopps's Rd 8 BD20 ....187 E8
Horn La BD20 ....187 E7
Hornbeam Cres HG2 ....222 F8
Hornbeam Park Ave
  HG2 ....222 F7
Hornbeam Park Sta
  HG2 ....222 F7
Hornbeam Sq N HG2 ....223 A7
Hornbeam Sq S HG2 ....223 A7
Hornbeam Sq W HG2 ....222 F7
Hornblower Cl 5 HG4 ....113 D2
Hornby Castle* DL8 ....62 C8
Hornby Cl 1 DL2 ....3 E1
Hornby Rd
  Appleton Wiske DL6 ....24 A3
  Roxburndale LA2 ....128 A2
  Wray-with-Botton LA2 ....128 A6
Horndale Rd 8 YO14 ....101 B4
Horne Rd DL9 ....40 F4
Horner Ave YO61 ....144 A5
Horner Cl YO61 ....144 A5
Horner St YO30 ....228 B7
Hornsea Rd TS8 ....6 E5
Hornsey Garth 25 YO32 ....166 E5
Horse Bell Gate LA6 ....103 D4
Horse Course La YO17 ....122 E1
Horse Mill La HG3 ....139 D5
Horsefair 2 YO51 ....141 B5
Horseman Ave YO23 ....230 A3
Horseman Cl 2 YO23 ....230 A3
Horseman La YO23 ....230 A3
Horsemarket Rd YO17 ....215 B4
Horseshoe Cave*
  BD24 ....132 A3
Horseshoe The YO24 ....230 E7
Horseway Gn YO18 ....49 D4
Horsfield Way YO19 ....184 F7
Horsman Ave YO10 ....233 C1
Horton in Ribblesdale C of E
  Prim Sch BD24 ....105 C3
Horton in Ribbleside Sta
  BD24 ....105 C3
Hospital Fields Rd
  YO10 ....228 D1
Hospital La YO8 ....197 B4
Hospital Rd YO17 ....215 B4
Hospitium The* YO1 ....233 A3
Hostess La YO18 ....72 E4
Hotham Ave YO26 ....227 B2
Hotfield Street Jun Sch
  BD20 ....174 C1
Houghton Ave YO41 ....201 D2
Houndgate DL1 ....3 C5
Houndsway 6 YO24 ....230 B8
House of Correction Mus*
  HG4 ....214 D5
Hovingham C of E Prim Sch
  YO62 ....119 E6
Hovingham Dr YO12 ....212 B4
Hovingham Hall*
  YO62 ....119 E6
How Hill Rd HG4 ....139 B6
How Stean Gorge*
  HG3 ....110 A4
Howard Dr YO30 ....224 E2
Howard Link YO30 ....224 D2

Howard Rd
  Catterick Garrison DL9 ....209 E1
  Towthorpe YO32 ....167 B6
Howard St
  8 Scarborough YO12 ....213 A7
  York YO10 ....228 D2
Howden Dike TS15 ....5 E2
Howden La YO19 ....231 E1
Howden Rd
  4 Barlby YO8 ....198 B4
  Romanby DL7 ....210 B2
  Silsden BD20 ....174 C1
Howdenshire Way
  DN14 ....205 F6
Howlands La HG4 ....140 E7
Howe Ave DL10 ....41 E3
Howe Bank YO21 ....29 B7
Howe End YO62 ....70 B1
Howe Field Rd YO26 ....142 A2
Howe Hill Bank TS8 ....7 B2
Howe Hill Cl YO26 ....227 E4
Howe Hill La DL10 ....41 C6
Howe Hill Rd YO26 ....227 E4
Howe La YO41 ....170 A5
Howe Rd Malton YO17 ....122 A6
  Norton YO17 ....215 E3
Howe St YO24 ....227 D3
Howes Rd 8 YO14 ....127 A8
Howgate DL8 ....60 D7
Howgill La
  Barden BD23 ....157 E6
  Rimington BB7 ....171 A1
Howhill Quarry Rd
  HG3 ....178 B7
Howkills Rd HG3 ....178 B8
Howl La YO62 ....116 F2
Howl Gate YO41 ....185 E8
Howlbeck Rd TS14 ....8 E7
Howldale La
  Appleton-le-Moors YO62 ....70 F4
  8 Beadlam YO62 ....93 D7
Howlgate La YO21 ....13 A1
Howsham Gates*
  YO60 ....146 F2
Howsham Hall Prep Sch
  YO60 ....146 F2
Howson La BD24 ....131 E4
Hoylake Rd TS4 ....6 F8
Hoylake Way TS16 ....5 E4
Hubert St 8 YO23 ....228 B1
  8 Ruby Prim Sch YO8 ....144 A4
  Ruby Rd YO61 ....144 B3
Hudgin La Lockton YO18 ....72 E4
  Wykeham YO13 ....98 D4
Hudson Cl
  Malton YO17 ....215 C6
  Stamford Bridge YO41 ....168 D2
  2 Tadcaster LS24 ....189 E6
Hudson Cres 2 YO30 ....228 A7
Hudson St
  Whitby YO21 ....208 D7
  2 York YO30 ....228 A7
Hudson View 1 LS24 ....189 E6
Hudson Way LS24 ....189 E6
Hugden Cl YO18 ....96 A6
Huggan Way YO12 ....212 A8
Huggate Hill YO17 ....170 E7
Hugh Field La YO8 ....199 A8
Hugh Field North La
  YO8 ....193 A1
Hugh St WF10 ....200 E4
Hugo Rd Cliffe YO8 ....198 E2
Hemingbrough YO8 ....199 B1
Heslington YO19 ....229 A1
Humber Dr 5 YO32 ....167 B6
Humber Rd TS17 ....6 B7
Humbersknott Ave DL3 ....3 A5
Hummersmoor Comp Sch
  DL3 ....3 A4
Humphrey Balk La
  YO7 ....114 D8
Humphrey Hill DL8 ....58 D1
Hundale Rd 8 TS15 ....25 C5
Hunday Field Rd YO51 ....141 E2
Hundens Day Hospl DL1 ....3 E5
Hundens La DL1 ....3 E5
Hungate
  Bishop Monkton HG3 ....140 A5
  Brompton YO13 ....98 C5
  Pickering YO18 ....95 F7
  York YO1 ....233 C2
Hungate Cl LS24 ....195 D8
Hungate Ct 10 YO14 ....126 F8
Hungate Cty Prim Sch
  LS25 ....195 F4
Hungate La YO14 ....126 F8
Hungate Rd LS25 ....195 F4
Hunger Hill LS29 ....218 C7
Hungerhill La YO62 ....93 F6
Hunmanby CP Sch
  YO14 ....126 F8
Hunmanby Rd
  Burton Fleming YO25 ....126 E3
  Reighton YO14 ....127 C6
Hunmanby Sta YO14 ....127 A7
Hunt Ct YO31 ....233 C3
Hunt House Rd YO22 ....51 B6
Hunt St WF10 ....200 D4
Hunter St 8 YO21 ....208 D7
Hunters Cl
  Dunnington YO19 ....184 E7
  11 Easingwold YO61 ....143 C8
  10 Haxby YO32 ....225 C8
  4 Hurworth-on-Tees DL2 ....3 D1
Hunters Gn DL2 ....4 C3

Hunters Ride DL6 ....24 B3
Hunters Row 6 YO51 ....141 B4
Hunters Way
  Norton YO17 ....215 D2
  Selby YO8 ....232 B4
  York YO24 ....230 F7
Hunters Wlk
  Barlow YO8 ....204 D7
  Kirk Hodgson LS22 ....180 C4
Hunters Wood Way 21
  YO19 ....184 F7
Huntington Prim Sch
  YO32 ....225 F4
Huntington Rd YO32 ....233 C4
Huntington Sch YO32 ....225 E3
Hunton CP Sch DL8 ....61 F7
Hunton Rd DL8 ....40 E1
Huntriss Row YO11 ....213 A6
Huntsmans La YO41 ....168 C2
Huntsman's Wlk YO24 ....227 B1
Hurdle Cl YO17 ....215 D3
Hurgill Rd DL10 ....209 A7
Hurn Rd YO61 ....144 A4
Hurns La YO30 ....224 A7
Hurrell La YO18 ....96 E5
Hurricane Way YO30 ....224 E3
Hurrs Rd 8 BD23 ....217 B4
Hurst Hill HG3 ....159 F7
Hurstleigh Terr HG1 ....220 A3
Hurst's Yd YO1 ....233 C2
Hurworth Comp Sch
  DL2 ....22 D8
Hurworth Cty Inf Sch
  DL2 ....3 E1
Hurworth House Sch
  DL2 ....3 E1
Hurworth Rd
  Hurworth-on-Tees DL2 ....22 D8
  Neasham DL2 ....4 A1
Hussars Ct 8 YO12 ....75 F5
Husthwaite C of E Prim Sch
  YO61 ....117 B5
Husthwaite Rd
  Coxwold YO61 ....117 D7
  Easingwold YO61 ....117 B2
Hutchinson Dr DL6 ....210 E3
Hutchinson's Rd YO61 ....117 A4
Hutton Ave DL1 ....3 E7
Hutton Bank
  8 Hutton Rudby TS15 ....25 D5
  Rudby HG4 ....214 D7
Hutton Cl YO26 ....224 A2
Hutton Cross Rd YO13 ....98 E8
Hutton La
  Guisborough TS14 ....8 A5
  Hutton Conyers HG4 ....114 A4
  Sharow HG4 ....214 E8
  Hutton Rae La YO7 ....116 D7
Hutton Rudby CP Sch
  TS15 ....25 C5
Hutton St YO26 ....182 A5
Hutton View Rd HG4 ....214 C7
Hutton Village Rd TS14 ....8 F5
Hutton's Mon* DL11 ....39 C6
Hutts La HG4 ....112 C7
Hyde Park Rd
  Harrogate HG1 ....219 E3
  Knaresborough HG5 ....221 B8
Hydro Cl LS29 ....218 F3
Hyrst Gr YO31 ....228 E6

I

Ian St TS17 ....6 B8
l'anson Cl DL8 ....60 D6
l'anson Rd DL8 ....60 D6
Ibbetson Cl 18 HG4 ....86 C3
Iburndale La YO22 ....32 A6
Iddison Dr DL8 ....63 A2
Ikin Way YO32 ....225 F6
Ilkeston Ave DL1 ....205 F3
Ilkley Gr TS14 ....8 E5
Ilkley Gram Sch LS29 ....218 C3
Ilkley Hall Mews 8
  LS29 ....218 B3
Ilkley Hall Pk 4 LS29 ....218 B3
Ilkley Rd
  Addingham LS29 ....175 A4
  Ilkley LS29 ....176 C1
Ilkley Sch LS29 ....218 E5
Ilkley Sta LS29 ....218 B4
Ilkley Swimming Baths
  LS29 ....218 C5
Ilton Bank HG4 ....85 E1
Ilton Garth YO30 ....225 A2
Imperial Athletic Club
  HG2 ....222 F8
Imperial Ave TS17 ....6 B8
In Moor La HG3 ....109 C6
Ingdale Howl YO62 ....92 C2
Ingdale La YO7 ....66 C3
Ingfield La BD24 ....131 D2
Ingham Cl YO22 ....32 A6
Ingleborough Ave
  YO10 ....229 B4
Ingleborough Dr 4
  BB18 ....171 D1
Ingleborough Park Cl
  LA6 ....103 D3
Ingleborough Park Dr
  LA6 ....103 D3
Ingleby Arncliffe C of E Prim
  Sch DL6 ....45 A8
Ingleby Dr LS24 ....189 E6

Ingleby Greenhow C of E
  Prim Sch TS9 ....27 C5
Ingleby Manor* TS9 ....27 C4
Ingleby Mill Prim Sch
  TS17 ....6 A4
Ingleby Rd
  Great & Little Broughton
    TS9 ....26 E5
  Great Broughton TS9 ....26 E5
Ingleby Way TS17 ....6 B5
Ingleton CP Sch LA6 ....103 D3
Ingleton Dr 18 YO30 ....143 D8
Ingleton Ind Est LA6 ....103 D3
Ingleton Mid Sch LA6 ....103 D3
Ingleton Wlk YO10 ....229 A5
Ingman Lodge Rd BD24 ....78 F1
Ingram Ave YO30 ....228 C5
Ingramgate YO7 ....211 C3
Ingrish La YO23 ....182 C1
Ings Cl 6 Pickering YO18 ....95 F6
  5 Willerby YO12 ....99 D2
Ings CP Sch BD23 ....216 D3
Ings Ct DN14 ....202 F4
Ings Dr
  Low Bradley BD20 ....173 E3
  Mickletown LS26 ....200 C6
Ings Field Rd 8 YO26 ....142 A3
Ings La
  Ainderby Quernhow YO7 ....88 D4
  Beal DN14 ....202 D4
  Bishop Monkton HG3 ....140 B5
  Bishop Wilton YO42 ....169 D2
  Bradleys Both BD20 ....173 E3
  Brompton YO13 ....98 C4
  Carlton DN14 ....204 E2
  Cawood YO8 ....197 D8
  Cononley BD20 ....173 D2
  Cottingwith YO42 ....193 C5
  Crakehall DL8 ....62 F5
  Ebberston & Yedingham
    YO13 ....97 E4
  Great Preston WF10 ....200 E6
  Harome YO62 ....93 D4
  Hensall DN14 ....203 D2
  Husthwaite YO61 ....117 A6
  Hutton Buscel YO13 ....99 A3
  Kellington DN14 ....202 F4
  21 Kirkbymoorside YO62 ....70 B1
  Kirkbymoorside YO62 ....70 B1
  Lastingham YO62 ....70 F5
  Lillings Ambo YO60 ....145 C2
  Nether Poppleton YO26 ....224 B1
  Pickering YO18 ....95 E4
  Riccall YO19 ....197 E8
  Skipton BD23 ....216 D2
  Snape with Thorp DL8 ....87 A7
  Stillington YO61 ....144 A6
  Thorganby YO19 ....193 B5
  Thorp Arch LS23 ....189 A8
  Tollerton YO61 ....143 B2
  Welburn YO62 ....94 A5
  Wheldrake YO19 ....193 B7
  Wighill LS24 ....189 D8
  4 Willerby YO12 ....99 D2
  Wistow YO8 ....198 A6
Ings Mere Ct 11 YO61 ....201 C6
Ings Rd Cliffe YO8 ....198 D2
  Dunsforths YO26 ....142 A3
  Snaith DN14 ....204 C1
  Thorganby YO19 ....193 B4
  Ulleskelf LS24 ....190 C3
  West Ayton YO13 ....99 B6
  Wilberfoss YO41 ....185 E6
Ings Terr YO22 ....31 C4
Ings View 2 Bedale DL8 ....63 B3
  Castleford WF10 ....201 A4
  Mickletown LS26 ....200 C6
  York YO30 ....224 D2
Ingsgarth YO18 ....95 F6
Ingthorns La LS25 ....195 F1
Ingthorpe La
  Mansfield BD23 ....171 E7
  Monk Fryston LS25 ....196 A1
Inhams La YO26 ....141 F2
Inholmes La
  Tadcaster LS24 ....189 D6
  Walton LS23 ....181 B2
Inman Gr HG5 ....221 B8
Inman Terr YO26 ....227 D4
Inman Wlk HG5 ....221 B8
Inn La 10 YO61 ....143 C8
Innisfree Cl HG2 ....220 B1
Institute St 4 BD20 ....187 E7
Intake Ave YO30 ....228 C8
Intake La
  Acaster Malbis YO23 ....191 C7
  Beal WF11 ....202 D5
  Carlton Miniott YO7 ....89 C4
  Dunnington YO19 ....184 F7
  Grassington BD23 ....134 E3
  Habton YO17 ....121 E7
  Heck DN14 ....207 C8
  Tollerton YO61 ....143 B4
  West Haddlesey YO8 ....202 F6
  Intakefield Rd YO8 ....199 D7
  Invicta Ct YO24 ....230 B8
  Ireby Rd LA6 ....102 F3
  Ireton St 8 YO23 ....228 B1
  Iron Moor La YO22 ....212 A1
  Irwin Ave YO31 ....228 E6
  Islebeck La YO7 ....115 F8
  Iver Cl YO26 ....227 B3
  Ivy Cl HG3 ....223 F5
  Ivy Cres 62 B4
  Ivy House Cl 5 YO11 ....100 B6
  Ivy House Gdns BD23 ....155 D1

Ivy La LS23 ....1...

J

Jack Field La BD20 ....1...
Jack Hill La LS21 ....1...
Jack Hole YO61 ....1...
Jack La Crayke YO61 ....1...
  Stillington YO61 ....1...
  Wigglesworth BD23 ....1...
Jackson Cl YO11 ....1...
Jackson Dr TS9 ....1...
Jackson La YO41 ....1...
Jackson St
  32 Glusburn BD20 ....1...
  York YO31 ....1...
Jackson's La
  Bradleys Both BD20 ....1...
  Eastfield YO11 ....1...
  Scarborough YO18 ....1...
Jackson's Wlk YO23 ....1...
Jacobi Cl YO30 ....2...
Jacques Gr BD20 ....1...
Jaffa Rd DL9 ....2...
Jagger La DL10 ....1...
Jagoe Rd 8 BB18 ....1...
James Backhouse Pl
  YO24 ....2...
James Cl LS25 ....1...
James Ct DL10 ....2...
James La DL10 ....2...
James Nicholson Way
  YO30 ....2...
Jameson Cres YO12 ....2...
Jamesville Way YO7 ....1...
Jamieson Terr YO23 ....2...
Janet's Foss* BD23 ....1...
Jasmine Cl
  10 Snaith DN14 ....2...
Jasper La HG3 ....1...
Jay Ave TS17 ....1...
Jaywick Cl 8 YO32 ....1...
Jedburgh Dr DL3 ....
Jedwell Cl YO32 ....2...
Jennifer Gr 4 YO24 ....2...
Jenny Field Dr HG3 ....2...
Jenny Frisk Rd YO22 ....3...
Jenny Gill Cres BD23 ....2...
Jenny La DL10 ....4...
Jerry Carr Bank YO62 ....
Jerry Croft 8 BD23 ....2...
Jerry La BD20 ....1...
Jersey Ct YO12 ....
Jervaulx Abbey* HG4 ....2...
Jervaulx Dr HG5 ....2...
Jervis Rd YO24 ....2...
Jesmond Ct YO17 ....2...
Jesmond Gr 5 TS18 ....
Jesmond Rd
  Darlington DL1 ....
  Harrogate HG1 ....2...
Jew Leys La YO23 ....1...
Jewbury YO31 ....2...
Jewitt La LS22 ....1...
Jin-Whin Hill WF10 ....2...
Jobbing Cross YO61 ....1...
Jockey La
  Huntington YO32 ....2...
  5 Knaresborough HG5 ....2...
Joffre Ave WF10 ....2...
John Breckon Rd YO21 ....3...
John Dixon La DL1 ....
John of Gaunt's Castle*
  HG3 ....1...
John St Darlington DL1 ....
  11 Earby BB18 ....1...
  38 Filey YO14 ....1...
  Great Ayton TS9 ....
  11 Harrogate HG1 ....2...
  Selby YO8 ....2...
  Whitby YO21 ....2...
  York YO31 ....2...
Johnson Cl 11 YO7 ....2...
Johnson St YO8 ....2...
Jolby La Cleasby DL10 ....
  Croft-on-Tees DL2 ....
  Newton Morrell DL10 ....
Jonah's La HG3 ....1...
Jonathan Garth 17 LS29 ....2...
Jorvik Viking Ctr*
  YO1 ....2...
Joseph Rowntree Sch
  YO32 ....2...
Jowett's La BD22 ....1...
Jowland Winn La YO8 ....2...
Jubbergate YO1 ....2...
Jubilee Bank TS7 ....
Jubilee Cave* BD24 ....1...
Jubilee Rd
  Norton YO17 ....2...
  5 Stokesley TS9 ....
Jubilee Terr YO26 ....2...
Julia Ave YO32 ....2...
Junction Farm Prim Sch
  TS16 ....

...er Cl YO32 ....225 D3
...er Gr TS21 ....5 C8
...er Way 28 HG3 ...161 B3
...Dr DL1 ....3 E8
...d YO26 ....9 A4
...nd Rd DL9 ....209 C2

...Ave TS5 ....6 D7
...Prim Sch TS5 .....6 E7
...a B023 ....156 F8
...el Cl HG4 ....214 C3
...en Ave 8 YO12 ....99 E6
...yn Ave YO32 ......226 A2
...House La TS15 ....24 D5
... Dr YO8 ....198 B4
...Bank YO61 ....117 C5
...gley Cl TS14 .....179 B1
...sley Rd HG4 ......214 B7
...ield DL11 ....37 D6
...den Rd LA2 ....130 A3
...s Cl
...ontefract WF8 ....201 B1
...on YO30 ....227 F8
...s Wlk HG1 ....219 E7
...e Cl YO23 ....231 B3
...e Garth LS25 .....194 E1
...e Gdns YO23 ......231 B2
...e Park Cres YO23 .231 A2
...e Pk N YO23 ......231 A3
...e Pk S YO23 ......231 A2
...er's Cl YO61 .....118 A1
...ers Gate 18 YO18 .95 F6
...er's Hill YO25 ...150 A1
...ers Way 11 YO19 ..184 F7
...nley Rd
...leys Both BD20 ...173 D3
...dine B88 ....186 A3
...ding BD22 ....187 B6
...lusburn BD20 .....187 F7
...y LS29 ....231 A8
...rshaw Bridge B88 .186 D3
...ton BD23 ....216 F2
...den Forest B88 ...186 B3
...ner Rise TS8 .....6 F5
...r Ave YO32 ....226 A4
...Rook TS4 ....6 F8
...rk Prim Sch
...................186 A7
...rook Rd BB18 .....171 D1
...par Cl LS24 ......189 D6
...bar Hill LS24 ....189 D6
...ar Way LS24 ......189 D6
...nave Caves* BD24 .131 D3
...Bank HG4 ....85 E3
...nert Cl YO12 .....95 E7
...dns YO12 ....212 B8
...Head Orch 11 .....70 A1
...Head Rd YO42 .....70 A1
...rds C of E Prim Sch
...................85 E3
...Beck 11 LS21 .....176 F1
...Syke La B023 .....155 A6
...ington La DN14 ...202 F2
...ington Prim Sch
...................202 F3
...mel Cl DL9 ....40 E2
...oton Cl YO24 .....227 D1
...oton Ct 16 DL1 ...3 F6
...mal Cl
...Dunnington YO19 ..184 F7
...Richmond DL10 ....154 B3
...mal Dr WF10 ......201 B4
...mal Gdns YO26 ....181 D7
...mal La YO26 ......181 D7
...mal Rd
...ington HG1 ....220 B3
...Preston BD23 .....154 A3
...almans 8 BD24 ...131 D2
...drew Cl 11 Bedale DL8 .63 A2
...ork YO32 ....225 F3
...orth Ave HG2 .....222 D7
...mfisher Cl
...arby BB18 ....172 A1
...ay BB18 ....186 A8
...ay Cl YO32 ....225 D4
...eedy Dr 82 YO32 ..166 E5
...nels La LS14 .....188 A4
...e La LS25 ....194 D3
...ion Ct 2 HG2 .....220 B3
...ion Rd HG2 ....220 B3
...ick Pl 8 YO26 ....227 B5
...r Rise 1 YO26 ....228 D2
...ington Ave
...n South Bank TS6 .7 E8
...ner LS14 ....188 A3
...ington Ct 1 YO42 .230 F8
...ington Gdns DL1 ..3 E5
...ington Rd YO30 ...224 D2
...ington Sq 18 HG2 .219 C2
...ington St YO23 ...228 B1
...Ave HG1 ....219 B3
...d Cl HG4 ....214 A2

Kent Cl YO32 ....225 D3
Kent Dr HG1 ....219 B3
Kent Rd Goole DN14 .205 F2
Guisborough TS14 ...8 B5
Harrogate HG1 .....219 B3
Selby YO8 ....232 A6
Kent Rd N HG1 .....219 A2
Kent St YO10 ......233 C1
Kentmere Dr YO30 .224 F1
Kenton Cl 4 TS18 ..5 E8
Kershaw Ave WF10 .201 A4
Kerver La YO19 ....184 F7
Kesteven Rd TS4 ...7 A7
Kestrel Dr 7 TS9 ..40 F2
Kestrel View 2 YO12 .99 E6
Kestrel Wood Way
...................225 D3
Keswick Dr WF10 ..201 C5
Keswick Rd TS5 ....6 D7
Keswick Way 5 YO32 .225 F5
Kettle Spring La HG3 .139 B1
Kettlebeck Brow LA2 .130 C5
Kettlestring La YO30 .225 A3
Kettlewell CP Sch
...................108 A3
Kettlewell La DL8 ..57 A5
Kex Gill Rd HG3 ...158 F2
Kexby Ave YO10 ...228 F3
Kexby Bridge* YO41 .185 C6
Kexby House* YO41 .185 A5
Kexby Stray YO41 .185 A5
Key La YO61 ....118 A1
Key Way YO19 .....231 F5
Keys Beck Rd YO18 .71 F4
Khyber Pass YO21 .208 D7
Kiddal La LS15 ....188 C2
Kidstones Bank DL8 .81 E3
Kielder Dr DL1 ....3 E7
Kielder Oval HG2 ..220 D2
Kilburn Rd YO10 ..228 D2
Kildale Stp YO21 ..27 E8
Kildare Garth 5 YO62 .70 C1
Kildwick C of E Prim Sch
BD20 ....187 F8
Kilgram La HG4 ....85 E8
Kilham Rd YO25 ...151 D5
Killerby Dr 2 DL10 .41 E4
Killerby La YO11 ..100 C5
Killin Rd DL1 .....3 E7
Killinghall C of E Prim Sch
HG3 ....161 C5
Kilmarnock Rd DL1 .3 E8
Kiln Hill La
Langcliffe LA2 .....131 A6
Silsden BD20 ....187 F8
Kiln La LA2 ....128 A6
Kilners Croft 18 LS29 .174 F4
Kilnsey Fold BD23 .174 B2
Kilnwick Ct DL7 ...210 D3
Kilton La TS12 ....10 F2
Kilton Thorpe La TS13 .10 B8
Kimberlows Wood Hill 8
YO10 ....229 C3
King Edward Ave
WF10 ....200 C7
King Edward Rd HG4 .214 C3
King Edward St
27 Glusburn BD20 ..187 F7
Normanton South WF6 .200 A1
King Edward's Dr
HG1 ....219 D5
King George Rd 11 HG4 .214 C3
King Hill YO14 ....101 A2
King James Rd HG5 .221 B5
King James's Gram Sch
HG5 ....221 B5
King Rudding Cl 6
YO19 ....198 A8
King Rudding La YO19 .198 B8
King St
Castleford WF10 ...200 F3
6 Cawood YO8 ....197 B8
Muston YO14 ....100 F2
Normanton South WF6 .200 A1
Pateley Bridge HG3 ..137 B4
Richmond DL10 .....209 C6
Ripon HG4 ....214 C4
Scarborough YO11 ..213 A6
York YO1 ....233 B2
Kingfisher Cl 7 YO12 .99 F6
Kingfisher Ct 8 DL9 .40 F2
Kingfisher Dr
8 Bedale DL8 ....63 B3
Guisborough TS14 ..8 D6
14 Pickering YO18 ..95 F6
Whitby YO22 ....208 E3
Kingfisher Reach
17 Boroughbridge YO51 .141 B5
5 Collingham LS22 .180 A1
Kings Acre YO31 ..229 B6
Kings Ave 2 LS29 ..218 A4
Kings Cl 8 YO8 ....198 B5
Kings Cl 5 DL8 ....41 D5
Kings Cl 9 LS29 ...175 C2
Kings Gate LS24 ..130 D3
Kings Gdns YO7 ...211 B3
Kings Keld Bank DL8 .86 F8
Kings La YO13 .....97 D5
Kings Lea YO8 ....199 A8

Kings Rd continued
Knaresborough HG5 ..221 C6
King's Sq YO1 .....233 C2
King's St BD23 ...217 B4
Kingsclere YO32 ..225 F5
Kingsland Terr 1 YO26 .227 F5
Kingsley Ave WF11 .201 D3
Kingsley Cl HG1 ..220 C3
Kingsley Dr
Harrogate HG1 .....220 A4
2 Middleham DL8 ...60 E2
Kingsley Park Mews 1
...................220 A4
Kingsley Park Rd HG1 .220 C3
Kingsley Rd
Harrogate HG1 .....220 B5
Trawden Forest B88 .186 B3
Kingsthorpe YO24 .227 D2
Kingston Ave HG4 ..214 C3
Kingston Cres YO8 .196 F2
Kingston Dr
Hambleton YO8 .....196 E1
10 Normanton WF6 ..200 B1
Kingston Garth 2 YO22 .33 C3
Kingston Gr 5 YO12 .212 B7
Kingstona Gdns 3
...................227 D2
Kingsway
Garforth LS25 ......194 B3
Harrogate HG1 .....219 E3
Pontefract WF8 ....201 B2
Scalby YO12 ....212 C8
Skipton BD23 ......217 B4
8 Stamford Bridge YO41 .168 D2
Weeton LS17 ....178 B2
Kingsway Dr
Harrogate HG1 .....219 E2
4 Ilkley LS29 ......218 A4
Kingsway Jun Sch
YO30 ....228 B7
Kingsway N YO30 ..228 B7
Kingsway W YO24 ..227 D1
Kingswood Gr YO24 .227 D3
Kinloss Cl TS17 ...6 A7
Kinsey Cave* BD24 .131 C4
Kiplin Hall* DL10 .42 B4
Kipling Gr WF8 ...201 B2
Kippax Greenfield Prim Sch
LS25 ....194 D1
Kippax Inf Sch LS25 .194 D1
Kippax Leisure Ctr
LS25 ....200 D8
Kippax North Jun & Inf Sch
LS25 ....194 C2
Kir Cres YO23 ....227 C3
Kirby Hill C of E Prim Sch
YO51 ....141 B7
Kirby La
Ebberston & Yedingham
...................97 E1
Skelton YO25 ......150 A4
Kirby Misperton La
YO17 ....121 C7
Kirby Misperton Rd
YO17 ....95 F1
Kirk Balk YO17 ....169 E8
Kirk Balk La YO60 ..168 B7
Kirk Bank
Conistone with Kilnsey
...................134 B4
Kirkby Malzeard HG4 .112 A5
Kirk Fenton C of E Prim Sch
LS24 ....196 B8
Kirk Gate
Bromton YO13 .....98 C7
Silpho YO13 ....74 E6
Kirk Hammerton C of E Prim
Sch YO26 ....164 C2
Kirk Hammerton La
...................164 C3
Kirk Hills LS14 ....188 A3
Kirk Ings La YO7 ..66 B7
Kirk La
Embsay with Eastby
BD23 ....217 E8
Tockwith YO26 .....181 C7
Kirk Rd Eaglescliffe TS16 .5 F2
Northallerton DL7 ..210 B3
Kirk Smeaton C of E Prim
Sch WF8 ....206 B3
Kirk Syke La BD23 .155 A5
Kirk View 1 YO23 ..227 C3
Kirkbank Rd YO13 ..75 D5
Kirkby & Great Broughton C
of E Prim Sch TS9 ..26 E5
Kirkby Ave HG4 ...214 A6
Kirkby Cl HG4 .....214 A6
Kirkby Dr HG4 .....214 A6
Kirkby Fleetham C of E Prim
Sch DL7 ....42 C1
Kirkby La
Gillamoor YO62 ....70 A3
Kearby with Netherby
...................179 B2
Kirkby TS9 ....26 D6
Kirkby Fleetham with Fencote
DL7 ....42 C2
Sicklinghall LS22 ..179 D3
Kirkby Malzeard C of E Prim
Sch HG4 ....112 A5
Kirkby Overblow C of E Prim
Sch HG3 ....179 A4
Kirkby Rd
North Stainley with Sleningford
HG4 ....113 C4

Kirkby Rd continued
Ripon HG4 ....214 A6
Selby YO8 ....232 B7
Kirkbymoorside Com Prim
Sch YO62 ....70 B1
Kirkbymoorside CP Sch
YO62 ....70 A1
Kirkcroft YO32 ....225 D8
Kirkdale La YO62 ..93 F8
Kirkdale Manor YO62 .93 D8
Kirkdale Rd YO10 ..229 D4
Kirkfield Ave LS14 ..188 A3
Kirkfield Cres LS14 ..188 A3
Kirkfield La LS14 ..188 A3
Kirkfield Rd DL3 ...3 D8
Kirkgate
Knaresborough HG5 ..221 A6
2 Middleham DL8 ...60 E2
6 Ripon HG4 ....214 C5
Settle BD24 ....131 D2
Sherburn in Elmet LS25 .195 E4
Silsden BD20 ....174 C1
Thirsk YO7 ....211 B3
Kirkgate La YO62 ..70 F4
**Kirkham Augustinian Priory
(rems of)*** YO60 ...146 F4
Kirkham Bridge*
...................146 F4
Kirkham Cl 6 YO30 .208 C6
Kirkham Cl 5 HG5 ..221 C4
Kirkham Gr YO30 ..219 F6
Kirkham Pl HG1 ...219 F6
Kirkham Rd
Harrogate HG1 .....219 F6
Middlesbrough TS7 ..7 D6
Whitby YO21 ....208 D6
Kirkham View YO60 .147 B4
Kirkham La WF11 ..201 D4
Kirkland Cl YO8 ...232 D4
Kirklands YO32 ....167 B6
Kirklands La YO41 ..169 C2
Kirkleatington Cty Prim Sch
TS15 ....24 F8
Kirkstall Dr BB18 ..171 E2
Kirkstone Dr YO31 ..229 A6
Kirkstone Rd HG1 ..220 B4
Kirkwell YO23 .....230 B3
Kit La BD20 ....174 B3
Kitchen Dr YO8 ...232 D4
Kitchener Rd
Ripon HG4 ....113 D3
Scotton DL9 ....40 E4
Kitchener St Selby YO8 .232 B6
York YO31 ....228 D7
Kitemere Pl 2 YO24 .230 B8
Kitter La YO21 ....31 C8
Kitty Garth YO19 ..197 A7
Knapping Hill HG1 ..219 C5
Knapton Cl 1 YO32 ..167 B6
Knapton La YO26 ..227 B4
Knapton Wold Rd
YO17 ....123 C5
Knaresborough Ave TS7 .7 D5
Knaresborough Castle*
...................221 A5
Knaresborough Rd
Bishop Monkton HG3 ..140 B4
Harrogate HG2 .....219 F2
Little Ribston LS22 ..180 A8
Ripon HG4 ....214 C6
Knaresborough Sta
HG5 ....221 A6
Knaresborough Swimming
Pool HG5 ....221 B5
Knavesmire Cl YO62 ..93 C5
Knavesmire Cres
YO23 ....228 B1
Knavesmire Prim Sch
YO23 ....228 A1
Knavesmire Rd YO23 ..228 A1
Knayton C of E Prim Sch
YO7 ....65 E3
Kneeton La DL10 ..21 C5
Knightsway LS25 ..194 B3
Knipe Point Dr 8 YO11 .100 B8
Knoll The
3 Bramham LS23 ....188 E6
York YO24 ....227 B2
Knolls Cl 11 YO11 ..100 B7
Knolls La HG4 .....67 F5
Knot La B87 ....171 A5
Knott La
Easingwold YO61 ...143 C8
Steeton with Eastburn
BD20 ....187 F7
Knott Rd YO18 .....49 D5
Knottingley England Lane
Jun & Inf Sch WF11 ..202 A2
Knottingley High Sch
WF11 ....202 A2
Knottingley Rd WF8 ..201 D1
Knottingley Rugby Union
Club WF11 ....202 A3
Knotto Bottom Cl DL6 .210 F3
Knotto Bottom Way
DL6 ....210 F3
Knotts La BD23 ....152 E1
Knowle La
Ilton-cum-Pott HG4 ..85 D1
Kirkby Knowle YO7 ..66 C2
Knowles Cl 18 TS15 ..24 E8
Knox Ave HG1 .....219 C5
Knox Chase HG1 ..219 C6
Knox Cl HG1 ....219 C6
Knox Dr HG1 ......219 C6
Knox Gdns HG1 ...219 C6

Knox Gr HG1 ....219 C6
Knox La Harrogate HG1 .219 D6
Scarborough YO11 ..213 B1
Knox Mill Bank HG1 ..219 B7
Knox Mill Cl HG3 ...219 B7
Knox Mill La HG3 ...219 B7
Knox Pk HG1 ....219 C6
Knox Rise HG1 ....219 C6
Knox Way HG1 ....219 C5
Kyle Cl 3 YO61 ....143 B3
Kyle Way YO26 ....227 B8
Kyme Castle* LS24 .189 C7
Kyme St YO1 ......233 B1

L

La Bassee Rd DL9 ...209 D1
Laburnum Ave
Fylingdales YO22 ...33 C4
Thornaby TS17 .....6 B7
Laburnum Cl
5 Catterick Garrison DL9 .209 B1
Rufforth YO23 .....182 C6
2 Snaith DN14 .....204 C1
8 Thorpe Willoughby YO8 .197 B1
Laburnum Dr HG3 ..140 A5
Laburnum Garth 6
YO31 ....228 F8
Laburnum Gr
Harrogate HG1 .....219 E6
Burton DL10 ....209 D8
Stillingfleet YO19 ..191 D4
Whitby YO21 ....208 B6
Laburnum Rd TS7 ...7 D8
Lacey Ave YO12 ...99 D7
Lachman Rd B88 ...186 A2
Lack La YO62 ......93 C2
Lackon Bank HG3 ..160 C8
Lacy Gr LS22 ......180 C2
Ladgate La TS5 ....6 F6
Lady Balk La WF8 ..201 B1
Lady Edith's Ave YO12 .212 B6
Lady Edith's Cres
YO12 ....212 B6
Lady Edith's Dr YO12 .212 A6
Lady Edith's Pk YO12 .212 B7
Lady Elizabeth Hastings C of
E Sch
Collingham LS22 ...180 A1
Thorp Arch LS23 ...180 F1
Lady Grace's Ride
YO12 ....212 A3
Lady Hamilton Gdns
YO24 ....227 E2
Lady Hullocks Ct LS29 .218 C7
Lady La HG3 ....222 A5
Lady Lumleys Sch YO18 .95 F7
Lady Rd YO30 .....228 B7
Ladycarr La YO61 ..143 E8
Ladysmith Ave YO22 .208 C7
Ladysmith Mews 15
YO32 ....167 A7
Ladysmith Rd DL9 ..40 C4
Ladywell La YO51 ..141 C5
Ladywell Rd YO51 ..141 A5
Lairs Cres YO13 ...98 A5
Lairs La YO13 .....98 A5
Lairum Rise LS23 ..188 E7
Laith Staid La LS25 .195 D4
Laithbutts La LA2 ..130 B8
Lakeber Ave LA2 ..130 C8
Lakeber Dr LA2 ...129 A8
Lakeber Dr LA2 ...129 A8
Lakeside
Acaster Malbis YO23 ..191 C7
Darlington DL1 .....3 C4
Hunmanby Sands YO14 ..101 B1
Lakeside Cl LS29 ..218 A5
Lakeside Gr 1 YO32 .167 B8
Lakeside Mdws 1 WF8 .201 B2
Lakeside Prim Sch
YO30 ....224 F2
Lakeside Way YO17 .215 D2
Laking La YO25 ...126 A3
Lamb Inn Rd 9 WF11 .202 A2
Lamb La TS17 .....6 A4
Lambert Cl YO10 ..233 B1
Lambert Meml Hospl
YO7 ....211 B2
Lambert St
1 Skipton BD23 ....217 A3
2 York YO30 ....186 B1
Lambeth St B88 ...186 A3
Lambourne Dr TS17 ..7 C6
Lamb's La TS9 .....27 B4
Lambs La 12 YO19 ..99 F7
Lamel St YO10 ....229 C4
Lamplugh Cres YO23 .231 B3
Lanacar La DL8 ...56 A4
Lancar Cl 18 YO22 ..166 D5
Lancaster Cl 9 YO13 .75 D5
Lancaster Park Rd
HG2 ....220 A3
Lancaster Rd
Harrogate HG2 .....219 C1
North Cowton DL7 ..22 C2
Ripon HG4 ....214 A6
Lancaster Way
17 Scalby YO13 .....75 D5
York YO30 ....225 A1
Lancers Ct 4 YO12 ..75 F5
Landalewood Rd YO30 .224 F2
Landau Cl YO30 ...227 F8

Landing La
Asselby DN14 ... 205 D6
Barlby with Osgodby
YO8 ... 232 F8
22 Howden DN14 ... 166 F5
Haxby YO32 ... 225 E7
Hemingbrough YO8 ... 204 F8
Riccall YO19 ... 197 F8
York YO26 ... 227 E6
Landing Rd YO8 ... 203 A7
Landings The 7 YO32 ... 166 F5
Lands La HG5 ... 220 E7
Lane Ends La BD22 ... 187 B7
Lane Foot Rd HG3 ... 159 E8
Lane House La BB8 ... 186 B1
Lane House Rd BD22 ... 187 A6
Lane The
Gate Helmsley YO41 ... 168 B2
Mickleby TS13 ... 12 A4
Lanehead La DL11 ... 18 H8
Lanehouse Rd TS17 ... 6 B8
Laneshawbridge CP Sch
BB8 ... 186 B3
Lang Ave YO10 ... 229 A4
Lang Gate YO13 ... 74 E4
Lang Kirk Cl 2 BD20 ... 173 F1
Lang Rd
Bishopthorpe YO23 ... 230 F4
York YO32 ... 225 F6
Langbar Rd DL8 ... 61 A6
Langbaurgh Cl TS9 ... 8 A2
Langber Rd TS15 ... 25 C4
Langber End La LA6 ... 103 B1
Langber La BD23 ... 154 A6
Langbourne Rd YO21 ... 208 D6
Langburn La YO21 ... 29 A7
Langburn's Bank YO21 ... 29 F7
Langcliffe Ave HG2 ... 222 F8
Langcliffe Ave E HG2 ... 222 E8
Langcliffe CP Sch
BD24 ... 131 E4
Langcliffe Garth BD23 ... 108 B3
Langcliffe Rd BD24 ... 131 D3
Langdale TS14 ... 8 D6
Langdale Ave
3 Pontefract WF6 ... 200 A2
York YO10 ... 229 A4
Langdale Dr 2 WF6 ... 200 A2
Langdale Gr YO8 ... 232 B3
Langdale Mews 6 WF6 ... 200 A2
Langdale Rd 3 YO12 ... 212 F7
Langer Hill La HG3 ... 160 B5
Langford Cl 7 LS29 ... 176 C1
Langford Ct 8 LS29 ... 176 C1
Langford La LS29 ... 176 C1
Langford Mews 10 LS29 ... 176 C1
Langford Rd LS29 ... 176 C1
Langford Ride 9 LS29 ... 176 C1
Langholm Cres DL3 ... 3 A5
Langholme Dr YO26 ... 227 C6
Langhorne Dr 2 DL11 ... 38 B6
Langley Cl 1 YO32 ... 225 F6
Langley Dr YO17 ... 215 D1
Langleys Rd 8 DN6 ... 206 E1
Langrickgate La YO42 ... 193 C5
Langsett Gr 7 YO42 ... 101 A3
Langsett Gr YO30 ... 224 F3
Langstrothdale Rd
BD24 ... 105 D7
Langthwaite La DL8 ... 59 C3
Langtoft CP Sch YO25 ... 151 C5
Langton CP Sch YO17 ... 147 F5
Langton Crossroads
YO17 ... 148 B6
Langton Ct 1 YO32 ... 167 A6
Langton La YO17 ... 148 C8
Langton Rd
Langton YO17 ... 148 A7
Norton YO17 ... 215 E2
Langwith Ave LS22 ... 188 A8
Langwith Stray YO10 ... 184 C2
Lansdown Rd DN14 ... 205 F2
Lansdown Way 7 YO32 ... 166 F5
Lansdowne Rd TS15 ... 5 E3
Lansdowne Terr 5
YO10 ... 228 E3
Lanshaw Bank BD23 ... 175 A7
Lanshaw Croft YO30 ... 224 F1
Lantsbury Dr TS13 ... 10 D8
Larch Gr 1 Filey YO14 ... 101 B4
Pannal HG3 ... 222 E2
Larch Rd YO7 ... 89 A1
Larch Rise 4 YO61 ... 117 D1
Larchfield YO31 ... 229 C7
Larchfield Com TS8 ... 6 E4
Larchfield Sports Ctr
DL3 ... 3 C5
Larchfield St DL3 ... 3 D6
Lark Hill Cl HG4 ... 214 A7
Lark Hill Cres 16 HG4 ... 214 B2
Lark Hill Dr HG4 ... 214 A6
Lark La HG4 ... 214 A6
Larkfield Cl
1 Copmanthorpe YO23 ... 230 A3
Pannal HG2 ... 222 A7
Larkfield Dr HG2 ... 222 A7
Larkfield Rd
Harrogate HG2 ... 222 A7
Selby YO8 ... 232 A4
Larkfield Way HG2 ... 222 A7
Larkhill Cl HG4 ... 214 A6
Larkspur Gr 14 HG3 ... 161 B3
Larkspur Rd DL1 ... 3 E7
Larpool Cres YO22 ... 208 E4
Larpool Dr YO22 ... 208 D3

Larpool La YO22 ... 208 D4
Larsen Rd DN14 ... 205 F2
Larun Beat The TS15 ... 5 E2
Lascelles Ct DL6 ... 210 E4
Lascelles Gr HG2 ... 219 B1
Lascelles La
Malton YO17 ... 215 E6
Northallerton DL6 ... 210 E4
Lascelles Rd HG2 ... 222 B8
Latimer La TS14 ... 8 E6
Latimer Rd DL1 ... 3 E7
Lauderdale Dr TS14 ... 8 F6
Laughton Ave YO12 ... 212 C5
Laundry La LA6 ... 103 D3
Laundry Rd
4 Filey YO14 ... 101 B3
3 Harrogate HG1 ... 220 C4
Lauradale La BD23 ... 134 D1
Laurel Ave TS4 ... 7 A8
Laurel Ct Burniston YO13 ... 75 D8
Gateforth YO8 ... 197 B1
Laurel Croft BD23 ... 217 D8
Laurels Garth YO60 ... 145 C5
Laurels The 6 DL6 ... 210 E2
Laurence Jackson Sch
TS14 ... 9 F8
Lavender Ct 21 DL9 ... 41 A5
Lavender Gr YO26 ... 227 E5
Laveracks Ind Est
YO41 ... 185 B3
Laverton Gdns 4 HG3 ... 219 A4
Law La HG3 ... 138 F1
Lawn Ave LS29 ... 176 C1
Lawn La DN6 ... 207 E3
Lawn Rd 8 LS29 ... 176 C1
Lawnfield Dr HG3 ... 140 B5
Lawnfield Rd HG3 ... 140 B5
Lawns Rd YO21 ... 29 E6
Lawns The HG2 ... 222 C8
Lawnswood Dr YO30 ... 227 F8
Lawnway YO31 ... 229 A7
Lawrence Cl YO12 ... 212 A8
Lawrence Cres DL10 ... 209 F8
Lawrence Gr YO12 ... 212 A8
Lawrence St YO10 ... 228 D3
Lawsings Brow LA2 ... 130 B5
Lawson Ave 1 YO51 ... 141 B4
Lawson Rd YO24 ... 230 F7
Lawsons Cl YO14 ... 126 F7
Layerthorpe YO31 ... 233 C3
Layfield Prim Sch TS15 ... 5 D2
Lazenby Dr 6 LS22 ... 180 B3
Lazenby Moor La HG5 ... 141 C3
Le Cateau Cl DL9 ... 40 F4
Le Cateau Rd DL9 ... 40 E4
Lea Croft LS23 ... 188 E7
Lea La YO61 ... 143 F4
Lea Way YO32 ... 226 A4
Lead La Brompton DL6 ... 43 F3
Nether Silton YO7 ... 66 B7
Ripon HG4 ... 214 B1
Westerdale YO21 ... 28 E4
Lead Mill La YO1 ... 233 C1
Leadhall Ave HG2 ... 222 D6
Leadhall Cl HG2 ... 222 D6
Leadhall Cres HG2 ... 222 D6
Leadhall Dr HG2 ... 222 D6
Leadhall Gdns HG2 ... 222 D6
Leadhall Gr HG2 ... 222 D6
Leadhall La HG2 ... 222 D6
Leadhall Rd HG2 ... 222 D6
Leadhall View HG2 ... 222 C5
Leadhall Way HG2 ... 222 C6
Leading Post St 8
YO11 ... 213 B6
Leadley Croft YO23 ... 230 A1
Leafield Rd DL1 ... 3 D4
Leahope Ct TS17 ... 6 C6
Leahurst Cl YO17 ... 215 E2
Leake La YO7 ... 65 F6
Leake St
Castleford WF10 ... 200 F4
York YO10 ... 228 E3
Lealholm C of E Sch
YO21 ... 30 C6
Lealholm Cres TS3 ... 7 C8
Lealholm La YO21 ... 30 B5
Lealholm Sta YO21 ... 30 B6
Leamington Rd LS29 ... 218 C5
Leamington Terr LS29 ... 218 C5
Leas Head Rd YO22 ... 32 B2
Leas La YO18 ... 95 F5
Leas The
11 Brafferton YO61 ... 115 F1
Darlington DL1 ... 3 D8
8 Eastfield YO11 ... 99 F7
Lease Rigg La YO21 ... 31 A3
Leases La DL10 ... 41 E4
Leases Rd DL7 ... 63 C5
Leasmires Ave 10 YO61 ... 143 D8
Leat Cl YO17 ... 215 D2
Leather Bank LS29 ... 176 C1
Leathley La LS21 ... 177 D1
Leavening CP Sch
YO17 ... 147 E1
Leck C of E Sch LA6 ... 102 E7
Leconfield Garth HG3 ... 223 F5
Ledbury Way TS14 ... 8 D6
Ledesway 1 BD23 ... 134 E3
Ledgate La LS25 ... 201 E6
Ledston Ave LS25 ... 194 D3
Ledston Hall* WF10 ... 200 F8
Ledston Mill La WF10 ... 200 F8
Leech La DL10 ... 41 E4
Leeds Barnsdale Rd
WF10 ... 200 D3
Leeds La LS26 ... 194 A3

Leeds Rd
Allerton Bywater WF10 ... 200 D7
Barwick in Elmet & Scholes
LS15 ... 194 B8
Castleford WF10 ... 200 E3
Collingham LS22 ... 188 A8
Great Preston WF10 ... 200 C7
Harrogate HG2 ... 219 D1
Ilkley LS29 ... 218 D5
Kippax LS25 ... 194 C2
Micklethwaite YO26 ... 227 B1
Mickletown LS26 ... 200 A6
Pannal HG3 ... 222 F3
Selby YO8 ... 232 A4
Tadcaster LS24 ... 189 D5
Leeman Rd YO26 ... 233 A2
Leeming & Londonderry CP
Sch DL7 ... 63 D4
Leeming La
Brough with St Giles
DL10 ... 41 D5
Burneston DL8 ... 87 F8
4 Burton in Lonsdale LA6 ... 102 F3
Catterick DL10 ... 41 C4
Kirklington-cum-Upsland
YO7 ... 88 A6
Langthorpe YO51 ... 141 B6
Leeming DL7 ... 63 C4
Melmerby HG4 ... 114 D8
Theakston DL7 ... 63 E1
Thornthwaite with Padside
HG3 ... 159 C6
Lees La DL7 ... 210 B1
Leeside YO24 ... 230 E8
Legion St LS25 ... 195 F2
Legram La YO26 ... 163 D8
Legram Rd YO26 ... 163 D8
Leicester Way
Aislaby TS16 ... 5 D4
York YO1 ... 233 C1
Leighton Cl YO12 ... 99 E6
Leighton Croft 3 YO30 ... 224 F1
Leighton Rd 6 TS18 ... 5 D8
Leith Rd DL3 ... 3 A5
Lendal YO1 ... 233 B2
Lendales La YO18 ... 95 E3
Lennerton La LS25 ... 196 C3
Lennox Ave DL10 ... 209 D7
Lennox Cl 2 YO14 ... 127 A8
Lennox Pl HG4 ... 113 D3
Leonard St 5 BB18 ... 171 D1
Leppington Dr YO12 ... 212 C4
Leppington La YO17 ... 147 D1
Lerecroft Rd YO24 ... 230 D8
Lesley Ave YO10 ... 231 E8
L'espec St DL7 ... 210 D3
Leven Bank Rd TS15 ... 5 F2
Leven Cl TS16 ... 5 D4
Leven Ct TS9 ... 8 A1
Leven Rd Eaglescliffe TS15 ... 5 E3
Stokesley TS9 ... 26 B7
York YO24 ... 230 D7
Leven Wynd 9 TS9 ... 26 C7
Levendale 6 TS15 ... 25 C5
Levendale Prim Sch
TS15 ... 25 C5
Levens Cl HG3 ... 161 B3
Levenside Great Ayton TS9 ... 7 F1
4 Hutton Rudby TS15 ... 25 D5
Stokesley TS9 ... 26 C7
Levick Cres TS5 ... 6 D8
Levisham St YO10 ... 228 D2
Levisham Sta YO18 ... 72 B5
Lewes Rd DL1 ... 3 D4
Lewis Cl
1 Croft-on-Tees DL2 ... 22 C8
Northallerton DL6 ... 210 F5
Lewis Rd DL6 ... 210 F5
Lexden Ave TS5 ... 6 D8
Leyburn Com Prim Sch
DL8 ... 60 D5
Leyburn Gr 1 TS18 ... 5 D8
Leyburn Pl 8 YO14 ... 101 A3
Leyburn RC Prim Sch
DL8 ... 60 D5
Leyburn Rd Askrigg DL8 ... 57 F6
Darlington DL1 ... 3 D7
Masham HG4 ... 86 B4
Middleham DL8 ... 60 E3
Scotton DL9 ... 40 C4
Leyes The YO10 ... 229 C4
Leyfield Cl 1 YO32 ... 167 A7
Leyland Rd
Darlington DL1 ... 3 D1
Harrogate HG2 ... 220 A3
York YO31 ... 229 A5
Leys La
Boston Spa LS23 ... 188 D8
Darrington WF11 ... 206 A8
Glusburn BD20 ... 187 B8
Knottingley WF11 ... 201 F1
Little Smeaton WF8 ... 206 B4
Leys Rd WF11 ... 201 E4
Leysthorpe La YO62 ... 93 B2
Liardet Rd DL10 ... 41 A4
Lichfield Ct 6 YO23 ... 228 B1
Lichfield Gr HG3 ... 219 A4
Lickley St HG4 ... 214 C5
Lidget La HG5 ... 163 B5
Lidget Rd BD20 ... 173 E3
Lidgett Gr YO26 ... 227 B6
Lidgett Grove Sch
YO26 ... 227 B6
Lidgett La
Garforth LS25 ... 194 C3
Lidice Rd DN14 ... 205 E2
Lidsty Hill YO62 ... 70 E5
Lifeboat Mus* YO11 ... 208 D7
Light Bank La BD20 ... 174 C2

Light La DL8 ... 59 E5
Lightfoots Ave YO12 ... 212 D3
Lightfoots Cl YO12 ... 212 D3
Lightfoot's La YO12 ... 212 D3
Lightfoots Rd YO12 ... 212 D3
Lightmire La YO26 ... 142 A1
Lightwater Valley Miniature
Rly* HG4 ... 113 C6
Lightwater Valley Theme
Pk* HG4 ... 113 C6
Lilac Ave
Appleton Roebuck YO23 ... 190 F5
Thornaby TS17 ... 6 B7
York YO10 ... 229 B3
Lilac Cl 12 LS29 ... 175 A4
Lilac Gr Harrogate HG1 ... 219 E6
New Earswick YO32 ... 225 D4
Lilac Rd TS7 ... 7 D7
Lilac Wlk YO12 ... 212 D7
Lilbourne Dr YO30 ... 228 A8
Lile Cl DL10 ... 209 C7
Lilla Cl YO24 ... 208 A6
Lilling Ave 3 YO31 ... 228 E8
Lilling La YO60 ... 145 C5
Lilling Low La YO60 ... 145 C2
Lilly Gate La HG3 ... 162 A8
Limber Hill YO21 ... 30 E4
Lime Ave YO31 ... 228 F7
Lime Chase 10 YO62 ... 70 B1
Lime La HG4 ... 114 C6
Lime Gr Harrogate HG1 ... 219 F3
4 Whitby YO21 ... 208 C6
Lime Kiln La LS22 ... 180 B5
Lime La DL8 ... 87 F2
Lime Rd Eaglescliffe TS16 ... 5 E6
Guisborough TS14 ... 8 F7
Sinnington YO62 ... 94 D8
Lime St HG1 ... 219 F3
Lime Tree Ave
8 Easingwold YO61 ... 117 D1
Malton YO17 ... 215 D6
York YO32 ... 225 D3
Lime Tree Gr YO8 ... 198 B4
Lime Tree Mews 15
YO19 ... 184 F7
Limber Bank Rd
YO51 ... 141 D1
Limebar La YO51 ... 141 C2
Limegarth 10 YO26 ... 165 F1
Limehouse La BD23 ... 216 E1
Limekiln Bank HG4 ... 113 C1
Limekiln Hill YO25 ... 150 B3
Limekiln La
Burton Leonard HG3 ... 140 A1
East Layton DL11 ... 1 B1
8 Eastfield YO11 ... 100 B6
Folkton YO11 ... 100 A2
Halton West BD23 ... 154 A1
North Stainley with Sleningford
HG4 ... 113 C5
Snape with Thorp HG4 ... 86 D5
Limekiln Rd YO7 ... 65 F5
Limes The
Burniston YO13 ... 75 C8
Helmsley YO62 ... 92 F6
Stockton on the Forest
YO32 ... 167 D2
Limestone Gr YO13 ... 75 C8
Limestone La YO13 ... 75 A5
Limestone Rd YO13 ... 75 B7
Limestone Way YO13 ... 75 C8
Limetree Cl 2 YO8 ... 197 B1
Lime-Tree Cres LS25 ... 194 E1
Limetrees WF8 ... 201 D2
Limpsey Gate La YO18 ... 72 D6
Limpton Gate TS15 ... 5 E2
Linacre Gr HG2 ... 220 D2
Lincoln Gr HG3 ... 219 A5
Lincoln Rd BB18 ... 172 A1
Lincoln St YO26 ... 227 F5
Lindale 2 YO24 ... 230 C7
Linden Ave Darlington DL3 ... 3 B5
Great Ayton TS9 ... 7 F1
4 Hutton Rudby TS15 ... 25 C4
Sleights YO22 ... 32 B7
Linden Cl
Great Ayton TS9 ... 7 F1
5 Hutton Rudby TS15 ... 25 C4
Middlesbrough TS7 ... 7 B6
Linden Dr Harworth DL2 ... 3 D1
7 Hurworth-on-Tees DL2 ... 22 D8
Linden Gdns DL10 ... 209 D7
Linden Gr Great Ayton TS9 ... 7 F1
York YO30 ... 224 F1
Thornaby TS17 ... 6 B8
Linden Rd 3 Earby BB18 ... 172 A1
Great Ayton TS9 ... 7 F1
Northallerton DL6 ... 210 E4
Scalby YO12 ... 212 A8
Linden Way
1 Thorpe Willoughby YO8 ... 197 B2
Wetherby LS22 ... 180 B4
Lindhead CP Sch YO13 ... 75 C8
Lindhead Rd YO13 ... 75 B8
Lindisfarne Rd TS3 ... 7 C8
Lindley Rd YO30 ... 224 F1
Lindley St Skipton BD23 ... 216 F2
York YO24 ... 227 F3
Lindley Wood Gr
YO30 ... 224 E3
Lindon Rd DL10 ... 209 F3
Lindrick Cl 3 HG4 ... 214 B2
Lindrick Way HG3 ... 219 A4
Lindsay Rd LS25 ... 194 C3
Lindsey Ave YO26 ... 227 E5
Ling Croft LS23 ... 188 D8

Ling Hill YO12 ... 212
Ling La YO41 ... 18
Ling Trod YO17 ... 12
Lingcrag Gdns BD22 ... 18
Lingcroft Cl YO8 ... 20
Lingcroft La
Naburn YO19 ... 23
Tockwith LS22 ... 18
Lingdale Prim Sch TS12 ...
Lingdale Rd
Lockwood TS12 ...
Thornaby TS17 ...
Lingerfield Prim Sch
HG5 ... 16
Lingfield Ash TS8 ...
Lingfield Cl DL1 ...
Lingfield Prim Sch TS7 ...
Lingfield Way DL1 ...
Lingham La YO7 ... 11
Linghaw La LA2 ...
Lingholm Cres 9 YO11 ... 9
Lingholm La YO11 ... 10
Lingmoor La YO62 ...
Lingrow Cl 8 TS13 ...
Link Ave YO30 ... 22
Link Rd YO31 ... 22
Link The
Copmanthorpe YO23 ... 23
Middlesbrough TS3 ...
Northallerton DL7 ... 21
Northallerton DL6 ... 21
Selby YO8 ... 23
York YO10 ... 23
Link Wlk 8 YO11 ... 10
Linkfoot La YO62 ...
Links Cl HG2 ... 22
Links Dr LA2 ... 12
Links Prim Sch The
HG5 ...
Links The
7 North Featherstone
WF7 ... 20
Tadcaster LS24 ... 18
Links Way HG2 ... 22
Linkway DN6 ... 2
Linnburn Mews 1 LS29 ... 21
Linnet Way YO24 ... 23
Linton Ave 9 LS22 ... 18
Linton Cl
Cloughton YO13 ...
9 Filey YO14 ... 10
Linton Comm LS22 ... 17
Linton Falls 7 BD23 ...
Linton Falls 1 BD23 ... 13
Linton La 7 YO30 ... 16
Linton Mdw 8 YO30 ... 16
Linton Mdws 7 LS22 ... 18
Linton Pl 4 YO30 ... 16
Linton Rd
Collingham LS22 ... 18
Poppleton YO26 ... 2
Wetherby LS22 ... 18
Linton Rise 17 DL9 ...
Linton St 5 YO26 ... 22
Linton Woods YO30 ... 16
Linton Woods La
YO30 ...
Linton-on-Ouse CP Prim S
YO30 ... 1
Linwith La DN14 ... 20
Linwood Ave TS9 ...
Lisheen Ave WF10 ... 20
Lismore Rd YO12 ... 21
Lismore Rd YO12 ... 21
Lister Hill 5 BD20 ... 18
Lister St LS29 ... 21
Lister Way YO30 ... 22
Lisvane Ave YO7 ...
Litley Bank YO7 ...
Little Ave YO30 ... 22
Little Ayton La TS9 ...
Little Beck Bank YO22 ...
Little Beck La YO22 ... 3
Little Catterton La
LS24 ... 19
Little Church La LS26 ... 20
Little Comm La DN14 ... 20
Little Croft HG3 ... 13
Little Crossing HG4 ... 2
Little Field La YO18 ... 7
Little Garth YO26 ... 22
Little Hallfield Rd
YO31 ... 22
Little Harries La HG4 ... 21
Little Heck Comm La
DN14 ...
Little Hutton La TS15 ...
Little Ings Cl 5 YO51 ... 14
Little Ings La YO51 ... 14
Little King St 1 BD23 ...
Little La Brompton DL6 ...
8 Easingwold YO61 ... 11
Ellerton YO42 ... 19
11 Haxby YO32 ... 16
Ilkley LS29 ... 21
Little Smeaton DN6 ... 20
North Stainley with Sleningford
HG4 ...
Little Mdws YO32 ... 22
Little Moor Cl YO13 ... 5
Little Moor La YO8 ... 23
Little Stonegate YO1 ... 23
Little Studley Cl HG4 ...
Little Studley Rd HG4 ... 21
Little Westfield YO7 ...
Little Wood St YO17 ... 21
Littlebeck Dr DL1 ...

eboy Dr TS17 .....6 C8
edale YO18 .....95 F7
efield Cl 5 YO26 .....165 F1
eside DL8 .....37 E7
ethorpe Cl HG3 .....219 A4
ethorpe La HG4 .....214 D2
ethorpe Pk HG4 .....214 E3
ethorpe Rd HG4 .....214 B5
ondale Ave HG5 .....221 D6
erton La TS13 .....10 D6
erton Mill Bank 10 B6
erton Rd TS13 .....10 D7
ngstone Rd YO22 .....212 E6
ngstone St YO26 .....227 C5
La YO41 .....229 B1
La YO41 .....168 D2
hrin Pl 7 YO26 .....227 B4
kton Pl DN14 .....207 F6
k La
 castleford WF10 .....200 E5
 ermanton WF6 .....200 A3
k Lane Sports Ctr
 10 .....10 B8
k Wlk DL10 .....41 E4
ker La HG4 .....214 C4
key Croft YO32 .....225 C8
kfield Dr BB18 .....171 E2
kgate Rd DN14 .....207 C4
kheed Cl TS18 .....5 F7
kton Cres TS17 .....6 A6
kton La YO18 .....72 E4
kton Rd YO18 .....208 A6
kwood Chase YO13 .....54 D1
kwood Prim Sch 9 D7
kwood Dr YO31 .....233 C3
lers Gn
 Eastfield YO11 .....99 F6
 Scarborough YO11 .....100 A6
ge Cl 7 YO11 .....100 B6
ge Gdns
 stithorpe YO14 .....100 E4
 Snaith DN14 .....204 C1
ge La 5 Brompton DL6 .....43 F3
 mby YO21 .....29 B7
 wdall DN14 .....203 F1
 wby with Mulwith
 4 .....140 E6
 nnington LA2 .....102 B1
ge Rd
 tton-le-Hole YO62 .....70 C5
 turs YO12 .....12 E3
ge Rd DN14 .....153 E8
ore Gr TS5 .....6 E6
thouse Endowed Prim Sch
 3 .....110 B4
thouse La YO41 .....185 D7
tus Cl YO12 .....212 B4
baurs Wynd DL10 .....209 C7
desborough Gr 8 .....197 B2
desborough Pk 10
 2 .....99 D6
desborough Rd
 2 .....212 E4
desborough St 5 .....232 C5
adon La DN6 .....207 D1
lg Acre Wlk HG3 .....222 C2
lg Ashes Leisure Ctr
 23 .....134 B3
lg Band DL8 .....58 A8
lg Bank DL11 .....19 C6
lg Bank La BD23 .....153 E1
lg Causeway Rd
 mby YO21 .....29 E3
lg Close La YO13 .....99 A4
lg Crag View 1 HG3 .....161 B2
lg Cswy
 alton East BD23 .....174 B8
 irkleby High & Low
 ith Osgodby YO7 .....90 D1
lg Furrow YO22 .....225 C8
lg Gate BD22 .....187 D4
lg Gn 7 BB18 .....172 B1
lg Heads La LS29 .....195 F1
lg Hill End BD23 .....187 B5
lg Ing La BB18 .....171 E1
lg La
 rwick in Elmet LS15 .....194 C7
 rroby YO7 .....65 E5
 ompton DL6 .....44 A6
 YO41 .....185 D6
 wood YO8 .....197 A6
 wling BD22 .....187 A8
 st Ayton YO13 .....99 B7
 rnby YO42 .....193 F1
 rndale East YO62 .....48 A7
 lifiscliffe HG3 .....160 E3
 ayles DL11 .....19 E6
 ck DN14 .....207 D8
 slington YO10 .....184 C3
 lk Smeaton WF8 .....206 B1
 eshaw Bridge BB8 .....186 B4
 ckwood TS12 .....10 B5
 rmanby YO62 .....94 F5
 ucliffe TS15 .....24 E6
 amer YO12 .....99 E6
 ngsby YO62 .....120 D6
 tham LA2 .....128 E7
lg La DL8 .....87 C4
lg Level LA6 .....102 C8
lg Mann Hills Rd 232 B4

Long Marston C of E Prim Sch YO26 .....182 A6
Long Mdw 19 Colne BB8 .....186 A3
 Skipton BD23 .....217 B5
Long Mdw Gate LS25 .....194 C2
Long Mdws
 Garforth LS25 .....194 C3
 6 Ilkley LS29 .....176 C1
 Rillington YO17 .....122 F5
Long Newton La TS21 .....5 A6
Long Preston Endowed Prim Sch BD23 .....153 F5
Long Preston Sta BD23 .....153 F4
Long Rampart YO42 .....193 D3
Long Riddings LS29 .....174 F5
Long Ridge Dr YO24 .....224 A1
Long Ridge La YO24 .....224 A1
Long Royd Rd BB18 .....172 A1
Long St Asenby YO7 .....115 B6
 Easingwold YO61 .....143 C8
 Thirsk YO7 .....211 C3
 Topcliffe YO7 .....115 C6
Long Stoop Standing Stone* HG3 .....160 A2
Long Swales La HG4 .....112 D5
Long Trods 5 YO8 .....232 C6
Long Wlk
 Knaresborough HG5 .....221 A6
 Scarborough YO12 .....212 D7
Longacre WF10 .....200 E3
Longbank Rd TS7 .....7 D7
Longber La LA6 .....102 D4
Longcroft 7 YO32 .....166 E5
Longcroft Rd 1 LS29 .....218 E3
Longdale Ave 18 BD20 .....131 D2
Longdike La
 Kippax LS25 .....200 E8
 Thornton Steward HG4 .....61 E1
Longfield Comp Sch DL3 .....3 C8
Longfield Ct 20 BB18 .....171 D1
Longfield Rd DL3 .....3 C7
Longfield Terr YO30 .....233 A3
Longgate La LA2 .....164 A3
Longlands Field Rd YO26 .....163 D8
Longlands La
 Boroughbridge YO51 .....141 A3
 Danby YO21 .....29 B6
 Hetton BD23 .....155 E1
 Sicklinghall LS22 .....179 E3
 Thornton-le-Dale YO18 .....96 E5
Longlands Rd YO17 .....123 B3
Longmans Hill CP Sch YO8 .....232 C3
Longtons La BD23 .....152 F4
Longwestgate YO11 .....213 B6
Longwood Bank DL10 .....209 D5
Longwood Link 6 YO30 .....224 E3
Longwood Rd YO30 .....224 E3
Lonsdale Mdws LS23 .....188 E8
Lonsdale Pl 12 YO13 .....99 B8
Lonsdale Rd YO11 .....213 A3
Loos Rd DL9 .....40 F3
Loraine Cres DL1 .....3 C4
Lord Ave TS17 .....6 B5
Lord Mayor's Wlk YO31 .....233 B3
Lord's Close Rd LA2 .....129 B3
Lords La DL8 .....61 C2
Lords La DL8 .....63 C2
Lords La DL8 .....62 E8
Lords Moor La YO7 .....167 C2
Lordship La YO8 .....232 D8
Loriners Dr 7 YO23 .....230 B3
Loring Rd YO13 .....54 A7
Lorne St YO23 .....228 B1
Lorraine Ave 3 YO41 .....185 B2
Loscoe Cl WF6 .....200 C2
Loscoe La WF7 .....200 C1
Loshpot La LS22 .....180 C5
Lothersdale CP Sch BD20 .....186 F8
Lothersdale Rd 7 BB18 .....187 B8
Lotherton La LS25 .....195 A7
Lotherton Way LS25 .....194 C4
Louisa St DL1 .....3 D5
Lousy Hill La YO22 .....32 D5
Louvain St 5 BB18 .....171 D2
Love La Brawby YO17 .....94 F1
 Castleford WF10 .....200 E3
 Easby DL10 .....209 E4
 8 Leyburn DL8 .....60 D5
 Whitby YO21 .....208 A7
 York YO24 .....228 A2
Love La DL7 .....64 F2
Low Bank
 Embsay BD23 .....217 E8
 Over Silton DL6 .....66 A8
Low Bentham CP Sch LA2 .....128 F8
Low Bentham Rd LA2 .....128 F8
Low Catton Rd YO41 .....185 C8
Low Cl LS29 .....218 A5
Low Croft 6 YO32 .....167 A7
Low Demesne LA6 .....103 D3
Low Demesne Cl LA6 .....103 D3
Low Farm LS26 .....200 C8
Low Farm Cl YO41 .....190 D4
Low Field La
 Cold Kirby YO7 .....91 D7
 Goldsborough HG5 .....163 A1
 Marton cum Grafton YO51 .....141 E2
 Staveley HG5 .....140 E1
Low Fields Dr YO24 .....227 C3
Low Fold BB18 .....186 A7

Low Garth YO22 .....32 A6
Low Garth Link 17 LS25 .....195 F4
Low Garth Rd LS25 .....195 F4
Low Gate DL8 .....57 F5
Low Gate La HG4 .....138 F7
Low Gn Catterick DL10 .....41 D4
 Copmanthorpe YO23 .....230 B2
 12 Knottingley WF11 .....202 A2
 Menwith with Darley HG3 .....160 A6
Low House La
 Carlton Miniott YO7 .....89 C2
 Dishforth YO7 .....115 B2
Low Hutton Pk YO60 .....147 C6
 Carperby-cum-Thoresby DL8 .....58 B4
 Cononley BD20 .....173 C2
 Cowling BD22 .....187 A8
 Cropton YO18 .....71 B4
 Dalby-cum-Skewsby YO60 .....119 B2
 Dalton DL11 .....19 D7
 Embsay with Eastby BD23 .....217 E8
 Grassington BD23 .....134 E3
 Grinton DL11 .....37 E5
 Grinton DL11 .....38 C5
 Heslington YO10 .....229 D1
 Hovingham YO62 .....119 F6
 Hunton-Sessay YO7 .....116 B7
 Leck LA6 .....102 D7
 Leyburn DL8 .....60 C4
 Maltby TS17 .....6 B3
 Menwith with Darley HG3 .....159 F6
 Mickleby TS13 .....12 A3
 Middlesbrough TS5 .....6 E6
 Muker DL11 .....36 C4
 Newsham DL11 .....18 F7
 Reeth, Fremington & Healaugh DL11 .....37 F5
 Silsden BD20 .....174 B3
 Spofforth with Stockeld LS22 .....179 C4
 Stainburn LS21 .....177 F3
 Sutton-under-Whitestonecliffe YO7 .....90 E6
 Swinton YO17 .....121 C4
 Thirkleby High & Low with Osgodby YO7 .....90 C1
 West Rounton DL6 .....24 D3
 Westow YO60 .....147 C4
 Wigglesworth BD23 .....153 D3
Low Mdw YO8 .....232 C6
Low Mill Cl YO10 .....229 C4
Low Mill La LS29 .....175 A4
Low Moor Ave 3 YO10 .....231 F8
Low Moor La
 Askham Richard YO23 .....182 D3
 Brearton HG5 .....162 B7
 East Harlsey DL6 .....44 C7
 Fearby HG4 .....85 F3
 Hessay YO26 .....182 C8
 Rillington YO17 .....122 D6
Low Moor Rd YO18 .....71 F5
Low Moor S La YO7 .....122 D6
Low Moorgate YO17 .....122 F5
Low Ousegate YO1 .....233 B2
Low Park Rd LS29 .....176 A3
Low Peter La HG3 .....140 A3
Low Peterate YO1 .....233 B3
Low Poppleton La YO26 .....227 B7
Low Rd Gainford DL2 .....1 C7
Low Rd DL8 .....204 A1
 Irton YO12 .....75 B3
 Kellington DN14 .....202 F4
 Kirby Grindalythe YO17 .....149 F7
 Newby & Scalby YO12 .....212 A6
 Thirkleby High & Low with Osgodby YO7 .....116 E8
Low Skellgate HG4 .....214 C5
Low Sleights Rd LA6 .....104 B7
Low St Aiskew DL7 .....63 C6
 Austwick LA2 .....130 E6
 Burton in Lonsdale LA6 .....102 F3
 Carlton DN14 .....204 C2
 Husthwaite YO61 .....117 B6
 Kirkby Fleetham with Fencote DL10 .....41 F2
 Knottingley WF11 .....201 E4
 Nunnington YO62 .....93 E2
 Oswaldkirk YO62 .....92 F3
 Ripon HG4 .....214 B5
 Scalby YO13 .....75 D5
 Sherburn in Elmet LS25 .....195 F4
 Thornton-le-Clay YO60 .....146 A4
Low Stanghow Rd TS12 .....9 F6
Low Town Bank Rd YO61 .....91 B4
Low Tun Way YO30 .....69 A2
Low Wath Rd HG3 .....137 B4
Low Way 5 LS23 .....188 E5
Low Well Pk YO19 .....192 F7
Low Westfield Rd YO23 .....230 A1
Low Wood La
 Glaisdale YO21 .....30 C6
 Leyburn DL8 .....60 C4
Low Wood Rise LS29 .....218 A3
Lowcroft 6 LS22 .....188 A8
Lowcross Ave TS14 .....8 E6
Lowcross Dr TS14 .....26 E5
Lowdale Ave 4 YO22 .....32 A6

Lower Clark St
 2 Scarborough YO12 .....212 F6
 13 Scarborough YO12 .....213 A7
Lower Constable Rd 218 D3
Lower Croft St YO8 .....172 A1
Lower Darnborough St YO23 .....233 B1
Lower Derwent Valley Nature Reserve* YO42 .....199 C8
Lower Flat Cliffs YO14 .....101 C1
Lower Friargate YO1 .....233 B2
Lower Greenfoot 18 BD23 .....131 D2
Lower Mickletown LS26 .....200 C6
Lower Oxford St WF10 .....200 E4
Lower Priory St YO1 .....233 A1
Lower Station Rd 8 WF8 .....201 A1
Lower Union St BD23 .....216 F3
Lower Wellington Rd LS29 .....218 B4
Lower William St 3 YO12 .....212 F6
Loweswater Rd 5 YO30 .....224 E1
Lowfield
 3 Eastfield YO11 .....100 A6
 Hawes DL8 .....56 C4
Lowfield Dr YO32 .....166 E5
Lowfield La
 Beamsley BD23 .....174 F7
 Kirkby Fleetham with Fencote DL7 .....42 D2
 Langthorpe YO51 .....141 A6
 Rufforth YO26 .....227 A4
 Sharow HG4 .....214 F6
 Snape with Thorp DL8 .....87 A7
Lowfield Rd
 Barlby with Osgodby YO8 .....198 B5
 Hillam LS25 .....202 C8
 Malton YO17 .....215 C6
Lowfield Sch YO24 .....227 D3
Lowfields 2 YO12 .....99 D2
Lowfields Ave TS17 .....6 A5
Lowfields La YO7 .....88 C6
Lowgate DL8 .....207 D5
Lowgill La LA2 .....128 F4
Lowick YO24 .....230 C7
Lowkber La LA6 .....103 E2
Lowlands Dr DL7 .....63 C5
Lowmoor Rd YO8 .....198 E6
Lown Hill YO24 .....227 C2
Lowna Rd YO62 .....70 B5
Lownorth Rd YO13 .....52 C6
Lowskellgate HG4 .....214 C5
Lowther Cres 3 LS26 .....194 A1
Lowther Ct YO31 .....233 C4
Lowther Dr
 Garforth LS25 .....194 C3
 5 Selby YO8 .....232 E3
 2 Swillington LS26 .....194 A1
Lowther Terr YO24 .....228 A3
Loxley Cl YO30 .....224 E3
Loyne Pk LA6 .....102 A7
Lucas Ave YO30 .....228 C8
Lucas Gr N YO26 .....181 C7
Lucas Gr S YO26 .....181 C7
Lucas Rd YO26 .....181 C7
Lucerne Dr TS14 .....8 E6
Lucia La TS14 .....8 E6
Lucky La YO7 .....89 E8
Lucombe Way YO32 .....225 D4
Luddith Rd YO17 .....148 D5
Ludlow Ave LS25 .....194 C4
Luke La TS17 .....6 C7
Lumb Gill La LS29 .....175 A3
Lumb La BD22 .....187 A5
Lumb Mill Way BD23 .....157 E7
Lumley Cl YO62 .....92 F6
Lumley La Azerley HG4 .....112 D2
 Kirkby Fleetham with Fencote DL7 .....42 B1
Lumley Rd YO30 .....228 B7
Lumley St WF10 .....200 D3
Lunar Pk* YO12 .....213 C6
Luncarr La HG4 .....114 B2
Lund Cl YO32 .....225 C8
Lund Head La HG3 .....179 B2
Lund La Bubwith YO8 .....199 C4
 Cliffe YO8 .....198 D4
 Hampsthwaite HG3 .....161 A5
Lund Rd YO62 .....70 B7
Lund Sand La
 Easingwold YO61 .....143 A8
 Raskelf YO61 .....117 A1
Lund Sike La LS25 .....195 F2
Lundgreen La YO61 .....143 A8
Lund's Twr* BD20 .....187 C6
Lundy Cl 10 YO30 .....225 A1
Lunebeck Wlk TS17 .....6 C6
Lunedale Ave
 Harrogate HG5 .....221 C5
 Middlesbrough TS5 .....6 E8
Lunedale Rd DL3 .....3 A6
Lunn La DN14 .....202 D3
Lunnfields La WF11 .....201 E6

Lupton Bank HG3 .....137 D3
Lupton Cl HG3 .....137 D3
Lutton La YO17 .....123 F4
Luttons CP Sch YO17 .....150 B8
Lutyens The 22 LS29 .....175 C2
Lycett Rd YO24 .....230 F6
Lych Gate BD22 .....3 E1
Lydford Rd 18 DL10 .....41 E4
Lydham Ct 2 YO24 .....230 C8
Lyell St YO12 .....212 E6
Lynbeck Cl YO7 .....211 B4
Lyndale LS25 .....200 D8
Lyndale Ave YO10 .....229 C3
Lyndale Rd 11 WF6 .....200 B1
Lynden Way YO24 .....227 D3
Lyndhurst Cl
 2 Norton DN6 .....206 F2
 7 Whitby YO21 .....208 D6
Lyndhurst Dr 1 DN6 .....206 F2
Lyndhurst Rise 3 DN6 .....206 F2
Lyndon Ave
 Bramham LS23 .....188 E6
 Garforth LS25 .....194 C4
Lyndon Cl 1 LS23 .....188 E6
Lyndon Cres 4 LS23 .....188 E6
Lyndon Rd LS23 .....188 E6
Lyndon Sq 1 LS23 .....188 E6
Lyndon Way LS23 .....188 E6
Lynmouth Cl TS8 .....6 E5
Lynndale Ave 6 BD20 .....187 F8
Lynton Ave LS23 .....188 E8
Lynton Cl YO8 .....232 B1
Lynton Gdns
 Brayton YO8 .....232 B1
 Darlington DL1 .....3 E5
 Harrogate HG1 .....220 A3
Lynton Way DL6 .....210 D3
Lynwith Cl DN14 .....204 C3
Lynwith Ct DN14 .....204 C3
Lynwith Dr DN14 .....204 C3
Lynwood Ave 3 YO23 .....230 A3
Lynwood View 4 YO23 .....230 A3
Lynx La DL10 .....209 C8
Lyon Rd YO26 .....187 F7
Lyonette Rd DL1 .....3 E7
Lyons Rd DL10 .....209 C8
Lys Cres DL9 .....209 D1
Lysander Cl YO30 .....225 A3
Lytham Cl BD23 .....217 C3
Lytham Gdns BD23 .....217 C3
Lytham Rd DL3 .....3 D8
Lythe Bank Lythe YO21 .....12 F4
 Sutton with Howgrave 87 C2
Lythe C of E Prim Sch YO21 .....12 E3
Lythe Fell Rd LA2 .....129 B2
Lythe La LA2 .....129 A2

M

M62 Trad Est DN14 .....205 F2
Mac Arthur Cl YO7 .....211 B2
Macdonell Cl 1 DL9 .....209 C1
Mackeridge La YO62 .....48 F4
Mackie Dr TS14 .....8 E6
Mackinnon Ave 1 WF6 .....200 B2
Maclagan Rd YO23 .....230 F4
Mafeking St HG1 .....219 F4
Magazine La YO8 .....198 B3
Magazine Rd YO8 .....198 B4
Magdalen's Cl HG4 .....214 D6
Magdalen's Rd HG4 .....214 D6
Magister Rd TS17 .....6 B7
Magnolia Gr YO32 .....225 D2
Maida Gr YO10 .....228 D1
Maiden Bower (Motte & Bailey)* YO7 .....115 D5
Maiden Castle* DL11 .....38 A5
Maiden Greve YO17 .....215 A4
Maidensgrave Henge* 126 F1
Maidstone Dr TS7 .....7 C6
Main Ave YO31 .....228 F5
Main Rd Drax YO8 .....204 F5
 Gainford DL2 .....1 D7
 Hambleton YO8 .....196 E1
 Hellifield BD23 .....154 B3
 Stainforth BD24 .....131 E6
 Steeton with Eastburn BD20 .....187 F7
 Weaverthorpe YO17 .....124 E1
Main St Aberford LS25 .....194 F8
 Addingham LS29 .....174 F4
 Allerston YO18 .....97 B5
 Aine YO61 .....142 F4
 Amotherby YO17 .....121 A4
 Appleton Roebuck YO23 .....190 F5
 Askham Bryan YO23 .....182 F3
 Askrigg DL8 .....57 E6
 Asselby DN14 .....205 D7
 Austwick LA2 .....130 E7
 Aysgarth DL8 .....58 E3
 Barkston Ash LS25 .....194 E6
 Barwick in Elmet LS15 .....194 B8
 3 Beal DN14 .....202 D4
 Bentham LA2 .....128 E8
 Bilbrough YO23 .....182 F1
 Bilton-in-Ainsty with Bickerton LS22 .....181 A5
 Bishop Monkton HG3 .....140 B5
 Bishopthorpe YO23 .....231 A4
 Boroughbridge YO51 .....141 A3
 4 Brafferton YO61 .....115 F1

Main St continued
Brafferton YO61 ... 141 F8
Bubwith YO8 ... 199 C7
Bugthorpe YO41 ... 169 D4
Burley in Warfedale
 LS29 ... 176 C1
Burton Salmon LS25 ... 201 F6
Church Fenton LS24 ... 196 B7
Cliffe YO8 ... 198 E2
Cononley BD20 ... 173 D1
Copmanthorpe YO23 ... 230 A2
Cottingwith YO42 ... 193 C5
Darley HG3 ... 160 A6
Deighton YO19 ... 192 A7
Earby BB18 ... 186 A8
East Ayton/West Ayton
 YO13 ... 99 A7
Eastfield YO11 ... 100 B6
Ebberston & Yedingham
 YO13 ... 97 D5
Ellerton YO42 ... 193 C1
Elvington YO41 ... 185 C2
Embsay BD23 ... 217 E8
Escrick YO19 ... 192 B5
Farnhill BD20 ... 173 E1
Folkton YO11 ... 100 A2
Follifoot HG3 ... 223 F5
Ganton YO12 ... 125 A8
Garforth LS25 ... 194 C3
Gillamoor YO62 ... 70 A4
Gilling East YO62 ... 118 F7
Glusburn BD20 ... 187 E7
Gowdall DN14 ... 204 A1
[18] Grassington BD23 ... 134 E3
Great Ouseburn YO26 ... 164 B8
Great Preston WF10 ... 200 D6
Gristhorpe YO14 ... 100 E4
Harome YO62 ... 93 C5
Healaugh LS24 ... 181 F2
Hebden BD23 ... 135 A1
Heck DN14 ... 207 C8
Helperby YO61 ... 142 A8
Hemingbrough YO8 ... 198 F1
Hensall DN14 ... 203 D2
Hessay YO26 ... 182 B8
High Bentham LA2 ... 129 A8
Hovingham YO62 ... 119 E6
Huby YO61 ... 144 A4
Ingleton LA6 ... 103 D3
Irton YO12 ... 99 C6
Kelfield YO19 ... 191 D1
Kellington DN14 ... 202 F3
Kirk Deighton LS22 ... 180 B5
Kirk Smeaton WF8 ... 206 B3
Kirkby Malham BD23 ... 154 F8
Kirkby Malzeard HG4 ... 112 C5
Langcliffe BD24 ... 131 E4
Ledston WF10 ... 200 F7
Linton LS22 ... 180 A1
Little Ouseburn YO26 ... 164 A7
Long Preston BD23 ... 153 F5
Low Bradley BD20 ... 173 E3
Menwith with Darley
 HG3 ... 160 A4
Mickletown LS26 ... 200 B6
Middleton YO18 ... 95 E8
Monk Fryston LS25 ... 201 F8
[1] Naburn YO19 ... 191 D8
Newton Ayme cum Toulston
 LS24 ... 189 C7
North Duffield YO8 ... 199 A8
Pannal HG3 ... 222 D3
Pollington DN14 ... 207 F6
Poppleton YO26 ... 165 F1
Rathmell BD24 ... 153 C6
Reighton YO14 ... 127 E5
Riccall YO19 ... 198 A8
Rythar cum Ossendyke
 LS24 ... 190 E2
Saxton with Scarthingwell
 LS24 ... 195 D7
Scholes LS15 ... 194 A7
Scotton HG5 ... 162 A6
Seamer YO12 ... 99 D6
Sheriff Hutton YO60 ... 145 D5
Shipton YO30 ... 165 F5
Sicklinghall LS22 ... 179 D3
Sinnington YO62 ... 95 A8
Stainforth BD24 ... 131 E6
Stamford Bridge YO41 ... 168 D2
Staveley HG5 ... 140 E1
Stillington YO61 ... 144 C6
Threshfield BD23 ... 134 C2
Thwing YO25 ... 126 B3
Tollerton YO61 ... 143 A3
Ulleskelf LS24 ... 190 C3
Walton LS23 ... 181 A2
Wath HG4 ... 114 A8
Weeton LS17 ... 178 C1
West Tanfield HG4 ... 87 A1
Westow YO60 ... 147 B4
Wheldrake YO19 ... 192 F7
Whittington LA6 ... 102 A7
Wilberfoss YO41 ... 185 D6
Womersley DN6 ... 206 C6
Wray-with-Botton LA2 ... 128 A6
York YO26 ... 227 A5
York YO26 ... 229 B1
York YO10 ... 231 D8
Mains La YO60 ... 146 D5
Mains The BD24 ... 131 D3
Mainsfield Cl [1] BD24 ... 131 D3
Mainsfield Rise [2]
 BD24 ... 131 D3

Maison Dieu DL10 ... 209 D7
Major St DL3 ... 3 C6
Malais La BD20 ... 187 D7
Malbys Gr YO23 ... 230 B2
Malden Rd HG1 ... 220 B3
Malham Gr YO31 ... 229 B5
Malham Moor La
 BD23 ... 133 F4
Malham Rakes BD23 ... 133 A2
Malham Tarn Field Ctr*
 BD24 ... 133 A1
Malham Visitor Ctr*
 BD23 ... 133 A1
Malham Way HG5 ... 221 D6
Malim Rd DL1 ... 3 F5
Mallard Cl [8] Filey YO14 ... 101 A4
 [12] Pickering YO18 ... 95 F6
Mallard Rd [4] DL8 ... 40 F2
Mallard Way YO17 ... 215 D2
Mallard Way
 [4] Eastfield YO12 ... 99 F6
 [11] Haxby YO32 ... 166 F5
Mallard Wlk [14] YO11 ... 141 B5
Mallinson Cl HG2 ... 222 D6
Mallinson Cres HG2 ... 222 E6
Mallinson Gate HG2 ... 222 E6
Mallinson Gr HG2 ... 222 D6
Mallinson Oval HG2 ... 222 D6
Mallinson Way HG2 ... 222 D6
Mallison Hill Dr [8]
 YO61 ... 117 D1
Mallorie Cl HG4 ... 214 A5
Mallorie Ct HG4 ... 214 B5
Mallorie Park Dr HG4 ... 214 A4
Mallory Cl YO32 ... 225 D4
Mallory Ct DL10 ... 3 F6
Mallowdale TS7 ... 7 C5
Malltraeth Sands TS17 ... 6 D6
Malpas Dr DL7 ... 210 D4
Malpas Rd
 Brompton YO13 ... 98 C4
 Northallerton DL7 ... 210 D3
Malsis Prep Sch BD20 ... 187 C7
Malt Dubs Cl LA6 ... 103 D3
Malt Kiln La YO23 ... 190 F5
Malt Kiln Terr LS24 ... 189 D4
Maltby Rd TS8 ... 6 D4
Malthouse La HG3 ... 143 A5
Maltings Ct Alne YO61 ... 143 A5
Maltings The
 [8] Brafferton YO61 ... 115 F1
 [15] Pontefract WF8 ... 201 B1
 Thirsk YO7 ... 211 B2
Maltkiln La
 Castleford WF10 ... 200 F4
 Killinghall HG3 ... 161 C6
Malton Ave YO31 ... 228 D8
Malton CP Sch YO17 ... 215 D5
Malton Gate YO18 ... 96 D5
Malton La
 Allerston YO18 ... 97 B4
 Flaxton YO60 ... 146 A1
 Kirby Grindalythe YO17 ... 150 A8
Malton Mus* YO17 ... 215 C4
Malton Norton & District
 Hospl YO17 ... 215 B4
Malton Rd
 Hunmanby YO14 ... 126 F8
 Huntington YO32 ... 226 A1
 Leavening YO17 ... 147 E2
 Pickering YO18 ... 95 F6
 Rillington YO17 ... 122 E4
 Scampston YO17 ... 123 B7
 Slingsby YO62 ... 120 B5
 Swinton YO17 ... 121 C4
 York YO31 ... 228 F7
Malton Rugby Club
 YO17 ... 215 E5
Malton St Marys RC Prim Sch
 YO17 ... 215 A5
Malton Sch YO17 ... 215 A5
Malton St YO61 ... 117 D6
Malton Sta YO17 ... 215 C3
Malton Way YO30 ... 227 F8
Malvern Ave YO26 ... 227 D5
Malvern Cl
 Huntington YO32 ... 226 A5
 [8] Hurworth-on-Tees DL2 ... 3 E1
 Stokesley TS9 ... 26 C7
Malvern Cres
 Darlington DL3 ... 2 F7
 Scarborough YO12 ... 212 D5
Malvern Dr
 Middlesbrough TS5 ... 6 F6
 Stokesley TS9 ... 26 C7
Malvern Rd WF11 ... 201 F2
Manchester Rd BB18 ... 171 D1
Mancroft YO32 ... 225 C8
Mandale Mill Prim Sch
 TS17 ... 6 B8
Mandale Rd TS5 ... 6 D8
Manfield C of E Prim Sch
 DL2 ... 2 B4
Mangrill La LS14 ... 188 C3
Manham Hill YO11 ... 99 F7
Mankin La HG4 ... 214 D1
Manley Cl YO32 ... 225 D4
Manley Dr LS22 ... 180 A3
Manley Gr LS29 ... 218 B4
Manley Rd LS29 ... 218 B4
Manley Rise LS29 ... 218 A4
Manor Beeches The [3]
 YO19 ... 184 E7
Manor C of E Sch
 YO26 ... 227 A5
Manor Chase YO26 ... 181 F6

Manor Cl
 Burton in Lonsdale LA6 ... 102 F3
 [5] Hemingbrough YO8 ... 198 F1
 Ingleton LA6 ... 103 D3
 Kirk Smeaton WF8 ... 206 B3
 [8] Kirkbymoorside YO62 ... 70 B1
 Low Worsall TS15 ... 24 B8
 [5] North Duffield YO8 ... 199 A7
 [8] Norton DN6 ... 206 E2
 [5] Stokesley TS9 ... 26 C7
 Topcliffe YO7 ... 115 C6
 Wath HG4 ... 114 B7
Manor Cres HG5 ... 221 C6
Manor Ct
 [6] Bubwith YO8 ... 199 D7
 Fairburn WF11 ... 201 D7
 Follifoot HG3 ... 223 F5
 Kirkby Malzeard HG4 ... 112 C5
 Knaresborough HG5 ... 221 B5
 [2] York YO32 ... 225 D7
Manor Dr
 [2] Brafferton YO61 ... 115 F1
 Camblesforth YO8 ... 204 C4
 [4] Dunnington YO19 ... 184 E7
 Harrogate HG2 ... 222 C8
 Hilton TS15 ... 6 C2
 Kirby Hill YO51 ... 141 A7
 Knaresborough HG5 ... 221 C6
 [8] North Duffield YO8 ... 199 A7
 North Featherston
  WF7 ... 200 E1
 Pickering YO18 ... 95 F7
 Scotton HG5 ... 162 A6
Manor Dr N YO26 ... 227 D4
Manor Dr S YO26 ... 227 D4
Manor Farm Cl
 [1] Brayton YO8 ... 232 A1
 Carlton DN14 ... 204 C2
 Copmanthorpe YO23 ... 230 A2
 Kellington DN14 ... 202 F3
Manor Farm Ct YO8 ... 203 C4
Manor Farm Way TS8 ... 6 F5
Manor Fold HG4 ... 223 F5
Manor Garth
 Haxby YO32 ... 225 B8
 Kellington DN14 ... 202 F3
 [2] Kirklevington TS15 ... 24 E8
 Ledsham LS25 ... 201 B8
 [7] Norton DN6 ... 206 F2
 [2] Riccall YO19 ... 198 A8
 [5] Spofforth HG3 ... 179 E6
Manor Garth Rd LS25 ... 194 E1
Manor Gdns
 [8] Hunmanby YO14 ... 127 A8
 Killinghall HG3 ... 161 C5
 Scarborough YO12 ... 212 E6
 Thorner LS14 ... 188 A3
Manor Gn DL8 ... 62 C6
Manor Gr Colburn DL9 ... 40 F5
 Great Broughton TS9 ... 26 E5
Manor Heath YO23 ... 230 A3
Manor House Art Gall &
 Mus* LS29 ... 218 B4
Manor Inf Sch The
 HG5 ... 221 B6
Manor La
 Healaugh LS24 ... 181 E1
 Rawcliffe YO30 ... 224 D2
Manor Orchards HG5 ... 221 B6
Manor Park Ave
 Great Preston WF10 ... 200 D7
 Pontefract WF8 ... 201 C2
Manor Park Cl YO30 ... 224 E2
Manor Park Gr YO30 ... 224 E2
Manor Park Rd YO30 ... 224 E2
Manor Pk
 Arkendale HG5 ... 163 A7
 Cowling BD22 ... 187 B6
 Ledston WF10 ... 200 F7
 Swinton YO17 ... 121 C4
Manor Rd Beal DN14 ... 202 C4
 Darlington DL3 ... 3 B6
 Easingwold YO61 ... 117 C1
 Fylingdales YO22 ... 33 C1
 Harrogate HG2 ... 222 B8
 Hurworth-on-Tees DL2 ... 3 E1
 Killinghall HG3 ... 161 C5
 Knaresborough HG5 ... 221 B6
 Scarborough YO12 ... 212 E5
 Stutton with Hazlewood
  LS24 ... 189 D4
Manor Rise LS23 ... 188 E5
Manor Vale [28] YO62 ... 70 B1
Manor View
 Oswaldkirk YO62 ... 93 A1
 Scarborough YO11 ... 212 F3
Manor View Rd YO11 ... 100 D5
Manor Way
 Glusburn BD20 ... 187 E6
 York YO30 ... 224 E2
Manse La HG5 ... 221 E5
Maple Ave
 Bishopthorpe YO23 ... 231 A3
 Malton YO17 ... 215 D6
Maple Cl [5] Colburn DL9 ... 40 F5

Maple Cl continued
 Hambleton YO8 ... 197 B1
 Knaresborough HG1 ... 220 D5
 [5] South Milford LS25 ... 195 F2
Maple Croft YO61 ... 144 A5
Maple Ct YO10 ... 231 E6
Maple Dr YO12 ... 212 D7
Maple Gr [2] Brayton YO8 ... 197 D1
 [7] Linton-on-Ouse YO30 ... 164 F7
 York YO10 ... 228 D1
Maple La YO61 ... 144 A5
Maple Rd DL10 ... 209 A8
Maple Tree Ave YO8 ... 198 B4
Maplewood Paddock [2]
 YO24 ... 227 C1
Mar Head Balk HG5 ... 163 A7
Marage Rd YO7 ... 211 B3
Marazion Dr DL3 ... 3 C8
Marbeck La HG5 ... 140 F2
March St
 Normanton South WF6 ... 200 A1
 York YO31 ... 233 C4
Marchlyn Cres TS17 ... 5 F4
Marcus St DN14 ... 205 F2
Marderby La YO7 ... 90 C7
Maresfield Rd YO4 ... 40 E3
Margaret Rd HG2 ... 219 B1
Margaret St YO10 ... 228 E3
Margerison Cres LS29 ... 218 E3
Margerison Rd LS29 ... 218 E3
Maria St [8] LS29 ... 176 C1
Marias Ct [9] YO11 ... 213 A6
Marigold Cl YO8 ... 232 C2
Marina Ave [3] DN14 ... 204 B1
Marina Cres BD23 ... 216 D3
Marina Rd DL3 ... 3 D8
Marina Way HG4 ... 214 A2
Marine Dr YO11 ... 213 C7
Marine Espl YO13 ... 54 A8
Marine Villa Rd WF11 ... 201 F2
Mariner's Terr [8] YO14 ... 101 B3
Marion Ave TS15 ... 5 D4
Marishes La
 Allerston YO17 ... 97 A2
 Thornton-le-Dale YO17 ... 96 E1
Marishes Low Rd
 YO17 ... 122 B8
Mark House La BD23 ... 155 C1
Mark La
 Fylingdales YO22 ... 33 C3
 Kirk Deighton LS22 ... 180 B5
Markenfield Hall*
 HG4 ... 139 D6
Markenfield Rd HG3 ... 219 B5
Market Flat La HG5 ... 162 C6
Market Hill [8] YO51 ... 141 B6
Market La YO8 ... 232 C5
Market Pl [4] Bedale DL8 ... 63 A3
 [2] Cawood YO8 ... 197 B8
 [7] Easingwold YO61 ... 143 C8
 [1] Helmsley YO62 ... 92 F6
 [8] Helmsley YO62 ... 92 F6
 [2] Kirkbymoorside YO62 ... 70 B1
 [8] Knaresborough HG5 ... 221 B6
 Malton YO17 ... 215 C4
 [8] Masham HG4 ... 86 C3
 [6] Middleham DL8 ... 60 E2
 [8] Normanton South WF6 ... 200 A1
 [2] Pickering YO18 ... 95 F7
 [8] Settle BD24 ... 131 D2
 [3] Snaith DN14 ... 204 C1
 Thirsk YO7 ... 211 B3
 [2] Wetherby LS22 ... 180 C3
 [8] Whitby YO21 ... 208 D7
Market Pl E [8] HG4 ... 214 C5
Market Pl N [8] HG4 ... 214 C5
Market Pl S [21] HG4 ... 214 C5
Market Pl W [2] HG4 ... 214 C5
Market St Malton YO17 ... 215 C4
 [8] Normanton South WF6 ... 200 A1
 [4] Scarborough YO11 ... 213 A6
 York YO1 ... 233 B2
Market Way [22] YO11 ... 213 A6
Market Weighton Rd
 YO8 ... 198 B6
Markham Cres YO31 ... 233 B4
Markham St YO31 ... 233 B4
Markington C of E Prim Sch
 HG3 ... 139 C3
Marl Hill La BD20 ... 186 D8
Marlborough Ave
 [3] Byram WF11 ... 201 F4
 Tadcaster LS24 ... 189 D5
 [3] Whitby YO21 ... 208 B7
Marlborough Cl YO30 ... 224 D2
Marlborough Dr
 Darlington DL1 ... 3 C4
 Tadcaster LS24 ... 189 D5
Marlborough Gr
 Ilkley LS29 ... 218 D3
 Ripon HG4 ... 214 B6
 York YO10 ... 228 D2
Marlborough Rd HG1 ... 219 E2
Marlborough Sq LS29 ... 218 D3
Marlborough St [1]
 YO12 ... 213 A7
Marmaduke Dr [3] HG2 ... 167 D2
Marmion Ct HG4 ... 87 A1
Marmion Twr* HG4 ... 87 A1
Marne Cl [1] DL9 ... 209 B1
Marne Rd DL9 ... 209 D1
Marr The YO14 ... 101 B3
Marrick Priory (rems of)*
 DL11 ... 38 E4
Marrick Rd TS18 ... 5 D8
Marridales DL8 ... 56 D4

Marriforth La HG4 ... 61
Mars La TS13 ... 11
Marset La DL8 ... 57
Marsh Croft WF11 ... 203
Marsh End WF11 ... 202
Marsh La Asselby DN14 ... 205
 Barlow YO8 ... 204
 [2] Beal DN14 ... 202
 Bolton Percy YO23 ... 190
 Byram cum Sutton WF11 ... 202
 Cawood YO8 ... 197
 Ingleby Greenhow TS9 ... 27
 Knottingley WF11 ... 202
 West Haddlesey YO8 ... 203
Marsh Lane Gdns
 DN14 ... 202
Marsh Rd WF10 ... 200
Marshall Dr YO18 ... 96
Marshfield Rd [7] BD24 ... 131
Marston Ave YO26 ... 227
Marston Bsns Pk
 YO26 ... 181
Marston Cres YO26 ... 227
Marston La YO26 ... 182
Marston Moor Rd DL1 ... 3
Marston Rd YO26 ... 181
Marston Way [3] LS22 ... 180
Marten Cl [2] YO30 ... 228
Martin Cheeseman Ct [3]
 YO24 ... 230
Martindale Rd DL1 ... 3
Martinet Rd TS17 ... 6
Marton Abbey (Priory)*
 YO61 ... 144
Marton Ave TS4 ... 7
Marton Cum Grafton C of E
 Prim Sch YO51 ... 141 [14]
Marton La
 Arkendale HG5 ... 163
 Marton-in-the-Forest YO61 ... 95
Marton Manor Prim Sch
 TS7 ... 7
Marton Moor Rd TS7 ... 7
Marton Rd
 Coulby Newham TS4 ... 7
 Gargrave BD23 ... 172
 Marton YO62 ... 94
 Sinnington YO62 ... 95
Marton St BD23 ... 216
Marton Sta TS7 ... 7
Martonside Way TS4 ... 7
Marvell Rise HG1 ... 219
Marwood Dr TS9 ... 7
Marwoods C of E Inf Sch
 TS9 ... 7
Mary La YO16 ... 14
Mary St [3] BD20 ... 173
Marygate Barton DL10 ... 21
 York YO30 ... 233
Marygate La YO30 ... 233
Marykirk Rd TS17 ... 6
Masefield Cl HG1 ... 219
Masham Bank HG4 ... 85
Masham C of E Prim Sch
 HG4 ... 86
Masham Cl HG2 ... 220
Masham La DL8 ... 87
Masham Rd Firby DL8 ... 62
 Harrogate HG2 ... 220
 Snape with Thorp DL8 ... 86
Mask La YO41 ... 185
Masongill Fell La LA6 ... 103
Masonic La YO7 ... 211
Maspin Moor Rd LS25 ... 202
Massa Flatts Wood
 BD23 ... 216
Massey St YO8 ... 232
Master Rd TS17 ... 6
Master's Gate YO18 ... 49
Mastil Cl DL8 ... 62
Mastiles La BD23 ... 134
Matfen Ave TS7 ... 7
Matthew La
 Bradleys Both BD20 ... 173
 Green Hammerton YO26 ... 164
Mattison Way YO24 ... 227
Maud La LS21 ... 177
Maude Rd DL9 ... 209
Maudon Ave YO18 ... 96
Maudon Gr YO17 ... 215
Maufe Way [3] LS29 ... 218
Maunby La YO7 ... 64
Mawson Gr DL6 ... 65
Mawson La HG4 ... 214
Maxim Cl [5] DL9 ... 40
Maxwell Rd LS29 ... 218
May Beck Farm Trail
 YO22 ... 32
Mayfair Ave TS6 ... 7
Mayfair Rd DL1 ... 3
Mayfield DL7 ... 64
Mayfield Ave
 Ilkley LS29 ... 218
 [3] Scalby YO12 ... 75
Mayfield Cl
 [3] Glusburn BD20 ... 187
 Ilkley LS29 ... 218
Mayfield Cres TS16 ... 5
Mayfield Dr
 [3] Brayton YO8 ... 232
 [4] Seamer YO12 ... 99
Mayfield Gdns LS29 ... 218
Mayfield Gr
 Harrogate HG1 ... 219
 [3] Whitby YO21 ... 208
Mayfield Pl
 Harrogate HG1 ... 219
 [3] Whitby YO21 ... 208

field Rd
yton YO8 ....232 A1
ey LS29 ....218 C4
idlesbrough TS7 ....7 D6
tby YO21 ....228 B5
field Terr HG1 ....219 D3
pole Gdns YO8 ....197 B8
pole Gr YO19 ....191 D8
pole Mews LS15 ....194 B8
thorn Rd YO12 ....223 C2
thorpe YO23 ....182 C6
ville Ave YO12 ....212 E6
onald Rd YO4 ....113 D3
null Rd DL1 ....3 E6
ed Cres TS17 ....6 C8
adlands YO21 ....229 B6
dow Ave [5] HG4 ....214 B2
dow Brook Chase [16]
6 ....200 B1
dow Cl
rpole BD20 ....173 D2
Eastfield YO11 ....100 A6
mpsthwaite HG3 ....160 F5
thallerton DL7 ....210 D2
rpe Willoughby YO8 ....197 C2
dow Croft
8 ....232 A2
onley BD20 ....173 C2
dow Ct
ington YO17 ....122 F5
thallerton DL7 ....63 E7
Willerby YO12 ....99 D2
York YO24 ....230 E8
dow Dale Ct TS12 ....9 F7
dow Dr
East Ayton/West Ayton
3 ....99 88
rrogate HG1 ....219 E7
thallerton DL7 ....63 E7
rpe Willoughby YO8 ....197 B2
dow Garth
Tadcaster LS24 ....189 F6
rpe Willoughby YO8 ....197 C2
dow Gate HG1 ....219 E6
dow Gn DL8 ....63 A2
dow La
onley BD20 ....173 C2
Darley HG3 ....160 A6
Eastfield YO11 ....100 A6
Haxby YO32 ....225 D8
thallerton DL6 ....210 E6
pe DL8 ....87 A7
dow Lea [4] BD20 ....187 E7
dow Pl [5] YO8 ....232 B6
dow Rd
forth LS25 ....194 D4
restorough HG5 ....221 B7
Pickering YO18 ....95 F7
dow Rise
rrogate HG1 ....219 E7
Skipton BD23 ....217 B5
dow Spring Ba [3]
3 ....143 D8
dow Springs Way [3]
3 ....143 D8
dow Vale
en Hammerton YO26 ....164 C3
Ripon HG4 ....214 B2
dow View
wick in Elmet & Scholes
5 ....194 88
rrogate HG1 ....219 E6
rburn in Elmet LS25 ....195 F4
dow Way
noldswalk BB18 ....171 E2
rrogate HG1 ....219 E7
dcaster LS24 ....189 F6
k YO31 ....228 F7
dowbank Rd TS7 ....7 D7
dowbeck Cl YO10 ....229 B4
dowcroft
ington BD23 ....174 B7
rrogate HG1 ....219 E6
dowcroft Dr HG3 ....140 A5
dowfield
otherby YO17 ....121 A4
Bedale DL8 ....63 B3
Subwith YO8 ....199 D7
k YO21 ....13 A3
Stokesley TS9 ....26 C8
dowfield Dr TS16 ....5 D5
dowfield Rd
Colburn DL9 ....41 A5
ington DL3 ....3 A7
dowfields YO21 ....208 C6
dowfields Cl [9]
3 ....143 D8
on 21 ....208 D6
dowfields Dr
dowings The TS15 ....5 D2
dowlands Cl [2] TS13 ....11 A8
dows The
ton DN14 ....204 C3
iby Newham TS8 ....7 B5
rough HG1 ....219 E6
dowside St George DL2 ....4 C4
Monk Fryston LS25 ....202 A8
all YO19 ....197 F8
mond DL10 ....209 E7
by YO12 ....212 B7
Skelton YO30 ....224 B5
rth Milford LS25 ....195 F2
dowside CP Sch
5 ....221 C7
ds La YO12 ....99 E5

Meads The
[3] Eastfield YO11 ....99 F6
[9] Eastfield YO11 ....100 A6
Meadway YO8 ....197 D2
Meadway Dr YO8 ....197 D2
Meagill La LS21 ....159 E2
Meagill Rise LS21 ....176 E1
Meanee Rd [11] DL9 ....40 F2
Medbourne Gdns TS5 ....6 E6
Megson Rd YO7 ....211 C4
Melander Cl YO30 ....225 A3
Melander Gdns [5] YO32 ....225 D7
Melbourne Dr YO7 ....90 E5
Melbourne Pl YO7 ....211 B2
Melbourne St YO7 ....211 B2
Melcombe Ave [11] YO32 ....167 A7
Meldyke La TS8 ....6 D5
Mellersh Rd [16] DL10 ....41 E4
Melling with Wrayton C of E
Sch LA6 ....102 A2
Melltown's Gn YO7 ....88 C6
Melmerby Green La
HG4 ....114 C6
Melmerby Green Rd
HG4 ....114 B6
Melmerby Ind Est
HG4 ....114 B6
Melrose Cl [1] YO31 ....229 A5
Melrose Cres
Bishop Monkton HG3 ....140 A5
Guisborough TS14 ....138 A8
Melrose Dr [1] LS29 ....176 C1
Melrose Rd HG4 ....140 A5
Melrose St [4] YO12 ....212 F6
Melrosegate YO31 ....228 F5
Melsonby Methodist Prim
Sch DL10 ....20 F7
Melton Ave YO30 ....227 F8
Melton Dr
Bishopthorpe YO23 ....231 A3
York YO30 ....227 F8
Melville Gr [1] LS29 ....176 C1
Melville Terr [5] YO14 ....101 B3
Melwood Gr YO26 ....227 B5
Mendip Cl [2] YO32 ....225 F5
Menethorpe La YO17 ....147 D7
Menin Rd DL9 ....209 B1
Menwith Hill Rd [4] HG3 ....159 D4
Mercer Art Gall *
HG2 ....219 C3
Mercer Dr DL9 ....209 C1
Merchant Adventurers Hall *
YO1 ....233 C2
Merchant Taylors Hall *
YO31 ....233 C3
Merchant Way YO23 ....230 B3
Merchantgate YO1 ....233 C2
Merchant's Row [6]
YO11 ....213 B6
Mercury Rd DL10 ....209 A8
Mere La YO11 ....212 F1
Mere View Gdns YO11 ....99 F8
Merewood Rd WF10 ....200 C4
Merlin Covert [4] YO31 ....225 F3
Merlinwood BD23 ....172 B4
Merrington Ave TS17 ....6 D6
Merry Dale YO11 ....100 A7
Merrybank La LS17 ....178 A3
Merrybent Dr [2] DL2 ....3 A3
Merryfield HG2 ....222 B7
Mesnes La DL8 ....59 D3
Messines Rd DL9 ....40 E3
Metcalfe La YO19 ....229 C5
Metes La YO12 ....99 E5
Methley Cty Jun Sch
LS26 ....200 B6
Methley La LS26 ....200 A6
Methley Park Hospl
LS26 ....200 A6
Methley Rd WF10 ....200 D4
Methodist Prim Sch
DL11 ....36 E5
Meuse Ct [4] DL9 ....209 C1
Mewburn Rd DL3 ....3 C8
Mewith La LA2 ....129 B6
Mews The WF10 ....200 A2
Meynell Rd DL3 ....3 C7
Michael Mount Rd
YO11 ....213 C1
Michael Syddall C of E Prim
Sch DL10 ....41 E5
Micklebury La HA4 ....86 A3
Mickleby Dr YO21 ....208 B6
Mickleby La TS13 ....11 F4
Mickledale La YO26 ....163 D8
Micklefield C of E Sch
LS25 ....195 A4
Micklefield Sta LS25 ....195 A3
Micklegate
[17] Pontefract WF8 ....201 B1
[1] Selby YO8 ....232 D5
York YO1 ....233 A2
Micklegate Bar Mus *
YO1 ....233 A1
Micklethwaite View
LS22 ....180 C2
Mickletown Rd LS26 ....200 B6
Middle Bank Rd TS7 ....7 D7
Middle Banks [24] YO32 ....166 E5
Middle Head Rd HG3 ....71 E8
Middle La Brayton YO8 ....232 C1
Brompton YO13 ....98 C2
Collingham LS22 ....180 B1
Hutton Buscel YO13 ....74 E1
Kettlewell with Starbotton
BD23 ....108 A3
[14] Knottingley WF11 ....202 A2
Snainton YO13 ....97 F4

Middle Moor La DL11 ....39 F5
Middle Oxford St
WF10 ....200 E4
Middle Rd TS17 ....6 A5
Middle St Gayles DL11 ....19 E6
Swinton YO17 ....121 B4
Wilberfoss YO41 ....185 F5
Middle Way [4] YO12 ....212 E7
Middlebrook Gdns
DL8 ....232 A2
Middlecave Cl YO17 ....215 A4
Middlecave Dr YO17 ....215 A4
Middlecave Rd YO17 ....215 B4
Middlecroft Dr YO32 ....167 A7
Middlecroft Gr [2] YO32 ....167 B7
Middlefield Cl YO17 ....124 E1
Middlefield La
Kirk Smeaton WF8 ....206 A2
Melmerby DL8 ....84 A8
Middleham Ave YO31 ....228 E8
Middleham C of E Prim Sch
DL8 ....60 E2
Middleham Castle *
DL8 ....60 E2
Middlesbrough Coll TS5 ....6 E8
Middlesbrough Rd TS7 ....7 E6
Middlesbrough Rugby &
Cricket Clubs TS5 ....6 E8
Middlethorpe Dr
YO24 ....230 E7
Middlethorpe Gr YO24 ....230 F7
Middleton Ave
Ilkley LS29 ....218 B6
Thornaby TS17 ....6 B6
Middleton Carr La
YO18 ....95 D7
Middleton Cl [3] YO41 ....122 D1
Middleton La
Middleton YO18 ....95 E8
Middleton St George DL2 ....4 C3
Middleton Rd
Hutton Rudby TS15 ....25 D6
Ilkley LS29 ....218 A4
Pickering YO18 ....95 E7
Sadberge DL2 ....4 C7
York YO24 ....227 C2
Middleton St George Cty
Prim Sch DL2 ....4 D5
Middleton Tyas C of E Prim
Sch DL10 ....21 C5
Middleton Tyas La
DL10 ....21 B4
Middleway BD20 ....174 C1
Middlewood Cl
[5] Fylingdales YO22 ....33 C3
Rufforth YO23 ....182 C6
Middlewood Cres [5]
YO22 ....33 C3
Middlewood Garth [4]
YO22 ....33 C3
Middlewood La YO22 ....33 C3
Midgeley Bank YO22 ....33 D6
Midhedge Bank DL10 ....40 D4
Midge Hall Cl [8] LS29 ....176 C1
Midgeley Gate HG5 ....162 F2
Midgley Cl
[4] Embsay BD23 ....217 C7
[2] Stamford Bridge YO41 ....168 D2
Midgley Rd LS29 ....176 C1
Midgley Rise [2] WF8 ....201 B2
Midhope Way [4] YO41 ....101 A3
Midland St BD23 ....216 E3
Midway Ave YO26 ....224 A1
Mightens' Bank DL8 ....60 D4
Milbank Rd DL3 ....3 B5
Milburn La YO7 ....89 D3
Mildred Gr [5] YO24 ....227 F2
Mildred Sylvester Way
WF6 ....200 B1
Mile Hill Coldhill La
LS25 ....195 E5
Mile Planting DL10 ....209 F8
Milestone Ave YO23 ....182 C6
Milford Mews [7] YO32 ....167 B8
Milford Rd LS25 ....195 F3
Milford Way [8] YO32 ....225 D7
Milking Hill YO61 ....118 B4
Mill Bank
Bishop Thornton HG3 ....138 F1
Fylingdales YO22 ....33 D2
Lindrick with Studley
Royal & Fountains HG4 ....113 A3
Mill Bank Rd HG3 ....72 D5
Mill Bridge BD23 ....216 F4
Mill Brow LA2 ....128 E2
Mill Brow BD23 ....172 B1
Mill Cl
Monk Fryston LS25 ....202 A8
Ravensworth DL11 ....19 F6
Settle BD24 ....131 D2
[6] Spofforth HG3 ....179 E6
Mill Croft
Cowling BD22 ....187 B6
Richmond DL10 ....209 A7
Mill Dam LS23 ....188 F7
Mill Dam La WF8 ....201 C1
Mill Dike La YO7 ....116 F8
Mill Field La WF11 ....201 E8
Mill Field Rd YO8 ....203 B5
Mill Flats La DL8 ....60 F3
Mill Garth
Gilling with Hartforth & Sedbury
DL10 ....20 E3
Harrogate HG1 ....219 C7
Knayton with Brawith YO7 ....65 E2

Mill Green Way The
YO22 ....51 D8
Mill Hill Escrick YO19 ....192 B5
[10] Normanton South WF6 ....200 A1
Mill Hill Ave YO21 ....208 C7
Mill Hill Cl DL6 ....210 E4
Mill Hill Cres DL6 ....210 E3
Mill Hill Dr YO32 ....225 F4
Mill Hill La
Giggleswick BD24 ....131 C3
Northallerton DL6 ....210 E3
Mill Hills La DL11 ....38 E4
Mill House YO7 ....65 D1
Mill La
Acaster Malbis YO23 ....191 C8
Ampleforth YO62 ....118 C8
Askham Richard YO23 ....182 D2
Askrigg DL8 ....57 E6
Aysgarth DL8 ....58 E3
Barlow YO8 ....204 B7
Bellerby DL8 ....60 E8
Bentham LA2 ....128 F7
Beverley Marys HG3 ....137 B4
Boroughbridge YO51 ....141 B5
Brayton YO8 ....203 C8
Buckton/Bempton YO13 ....97 D5
Burniston YO13 ....75 C8
Burton Leonard HG3 ....140 B2
Carlton DN14 ....204 D3
Castleford WF10 ....200 E5
Cayton YO11 ....100 C6
Constable Burton DL8 ....61 C5
Darlington DL1 ....3 F6
Farby BB18 ....172 B1
Easingwold YO61 ....117 D1
East Ayton/West Ayton
YO13 ....99 A7
Eskdaleside cum Ugglebarnby
YO22 ....32 B6
Exelby, Leeming & Newton
DL7 ....63 D3
Faceby TS9 ....25 F2
Farndale East YO62 ....48 E4
Farndale West YO62 ....48 F1
Great Ouseburn YO26 ....164 C8
Hambleton YO8 ....196 F1
Haxby YO32 ....166 D5
Hebden BD23 ....135 A1
[2] Hemingbrough YO8 ....198 F1
Hessay YO23 ....182 B7
High Coniscliffe DL2 ....2 C6
Kearby with Netherby
LS22 ....179 C2
Kirk Hammerton YO26 ....164 C2
Knaresborough HG5 ....221 F8
Langtoft YO25 ....151 C7
Leyburn DL8 ....60 E4
[6] Linton-on-Ouse YO30 ....164 F7
Long Preston BD23 ....153 F4
Longnewton DL2 ....4 F6
Low Bradley BD20 ....173 D6
Micketown LS26 ....200 B6
Middleton St George DL2 ....4 D5
Muston YO14 ....101 A2
Nether Silton YO7 ....66 B6
Newland YO8 ....205 A3
Pannal HG3 ....222 E2
Pickering YO18 ....95 F6
Pontefract WF8 ....201 C2
Rawcliffe DN14 ....204 F1
Redmire DL8 ....59 C5
[1] Riccall YO19 ....192 A1
Ryther cum Ossendyke
LS24 ....190 E1
[1] Scarborough YO12 ....212 E3
Scruton DL7 ....63 E5
Sherburn in Elmet LS25 ....195 F2
Skipton BD23 ....216 F3
Sledmere YO25 ....149 F3
Snape with Thorp DL8 ....87 B7
South Milford LS25 ....195 F2
Spofforth with Stockeld
HG3 ....179 E6
Stillington YO61 ....144 C6
Stutton with Hazlewood
LS24 ....189 E4
Swinden BD23 ....154 B1
Threlkeld High & Low
with Osgodby YO7 ....90 D2
Thormanby YO61 ....116 E5
Thornton WF10 ....63 F8
Whitwood WF10 ....200 B2
York YO31 ....228 E6
Youlton YO61 ....142 F2

Mill Lane Ave YO60 ....145 C5
Mill Mount YO24 ....228 A3
Mill Mount Ct YO24 ....228 A3
Mill Race The [4] DL2 ....22 C8
Mill Rd
Burton Fleming YO25 ....126 D4
Gillamoor YO62 ....70 A5
Goldsborough HG5 ....221 F2
[1] Riggs TS9 ....26 D7
Mill Rise YO8 ....203 B5
Mill Row BD20 ....187 F7
Mill St
[6] Barnoldswick BB18 ....171 D1
Glusburn BD20 ....187 F7
Guisborough TS14 ....8 F6
Harome YO62 ....93 C4
Norton YO17 ....215 E3
Scarborough YO12 ....212 F5
York YO1 ....233 C1
Mill View
[5] Burley in Wharfedale
LS29 ....176 C1

Mill View continued
Knottingley WF11 ....201 D2
Mill Wynd TS16 ....5 E3
Millbank Ct YO7 ....89 C4
Millbank La TS17 ....6 B7
Millbeck Gn LS22 ....188 A8
Millenium Rd YO7 ....211 D3
Millers Cl YO17 ....215 D2
Millers Croft [6] YO23 ....230 B3
Millers La TS12 ....9 F6
Millers Rd [2] YO7 ....211 C3
Millfield YO11 ....141 D2
Millfield Ave
Northallerton DL6 ....210 E3
York YO10 ....228 F3
Millfield Cl
Eaglescliffe TS16 ....5 D4
[1] Leeming DL7 ....63 D4
Pickering YO18 ....95 F6
Wilberfoss YO41 ....185 E5
Millfield Cres DL6 ....210 E3
Millfield Dr YO8 ....204 D4
Millfield Gdns YO26 ....224 A2
Millfield Glade HG2 ....220 D4
Millfield La
Easingwold YO61 ....117 C1
Nether Poppleton YO26 ....227 B8
Poppleton YO26 ....224 A2
York YO26 ....224 A2
Millfield Rd
[7] Hemingbrough YO8 ....198 F1
Hemingbrough YO8 ....204 F8
York YO10 ....228 F3
Millfield St HG3 ....137 B4
Millfield Rise YO61 ....117 C1
Millfields BD20 ....174 B1
Millgarth Ct LS22 ....188 A8
Millgate [10] Masham HG4 ....86 C3
Richmond DL10 ....209 C6
Selby YO8 ....232 C6
Thirsk YO7 ....211 B3
Millgates YO26 ....227 C6
Millholme Rise BD23 ....217 C8
Millings La YO51 ....141 B7
Millrace Cl YO10 ....215 D2
Millside YO17 ....215 D2
Millthorpe Sch YO23 ....228 B2
Millway YO17 ....92 C1
Milner La LS24 ....195 D8
Milner Rd DL1 ....3 D4
Milner St YO24 ....227 D3
Milners La HG1 ....219 F7
Milnthorpe [13] LS23 ....188 E6
Milnthorpe Garth [7]
LS23 ....188 E6
Milnthorpe Gdns [5]
LS23 ....188 E6
Milnthorpe La LS23 ....188 D5
Milnthorpe Way LS23 ....188 D5
Milson Gr YO10 ....229 A3
Milton Ave
Malton YO17 ....215 D5
Scarborough YO12 ....212 E3
Milton Carr [8] YO30 ....224 E1
Milton Cl HG1 ....219 F7
Milton Gr [1] BB18 ....171 D2
Milton Rd Malton YO17 ....215 C6
Pannal HG3 ....222 E3
Milton St Darlington DL1 ....3 E5
[4] Skipton BD23 ....217 A3
York YO10 ....228 F3
Milton Terr YO30 ....225 B1
Mine Mus * BB18 ....172 A2
Minors Cres DL3 ....3 A7
Minskip Rd HG5 ....140 F2
Minster Ave YO31 ....225 F2
Minster Cl
[3] Haxby YO32 ....225 C8
[2] Ripon HG4 ....214 C5
Minster Gr HG4 ....214 C5
Minster Sch The YO1 ....233 B3
Minster View YO32 ....225 C8
Minster Wlk [12] DL2 ....3 E1
Minster Yd YO1 ....233 B3
Minsterley Dr TS5 ....6 D7
Minster Cl [2] YO7 ....211 D3
Mire Bank La DL8 ....56 F4
Mire Close La BD22 ....187 A8
Mire Ridge BD20 ....186 A2
Mire Syke La HG5 ....162 A5
Mires La Carthorpe DL8 ....87 D6
Ulleskelf LS24 ....190 B1
Mirkhill Rd YO8 ....232 B6
Miry La LS15 ....188 C1
Missies La HG4 ....112 C3
Mistral Ct YO31 ....228 E8
Mitchell Ave TS5 ....6 B7
Mitchell La Aline YO41 ....142 F4
Catton YO41 ....185 D8
Settle BD24 ....131 E1
Mitchell's La YO10 ....231 F8
Miterdale [6] YO11 ....100 B8
Mitford Cl [3] YO14 ....126 F8
Mitford Rd [2] YO14 ....126 F8
Mitford St [2] YO14 ....101 B3
Mitton La BD20 ....172 C1
Moat Field YO10 ....229 C4
Moat Way YO7 ....197 D1
Moatside Ct YO31 ....233 B3
Mock Beggar Hall *
YO10 ....157 D7
Moiser Cl YO32 ....225 D4
Mole End [8] YO18 ....95 F6
Monash Ave DL9 ....209 C1
Monckton Dr WF10 ....201 B3

Monk Ave YO31 ....228 F7
Monk Bar DL8 ....233 B3
Monk Bar Mus* YO31 ....233 C3
Monk Fryston C of E Prim
  Sch LS25 ....202 A8
Monk Fryston Prim Sch
  LS25 ....202 A8
Monk Gardens La YO62 ...93 A7
Monk Gn YO31 ....142 F4
Monk Ing Rd HG3 ....159 E8
Monk La YO8 ....232 C7
Monkbridge St YO31 .....233 C4
Monket House Bank
  YO62 ....48 C4
Monkgate YO31 ....233 C3
Monkgate Cloisters
  YO31 ....233 C3
Monkhill Ave WF8 ....201 B1
Monkhill Dr WF8 ....201 B1
Monkhill La WF8 ....201 B2
Monkhill Mount WF8 .....201 B1
Monkholme La BD23 .....134 C2
Monkroyd Ave BB18 .....171 D1
Monks Cross Dr YO32 ...226 A3
Monks Cross Link
  YO32 ....226 B4
Monk's Rd BD23 ....107 D2
Monkswell Pk HG5 ....221 D5
Monkton Rd
  5 York YO31 ....225 F1
  York YO31 ....228 E8
Monmouth Dr TS16 ....5 E5
Monmouth St DL8 ....186 A3
Mons Ct 3 DL9 ....209 B1
Mons Rd
  Catterick Garrison DL9 ...209 D1
  Colburn DL9 ....40 F4
Montague Cres LS25 ....194 D4
Montague Rd YO23 ....231 A3
Montague St YO23 ....228 C1
Montague Wlk YO26 .....165 F1
Montagu's Harrier TS14 ..8 D6
Montgomery Rd DL9 .....209 C2
Montgomery St BD23 ....217 A3
Montpellier Gdns 2
  HG1 ....219 C2
Montpellier Hill HG2 .....219 C2
Montpellier Mews 3
  HG1 ....219 C2
Montpellier Rd 1 HG1 ...219 D2
Montpellier Sq 3 HG1 ...219 D2
Montpellier St 4 HG1 ...219 C2
Montrose Ave YO31 ......228 D8
Moody Sty La 4 BD23 ...134 E3
Mook St YO60 ....98 A8
Moor Ave 1 LS23 ....188 E7
Moor Carr La YO8 ....198 B5
Moor Cl Killinghall HG3 ..219 A8
  10 Kirklevington TS15 ....24 E8
  Lockwood TS12 ....10 B5
  Wheldrake YO19 ....192 F8
Moor Cres BD23 ....217 B4
Moor Croft 8 BD23 ......134 E3
Moor End La
  Crakehall DL8 ....62 C3
  Sowerby YO7 ....90 A2
Moor End Rd YO13 ....53 F2
Moor Gn TS7 ....7 D5
Moor Gr YO24 ....230 E8
Moor Hill YO17 ....147 E7
Moor House La YO61 ....116 B1
Moor La
  Addingham LS29 ....174 D5
  Aislaby YO21 ....31 F7
  Aldfield HG4 ....138 F8
  Arkendale HG5 ....162 F7
  Arrathorne DL10 ....41 A2
  Askwith LS21 ....176 D4
  Bagby YO7 ....90 C4
  6 Barlby YO8 ....198 B5
  Bilton-in-Ainsty with Bickerton
    YO26 ....181 D5
  Bishopthorpe YO23 ......230 E2
  Borrowby TS13 ....11 C6
  Brawby YO17 ....94 F2
  Broughton YO17 ....121 C4
  Burton Leonard HG3 .....140 B4
  Carthorpe DL8 ....87 D4
  Catterton LS24 ....190 A8
  Cleasby DL2 ....2 F2
  Cliffe YO8 ....198 F4
  Cloughton YO13 ....54 C1
  Collingham LS23 ....188 C8
  Coneythorpe & Clareton
    HG5 ....163 B6
  Copmanthorpe YO23 .....230 A1
  Cropton YO18 ....71 B6
  Crosby DL6 ....65 C5
  Dalton DL11 ....19 C6
  Dalton YO7 ....116 B8
  Dishforth YO7 ....114 E3
  Earswick YO32 ....226 C8
  East Ayton/West Ayton
    YO13 ....99 B8
  East Layton DL11 ....20 B8
  Eastfield YO11 ....100 A6
  Elslack BD23 ....172 D3
  Embsay with Eastby
    BD23 ....156 F1
  Full Sutton YO41 ....168 F1
  Grassington BD23 ....134 E3
  Great Ouseburn YO26 ...163 D7
  Great Ribston with Walshford
    LS22 ....180 E8

Moor La continued
Halton East BD23 ....157 B1
Haxby YO32 ....166 D7
Hunton DL8 ....61 E8
Hutton-le-Hole HG6 ....70 C5
Kearby with Netherby
  HG3 ....179 B2
Kelfield YO19 ....191 E2
Kirby Hill HG4 ....140 F8
Long Preston BD23 ....153 F5
Milby YO51 ....141 C7
Murton YO19 ....229 F8
Myton-on-Swale YO61 ...142 B5
Naburn YO19 ....191 D8
Nether Silton DL6 ....66 A4
Newsham DL11 ....19 A7
Newsham with Breckenbrough
  YO7 ....65 A1
Newton-on-Ouse YO30 ...165 C7
Rufforth YO23 ....182 E6
Ryther cum Ossendyke
  LS24 ....196 E8
Scalby YO12 ....212 A8
Settrington YO17 ....122 C1
Sherburn in Elmet LS25 ..195 F4
Skelton YO30 ....224 D6
Snape with Thorp DL8 .....86 E6
Steeton with Eastburn
  BD20 ....187 F7
Stillington YO61 ....143 F6
Strensall YO32 ....167 B7
Sutton with Hazlewood
  LS24 ....189 D4
Thirkleby High & Low with
  Osgodby YO7 ....90 C1
Thirsk YO7 ....89 D5
Thorlthorpe YO61 ....142 D6
Thornaby YO61 ....116 E5
Thornton Steward HG4 ...61 E2
Thornton-le-Clay YO60 ...145 F2
Thorp Arch LS23 ....180 E3
Threshfield BD23 ....134 B2
Welburn YO62 ....94 A5
West Tanfield HG4 ....87 B2
Weston LS21 ....176 E2
Wilstrop YO26 ....181 D8
Yafforth DL7 ....43 B2
York YO24 ....230 C6
Moor Lane Trad Est
  LS25 ....196 A3
Moor Lee La
  Eggborough DN14 ....207 B8
  Heck DN14 ....203 B1
Moor Park Cl
  2 Addingham LS29 ...174 E4
  Pannal HG3 ....178 A8
Moor Park Cres LS29 ...174 E4
Moor Park Dr LS29 ......174 E4
Moor Park Gr 2 LS29 ...174 F4
Moor Park Way 1 LS29 .174 F4
Moor Pk TS7 ....7 D5
Moor Rd Askrigg DL8 .....57 E6
  Bishop Monkton HG3 ....139 F5
  Filey YO14 ....101 B1
  Hunmanby YO14 ....127 B7
  Ilkley LS29 ....218 F1
  Knayton with Brawith YO7 ..65 F3
  Leyburn DL8 ....60 C5
  Marton cum Grafton
    YO51 ....141 C2
  Melsonby DL10 ....20 F6
  Muston YO14 ....101 A2
  1 Sherburn in Elmet LS25 195 F4
  Stamford Bridge YO41 ...168 D2
  Wykeham YO13 ....74 B4
Moor Side LS23 ....188 D8
Moor View 3 TS13 ....11 F7
Moor Way YO32 ....166 D5
Moorber La BD23 ....171 F8
Moorberries TS15 ....6 C2
Moorbridge Croft 6
  LS25 ....196 A4
Moorcock La HG3 ....159 F5
Moorcroft Rd YO24 ......230 D7
Moore Ave YO10 ....229 B4
Moorfield Dr YO41 ......185 E6
Moorfield Rd LS29 ......218 F4
Moorfield Sch LS29 .....218 C3
Moorfield Way YO41 ....185 E6
Moorfields
  Raskelf YO61 ....116 F2
  3 Wistow YO8 ....197 D6
Moorfields La YO62 ......93 E5
Moorland La BD20 ......173 D2
Moorgarth Ave
  10 York YO24 ....227 F2
  3 York YO24 ....228 A2
Moorgate YO24 ....227 F2
Moorgate Dr LS25 ....194 D1
Moorgate Rd LS25 ......194 D2
Moorhill La YO17 ....147 E6
Moorhouse Cl 3 WF6 ...200 B2
Moorhouse La YO7 ....89 E8
Moorland Ave 6 BB18 ..172 B1
Moorland Cl
  8 Embsay BD23 ....217 E8
  Harrogate HG2 ....220 D4
Moorland Dr YO23 ......167 A7
Moorland Rd
  Harrogate HG2 ....220 D4
  York YO10 ....231 D8
Moorland Rise BD23 ....217 E8
Moorland View HG2 ......220 D4
Moorlands Ilkley LS29 ..218 A2
  Skelton YO32 ....166 B5

Moorlands La
  Skelton YO30 ....224 C6
  1 Tollerton YO61 ......143 B3
Moorlands Pk YO21 ....29 A6
Moors Ctr The* YO21 ....29 D7
Moorsholm La TS13 ......10 C6
Moorside
  Melling-with-Wrayton
    LA6 ....102 A2
  Scalby YO12 ....212 A8
Moorside Ave HG4 ....214 B2
Moorside Cl LA6 ....102 A2
Moorside Cty Jun & Inf Sch
  HG4 ....214 B3
Moorside Dale 6 HG4 ...214 B2
Moorside La
  Addingham LS29 ....175 A2
  Askwith LS21 ....176 C4
Moorside Rd DL10 ....209 E8
Moorside View HG4 .....214 C2
Moorview Rd
  Northallerton DL6 ....210 F5
  Skipton BD23 ....217 B3
Moorview Way BD23 ....217 B4
Morehall Cl YO30 ....229 F7
Morgan Dr TS14 ....8 E6
Morgan St 4 YO12 ......212 F5
Morley Dr 10 YO13 ......99 A7
Morley Gate DL11 ....37 E5
Mornington Cres HG1 ...219 A4
Mornington Rd LS29 ....218 C4
Mornington Terr HG1 ...219 E3
Morpeth Ave
  Coulby Newham TS4 ....7 A7
  Darlington DL1 ....3 E7
Morpeth Gate DL8 ....58 F1
Morrets La YO8 ....197 A1
Morrison Rd TS14 ....8 F7
Morritt Cl 3 YO31 ....228 F8
Morton Carr La TS7 ....7 E6
Morton La YO8 ....184 A8
Morton Rd DL1 ....4 A5
Mosber La BD23 ....172 C8
Moss Arc HG4 ....214 C5
Moss End La BD22 ......186 F5
Moss Green La
  Brayton YO8 ....232 A2
  Hirst Courtney YO8 ......203 F3
Moss Haven DN6 ....207 D1
Moss Hill La YO26 ......164 D5
Moss Rd DN6 ....207 B1
Moss Side BB18 ....171 E1
Moss St YO24 ....233 A1
Moss Way TS18 ....5 F7
Mossburn Dr YO62 ....119 E6
Mossdale Gr TS14 ....8 D6
Mossra La HG4 ....85 F4
Mosswood Cres TS5 ......6 D7
Mosswood La YO41 ......118 A1
Mossy La DL8 ....56 C4
Moulton Hall* DL10 .....21 D2
Moulton La DL7 ....22 C3
Mounstrall La DL7 ....43 C1
Mount Ave YO8 ....232 B3
Mount Bank YO61 ....45 A5
Mount Cres YO17 ....215 B5
Mount Dr DL6 ....60 D5
Mount Ephraim 6
  YO24 ....228 A3
Mount Farm Cl YO22 ....208 E3
Mount Gdns LS22 ....222 E7
Mount Gr YO8 ....232 B3
Mount Grace Priory* 45 B5
Mount Leven Rd TS15 ....5 F3
Mount Par
  6 Harrogate HG1 ......219 D3
  York YO24 ....228 A3
Mount Park Ave YO12 ...212 E5
Mount Park Rd 2 YO12 .212 E4
Mount Pk YO19 ....198 A8
Mount Pleasant
  8 Addingham LS29 ....174 F4
  High Bentham LA2 ....129 A8
  Kippax LS25 ....200 D8
  Newby & Scalby YO13 .....75 C5
Mount Pleasant Cl 6 DL2 ..4 C4
Mount Pleasant E 2
  YO22 ....33 D4
Mount Pleasant Grange
  TS18 ....6 A8
Mount Pleasant N 1
  YO22 ....33 D4
Mount Pleasant Prim Sch
  DL3 ....3 A7
Mount Pleasant S 3
  YO22 ....33 D4
Mount Rd Malton YO17 ..215 B5
  Northallerton DL6 ....210 F6
  Mount Sch The YO24 ....228 A3
Mount St HG2 ....222 E7
Mount The
  Barwick in Elmet & Scholes
    LS15 ....194 B7
  Castleford WF10 ....201 B4
  Malton YO17 ....215 B4
  Selby YO8 ....232 B3
  6 Thornton Dale YO18 ..96 D5
  York YO24 ....228 A3
Mount Vale YO24 ....228 A2
Mount Vale Dr YO24 .....228 A2
Mount View HG4 ....214 C5
Mount View YO11 ....100 A2
Mount View Ave 5 YO12 212 E3
Mount View Rd 8 YO11 100 B6
Mountside YO11 ....212 F3
Mouseman Visitor Ctr*
  YO61 ....91 B2

Moorlands La cont.
Mowbray Castle (site of)*
  HG4 ....112 D5
Mowbray Cres
  3 Bedale DL8 ....63 A2
  Hovingham YO62 ....119 E6
  Kirkby Malzeard HG4 ...112 D5
Mowbray Dr
  4 Hurworth-on-Tees DL2 ..3 E1
  5 York YO7 ....227 C4
Mowbray Pl YO7 ....211 B2
Mowbray Rd
  5 Catterick DL10 ....41 D5
  Northallerton DL6 ....210 E6
  Mowbrays Sch DL8 ....63 A2
  Mowbray Sq HG1 ....219 E3
  Mowbray Terr HG4 ....87 A2
  Mowden Inf Sch DL3 ......3 A6
Mowthorp Rd YO12 ....75 A3
Mowthorpe La YO60 ....145 F8
Mowthorpe Medieval
  Village* HG4 ....149 C6
Moxby La YO61 ....144 D5
Moxby Priory* YO61 ....144 D5
Muddy La LS22 ....180 A1
Muff La TS8 ....7 A3
Muirfield TS7 ....7 D5
Muirfield Ave WF7 ....200 E1
Muirfield Rd TS16 ....5 E5
Muirfield Way 6 YO26 ..227 B5
Mulberry Ct YO12 ....212 C5
Mulberry Dr 7 YO12 ....166 E5
Mulberry Garth LS23 ...188 F8
Mulgrave Castle*
  ....12 E2
Mulgrave Cres YO21 ....208 B8
Mulgrave Dr 6 DL7 ......210 D2
Mulgrave Pl YO11 ....213 B7
Mulgrave Rd YO21 ......208 A8
Mulgrave View YO22 .....32 F7
Mulberry Gdns DL10 .....41 D5
Mulwith Cl YO31 ....229 A6
Mulwith La HG4 ....140 E6
Muncaster Way YO22 ...208 E3
Muncastergate YO31 ....228 E7
Murchison Pl 8 YO12 ...212 C6
Murchison St YO12 ......212 E6
Murray St 8 Filey YO14 101 B3
  York YO24 ....227 F3
Murray Wlk DL3 ....3 A6
Murrayfield Way 6 DL1 ..3 F6
Murrough Wilson Pl 3
  YO31 ....228 C7
Murton Bank YO62 ....67 E3
Murton Garth YO19 .....229 F6
Murton La YO19 ....184 D7
Murton Way YO19 ....229 E5
Muscoates La YO62 ......67 E5
Museum of Craven Life*
  BD24 ....131 E2
Musham St YO10 ....233 B2
Musham Bank Rd YO11 ..99 F7
Music in Miniature Ex*
  ....33 D3
Musterfield La HG4 ......113 B7
Muston Rd Filey YO14 ..101 A3
  Muston YO14 ....100 F4
Mutton Scalp Rd TS12 ....9 F7
My Love La HG3 ....159 C5
Myers Green La HG3 ....161 B5
Myers La DL7 ....64 A8
Myra Bank La YO61 .....117 F3
Myrtle Ave
  Bishopthorpe YO23 ......231 B3
  Selby YO8 ....232 B3
Myrtle Gdns DL1 ....3 D8
Myrtle Rd
  Eaglescliffe TS16 ....5 E6
  3 Harrogate HG2 ......219 E3
Myrtle Sq 2 HG2 ....219 E3
Myson Ave WF8 ....201 C2
Myton La YO61 ....142 C5
Myton Rd TS17 ....6 A4

N

Nab Wood BD20 ....174 C2
Nabs View YO12 ....212 A7
Naburn La
  Deighton YO19 ....192 A7
  Fulford YO19 ....231 D4
Naburn Park Mews
  YO19 ....191 E8
Nairn Cl YO24 ....230 C6
Nairnhead Cl TS8 ....6 E5
Nalton Cl YO23 ....230 A1
Nalton St YO8 ....232 C5
Nanny Goat La
  Barwick in Elmet & Scholes
    LS25 ....194 B4
  Hunton DL8 ....61 F8
Nanny La LS24 ....190 C7
Nansen St YO12 ....212 E6
Nap Cote La HG4 ....112 E4
Napier Cres YO24 ....99 D7
Napier Rd HG4 ....113 D3
Nares St YO12 ....212 E6
Narrow La YO42 ....193 D7
Narrowfield 8 YO22 ......32 A6
Naseby Garth YO26 ......162 F5
Nasterfield Nature Reserve*
  HG4 ....86 B3
Nat La LS17 ....178 A3
National Riv Mus*
  YO26 ....165 E1
Nattrass Wlk 7 DL8 ....63 B2
Navigation Rd YO1 ....233 C2
Nawton Cty Sch YO62 ...93 D7

Nawton Rd YO62 ....93 E7
Neasham Ct TS9 ....26 C1
Neasham Hill DL2 ....4 E1
Neasham Rd
  Darlington DL1 ....3 D1
  Low Dinsdale DL2 ....4 F1
Neile Cl DL1 ....210 E1
Nell Bank Ctr* LS29 .....218 E1
Nelson Rd LS29 ....218 B4
Nelson St
  7 Normanton South WF6 200 A1
  Scarborough YO12 ....212 F4
  Skipton BD23 ....217 A3
  York YO1 ....233 C1
Nelson's La YO24 ....230 E6
Nesfield Cl
  11 Eastfield YO11 ......100 B7
  Harrogate HG1 ....219 B5
Nesfield Rd LS29 ....218 A4
Nesfield View LS29 .....175 C2
Ness La
  Pickhill with Roxby YO7 ...88 B4
  Tockwith YO26 ....181 C6
Ness Rd YO8 ....232 A4
Nessgate YO1 ....233 B2
Nesfield Cl WF8 ....201 B1
Nether Way 10 YO26 ....165 F1
Netherby Cl 6 YO22 ......32 A6
Netherby La
  Huttons Ambo YO60 .....147 A7
  Sinnington YO62 ....71 F4
Netheredge Cl HG5 .....220 D5
Netheredge Dr HG5 .....220 D5
Netherfield Cl WF10 ....200 E3
Nethergill La BD20 ......173 A1
Netherside Hall Sch
  BD23 ....134 A3
Netherwindings 18
  YO32 ....166 E5
Netherwoods 8 YO32 ...166 E5
Nettledale Cl 1 TS13 ....12 B1
Nettledale La YO13 ....53 B1
Nevern Cres TS17 ....5 F4
Neville Cres BD23 ......155 D1
Neville Dr YO23 ....231 A4
Neville Gr LS26 ....194 A1
Neville Pits La DN14 ....207 A7
Neville Rd Darlington DL3 ..3 A5
  Gargrave BD23 ....155 D1
Neville St
  7 Normanton South WF6 200 A1
  Skipton BD23 ....217 A3
  York YO31 ....233 C4
Neville Terr YO31 ....233 C4
Neville Wlk DL10 ....209 F8
Nevinson Gr YO10 ....231 E7
Nevis Way YO24 ....230 B1
Nevison Ave WF8 ....201 C2
New Brook St LS29 .....218 B4
New Close La LA2 ....130 C1
New Dales La BD20 ......173 D3
New Earswick Prim Sch
  YO32 ....225 E4
New Fen La YO8 ....197 B2
New Forge Ct 18 YO32 ..166 E5
New House La BD23 .....153 B3
New Ings La YO18 ....96 B3
New Inn La DL8 ....87 F3
New La Aislaby YO18 .....95 B4
  Beal DN14 ....202 D4
  Bishopthorpe YO23 ......231 A3
  Burton Salmon WF11 ....201 F6
  Green Hammerton YO26 164 C3
  Hawes DL8 ....56 E4
  Huntington YO32 ....226 A5
  Kildwick BD20 ....172 D5
  Lillings Ambo YO60 ......145 D5
  Little Ouseburn YO26 ....164 B6
  Long Marston YO23 ......182 B5
  Neasham DL2 ....4 D1
  Newland YO8 ....207 C2
  Ravensworth DL11 ....19 C6
  Selby YO8 ....232 D3
  Sherburn in Elmet LS25 ..195 F4
  Sheriff Hutton YO60 .....145 C5
  Stainburn LS21 ....177 B2
  Stensall YO32 ....167 B8
  West Tanfield DL8 ....87 B1
  York YO24 ....225 F2
  York YO24 ....230 E8
New Laithe Cl 5 BD23 ..217 E8
New Lennerton La
  LS25 ....196 C3
New Mill La LS23 ....188 E5
New Millgate YO8 ....232 D6
New Park CP Sch
  HG1 ....219 C5
New Park Rd 4 YO12 ....212 E4
New Park Row HG1 ......219 D5
New Parks Cres 8
  YO12 ....212 E5
New Potter Grange Rd
  DN14 ....205 F3
New Quay Rd YO21 ......208 D6
New Queen St 10 YO12 .212 F6
New Rd Allerston YO13 ...97 F6
  Allerton Mauleverer
    with Hopperton HG5 ...163 F6
  Appleton Roebuck YO23 ..190 E4
  Appletreewick BD23 ......139 A8
  Beningbrough YO30 ....165 A6
  Birstwith HG3 ....160 A5
  Bramham LS23 ....188 E6
  Earby BB18 ....172 A1
  Fylingdales YO22 ....33 C4
  Glaisdale YO21 ....30 D4
  Guisborough TS14 ....8 D6

w Rd continued
ck DN14 ....203 D1
ssay YO26 ....182 C8
nmanby YO14 ....126 F7
by HG1 ....188 B6
kbymoorside YO62 ....70 B1
ottingley WF11 ....201 D3
stham LS25 ....201 B8
ings Ambo YO60 ....145 D3
ing Drax YO8 ....204 E6
sham DL11 ....18 J8
arth Stainley with Sleningford
4 ....113 B8
ton YO6 ....206 F2
inton with Newby YO7 ..114 E6
skelf YO61 ....116 E3
ighton YO14 ....127 E5
chmond DL10 ....209 C6
sedale East Side YO18 ..49 E3
fton HG5 ....162 A5
rington YO17 ....122 D1
uton YO62 ....70 E5
apleton WF8 ....206 B5
rlington YO60 ....119 E2
rnton in Lonsdale
 ....103 B4
eskelf LS24 ....190 B3
esterdale YO21 ....28 F6
neldrake YO19 ....192 C7
axley YO24 ....164 A4
w Row
Boroughbridge YO51 ...141 B5
pleby DL11 ....1 D4
wden Forest BB8 ....186 B2
w St Carleton BD23 ...173 B4
ngon HG5 ....162 A5
ngcliffe BD24 ....131 E4
icaster LS24 ....189 E6
rk YO1 ....233 B2
w Sturton La LS25 .....194 D4
w Walk Terr YO10 .....228 D2
w Way YO21 ....29 C4
wall Ave LS21 ....176 F1
wall Carr Rd LS21 .....176 F1
wall Hall Pk LS21 ....177 A1
wbigin
nchmond DL10 ....219 B5
chmond DL10 ....209 B6
wborough YO11 ....213 A6
wborough St YO30 .....233 A4
wbridge La BD23 ....174 B8
wburgh Priory*
 ....117 E7
wbury Ave YO24 ....227 D1
wby Cl HG4 ....214 C4
wby CP Sch YO12 ......212 B8
wby Cres HG6 ....219 A4
wby Farm Cl WF6 .....200 B1
wfield Cl WF6 ....200 B1
wfield Cres
 ....6 D7
ddlesbrough TS17 ....6 D7
rmanton South WF6 ....200 B1
wfield Cl WF6 ....200 B1
wgate Malton YO17 ...215 C4
rk YO1 ....233 B2
wgate Bank YO62 ....68 A4
wgate Rd YO1 ....233 B2
wham Bridge Prim Sch
 ....7 B5
wham Way TS8 ....7 B5
whay La YO8 ....198 E1
whold LS25 ....194 D4
wington Rd TS4 ....7 A8
wland DL8 ....57 D5
wlaithes Cres WF6 ...200 B1
wland Ave HG2 ....220 A1
wland Park Cl
 ....229 A3
wland Park Dr
 ....228 F3
wlands DL6 ....210 F4
wlands Ave
carborough YO12 ....212 E8
 Whitby YO21 ....208 C7
 York YO21 ....211 D3
wlands Dr
 Glusburn BD20 ....187 F8
pon HG4 ....214 B3
rk YO26 ....227 B6
wlands La
rper Poppleton YO26 ..182 E8
ntringham YO17 ....123 F3
wlands Park Ave
 ....212 D8
wlands Park Cres
 ....212 D8
wlands Park Dr
 ....212 D8

Newlands Park Gr 2
YO12 ....212 D8
Newlands Park Rd
YO12 ....212 D8
Newlands Rd
Bishopthorpe YO23 .....230 F4
Darlington DL3 ....3 B6
Newlands Sch TS4 ....6 F7
Newlyn Dr DL3 ....3 C8
Newmarket St BD23 ...217 A4
Newnham St HG2 ....220 A3
Newnham Terr HG2 .....220 A3
Newport Ave YO8 .....232 B4
Newport St
Goole DN14 ....205 F2
 6 Pontefract WF8 .....201 B1
Newsham Hill DL11 .....18 J8
Newsham La
Barugh (Great & Little)
YO17 ....95 A1
 Habton YO17 ....121 A8
Newsham Rd YO7 ......211 A3
Newsham Way DL10 ...210 B1
Newstead La HG4 ......85 C7
Newstead Prim Sch
TS14 ....8 E5
Newstead 12 DL8 ....63 B3
Newthorpe Rd 2 DN6 .206 E2
Newton Cres 4 DL7 ...63 D4
Newton Dr TS17 ....6 B6
Newton House Ct
YO61 ....144 C3
Newton La
Archdeacon Newton DL2 ..2 F8
Ledsham WF10 ....201 A6
Newton Mulgrave TS13 ..11 F6
Newton Pk YO30 ......165 B7
Newton Rd
Great Ayton TS9 ....8 A2
Tollerton YO61 ....143 B3
Newton St YO21 ....208 D6
Newton Terr YO11 ....233 B1
Newtondale Cl HG5 ....221 D6
Newtondale Forest Dr
YO18 ....51 D1
Newtondale Halt YO18 .51 D1
Nicholas Gdns YO10 ...228 F3
Nicholas St YO10 .....228 F3
Nichols Way LS20 ....180 A3
Nicholson Ave HG4 ...113 D3
Nickey Nackey La YO8 .197 B8
Nicklaus Dr TS16 ......5 D5
Nickstream La DL3 .....3 A7
Nidd Bank HG5 ....220 F7
Nidd Cl YO26 ....227 B8
Nidd Dr HG3 ....160 E6
Nidd Gr YO24 ....230 E8
Nidd La Birstwith HG3 .160 B6
Ripley HG3 ....161 D7
Nidd Rise HG3 ....160 A6
Nidd Viaduct* HG3 ...219 E8
Nidd Wlk HG3 ....137 B4
Nidderdale Dr HG5 ....221 D5
Nidderdale Lodge
HG5 ....221 E5
Nidderdale Mus*
HG3 ....137 B4
Nidderdale Recn Ctr
 ....137 A5
Nidside HG3 ....160 A6
Niffany Gdns 7 BD23 ..216 D3
Nigel Gr 7 YO12 ....225 E1
Nightingale Dr HG2 ..220 B3
Nightingale La 9 YO12 ..99 F6
Nile Rd LS25 ....218 B4
Ninelands La LS25 ...194 D3
Ninelands Lane CP Sch
LS25 ....194 D4
Ninevah La WF10 .....200 C7
Ninth Ave YO31 ......228 F5
No Man's Moor La DL8 ..61 B6
Noel's Ct DL10 ....41 E5
Nook The LS25 ....195 F2
Nooking The YO61 ....117 B6
Nora Ave HG5 ....221 C6
Norby YO7 ....211 B3
Norby Front St YO7 ..211 B3
Norfolk Cl WF11 ......201 E4
Norfolk Cres TS3 ....7 C8
Norfolk Gdns YO26 ...181 C7
Norfolk Rd HG2 ....222 D7
Norfolk St YO23 .....228 C2
Norman Cl
 2 Pickering YO18 .....95 F7
 7 Thorpe Willoughby YO8 ..197 B1
Norman Cres YO14 ...101 B3
Norman Dr YO26 .....227 B6
Norman Rd Aske DL10 ..20 D1
Catterick Garrison DL9 ..209 E1
Richmond DL10 ....209 C8
Norman Sq DL10 ......209 D8
Norman St 5 YO10 ...229 B3
Normanby Rd
Middlesbrough TS7 ......72 B6
Northallerton DL7 .....210 D2
Normandy Cl 4 YO8 ..232 B6
Normanton Comm Sch
WF6 ....200 B2
Normanton Freeston High
Sch WF6 ....200 A1
Normanton Ind Est
WF6 ....200 A1
Normanton Public Baths
WF6 ....200 A1
Normanton Sta WF6 ..200 A2

Normanton Town Mid Sch
WF6 ....200 A1
Norseman Cl 7 YO19 ..197 F8
Norseway 2 YO41 ...168 D1
North & South Cowton CP
Sch DL7 ....22 C2
North App LS24 ....189 A2
North Ave
Castleford WF10 ....200 C4
 6 Glusburn BD20 .....187 E6
North Back La YO60 ..119 E1
North Baileygate WF8 ..201 B1
North Bay Rly* YO12 ..212 F8
North Burton La YO14 .127 B4
North Cl 5 WF7 ......200 E1
North Cliff Ave YO12 ...75 F5
North Cliff Cty Pk*
YO14 ....101 C4
North Cotes Rd
Hunmanby YO25 ....126 C5
 Reighton YO14 ....125 E5
North Cres LS25 ......195 F5
North Croft Grove Rd 1
LS29 ....218 A4
North Dr Kippax LS25 .194 D2
Sherburn in Elmet LS25 ..195 F5
North Duffield CP Sch
YO8 ....199 A8
North End Bedale DL8 ..63 A3
 2 Hutton Rudby TS15 ..25 C5
Osmotherley DL6 ....45 B4
North Field Ave YO25 .190 F5
North Field Cl YO23 ..190 F5
North Field La
Askham Bryan YO23 ....182 F3
Upper Poppleton YO26 ..182 F7
North Field Way YO23 .190 F5
North Field Way YO26 ..227 B5
North Garth La YO60 ..145 D5
North Gr 2 LS22 ....180 C3
North Grove Ave 6
LS22 ....180 C4
North Hill Rd YO12 ...115 B2
North La Eastfield YO11 .100 B6
Gainford DL2 ....1 D8
Great Timble LS21 .....176 E8
Huntington YO32 ......226 D5
 Hutton Hang DL8 ....61 D3
 Wheldrake YO19 ......192 F7
York YO30 ....225 F5
North Leas Ave YO12 ..212 D8
North Lodge Ave 2
HG1 ....219 C5
North Marine Rd
YO12 ....212 F7
North Moor YO32 ....225 F5
North Moor Gdns
YO32 ....225 F5
North Moor La YO61 ..118 C5
North Moor Rd
Easingwold YO61 ......117 B2
York YO32 ....225 F5
North Par
 8 Burley in Warfedale
LS29 ....176 C1
 Ilkley LS29 ....218 C4
Skipton BD23 ....216 F4
North Park Rd HG1 ...219 E2
North Prom YO21 .....208 C7
North Rd Darlington DL1 ..3 D7
 5 Fairburn WF11 ....201 D6
Glusburn BD20 ....187 E7
Grosmont YO22 ....53 A7
Hackforth DL8 ....62 E8
 8 Middleham DL8 ......60 E2
Norton YO17 ....215 E3
Ripon HG4 ....214 C6
Stokesley TS9 ....26 C6
Whitby YO21 ....208 D6
North Road Prim Sch
DL1 ....3 D6
North Road Sta DL1 ....3 D6
North Ribblesdale RUFC
BD24 ....131 D2
North Rigton C of E Prim Sch
LS17 ....178 C4
North Side TS15 ......25 C5
North St
Addingham LS29 ....175 A4
Barmby on the Marsh
DN14 ....205 A4
Barnoldswick BB18 ....171 D1
Castleford WF10 ....201 B6
Folkton YO11 ....100 A2
Gargrave BD23 ....155 D1
 3 Glusburn BD20 .....187 E7
 6 Glusburn BD20 .....187 E8
Newby & Scalby YO13 ..75 C6
Ripon HG4 ....214 C6
Scarborough YO11 ....213 A6
Silsden BD20 ....174 C1
Wetherby LS22 ....180 C3
York YO1 ....233 B2
North Stainley C of E Prim
Sch HG4 ....113 C8
North Street La
YO11 ....213 A6
North Terr Gainford DL2 ..1 D7
 4 Scarborough YO11 ..213 A6
Whitby YO21 ....208 C7
North View
Knottingley WF11 ......201 F2
 Little Ribston LS22 ...180 A8
North York Craven Inst of
Further Ed BD23 ......217 A4

North Yorkshire Moors Rly*
YO18 ....95 F7
Northallerton Coll
DL6 ....210 E4
Northallerton Rd
Brompton DL6 ....210 E7
Dalton-on-Tees DL2 ....22 E6
Leeming DL7 ....63 C4
Thirsk YO7 ....211 A6
Thornaby TS17 ....6 B7
Northallerton Rigg 6 DL6 ..43 D4
Northallerton Rugby Club
DL6 ....210 D8
Northallerton Sta DL6 .210 C3
Northcarrs La YO61 ..144 A4
Northcliffe Ct TS15 ...25 C5
Northcote Ave 2 DL3 ..3 C4
Northcote Fold 3 LS22 ..180 A1
Northcroft YO23 .....166 F5
Northfield 6 YO8 ...198 B5
Northfield Cl
Stokesley TS9 ....26 C7
Womersley DN6 ....206 C6
Northfield Ct LS24 ...196 B8
Northfield Dr
Pontefract WF8 ....201 C1
Stokesley TS9 ....26 C8
Northfield La
Church Fenton LS24 ...196 B8
Pockley YO62 ....69 B2
 8 Riccall YO19 ......197 F8
South Milford LS25 ...195 E2
Womersley DN6 ....206 C7
Northfield Pl LS22 ...180 C3
Northfield Rd YO8 ...199 E8
Northfield Way YO26 .227 B5
Northfield Way YO26 ...75 D6
Northfields
 8 Hutton Rudby TS15 ..25 C5
 5 Strensall YO32 ....167 B8
Northfields Ave 4
BD24 ....131 D3
Northfields Cres 5
BD24 ....131 D3
Northfields La HG4 ...142 C6
Northgate Darlington DL1 ..3 C5
Guisborough TS14 ......8 D6
Humanby YO14 ....126 F8
Muston YO14 ....100 F1
Pontefract WF8 ....201 B1
 4 Northallerton DL7 ..210 C3
Northgate Jun Sch TS14 ..8 F7
Northgate La
 8 Linton LS22 ....180 A1
Warthill YO41 ....168 A3
Northgate Lodge 11
WF8 ....201 B1
Northgate Rise 2 LS22 ..180 A1
Northlands Ave YO32 .225 F7
Northleach Dr TS8 .....7 A5
Northminster Bsns Pk
YO26 ....182 F7
Northolme YO30 .....224 E1
Northstead Cty Prim Sch
YO12 ....212 D8
Northstead Manor Dr
YO12 ....212 E7
Northumberland Ct 8
HG1 ....219 D2
Northumberland Rd
TS17 ....6 B8
Northway Pickering YO18 ..95 E7
 12 Scarborough YO12 ..212 F6
 6 Whitby YO21 ......208 B7
Northwell Gate LS21 ..176 F1
Northwold Rd YO11 ..100 A7
Norton & Kirk Smeat
WF8 ....206 C3
Norton Back La DL2 ....4 D1
Norton Cl HG4 ....114 A8
Norton Comm La 2 DN6 ..206 F2
Norton Comm Rd
DN6 ....207 A1
Norton Comp Sch
YO17 ....215 E2
Norton Cres YO17 ...215 E3
Norton Ct DL2 ....4 D1
Norton Cty Jun & Inf Sch
DN6 ....206 E2
Norton Grove Ind Est
YO17 ....215 F3
Norton Mill La DN6 ...206 E2
Norton Priory DN6 ...206 E2
Norton Rd
Norton YO17 ....215 C3
Sadberge DL2 ....4 C7
Norton Twr* BD23 ...156 B6
Norway Dr YO10 .....231 D8
Norwich Cl YO13 ......75 D6
Norwich Dr HG3 .....219 A5
Norwood Ave LS29 ..176 C1
Norwood Bottom Rd
LS21 ....177 A5
Norwood Cl
 5D Burley in Warfedale
LS29 ....176 C1
 12 Knaresborough HG5 ..221 B8
Norwood Dr HG3 .....219 A5
Norwood Gr HG3 .....219 B4
Norwood La
Glusburn BD20 ....187 B8
Pannal HG3 ....177 E2
Norwood Pl 8 YO12 ..212 F5
Norwood St
Normanton WF6 ......200 B2
Scarborough YO12 ....212 F5

Nossill La DL8 ....59 C3
Nosterfield Rd HG4 ...87 B2
Notagreen Rd DL11 ...39 F6
Nought Bank Rd HG3 .137 B3
Nought Moor Rd HG3 .137 B2
Nova Scotia Way 4
YO19 ....198 A8
Nun Monkton Prim Sch
YO26 ....165 A5
Nuneaton Dr TS8 ......6 E5
Nunmill St YO23 .....228 C2
Nunnery La
Darlington DL3 ....3 A5
York YO23 ....233 B1
Nunnington Cres HG3 .219 A5
Nunnington Hall*
YO62 ....93 F2
Nuns Green La YO21 ..29 E3
Nunthorpe Ave YO23 .228 B2
Nunthorpe Cres YO23 .228 B1
Nunthorpe Gr YO23 ..228 B2
Nunthorpe Prim Sch
TS7 ....7 E6
Nunthorpe Rd YO23 ..233 A1
Nunthorpe Sta TS7 ....7 E6
Nurseries The
 3 Easingwold YO61 ...143 C8
East Ayton YO13 ....99 C8
 10 Leyburn DL8 ....60 D5
 3 Whitby YO21 ......208 B6
Nursery Ct YO24 .....224 A2
Nursery Dr YO24 .....227 E3
Nursery Gdns YO10 ..229 C5
Nursery La 4 LS29 ..175 A4
Nursery Rd YO26 .....224 A2
Nursery Way 8 LS23 .188 E2
Nutgill La Bentham LA2 .129 D8
Ingleton LA2 ....103 D1
Nutwith La HG4 ......112 B8
Nydd Vale Rd HG1 ...219 D3

O

Oak Ave
Appleton Roebuck YO23 ..190 E3
Garforth LS25 ....194 C4
Killinghall HG3 ....161 B2
Oak Beck Rd HG1 ....219 B6
Oak Beck Way HG1 ...219 B6
Oak Busk La YO60 ...145 F1
Oak Cl Filey YO14 ....101 B4
 8 Garforth LS25 .....194 C4
Oak Cres LS25 ....194 C4
 5 Thorpe Willoughby YO8 ..197 B1
 Topcliffe YO7 ....89 A1
Oak Field YO8 ....232 A1
Oak Field Ave YO22 ..51 D8
Oak Glade YO31 .....225 F3
Oak Gr TS7 ....7 D6
Oak Hill TS8 ....159 F8
Oak Rd Eaglescliffe TS16 ..5 E6
Garforth LS25 ....194 C4
Guisborough TS14 ......9 F4
 2 North Duffield YO8 ..199 A7
Ripon HG4 ....214 B2
Scarborough YO12 ....210 D4
Tockwith LS22 ....180 E7
Whitby YO21 ....208 B6
Oak Ridge 6 LS25 ...180 B3
Oak Rise 4 YO26 ...227 C3
Oak St 3 YO26 ......227 E5
Oak Terr HG2 ....219 C2
Oak Tree Cl
 2 Bedale DL8 ....63 A2
 6 Strensall YO32 ....167 B7
Tees-side Airport DL2 ...4 E4
Oak Tree Dr YO8 .....199 D7
Oak Tree Gr YO32 ...225 D3
Oak Tree La YO32 ...225 C7
Oak Tree Rd DL8 .....63 A2
Oak Tree Way 8 DL8 ..63 A2
Oak Wood Rd LS22 ..180 A4
Oakbank HG1 ....219 C4
Oakburn Rd LS29 ....218 A3
Oakbusks La YO61 ...142 F4
Oakdale HG1 ....219 A3
Oakdale Ave HG1 ....219 A3
Oakdale Glen HG1 ...219 B3
Oakdale Manor HG1 ..161 B2
Oakdale Pl HG1 ......219 A3
Oakdale Rd YO30 ....224 F2
Oakdale Rise HG1 ...219 C4
Oaken Grove Sch
YO32 ....166 F5
Oakenshaw Dr TS5 ....6 E7
Oaker Bank HG3 .....161 B2
Oakfield Cl DL8 ......60 D5
Oakhill Cres LS14 ...201 A8
Oakhill Ct YO32 .....167 A6
Oakland Ave YO31 ..229 A7
Oakland Dr YO31 ....229 A7
Oakland
Camblesforth YO8 ....204 C5
 8 Great Ayton TS9 ....8 A2
 8 Ilkley LS29 ....218 A3
 5 Pickering YO18 .....96 A6
 8 Strensall YO32 ....167 B7
Oaklands Cres YO8 ..204 C5
Oaklands Rd 7 ....7 F8
Oaklands Sch YO24 ..227 C2

Oaklands Small Sch
DN14 ....205 E4
Oaklands Sports Ctr
YO24 ....227 C2
Oaklands The DL2 .....A03
Oakley Bank YO22 ....208 B2
Oakley CI TS14 ....8 F5
Oakley Rd TS12 ....9 F7
Oakney Wood Dr YO8 .232 D1
Oakridge Cty Prim Sch
TS13 ....11 F7
Oakridge View 图 HG3 ..161 B3
Oaks La LS23 ....188 E8
Oaks The
Coulby Newham TS8 ....6 E5
Dalton YO7 ....115 F7
 Masham HG4 ....86 C3
Oaksfield LS26 ....200 B5
Oaktree Ave DL9 ....40 E2
Oaktree Bank YO7 ....65 F3
Oaktree Dr DL7 ....210 C1
Oaktree Gr 图 TS18 ....5 D8
Oaktree Hill DL6 ....43 D6
Oaktree Junc DL2 ....4 A4
Oakville Ave YO12 .....212 E6
Oakwood CI LS24 ....196 B7
Oakwood Pk DN14 .....207 F6
Oatlands Cty Inf Sch
HG2 ....222 E7
Oatlands Cty Jun Sch
HG2 ....227 F7
Oatlands Dr
Harrogate HG2 ....222 F8
 Otley LS21 ....177 A2
Oatlands Gr 图 TS13 ....11 A8
Occaney La HG3 ....162 D8
Occupation La LS24 ...188 E2
Occupation Rd TS6 ......7 F8
Ocean Rd YO21 ....208 C7
Ocean Terr YO14 ....100 F6
Ochrepit Hill YO42 ....170 A2
Oddie's La LA6 ....103 D5
Offerton Dr TS8 ....5 D4
Ogleforth YO31 ....233 B3
Okehampton Dr TS7 ....7 D6
Olav Rd DL10 ....209 C7
Old Barber HG1 ....219 D6
Old Boys Sch La 图 YO8 .197 B8
Old Brewery Gdns 图
LS24 ....189 F6
Old Bridge Rise 图 LS29 .218 A4
Old Chapel CI 图 HG3 .161 B2
Old Church Gn YO26 ..164 C2
Old Coach La 图 HG3 ..137 C4
Old Church St DL8 .....60 D2
Old Coach Rd HG3 ....137 F2
Old Coppice 图 YO32 .166 E5
Old Courthouse Museum*
HG5 ....221 A5
Old Dike Lands YO32 .225 C8
Old Farm CI 图 YO18 ....95 F7
Old Farm Way YO8 ....232 B2
Old Garth Croft 图
WF11 ....201 D6
Old Gayle La DL8 ....56 D4
Old Great North Rd
WF11 ....201 E4
Old Hall CI BD20 ......187 D7
Old Hall Croft BD23 ..155 D1
Old Hall La
Gilling with Hartforth & Sedbury
DL10 ....
Kexby YO41 ....185 C5
Old Hall Rd BD20 .....187 D7
Old Hall Way BD20 ...187 D7
Old La Addingham LS29 .175 B3
Broughton BD23 ....172 D5
Cowling BD22 ....187 B5
Earby BB18 ....172 A2
Hambleton YO8 ....196 E1
Hirst Courtney YO8 ....203 F3
Horton in Ribblesdale
BD24 ....105 A7
Ilkley LS29 ....218 D3
Kelbrook & Sough BB18 ..186 A6
Long Marston YO26 ...182 A6
Old Lane CI LS24 ......190 E7
Old London Rd LS24 ..189 D3
Old Malton Rd
Malton YO17 ....215 D5
 Willerby YO12 ....99 D2
Old Maltongate YO17 .215 C4
Old Market PI 图 HG4 .214 C5
Old Mill CI 图 LS29 ....176 C1
Old Mill Row 图 YO7 ..211 C3
Old Mill View YO60 ...145 C5
Old Mill Wynd YO7 .....9 E3
Old Moor La YO24 .....230 E7
Old Moor Rd LA2 ......128 B8
Old Oliver La BD24 ...152 F6
Old Orch YO32 ....225 D8
Old Orch The
 Easingwold YO61 ..143 C8
Fulford YO10 ....231 E7
Shipton YO30 ....165 F5
Old Park La YO21 ....31 D6
Old Park Mews 图 HG4 .214 B5
Old Quarry La LS25 ...195 E1
Old Raike BD23 ....152 F4
Old Rd
Appleton Roebuck YO23 .190 F6
Clapham LA2 ....130 C8
Garsdale LA10 ....55 A6
Ingleton LA6 ....103 E3
Kirkby Overblow LS17 .178 E1

Old Rd continued
Kirkbymoorside YO62 ...70 B1
Thornton in Craven
BD23 ....172 A3
Old Sawmill The BD24 .135 E7
Old Sch The LS23 .....188 E7
Old School Hall LS29 .174 F4
Old School La YO8 ....198 B5
Old St The LS24 ....190 C8
Old Station Rd 图 YO8 .232 C6
Old Station Way 图
LS29 ....174 F4
Old Station Yd* YO8 ....92 F6
Old Stone Trough La
BB18 ....186 A6
Old Stubble The 图 TS13 .13 K2
Old Sutton Rd YO7 ...211 A3
Old Trough Way HG1 .219 C6
Old Vicarage La 图
LS25 ....202 A7
Old Village The YO32 .225 F5
Old Wife's Way YO18 ...73 A8
Olde Mkt The TS16 .....5 D3
Oldfield La
Collingham LS22 ....180 C1
Spaunton YO7 ....70 E4
Sutton BD22 ....187 F1
Oldgate La LS25 ....195 D6
Oldham CI TS12 ....9 D8
Oldham St TS12 ....9 D7
Oldstead Rd YO61 ....91 B3
Olicana Pk LS29 ....218 B5
Olive Gr HG1 ....220 B4
Olive Way HG1 ....220 B4
Oliver La YO17 ....121 C8
Oliver St 图 YO11 ....213 A4
Oliver's CI 图 YO14 ....126 F8
Oliver's Mount Rd
YO11 ....212 F2
Olliver La DL10 ....20 F1
Olliver Rd DL10 ....209 E8
Olympia Cres YO8 ....232 B4
Omega St 图 HG1 ......219 C5
Onams La YO62 ....92 B1
One Acre Garth 图 YO8 .196 E1
Onhams La YO60 ....146 E4
Oran La DL10 ....41 E4
Orcaber La LA2 ....130 E6
Orchard CI
Appleton Roebuck YO23 ..190 F5
Barkston Ash LS24 ....195 E7
Dalton-on-Tees DL2 ....22 D7
 Great Ayton TS9 ....8 A2
 Hartwith cum Winsley
HG3 ....137 F1
 Knaresborough HG5 .221 B8
 Monk Fryston LS25 ..202 A7
 Norton DN6 ....206 E2
Selby YO8 ....232 A4
Sharow HG4 ....214 F6
South Milford LS25 ...195 F2
York YO24 ....227 E1
Orchard Cotts 图 YO19 .184 E7
Orchard Ct
Bramham cum Oglethorpe
LS23 ....188 E5
 Knaresborough HG5 .221 B5
Orchard Dr
Fairburn WF11 ....201 D7
Hambleton YO8 ....196 F2
Linton LS22 ....180 A2
Orchard Gdns YO31 ..225 E2
Orchard Gr 图 DL6 ......4 F3
Orchard Head Cres
WF8 ....201 C2
Orchard Head Jun & Inf
WF8 ....201 C2
Orchard Head La WF8 .201 B2
Orchard La
 Addingham LS29 ......175 A4
Barkston Ash LS24 ....195 F6
Hebden BD23 ....135 A2
Ripley HG3 ....161 C7
Thirsk YO7 ....211 B1
Orchard Paddock
图 Haxby YO32 ....166 E5
图 Haxby YO32 ....225 D8
Orchard Rd
Malton YO17 ....215 B4
Selby YO8 ....232 A4
 Sleights YO22 ....32 A6
Upper Poppleton YO26 ..224 A1
Orchard The
 Ampleforth YO62 .....92 C1
Burniston YO13 ....75 D8
 North Featherstone
WF7 ....200 E1
Sadberge DL2 ....4 C7
Sadgill YO12 ....212 C7
Snainton YO13 ....98 A4
Thirsk YO7 ....211 C4
Tholthorpe YO61 ....142 D5
Orchard View
Markington with Wallerthwaite
HG3 ....139 E3
图 Skelton YO30 ....224 B5
Orchard Way
Hensall DN14 ....203 C2
Middlesbrough TS7 .....7 D8
Selby YO8 ....232 A4
 Strensall YO32 ....167 B7
Thorpe Willoughby YO8 ..197 B2
York YO24 ....227 E1
Orchards The
 Beadlam YO62 ....93 D7
 Brafferton YO61 .....115 F1

Orchards The continued
Leavening YO17 ....147 E1
Mickletown LS26 ......200 B5
Ripon HG4 ....214 C6
Westow YO60 ....147 B4
Orchid Dr 图 HG3 ......161 B3
Orchid Way 图 HG3 ...161 B3
Ordmerstones La YO18 ..96 C4
Ordnance La YO10 ....228 D1
Oriel Bank YO11 ....212 F3
Oriel CI YO11 ....212 F3
Oriel Cres YO11 ....212 F3
Oriel Gr YO30 ....228 A8
Ormesby Bank TS7 .....7 D7
Ormesby Cres DL7 ....210 D2
Ormesby Cty Modern Sch
TS3 ....7 E8
Ormesby Prim Sch TS7 ..7 D8
Ormesby Rd TS3 ....7 D8
Orms Gill Green La
BD23 ....154 D6
Orpington Rd TS3 ......7 D8
Orrin CI YO24 ....230 B7
Osbaldwick La YO10 ..229 B4
Osbaldwick Link Rd
YO19 ....229 D4
Osbaldwick Prim Sch
YO10 ....229 C4
Osbaldwick Village
YO10 ....229 C4
Osborne CI HG1 ....219 D4
Osborne Gdns HG1 ..219 D4
Osborne Pk YO12 ......212 D5
Osborne Rd HG1 ....219 D4
Osborne Wlk HG1 .....219 D4
Osbourne Dr 图 YO30 .224 E3
Osgodby CI 图 YO11 ..100 B8
Osgodby Cres YO11 ..100 B8
Osgodby Gr 图 YO11 .100 B8
Osgodby Hall Rd YO11 .100 B7
Osgodby Hill YO11 ....100 B7
Osgodby La 图 YO11 ..100 B8
Osgodby Way 图 YO11 .100 B8
Osgodby Bank YO7 ....92 F6
Osmington Gdns 图
YO32 ....167 A7
Osmotherley CP Sch
DL6 ....45 B4
Osprey CI
 Collingham LS22 .....180 A1
Guisborough TS14 ....8 D6
 Scotton DL9 ....40 F2
 Wilton YO24 ....230 B8
Osprey Garth 图 YO12 ..99 E6
Ostler's CI YO23 ....230 C3
Ostman Rd YO26 ......227 C5
Oswaldene DL6 ....45 A6
Oswaldkirk Bank YO62 .93 A1
Oswestry Gn TS4 ....7 A7
Oswin Gr DL10 ....204 E4
Oswy St 图 YO21 ....208 D5
Otley Rd
Harrogate HG2 ....222 B8
Killinghall HG3 ....161 B4
Pannal HG3 ....178 A7
Skipton BD23 ....217 B4
Otley St BD23 ....217 A4
Otter Cl 图 YO18 ....95 F6
Otter Way TS17 ....6 A5
Otterbeck Way 图 DL8 ..63 B3
Otterwood Bank 图
YO24 ....227 B1
Otterwood La YO24 ...227 B1
Otterwood Paddock
YO41 ....168 C2
Oucher La 图 HG3 .....140 B2
Oughtershaw Rd BD23 ..80 B6
Oulston Rd YO61 ....117 B1
Our Ladys RC Prim Sch
YO24 ....227 E1
Ouse Acres YO26 ......227 D6
Ouse Bank YO8 ....232 E5
Ouseburn Ave YO26 ..227 C6
Ousecliffe Gdns YO30 .228 A6
Ousegate YO8 ....232 D5
Ouston CI LS24 ....189 F6
Ouston La LS24 ....189 F6
Out Gang La BD23 ...107 F1
Outgaits CI 图 YO14 ..126 F8
Outgaits La
Hunmanby YO14 ....127 A8
Muston YO14 ....100 F1
Outgang La
Osbaldwick YO19 ......229 D6
图 Pickering YO18 ......95 F6
Thornton-le-Dale YO18 ..96 E6
Outgang Rd
Malton YO17 ....215 B5
Pickering YO18 ....96 A6
Outgang The YO17 ...122 C4
Outgate Cnr DL6 ....23 F4
Outwood La LS24 .....190 C2
Oval The
Harrogate HG2 ....222 D8
Hurworth DL2 ....3 D1
Kellingley DN14 ....202 C3
Middlesbrough TS5 .....6 E8
Otley LS21 ....176 F1
 Scruton DL7 ....63 C7
Over Nidd HG1 ....219 C6
Overburn Rd 图 BD20 .187 E6
Overdale
Overdale CI YO24 .....230 D8
Overdale CP Sch
YO11 ....100 A7

Overdale Ct BD23 .....217 A5
Overdale Grange 图
BD23 ....217 B5
Overdale Rd TS3 ....7 C8
Overgreen CI YO13 ....75 D8
Overgreen Dr YO13 ...75 D8
Overgreen View YO13 .75 D8
Overscar La YO18 ......72 E3
Overton Rd YO30 ......165 F3
Ovington La DL11 ....1 A6
Ovington Terr YO23 ..228 B2
Owler Park Rd LS29 ..175 C3
Owlwood Ct 图 YO19 ..184 E7
Owlwood La 图 YO19 .184 E7
Owmen Field La YO62 .93 C5
Owston Ave 图 YO10 ..229 A3
Owston Rd 图 YO14 ..126 F8
Ox Calder CI 图 YO19 .184 F7
Ox Carr La YO32 ....167 B6
Ox CI YO41 ....168 D2
Ox Close La
Eldmire with Crakehill
YO7 ....115 C5
Myton-on-Swale YO61 ..141 F5
North Deighton LS22 ..180 B7
Whixley YO26 ....163 F5
Ox Moor La
Cattal YO26 ....164 A1
Hunsingore LS22 ....180 E8
Oxcliff YO12 ....212 C8
Oxclose La Huby YO61 .144 B4
Hutton-le-Hole YO62 ...70 C4
Oxcroft 图 YO62 ....70 B1
Oxen La YO8 ....198 E3
Oxenby PI 图 YO61 ....117 D1
Oxford Dr LS25 ....194 D1
Oxford PI 图 HG1 ......219 D2
Oxford St
Harrogate HG1 ....219 D2
 Normanton South WF6 .200 A2
Scarborough YO12 ....212 F6
Skelton & Brotton TS12 ..9 D7
 York YO24 ....228 A3
Oxford Terr 图 HG1 ...219 D2
Oxmoor La LS24 ....196 D7
Oxpasture CI YO12 ...212 C4
Oxton Dr LS24 ....189 F6
Oxton La LS24 ....189 F6
Oyster Park Inf Sch
WF10 ....201 B4
Oyster Park Mid Sch
WF10 ....201 B4

P

Packhorse Bridge*
Dacre HG3 ....159 D6
Romanby DL7 ....210 B4
Pad Cote La BD22 .....187 A5
Padbury Ave 图 YO11 .101 B3
Padbury CI 图 YO11 ...101 B3
Paddock CI
Copmanthorpe YO23 .230 A2
Norton YO17 ....215 D3
 Pickering YO18 ....95 F6
Paddock Hill YO17 ....215 A4
Paddock House La
LS22 ....179 E1
Paddock Rise 图 YO61 .117 D1
Paddock The
 Appleton Wiske DL6 ..24 B3
Burton Salmon LS25 ..201 F6
 Knaresborough HG5 .221 C5
 Linton-on-Ouse YO30 .164 F8
Melmerby HG4 ....114 B7
Middleton St George DL2 ..4 C1
Newby Wiske DL7 ....64 E2
Normanton South WF6 .200 A2
 Selby YO8 ....232 C6
Stokesley TS9 ....26 C8
 Whitby YO21 ....208 D7
Wilberfoss YO41 ....185 E5
York YO24 ....227 C6
Paddock Way YO26 ..227 C6
Paddocks The HG3 ...223 F4
Page La YO62 ....93 E6
Pagnell Ave YO8 ......197 D7
Painsthorpe La YO41 .170 B5
Painter La YO8 ....196 E2
Palace Rd HG4 ....214 B7
Pale La Carleton BD23 .216 E1
Gateforth YO8 ....207 F7
Paley Green La BD24 .131 B2
Pallet Hill 图 DL10 ....41 C5
Palmer Gr YO8 ....232 A3
Palmer La YO1 ....233 C2
Palmes CI YO19 ....191 E8
Pannam La YO19 ....184 F8
Pannal Ash CI HG2 ...222 C8
Pannal Ash Cres HG2 .222 B7
Pannal Ash Dr HG2 ..222 B7
Pannal Ash Gr HG2 ..222 B7
Pannal Ash Rd HG2 ..222 B7
Pannal Ave HG3 ....222 E2
Pannal CP Sch HG3 ..178 A8
Pannal CI 图 YO21 ....208 B5
Pannal Gn HG3 ....222 E3
Pannal Gr HG3 ....222 E3
Pannal Rd HG3 ....178 B8
Pannal Sta HG3 ....222 E2
Pannett Way 图 YO21 .208 D6
Pannierman La TS9 ...7 D1
Panorama CI 图 HG3 .137 C4
Panorama Dr LS29 ...175 C1
Panorama Wlk YO21 .137 C4
Pant La LA2 ....130 E2

Parade Ct YO31 ....228 ...
Parade The HG1 ....219 ...
Paradise YO11 ....213 ...
Paradise Cotts YO17 .170 ...
Paradise Field Est 图
HG1 ....143 ...
Paradise La Dalton YO7 .119 ...
Stutton with Hazlewood
LS24 ....189 ...
Paradise Rd YO7 ....67 ...
Paragon St YO10 ......233 ...
Parish Ghyll Dr LS29 .218 ...
Parish Ghyll La LS29 .218 ...
Parish Ghyll Rd LS29 .218 ...
Parish Ghyll Wlk LS29 .218 ...
Park Ave Barlow YO8 .204 ...
Castleford WF10 ....200 ...
Glusburn BD20 ....187 ...
Great Preston WF10 ..200 ...
Harrogate HG2 ....219 ...
Kippax LS25 ....194 ...
Knaresborough HG5 ..221 ...
New Earswick YO32 ..225 ...
Normanton South WF6 .200 ...
Scarborough YO12 ....212 ...
Sherburn in Elmet LS25 .195 ...
Skipton BD23 ....216 ...
Swillington LS26 ....194 ...
Thornaby TS17 ....6 ...
Park Ave S HG2 ....222 ...
Park Bank YO21 ....29 ...
Park Chase
Harrogate HG1 ....219 ...
Hornby DL8 ....62 ...
Park CI 图 Airmyn DN14 .205 ...
 Easingwold YO61 ....143 ...
 Knaresborough HG5 .221 ...
Skelton YO30 ....224 ...
Park Cres
图 Addingham LS29 ...175 ...
Castleford WF10 ....201 ...
Darlington DL1 ....3 ...
Embsay BD23 ....217 ...
Hellifield BD23 ....154 ...
York YO31 ....233 ...
Park Crest HG5 ....221 ...
Park Dale WF10 ....200 ...
Park Dr Campsall DN6 .206 ...
Glusburn BD20 ....187 ...
 Harrogate HG2 ....219 ...
Harrogate HG2 ....222 ...
Knaresborough HG5 ..221 ...
 Masham HG4 ....86 ...
Park Edge HG2 ....222 ...
Park End Prim Sch TS3 ..7 ...
Park Gate
Knaresborough HG5 ..221 ...
Strensall YO32 ....167 ...
Park Gr
Knaresborough HG5 ..221 ...
Norton YO17 ....215 ...
Selby YO8 ....232 ...
Swillington LS26 ....200 ...
York YO31 ....233 ...
Park Grove Sch YO31 ..233 ...
Park Hill BD23 ....17 ...
Park House Gn
Harrogate HG1 ....219 ...
图 Spofforth HG3 ....179 ...
Park House La LA2 ...128 ...
Park La Balne DN14 ..207 ...
Barlow YO8 ....204 ...
Bishop Wilton YO42 ..169 ...
Borrowby YO7 ....65 ...
Buckden BD23 ....81 ...
Burn YO8 ....203 ...
Carleton BD23 ....173 ...
Cowling BD22 ....186 ...
Darlington DL1 ....3 ...
 Easington TS13 ....11 ...
Glusburn BD20 ....187 ...
Great Preston WF10 ..200 ...
Guisborough TS14 ......8 ...
Kippax LS25 ....200 ...
Kirkbymoorside YO62 .70 ...
Ledsham LS25 ....200 ...
Luttons YO17 ....150 ...
Micklefield LS25 ....194 ...
 Middleham DL8 ....60 ...
North Stainley with Sleningford
HG4 ....11 ...
Spofforth with Stockeld
HG3 ....179 ...
Tatham LA2 ....128 ...
West Tanfield HG4 ....87 ...
Wilberfoss YO41 ....185 ...
Womersley DN6 ....206 ...
York YO24 ....227 ...
Park Lands 图 HG3 ....161 ...
Park Lane CI YO42 ...170 ...
Park Lane Inf Sch TS14 ..8 ...
Park Mount 图 HG2 ...219 ...
Park Nook Rd YO8 ....199 ...
Park Par
Harrogate HG1 ....219 ...
Knaresborough HG5 ..221 ...
Park PI Darlington DL1 ..3 ...
Harrogate HG1 ....219 ...
 Knaresborough HG5 .221 ...
Park Rd Airmyn DN14 .205 ...
Asenby YO7 ....115 ...
Barlow YO8 ....204 ...
Castleford WF10 ....200 ...
Cowling BD22 ....187 ...
Glusburn BD20 ....187 ...

k Rd *continued*
Harrogate HG2 ... 219 D1
rrogate HG2 ... 222 D8
rton-on-Derwent
17 ... 215 C3
ntefract WF8 ... 201 A1
Scarborough YO12 ... 212 E4
offorth HG3 ... 179 E5
k Rise 17 YO14 ... 126 F8
k Row
aresborough HG5 ... 221 B5
by YO8 ... 232 D5
k Side BB18 ... 186 A8
k Sq
Knaresborough HG5 ... 221 B6
Ripon HG4 ... 214 C4
k St 16 Glusburn BD20 ... 187 E8
Harrogate HG1 ... 219 C5
vingham YO62 ... 119 E6
sham HG4 ... 86 C3
kering YO18 ... 95 F7
on HG4 ... 214 B5
arborough YO12 ... 212 D4
by YO8 ... 232 D5
Skipton BD23 ... 216 F4
k YO24 ... 233 A1
k Terr YO21 ... 208 D6
k The 14 YO13 ... 75 D5
k View
stleford WF10 ... 201 B3
aisdale YO21 ... 30 D4
rrogate HG1 ... 219 E2
Leyburn DL8 ... 60 D5
ddleton Tyas DL10 ... 21 C4
pton BD23 ... 216 D4
illington LS26 ... 194 A1
k View Dr BD23 ... 134 B3
k Way
k Hammerton YO26 ... 164 C2
aresborough HG5 ... 221 B8
k Wood BD23 ... 216 D5
k Wood Cl BD23 ... 216 E5
k Wood Cres BD23 ... 216 D5
k Wood Way BD23 ... 216 D5
k Wynd DL10 ... 209 C6
ker Ave YO26 ... 227 B2
ker Dr 21 DL8 ... 63 A2
ker La YO26 ... 164 C3
ker St 15 BD20 ... 187 E8
kers Mount 20 YO62 ... 70 B1
kfield Ave TS5 ... 6 E8
kfield Cl YO12 ... 212 D4
kfield Gdns YO12 ... 212 D4
kfield La WF7 ... 200 E1
kgate DL1 ... 3 D5
kgate La DL10 ... 41 B7
kin Ave YO8 ... 232 E4
kinson App LS25 ... 194 C4
kinson's La LS21 ... 159 E2
kinson's Yd 5 DL10 ... 209 C6
kland Dr
rlington DL3 ... 3 A6
dcaster LS24 ... 189 F6
kland Way YO32 ... 225 D8
klands
stleford WF10 ... 200 F4
ley LS29 ... 218 D4
klands The
Ingleby Arncliffe DL6 ... 45 A7
ruton DL7 ... 63 D7
kshill Ct DL10 ... 20 F7
kside DL1 ... 3 C4
kside Cl YO24 ... 227 E3
kside Prim Sch
14 ... 205 F3
kway The YO12 ... 212 B7
kways YO8 ... 232 B3
kwood Dr 6 TS18 ... 5 E8
liament Ave YO17 ... 215 E4
liament St
rrogate HG1 ... 219 C3
rton YO17 ... 215 E3
rk YO1 ... 233 B2
liament Terr 2 HG1 ... 219 D2
lington Ct LS15 ... 194 C8
lington Dr LS25 ... 194 E8
lington La LS25 ... 194 E7
lington Mdw LS15 ... 194 C7
lington Villas LS25 ... 194 E8
rock St 7 BB18 ... 171 D1
son Back La DL6 ... 25 B2
sonage Rd LS26 ... 200 C6
sonage The 11 HG5 ... 221 A6
sons Cl 10 DN14 ... 205 E4
son's Cl YO21 ... 208 A7
sons Close La
24 ... 131 A2
son's La
Addingham LS29 ... 174 E4
tton Rudby DL6 ... 25 A2
sons La YO26 ... 165 E1
son's Wlk 11 DN14 ... 205 E4
sley Rd HG4 ... 113 D3
sture Ave LS25 ... 196 A4
sture Cl
rnoldswick BB18 ... 171 E2
Sherburn in Elmet
25 ... 196 A4
elton YO30 ... 224 B5
ipton BD23 ... 217 B5
Strensall YO32 ... 167 B6
stow YO8 ... 197 D6
sture Cres
ey YO14 ... 101 A4
Knaresborough HG5 ... 221 B7
sture Ct LS25 ... 195 F4
sture Dr Bedale DL8 ... 63 A2
stleford WF10 ... 200 D3

Pasture Farm Cl YO10 ... 231 D6
Pasture Field La YO22 ... 32 C5
Pasture Fold 4 LS29 ... 176 C1
Pasture Hill YO17 ... 169 E8
Pasture La
Ellerton YO42 ... 193 C1
Helperby YO61 ... 142 B8
Heworth YO31 ... 229 B8
Hovingham YO62 ... 119 E6
Kearby with Netherby
LS22 ... 179 C1
Malton YO17 ... 215 C5
Marton-le-Moor HG4 ... 140 D8
2 Seamer YO12 ... 99 D6
Pasture Rd
Embsay with Eastby
BD23 ... 217 C8
Lockton YO18 ... 73 A5
Pasture View LS25 ... 195 F4
Pasture Way
Castleford WF10 ... 200 D3
Sherburn in Elmet LS25 ... 195 F4
Wistow YO8 ... 197 D6
Pastures The
Carlton DN14 ... 204 C3
Coulby Newham TS8 ... 7 B5
16 Eastfield YO11 ... 100 B6
Sherburn YO17 ... 124 D7
4 York YO24 ... 230 E8
Pateley Moor Cres DL2 ... 3 E3
Pately Pl 1 YO26 ... 227 D4
Paterson Cres DL6 ... 210 E4
Patience La HG4 ... 114 D3
Patrick Pool YO1 ... 233 B2
Patterdale Dr YO30 ... 224 E1
Patterham La DL8 ... 59 D4
Paul's Row 5 YO17 ... 215 C4
Pavement YO1 ... 233 B2
Paver La YO1 ... 233 C2
Pavilion Sq 7 HG2 ... 219 C1
Peacock's Cl DL7 ... 63 E7
Peacocks Cl TS9 ... 26 C8
Peak Scar Rd YO62 ... 67 C3
Pear Tree Acre LS23 ... 180 F1
Pear Tree Ave
Long Drax YO8 ... 204 F7
8 Poppleton YO26 ... 165 F1
Pear Tree Cl
Skeeby DL10 ... 20 F1
York YO32 ... 225 F4
Pear Tree Wlk YO17 ... 215 B4
Pearl Rd TS17 ... 6 B8
Pearl St HG1 ... 220 C4
Pearson Garth YO13 ... 99 A7
Pearson St WF6 ... 200 A3
Peart La BD23 ... 154 C8
Peartree Ct YO1 ... 233 C3
Pease Ct
Guisborough TS14 ... 8 D5
4 Lingdale TS12 ... 9 F7
Pease St Darlington DL1 ... 3 E5
6 Lingdale TS12 ... 9 F7
Peasey Hills Rd YO17 ... 215 C5
Peasholm Ave YO12 ... 212 F7
Peasholm Cres YO12 ... 212 F7
Peasholm Dr YO12 ... 212 E7
Peasholm Gap YO12 ... 212 F8
Peasholm Gdns YO12 ... 212 F7
Peasholm Rd YO12 ... 212 F8
Peasholme Bridge
YO12 ... 212 E7
Peasholme Gn YO1 ... 233 C2
Peasland La YO7 ... 66 B5
Peaslands La YO18 ... 96 D5
Peat La HG3 ... 137 B3
Peatmoor La DL8 ... 58 E5
Peckett's Holt HG1 ... 219 D7
Peckett's Way HG1 ... 219 D7
Peckfield HG4 ... 214 C2
Peckfield Cl HG3 ... 160 F5
Peckitt St YO1 ... 233 B1
Peel Cl YO10 ... 229 A1
Peel Gn BD23 ... 154 B2
Peel Pl 11 LS29 ... 176 C1
Peel St Thornaby TS17 ... 6 B8
York YO1 ... 233 C1
Pefham La YO17 ... 170 F4
Pegman Cl TS14 ... 8 F7
Peirse Cl DL8 ... 63 A2
Pelham Pl 15 YO32 ... 167 A7
Pellentine Rd HG3 ... 223 F4
Pemberton Cres TS4 ... 7 A8
Pemberton Rd WF10 ... 201 A4
Pembroke St
10 Skipton BD23 ... 216 F3
York YO30 ... 228 B7
Pembroke Way YO21 ... 208 C5
Pembury Mews DL10 ... 41 B6
Penders La TS15 ... 5 E1
Penderyn Cres TS17 ... 5 F4
Pendle St 4 BD23 ... 216 D3
Pendleton Rd DL1 ... 3 D7
Pendragon Castle*
CA17 ... 14 A1
Penhill Ct DL7 ... 210 C1
Penhowe La YO17 ... 147 D4
Penistone Rd TS3 ... 7 C8
Penley's Grove St
YO31 ... 233 C4
Penn La DL8 ... 56 D4
Penn Rd DL10 ... 209 B7
Pennine Way BD20 ... 172 E2
Pennine Cl YO32 ... 225 F4
Pennine View
Burneston DL8 ... 87 E8
Northallerton DL7 ... 210 B2
Pennine Way
11 Barnoldswick BB18 ... 171 D1

Pennine Way *continued*
Ingleby TS17 ... 6 A4
Penniston La YO13 ... 97 C4
Penny Gn BD24 ... 131 D1
Penny La
1 Easingwold YO61 ... 117 D1
Ripon HG4 ... 214 C7
Penny Pot Gdns 4 HG3 ... 161 B2
Penny Pot La
Felliscliffe HG3 ... 160 D2
Killinghall HG3 ... 161 A2
Penny Royal Cl 7 HG3 ... 161 B3
Pennycarr La YO61 ... 143 D7
Pennyman Prim Sch
TS3 ... 7 D8
Pennypot La TS18 ... 5 E7
Pennywort Gr 16 HG3 ... 161 B3
Penrith Cres WF10 ... 201 B5
Penrith Rd TS3 ... 7 B8
Pentland Dr YO32 ... 225 E3
Penton Rd 20 YO11 ... 100 B6
Penyghent Ave YO31 ... 229 A5
Pen-y-Ghent Way 5
BB18 ... 171 D1
Penyghent Way TS17 ... 6 A3
Peppercorn Cl 6 YO26 ... 227 E4
Peppergarth The DL7 ... 210 B3
Peppermint Dr 15 DL9 ... 41 A5
Peppermint Way YO8 ... 232 A5
Per Ardua Way 6 DL10 ... 41 E4
Percy Cross Rigg YO21 ... 9 A1
Percy Dr 4 DN14 ... 205 E4
Percy Rd Darlington DL3 ... 3 C7
14 Hunmanby YO14 ... 127 A8
Percy St YO31 ... 233 B3
Percy's La YO1 ... 233 C2
Perie Ave HG4 ... 113 D3
Perry Ave TS17 ... 6 B5
Peter Hill Dr YO30 ... 228 A8
Peter La
Burton Leonard HG3 ... 140 A2
York YO1 ... 233 B2
Petercroft Cl 5 YO19 ... 184 F7
Petercroft La YO19 ... 184 F7
Peterhouse Cl DL1 ... 3 D7
Petersbottom La LA2 ... 129 B4
Petersway YO30 ... 233 A4
Petre Ave YO8 ... 232 E3
Petty Whin Cl 25 HG3 ... 161 B3
Petyt Gr BD23 ... 217 A4
Pheasant Dr 5 YO24 ... 230 B8
Philadelphia Terr 2
YO23 ... 228 B2
Philip La YO8 ... 196 E2
Philippa's Dr HG2 ... 222 D8
Philpin La LA6 ... 104 C8
Phlashetts La DL8 ... 87 A4
Phoenix Pk TS8 ... 6 F6
Piave Rd DL9 ... 40 D4
Piccadilly YO1 ... 233 C2
Pick Haven Garth
DN14 ... 202 F3
Pickard Cl BB18 ... 171 E2
Pickard La BD20 ... 174 C1
Pickering Castle*
YO18 ... 95 F7
Pickering Cty Inf Sch
YO18 ... 96 A7
Pickering Cty Jun Sch
YO18 ... 95 F7
Pickering Rd
East Ayton/West Ayton
YO13 ... 99 A7
Thornaby TS17 ... 6 B8
Thornton-le-Dale YO18 ... 96 C6
Pickeringmoor La YO7 ... 64 C2
Pickhill C of E Prim Sch
YO7 ... 88 C6
Picking Croft La HG3 ... 161 B5
Pickrowfield La LS25 ... 196 C6
Pickwick Cl YO17 ... 215 C5
Piece Croft 2 BD23 ... 134 D2
Piece Fields 4 BD23 ... 134 D2
Pier Rd YO21 ... 208 D7
Piercy End YO62 ... 70 B1
Pierremont Rd DL3 ... 3 B6
Piggy La DL2 ... 1 C7
Pighill Nook Rd LS25 ... 202 C7
Pike Hills Mount
YO23 ... 230 A3
Pike La BD24 ... 131 E4
Pike Rd 8 YO18 ... 95 F6
Pikepurse La DL10 ... 209 D8
Pilgrim St YO31 ... 233 B4
Pill White La LS21 ... 177 C3
Pilmoor Cl DL10 ... 209 E8
Pilmoor Dr DL10 ... 209 E8
Pindar Leisure Ctr
YO11 ... 100 A6
Pindar Rd YO11 ... 100 A6
Pindar Sch YO11 ... 100 A6
Pinders Cres WF11 ... 201 E3
Pinders Gn LS26 ... 200 B4
Pinders Green Ct
LS26 ... 200 B5
Pinders Green Dr
LS26 ... 200 B5
Pinders Green Fold
LS26 ... 200 B5
Pine Cl
Castleford WF10 ... 200 F3
Skipton BD23 ... 216 E4
Pine Croft HG4 ... 112 F2
Pine Gr 1 DL6 ... 210 E3
Pine Hill TS8 ... 7 B5
Pine Rd Guisborough TS14 ... 8 E7
Middlesbrough TS7 ... 7 D8
Pine St HG1 ... 219 E5

Pine Tree Ave YO17 ... 122 F5
Pine Tree Cl YO8 ... 197 B2
Pine Tree La 1 LS25 ... 202 A7
Pinelands 4 YO32 ... 225 D7
Pinelands Way YO10 ... 229 C3
Pines Gdns 23 LS29 ... 175 C2
Pines The LS17 ... 178 B2
Pinetree Gr DL2 ... 4 C4
Pinewood Ave YO14 ... 101 B4
Pinewood Cl
5 Easington TS13 ... 11 A8
2 Ilkley LS29 ... 218 A3
5 Whitby YO21 ... 208 C6
Pinewood Dr
Camblesforth YO8 ... 204 D4
Scarborough YO12 ... 212 D5
Pinewood Gate HG2 ... 222 A7
Pinewood Gr
13 Bedale DL8 ... 63 A2
6 York YO31 ... 225 E2
Pinewood Hill 4 YO10 ... 229 C3
Pinewood Rd TS7 ... 7 C6
Pinewood Wlk 7 TS9 ... 26 C8
Pinfold Ave LS25 ... 195 F4
Pinfold Cl
Bilton-in-Ainsty with Bickerton
LS22 ... 181 B5
5 Riccall YO19 ... 192 A1
3 Sherburn in Elmet LS25 ... 195 F4
Pinfold Ct
Kirkby Malzeard HG4 ... 112 D5
4 Sherburn in Elmet LS25 ... 195 F4
4 York YO30 ... 228 A7
Pinfold Dr DL6 ... 210 E5
Pinfold Garth
Malton YO17 ... 215 A4
6 Sherburn in Elmet LS25 ... 195 F4
1 Sherburn in Elmet
LS25 ... 196 A4
Pinfold Gn HG5 ... 140 E1
Pinfold Hill YO8 ... 197 D6
Pinfold La
Asselby DN14 ... 205 F6
Kirk Smeaton WF8 ... 206 B3
Mickletown LS26 ... 200 C5
Moss DN6 ... 207 D1
Norton DN6 ... 206 E2
Norwood HG3 ... 177 A8
Pollington DN14 ... 207 F6
Pinfold Rise LS25 ... 194 F8
Pinfold The 5 BD23 ... 216 D4
Pinfold View DN14 ... 207 F6
Pinfold Way
5 Sherburn in Elmet LS25 ... 195 F4
2 Sherburn in Elmet
LS25 ... 196 A4
Pinhaw Rd BD23 ... 217 A2
Pinnacle View BD22 ... 187 A5
Pioneer Way WF10 ... 200 C2
Piper Hill 1 WF11 ... 201 D6
Piper La Cowling BD22 ... 187 B5
Thirsk YO7 ... 211 C3
Piper Rd DL6 ... 45 F6
Pipers Acre 4 YO18 ... 95 F7
Pipers La YO26 ... 141 F1
Pippin Rd YO17 ... 215 B4
Pippin's App 17 WF6 ... 200 A2
Pit Ings La YO7 ... 115 F6
Pit La Micklefield LS25 ... 195 A4
Mickletown LS26 ... 200 B6
Pitman Rd YO17 ... 215 C5
Place Hill DL11 ... 38 B6
Plane Tree Way YO14 ... 101 A4
Planetree La
Kirkby Fleetham with Fencote
DL7 ... 42 A1
Thornville YO26 ... 164 A1
Plantation Ave HG3 ... 222 A8
Plantation Cl HG2 ... 222 A8
Plantation Dr
Barlby with Osgodby
YO8 ... 198 B5
York YO26 ... 227 C6
Plantation Gr YO26 ... 227 C6
Plantation Rd HG2 ... 222 A8
Plantation Terr HG2 ... 222 A8
Plantation The BD23 ... 152 E3
Plantation Way 23 YO32 ... 166 E5
Pleasance The 6 LS26 ... 194 A1
Pleasant Mount YO22 ... 208 F3
Pleasant View 5 BB18 ... 172 B1
Plews Way DL7 ... 63 C5
Plompton Cl HG2 ... 220 D1
Plompton Dr HG2 ... 220 D2
Plompton Gr 3 HG2 ... 220 D2
Plompton Rd HG3 ... 223 F5
Plompton Way 1 HG2 ... 220 D2
Plompton Wlk 2 HG2 ... 220 D2
Plough Garth The
DN14 ... 202 F3
Ploughlands 1 YO32 ... 225 C7
Ploughman's Cl YO23 ... 230 C3
Ploughmans Ct 14 YO11 ... 100 B7
Ploughmans' La YO32 ... 225 C7
Plover Gdns 1 YO12 ... 99 F6
Plum St YO17 ... 215 D3
Plumer Ave YO31 ... 229 A5
Plumer Rd DL9 ... 209 B1
Plumpton La HG4 ... 139 D8
Plumpton Pk HG2 ... 220 D3
Plumpton Rocks*
HG5 ... 179 D8
Pluntrain Dale La YO18 ... 96 B7
Pocklington La YO42 ... 169 F2
Pockthorpe La YO25 ... 151 F2
Pocock Pl DL10 ... 41 E4
Polam Hall Sch DL1 ... 3 C4
Polam La DL1 ... 3 C4

Pole Rd BD22 ... 187 F4
Pollard Cl YO32 ... 225 E3
Pollard Gdns YO12 ... 212 C4
Pollington Balne C of E Sch
DN14 ... 207 F6
Polperro Cl 21 WF6 ... 200 A2
Pond Farm Cl TS13 ... 11 F7
Pond Field Cl DL3 ... 3 A4
Pond St 3 YO8 ... 232 D6
Pondfields Dr LS25 ... 194 D1
Pontefract C of E Sch
WF8 ... 201 B1
Pontefract Castle*
WF8 ... 201 C1
Pontefract Monkhill Sta
WF8 ... 201 B1
Pontefract Mus*
WF8 ... 201 B1
Pontefract New Coll
WF8 ... 201 A1
Pontefract Park Race
Course* WF8 ... 200 F2
Pontefract Rd
Castleford WF10 ... 200 F4
Knottingley WF11 ... 201 D2
Normanton South WF6 ... 200 B2
Pool Ct 20 YO18 ... 95 F6
Pool La YO26 ... 164 E4
Poole La LS25 ... 201 F6
Pope St WF6 ... 200 B3
Poplar Ave
Castleford WF10 ... 201 B4
6 Hutton Rudby TS15 ... 25 D5
4 Kirkbymoorside YO62 ... 70 B1
3 Wetherby LS22 ... 180 C4
Poplar Cres
Harrogate HG1 ... 219 F6
Northallerton DL7 ... 210 C2
Poplar Dr WF6 ... 200 A3
Poplar Gdns YO8 ... 204 F5
Poplar Gn HG5 ... 162 A6
Poplar Gr
Harrogate HG1 ... 219 F6
York YO32 ... 225 E3
Poplar Pl TS14 ... 8 E7
Poplar Row 6 YO21 ... 208 D7
Poplar St YO26 ... 227 E5
Poplar Way HG1 ... 219 F6
Poplars La YO17 ... 123 A7
Poplars The
11 Brayton YO8 ... 197 D1
2 Glusburn BD20 ... 187 E6
Knottingley WF11 ... 202 A1
Poppleton Hall Gdn
YO26 ... 224 A3
Poppleton Rd YO26 ... 227 E4
Poppleton Road Prim Sch
YO26 ... 227 E5
Poppleton Sta YO26 ... 182 F8
Poppy Cl YO8 ... 232 C2
Poppy Ct 16 DL9 ... 41 A5
Porch Farm Cl YO62 ... 120 B5
Porch The DL10 ... 21 D7
Pornic Ave YO13 ... 75 D5
Porritt La YO12 ... 99 D7
Portal Rd YO26 ... 227 B6
Portholme Cres 7 YO8 ... 232 C5
Portholme Dr YO8 ... 232 C4
Portholme Rd YO8 ... 232 C5
Portisham Pl 12 YO32 ... 167 A7
Portland St YO31 ... 233 B4
Portland Way DL7 ... 63 C5
Portman Rise TS14 ... 8 F5
Post Office Row DN14 ... 205 A1
Postern Cl YO23 ... 233 B1
Postern La YO42 ... 193 D6
Pot Bank HG3 ... 178 A8
Potlands DL7 ... 63 C4
Pott Bank HG4 ... 85 A1
Pott Moor High Rd
HG4 ... 110 F8
Potter Hill 11 YO18 ... 95 F7
Potter La DL7 ... 64 A5
Pottergate
Gilling East YO62 ... 118 F7
14 Helmsley YO62 ... 92 F6
Richmond DL10 ... 209 C7
Potters Dr 4 YO23 ... 230 B3
Potter's Side La YO21 ... 9 D1
Potterton Cl LS15 ... 194 C8
Potterton La
Barwick in Elmet LS15 ... 194 C8
Barwick in Elmet & Scholes
LS15 ... 188 C1
Pottery La
Bishop Monkton HG4 ... 140 A6
Knottingley WF11 ... 201 E3
Littlethorpe HG4 ... 214 E1
York YO31 ... 228 E7
Pottery St WF10 ... 200 D4
Potticar Bank YO62 ... 119 D4
Pounteys Cl 4 DL2 ... 4 C4
Powell St
Harrogate HG1 ... 219 F4
Selby YO8 ... 232 B6
Prail Cl 13 WF8 ... 201 C1
Precentor's Ct YO31 ... 233 B3
Preen Dr TS5 ... 6 D8
Premier Rd TS7 ... 7 D7
Premiere Pk 30 LS29 ... 175 C2
Preston Field Cross Rd
YO13 ... 74 E1
Preston Hall Mus* TS18 ... 5 F6
Preston La
Great Preston WF10 ... 200 C7

Preston La continued
Preston-on-Tees TS18 ......5 E7
Preston Prim Sch TS16 .....5 E6
Preston View G26 ....194 A1
Preston Way TS9 ....26 C8
Prestwick Ct
 Middleton St George DL2 ..4 C4
Rufforth YO26 ....227 B5
Pretoria St WF10 ....200 F4
Price's La YO23 ....233 B1
Priest Bank DL8 ....57 B4
Priest Bank Rd BD20 ...173 F1
Priest Cl YO14 ....126 F8
Priest Gill Bank DL11 ...19 F5
Priest La
Dunnington YO19 ....184 F5
Ripon HG4 ....214 D4
Priestcart La YO26 ....163 D8
Primrose Ave
Hunmanby Sands YO14 ....101 B1
Swillington LS26 ....194 A1
Primrose Cl
Guisborough TS14 ....8 E6
 Killinghall HG3 ....161 B3
Ripon HG4 ....214 C6
Primrose Ct YO13 ....41 A5
Primrose Dene WF11 ..201 E4
Primrose Dr
Filey YO14 ....101 B1
Ripon HG4 ....214 C6
Primrose Gr YO8 ....232 A6
Primrose Hill
 Knottingley WF11 ......202 A3
 Skipton BD23 ....216 E2
Primrose Hill Cl LS26 ..194 A1
Primrose Hill Dr
Great & Little Preston
 LS26 ....200 A8
 Swillington LS26 ....194 A1
Primrose Hill Garth
 LS26 ....200 A8
Primrose Hill Gdns
 LS26 ....194 A1
Primrose Hill Gn LS26 .200 A8
Primrose Hill Gr
 LS26 ....194 A1
Primrose La LS23 ....188 E8
Primrose Vale WF11 ..202 A2
Primrose Valley Rd
YO14 ....101 B1
Prince Henry Rd LS21 ..177 A1
Prince Henrys Gram Sch
LS21 ....177 A1
Prince of Wales Terr
YO11 ....213 A4
Prince Rupert Dr
YO26 ....181 C7
Princes St WF10 ....200 C8
Princes Cres BD23 ....217 B4
Prince Dr BD23 ....217 A4
Princes Sq
 Harrogate HG1 ....219 D2
Thornaby TS17 ....6 B6
Princes Villa Rd HG1 ..219 E2
Princess Ave HG5 .....221 C6
Princess Ct HG4 ....214 C6
Princess Ct WF6 ....200 B1
Princess Dr HG5 ....221 C5
Princess Gr HG5 .....221 C5
Princess La YO11 ......213 B6
Princess Mead HG5 ...163 A3
Princess Mount HG5 .221 C5
Princess Pl YO21 .....208 D6
Princess Rd
Darlington DL3 ....3 D8
Ilkley LS29 ....218 A3
Malton YO17 ....215 C4
Ripon HG4 ....214 C6
Strensall YO32 ....167 B7
Princess Royal La
YO11 ....212 F3
Princess Royal Pk
YO11 ....213 A3
Princess Royal Rd
HG4 ....214 C3
Princess Royal Terr
YO11 ....213 A3
Princess Royal Way
HG3 ....219 A4
Princess Sq YO11 ....213 B6
Princess St
Castleford WF10 ....200 F5
Normanton South WF6 ....200 A1
Scarborough YO11 ....213 B6
Prior Ave DL10 ....209 B7
Prior Pursgrove Coll
TS6 ....7 F8
Prior Wath Rd YO13 ....54 A5
Priorpot Way YO17 ....215 F4
Prior's La BD23 ....174 C8
Prior's Wlk YO26 ......227 D6
Priorwood Gdns TS17 ...6 A4
Priory Cl
Guisborough TS14 ....8 F7
Northallerton DL6 ....210 E5
Wilberfoss YO41 ....185 F6
Priory La DN14 ....204 C1
Priory Park Cl LS25 ..202 A8
Priory Park Gr LS25 ..202 B8
Priory Pk YO21 ....31 C4
Priory Pl YO11 ....100 B7
Priory Rd DN6 ....206 E2
Priory St YO1 ....233 A1
Priory View BD23 ....217 E8

Priory Way
 Ingleby Arncliffe DL6 ....45 A7
 Snaith DN14 ....204 B1
Priory Wood Way
YO31 ....225 F2
Prissick Sports Ctr TS4 ..7 B8
Pritchett Rd TS3 ....7 C8
Promenade La HG1 .....219 C3
Prospect Ave
Normanton South WF6 ....200 A2
Sherburn in Elmet LS25 ...195 F4
Prospect Bank LS23 ...188 E8
Prospect Cl
Camblesforth YO8 ....204 D5
Harrogate HG2 ....220 C3
Pollington DN14 ....207 F6
Prospect Cres
 Harrogate HG1 ....219 D2
Scarborough YO12 ....212 D6
Prospect Ct LS24 ....189 E6
Prospect Dr LS24 ....189 E6
Prospect Field
 Fylingdales YO22 ....33 D4
Hawsker-cum-Stainsacre
 ....33 A6
Prospect Hill YO21 ....208 C5
Prospect Mount Rd
YO12 ....212 D6
Prospect Pk YO12 .....212 D6
Prospect Pl
Harrogate HG1 ....219 D2
Northallerton DL6 ....210 F4
 Scarborough YO11 .....213 A6
Skipton BD23 ....216 F4
Thornton-le-Dale YO18 .....96 D6
Wistow YO8 ....197 D6
Prospect Rd
Harrogate HG2 ....220 C3
 Scarborough YO12 .....212 F6
Prospect St BD20 ....187 E7
Prospect Terr
Fulford YO10 ....231 D6
 Lingdale TS12 ....9 F7
Micklefield LS25 ....195 A3
York YO1 ....233 B1
Prospect View DL6 ....210 E4
Prospect Way
 Leeming DL7 ....63 D4
Selby YO8 ....232 D4
Providence Gn WF8 ..201 C2
Providence Pl
 Filey YO14 ....101 B3
Micklefield LS25 ....200 D6
 Scarborough YO11 .....213 A6
Skipton BD23 ....217 A4
Providence Terr HG1 ..219 D4
Pry Hills La
Hartoft YO18 ....71 A8
Rosedale East Side YO18 ..49 F2
Pudding Hill Rd DL11 ....1 B6
Pudding La YO13 ....97 F5
Pudding Pie Hill*
 YO7 ....211 D1
Pulleyn Cl YO32 ......167 C8
Pulleyn Dr YO24 ....227 F1
Pump Hill HG5 ....221 A6
Pump La
Kirklevington TS15 ....24 F8
 Malton YO17 ....215 C4
Purey Court Nuffield Hospl
The YO31 ....233 B3
Pursglove Prior Coll
TS14 ....8 F7
Pye Busk Cl LA2 ....129 B8
Pye La HG3 ....160 F8

Q

Quaker Cl
 Reeth, Fremington &
Healaugh DL11 ....38 B6
Scarborough YO12 ....212 C5
Quaker Gn YO24 .....230 C7
Quaker La DL6 ....210 D5
Quaker's La DL6 ....44 D7
Quakers La DL10 ......209 B7
Quant Mews YO10 ....229 B3
Quarry Ave WF11 ....202 A2
Quarry Banks YO17 ....210 A5
Quarry Dr TS8 ....6 E5
Quarry Gate YO13 ....74 C1
Quarry Hill YO17 ....120 F4
Quarry Hill La LS22 ....180 B3
Quarry La
Harrogate HG1 ....219 C6
Osmotherley DL6 ....45 C5
Pateley Bridge HG3 ....137 C4
Quarry Moor La HG4 .....214 C3
Quarry Mount YO12 ....212 B3
Quarry Rd Norton DN6 .206 F2
Richmond DL10 ....209 B7
Ripon HG4 ....214 B2
Quay St YO11 ....211 D5
Quay The YO8 ....232 D6
Queen Anne's Ct DL8 ..63 A2
Queen Anne's Dr DL8 ..63 A2
Queen Anne's Rd
YO30 ....225 F3
Queen Elizabeth Dr
YO13 ....75 D5
**Queen Elizabeth Sixth Form
 Coll** DL3 ....3 C5
Queen Ethelburgas Coll
YO26 ....164 C6
Queen Ethelburga's Dr
HG3 ....161 B2

Queen Ethelburga's Pa
HG3 ....161 B2
Queen Margarets Ave
WF11 ....201 E4
Queen Margarets Cl
WF11 ....201 E4
Queen Margaret's Dr
WF11 ....201 E4
Queen Margaret's Rd
WF11 ....201 E4
Queen Margarets Sch
YO19 ....192 A5
Queen Marys Sch YO7 .115 A7
Queen Par HG1 ....219 E2
Queen St
 Cowling BD22 ....187 B6
Great Preston LS26 ....200 C7
Normanton South WF6 ....200 A1
 Ripon HG4 ....214 C5
Skelton & Brotton TS12 ...213 A6
 Whitby YO21 ....208 C6
Queen Street Jun & Inf Sch
WF6 ....200 A1
Queen Victoria St
YO23 ....228 B1
Queens Ave DL9 ....40 E3
Queen's Cl HG2 ....219 C1
Queen's Dr LS29 .....218 A3
Queens Dr
 Stokesley TS9 ....26 C8
 Whitby YO21 ....208 C6
Queens Drive La LS29 ..218 A3
Queens Garth BD23 ...172 A3
Queen's Gdns
 Ilkley LS29 ....218 A3
Tadcaster LS24 ....189 E6
Queen's Par YO12 .....213 A7
Queen's Park Dr
WF10 ....201 A4
Queen's Rd
Harrogate HG2 ....219 C1
 Ilkley LS29 ....218 A3
Queens Rd
Knaresborough HG5 ....221 C6
Richmond DL10 ....209 C7
Queen's St BD23 .....216 F4
Queen's Staith Rd
YO1 ....233 B2
Queen's Terr
 Filey YO14 ....101 B3
Scarborough YO12 ....213 A7
Queen's Way YO10 ....213 A7
Queensbury Ct WF6 ..200 B1
Queensway WF8 ....201 C1
Queenswood Gr YO24 ..227 D2
Quentin Rd BD18 ......40 A4
Quernmore Dr BB18 ...186 A7

R

Rabbit La YO17 ....215 F8
Raby La DL7 ....22 E3
Raby Pk LS22 ....180 B3
Raby Terr DL3 ....3 C5
Racca Ave WF11 .....202 A2
Racca Gn WF11 ....202 A2
Race La Carlton YO8 ...204 B4
Sessay YO61 ....116 C4
Racecourse Cl DL10 ...209 A8
Racecourse La DL7 ....210 D3
Racecourse Mews
YO17 ....211 A2
Racecourse Rd
East Ayton/West Ayton
YO13 ....99 B8
Irton YO12 ....212 A1
Richmond DL10 ....209 B8
York YO23 ....231 B8
Rachel La DL11 ....208 F8
RAF Leeming CP Sch
DL7 ....63 F3
Rag Robin Turn YO7 ....66 D6
Raghill La YO61 ....142 A8
Raglan St HG1 ....219 D2
Raglan Terr HG1 .....208 D5
Raikes Ave BD23 ....216 F5
Raikes La BD23 ....156 A6
Raikes' La YO22 ....32 E3
Raikes Rd BD23 ....216 F5
Raikes The HG3 ....137 E3
Raikeswood Cres
BD23 ....216 F5
Raikeswood Dr BD23 ...216 F5
Raikeswood Rd BD23 ..216 F5
Railer Bank HG4 ....112 E6
Railway Ave WF8 ......201 B1
Railway Rd
Follifoot HG3 ....223 A4
 Ilkley LS29 ....218 B4
Railway St Leyburn DL8 .60 D5
Norton YO17 ....215 C3
Slingsby YO62 ....120 B5
Railway Terr
Hurworth-on-Tees DL2 ....22 D8
 Normanton South WF6 ..200 A1
Thirsk YO7 ....211 B2
York YO24 ....228 A4
Railway View DL7 .....210 D3
Raincliffe Ave
 Filey YO14 ....101 B3
Scarborough YO12 ....212 C5
Raincliffe Cres YO12 ...212 C5
Raincliffe Cl YO12 .....212 C5
Raincliffe Sch YO12 ...212 B6
Raincliffe St YO8 ....232 C5
Raindale Rd YO18 ....71 F6

Raines Dr BD20 ......173 E3
Raines La BD23 ....134 D3
Raines Lea BD23 ....134 D3
Raines Mdws BD23 ..134 D2
Raines Rd BD24 ....131 C1
Rainford Cl YO12 ......99 D6
Rainhall Cres BB18 ....171 E1
Rainhall Rd BB18 ....171 D1
Rainham Cl TS17 ....6 B4
Rainhill Road Cty Prim Sch
BB18 ....171 D1
Rainsborough Way
YO30 ....228 A8
Rainsburgh La YO25 ...126 A3
Raisdale Rd TS9 ....26 D1
Rake La YO21 ....30 C6
Rakehill Rd LS15 ......194 B8
Raker Cl YO19 ....192 F7
Rakes BD23 ....134 C1
Rakes La BD23 ....171 B5
Raleigh St YO12 ....212 E5
Ralph Butterfield Sch
YO32 ....166 F5
Ralph Garth YO26 .....181 D7
Rampart The YO23 ....190 D4
Ramsay Cl YO31 ....233 C4
Ramsden Cl WF11 .....201 D4
Ramsden St LS25 ......200 C8
Ramsey Ave YO23 .....231 B3
Ramsey St YO12 ......212 E6
Ramshaw Dr BD23 ....217 A1
Ramshill Rd YO11 ......213 A4
Randal La HG3 ....160 D4
Range Rd HG4 ....40 A2
Rankin's Well Rd
BD23 ....217 B4
Rantreefold Rd LA2 ...128 F4
Rape Close La YO62 ...118 E4
Rape La YO62 ....117 B3
Raper La YO61 ....117 B3
Raper View LS25 ......194 F8
Rarber Top La LA6 ....103 D2
Rarey Dr YO17 ....124 E1
Raskelf Rd
 Brafferton YO61 ....115 F1
Easingwold YO61 ....117 B1
Ratcliffe St YO30 .....228 A7
Ratcliffe Ct WF10 .....200 F3
Rathmell La YO26 .....164 C2
Rathmell C of E Prim Sch
BD24 ....153 B7
Rattan Row YO25 .....151 C6
Rattle Row Huddswell DL8 .61 E7
Seamer YO12 ....99 C5
Raven Cl Eastfield YO12 .99 F6
Featherstone WF7 ....200 D1
Raven Gr YO26 ....227 C4
Raven Hall Rd YO13 ...153 F7
Ravens Close Brow
LA2 ....102 C1
Ravenscroft Way
BB18 ....171 E2
Ravensdale Rd BD23 ....3 B4
Ravensthorpe Prep Sch
DL3 ....3 B4
Ravensville YO22 ......187 F7
Ravenswick C of E Prim Sch
DL11 ....200 E4
Ravensworth Castle*
 ....20 A6
Ravine Hill YO14 ......101 B4
Ravine Rd YO14 ....101 B4
Ravine Terr YO14 ...101 B3
Raw Bank DL11 ....37 E8
Raw La Fylingdales YO22 ..33 A4
Newland YO8 ....199 B6
Raw Pasture Bank
YO22 ....33 B5
Raw Pasture La YO22 ...33 C5
Rawcliff Rd YO18 ....72 A5
Rawcliffe Ave YO30 ...227 F8
Rawcliffe Cl YO30 .....222 F2
Rawcliffe Croft YO30 ..224 D2
Rawcliffe Dr YO30 .....222 F2
Rawcliffe in Snaith Prim Sch
DN14 ....205 A2
Rawcliffe Inf Sch
YO30 ....224 E1
Rawcliffe La YO30 .....224 F1
Rawcliffe Rd DN14 ....205 D2
Rawcliffe Way YO30 ...224 E2
Rawdon Ave YO10 ....228 F4
Rawfield La WF11 .....201 D7
Rawlinson Rd DL9 .....209 D2
Rawson St HG1 ....219 E5
Ray Bridge La BD23 ...155 D1
Ray Dike Cl YO32 ......225 C7
Ray La HG4 ....113 A1
Raydale Cl HG5 ......221 D5
Raygill La BD20 ....186 E8
Rayleigh Rd HG2 ......222 E8
Raylton Ave TS7 ....7 B5
Rayner St HG4 ....214 C5
Read Cl YO8 ....204 F5
Read Sch YO8 ....204 F5
Real Aeroplane Mus The*
 ....199 D5
Reas La YO51 ....141 D1
Reasty Hill YO13 ....53 E1
Reasty Rd YO13 ....53 D1
Recreation Rd
 Pickering YO18 ....95 F6
 Selby YO8 ....232 D6
Rectory Cl
Bolton Percy YO23 ....190 D4

Rectory Cl continued
Hesterton YO17 12
Rectory Gdns YO23 22
Rectory La
Guisborough TS14 8
 Hurworth-on-Tees DL2 ...2
Longnewton TS21 ....
Skipton BD23 21
Thornton-le-Dale YO18 9
Red Bank Cl HG4 21
Red Bank Dr HG4 21
Red Bank La HG4 21
Red Barnes Way DL1 ....
Red Brae Bank HG3 ...13
Red Brow YO13 7
Red Gate DL8 5
Red Hall La TS15 19
Red Hills La HG3 14
Red Hall Prim Sch DL1 ..
Red Hill La LS25 1
Red Hills La HG3 14
Red Hills Rd HG4 21
Red House Prep Sch
YO26 16
Red La
Green Hammerton YO26 ..16
 Masham HG4 8
Red Lion St BB18 17
Red Scar Dr YO12 23
Red Scar La
Newby & Scalby YO12 7
Scalby YO12 21
Red Tower* YO1 22
Red Way Brompton DL6 ..4
Danby YO21 2
Farndale East YO62 4
Nether Silton DL6 ....
Redcap La YO42 19
Redcar Rd
Guisborough TS14 ....
Thornaby TS17 ....
Redcliff Cl YO11 10
Redcliffe Ct YO12 21
Redcliffe Gdns YO12 ...21
Redcliffe La YO12 ......
Redcliffe Rd YO12 21
Redcoat W YO24 23
Redeness St YO31 22
Redhill Ave WF10 20
Redhill Cl HG1 2
Redhill Dr WF10 20
Redhill Field La YO23 ..18
Redhill Inf Sch WF10 ...20
Redhill Rd
Castleford WF10 20
Harrogate HG1 2
Redhouse La YO8 20
Redlish Rd HG3 1
Redman Cl YO10 22
Redmayne Sq YO32 16
Redmires Cl YO30 22
Redruth Dr WF6 20
Redshaw Cl HG4 21
Redshaw Gr YO24 23
Redthorn Dr YO31 22
Redwood Dr YO32 ...16
Reebys La LA2 12
Reedshaw La BD22 1
Reeth Rd
Middlesbrough TS5 ....
Richmond DL10 20
 Stockton-on-Tees TS18 ..
Reeval Cl BB18 17
Reeves The YO24 22
Regency Ave TS6 ....
Regency Ct
 Ilkley LS29 21
Northallerton DL6 ....
Regency Mews YO24 .23
Regency Pk TS17 ....
Regent Ave
Harrogate HG1 2
Skipton BD23 2
Regent Cres BD23 2
Regent Dr BD23 2
Regent Gr HG1 2
Regent Mount HG1 ...2
Regent Par HG1 2
Regent Pl HG1 2
Regent Rd Ilkley LS29 ...2
Skipton BD23 2
Regent St
Castleford WF10 20
Harrogate HG1 2
Normanton WF6 20
 Scarborough YO12 21
York YO10 22
Regent Terr HG1 2
York YO10 2
Regents Ct YO26 22
Reginald Gr YO23 2
Reid Street Prim Sch
DL3 ....
Reid Terr TS14 ....
Reighton Ave YO30 2
Reighton Dr YO30 2
Rein Ct LS25 19
Reins HG5 16
Reivaulx Dr TS5 ....
Renfield Gr WF6 20
Renshaw Gdns YO26 .22
Renton Cl HG4 1
Reservoir La YO11 ...10
Residence La HG4 ......
Resolution Way YO21 ...
Retreat Hospl The
YO10 2
Reygate Gr YO23 2
Reynard Crag La HG3 ..16
Reynolds St YO14 10

e's Hill La LS23 . . . .188 F6
les La LS23 . . . . . . .188 D7
les St W10 . . . . . . .200 D4
dings Gdns LS29 . . .218 D4
oor La YO17 . . . . . .215 C6
e Dr DL1 . . . . .3 C3
ehead Sta LA6 . . . . .78 E1
ehead Viaduct* 78 D2

on Rd
e Ribston LS22 . . . .180 A7
orth with Stockeld
. . . . .179 F6
one Gr YO31 . . . . . .229 B6
al Dr
imsley YO62 . . . . . . .92 F6
ons Ambo YO17 . . . .121 C1
al Moor La YO62 . . . .93 E4
all CP Sch YO19 . . . .191 F1
all La YO19 . . . . . . .191 D1
Gate YO13 . . . . .74 D8
e YO13 . . . . .74 D8
La Aldwark YO61 . . .142 C2
on YO60 . . . . .145 F2
ard St YO8 . . . . . . .232 B5

Ripley Cl
Kirkbymoorside YO62 . .70 B1
Normanton South WF6 . .200 B1

Ripley Dr
Harrogate HG1 . . . . .219 C6
Normanton South WF6 . .200 B2

Ripley Endowed Prim Sch
HG3 . . . . .161 C7

Ripley Gr ⑧ YO32 . . .166 E5

Ripley Rd
Knaresborough HG5 . .220 E8
Nidd HG3 . . . . .161 E6
Scotton HG5 . . . . . . .162 A5

Ripley Way HG1 . . . . .219 C6
Ripley's Rd YO13 . . . . .54 B1

Ripon & District Hospl
HG4 . . . . .214 B5

Ripon By-Pass HG4 . .214 C2
Ripon Cath HG4 . . . . .214 C5

Ripon Cathedral Choir
HG4 . . . . .214 A3

Ripon Coll HG4 . . . . . .214 A5
Ripon Dr DL1 . . . . .3 D4
Ripon FC HG4 . . . . . .214 B5
Ripon Greystone CP Sch
HG4 . . . . .214 C2

Ripon Horn The* 214 C5
Ripon Leisure Ctr
HG4 . . . . .214 B5

Ripon Race Course*
. . . . .214 D2

Ripon Rd
Harrogate HG3 . . . . .219 A7
Middlesbrough TS7 . . . . .7 E6
Ripley HG3 . . . . .161 D8
South Stainley with Cayton
HG3 . . . . .139 E2

Ripon Rugby Club
HG4 . . . . .214 B5

Ripon Swimming Baths
HG4 . . . . .214 B5

Ripon Way
Carlton Miniott YO7 . . .89 C4
Harrogate HG1 . . . . .219 C5

Rise Carr Prim Sch DL3 . . .3 C7
Rise Richmond DL7 . . .210 C3

Rise The
Huttons Ambo YO60 . .147 C6
Knottingley WF11 . . . .201 E4
Leavening YO17 . . . . .147 E1
Thornton Dale YO18 . . .96 C5

Riseber DL8 . . . . .60 C5
Risedale Rd DL9 . . . .209 B1
Risedale Sch DL9 . . . .209 F1
Risewood YO41 . . . . .168 B2
Rishworth Gr YO30 . . .224 F2
Rivadale View LS29 . .218 B5

Rivelin Way
⑯ Filey YO14 . . . . . .101 A3
York YO30 . . . . .224 F2

Rivendell BD23 . . . . .134 B3
River Cl ② YO8 . . . . .198 B5

River La
Brompton-on-Swale DL10 . .41 B6
Kilburn High & York HG . . .91 B2
West Haddlesey YO8 . .203 A5

River Pl YO61 . . . . . .155 D1
River Rd YO61 . . . . . . .91 C2
River St ① Selby YO8 . .232 D6
Trawden BB8 . . . . . .186 B2
York YO1 . . . . .233 B1

River View
① Barlby YO8 . . . . . .198 B5
Boston Spa LS23 . . . .188 F8
River View Rd HG4 . . .214 C7
Riverdale DN14 . . . . .202 D4
Rivergarth DL1 . . . . . . .3 F7
Riversdale
① Haxby YO32 . . . . .166 F5
⑥ Settle BD24 . . . . .131 D2
Riverside TS9 . . . . . . .26 B7
Riverside Ave ⑦ YO26 .165 F1
Riverside Cl
① Elvington YO41 . . .185 C2
Farnley LS21 . . . . . . .177 A1
Riverside CP Sch
LS24 . . . . .189 E6
Riverside Cres
⑤ Otley LS21 . . . . . .177 A1
York YO12 . . . . .212 F5

Rievaulx Terr* YO62 . . .92 B7
Rievaulx Way TS14 . . . . .8 F6
Riffa La LS21 . . . . . . .177 E2
Rigg Bank HG4 . . . . . . .85 E3
Rigg The TS15 . . . . .5 E2
Rigg Way YO22 . . . . . . .32 F7
Riggs Rd YO17 . . . . . .121 F5
Riggs Spring ⑧ HG3 . .137 F1
Rigton Hill YO17 . . . . .178 B4
Riley St ⑱ BD23 . . . . .172 A1
Rillington CP Sch
YO17 . . . . .122 F5
Rimington Ave DL10 . .209 D6
Rimington Way YO11 .100 B7
Ringing Keld Hill YO13 . .54 A3
Ringstone Rd YO30 . . .224 F3
Ringstones La LA2 . . .129 A4
Ringway LS25 . . . . . .194 B3
Ringway Gr ⑪ DL2 . . . . .4 C4
Ringwood Rd DL9 . . . . .40 F3
Ripley Bank HG3 . . . .137 C4
Ripley Castle* HG3 . . .161 C7

Ripley Castle* 209 C6
Ripon Garth HG4 . . . .112 C5
Ripon Holt HG3 . . . .
Ripon Methodist Prim
DL10 . . . . .209 E7
Ripon Pl LS29 . . . . . .218 C3
Robson Ave TS17 . . . . . .6 B5
Roche Ave
Harrogate HG1 . . . . .219 F6
York YO31 . . . . .228 E8
Rock Hill WF10 . . . . . .201 A3
Rockingham Ave
YO31 . . . . .229 A5
Rockingham Cl YO17 . .215 A3
Rockingham Dr LS24 . .189 E2
Rockingham Dr YO12 . .212 B7
Rockland Gdns YO12 . .212 D5
Rockley Grange Gdn
YO31 . . . .
Rocks La YO13 . . . . . . .75 D7
Rocks La Cl YO13 . . . . .75 D7
Rockville Dr BD23 . . .217 C8
Rockwell Ave DL1 . . . . . .3 E7
Rockwood Cl ① BD23 .216 E5
Rockwood Dr BD23 . . .216 E5
Rockwood Terr ⑯ HG4 . .86 C3
Rockwood Way YO30 . . . . . .
Roe La LS25 . . . . .202 C7
Roebuck La LS21 . . . .176 F2
Rocliffe C of E Prim Sch
YO51 . . . . .140 F4
Roecliffe La YO51 . . . .141 B5
Roedean Dr TS16 . . . . . .5 E4
Roger La TS8 . . . . .6 C4
Rogerley Cl HG1 . . . . .219 E4
Rolston Ave ⑨ YO31 . .225 E2
Roman Ave N ④ YO41 .168 D2
Roman Ave S ④ YO41 .168 D1
Roman Cl
Newby & Scalby YO12 . .212 A7
④ Tadcaster LS24 . . .189 E6
Roman Cres DL9 . . . . .209 C1

Riverside Ct DN14 . . . .205 A2
Riverside Dr ③ LS21 . .177 A1
Riverside Gdns
② Boroughbridge YO51 .141 B6
⑧ Elvington YO41 . . .185 C2
⑧ Poppleton YO26 . . .165 F1
Riverside Mews ⑥ YO7 .211 C3
Riverside Pk ④ LS21 . .177 A1
Riverside Rd DL10 . . . .209 C6
Riverside View YO17 . .215 B3
Riverside Way DL1 . . . . .3 E7
Riverside Wlk
Airton BD23 . . . . .155 A6
Ilkley LS29 . . . . .218 A5
② Poppleton YO26 . . .165 F1
⑤ Strensall YO32 . . .167 A7
Riverslea TS9 . . . . .26 B7
Riverslade Dr ②① YO26 .165 F1
RNLI Mus* YO21 . . . .208 D7
Roach Grange Ave
LS25 . . . . .194 D2
Roall La DN14 . . . . . . .202 F4
Robert St HG1 . . . . . .219 D1
Robert Wilkinson Prim Sch
YO32 . . . . .167 A7
Roberts Cres DL3 . . . . . .3 A6
Robertson Rd
Colburn DL9 . . . . .40 F4
Ripon HG4 . . . . .113 D3
Robin Cl ⑥ WF8 . . . . .201 B2
Robin Hood Cl YO21 . . .29 A6
Robin Hood Rd YO13 . . .53 F8
Robin Hood's Bay Rd
YO22 . . . . .33 A3
Robin La Bentham LA2 . .103 A1
High Bentham LA2 . . .129 A8
Huby YO61 . . . . .144 A4
Robinson Dr
Harrogate HG1 . . . . .219 F6
York YO24 . . . . .227 B2
Robinson Rd ⑱ DL10 . . .41 E4
Robinson St WF10 . . . .200 D6

Rose Ave
Sherburn in Elmet LS25 . .195 F3
Whitby YO21 . . . . . . .208 B7
Rose Cres
Richmond DL10 . . . . .209 B7
Sherburn in Elmet LS25 . .195 F3
Rose Ct LS25 . . . . . . .194 D4
Rose Hill Dr ③ TS9 . . . .26 C7
Rose Hill Way TS9 . . . .26 C7
Rose La ② LS25 . . . . .196 A2
Rose La Cl ② LS25 . . .202 A7
Rose St YO31 . . . . . . .228 C7
Rose Tree Gr YO32 . . .225 D4
Rose Wood Prim Sch
TS8 . . . . .7 A4
Roseberry Ave
Great Ayton TS9 . . . . .8 A2
Stokesley TS9 . . . . . . .26 D8
Roseberry CP Sch TS9 . .8 A2
Roseberry Cres ⑤ TS9 . .8 A2
Roseberry Dr ④ TS9 . . .8 A2
Roseberry Gr HG4 . . .113 C7
Roseberry Gr YO30 . . .224 F3
Roseberry La
Guisborough TS9 . . . . .8 B3
② Great Ayton TS9 . . .8 A2
Roseberry Mount TS14 . .8 E6
Roseberry Rd TS9 . . . . .8 A2
Roseberry Topping*
TS9 . . . . .8 C3
Roseberry Ave YO12 . .212 C3
Roseberry St YO26 . . .227 F6
Rosecomb Way ⑥
. . . . .225 D7
Rosecroft Ave TS13 . . .10 D8
Rosecroft La TS13 . . . .10 D7
Rosecroft Sch TS13 . . .10 D7
Rosecroft Way YO30 . .227 B8
Rosedale
Guisborough TS14 . . . . . . .49 E2
Rosedale Ave YO26 . .227 C4
Rosedale Abbey CP Sch
YO18 . . . . .49 E2
Rosedale Chy Bank
YO18 . . . . .49 E1
Rosedale Cl
Pannal HG3 . . . . .222 D3
④ Whitby YO21 . . . . .208 C6
Rosedale Cres
Darlington DL3 . . . . .3 A6
Guisborough TS14 . . . . . . .8 E7
Rosedale La
Hinderwell TS13 . . . . .11 F8
Staithes TS13 . . . . . . .13 L1
Rosehill Sq ⑪ HG5 . . .221 B5
Rosehurst Gr HG3 . . .222 E2
Roseland Dr TS7 . . . . . . .7 C7
Rosemary Ct
② Easingwold YO61 . .143 C8
⑱ Tadcaster LS24 . . .189 E6
Rosemary La ① LS24 . .189 E6
Rosemary Pl YO1 . . . .233 C2
Rosemary Row ⑤ LS24 .189 E6
Rosemoor Cl
Coulby Newham TS8 . . .7 B5
⑯ Hunmanby YO14 . .126 F8
Rosemount Rd ② YO21 .208 C5
Rosendale Ave YO17 . .215 F2
Roseville Ave
Harrogate HG1 . . . . .220 A3
② Harrogate HG1 . . .220 A3
Roseville Dr HG1 . . . .220 A3
Roseville Rd HG1 . . . .220 A3
Roseway HG1 . . . . . . .219 E5
Rosley St BB8 . . . . . . .186 A3
Roslyn Rd HG2 . . . . . .220 A2
Rossett Ave HG2 . . . .222 C6
Rossett Beck HG2 . . . .222 C6
Rossett Cres HG2 . . . .222 C6
Rossett Dr HG2 . . . . . .222 C6
Rossett Garth HG2 . . .222 C6
Rossett Gdns HG2 . . .222 C6
Rossett Green La HG2 .222 C7
Rossett Holt Ave HG2 .222 C7
Rossett Holt Cl HG2 . .222 C7
Rossett Holt Dr HG2 . .222 C7
Rossett Holt Gr HG2 . .222 C7
Rossett Holt View
HG2 . . . . .222 C7
Rossett Park Rd HG2 . .222 C6
Rossett Sch HG2 . . . . .222 B6
Rossett Way HG2 . . . .222 C7
Rossiter Dr WF11 . . . .201 E2
Rossway DL1 . . . . .3 F8
Rostle Top Rd ⑩ BB18 .172 A1
Rotary Way HG4 . . . . .214 B3
Roth Hill La YO19 . . . .192 E3
Rothbury Cl HG2 . . . .220 D2
Rothbury St YO12 . . . .212 E5
Rothermere Cl TS7 . . . .7 D6
Rothwell Methley CP Inf Sch
LS26 . . . . .200 B5
Rotunda Mus* YO11 . .213 A5
Rough Rd HG4 . . . . . .112 D3
Roughaw Cl BD23 . . .216 F2
Roughaw Rd BD23 . . .217 A2
Roughley Bank DL7 . . .63 C5
Rougier St YO1 . . . . . .233 A2
Round Hill Link YO30 . .224 F2
Roundel Cl BD23 . . . .216 F3
Roundhill Ave BB18 . . .171 E2
Roundhill Cl BD23 . . . . .5 F4
Roundhill Jun Sch
WF11 . . . . .201 D3

Roundhill Rd DL2 . . . . . . .3 E1
Rounth Wlk ⑤ YO21 . .208 D7
Rowan Ave
⑧ Filey YO14 . . . . . .101 A4
Malton YO17 . . . . . . .215 D6
York YO32 . . . . .225 D4
Rowan Ct
Gateforth YO8 . . . . . .197 B1
Scarborough YO12 . . .212 C6
Rowan Dr ⑧ DL10 . . . .41 D5
Rowan Dr ⑤ TS9 . . . . .8 A2
Rowan Fields YO12 . . . .99 F7
Rowan Garth ② BD20 .187 E7
Rowan Lea HG2 . . . . .222 B7
Rowan Rd YO32 . . . . .225 D4
Rowan Sq ⑥ DL9 . . . .209 B1
Rowans The YO7 . . . . .115 F7
Rowans Way DL7 . . . .210 B4
Rowan La HG5 . . . . . .160 F5
Rowen Ave ④ YO61 . .117 D1
Rowland Keld TS14 . . . .8 E5
Rowland St ⑱ BD23 . .217 A3
Rowlandhall La DN14 . .199 E1
Rowley Cr ② YO32 . . .225 F7
Rowley Dr LS29 . . . . .218 F3
Rowmans The YO30 . .224 C4
Rowntree Ave YO30 . .228 B7
Rowughay Dale YO30 . .200 C1
Roxby Ave ⑭ 8 E5
Roxby Gdns
④ Eastfield YO12 . . . . .99 F7
⑧ Thornton Dale YO18 . .96 D5
Roxby La Roxby TS13 . .11 C7
Staithes TS13 . . . . . . .13 J1
Roxby YO18 . . . . .96 D5
Roxby Terr ⑥ YO18 . . .96 D5
Royal Albert Dr YO12 . .212 F8
Royal Ave YO11 . . . . .212 F4
Royal Chase YO24 . . .230 F8
Royal Cres YO21 . . . .208 C7
Royal Crescent La ⑬
YO11 . . . . .212 F4
Royal Dragoon Guard
Association Regimental
Mus* YO1 . . . . .233 B2
Royal George Dr TS16 . .5 D5
Royal Hall* HG1 . . . . .219 C3
Royal Par ⑧ HG1 . . . .219 C2
Royal Pump Room Mus*
HG2 . . . . .219 C2
Royd Cl ⑱ BD20 . . . .187 E7
Royd The TS15 . . . . . . .5 D2
Royds Ave WF10 . . . . .201 B4
Royd's Rd YO8 . . . . . .202 F6
Ruby St ⑧ YO23 . . . .228 B1
Rudbeck Cl HG2 . . . . .220 C1
Rudbeck Cres HG2 . . .220 C1
Rudbeck Dr HG2 . . . . .220 C1
Rudby Bank TS15 . . . . .25 D5
Rudby Lea TS15 . . . . . .25 D6
Rudcarr La YO19 . . . . .167 E1
Rudda Rd YO13 . . . . . .53 F6
Rudding Dower HG3 . .223 C7
Rudding La
Follifoot HG3 . . . . . . .223 C5
North Rigton HG3 . . .222 A3
Ruddings YO19 . . . . . .193 A8
Ruddings Cl ⑧ YO32 . .225 C8
Ruddings La
Cowesby YO7 . . . . .66 C4
Crakehall DL8 . . . . . . .62 D4
Ellerton YO42 . . . . . .193 C2
Ruddings Rd YO18 . . . .72 B3
Ruddings The YO8 . . .232 A4
Rudgate
Bilton-in-Ainsty with Bickerton
YO26 . . . . .181 B6
Newton Kyme cum Toulston
LS24 . . . . .189 B6
Walton LS23 . . . . . . .181 B1
Rudgate Gr YO26 . . . .164 A4
Rudgate Pk LS23 . . . .181 A2
Rudstone Gr LS25 . . . .195 F4
Ruebury La DL6 . . . . . .45 B4
Rue La LS24 . . . . .176 C8
Ruff La YO61 . . . . . . .142 B5
Ruffa La YO18 . . . . . . .96 A6
Ruffhams Cl YO19 . . .192 F8
Ruffin La YO17 . . . . . .147 D5
Rufford Cl TS14 . . . . . .8 F5
Rufforth Prim Sch
YO23 . . . . .182 C6
Rumford Way DL8 . . . . .60 D6
Rumple Croft ④ LS21 .176 F1
Runnymede TS7 . . . . . . .7 D5
Runs Bank HG3 . . . . . .60 D8
Runswick Ave
Middlesbrough TS5 . . . .6 E6
Whitby YO21 . . . . . . .208 B6
York YO26 . . . . .227 B4
Runswick La TS13 . . . .11 F7
Rupert Rd LS29 . . . . .218 A3
Rushmere TS8 . . . . .7 B5
Rusholme La ⑧ BD20 .172 A1
Rushwood Cl ⑥ YO32 .166 F5
Ruskin Ave
Middlesbrough TS5 . . . .6 D7
⑧ Skipton BD23 . . . .216 D3
Ruskin Cl DL2 . . . . .4 D3
Ruskin Dr WF10 . . . . .201 A4
Russell St
Harrogate HG2 . . . . .222 E7
Skipton BD23 . . . . . .217 A3

Russell St *continued*
York YO23 228 B2
Russet Dr YO31 229 B5
Russet Gr YO12 212 C8
Russett Rd YO17 215 B4
Ruston La YO13 98 D7
Ruswarp Bank YO21 208 B3
Ruswarp C of E Prim Sch YO21 208 B3
Ruswarp La YO21 208 B4
Ruswarp Sta YO22 208 C3
Rutland Cl
Copmanthorpe YO23 230 A3
Harrogate HG1 219 A2
Rutland Dr HG1 219 A2
Rutland Pl 4 YO62 92 F7
Rutland Rd HG1 219 B2
Rutland St 38 YO14 101 B3
Rutmoor Rd YO18 71 E8
Rutson Hospl DL7 210 D5
Ryburn Cl YO30 224 F2
Rycroft Rd 3 YO12 75 E5
Rydal Ave
Middlesbrough TS5 6 E8
York YO31 229 A6
Rydal Cl 2 YO7 89 C4
Rydal Cres 7 YO12 99 F7
Rydal Pl 3 BB8 186 A3
Rydal Rd Darlington DL1 3 E4
Harrogate HG1 220 B3
Ryder Cres 3 YO62 70 B1
Ryder's Wynd 3 DL10 209 C6
Rye Cl Haxby YO32 225 C8
Huttons Ambo YO17 121 C1
Rye Hill Way TS8 7 B4
Ryecroft 7 YO32 167 A6
Ryecroft Ave
10 Norton DN6 206 E2
York YO24 230 C7
Ryecroft Cl YO31 229 C8
Ryecroft Gdns DN14 203 A2
Ryecroft Rd
Glusburn BD20 187 D8
Norton DN6 206 E1
Ryecroft Way 2 BD20 187 E8
Ryedale Cl
Helmsley YO62 92 F7
Norton YO17 215 F1
Pontefract WF6 200 A3
Ulleskelf LS24 190 B2
Ryedale Folk Mus* YO62 70 C5
Ryedale Indoor Bowls Ctr YO17 215 E4
Ryedale Leisure Ctr YO18 95 F7
Ryedale Pk LS29 218 D3
Ryedale Pl WF6 200 A3
Ryedale Sch YO62 93 D7
Ryedale Swimming Pool YO62 93 D4
Ryedale View 2 YO62 70 B1
Ryedale Way YO8 232 C3
Ryefield Cl 12 YO11 99 F7
Ryefield Rd 1 YO11 100 A6
Ryegate 13 YO62 92 F6
Ryehill Cl YO32 225 D5
Ryeland St 9 BD20 187 E8
Ryelands Pk 1 TS13 11 A8
Ryemoor Rd YO32 225 C8
Rylatt Pl YO26 227 B3
Rylstone Dr 1 BB18 171 D1
Rymer Way 4 YO7 211 C3
Ryndle Cres YO12 212 E8
Ryndle Wlk YO12 212 E8
Ryndleside YO12 212 E7
Ryngwoode Dr YO17 215 C6
Ryton Old La YO17 121 F5
Ryton Old Rd YO17 122 A5
Ryton Stile Rd YO17 215 C7

S

Sackville Rd BD20 174 C1
Sackville St
20 Barnoldswick BB18 171 D1
Skipton BD23 217 A3
Sacred Heart Cath Prim Sch LS29 218 D4
Sacred Heart RC Prim Sch DL7 210 D2
Sadberge C of E Sch DL2 4 C8
Sadberge Ct YO10 229 C3
Sadberge Rd DL2 4 C5
Saddle Cl YO17 215 D2
Saddlers Cl
1 Copmanthorpe YO23 230 B3
Huntington YO32 225 F2
Saddlers Croft 8 LS29 218 A4
Saddlers La WF11 201 E5
Saddlers Way YO26 182 A6
Sadler Dr TS7 7 B6
Sadler Forster Way TS17 6 B5
Sadlers Ct YO61 143 A5
Saffron Dr 6 DN14 204 C1
Saffron Mdw 19 HG3 161 B3
Sails Dr YO10 229 B3
St Aelreds Cl YO31 228 F4
St Aelreds RC Prim Sch YO31 229 B5
St Aidans C of E High Sch HG2 219 F1
St Aidan's Rd DL9 209 D1
St Aidans Rd LS26 200 C8
St Alkelda's Rd 1 DL8 60 E2
St Andrew Pl YO1 233 C2
St Andrewgate YO1 233 B2
St Andrew's Ave HG2 220 A3
St Andrew's Cres HG2 220 A3
St Andrews Dr WF7 200 E1
St Andrews Gate HG4 112 D5
St Andrew's Gr 1 HG2 220 B2
St Andrews Gr 2 DL7 210 D2
St Andrew's Par 3 HG2 220 A2
St Andrew's Pl 2 HG2 220 A2
St Andrew's Rd
Castleford WF10 201 B5
4 Harrogate HG2 220 B3
St Andrews Rd YO21 208 B5
St Andrew's St 1 HG2 220 A2
St Andrew's Wlk HG2 220 A2
St Anne's Cres 3 DL10 41 E4
St Annes Gdns DL2 4 C3
St Ann's Ct YO10 228 D2
St Ann's Staith 13 YO21 208 D7
St Anthonys Ave 2 DL7 210 E2
St Athan's Wlk HG2 222 D7
St Aubyn's Pl YO24 228 A2
St Augustines RC Jun & Infants Sch DL3 3 C5
St Augustines RC Prim Sch TS8 7 B5
St Augustines RC Sch YO12 212 C4
St Barnabas Ct 18 YO26 227 F5
St Bedes Ave 4 DL7 210 D2
St Bedes RC Prim Sch DL1 3 D8
St Benedict Rd YO23 233 A1
St Bernadettes RC Prim Sch TS7 7 D6
St Boltophs Cl 4 WF11 202 A2
St Catherines YO30 224 D6
St Catherines Cl YO30 224 C5
St Catherine's Rd HG2 219 F1
St Chads Wharf YO23 231 C8
St Christopher Cl 3 DL7 210 D2
St Christophers Dr 27 LS29 174 F4
St Clares Abbey DL3 3 B5
St Clares RC Prim Sch TS5 6 D6
St Clement's Gr YO23 228 C2
St Clement's Rd HG2 220 A2
St Cuthbert Dr DL7 210 B3
St Cuthbert's Ave 4 DL9 41 A5
St Cuthberts C of E Prim Sch HG3 137 B4
St Cuthbert's Gn DL10 21 D8
St Davids Gr TS17 5 F4
St Davids Rd LS21 176 F1
St Davids Sec Sch TS5 6 E7
St David's View 9 DN14 205 E4
St Denys' Rd YO1 233 C2
St Edmunds Cl 1 DL10 41 C6
St Edwards Cl 2 WF11 201 F4
St Edward's Cl YO24 230 F8
St Edward's RC Prim Sch LS23 188 E8
St Edwin's Cl DL2 2 C6
St Francis Xavier Sch DL10 209 E8
St Gabriels RC Prim Sch TS7 7 D8
St George's Ave HG2 222 D7
St Georges Gr 3 DL7 210 E2
St George's Pl YO24 227 F2
St Georges RC Prim Sch
Eastfield YO11 100 A7
York YO10 228 D2
St George's Rd HG2 222 D7
St George's Wlk HG2 222 D6
St Giles' Cl 1 DL9 41 A5
St Giles Cl YO7 211 C3
St Giles Ct YO31 233 B3
St Giles Rd YO30 224 B5
St Giles Way YO23 230 A2
St Gregory's Cl DL8 62 E4
St Heddas RC Prim Sch YO21 31 A4
St Helena 11 YO51 141 B5
St Helens Cl DL7 64 A7
St Helen's Dr LS25 194 F4
St Helens Dr DL7 64 A7
St Helen's La
Borrowby YO7 65 E4
Reighton YO14 127 C6
St Helen's Rd
Harrogate HG2 223 A8
5 York YO24 230 E8
St Helen's Rise YO19 193 A7
St Helen's Sq
26 Scarborough YO11 213 A6
York YO1 233 B2
St Helen's Way LS29 218 D4
St Hilary Cl DL10 209 B7
St Hilda's Bsns Ctr YO22 208 E6
St Hildas C of E Sch YO62 92 C1
St Hilda's Cres YO17 124 E8
St Hilda's Gdns 4 YO21 208 C7
St Hildas RC Prim Sch YO21 208 D5
St Hilda's Rd HG2 219 F1
St Hildas Rd 5 DL7 210 D2
St Hilda's St YO17 124 D7
St Hilda's Terr YO21 208 D6
St Hilda's Wlk 6 YO62 92 C1
St Ians Croft 32 LS29 174 F4
St Ives Cl 3 WF8 201 B2
St Ives Cres WF10 201 B3
St James C of E Sch LS22 180 C3
St James Cl
Melsonby DL10 20 F7
York YO30 224 E3
St James Ct DN14 205 A1
St James' Dr HG2 222 E8
St James Dr DL7 210 D2
St James Gn 9 YO7 211 C3
St James' Mdw 16 YO51 141 B5
St James Mount YO24 228 A2
St James Pl 5 YO24 227 D1
St James' Rd LS29 218 A3
St James Rd
Northallerton DL7 210 B2
Scarborough YO12 212 E4
St James Terr YO8 232 C5
St James's St 7 LS22 180 C3
St John Fisher RC High Sch HG2 223 A8
St John Mews YO8 232 B7
St John of God Hospl DL10 41 F7
St John St
Harrogate HG1 219 D2
York YO31 233 B3
St John the Baptist RC Aided Prim Sch WF6 200 B1
St Johns Ave 25 LS29 174 F4
St John's Ave
42 Filey YO14 101 B3
Milby YO51 141 B7
Scarborough YO12 212 E5
St Johns C of E Prim Sch DL1 3 E4
St John's Cl
Aberford LS25 188 F1
Bishop Monkton HG3 140 B5
St Johns Cl
Northallerton DL6 210 E2
Sharow HG4 214 F7
St John's Cres
Bishop Monkton HG3 140 A5
Harrogate HG1 219 D5
3 Leeming DL7 63 D4
York YO31 233 C4
St Johns Ct LS24 190 C3
St John's Dr
Harrogate HG1 219 D6
North Rigton LS17 178 B4
St John's Garth LS25 194 F8
St John's Gr HG1 219 C5
St Johns Pk DL11 2 A1
St John's Rd
Bishop Monkton HG3 140 A5
Clifford LS23 188 E7
Harrogate HG1 219 D5
Ilkley LS29 218 E4
2 Leeming DL7 63 D4
Scarborough YO12 212 E5
Scotton HG5 162 A6
9 Stamford Bridge YO41 168 D2
St Johns Rd DL9 209 F1
St Johns Residential Sch for the Deaf LS23 188 E8
St John's St BD20 173 C1
St John's View LS23 188 E8
St John's Way
Bishop Monkton HG3 140 A5
Harrogate HG1 219 D6
St John's Wlk
Harrogate HG1 219 D6
Milby YO51 141 B7
St Joseph's Cl 2 YO12 212 C8
St Josephs RC Prim Sch
Harrogate HG1 219 C5
Loftus TS13 10 D8
Pickering YO18 95 F7
Tadcaster LS24 189 E6
Wetherby LS22 180 C3
St Josephs RC Sch
Barnoldswick BB18 171 D2
Castleford WF10 200 F4
St Joseph's St LS24 189 E6
St Lawrences C of E Prim Sch YO10 228 E3
St Leonards Ave YO8 198 B4
St Leonards Cl 30 LS29 174 F4
St Leonard's Cl
1 Harrogate HG2 220 B1
8 Malton YO17 215 C4
St Leonard's Cres YO12 212 D8
St Leonard's Oval HG2 220 A1
St Leonard's Pl YO30 233 B3
St Leonards Rd TS14 8 E6
St Leonard's Rd HG2 220 A1
St Luke's Cl
6 Boston Spa LS23 188 E7
Harrogate HG1 219 D4
St Lukes Cl DL7 22 C2
St Luke's Cres YO12 212 C6
St Luke's Gr YO30 228 B7
St Lukes Hospl TS4 7 A8
St Luke's Mount HG1 219 D4
St Margaret's Ave LS26 200 B6
St Margaret's Cl 3 HG5 221 A6
St Margarets Cl DL2 4 C3
St Margaret's Garth 2 HG5 221 A6
St Margaret's Gdns 1 HG5 221 A6
St Margaret's Rd
Knaresborough HG5 221 A6
St Margaret's Rd *continued*
Mickletown LS26 200 B6
St Margaret's Terr
6 Ilkley LS29 218 B3
York YO1 228 E4
St Mark's Ave HG2 222 D7
St Mark's Cl 1 YO12 212 C8
St Mark's Gr YO30 224 E2
St Martins Ave 2 LS21 176 F1
St Martin's Ave YO11 213 A4
St Martins C of E Prim Sch YO11 213 C1
St Martins Cl 15 DL9 40 E4
St Martin's La YO1 233 A2
St Martin's Pl 10 YO11 213 A4
St Martin's Rd 9 YO11 213 A4
St Martin's Sq 5 YO11 213 A4
St Martins Way 11 TS15 24 E8
St Marygate HG4 214 D5
St Mary's YO30 233 A3
St Mary's App YO8 196 F1
St Mary's Ave
Barnoldswick BB18 171 E2
Harrogate HG2 219 C2
12 Hemingbrough YO8 198 F1
14 Swillington LS26 194 A1
Thirsk YO7 211 C4
St Marys C of E Prim Sch
Askham Richard YO23 182 D3
Longnewton TS21 5 A7
St Marys Cath TS8 7 B5
St Mary's Cl DL10 21 D7
St Marys Cl YO42 193 C5
St Mary's Cl
15 Haxby YO32 166 E5
Ilkley LS29 218 C4
South Cowton DL7 22 E2
Thirsk YO7 211 C4
St Mary's Cres YO22 208 E6
St Mary's Ct
Allerton Bywater LS26 200 D6
York YO24 233 A1
St Mary's Dr YO7 211 C4
St Mary's Gdns BD23 173 B4
St Mary's Gr YO10 229 C4
St Marys Hospl YO12 212 F6
St Marys RC Prim Sch
Knaresborough HG5 221 A7
Richmond DL10 209 E7
Selby YO8 232 B2
St Marys Sixth Form Coll TS4 6 F7
St Mary's St 6 YO11 213 B6
St Mary's Terr YO30 233 A3
St Mary's Way YO7 211 C4
St Mary's Wlk
Harrogate HG2 219 C1
Micklefield LS25 194 F4
Middlesbrough TS5 6 E8
Scarborough YO11 213 A7
Thirsk YO7 211 C4
St Matthew's Cl
20 Leyburn DL8 60 D5
4 Naburn YO19 191 D8
St Maurice's Rd YO31 233 C3
St Michael St 6 YO17 215 C4
St Michaels Ct 1 DL7 210 D2
St Michaels Gn 15 WF6 200 A1
St Michael's La YO11 213 C1
St Michael's Mead HG4 138 E6
St Michaels Way 29 LS29 174 F4
St Monica Hospl YO61 143 C8
St Monicas Ct 4 YO61 143 D8
St Nicholas Cl
Copmanthorpe YO23 230 A3
Richmond DL10 209 F8
St Nicholas Cliff 5 YO11 213 A5
St Nicholas Cres YO23 230 A3
St Nicholas Croft YO23 182 E3
St Nicholas Dr DL10 209 F7
St Nicholas Gdns TS15 5 F2
St Nicholas Pl 1 YO10 228 F3
St Nicholas Rd
Copmanthorpe YO23 230 A3
Harrogate HG2 220 B2
Ilkley LS29 218 A5
St Nicholas St
Norton YO17 215 D3
Scarborough YO11 213 A6
St Nicholas Way 22 YO32 166 E5
St Olave's Cl HG4 214 A3
St Olave's Rd YO30 233 A4
St Olave's Sch YO30 233 A3
St Oswalds C of E Prim Sch YO10 231 E7
St Oswalds Cl 14 DL9 40 E4
St Oswald's Cl
Catton YO41 185 F6
Oswaldkirk YO62 93 A1
St Oswalds Cl YO7 89 F3
St Oswalds Ct 6 YO14 101 B3
St Oswalds Rd 18 DL9 40 E4
St Oswald's Rd YO10 231 D8
St Patricks RC Comp Sch TS17 6 C7
St Patricks RC Prim Sch TS17 6 B8
St Patrick's Way HG2 220 B2
St Paulinas RC Prim Sch TS14 8 D6
St Paulinus Dr DL7 210 B3
St Pauls C of E Prim Sch YO24 2…
St Paul's Cl DL10
St Pauls Cl 4 DL7 2…
St Pauls Ct 3 WF8 2…
St Paul's Dr DL10
St Paul's Gr LS29 2…
St Pauls Mews YO24 2…
St Paul's Rd TS17
St Pauls Rise LS29 1…
St Paul's Sq YO24 2…
St Paul's Terr
Darlington DL3
York YO24 2…
St Peter St YO17 2…
St Peters C of E Prim Sch HG2 2…
St Peter's Cl 2 DL9
St Peters Cl YO26 2…
St Peter's Cres YO17 2…
St Peters Ct 31 LS29 1…
St Peter's Ct YO22 2…
St Peter's Garth LS14 1…
St Peter's Gr YO30 2…
St Peters RC Prim Sch YO12 2…
St Peter's Rd Drax YO8 2…
Whitby YO22 2…
St Peters Sch YO30 2…
St Peter's Sq 7 HG2 2…
St Philip's Gr YO30 2…
St Philip's Way 33 LS29 1…
St Princes Sq 14 HG1 2…
St Richards Rd 3 LS21 1…
St Robert's Gdns HG5 2…
St Roberts Mews 4 HG1 2…
St Roberts RC Prim Sch HG1 2…
St Robert's Rd HG5 2…
St Ronan's Cl 3 HG2 2…
St Ronan's Rd 2 HG2 2…
St Sampsons Sq YO1 2…
St Saviourgate YO1 2…
St Saviour's Pl YO1 2…
St Sepulchre St 7 YO11 2…
St Simon's Chapel (rems of)* DL8
St Stephen's Cl BD23 2…
St Stephens Gdns 1 DL7 2…
St Stephens RC Prim Sch BD23 2…
St Stephen's Rd YO24 2…
St Stephen's Sq YO24 2…
St Swithin's Wlk YO26 2…
St Teresa's RC Prim Sch DL1
St Thomas' Pl YO31 2…
St Thomas St YO11 2…
St Thomas's Cl 2 YO10 2…
St Thomas's Way YO26 1…
St Trinians Cl DL10 2…
St Trinians Dr DL10 2…
St Wilfred Dr DL7 2…
St Wilfrids Cath High Sch WF7 2…
St Wilfrid's Cl 7 YO32 1…
St Wilfrid's Cres 9 YO8 1…
St Wilfrid's Gdns HG4 2…
St Wilfrid's Pl 2 HG4 2…
St Wilfrids RC Prim Sch
Ripon HG4 2…
York YO31 2…
St Wilfrid's Rd
1 Ripon HG4 2…
8 Strensall YO32 1…
St Williams Coll YO31 2…
St Winifred's Ave HG2 2…
St Winifred's Cl HG2 2…
St Winifred's Rd HG2 2…
St Wulstan Cl YO31 2…
Salents La YO17 1…
Salerno Cl 6 DL9 2…
Salisbury Cl 15 WF6 2…
Salisbury Dr 9 HG3 1…
Salisbury Rd YO26 2…
Salisbury St
Scarborough YO12 2…
Skipton BD23 2…
Sallow Heath 16 HG3 1…
Salmon La DL8
Salmond Rd 5 YO24 2…
Salt Pans Rd YO13
Saltburn Rd TS17
Salter Rd YO11
Salterforth La BB18 1…
Salterforth Rd BB18 1…
Saltergate Bank YO18
Saltergate Cty Jun & Inf S…
HG3 2…
Saltergate Dr HG3 1…
Saltergill La TS15
Saltergill Sch TS15
Salters Ave DL1
Salters La DL1
Salters La N DL1
Salters La S DL1
Saltersgill Ave TS4
Salton La
Nunnington YO62
Salton YO62
Salutation Rd DL3
Sam La YO61 1…
San Carlos Cl 1 DL9

Hutton C of E Prim Sch 168 B5
Hutton Cl Y041 ...168 B5
.a
with Osgodby 198 B4
ton Y08 ...199 D5
ton Y017 ...123 F7
...144 A5
Milford LS25 ...195 F2
gton Y061 ...144 A6
Way ...197 E6
eck Cl DL10 ...209 C5
eck Ind Est
eck La LS22 ...180 C4
eck Way LS22 ...180 C4
oft Cl 4 Y024 ...230 D8
roft Rd Y024 ...230 D8
rson Rd DL2 ...3 F1
eld La Y07 ...188 D4
eld Terr 4 LS24 ...189 F6
ate 2 LS25 ...194 D1
ate Dr LS25 ...194 D1
ate La LS25 ...194 E2
ate Rise LS25 ...194 D1
ate Terr LS25 ...194 E1
ill Bank Y021 ...9 E1
ill Cl
gate HG1 ...219 F6
frazr WF8 ...201 B2
ill Dr HG1 ...219 F6
ill La Bedale DL8 ...63 B3
on Y08 ...197 D2
t upon Derwent 185 E2
ill Way HG1 ...219 F6
olme 2 Y032 ...166 F5
olme Cl
singwold Y061 ...143 D8
ttle BD24 ...131 D2
olmes La Y07 ...89 E3
urst Gdns 4 ....212 B7
utton La Y07 ...89 B4
acres 8 Y08 ...197 D1
martin Ct Y024 ...230 D8
noor Cl 5 Y021 ...208 B5
own Cl Bagby Y07 ...90 B3
........227 E2
aiper Cl
astfield Y012 ...99 A5
ter Y014 ...101 A3
ar La Y062 ...69 B1
iggs DL3 ...3 B7
ringham Ct Y032 ...225 C7
ringham Rd
m cum Sutton WF11 ...201 E4
wood TS12 ...9 F6
sbrough TS3 ...7 B8
pon HG4 ...214 C3
sprout La LS22 ...180 C3
ringham St
arborough Y012 ...212 F7
........228 D2
ock Rd 3 WF8 ...201 C1
s Cl Y014 ...127 D7
La
nanby Y014 ...127 A8
ton Y017 ...122 F5
g Rd Y014 ...127 B7
send Rd
holm-cum-Dunsley 13 A3
le Y021 ...208 A8
side Y011 ...213 B6
sprunt La Y013 ...75 D7
stock Rd Y031 ...229 B7
rrath La LS24 ...196 A8
way Ave 12 Y08 ...197 B1
way Cl 11 Y08 ...197 B1
way Dr
olesforth Y08 ...204 D4
orpe Willoughby Y08 ...197 B1
th La Y08 ...204 B4
wood Pk TS14 ...8 D5
t Bank
nallerton DL6 ...210 F3
nby DL6 ...65 A7
y Flatts La TS5 ...6 F6
r Gap Y022 ...225 C7
y Gate HG3 ...159 A6
y La Aine Y061 ...143 A4
on Y017 ...116 A8
mbsay BD23 ...217 C7
on Y060 ...168 B8
axby Y032 ...166 E5
& Low Bishopside 137 D3
berton Y011 ...141 D8
n Duffield Y08 ...198 F8
Rd ...214 B2
apston Y017 ...123 B5
xton on the Forest 167 E4
y Leas La TS21 ...5 A8
y Rise Y08 ...232 C3
ybed Cres Y012 ...212 C4
y Rd
sborough Y012 ...212 C4
eham Y013 ...98 F6
nyforth La BD22 ...186 E5

Sandyland 28 Y032 ...166 E5
Sandyridge Y036 ...224 A1
Sark's Croft BD23 ...155 A1
Sargent Ave Y023 ...230 F4
Saunters Way WF6 ...200 A2
Savile Rd
Castleford WF10 ...200 C4
Mickletown LS26 ...200 B6
Saville Gr Y030 ...228 A8
Saville St 7 Y017 ...215 C4
Saw Wells La LS24 ...195 F6
Sawley Cl BD23 ...171 D2
Sawley Moor La HG4 ...138 D6
Sawmill La Y062 ...92 C1
Sawyer's Cres Y023 ...230 C2
Sawyers Garth 8 LS29 ...175 A4
Sawyers Wlk 9 Y019 ...184 F7
Saxford Way Y032 ...166 D5
Saxon 4 Thorpe Willoughby Y08 ...197 B1
Saxon Dr Y017 ...122 E5
Saxon Pl Y031 ...228 C7
Saxon Rd
Catterick Garrison DL9 ...209 E1
Ripon HG4 ...214 D5
Stamford Bridge Y041 ...168 D2
Bellerby DL23 ...108 B7
Saxon Vale Y030 ...165 F5
Saxonfield TS8 ...7 A6
Saxton C of E Prim Sch 195 D7
Saxton Ct LS24 ...195 D8
Saxton La LS24 ...195 D8
Saxty Way Y07 ...211 A1
Scabbate Gate BD23 ...108 B3
Scackleton Bank Y062 ...119 C4
Scackleton La Y062 ...119 C3
Scafell Cl 9 Y030 ...224 E1
Scagglethorpe La Y017 ...122 C4
Scaife Gdns Y031 ...228 C7
Scaife Shay La Y07 ...116 A7
Scaife St Y031 ...228 C7
Scalby Ave Y012 ...212 C8
Scalby Beck Rd 17 Y013 ...75
Scalby City Mdws Y012 ...212 B8
Scalby Mills Rd Y012 ...75 F5
Scalby Rd Y012 ...212 D5
Scaldhill La Y051 ...141 C7
Scale Hill LS21 ...177 D2
Scale The BD23 ...172 B2
Scallow Bank La DL8 ...59 B6
Scalm La
Hambleton Y08 ...196 F2
Selby Y08 ...197 A4
Scampton Cl TS17 ...6 A6
Scar Close Nature Reserve*
LA6 ...104 D8
Scar Field 8 BD23 ...134 E7
Scar Hos LA1 ...35 F5
Scar Rd BD23 ...171 C6
Scar St BD23 ...134 E2
Scarah Bank HG3 ...161 B8
Scarah La HG3 ...140 A2
Scarbeck Bank DL11 ...19 D7
Scarborough Art Gall*
Y011 ...213 A5
Scarborough Castle*
Y011 ...213 C7
Scarborough Coll
Y011 ...213 A2
Scarborough Football Club
Y012 ...212 B2
Scarborough General Hospl
Y012 ...212 B6
Scarborough Indoor Pool*
Y012 ...213 A2
Scarborough RUFC
Y012 ...212 A8
Scarborough Sixth Form Coll
Y012 ...212 C4
Scarborough Sports Ctr
Y011 ...213 A2
Scarborough Sta Y011 ...212 F5
Scarborough Terr
Y030 ...233 B4
Scarcroft Hill Y024 ...228 B2
Scarcroft La Y023 ...233 A1
Scarcroft Prim Sch
Y023 ...233 A1
Scarcroft Rd Y024 ...233 A1
Scardale Cres Y012 ...212 E8
Scardale Ct Y012 ...232 A2
Scarer's La Y026 ...142 B2
Scargill Rd HG1 ...219 B4
Scarhouse La DL11 ...17 E2
Scarlet Balk La Y017 ...122 C1
Scarth Cl 3 TS12 ...9 F7
Scarth Nick
Preston-under-Scar DL8 ...59 E6
Whorlton DL6 ...45 D6
Scarthingwell Cres 195 D8
Scarthingwell La LS24 ...195 E8
Scate Moor La Y026 ...163 F3

Scaudercroft 5 Y019 ...184 F7
Scawling End Rd Y061 ...91 C3
Scawton Ave 11 Y031 ...225 E2
Scholes La BD22 ...187 F1
Scholes Park Ave 3
Y012 ...75 F5
Scholes Park Cliff 1
Y012 ...75 F5
Scholes Park Dr 2 Y012 ...212 E3
Scholes Park Rd Y012 ...75 F5
Scholes Rd WF10 ...201 B5
Scholla La DL6 ...210 F5
Scholla View DL6 ...210 F5
School Cl Huby Y061 ...144 A4
Selby Y08 ...232 B3
School 10 Stamford Bridge Y041 ...168 D2
School Croft WF11 ...201 E4
School Fields BB18 ...172 A2
School Garth Y07 ...89 E3
School Hill
Bainbridge DL8 ...57 D5
Settle BD24 ...131 D3
School House Dr Y012 ...99 D6
School La
Addingham LS29 ...174 F5
Askham Richard Y023 ...182 D3
Bishopthorpe Y023 ...231 A4
Burton Fleming Y025 ...126 E3
Cawood LS25 ...188 A8
Copmanthorpe Y023 ...230 A2
Earby BB18 ...172 A1
Easington BB7 ...152 B3
Eppleby DL11 ...1 D4
Great Ayton TS9 ...8 A1
Laneshaw Bridge BB8 ...186 C3
Lawkland LA2 ...130 D3
Lotherton cum Aberford 194 F8
Malton Y017 ...215 C4
4 Nawton Y062 ...93 D7
Newton-le-Willows DL8 ...62 B4
Osmotherley DL6 ...45 B4
22 Poppleton Y026 ...165 F1
South Milford LS25 ...195 F2
13 Spofforth HG3 ...179 E6
Thornton-le-Beans DL6 ...65 B5
Walton LS23 ...180 F2
Wray-with-Botton LA2 ...128 A6
York Y010 ...231 E7
York Y010 ...231 E7
School Rd
Hemingbrough Y08 ...198 F1
Wetherby LS22 ...180 C3
School St
Castleford WF10 ...200 F5
2 Earby BB18 ...186 A7
York Y024 ...227 D3
Schoolgate LS15 ...194 C8
Scoreby La Y041 ...168 B1
Scoresby Terr 2 Y021 ...208 D5
Scotch Cnr
Middleton Tyas DL10 ...21 B4
Oldstead Y061 ...91 C4
Scotch George La
HG5 ...221 A7
Scotchman La Y060 ...168 A8
Scotpit La DL6 ...45 C3
Scots Dike Terr DL10 ...209 D6
Scots Dyke Ct DL10 ...20 F7
Scott Cl
88 Glusburn BD20 ...187 E7
35 Swillington LS26 ...194 A1
Scott Moncrieff Rd
Y032 ...167 B6
Scott Rd Y08 ...232 C6
Scotton Bank DL8 ...40 D2
Scotton Ct HG5 ...162 A6
Scotton Dr HG5 ...220 C8
Scotton Gdns 8 DL9 ...40 E3
Scotton Gr
Knaresborough HG5 ...220 C8
Scotton HG5 ...162 A5
Scotton Pk DL9 ...40 E3
Scotton Rd DL9 ...40 E3
Scriftain La LS22 ...180 C5
Scriven Gr 8 Y032 ...166 F5
Scriven Rd HG5 ...221 B8
Scrogs La DL8 ...86 E7
Scrope Ave 4 Y031 ...228 E5
Scugdale Rd DL6 ...45 E8
Scurragh House La 21 C1
Scurragh La DL10 ...21 B2
Sea App Y014 ...127 A8
Sea Cliff Cres Y011 ...213 B2
Sea Cliff Rd Y011 ...213 B2
Sea Life Ctr* Y012 ...75 F5
Sea View La Y011 ...101 C1
Sea View Cl Y011 ...100 B8
Sea View Cres Y011 ...100 B8
Sea View Dr 18 Y011 ...100 B8
Sea View Gdns 6 Y011 ...100 B8
Sea View Gr 6 Y011 ...100 B8
Seafield Ave 1 Y011 ...100 B7
Seafire Cl Y030 ...225 A3
Seagram Cres DL10 ...209 C8
Seakel La Y023 ...182 C2
Seal Bank BD23 ...81 D1
Seamer & Irton CP Sch
Y012 ...99 D6

Seamer Moor Hill
Y012 ...212 B1
Seamer Moor La Y012 ...212 B1
Seamer Rd
East Ayton Y013 ...99 B7
Eastfield Y012 ...99 F8
Hilton TS15 ...6 C2
Maltby TS8 ...6 D5
Scarborough Y012 ...212 E3
Seamer St Y011 ...213 A3
Seamer Sta Y011 ...99 F6
Seaton Cl Y010 ...229 C4
Seaton Cres TS13 ...13 K2
Seaton Cnty Prim Sch
TS13 ...13 K2
Seaton Garth TS13 ...13 K2
Seave Cl La Y061 ...164 D2
Seavegate 4 Y013 ...99 B8
Seavegate Cl Y013 ...99 B8
Seaview Ave 8 Y012 ...75 E5
Seavy Rd DN14 ...205 F2
Second Ave
Menwith with Darley
HG3 ...160 A4
8 Pickering Y018 ...95 F7
York Y031 ...228 F5
Second Common La
Y08 ...197 C4
Sedber La 6 BD23 ...134 E2
Sedbergh Dr LS29 ...218 B3
Sedbergh Pk LS29 ...218 B3
Sedbusk La DL8 ...56 D6
Sedge Rise LS24 ...189 D5
Sedgefield Rd TS5 ...6 E6
Sedley Cl HG1 ...219 E7
Seed Hill LA6 ...103 D4
Sefton Ave Y031 ...228 F8
Sefton Dr LS29 ...218 B3
Sefton Way TS15 ...5 D2
Seg La Y08 ...204 F3
Seggans Rd Y026 ...142 A1
Segrave Rd Y026 ...227 A3
Segrave Wlk 10 Y026 ...227 E4
Selbourne 9 BB18 ...172 B1
Selby Abbey Y08 ...232 D5
Selby Abbey Prim Sch
Y08 ...232 C5
Selby Coll Y08 ...232 F3
Selby Cres DL3 ...3 A7
Selby High Sch Y08 ...232 B4
Selby Rd
Eggborough DN14 ...202 F1
Fulford Y019 ...231 E6
Garforth LS25 ...194 B3
Ledston LS25 ...195 A2
Riccall Y019 ...198 A8
Snaith DN14 ...204 C1
Swillington LS15 ...194 A3
Wistow Y08 ...197 D6
Womersley DN14 ...207 A4
York Y08 ...232 D5
Selby Town Football Club
Y08 ...232 B5
Seldon Rd Y026 ...227 E5
Self Gdns Y062 ...70 F3
Selside Shaw BD24 ...105 A7
Selstone Cres 7 Y022 ...32 A6
Seph Way Y017 ...215 B3
Sergeant Bank HG4 ...86 B8
Sessay C of E Prim Sch
Y07 ...116 C5
Sessions House Yd 10
Y01 ...233 B2
Settle C of E Prim Sch
WF8 ...201 B1
Settle Mid Sch BD24 ...131 E2
Settle High Sch BD24 ...131 D3
Settle Junc BD24 ...153 D8
Settle Mid Sch BD24 ...131 D3
Settle Rd BD23 ...155 A6
Settle Sta BD24 ...131 C3
Settle Swimming Pool
BD24 ...131 D3
Settrington C of E Prim Sch
Y017 ...122 D1
Settrington Rd Y012 ...212 B5
Seven St Y017 ...121 A4
Seven Wells Y017 ...121 A4
Seventh Ave Y031 ...228 F5
Seventh Ave Y031 ...228 F5
Severn Cl DN14 ...207 D2
Severn Dr
Garforth LS25 ...194 D3
Guisborough TS14 ...8 E6
Severus Ave Y026 ...227 C8
Severus St Y024 ...227 D3
Sewell's Cave* LA2 ...131 A7
Sewerbridge La WF7 ...200 C1
Sexhow La TS9 ...25 F4
Seymour Cres TS16 ...5 D4
Seymour Gr
Eaglescliffe TS16 ...5 D4
Garforth LS25 ...194 B6
Shackleton Cl Y021 ...208 C5
Shady La BD20 ...173 C2
Shaftesbury Ave
Goole DN14 ...205 F3
Kellingley DN14 ...202 C3
Shaker Stile Rd HG4 ...96 B7
Shakespeare Ave 2
DN6 ...206 E1
Shakespeare Cl 3 DL10 ...41 C7
Shallowdale La 11 Y030 ...229 C3
Shambles Y01 ...233 B2
Shambles La Y07 ...114 C5

Shambles The 2 Y017 ...215 B4
Shandon Pk TS8 ...7 B5
Shandy Hall* Y061 ...117 D8
Shannon Cl 26 LS29 ...175 C2
Shannon Lea DL2 ...4 D4
Sharow C of E Prim Sch
HG4 ...214 F7
Sharow La HG4 ...214 E6
Sharp Hill La Y08 ...204 F6
Sharphaw Ave BD23 ...217 A2
Sharphaw View BD23 ...155 D1
Shaw Ave Y06 ...200 B1
Shaw Barn La LS22 ...180 B3
Shaw Cl WF6 ...200 B1
Shaw Cres Y061 ...144 A5
Shaw Dr Y062 ...70 B1
Shaw La Farnham HG5 ...162 C7
Fenwick DN6 ...207 D2
North Rigton HG3 ...178 B6
Spofforth with Stockeld
HG3 ...179 D7
Shaw Rise WF6 ...200 B1
Shawclose La Y062 ...67 E4
Shawcroft Ct DL10 ...209 E8
Shawl Terr 11 DL8 ...60 D5
Shaws La
Barwick in Elmet & Scholes
LS15 ...194 B7
Shaw's Terr Y024 ...233 A1
Sheep Rake La Y025 ...151 F4
Sheep St 11 BD23 ...216 F4
Sheepcote La HG3 ...159 F5
Sheepdyke La Y014 ...127 A8
Sheepfoot Hill Y017 ...215 D4
Sheepwalk La
Castleford WF10 ...201 B3
Kirby Grindalythe Y017 ...150 B7
Sheepwash Bank Y07 ...66 D5
Sheepwash La DN14 ...207 A7
Sheldrake Cl 9 Y011 ...101 A4
Sheldrake Rd WF10 ...200 E3
Shelley Cl Y011 ...100 B8
Shelley Cres HG1 ...219 E7
Shelley Dr Y030 ...224 F1
Shelley Rd TS4 ...6 F8
Shelton Ave 2 Y013 ...99 B8
Shepherd Ct TS12 ...9 E7
Shepherd Gate La Y07 ...66 D6
Shepherd Hill DL6 ...45 D8
Shepherdfields La
Y060 ...146 E5
Sheerdies The HG4 ...113 C8
Shepherds Dr DL6 ...45 D8
Shepherd's Rd DL10 ...100 B7
Sherbrooke Cl 18 Y062 ...70 B1
Sherburn C of E Prim Sch
Y017 ...124 D7
Sherburn High Sch
LS25 ...195 F3
Sherburn Rd Y08 ...232 A8
Sherburn St 1 Y08 ...197 B8
Sherburn in Elmet Sta
LS25 ...196 A4
Sheridan Rd BB8 ...186 B3
Sheriff Hutton Castle (rems
of)* Y060 ...145 D5
Sheriff Hutton CP Sch
Y060 ...145 C5
Sheriff Hutton House*
Y060 ...145 D4
Sherringham Dr Y024 ...230 D8
Sherwood Brow BD24 ...131 E2
Sherwood Cl
Hutton DL8 ...61 E7
8 Norton DN6 ...206 E1
Sherwood Dr Y026 ...220 D2
Sherwood Gr
Huntington Y032 ...225 F1
York Y026 ...227 B6
Sherwood St 5 Y012 ...212 F5
Shetland Cl 8 Y032 ...225 F7
Shilton Garth Cl 3
Y032 ...225 F7
Shipton Low Rd Y030 ...165 E5
Shipton Rd
Clifton Y030 ...227 F8
Rawcliffe Y030 ...224 D2
Skelton Y030 ...224 A7
Shipton St 3 Y030 ...228 B7
Shipton Street Inf Sch
Y030 ...228 B7
Shipyard Rd Y08 ...232 E5
Shirbutt La Y026 ...142 A6
Shire Cl 18 Y011 ...100 B7
Shire Croft 17 Y011 ...100 B7
Shire Fold Y030 ...100 B6
Shire Garth DL6 ...24 B1
Shire Gr Y017 ...211 B4
Shirestone Ctr* Y011 ...54 C8
Shires Croft BD23 ...217 E8
Shires La BD23 ...217 D8
Shirley Ave Ripon HG4 ...214 B4
York Y026 ...227 B6
Shoebridge Ave BD20 ...187 F7
Shop Hill Y022 ...33 B4
Shop La Cowling BD22 ...187 A6
Danby Y021 ...29 B3
Middleton Y018 ...95 D8
Short La
Farndale East Y062 ...48 F4
West Haddlesey Y08 ...202 F6
Short Lee La Y021 ...216 F6

Short Rd YO7 ....115 B2
Shortacre La YO42 ....193 E2
Shortbank Cl BD23 ....217 B3
Shortbank Rd BD23 ....217 B3
Shortsill La HG5 ....163 B5
Shotel Cl YO30 ....202 C3
Showfield Cl LS25 ....195 F4
Showfield Dr ⑰ YO61 ......143 C8
Showfield La YO17 ....215 C6
Shrubberies The YO8 ....198 E2
Shute Rd DL9 ....209 E1
Shutt La DL8 ....56 E6
Shuttleworth St ⒅
  BB18 ....172 A1
Shuttocks Fold LS25 ......194 D2
Sicklinghall CP Sch
  LS22 ....179 D3
Sicklinghall Rd LS22 ......179 F3
Side Gate YO12 ....99 D1
Sidegate La BD20 ....186 F8
Sidgwick Ct ⑦ BD23 ....217 A3
Siding La YO8 ....198 B5
Sidings La YO61 ....143 B4
Sidings The
  Settle BD24 ....131 D2
  Skipton BD23 ....216 E3
Sidmouth St ⑨ DL9 ....40 E4
Signals Ct ⑦ YO12 ....75 F5
Sigston Castle* DL6 ....44 D2
Sike La YO7 ....115 B6
Sikelands La DL11 ....38 F4
Silicar La HG4 ....88 B1
Sills La YO30 ....165 B6
Silly La LA2 ....129 A2
Silsden Rd
  Addingham LS29 ....174 D4
  Low Bradley BD20 ......173 E3
Silver Garth DL10 ....21 C7
Silver Hill DL7 ....22 C2
Silver Mdws DL10 ....22 C1
Silver St Askrigg DL8 .....57 E5
  Barton DL10 ....21 C7
  Fairburn WF11 ....201 D6
  Hackforth DL8 ....62 E8
  ④ Knaresborough HG5 ..222 A5
  Masham HG4 ....86 C3
  Reeth, Fremington & Healaugh
    DL11 ....38 B6
  ⑧ Riccall YO19 ....198 A8
  ⑧ Scarborough YO11 ...213 A6
  Thirsk YO7 ....211 C1
  Whitby YO21 ....208 D7
  Whitley DN14 ....203 A1
  York YO1 ....233 B2
Silverdale Cl ⑥ HG3 .....160 A6
Silverdale Ct YO24 ....230 D7
Silverdale Rd BD24 ....131 F8
Silverfields Rd HG1 ....220 A3
Silverton Rd TS14 ....8 F5
Silverwood Ave ⑧
  YO14 ....101 A3
Sim Balk La YO24 ....230 E5
Simbach Cl BD23 ....217 B3
Simon Howe YO12 ....124 F6
Simpson Ave ⑧ YO14 .....126 F8
Simpson Cl BB18 ....171 E2
Simpson Lane Jun & Inf Sch
  WF11 ....201 E2
Simpsons La WF11 ....201 E2
Simpson's Yd ⑧ YO8 .....232 C6
Sinderby La YO7 ....88 B4
Sinks La DL8 ....62 C4
Sinnington Cl TS14 ....8 F6
Sinnington Cliff Rd
  YO62 ....95 A8
Sinnington CP Sch
  YO62 ....94 F8
Sinnington Rd TS17 ....6 B6
Sir John's La LS25 ....195 E4
Sirocco Ct YO31 ....228 D8
Sissy Bank DL8 ....59 D6
Sitwell Gr YO30 ....227 C5
Sitwell St YO12 ....212 E5
Siward St YO10 ....228 E3
Sixth Ave YO31 ....228 E5
Skates La YO61 ....144 B3
Sked Dale YO17 ....124 E6
Skeeby Cl ③ TS18 ....5 D8
Skegmer La YO60 ....145 F4
Skelda Rise LS29 ....218 B3
Skelder Rd YO21 ....31 E8
Skeldergate YO1 ....233 B2
Skelf St LS24 ....190 C1
Skelgate La DL11 ....38 B6
Skelbank HG4 ....214 B4
Skellbank Cl HG4 ....214 B4
Skelldale Cl HG4 ....214 C4
Skelldale View HG4 ......214 C4
Skellfield Terr HG4 ....214 C4
Skellgill La DL8 ....57 C6
Skelton Cl ⑧ YO30 ......228 A6
Skelton Ellers TS14 ....9 A8
Skelton La
  Givendale HG4 ....140 C8
  Marske DL11 ....39 B7
Skelton Prim Sch
  YO30 ....224 C5
Skelton Rd
  Skelton YO51 ....140 E6
  Thornaby TS17 ....6 B8
Skelton Windmill*
  YO51 ....140 F8
Skerne Park Cty Inf Sch
  DL1 ....3 D4

Skerne Park Cty Jun Sch
  DL1 ....3 C4
Skeugh Head La DL11 .....35 E6
Skeugh La YO61 ....144 D6
Skewsby Gr YO31 ....225 F1
Skibeden BD23 ....217 E6
Skibeden Ct ④ BD23 .....217 B5
Skidaw YO24 ....230 C7
Skiddaw Ct TS7 ....7 B6
Skinner La ⑭ WF8 ......201 B1
Skinner St YO21 ....208 D7
Skiplam Cl ④ YO12 ......212 B5
Skiplam Rd YO62 ....69 D2
Skipper La YO25 ....125 E3
Skipton Castle*
  BD23 ....217 A5
Skipton Cres HG1 ....219 D5
Skipton General Hospl
  BD23 ....216 F3
Skipton High Sch
  BD23 ....216 E5
Skipton Hospl BD23 ......216 E3
Skipton Old Rd BB8 ......186 A3
Skipton Parish Church Sch
  BD23 ....217 A3
Skipton Rd
  Addingham LS29 ....174 E5
  Barnoldswick BB18 .....171 E2
  Bradleys Both BD20 ....173 D4
  Colne BB8 ....186 A2
  Cononley BD20 ....173 C2
  Earby BB18 ....172 A2
  Embsay with Eastby
    BD23 ....217 C7
  Farnhill BD20 ....187 E8
  Fellscliffe HG3 ....160 E3
  Fewston LS21 ....159 D2
  Gargrave BD23 ....155 D1
  Glusburn BD20 ....187 F8
  Harrogate HG3 ....219 A4
  Hellifield BD23 ....154 B3
  Ilkley LS29 ....218 A4
  Silsden BD20 ....174 B1
  Skipton BD23 ....216 B6
  Skipton RUFC BD23 ...216 D3
  Skipton St HG1 ....216 B5
  Skipton Sta BD23 .....216 E3
Skipwith Comm Nature
  Reserve* YO8 ....198 E8
Skipwith Rd YO19 ....192 B6
Skirt Bank YO7 ....66 C7
Skottowe Cres TS9 ......7 F2
Skottowe Dr TS9 ....7 F1
Skuff Rd BD23 ....157 B8
Skurkhill La YO62 ....92 E7
Skyreholme Bank
  BD23 ....157 F7
Skyreholme La BD23 .....157 F7
Slack La HG3 ....160 B4
Slackgap La CA17 ....14 A8
Sladeburn Dr ② DL6 ....210 E3
Sladburn Rd LA2 ....129 B4
Slate Hill YO21 ....29 C4
Slates La LS29 ....218 B7
Slayde The TS15 ....5 E2
Sled Gates YO22 ....33 B3
Sled La DL10 ....41 F4
Sledgate YO17 ....122 F5
Sledgate Garth YO17 ....122 F5
Sledmere Rd YO25 ....151 B6
Sledmere Sch YO25 .....150 B3
Sleigh La YO60 ....120 A1
Sleightholme Dale Rd
  YO62 ....69 D5
Sleightholme Moor Rd
  DL11 ....16 D7
Sleights C of E Prim Sch
  YO22 ....32 A6
Sleights La
  Acklam YO17 ....169 E7
  Amotherby YO17 ....121 A4
  Birstwith HG3 ....160 C4
  Rainton with Newby YO7 114 A5
Sleights Rd Glaisdale 69 D6
Sleights Sta YO22 ....32 A7
Sleights The LS17 ....178 A2
Slessor Rd
  ⑧ Catterick DL10 ......41 E4
  York YO24 ....227 B1
Slice La LS24 ....190 A6
Slim Rd DL9 ....209 C2
Slingsby Ave HG5 ....221 A7
Slingsby Bank YO62 .....120 C4
Slingsby Castle (rems of)*
  YO62 ....120 B5
Slingsby Cres HG1 ......219 F4
Slingsby Cty Prim Sch
  YO62 ....120 B5
Slingsby Garth ⑲ YO41 ..70 B1
Slingsby Gdns DL7 ....210 B3
Slingsby Gr YO24 ....230 E8
Slip Inn Bank DL11 ......19 E6
Slippery Ford La BD22 ...187 E3
Smales' St YO1 ....233 B1
Smary La YO19 ....184 D7
Smawthorne Ave
  WF10 ....200 C4
Smawthorne Gr WF10 ...200 C4
Smawthorne La WF10 ...200 C4
Smay La YO22 ....33 D5
Smearbottoms La
  BD23 ....133 C3
Smeathorns Rd TS12 ....9 F4
Smeatley's La DN6 ......206 F4
Smeaton Gr
  ⑧ Swillington LS26 ....194 A1
  York YO26 ....227 C5
Smeaton Rd YO41 ....185 D7

Smiddy Hill
  ⑩ Pickering YO18 .....95 F6
  Walton LS23 ....181 A2
Smiddyfields ⑧ YO22 ...32 A6
Smirthwaite View ⑭
  WF6 ....200 A1
Smith Cl YO10 ....231 F8
Smith La HG4 ....88 A8
Smith St ⑩ BB18 ....171 D1
Smithfield Cl ⑦ HG4 ....214 B2
Smithfield Rd DL1 ....3 D4
Smithgutter La DL10 ....21 C4
Smithson Ave WF10 .....201 B3
Smithson Cl DL1 ....21 D2
Smithson Ct YO17 ....215 B5
Smithson Gr ④ YO51 ...141 B4
Smithson's La HG3 ......177 A8
Smithy Croft Rd BD23 ...155 D1
Smithy La Denton LS29 ..176 A4
  Scotton HG5 ....162 A6
  Thornton in Lonsdale
    LA6 ....103 A4
  Ulleskelf LS24 ....190 C2
Smuts Rd DL9 ....209 D1
Smythy La YO25 ....125 E3
Snainton C of E Prim Sch
  YO13 ....98 A5
Snainton La YO13 ....97 F7
Snaith Rd
  Pollington DN14 ....207 F7
  Rawcliffe DN14 ....205 A1
  Snaith Sta DN14 ......204 C1
Snaizeholme Rd DL8 ....55 E1
Snape Castle* DL8 ......87 A7
Snape CP Sch DL8 ......87 A7
Snape Hill YO62 ....93 F7
Snargate Hill YO61 ......118 E3
Sneaton La YO22 ....208 B1
Sneaton Thorpe La
  YO22 ....32 E5
Sneck Gate La TS8 ......7 B2
Sneck Yate Bank YO7 ...67 A2
Snipe Cl ⑧ YO14 ......101 A4
Snipe La Hurworth DL2 ..3 C3
  Loftus TS13 ....11 A6
Snowden Carr Rd
  LS21 ....176 E5
Snowden Cl ④ HG4 .....214 B2
Snowdon Cl YO23 ....182 D3
Snowfield La WF6 ....142 F5
Snydale Ave WF6 ....200 B1
Snydale Cl WF6 ....200 B1
Snydale Ct ⑩ WF6 .....200 B1
Snydale Gr WF6 ....200 B1
Snydale Rd WF6 ....200 A1
Sober Hall Ave TS17 ....6 A4
Socarrs La YO62 ....48 E1
Sockburn La DL2 ....23 B8
Somerset Cl ⑧ YO30 ...224 E3
Somerset Rd
  ② Harrogate HG2 .....219 C1
  York YO31 ....228 E8
Somerset Terr YO11 .....213 A5
Somme Barracks DL9 ...40 F3
Sommerset Pastures
  YO61 ....116 F2
Sorrel Gr ⑧ HG3 ....161 B3
Sorrell Gr TS14 ....8 D6
Sough La BB18 ....186 A8
Sour La BD23 ....216 B6
Sourby La LS21 ....176 D7
Soursikes Field Rd
  YO15 ....141 D5
South App
  Aberford LS25 ....188 F1
  Bramham cum Oglethorpe
    LS23 ....188 C5
  Stutton with Hazlewood
    LS24 ....189 A2
South Ave
  Castleford WF10 ....200 C4
  ⑳ Selby YO13 ....75 D5
South Back La
  Stillington YO61 ....144 C6
  Terrington YO60 ....119 E1
  Tollerton YO61 ....143 B2
South Baileygate WF8 ...201 B1
South Bank Ave WF8 ...201 B1
South Beech Ave HG2 ..220 C3
South Cleveland Hospl
  TS4 ....7 A8
South Cliff Dr YO14 .....101 B1
South Craven Sch
  BD20 ....187 E7
South Cres HG4 ....214 C4
South Crescent Ave ⑳
  YO14 ....101 B3
South Crescent Cl ⑧
  YO14 ....101 B3
South Crescent Rd
  YO14 ....101 B3
South Down La WF8 ....201 D7
South Down Rd ⑧ YO32 .225 F5
South Dr HG2 ....222 E8
South Duffield Rd
  YO8 ....198 C4
South End Bedale DL8 ...63 A2
  Burniston YO13 ....75 D7
  Osmotherley DL6 ......45 B3
South End Ave DL8 .....63 A2
South End La YO26 .....181 B6
South Esk DL9 ....40 C4
South End La YO7 ......88 D1
South Gate ⑱ YO62 ....92 F6
South Grange Rd HG4 ..214 B2

South Hawksworth St ⑦
  LS29 ....218 B4
South Ings La YO62 .....70 F3
South Kilvington C of E Prim
  Sch YO7 ....211 B4
South La
  Bishop Wilton YO42 ...169 F1
  Cawood YO8 ....197 B7
  Thornton Dale YO18 ...96 D6
South Milford CP Sch
  LS25 ....195 F2
South Milford Sta
  LS25 ....195 F2
South Moor La
  Garriston DL8 ....61 A2
  Sowerby YO7 ....89 F3
South Otterington C of E
  Prim Sch DL7 ....64 F2
South Par
  Hurworth-on-Tees DL2 ..3 E1
  Ilkley LS29 ....218 A4
  Northallerton DL7 .....210 D3
  Norton YO17 ....215 E3
  ⑩ Selby YO8 ....232 C5
  York YO24 ....233 A1
South Park Ave TS4 .....7 E8
South Park La LS22 .....180 A8
South Park Rd HG1 .....219 E1
South Ridge LS25 ....194 D1
South Ruddings La
  YO19 ....192 F7
South Side TS15 ....25 C5
South St
  Barmby on the Marsh
    DN14 ....205 A2
  Burton Fleming YO25 ..126 E2
  Scalby YO13 ....75 D5
  ⑦ Scarborough YO11 ..213 A4
  South Town La TS13 ...10 E8
  South Vale DL6 ....210 E2
South View
  Burniston YO13 ....75 D7
  Castleford WF10 ......201 B5
  ⑧ Glusburn BD20 ....182 A4
  Hunton DL8 ....61 E7
  ⑩ Leyburn DL8 ......60 D5
  Northallerton DL6 .....210 E6
  ② Ruddy TS15 ....25 D5
  South West Terr BD20 .174 B1
South Wood La ⑪ BD23 .134 E3
Southdean Dr TS8 ......6 F6
Southdene ⒁ YO14 .....101 B3
Southend Ave DL3 ......3 B6
Southend Gdns ⑧ YO21 .208 C6
Southey Way YO26 .....227 A3
Southey St ⑭ BD23 ....217 A3
Southfield YO17 ....122 D3
Southfield Ave HG4 ....214 B2
Southfield Cl
  ⑧ Hurworth-on-Tees DL2 .3 E1
  Rufforth YO23 ....182 D6
Southfield Cres ⑧
  YO24 ....230 E8
Southfield La
  ⑧ Addingham LS29 ...174 F4
  Kellington DN14 ....202 E2
Southfield Rd
  ② Addingham LS29 ...174 F4
  Burley in Warfedale
    LS29 ....176 C1
  Littlethorpe HG4 ......214 B2
Southfield Terr
  ② Addingham LS29 ...174 F4
  ⑦ Skipton BD23 ......216 F3
Southfields Rd YO32 ....167 B7
Southgate
  Eastfield YO12 ....99 E6
  Pickering YO18 ....95 F7
  Ripon HG4 ....214 C4
Southgate Ave HG4 .....214 C4
Southgate Ct ⑦ HG4 ...214 C4
Southlands
  ④ Haxby YO32 ....166 E5
  ⑩ Helmsley YO62 ....92 F6
  ⑥ Hemingbrough YO8 ..198 F1
  High & Low Bishopside
    HG3 ....137 B4
Southlands Cl
  Escrick YO19 ....192 B6
  ⑧ South Milford LS25 .195 F2
Southlands Gr ⑫ YO12 .212 B7
Southlands Rd YO23 ....228 B2
Southlea YO17 ....215 D2
Southmoor La WF11 ....202 B1
Southmoor Rd YO19 ...192 F5
Southolme Cl ⑳ YO51 ..141 B5
Southolme Dr YO30 ....224 F1
Southolme Wlk ⑳ YO51 141 B5
Southway
  Harrogate HG2 ....222 C8
  Ilkley LS29 ....218 D3
Southwold ⑧ YO11 .....100 B7
Southwold Cl ⑧ YO11 ..100 B7
Southwold Rise ⑧
  YO11 ....100 B7
Southwood TS8 ....7 B4
Southwood Cl WF6 .....193 C8
Sovereign Gdns ② WF6 .200 A1
Sovereign Pk HG1 ......219 B2
Sowarth Field ⑧ BD23 ..134 E3
Sowerby Cres TS9 ......26 B7
Sowerby Cty Prim Sch
  YO7 ....211 B1
Sowerby Rd Thirsk YO7 .211 B2
  York YO26 ....227 D4
Sowerby St WF8 ....201 B2
Sowerby Terr YO7 ......211 B2
Sowerby Way TS16 .....5 D6
Sowgate La WF8 ....201 D2

Spa Complex The*
  YO11 ....21?
Spa La Harrogate HG2 ...220
  Middleton YO18 99
Spa Rd Gainford DL2 ....
  Harrogate HG2 220
Spa St HG2 226
Spa St ⑧ HG2 226
Spalding Ave YO30 .....22?
Sparrington La YO61 14
Sparrow Hall Dr DL1 ....
Sparrow La TS14 ....
Spartal La LS25 20
Spaunton Bank YO62 ...
Spaunton La YO62 7
Spawd Bone La WF11 ...20
Speculation St YO1 22
Speedwell Rd WF10 20
Speeton Ave YO30 .....
Spellow Cres HG5 14
Spellow Gr HG5 14
Spen Brow LA2 12
Spen Common La
  LS24 18
Spen La YO1 23
Spence Ct ④ TS9 .....
Spenceley Pl DL11 ....
Spencer Cl BD20 18
Spencer St
  ⑳ Glusburn BD20 18
  ⑧ York YO23 23
Spencer Wlk BD23 ....
Spencer's Holt HG1 ...21
Spencer's Way HG1 ...21
Speng La YO26 ....
Spennithorne C of E Prim
  Sch DL8 ....
Spey Bank YO24 23
Spiker's Hill La YO13 ..
Spindle Cl YO24 23
Spink La WF8 20
Spinksburn La HG3 15
Spinner La HG3 16
Spinney The
  Darlington DL3 ......
  Draughton BD23 17
  ⑧ Easingwold YO61 ..14
  Knaresborough HG5 ..22
  ⑧ Scarborough YO12 .22
  Tees-side Airport DL2 ..
  York YO24 ....
Spinniker Dr ④ YO21 ..20
Spital Bridge YO22 20
Spital Field Ct ⑧ YO17 .22
Spital Rd YO12 ....
Spital St YO17 22
Spital The TS15 ......
Spitalcroft HG5 ......
Spitalfields TS15 ....
Spitfire Ct DL10 ......
Spitfire Way LS25 ....1?
Spitlands La HG5 16
Spittal Hardwick La
  WF10 20
Spittlerush La DN6 20
Spofforth Castle*
  HG3 ....
Spofforth Hill LS22 ...18
Spofforth La
  Follifoot HG3 ....
  North Deighton LS22 ..
Spofforth Prim Sch
  HG3 ....
Spofforth La YO51 ....
Spout La LA2 ....
Spring Bank YO12 ....
Spring Bank Cl HG4 ...2
Spring Bank Rd HG4 ..2
Spring Cl
  Garforth LS25 ......
  ⑧ Sleights YO22 ....
Spring Ct HG3 ....
Spring Field Garth
  YO17 2
Spring Gdns ⑩ YO11 ..2
Spring Gr
  Harrogate HG1 22
  Laneshaw Bridge BB8 ..1?
Spring Hall Garth
  YO17 2
Spring Hill
  Stonegrave YO62 ....
  Welbury DL6 ....
  Whitby YO21 20
Spring Hill Sch HG4 ..1
Spring Hill Terr ⑩
  YO21 20
Spring La Birdforth YO7 .1
  Kirkby Overblow HG3 ..
  Long Marston YO26 ..
  Pannal HG3 ....
  Weatherby LS22 .....
  York YO10 ....
Spring Mount ⑧ YO21 ..
Spring Rise BD23 2
Spring St
  ⑧ Easingwold YO61 ..1
  Whitby YO21 20
Spring Vale YO21 2
Spring Way TS18 ......
Spring Wlk YO8 2
Springbank
  Marton cum Grafton
    YO51 ....
  Swillington LS25 2
Springbank Ave YO19 ..2
Springfield
  Bentham LA2 ....

...field continued

...d LS23 ....188 E7
...arborough YO11 .....213 B6
...by DL10 ....21 A1
...tley TS9 ....26 C7

...field Ave

...by BB18 ....172 B1
...gate HG1 ....219 C3
...LS29 ....218 C4
...ntefract WF8 ....201 C1

...field Cl

...e with Osgodby
....198 B5
...roughbridge YO51 ...141 B5
...York YO31 ....229 C7
...iburn DL8 ....60 D2
...roughbridge HG3 ....137 C4
...HG4 ....212 B3
...YO7 ....211 B4

...field Cres

...m LA2 ....129 B8
...on LS17 ....129 E8
...cl LS23 ....134 C2
...sm in Elmet LS25 ......195 F5

...field Cty Prim Sch
....3 E7

...field Dr

...rlby YO8 ....198 B5
...roughbridge YO51 .....141 B5
...field Gdns ﹇1﹈ TS9 ...26 C7

...field Gr
...roughbridge YO51 .....141 B5

...field La
...roughbridge TS15 ......5 F1

...field Mews
....219 C3

...field Mount
....174 E7

...field Rd
...roughbridge YO51 .....141 B5
...pton DL1 ....3 E7
...sgodby YO26 ....165 F1
...sm in Elmet LS25 ......195 F5
...field Rise ﹇1﹈
....164 A8
...field Terr YO17 ....124 D7
...field Way
...eley Bridge HG3 ....137 C4
...031 ....229 B7

...fields
...ottingley WF11 ....202 A2
...apton BD23 ....217 B4
...field Ave ﹇7﹈
....202 A2

...ahead Specl Sch
....212 E2
...hill Cl YO12 ....212 E2
...hill Ct ﹇7﹈ LS24 ....189 E6
...hill La YO12 ....212 D3
...hill Rd YO12 ....212 E4
...mead Dr LS25 ....194 B3
...mount ﹇3﹈ BB18 ....172 B1
...rs La
...on-on-Swale DL10 ......41 F4
...LS25 ....218 C4
...BD23 ....180 F3
...ton DL11 ....20 B4
...s Leisure Ctr TS17 ....6 B8
...s The ﹇4﹈ DL8 ....60 E2
...well Ave HG2 ....220 D4
...well Ave ﹇6﹈ LS26 ....194 A1
...well Cl ﹇8﹈ BD22 ......187 B6

...well Gdns ﹇3﹈
....210 D4
...well La DL7 ....210 D4
...well Rd ﹇6﹈ LS26 ......194 A1
...well Terr ﹇1﹈
....210 D4
...well Terr W ﹇2﹈
....210 D4
...wood YO32 ....225 D7
...ce CI YO32 ....225 D2
...e Gill Ave ﹇4﹈ DL8 ...63 B3
...e Gill Dr ﹇5﹈ DL8 ...63 B3
...sty Rd HG1 ....219 C5
...Lightship*
....233 B1
...ergate YO1 ....233 B2
...e The
...n Spa LS23 ....188 F8
...on LA6 ....103 D4
...n LS25 ....194 D1
...ingley WF11 ....201 E3
...ng DL7 ....63 F3
...ncaster LS24 ....189 F6
...Rd YO8 ....204 D7
...r CI ﹇5﹈ YO32 ....166 D5
...rs Wlk
...York YO32 ....225 F7
...ntefract WF6 ....200 A2
...ds La LS23 ....188 F8
...ouse La
...swick BD24 ....131 D4
...ham DL2 ....130 F2
...urn Ave WF10 ....201 A3
...urn La LS21 ....177 E2
...ale CI YO30 ....224 E2
...rop St TS9 ....6 E7
...rop Rd DL3 ....3 A6
...d Glass Ctr*
....100 C5
...orth Gdns TS17 ....6 B5

Stainforth La BD24 ....131 D5
Stainforth Rd BD24 ....131 E4
Stainscare La
Hawsker-cum-Stainscare
YO22 ....32 F6
Whitby YO22 ....208 F3
Stainsby Rd TS6 ....6 D8
Stainton Rd TS9 ....6 F1
Stainton Way
Coulby Newham TS8 ....7 A5
Stainton & Thornton TS8 ...6 F5
Staithe St YO8 ....199 D7
Staithes Cl ﹇4﹈ YO26 ....227 B4
Staithes La TS13 ....13 K2
Stake Rd DL8 ....111 D2
Stakesby Com Prim Sch
YO21 ....208 B6
Stakesby Rd YO21 ....208 C6
Stakesby Vale YO21 ......208 C6
**Stamford Bridge Prim & Inf
Sch** YO41 ....168 D2
Stamford Bridge Rd
YO19 ....184 E7
Stamford Bridge W
YO41 ....168 C2
Stamford St E ﹇10﹈ YO26 ...227 F5
Stamford St W ﹇9﹈ YO26 ...227 F5
Stammergate YO7 ....211 C3
Stammergate La LS22 ...180 A1
Stamp Hill Cl ﹇1﹈ YO21 ...181 D7
Stan Valley ﹇2﹈ WF8 .....206 C3
Standard Way DL6 ....210 D6
Standard Way Ind Est
DL6 ....210 C6
Standridge Clough Lan
BB18 ....172 B1
Standroyd Dr BB8 ....186 A3
Standroyd Rd BB8 ....186 A3
Stang La
Arkengarthdale DL11 ....172 A1
Farnham HG5 ....162 C7
Hope DL11 ....18 A8
Stang Rd
Arkengarthdale DL11 ....172 A1
Hope DL11 ....18 A6
Stanghow Rd TS12 ....9 F8
Stangs La BD23 ....157 D6
Stanhope Dr HG2 ....220 B2
Stanhope Gr TS5 ....6 E8
Stanhope Rd N DL3 ....3 C5
Staniland Dr YO8 ....232 A5
Stanley Cl HG4 ....214 C6
Stanley Ct ﹇2﹈
Catterick Garrison DL9 ......40 E3
Eastfield YO11 ....100 B6
Stanley Gr Aske DL10 .....20 D1
Richmond DL10 ....209 D8
Stanley St
Castleford WF10 ....200 F4
﹇4﹈ Scarborough YO12 ...213 A7
York YO31 ....233 C4
Stansfield Brow BD20 ...187 D8
Stansfield Dr WF10 ....201 B4
Stansfield Rd WF10 ....201 A4
Stanstead Gr DL2 ....4 D4
Stanyforth Cres YO26 ...164 C2
Stape Rd YO18 ....71 F7
Stape Sch YO18 ....71 F7
Stapleton Bank DL2 ....3 A2
Stapleton Cl
﹇3﹈ Bedale DL8 ....63 B2
﹇1﹈ Seamer YO12 ....99 E6
Stapley La DL8 ....87 F4
Starbeck Cl ﹇4﹈ YO21 ...208 B5
Starbeck CP Sch HG2 ...220 D4
Starbeck Sta HG2 ....220 C4
Starbeck Swimming Baths
HG2 ....220 D3
Starfits La
Fadmoor YO62 ....69 F3
Welburn YO62 ....94 A8
Starkey Cres YO31 ....229 A5
Starkey La ﹇5﹈ BD20 .....173 F1
Starmire BD22 ....187 A6
Starra Field La YO26 ....163 F5
Station Ave
﹇2﹈ Filey YO14 ....101 B3
Filey YO14 ....101 B3
Harrogate HG1 ....219 E2
Whitby YO21 ....208 B7
York YO1 ....233 A2
Station Bridge HG1 ....219 D2
Station Cl Dacre HG3 ...159 E8
﹇6﹈ East Ayton/West Ayton
YO13 ....99 A7
Hambleton YO8 ....196 F2
Sharow HG4 ....214 D7
Station Dr HG4 ....214 D7
Station Fields LS25 ....194 C4
Station La
Barmby on the Marsh
DN14 ....205 B7
Burton Leonard HG3 ....139 F3
Cliffe YO8 ....198 E3
Cloughton YO13 ....54 D1
Gristhorpe YO14 ....100 E4
Morton-on-Swale DL7 ......64 A7
Shipton YO30 ....165 E5
Station Par HG1 ....219 D2
Station Rd
Ampleforth YO62 ....92 C1
Beadlam YO62 ....93 D7
Brompton DL6 ....43 F4
Brompton-on-Swale DL10 ..41 B6

Station Rd continued
Burley in Wharfedale
LS29 ....176 C1
Carlton DN14 ....204 C3
Castleford WF10 ....200 E4
Church Fenton LS24 ......196 B7
Clapham LA2 ....130 C7
Copmanthorpe YO23 .....230 B2
Danby YO21 ....29 A7
Fylingdales YO22 ....33 C4
Gainford DL2 ....1 C8
Gilling East YO62 ....118 F8
Glusburn BD20 ....187 E8
Goldsborough HG5 ....163 A3
Great Ayton TS9 ....8 C1
Great Preston WF10 ....200 E6
Hambleton YO8 ....196 F1
Haxby YO32 ....166 F5
Helmsley YO62 ....92 F5
Hensall DN14 ....203 C1
Heslerton YO17 ....97 D1
High Bentham LA2 ....129 A8
Hinderwell TS13 ....111 F7
Horton in Ribblesdale
....105 C3
Ilkley LS29 ....218 B4
Kildale YO21 ....27 E8
Kippax LS25 ....200 C8
Kirk Hammerton YO26 ...164 D2
Knaresborough HG5 ....221 A6
Long Preston BD23 ....153 F4
Menwith with Darley
HG3 ....160 A6
Mickletown LS26 ....200 A6
Middleton St George DL2 ..4 C5
Normanton WF6 ....200 A2
Norton DN6 ....206 F2
Nunnington YO62 ....93 E2
Pannal HG3 ....222 E2
﹇2﹈ Poppleton YO26 ......165 F1
Poppleton YO26 ....182 F8
Rawcliffe DN14 ....205 A1
Riccall YO19 ....198 A8
Richmond DL10 ....209 C7
Scalby YO13 ....75 D5
Scruton DL7 ....63 E6
Settle BD24 ....131 C2
Sleights YO22 ....32 A6
Snainton YO13 ....97 F4
South Otterington DL7 .....64 F2
Sowerby YO7 ....211 A2
Stainton Dale YO13 ....54 A8
Stokesley TS9 ....26 C7
Tadcaster LS24 ....189 D6
Thirsk YO7 ....211 B4
Threshfield BD23 ....134 D2
Tollerton YO61 ....143 B3
Wharram YO17 ....148 A5
Whixley YO26 ....164 A3
Wistow YO8 ....197 C6
Womersley DN6 ....206 D5
York YO1 ....233 A2
Station Rise YO1 ....233 A2
Station Sq
﹇1﹈ Strensall YO32 ....167 B7
﹇4﹈ Whitby YO21 ....208 D7
Station Terr
﹇4﹈ Boroughbridge YO51 ..141 B6
Great Preston WF10 ....200 E6
Station View
Cliffe YO8 ....198 D3
﹇1﹈ Harrogate HG1 ....220 C3
Seamer YO12 ....99 E7
﹇8﹈ Skipton BD23 ....217 C3
Station Way LS25 ....215 C3
Staupes Rd HG3 ....160 B8
Staveley CP Sch HG5 ....140 E1
Staxton Carr La YO12 ...99 B3
Staxton Hill YO12 ....125 C8
Staynor Ave YO8 ....232 E3
Stead La LS14 ....188 A3
Steelmoor La YO60 ....146 C2
Steeple Cl ﹇4﹈ YO32 .....166 D5
Steeton La LS24 ....190 D7
Steincroft Rd ﹇7﹈ LS25 ..195 F2
Stella Gdns ﹇9﹈ WF8 ...201 C1
Stelling Rd DL11 ....38 E7
Stephen Bank DL11 ....18 H8
Stephen's Wlk YO8 ....232 B2
Stephenson Cl
Knaresborough HG5 ....221 B4
York YO31 ....225 E1
Stephenson Rd ﹇2﹈ DL2 ...41 C7
Stephenson Way
Stephenson's La YO26 ...164 A2
Stephensons Way
LS29 ....218 C5
Stephenwath La YO41 ...169 C5
Stepin Turn YO62 ....49 B1
Stepney Ave YO17 ....215 B2
Stepney Cl YO12 ....212 D4
Stepney Dr YO12 ....212 D4
Stepney Gr YO12 ....212 D4
Stepney Hill YO12 ....212 D4
Stepney Rd YO12 ....212 D4
Stepney Rise YO12 ....212 D4
Sterne Ave YO31 ....229 A5
Sterne Way YO61 ....144 C3
Stewart La YO19 ....191 C4
Stillington Cty Prim Sch
YO61 ....144 C1

Stillington Rd
Easingwold YO61 ....143 D8
Huby YO61 ....144 A4
Stinton La
Boroughbridge YO51 ....141 C4
Helperby YO61 ....142 A8
Stirling Gr YO10 ....231 F8
Stirling Rd
Burley in Wharfedale
LS29 ....176 B1
York YO30 ....224 F3
Stirling Way TS17 ....6 B6
Stirrup Cl ﹇2﹈ Norton YO17 ..215 F2
York YO24 ....230 B8
Stirton La BD23 ....216 C5
Stirtonber BD23 ....216 A5
Stittenham Hill YO60 ....146 A6
Stobarts La TS15 ....5 B1
Stock Stile La HG3 ....160 D5
Stockdale Cl ﹇9﹈ HG5 ...221 B5
Stockdale Ct DL6 ....43 A4
Stockdale La BD24 ....131 F2
Stockdale Wlk HG5 ....221 B5
Stockeld La LS22 ....179 E3
Stockeld Rd LS29 ....218 A4
Stockeld Way LS29 ....218 A5
Stockfield La YO51 ....141 D2
Stockfield Park House*
LS22 ....179 F4
Stockhill Cl ﹇1﹈ YO19 ...184 E7
Stockholm Cl ﹇7﹈ YO10 ..231 D8
Stocking Hill TS9 ....25 E2
Stocking La
Hambleton YO8 ....196 E1
Hillam LS25 ....202 B7
Knottingley WF11 ....202 B2
Lotherton cum Aberford
LS25 ....195 A7
Stockings La YO62 ....92 F2
Stocks La ﹇1﹈ HG3 ....160 A6
Stockshill YO12 ....208 C8
Stockshott La BD20 ....173 C2
Stockton Football Club
TS17 ....6 C8
Stockton La
Heworth YO32 ....226 D1
York YO31 ....229 A7
**Stockton on the Forest CP
Prim Sch** YO32 ....167 D3
Stockton Rd
Darlington DL1 ....3 C3
Sadberge DL2 ....4 C1
South Kilvington YO7 ......211 B6
Stockwell Ave
Ingleby TS17 ....6 B5
Knaresborough HG5 ....221 B7
Stockwell Cres ﹇5﹈ HG5 ...221 B7
Stockwell Ct ﹇9﹈ HG5 ...221 B7
Stockwell Dr HG5 ....221 B7
Stockwell Gr HG5 ....221 B7
Stockwell La HG5 ....221 B7
Stockwell PI HG5 ....221 B7
Stockwell Rd HG5 ....221 B6
Stockwell View HG5 ......221 B6
Stockwith La YO8 ....204 A4
Stokelake Rd ﹇5﹈ HG1 ...219 E3
Stokesley CP Sch TS9 ...26 C7
Stokesley Leisure Ctr
TS9 ....26 D7
Stokesley Rd
Brompton DL6 ....44 A3
Coulby Newham TS7 ....7 B7
Guisborough TS14 ....8 C6
Middlesbrough TS7 ....7 B6
Northallerton DL6 ....210 E7
Stokesley Sch TS9 ....26 C7
Stone Bramble ﹇8﹈ HG3 ..161 B3
Stone Bridge Dr WF11 ...201 E5
Stone Cl ﹇3﹈ YO13 ....75 D5
Stone Dale YO42 ....170 D3
Stone Garth ﹇3﹈ YO62 ....92 F6
Stone Gate YO26 ....164 A4
Stone Head La ﹇2﹈ BB8 ..186 A4
Stone Man La DL11 ....19 E5
Stone Quarry Rd YO13 ...75 C8
Stone Riggs YO32 ....167 B3
Stone Rings Cl HG2 ....222 E5
Stone Rings Gr HG2 ......222 E5
Stone Rings La HG2 ....222 E5
Stone Stoup Hill TS9 .....27 C5
Stonebeck Ave HG1 ......219 B4
Stonebeck Gate La
YO21 ....29 D4
Stonebow The
Thornton-le-Beans DL6 .....65 B5
York YO1 ....233 C2
Stonebridge Ave ﹇4﹈ YO19 ..184 E7
Stonecrop Ave ﹇5﹈ HG3 ..161 B3
Stonecrop Dr ﹇1﹈ HG3 ...161 B3
Stonecross Rd YO21 ......208 A6
Stoned Horse La
YO26 ....164 C4
Stonefall Ave HG2 ....220 C3
Stonefall Dr HG2 ....220 B2
Stonefall Mews HG2 ......220 B2
Stonefall Pl ﹇8﹈ HG2 .....220 B2
Stonefield Ave ﹇4﹈ YO61 ..143 C8
Stonefield Garth ﹇9﹈
YO61 ....143 C8
Stonefield La ﹇4﹈ YO61 ...143 C8
Stonegate
Hunmanby YO14 ....126 F8
York YO1 ....233 B2
Stonehaven Way DL1 ......3 F8
Stonelands St ﹇2﹈ BD20 ..187 E7
Stonepit Balk YO17 ....149 C5
Stonepit Hill YO17 ....149 C5

Stonepit La
Birdsall YO17 ....148 D6
Gristhorpe YO14 ....100 E5
Stonesdale Cl ﹇3﹈ HG5 ..221 D5
Stonesdale La YO21 ....35 E8
Stonethwaite ﹇5﹈ YO24 ..230 C7
Stoney Bank Rd BB18 ...172 B1
Stoney Haggs Rd YO12 ...99 E7
Stoneyborough Cl
YO7 ....211 C4
Stoneybrough La YO7 ....211 C4
Stony Cross YO62 ....93 E7
Stony La
East Harlsey DL6 ....44 F5
﹇8﹈ Scalby YO13 ....75 D5
Stonygate Bank DL11 ....20 A5
Stoop Cl YO32 ....225 C8
Stoopdale Ave DL3 ....3 B7
Stoopes Hill ﹇8﹈ BB18 ...172 B1
Storey Cl ﹇2﹈ YO62 ....92 F6
Storiths La BD23 ....175 A8
Storking La YO41 ....185 F6
Storr La YO13 ....74 E5
Storth Gill La BD24 ....131 A1
Stourton Rd LS29 ....175 C3
Stow Ct YO32 ....225 D3
Strafford Rd ﹇13﹈ DL10 ..41 E4
Straight La
Addingham LS29 ....174 E3
Aldwark YO61 ....142 C3
Burton Leonard HG3 ....140 A3
Holtby YO19 ....184 F8
Middleham DL8 ....60 F2
Straights The DL8 ....5 B8
Strait La
Copt Hewick HG4 ....114 B2
Danby YO21 ....29 C6
Hurworth DL2 ....3 F1
Stainton & Thornton TS8 ...6 D5
Weeton LS17 ....178 B2
Well DL8 ....87 A3
Straits La YO11 ....99 A3
Stranglands La WF11 ....201 C3
Stratford Way YO32 ......225 F3
Strathmore Dr ﹇3﹈ TS15 ..28 H8
Strathmore Rd LS29 .....218 E4
Straw Gate DL2 ....3 A2
Strawberry Ct YO12 ......212 D4
Strawberry Dale Ave ﹇3﹈
HG1 ....219 D3
Strawberry Dale Sq ﹇1﹈
....219 D3
Strawberry Dale Terr ﹇2﹈
....219 D3
Strawgate Gr DL3 ....3 A3
Stray Garth YO31 ....225 F7
Stray Rd
Harrogate HG2 ....222 D8
York YO31 ....229 B6
Stray Rein HG2 ....219 E1
Stray The Darlington DL1 ..3 E5
Henderskelfe YO60 ....146 D8
Longnewton TS21 ....5 A2
Stray Wlk HG2 ....228 F8
Straylands Gr YO31 ......229 B7
Street 1 LS23 ....189 A1
Street 2
Thorp Arch LS23 ....181 A1
Walton LS23 ....181 A1
Street 3 LS23 ....181 A1
Street 4 LS23 ....181 A1
Street 5 LS23 ....181 A1
Street 6 LS23 ....181 A1
Street 7 LS23 ....181 A1
Street 8 LS23 ....181 A1
Street Head La BD22 .....187 F1
Street La Beverley HG3 ...137 B4
Bubwith YO8 ....199 F5
Colton LS24 ....190 D7
Glaisdale YO21 ....29 E3
Middleton YO18 ....95 E7
Pickhill with Roxby YO7 ...88 B6
Street The ﹇8﹈ LS29 ....174 E4
Strensall Dr ﹇11﹈ YO12 ...75 F5
Strensall Pk YO32 ....167 A5
Strensall Rd
Earswick YO32 ....226 A7
York YO32 ....225 F6
Stretton Dr WF7 ....200 D1
Strickland Rd ﹇4﹈ YO14 ..127 A8
Strikes La BD20 ....187 F6
Stripe La
Hartwith cum Winsley
HG3 ....160 B8
Skelton YO30 ....224 B5
Stripe The ﹇6﹈ TS9 ....26 C7
Stuart Ave DL10 ....209 C8
Stuart Cl
﹇4﹈ Scarborough YO11 ...100 B7
﹇4﹈ Strensall YO32 ....167 B7
Stuart Gr
Eggborough DN14 ....203 A2
﹇1﹈ Pontefract WF6 ....200 A2
﹇3﹈ Thorpe Willoughby YO8 ..197 B1
Stuart Rd
Pontefract WF8 ....201 A4
York YO24 ....227 C1
Stuart St
﹇10﹈ Barnoldswick BB18 ..171 F1
Pontefract WF8 ....201 B1
Stubbing La DL3 ....81 B1
Stubbing Nook La DL8 ....62 B2
Stubbs La
Cridling Stubbs WF11 .....206 A8
Norton DN6 ....206 E4

Stubbs La continued
Stainton Dale YO13 ....53 F5
Stubbs Rd DN6 ....206 D3
Stubden Gr YO30 ....224 F2
Stubham Rise LS29 ......218 A5
Stud Fold Bank HG3 ....110 B3
Studford Ring* YO62 .....92 C2
Studley Cl DL7 ....210 B2
Studley La HG4 ....113 C1
Studley Rd
Harrogate HG1 ....219 D3
Ripon HG4 ....214 A4
Studley Roger HG4 ....113 D1
Stumpcross Ct WF8 .....201 C2
Stumpcross La WF8 .....201 C2
Stumpcross Way █
WF8 ....201 C2
Stumps La HG3 ....160 A5
Stunstead Rd BB8 ....186 B2
Sturdee Gr YO31 ....228 D7
Sturdy House La
Marske DL11 ....19 E2
Whashton DL11 ....20 A4
Sturton Grange La
LS25 ....194 D4
Sturton La LS25 ....194 D4
Stuteville Cl █ YO62 ....70 C1
Stutton Rd LS24 ....189 D4
Stygate La DN6 ....206 E1
Sudforth La DN14 ....202 C1
Suffield Hill YO13 ....75 A5
Sugar Hill █ LS29 ....174 F4
Summer Hill Rd LS26 ...200 B6
Summerbridge CP Sch
HG3 ....138 A1
Summerfield Cl █
WF11 ....201 F4
Summerfield Dr WF11 ..201 F4
Summerfield La YO22 ...33 A7
Summerfield Rd YO24 ..230 C7
Sun La LS29 ....176 C1
Sun Lounge Theatre
YO14 ....101 B3
Sun St Cononley BD20 ..173 C1
█ Cowling BD22 ....187 B6
Thornaby S17 ....6 A8
Sunderland Rd BD20 ...173 E3
Sundew Heath █ HG3 ...161 B3
Sunmoor Dr BD23 ....217 A4
Sunningdale LS25 ....194 F4
Sunningdale Cl █ YO26 .227 B5
Sunningdale Dr TS16 ....5 E5
Sunningdale Gr █
YO21 ....208 B5
Sunningdales WF6 ......200 B1
Sunny Bank Rd █ WF11 .202 A2
Sunny Bank Rd BD20 ...187 E7
Sunnybank Rd LS25 ....195 A3
Sunnycrest Ave YO10 ..209 D8
Sunnydale █ YO32 .....225 D7
Sunnyside Prim Sch TS8 ..7 A6
Sunset Dr LS29 ....218 D5
Sunstar Gr TS7 ....7 B6
Sur Gate
Harwood Dale YO13 ....53 F1
Suffield-cum-Everley
YO13 ....74 F8
Surray Way YO30 ....227 F8
Surtees St Darlington DL3 .3 C6
York YO30 ....225 B2
Sussex Cl █ Bedale DL8 ..63 A2
York YO10 ....229 C2
Sussex Rd YO10 ....229 C2
Sussex St Bedale DL8 ....63 A2
█ Scarborough YO11 ....213 A6
Sussex Way █ YO32 ....167 A7
Sutcliffe Ct █ YO21 .....208 B5
Sutherland Rd YO18 .....71 C6
Sutherland St YO23 .....228 B1
Sutton Way
Middlesbrough TS4 ....6 F8
York YO30 ....228 B8
Sutton-on-the-Forest C of E
Prim Sch YO61 ....144 C3
Swadford St BD23 ....216 F4
Swain Ct DL6 ....210 D5
Swainby Abbey* DL8 ....88 B8
Swainby Ellers DL6 .....25 D1
Swainby La DL8 ....87 F7
Swainsea Dr █ YO18 ....95 F7
Swainsea La YO18 ....95 F8

Swainstead Raike
BD24 ....153 B8
Swainston Cl TS5 ....6 E7
Swale Ave YO24 ....230 E8
Swale Hall La DL11 ......38 B5
Swale La Catterick DL10 ..41 E5
Pickhill with Roxby YO7 ..88 C7
Swale Pasture La DL10 ..41 E5
Swale View YO7 ....115 B6
Swaledale Ave DL3 ......3 B6
Swaledale Rd █ DL9 ....40 E4
Swalegate DL10 ....209 C8
Swallow Cl TS14 ....8 D6
Swan Cl YO19 ....192 A7
Swan Farm Ct YO19 .....192 A7
Swan Hill Rd YO11 ......213 A6
Swan La YO7 ....165 B1
Swan Rd HG1 ....219 C2
Swan St BD23 ....173 B4
Swan Syke Dr █ DN6 ...206 F2
Swang Rd YO13 ....75 A6
Swanhills La YO13 ....98 F3
Swanland Rd YO62 ....92 F7
Swan St YO23 ....233 A1
Swarcliffe Rd HG1 ....220 B4
Swartha La BD20 ....174 D2
Swarthlands La YO13 ....75 D7
Swarthmoor La LS25 ....196 C1
Sweet Bits La HG5 ......221 C8
Sweet Briar
█ Harrogate HG3 ....161 B3
Harrogate HG3 ....219 A4
Sweetbecks Cl █ YO11 ..100 A6
Swillington La LS26 .....194 A2
Swillington Prim Sch
LS26 ....194 A1
Swinburn Ct █ HG4 .....86 C3
Swinburn Rd █ HG4 .....86 C3
Swinburne Cl HG1 ....219 E7
Swinburne Rd TS16 .....5 E6
Swindale La TS12 ....9 F5
Swindon La HG3 ....178 E4
Swinegate YO1 ....233 B2
Swinherd La YO62 ....70 C1
Swinneybeck Bank
HG4 ....85 E5
Swinsty Ct YO30 ....224 F1
Swinton Cl HG2 ....222 B8
Swinton La YO17 ....121 B3
Swire Way DL10 ....20 F7
Swires La BD20 ....173 C3
Swordfish Way LS25 ....196 B4

Sycamore Ave
█ Catton YO7 ....89 A1
Filey YO14 ....101 A4
Kippax LS25 ....194 C1
Knottingley WF11 ....201 E1
Malton YO17 ....215 D5
Richmond DL10 ....209 A8
York YO32 ....225 D4
Sycamore Cl
Bishop Monkton HG3 ....140 A5
Clint HG3 ....160 F8
█ Haxby YO32 ....166 E5
█ Hurworth-on-Tees DL2 ..3 E1
Selby YO8 ....232 A4
Skelton YO30 ....224 C5
Slingsby YO62 ....120 B5
Spennithorne DL8 ....60 F4
Sycamore Dr
█ Addingham LS29 ......175 A4
█ Bedale DL8 ....63 A2
Harrogate HG2 ....220 C3
Norton-le-Clay YO7 ......115 B1
Sycamore Gr BD20 .....187 F7
Sycamore La DL7 ....63 D4
Sycamore Pl YO30 ......233 A3
Sycamore Rd
Barlby with Osgodby
YO8 ....198 B5
Ripon HG4 ....214 B2
Sycamore Terr YO30 ....233 A3
Sycamore View █ YO26 .165 F1
Sycamore Way █ DL10 ..41 E4
Sydall's Way █ DL10 ....41 E4
Sydney St █ YO12 ....212 F7
Sykehead La YO62 ....93 D6
Sykes Barrel █ BD24 ...131 D3
Sykes Gr HG1 ....219 C5
Sykes La YO61 ....143 B3

T

Tabard Hamlet █ DN14 ..202 F2
Tabard La █ DN14 ....202 F2
Tabards The █ DN14 ....202 F2
Tadcaster Albion FC
LS24 ....189 E6
Tadcaster East CP Sch
LS24 ....189 F6
Tadcaster Gram Sch
LS24 ....189 B5
Tadcaster Leisure Ctr
LS24 ....189 E6
Tadcaster Rd YO24 ......230 F8
Tadcaster Road Dringhouses
YO23 ....230 E5
Tadcaster Sports & Leisure
Ctr LS24 ....189 E6
Talbot St WF6 ....200 A1
Tameside TS9 ....26 C8
Tamworth Rd █ YO30 ...225 A1
Tanfield Dr █ LS29 .....176 C1
Tanfield La HG4 ....114 A8

Tang Hall La YO31 ......229 A5
Tang Hall Prim Sch
YO31 ....228 F5
Tang Rd HG3 ....160 D4
Tanner Row YO1 ....233 A2
Tanner's Moat YO1 ......233 A2
Tannery Ct █ HG5 ....221 B5
Tannery La DL7 ....210 D5
Tanpit La
Easingwold YO61 ....143 C8
Walden Stubbs DN6 ......206 E3
Tanshelf Sta WF8 ....200 F1
Tansy Cl █ HG3 ....161 B3
Tansy Rd █ HG3 ....161 B3
Tanton Rd TS9 ....7 B1
Tarbard Ave █ HG4 ......113 D2
Tarbert Cres █ YO24 ....230 B8
Tarn Moor Cres BD23 ...216 E6
Tarr Steps TS7 ....6 A3
Tasmania Sq TS7 ....7 C6
Tate Cl YO8 ....197 D6
Tate Rd DL10 ....209 C8
Tatham Fells Sch LA2 ....128 F3
Tatton Cl YO30 ....225 A1
Taylor Cl LS26 ....200 C6
Taylor Hill YO18 ....71 F7
Taylor La LS15 ....194 A7
Taylor St █ BB18 ....171 D1
Teal Cl Castleford WF10 .200 E3
█ Filey YO14 ....101 A3
Teal Dr YO24 ....230 C8
Teal La █ YO18 ....95 F7
Teasel Gr █ HG3 ....161 B3
Tebay Cl TS7 ....7 D8
Tedder Ave TS17 ....6 B6
Tedder Prim Sch TS17 ..6 C6
Tedder Rd YO24 ....227 B1
Tedworth Cl TS14 ....8 F5
Tees Bank Ave TS18 ....5 E6
Tees Grange Ave DL3 ..3 A5
Tees View Hurworth DL2 .3 C1
Hurworth-on-Tees DL2 ..22 C8
Teesdale Ave DL3 ....3 A4
Teesdale Rd DL9 ....40 E4
Teesgate TS17 ....6 C8
Teesside Tertiary Coll
TS4 ....7 B8
Teesside High Sch TS16 .5 E5
Teesside Ind Est TS17 ..6 C5
Teesside International
Airport DL2 ....4 F4
Teesway DL2 ....4 A5
Telford Cl WF10 ....200 D4
Telford Terr █ YO24 ....228 B2
Templar Cl DN14 ....202 F1
Templar Gdns LS22 .....180 C4
Templar Way YO8 ....232 C2
Temple Ave YO10 ....229 B4
Temple Bank DL8 ....59 A3
Temple Garth YO23 .....230 C1
Temple La
Burton cum Walden DL8 ..82 D3
Copmanthorpe YO23 ....230 C1
Temple Manor* YO8 .....203 D4
Temple Rd YO23 ....230 F4
Temple St WF10 ....200 E4
Templemead YO31 ....228 E8
Tems Side █ BD24 ......131 D3
Tems St █ BD24 ....131 D2
Ten Thorn La YO26 ......227 A4
Tennant Cl DL7 ....210 B6
Tennant St YO8 ....232 B6
Tennant Rd YO24 ....227 B2
Tennis Court La YO61 ...143 A3
Tennyson Ave
█ Campsall DN6 ....206 C1
Harrogate HG1 ....219 E7
Scarborough YO12 ....212 F7
█ Selby YO8 ....232 D3
Tennyson Way █ WF8 ...201 B1
Tentergate Ave █ HG5 ..221 A7
Tentergate Cl █ HG5 ....221 A7
Tentergate Gdns █
HG5 ....221 A7
Tentergate La HG5 ......221 A7
Tentergate Rd █ HG5 ...221 A7
Tenters Cl WF11 ....201 E3
Tern Pk █ LS22 ....180 A1
Terrington Bank YO60 ..119 C2
Terrington C of E Prim Sch
YO60 ....119 C1
Terrington South Bank
YO60 ....119 D1
Terrington South Bank
YO60 ....119 D1
Terrington View YO60 ...145 C5
Terry Ave YO1 ....233 B1
Terry St YO23 ....228 C1
Tetherings La YO11 .....99 F6
Tewit Well Ave HG2 .....222 D8
Tewit Well Rd HG2 ....222 E7
Thackadale La YO17 .....121 A1
Thackeray Gr TS5 ....6 E8
Thacking La LA6 ....103 D4
Thames Ave
Guisborough TS14 ....8 E6
Thornaby TS17 ....6 A8
Thanet Rd YO24 ....227 D1
Theakston La DL8 ....62 D4
Thatch Cl YO8 ....232 C4
Thatchers Croft YO23 ...230 F3
Theakston Brewery Visitor
Ctr* HG4 ....61 C4
Theakston Hargill DL8 ..87 E8
Theakston La DL10 ......209 C6
Theresa Cl █ YO31 ......225 F1

Thickrash Brow LA2 .....129 A7
Thief La Barlow YO8 .....232 F1
York YO10 ....228 F3
Thiefgate La HG4 ....86 E3
Thiefhole La DL7 ....65 B3
Third Ave
█ Wetherby LS22 ....180 C3
York YO31 ....228 F5
Thirkleby Way YO10 ....229 C4
Thirlmere Cl █ YO7 .....89 C4
Thirlmere Dr YO31 ......229 A6
Thirsk Athletic Club
YO7 ....211 A3
Thirsk Bank
Angram Grange YO61 ....117 B8
Thornton-le-Moor DL7 ....65 B3
Thirsk Bsns Pk YO7 .....211 B2
Thirsk CP Sch YO7 ....211 C4
Thirsk Ind Pk YO7 ....211 D2
Thirsk Mus* YO7 ....211 B3
Thirsk Race Course*
YO7 ....211 A4
Thirsk Rd
Eaglescliffe TS15 ....5 E2
Easingwold YO61 ....117 B1
Kirkby TS9 ....26 C6
Romanby DL6 ....210 F1
Thirsk Sch YO7 ....211 B1
Thirsk Sta YO7 ....89 D4
Thirsk Swimming Pool
YO7 ....211 C2
Thirty Acre La HG5 ......163 A6
Thirwall Dr TS17 ....6 A4
Thistle Cl
Northallerton DL7 ....210 D1
Selby YO8 ....232 C2
Thistle Hill HG5 ....221 B3
Thistle Rise TS8 ....6 F6
Thistlebar Rd YO51 .....141 D2
Thomas Gill Rd █ HG2 ..137 F1
Thomas St █ Selby YO8 .232 D6
█ York YO10 ....228 E3
Thomason Foss (Waterfall)*
YO22 ....31 C1
Thompson Cl
█ Barlby YO8 ....198 B4
█ Selby YO8 ....75 D5
Thompson Dr █ YO32 ...166 B7
Thompson Pl █ YO26 ...227 E5
Thompson St E DL1 .....3 D7
Thompson St W DL3 .....3 C7
Thoresby La DL8 ....59 B5
Thoresby Rd YO24 ......227 B1
Thornborough Gdns TS17 .6 B8
Thorn Nook YO31 ....228 F8
Thorn Tree Ave █ YO14 .101 B4
Thorn Wath La YO62 ....48 E4
Thornaby Comn Sch TS17 .6 B7
Thornaby Rd TS17 ......6 B7
Thornaby Swimming Baths
TS17 ....6 A8
Thornaby Village Prim Sch
TS17 ....6 A8
Thornborough Cres █
DL8 ....60 D5
Thornburgh Rd DL6 .....210 E3
Thornburgh Rd YO11 ....99 F6
Thorncroft █ YO19 ......184 F7
Thorndale St BD23 ......154 B3
Thornden Bldgs YO8 ....232 D5
Thorndikes La HG5 ......141 A2
Thorne Cl DL8 WF6 ......200 B1
Thorner C of E Prim Sch
LS14 ....188 A3
Thorner Gr BD20 ....174 C2
Thorner La LS23 ....188 B5
Thorner Rd LS23 ....188 B4
Thornfield Ave
Dishforth YO7 ....115 A4
█ York YO31 ....228 F8
Thornfield Bsns Pk
DL7 ....210 B6
Thornfield Dr █ YO31 ...225 E2
Thornfield Gr TS5 ....6 E8
Thornfield Rd DL8 ....63 C1
Thornhill
█ Eastfield YO11 ....100 A6
Northallerton DL6 ....210 E3
Thornhill Rd WF10 ......200 F3
Thornhill Way HG1 ......219 B5
Thornlands █ YO61 .....117 D1
Thornley Ave DL7 ....210 D3
Thorns La YO51 ....140 F4
Thornthwaite Brow
HG3 ....159 E5
Thornton Cl
█ Easingwold YO61 .....143 D8
Stainton & Thornton TS8 ..6 D4
Thornton in Craven CP Sch
BD23 ....172 A3
Thornton La Dent LA10 ..78 A4
Marishes YO17 ....96 B1
Thornton in Lonsdale
LA6 ....103 C4
Thornton-le-Moor
YO7 ....117 D4
Thornton le Dale C of E Prim
Sch YO18 ....96 C5
Thornton Moor Cl
YO30 ....224 F2
Thornton Rd
Coulby Newham TS8 .....6 E5
Pickering YO18 ....96 A6
Thornton St
█ Burley in Warfedale
LS29 ....176 C1
Darlington DL3 ....3 C5
█ Skipton BD23 ....216 D3

Thornton Vale TS8 ....6 D4
Thornton Watlass C of E
Sch HG4 ....86 B8
Thorntree Gdns DL2 ....3 E1
Thorntree La DN14 ....6 F1
Thorntree Rd
Northallerton DL6 ....210 E3
Thornaby TS17 ....6 A8
Thornview Rd BD23 .....174 B1
Thornwood Ave TS17 ...6 A7
Thornwood Covert █
YO7 ....211 A3
Thorny Hill La YO51 ....141 B1
Thorp La YO42 ....193 C5
Thorp Arch Pk LS23 ....181 A1
Thorp Arch Trad Est
LS23 ....181 A2
Thorpe Bassett La
YO17 ....123 D6
Thorpe Chase HG4 ......214 B3
Thorpe Green Bank █
YO22 ....32 A6
Thorpe Green La
YO26 ....182 D8
Thorpe La
Ampleforth YO62 ....118 E2
Cawood YO8 ....197 A8
Cracoe BD23 ....156 B7
Fylingdales YO22 ....33 A4
Thorpe BD23 ....214 C8
Thorpe Rd HG4 ....214 B2
Thorpe St YO23 ....228 C1
Thorpe Willoughby Cty P
Sch YO8 ....197 B2
Threapland BD23 ....156 B5
Three Tuns Wynd █ TS9 .26 C7
Threshfield Prim Sch
BD23 ....134 D2
Thrintoft La DL7 ....64 D3
Thrintoft Moor La DL7 ..64 A4
Thrope La HG3 ....109 E3
Throstle Farm Sch
WF11 ....201 E3
Throstle Nest Cl LS21 ..177 A1
Throstle Nest Dr HG2 ...222 B5
Throxenby Gr █ YO12 ..212 A8
Throxenby La YO12 ......75 A8
Thruscross La HG3 ......159 A8
Thrussendale Rd
YO17 ....147 C4
Thurland Castle* LA6 ....102 D7
Thwaite Holme La DL8 ..61 A5
Thwaite La LA2 ....130 F8
Thwaites Ave LS29 ......218 C3
Thwaites La
Markington with Wallerthwaite
HG3 ....139 C2
Nether Silton YO7 ....66 B5
Thirkleby High & Low with
Osgodby YO7 ....90 D1
Thweng Way TS14 ......8 F6
Thwing Rd YO25 ....126 F5
Tib Garth LS22 ....188 A8
Tibby Butts █ YO13 ......75 D5
Tickergate La DL7 ....65 B6
Tidkin La TS14 ....8 F6
Tile Cl BD23 ....216 B3
Tillman Cl █ BD24 ....131 D2
Tilmire Cl █ YO10 ....231 D8
Timble Gr HG1 ....219 F6
Timmys La DL2 ....4 D5
Tindall St YO12 ....212 F6
Tinker La YO23 ....182 C2
Tinkers' La HG3 ....161 A3
Tinkingfield La LS22 ....180 E5
Tinkler La YO51 ....141 C5
Tinkler's La WF11 ......201 C6
Tinley Garth YO62 ....70 B1
Tinley Gdns █ YO62 ....70 B1
Tintagel Ct WF6 ....200 A3
Tippaty La WF11 ....201 A6
Tirril Way TS7 ....7 B6
Tisbury Rd YO26 ....227 E4
Tithe Barn Fold LS15 ...194 B8
Tithe Barn Rd █ WF8 ...201 B1
Tithe Barn Way DN14 ...202 F1
Tithe La HG4 ....113 C8
Tivoli Pl LS29 ....218 B4
Toadham La DN14 ....204 A1
Toby Ct YO32 ....225 C8
Toc La YO18 ....53 E5
Tockwith C of E Prim Sch
YO26 ....181 F6
Tockwith La YO26 ....181 C5
Tockwith Rd
Long Marston YO26 ......181 E6
Tockwith LS22 ....180 F4
Tod Holes La BD23 ......155 A5
Todd La DL7 ....42 D1
Toddcs Ct █ YO7 ....89 B1
Toddy Hall Rd BD22 ....187 B6
Todmanhaw La BD23 ...155 A1
Toft Gn YO1 ....233 A2
Toft Ings La YO61 ....143 D8
Tofta Rd YO13 ....54 B3
Tofting La YO17 ....147 E1
Tofts Cl TS15 ....5 D2
Tofts Fort The* DL11 ...18 H6
Tofts La Danby YO21 ....29 B6
Follifoot HG3 ....223 C5
Humberton YO61 ....141 F6
Pickering YO18 ....95 F7
Tholthorpe YO61 ....142 D5
Welbury DL6 ....24 E5
Tofts Rd YO18 ....95 F7
Toll Bar Cl █ YO8 ....204 F1

ar Rd WF10 ....200 C4
ar Way LS24 ....189 F7
'gate YO11 ....213 A7
'ton Rd YO30 ....165 B7
sby La TS7 ....7 B6
sby Rd TS5 ....6 F8
Cat La
n-in-Ainsty with Bickerton
....181 A5
all YO17 ....148 B4
Dando Cl WF6 ....200 C1
Hall Ct 12 DL8 ....63 A2
La Cowling BD22 ....186 E7
forths YO26 ....141 F3
Smith's Cross
....92 B4
hawk Trail WF10 ....200 F3
ill Bank DL8 ....58 E2
nson Way LS25 ....195 E4
old WF11 ....201 D6
ouse Farm Mews 2
....201 D6
a Colne BB8 ....186 B2
anthorpe YO23 ....230 B3
ood LS21 ....177 A6
tone Cl LS25 ....201 F6
iff Ct YO8 ....232 B7
iffe C of E Prim Sch
....115 C7
iffe Rd
rby YO7 ....89 E3
k YO7 ....211 B1
naby TS17 ....6 C7
nill Cl YO32 ....225 D4
nce Dr DL1 ....3 F8
on Pl YO24 ....230 B7
Rd HG1 ....220 A3
Ave YO26 ....227 C5
Cl 14 YO41 ....168 D2
ton La LS23 ....188 F5
Hill YO60 ....146 E5
car Rd LA6 ....103 C5
op La BD20 ....173 A1
Cres LS24 ....189 D6
Croft 7 YO61 ....117 D1
Rd Darlington DL3 ....3 B6
HG4 ....214 C6
St
gate HG1 ....219 D1
YO1 ....233 B1
Street Castle W 4
....209 C6
The* HG4 ....139 B6
View DN14 ....204 C2
rs Paddock
....201 A4
End Ave DN14 ....204 C3
End Cl
usburn BD20 ....187 E7
ckering YO18 ....96 A6
End Gdns 3
....166 D5
Farm Cl 15 YO62 ....70 B1
Green Dr TS9 ....26 E5
Head Ave 1
....131 E2
Head Way 14
....131 D2
Hill LS23 ....188 E5
St
p Thornton HG3 ....138 F1
sby-cum-Stearsby
....118 D3
n YO17 ....215 E6
HG3 ....161 E7
pston YO17 ....123 A6
ngton YO17 ....122 C1
end Ct 3 YO26 ....164 A8
end Pl 5 BD20 ....187 E7
end Rd YO42 ....193 D1
end St YO31 ....233 B4
head 2 BD24 ....131 E2
head Fold 12 LS29 ....174 F4
head La LA2 ....130 E8
orpe Moor La
....167 C5
orpe Rd YO32 ....166 F5
n Ave
rk YO24 ....227 F2
rk YO24 ....228 A2
us* YO12 ....212 F5
gar Ct 10 HG1 ....219 D1
gar Rd
arrogate HG1 ....219 D1
LS29 ....218 B4
gar Sq YO12 ....212 F7
gar St YO23 ....228 B1
gar St W YO12 ....212 F6
gar Terr YO12 ....212 F7
rd Ct 19 DL1 ....3 F6
rd Rd 4 DN6 ....206 E2
La 14 YO18 ....95 F7
y Ave YO10 ....229 D4
ire Cl YO7 ....211 D4
ore La DN14 ....203 B3
Wlk LS24 ....190 B1
r Rd TS4 ....6 F8
ing Hill HG3 ....110 C4
es Hill YO13 ....54 D2
lers Garth YO17 ....121 C1
en CP Sch BB8 ....186 A1
en Rd BB8 ....186 A3
dale Rd 1 HG2 ....219 C1
l Cl TS14 ....8 D6
l Dr 4 HG3 ....161 B3
l Wood TS7 ....7 B7
ar La YO61 ....91 A2
ard Ave TS17 ....6 B6

Trenchard Rd YO26 ....227 B6
Trenchard St 8 YO7 ....89 B1
Trenholme La TS15 ....25 B3
Trent Ave
Garforth LS25 ....194 D3
Pontefract WF6 ....200 A2
4 York YO32 ....225 F6
Trent Way YO24 ....230 D7
Trentholme Dr 2 YO24 ....228 A2
Trevine Gdns TS17 ....5 F4
Trevor Gr 8 YO24 ....227 F2
Trimdon Ave TS5 ....6 D6
Trinity Cl 1 YO11 ....212 F3
Trinity Gdns 2 YO11 ....212 F3
Trinity La Ripon HG4 ....214 B5
York YO1 ....233 A2
Trinity Pk HG4 ....214 B6
Trinity Rd Darlington DL3 ....3 C5
Harrogate HG2 ....219 D1
Scarborough YO11 ....212 F3
Trinket La LA2 ....128 B6
Trip Garth LS22 ....180 A1
Trip La Collingham LS22 ....180 A1
Sicklinghall LS22 ....179 F1
Triplins La HG4 ....113 B6
Troon Cl 2 YO26 ....227 B5
Trousdale Hill YO60 ....147 A7
Troutbeck 7 YO24 ....230 C7
Troutbeck Cl 11 YO18 ....95 F6
Troutsdale Ave YO30 ....224 E2
Trumfleet La DN6 ....207 D1
Trundles La 7 WF11 ....202 A2
Truro Cres 8 HG3 ....161 B3
Truro Dr 19 WF6 ....200 A2
Truro Rd 7 HG3 ....161 B3
Truro Wlk 23 WF6 ....200 A2
Trust Fold LS25 ....201 E6
Tudor Cl 10 YO8 ....197 B1
Tudor Rd
Richmond DL10 ....209 D7
York YO24 ....227 C2
Tudor Way YO32 ....167 C8
Tuke Ave YO10 ....229 B4
Tumbledown Cl 5 DL9 ....40 E3
Tune St YO8 ....198 B4
Tunstall Rd
Catterick DL10 ....41 D4
Harrogate HG2 ....220 B3
Turbary Rd LA6 ....103 B7
Turfy Hill DL8 ....56 C4
Turker Cl DL6 ....210 E5
Turker La DL6 ....210 F6
Turkey La YO7 ....114 F8
Turnberry Ave TS16 ....5 E4
Turnberry Dr YO26 ....227 B4
Turnberry Way TS8 ....7 C5
Turner Cl DL9 ....209 C2
Turner Cres 6 LS21 ....177 A1
Turner La 4 LS29 ....174 E4
Turner's Croft YO10 ....229 A1
Turners Sq 9 YO8 ....232 C5
Turnham La YO8 ....198 C2
Turnhead Cres YO8 ....198 B5
Turnhead Ct YO8 ....198 B6
Turnmire Rd 1 YO24 ....230 E8
Turnpike La LS22 ....181 B5
Turnpike Rd LS24 ....189 F7
Turnshaw Rd BD22 ....187 F1
Turpin La LS25 ....196 A2
Turton Rd TS15 ....5 D2
Turver's La WF11 ....202 C2
Tuscany Way WF6 ....200 A3
Tuthill 18 YO11 ....213 B6
Tutin Rd DL7 ....63 C5
Tweed Ave TS17 ....6 B7
Twelve Acre Bank DL8 ....40 E1
Twin Pike Way 14 YO32 ....166 D5
Twine Wlk 7 LA6 ....102 F3
Twizzie Gill View 7
TS13 ....11 A8
Two Laws Rd BB8 ....187 B1
Tyler Cl WF6 ....200 C1
Tyn Garth YO19 ....191 D8
Tyne Cres DL1 ....3 D3
Typhoon Cl DL10 ....41 F6
Tyseley Gr 4 BB18 ....172 A1
Tyson Pl HG2 ....220 B2

U

Uldale Cl 5 HG5 ....221 D5
Uldale Dr TS16 ....5 E4
Ulla Gn LS24 ....190 B1
Ulleskelf Sta LS24 ....190 B2
Ullswater YO24 ....230 D7
Ullswater Ave TS5 ....6 E8
Ullswater Dr LS22 ....180 B3
Ullswater Rise 5 LS22 ....180 B3
Ulnaby La DL2 ....2 C7
Under Cliffe 17 YO18 ....95 F7
Undercliffe Rise LS29 ....218 E2
Undercroft 7 YO19 ....184 F7
Underlands La HG4 ....114 C7
Underwit Rd YO8 ....204 C4
Union La YO8 ....232 C4
Union St 28 Filey YO14 ....101 B3
Harrogate HG1 ....219 D3
12 Knaresborough HG5 ....221 A5
2 Scarborough YO11 ....213 A6
Union Terr
5 Skipton BD23 ....216 F3
York YO31 ....233 B4
Unity Cl HG1 ....219 D5
Unity Gr HG1 ....219 D5
Unity St 1 BB18 ....186 A7
University Coll of Ripon &
York St John HG4 ....214 B6
University College of
Scarborough YO12 ....213 B1
University of York
Heslington YO10 ....228 F1
York YO10 ....228 E3
York YO10 ....229 B2
York YO30 ....233 A3
University Rd YO10 ....228 F2
Upgang La YO21 ....208 B7
Upgarth Cl 2 TS13 ....12 A7
Uplands BD23 ....217 B5
Uplands Ave 8 YO13 ....99 B8
Uplands Rd DL3 ....3 B5
Uplands The YO12 ....212 A7
Upper Carr La YO18 ....96 A4
Upper Green La TS18 ....6 A7
Upper Hanover St 6
YO26 ....227 F5
Upper Newborough St 1
YO30 ....228 C7
Upper Nidderdale High Sch
HG3 ....137 B4
Upper Poppleton Jun Sch
YO26 ....165 F1
Upper Price St YO23 ....233 A1
Upper Sackville St 5
BD23 ....217 A3
Upper St Paul's Terr
YO24 ....228 A4
Upper Union St BD23 ....216 F3
Upper Wharfdale Mus*
BD23 ....134 E2
Upper Wharfedale Sch
BD23 ....134 D2
Uppercommon La
DN14 ....202 F3
Uppercroft 4 YO32 ....225 C8
Uppergate LA6 ....103 D4
Upsall Dr DL3 ....3 C4
Upsall La
South Kilvington YO7 ....211 C7
Thornbrough YO7 ....90 A8
Upsall YO7 ....66 B1
Upwell Rd DL7 ....210 D4
Ure Bank HG4 ....214 D7
Ure Bank Terr HG4 ....214 C7
Ure Bank Top HG4 ....214 D7
Urlay Nook Rd TS16 ....5 C5
Usher La YO32 ....166 F6

V

Vale Ave WF11 ....201 E2
Vale Cres
Bishop Wilton YO42 ....169 F2
Knottingley WF11 ....201 E2
Vale Crest WF11 ....201 E2
Vale Sch WF11 ....201 E2
Vale The
10 Collingham LS22 ....188 A8
Middlesbrough TS5 ....6 F8
Skelton YO30 ....224 B5
Vale View HG4 ....114 B2
Valley Bridge Par
YO11 ....213 A5
Valley Dr
Barnoldswick BB18 ....171 E2
Eaglescliffe TS15 ....5 E3
Great Preston LS26 ....200 C8
Harrogate HG2 ....219 C1
Ilkley LS29 ....218 D4
Valley Gdns TS16 ....5 D4
Valley Gdns* HG2 ....219 C2
Valley Mount HG2 ....219 C2
Valley Rd
Barnoldswick BB18 ....171 E1
3 Darley HG3 ....160 A6
32 Earby BB18 ....172 A1
Harrogate HG2 ....219 C2
Ilkley LS29 ....218 D5
Kippax LS25 ....194 C2
Northallerton DL6 ....210 F3
Scarborough YO12 ....212 E4
Whitby YO21 ....208 A8
Valley Ridge LS25 ....194 C2
Valley St N DL1 ....3 D5
Valley View
3 Ampleforth YO62 ....92 C1
Clint HG3 ....160 F8
Danby YO21 ....29 C6
3 Glusburn BD20 ....187 E8
Wheldrake YO19 ....192 F7
Valuation La 1 YO51 ....141 B5
Vanbrugh Dr YO10 ....229 C3
Vane Ct TS21 ....4 F7
Vane Terr DL3 ....3 C5
Vasey Cl 5 DL8 ....63 B2
Vaughan Rd 10 DN6 ....206 E1
Vavasour Ct YO23 ....230 B2
Venables Rd TS14 ....8 E7
Vernon Cl YO23 ....231 A3
Vernon Gr 4 YO12 ....212 D8
Vernon Pl 3 YO11 ....213 A5
Vernon Rd
Harrogate HG2 ....222 E7
2 Scarborough YO11 ....213 A5
Trawden Forest BB8 ....186 B3
York YO30 ....224 E2
Vesper Dr YO24 ....227 B3
Vesper Wlk YO32 ....225 F6
Vicar Hill La YO7 ....116 D8
Vicarage Cl
2 Bubwith YO8 ....199 D7
12 Hunmanby YO14 ....126 F8
Seamer YO12 ....99 D6
Vicarage Gdns 1 YO10 ....229 C4
Vicarage La
Bishop Wilton YO42 ....169 F2
Bramham LS23 ....188 E5
10 Knaresborough HG5 ....221 A6
Naburn YO19 ....191 E8
Sherburn YO17 ....124 D8
Vicarage Rd
Barnoldswick BB18 ....171 E2
16 Catterick Garrison DL9 ....40 E4
3 Kelbrook & Sough
BB18 ....186 A7
Vicars Cl YO23 ....230 B2
Vicars Croft DL6 ....210 E5
Vicar's La YO61 ....144 C6
Vicars Terr WF10 ....200 D6
Vickers Rd 2 DL9 ....40 E4
Victor St YO1 ....233 B1
Victoria Ave
10 Filey YO14 ....101 B3
Harrogate HG1 ....219 D2
Ilkley LS29 ....175 C2
Knaresborough HG5 ....221 B8
Ripon HG4 ....214 D5
Thirsk YO7 ....211 B2
Victoria Cave* BD24 ....131 F4
Victoria Cl
Great Preston WF10 ....200 E6
Ilkley LS29 ....218 A4
Victoria Ct 15 YO26 ....227 F5
Victoria Dr 9 LS29 ....175 C2
Victoria Emb DL1 ....3 C4
Victoria Farm Cl YO23 ....182 C6
Victoria Gdns 17 LS29 ....175 C2
Victoria Gr
5 Ilkley LS29 ....175 C2
Ripon HG4 ....214 C5
Victoria Par 18 YO11 ....212 F5
Victoria Park Ave 2
YO12 ....212 F7
Victoria Park Mount
YO12 ....212 E7
Victoria Pk 1 YO12 ....212 F7
Victoria Pl 3 YO21 ....208 D6
Victoria Rd
1 Barnoldswick BB18 ....171 E1
28 Burley in Warfedale
LS29 ....176 C1
Cowling BD22 ....187 B6
Darlington DL1 ....3 C5
Earby BB18 ....172 A1
Glusburn BD20 ....187 E7
Harrogate HG2 ....219 C1
10 Ilkley LS29 ....175 C2
1 Malton YO17 ....215 B4
Richmond DL10 ....209 B7
Scarborough YO11 ....212 F5
Thornaby TS17 ....6 B8
Victoria St
24 Earby BB18 ....172 A1
Glusburn BD20 ....187 E7
Great Preston WF10 ....200 D6
Pontefract WF8 ....201 B2
Scarborough YO12 ....212 F6
Settle BD24 ....131 E2
10 Skipton BD23 ....216 F4
1 York YO23 ....233 B1
Victoria Terr
1 Harrogate HG1 ....220 C4
3 Skipton BD23 ....216 F4
Victoria Way 2 YO32 ....228 F8
Victoria Works Ind Est
BD20 ....187 F8
Victory Rd LS29 ....218 B4
Viewley Hill Ave TS8 ....6 F5
Viewley Hill Sch TS8 ....6 F5
Viking Cl 20 YO41 ....168 D2
Viking Dr 5 YO19 ....197 F8
Viking Rd
Stamford Bridge YO41 ....168 D2
York YO26 ....227 C5
Vikings Ct 6 DL6 ....43 F3
Villa Cl YO8 ....198 F1
Villa Fields 4 DN14 ....204 C1
Villa Gr 2 YO31 ....228 E6
Village Farm Ct 7
DN14 ....202 D4
Village Fold DL7 ....42 B1
Village Garth 1 YO32 ....166 E5
Village Paddock TS18 ....5 E8
Village Rd TS15 ....24 B8
Village St YO30 ....224 E3
Village The
Boston Spa LS23 ....180 F1
Haxby YO32 ....166 E5
Skelton YO30 ....224 B5
Stockton on the Forest
YO32 ....167 D3
Strensall YO32 ....167 B7
Village Wy DL7 ....42 B1
Villiers Ct 8 YO62 ....92 F6
Vimy Rd DL9 ....40 E3
Vincent St 9 YO12 ....213 A7
Vincent Way YO24 ....230 C8
Vine Cl TS14 ....8 F6
Vine Farm Cl YO26 ....164 A4
Vine St Darlington DL3 ....3 B6
Norton YO17 ....215 E4
6 Scarborough YO12 ....212 F6
York YO23 ....228 C2
Vinstra Cl DL10 ....209 D8
Virginia Gdns TS5 ....6 E6
Vivars Way YO8 ....232 D5
Vivers Pl 8 YO62 ....70 C1
Vivis La YO18 ....95 F6
Volta St YO8 ....232 E4
Vulcan Way TS17 ....6 B6
Vyner St Ripon HG4 ....214 D4
York YO31 ....228 C7

W

Waddington St 37 BB18 ....172 A1
Wade House La YO8 ....204 F4
Waggoners Dr 3 YO23 ....230 B3
Wain Cl
15 Eastfield YO11 ....100 B7
South Milford LS25 ....195 E2
Wain Gap LS25 ....195 F2
Waincroft 8 YO32 ....167 A6
Waindyke Way WF6 ....200 B1
Wainers Cl 5 YO23 ....230 B3
Wainfleet Rd HG1 ....219 D6
Waingates La YO51 ....140 F4
Wainman's Cl BD22 ....187 B6
Wain's Gr YO24 ....230 D7
Wain's La YO12 ....99 D2
Wain's Rd YO24 ....230 D8
Wainstones Cl TS9 ....7 F1
Wainstones Dr TS9 ....7 F1
Waite La YO13 ....53 F2
Waithwith Rd DL9 ....209 B1
Waitlands La DL11 ....20 A7
Wakefield Coll WF10 ....200 D3
Wakefield Rd
Garforth LS25 ....194 B3
10 Normanton South WF6 ....200 A1
Swillington LS26 ....194 A2
Wakeman Rd HG4 ....214 C3
Walburn Head DL11 ....39 D3
Walden Stubbs Rd
DN6 ....206 E2
Wales St DL3 ....3 C7
Walker Cl BD20 ....187 D7
Walker Dr YO24 ....230 C8
Walker La
Menwith with Darley
HG3 ....160 A6
Wheldrake YO19 ....192 F7
Walker St YO21 ....208 D6
Walker's La BD20 ....174 B4
Walkers Row TS14 ....8 F7
Walkerville Ave 22 DL9 ....41 A5
Walkington La YO30 ....165 B8
Wallgates La YO17 ....215 D4
Walmgate YO1 ....233 C2
Walmsley Gdns YO12 ....212 C5
Walney Rd YO31 ....229 A5
Walnut Cl
Saxton with Scarthingwell
LS24 ....195 D8
York YO10 ....229 A1
Walnut Gr HG1 ....219 E6
Walpole St YO31 ....228 D7
Walton Ave
Gargrave BD23 ....155 C1
Middlesbrough TS5 ....6 E8
Pannal HG3 ....222 F2
Walton Chase LS23 ....180 F2
Walton Cl
Gargrave BD23 ....172 C8
Huby YO61 ....144 A4
Walton Head La HG3 ....178 F4
Walton Pk HG3 ....222 E2
Walton Pl Pannal HG3 ....222 E2
York YO26 ....227 B3
Walton Rd
Walton LS23 ....181 A2
Wetherby LS22 ....180 E2
Walton St
5 Cowling BD22 ....187 B6
Skipton BD23 ....216 F1
Walworth Ave HG2 ....220 B3
Walworth St N 4 YO26 ....227 F5
Walworth St S 9 YO26 ....227 F5
Wand Hill TS12 ....9 E8
Wand La DN14 ....203 C3
Wandale La YO17 ....95 A2
Wandales Cl YO17 ....215 F3
Wandales Ct YO13 ....75 D8
Wandales Dr YO13 ....75 D8
Wandales La YO60 ....146 B6
Wandales Rd YO13 ....75 D8
Wandell Balk YO61 ....144 B6
Wandels La YO21 ....29 B6
Wandesford Gr DL9 ....209 F1
Wandhill 31 YO32 ....166 E5
Wandhill Gdns TS12 ....9 E8
Wandhill La YO7 ....66 D1
Wandle The YO26 ....227 A2
Wansbeck 3 YO24 ....230 B7
Wapping La YO62 ....94 C7
War Dike La YO13 ....54 B6
War Field La LS22 ....180 F6
Warbler Cl TS17 ....6 A5
Ward Ct YO23 ....233 B1
Ward St BD23 ....217 A4
Wardale Ave TS5 ....6 E6
Wardrop Rd DL9 ....209 C1
Wareham Rd YO11 ....99 F6
Warehill La YO61 ....143 C2
Warlbeck 23 LS29 ....175 C2
Warley Wise La BB8 ....186 D6
Warren Ave WF11 ....201 E2
Warren La
Bramham cum Oglethorpe
LS24 ....189 A5
Brearton HG3 ....162 A8
Kirkby Malzeard HG4 ....112 D4
Warren Pl HG1 ....219 D5
Warrener La DL10 ....20 C6
Warth La LA6 ....103 C3

Warthill C of E Prim Sch
YO19 ....167 F2
Warwick Cl YO60 ....145 D5
Warwick Dr 🟦 YO24 ....222 E8
Warwick Dr 🟦 BB18 ...172 A1
Wasdale Cl YO30 ......224 E1
Wash Beck La YO42 ....93 F6
Washbeck Cl YO12 .....212 E4
Washbrook Dr DL3 ......3 C8
Washburn Cl 🟩 YO14 ..101 A3
Washburn Dr 🟩 BD20 ..187 E8
Washfold La DL8 ....60 B6
Washford Cl TS17 ......6 A3
Washington Ave DL2 ...4 D4
Washington Cl HG4 ...214 E2
Wass Bank Rd YO61 ...91 F2
Wass Way TS16 ....5 D5
Waste La YO62 ....48 F2
Watchet Rd 🟦 DL9 ....40 E4
Water Bag Bank 🟦 HG5 .221 A6
Water End YO26 ....227 E5
Water Gap YO8 ....97 B5
Water Garth DL4 .....202 F4
Water Hill La YO8 ....232 D6
Water Houses BD24 ...132 E6
Water La
Camblesforth YO8 ....204 D5
🟦 Clifton YO30 ......225 A1
Dalton YO7 ....115 E7
Dunnington YO19 ....184 F7
Eggborough DN14 ...203 A2
Exelby, Leeming & Newton
DL7 ....63 D4
Hemingbrough YO8 ..198 F1
Huttons Ambo YO60 .147 C6
Kirby Grindalythe YO17 .149 B6
Kirby Underdale YO41 .170 A5
Kirk Smeaton WF8 ...206 C3
Knaresborough HG5 ..221 C8
Loftus TS13 ....10 E8
North Stainley with Sleningford
HG4 ....113 C6
🟦 Pontefract WF8 ...201 C1
South Stainley with Cayton
HG3 ....139 D2
Thorpe Bassett YO17 .123 A3
Walkern YO60 ....146 E7
Whitby YO21 ....208 B3
York YO30 ....228 A7
Water Skellgate HG4 .214 C5
Water Slack La YO26 .164 C4
Water St Earby BB18 .172 A1
Gargrave BD23 ....155 D1
Malton YO17 ....215 C4
Skipton BD23 ....216 F4
Water Street CP Sch
BD23 ....216 F4
Water Way Garth
DN14 ....207 F6
Water World York*
YO32 ....226 A2
Waterdale Rd 🟦 YO31 .225 E1
Waterfall Fold 🟦 WF8 .201 C2
Waterfalls Wlk LA6 ...103 D6
Watergate
Mickletown LS26 ....200 A5
🟦 Pontefract WF8 ...201 B1
Watergate Rd HG3 ....139 A4
Waterhouse La 🟦 YO11 .213 A6
Waterings 🟩 YO32 ...166 D5
Waterloo YO22 ....31 C4
Waterloo Cl WF10 ....200 C3
Waterloo Rd BB18 ...186 A7
Waterloo St
Harrogate HG1 ......219 E4
🟦 Richmond DL10 ...209 C6
Waterman Ct 🟦 YO24 .227 B1
Watermill Croft HG4 .113 C7
Watermill La HG4 ....113 C7
Waters End DL2 ....1 D7
Waters La DL10 ....20 E3
Watershed Mill Bsns Ctr
BD24 ....131 D3
Waterside
🟦 Boroughbridge YO51 .141 B6
Knaresborough HG5 ..221 A5
🟦 Ripon HG4 ....214 C4
🟦 Thirsk YO7 ....211 C3
Watersole La LS22 ...180 D2
Waterstead Cres 🟦
YO21 ....208 D5
Waterstead La YO21 ..208 C5
Waterways Mus & Adventure
Ctr The* DN14 ....205 F3
Watery La Airton BD23 .155 A5
Gigglesswick BD24 ...131 C1
Snape with Thorp DL8 ...66 A5
Wath La Catton YO41 .185 C8
Copgrove HG3 ....140 A7
🟦 Low Bishopside
HG3 ....137 B6
Humberton YO61 ....141 E8
Ulleskelf LS24 ....190 B2
Wath Rd HG3 ....137 B6
Wathcote Cl DL10 ....209 F8
Wathcote Pl DL10 ....209 F8
Wathgill Camp DL11 ...39 C3
Watlass La HG4 ....86 E8
Watlass Moor La HG4 ..86 D7
Watling Cl DL11 ......19 E6
Watling Rd WF10 ....201 C5
Watson Cl 🟦 YO14 ...127 A8

Watson St
🟦 Normanton South WF6 .200 A1
York YO24 ....228 A3
Watson Terr 🟦 YO24 ..228 A3
Watson's Houses 🟦
BD23 ....216 F4
Watson's La
Newton Kyme cum Toulston
LS24 ....189 B7
Norwood HG3 ....177 B8
Reighton YO14 ....122 D6
Wattle Syke LS22 ....180 B1
Wattlers Cl YO23 ....230 C3
Wattlesyke LS22 ......188 C8
Wavell Cty Jun Sch
DL9 ....209 D1
Wavell Rd DL9 ....209 D1
Wavell St YO8 ....232 A6
Waveney Gr YO30 ....228 B8
Waver La DL6 ....43 F8
Waverley Cl DN14 ....200 C2
Waverley Cres HG2 ...222 E8
Waverley St 🟦 YO31 ..233 C3
Waydale Cl YO62 .....70 A2
Wayfoot Gr 🟦 YO12 ...12 D7
Wayne Tarbard Cl 🟦
HG2 ....222 B7
Waynefleet Gr 🟦 YO10 .229 A3
Wayside Ave HG2 .....220 B1
Wayside Cl 🟦 HG2 ...220 B1
Wayside Cres HG2 ....220 A1
Wayside Dr HG2 ......220 B1
Wayside Terr LS17 ...178 B2
Wayside The DL2 ......3 E1
Wayside Wlk 🟦 HG2 ..220 B1
Weaponness Dr YO11 .213 A2
Weaponness La
Eastfield YO11 ....99 F8
Scarborough YO11 ...212 F1
Weaponness Pk YO11 .213 A2
Weaponness Valley Cl 🟦
YO11 ....212 F3
Weaponness Valley Rd
YO11 ....212 E3
Weardale TS14 ....8 D5
Weardale Rd 🟦 DL9 ...40 E4
Weary Bank TS15 .....25 B8
Weavers Cl YO23 ....230 B3
Weavers Ct 🟦 TS9 ...26 C7
Weavers Gn DL7 .....210 C3
Weaverthorpe C of E Prim
Sch YO17 ....124 E2
Webster Hill 🟦 HG4 ..200 A1
Weddall Cl YO24 .....227 F1
Wedderburn Ave HG2 .220 C2
Wedderburn Cl HG2 ..220 C2
Wedderburn Cty Inf Sch
HG2 ....220 B2
Wedderburn Dr HG2 ..220 B2
Wedderburn Lodge 🟦
HG2 ....220 B2
Wedderburn Rd HG2 ..220 B2
Weedling Gate LS24 .189 D4
Weeland Ct 🟦 WF11 ..202 A2
Weeland Rd Beal DN14 .202 E3
Hensall DN14 ....203 E2
Weeton La LS17 ......178 D1
Weeton Sta LS17 .....178 B2
Weets View BB18 ....172 A1
Welbeck Ave DL1 ......3 E7
Welborn Cl YO10 ....229 B4
Welborn Dr 🟦 YO12 ...99 E6
Welbourn Dr 🟦 YO12 ..99 D6
Welburn Cty Prim Sch
YO60 ....146 D6
Welburn Gr TS7 ....7 D7
Welburn Hall Sch YO62 .94 A7
Welburn La YO60 ....147 A8
Welbury Cl 🟦 BB18 ..172 B1
Welfare Ave LS15 ....194 C8
Welford Rd 🟦 YO14 ..101 B3
Welham Hill YO17 ...147 E7
Well Bank DL8 ....87 A4
Well Cl
Great & Little Preston
LS25 ....200 C8
🟦 Whitby YO21 ......208 D7
Well Close Terr 🟦
YO21 ....208 D7
Well La Kippax LS25 .194 D1
Redmire DL8 ....59 C5
Seamer TS9 ....6 F2
Snape with Thorp DL8 ...87 A6
South Milford LS25 ..195 F2
Yearsley YO61 ....118 C5
Welland Dr LS25 .....194 D3
Welland Rise YO26 ..227 D5
Wellbrook Cl TS17 ....6 B4
Wellesley Cl YO30 ..225 A2
Wellfield La 🟦 LS29 .176 C1
Wellhouse St 🟦 BB18 .171 E1
Wellington Cl 🟦 HG2 .219 C2
Wellington Mews 🟦
HG2 ....208 D7
Wellington Rd
Ilkley LS29 ....218 B4
Richmond DL10 .....209 C6
🟦 Whitby YO21 ......208 D6
Wellington Row YO1 .233 A2
Wellington Sq 🟦 HG2 .219 C2
Wellington St
🟦 Knaresborough HG5 .221 B5
🟦 Ripon HG4 ....214 B5
🟦 Skipton BD23 ....216 F3
🟦 York YO10 ....228 E3
Wellington Terr YO21 .208 D7
Wellington Way 🟦 DL10 .41 C7
Wellingtonia Dr DN6 .206 E1

Wells Cl YO8 ....232 A5
Wells La Barton DL10 .21 D7
Kellington DN14 ....202 E3
Malton YO17 ....215 C4
Wells Prom LS29 ....218 B4
Wells Rd LS29 ....218 B4
Wells Wlk Ilkley LS29 .218 B4
🟦 Pickering YO18 ....95 F7
Wellspring Cl TS17 ....6 D7
Welton Ave YO26 ....227 D6
Welwyn Dr YO10 ....231 E8
Wemyss Rd 🟦 HG4 ...113 D2
Wendel Ave LS15 ....194 B8
Wendy Ave HG4 .....214 B3
Wenham Rd YO24 ....230 C8
Wenlock Dr YO19 ....192 B6
Wenlock Terr YO10 ..228 D1
Wenning Ave LA2 ...129 A7
Wenning Bank LA2 ..130 A6
Wennington Hall Sch
LA2 ....102 A1
Wennington Rd LA2 .128 A6
Wennington Sta LA2 .128 B8
Wensley Gr HG2 ....222 D7
Wensley Rd
Harrogate HG2 ......222 D7
🟦 Leyburn DL8 ......60 D5
Northallerton DL7 ..210 B2
Wensleydale Ave 🟦
BD23 ....217 B4
Wensleydale Dr YO10 .229 D4
Wensleydale Rd 🟦 DL9 .40 E4
Wensleydale Rugby Club
DL8 ....60 C5
Wensleydale Sch DL8 .60 D5
Wentcliffe Dr BB18 ..172 A1
Wentdale 🟦 WF8 ....206 C3
Wentworth Ave YO61 .116 F5
Wentworth Cl
Camblesforth YO8 ...204 D4
Harrogate HG2 ......220 D4
Kellington DN14 ....203 A2
Wentworth Cres
Harrogate HG2 ......220 D3
🟦 Whitby YO21 ......208 B5
Wentworth Gate LS22 .180 A3
Wentworth Gr HG2 ..220 D3
🟦 Wentworth St YO17 .215 B5
Wentworth Way
Eaglescliffe TS16 .....5 E4
🟦 Hunmanby YO14 ..126 F8
Wescoe Hill La LS17 ..178 B1
Wesley Pl YO1 ....233 C2
Wesley Rd YO22 ....33 C4
Wesley Sq 🟦 TS13 ...13 K2
Wesson Cl 🟦 DL9 ....40 E4
West Acres 🟦 WF11 ..201 E4
West Acres Cl 🟦 YO13 .99 A7
West Auckland Rd DL3 ..3 A7
West Ave
Boston Spa LS23 ...180 E1
Eaglescliffe YO21 ...208 B5
🟦 Easingwold YO61 .143 D8
Filey YO14 ....101 B3
🟦 Scalby YO13 ....97 F5
West Bank
Scarborough YO12 ..212 E4
York YO24 ....227 E3
West Bank Rd BD23 ..216 E4
West Barnby La YO21 .12 B3
West Beck Way TS8 ...7 B6
West Burton C of E Prim Sch
DL8 ....58 F1
West Cam Rd BD23 ...79 E6
West Cl Carthorpe DL8 .87 E6
Normanton WF6 .....200 A1
Swinton YO17 ....121 B4
West Cliff Ave 🟦 YO21 .208 B7
West Cliffe Gr HG2 ..219 B1
West Cliffe Mews 🟦
HG2 ....219 C1
West Cliffe Mount
HG2 ....219 B1
West Cliffe Terr YO21 .219 B1
West Close Rd 🟦 BB18 .171 D2
West Craven High Sch
BB18 ....171 E1
West Craven Swimming Pool
BB18 ....171 E1
West Croft
🟦 Addingham LS29 ..174 F4
🟦 Glusburn BD20 ...187 E6
West Ct 🟦 YO19 .....197 F8
West Dale LS23 ......180 E1
West Dike Rd YO18 ...71 F5
West Edge Rd WF8 ..206 A3
West End
Boston Spa LS23 ...180 E1
Guisborough TS14 ....8 D6
Hurworth-on-Tees DL2 ..3 E1
Hutton Rudby TS15 ..25 C5
Kirkbymoorside YO62 ..70 B1
Muston YO14 ....100 F2
Osmotherley DL6 ....45 B4
Pollington DN14 ....207 F6
Rawcliffe DN14 ....205 A1
Sheriff Hutton YO60 .145 C5
Stokesley TS9 ....26 C7
Swinton YO17 ....121 B4
West End App LS26 .200 B3
West End Ave
Appleton Roebuck YO23 .190 F5
Harrogate HG2 ......222 D8
Richmond DL10 .....209 C7
West End Cl
North Duffield YO8 ..199 A8
🟦 Stensall YO32 ...167 B7
West End Ct 🟦 YO11 .100 B6

West End Gdns
Egglescliffe TS16 .....5 D4
Pollington DN14 ....207 F6
West End Rd DN6 ....206 E2
West End View 🟦 YO11 .100 B6
West End Way TS18 ...5 F8
West Field La
Arkendale HG5 ......163 A8
East Witton Town DL8 ..60 F1
Upper Poppleton YO26 .165 E1
West Field Rd 🟦 BB18 .171 D2
West Fields YO22 ......70 B1
West Garforth Jun Sch
LS25 ....194 C3
West Garth
Cayton YO11 ....100 B6
Sherburn YO17 .....124 D8
Ulleskelf LS24 ....190 B3
West Garth Gdns 🟦
LS25 ....194 C3
West Gate
Thornton-le-Dale YO18 ..96 C5
Wetherby LS22 ......180 B3
Wykeham YO13 ......98 D6
West Gr
Bishop Thornton HG3 ..139 A2
Swinton YO17 ....121 B4
West Grove Rd HG1 ..219 D4
West Hall La LS29 ...175 A5
West Heslerton C of E Prim
Sch YO17 ....123 F6
West Ing La BD23 ...171 A5
West Ings Cl 🟦 WF11 .202 A3
West Ings Cres 🟦
WF11 ....202 A3
West Ings Ct 🟦 WF11 .202 A3
West Ings La 🟦 WF11 .202 A3
West Ings Mews 🟦
WF11 ....202 A3
West Ings Way 🟦 WF11 .202 A3
West La
Appleton Wiske DL6 ..24 A3
Askwith LS21 ....176 C3
Azerley HG4 ....112 F3
Bewerley HG3 ......136 E4
Boston Spa LS23 ...180 E1
Burn YO8 ....203 C4
Burniston YO13 ......54 C1
Burton Fleming YO25 .126 E3
Caldwell DL11 ....1 B4
Caldwell DL11 ....1 D5
Cononley BD20 .....173 C2
Dalton-on-Tees DL2 ..22 D6
Danby YO21 ....29 C8
East Layton DL11 ...20 A8
Embsay BD23 ....217 D8
Hampsthwaite HG3 ..161 A4
Hutton Rudby TS15 ..25 D5
Littlethorpe HG4 ...214 A2
🟦 Low Bradley BD20 .173 E3
Melsonby DL10 ......21 C6
Mickleby TS13 ....12 A5
Nether Silton YO7 ....66 B7
North Deighton LS22 .179 F6
Snainton YO13 ......97 F5
Stillington YO61 ....143 F7
Sutton BD20 ....187 E6
Sykehouse DN14 ...207 F2
Whisley YO26 ....163 F5
West Lea Ave HG2 ...222 B7
West Lodge Gdns
YO17 ....215 A4
West Lund La YO62 ...70 B1
West Lund La YO62 ....94 B8
West Mead WF10 ....201 A4
West Moor La DL8 ....61 E4
West Moor Rd
Darlington DL2 ....3 E8
Raskelf YO61 ....116 E2
West Mount LS24 ....188 E8
West Oaks Sch LS23 .188 E8
West Par LS29 ....218 A4
West Parade Rd 🟦
YO12 ....212 F5
West Park Ave YO12 .212 C8
West Park Cres YO12 .212 C7
West Park Rd 🟦 YO13 .75 D5
West Park St 🟦 HG2 ..219 D1
West Pasture
Kirkbymoorside YO62 ..70 B1
🟦 Pickering YO18 ....95 F7
West Pk YO8 ....232 A4
West Rd Carleton BD23 .173 A4
🟦 Filey YO14 ....101 B3
Melsonby DL10 ......20 F7
West Row DL2 ....4 C7
West Side Rd YO13 ...53 A1
West Sq 🟦 YO11 ....212 F5
West St
Castleford WF10 ....200 E4
Egglescliffe TS15 .....5 D4
Gargrave BD23 .....155 D1
Gayles DL11 ....19 E6
Harrogate HG1 .....219 C5
Ilkley LS29 ....218 A4
Muston YO14 ....100 F2
Normanton South WF6 .200 A1
Scarborough YO11 ..213 A4
Swinton YO17 ....121 B4
West Tanfield C of E Prim
Sch HG4 ....87 A1
West Thorpe YO24 ..230 D8
West Vale 🟦 YO11 ..101 B3
West View
Airton BD23 ....155 A5
Carleton BD23 ......173 B4
Darlington DL3 ....3 A5
Draughton BD23 ...174 B7
Kippax LS25 ....194 D1

West View continued
Micklefield LS25 ....195 A4
North Deighton LS22 .179 F6
Sherburn in Elmet LS25 .195 F4
West View Rd 🟦 LS29 .176 C1
West View Rd 🟦 LS29 .176 C1
West View Terr TS16 ...5 D5
West Villa YO43 .....135 D5
West Way YO61 ....11 C1
West Wood La YO23 .182 D2
Westacres 🟦 DL2 .....4 C4
Westbeck Gdns TS5 ...6 E8
Westborough 🟦 YO11 ..212 F5
Westbourne Ave
Harrogate HG2 ....22 D3
Whitby YO21 ....8 F7
Westbourne Cl YO21 ..8 F7
Westbourne Cres
LS25 ....194 D1
Westbourne Gdns
YO8 ....232 C4
Westbourne Gr
🟦 Pickering YO18 ....95 F7
🟦 Ripon HG4 ....214 B5
🟦 Scarborough YO11 ..213 A2
Selby YO8 ....232 C4
Whitby YO21 ....8 F7
Westbourne Pk YO12 ..212 D5
Westbourne Rd
Scarborough YO12 ..212 D5
Selby YO8 ....232 C4
🟦 Whitby YO21 ....8 F7
Westbourne Terr 🟦 YO21 .8 F7
Westbury Cty Jun Sch
TS17 ....6 C8
Westbury St TS17 .....6 C8
Westcliff Prim Sch
YO21 ....8 F7
Westcroft La YO8 ...204 B1
Westdene HG2 ....222 B7
Westend DL1 ....3 D6
Westerdale 🟦 YO18 ..95 F7
Westerdale Ct 🟦 YO30 .225 A1
Western Ave WF8 ....201 B2
Western CP Sch HG2 ...2 D4
Western Gales Way
WF6 ....200 A1
Western Rd
Goole DN14 ....205 C3
Skipton BD23 ......216 F4
Western Way 🟦 YO18 ..95 F7
Westerns La HG3 .....160 A6
Westfield YO8 ....198 B4
Westfield Ave
Castleford WF10 ....201 A5
🟦 Eaglescliffe DN14 ..4 B8
Rawcliffe DN14 ....205 A1
🟦 Scalby YO12 ......75 E5
Selby YO8 ....232 A4
Westfield Cl
🟦 Eggborough DN14 .203 A1
🟦 Haxby YO32 ......166 E6
South Milford LS25 ..195 F1
Westfield Cres 🟦 LS24 ..1
Westfield Cty Inf Sch
YO26 ....227 E5
Westfield Cty Jun Sch
YO26 ....227 E5
Westfield Dr
Hurworth-on-Tees DL2 ..3 E1
🟦 Haxby YO32 ......166 E6
Westfield Gn 🟦 YO8 .199 A8
Westfield Gr
Allerton Bywater WF10 ..200 A1
🟦 Eggborough DN14 .203 A1
🟦 Haxby YO32 ......166 E6
Westfield La
Exelby, Leeming & Newton
DL8 ....62 F4
Kippax LS25 ....194 C2
Ledsham LS25 .....194 A1
Lockton YO18 ....72 E4
Normanby YO62 .....94 A3
Norton WF8 ....206 B1
South Milford LS25 ..195 F1
Thirsk YO7 ....211 B4
Thornton-le-Dale YO18 ..96 C5
Westfield Pl HG2 ....222 D8
Westfield 🟦 YO32 ...166 D5
Westfield Rd
🟦 Great Preston WF10 ..200 D7
Tadcaster LS24 .....189 D5
🟦 Thornton Dale YO18 ..96 C5
Westfield Way YO17 ..215 A4
Westfields
Castleford WF10 ....200 E4
Richmond DL10 .....209 C7
Scorton DL10 ....41 F6
🟦 Tadcaster LS24 ...189 E6
🟦 Stokesley TS9 .....26 C7
Tockwith YO26 ......179 D5
Westfields Sq 🟦 LS24 ..1
Westfield Terr
🟦 Great Preston WF10 ..2
Tadcaster LS24 .....189 D5
🟦 Thornton Dale YO18 ..9
Westgarth LS22 .....180 B3
Westgate
🟦 Barnoldswick BB18 ..1
Guisborough TS14 ....8 D6

...an YO17 ....215 E6
Weymouth Dr ....
rington YO18 ....95 E7
gton YO17 ....122 F5
eld YO4 ....214 C5
aster LS24 ....189 E6
e YO7 ....211 B2
gate Carr Rd
................95 D5
gate La
n YO17 ....215 D6
iton in Lonsdale
................103 C5
gate Rd DL3 ....3 87
nolme **10** TS15 ....25 C5
nolme Bank DL8 ....58 F2
nolme Cres **8** HG4 ....86 C3
nolme La **3** HG4 ....86 C3
nolme Dr YO30 ....224 C1
nolme Rd **1** HG4 ....86 C3
and Cl **8** BD20 ....187 F7
ands
e-in-Ainsty with Bickerton
................181 D5
nklevington TS15 ....24 E8
inghill YO 91 A4
esley TS9 ....26 B7
ands Ave **1** YO21 ....208 C7
ands Gr YO31 ....228 F7
ands La YO7 ....211 A4
ands Rd DL3 ....3 86
ands Cl HG3 ....222 C3
ninster Cres
................222 D2
ninster Dr HG3 ....222 D3
ninster Gate
................222 C3
ninster Gr HG3 ....222 D3
ninster Rd
ual HG3 ....222 C3
O30 ....228 A6
ninster Rise
................222 D2
moreland St
ington DL3 ....3 C7
arrogate HG1 ....219 E3
orough YO19 ....184 F7
wood Rd
HG4 ....214 A2
orough YO11 ....212 F4
wood Terr YO23 ....228 B1
wood Way LS23 ....188 E8
erby Bsns Pk
................180 C3
erby High Sch
................180 C3
erby Jun Sch
................180 C3
erby La LS22 ....180 B2
erby Leisure Ctr
................180 C2
erby Race Course*
................180 C1
erby Rd
arough HG2 ....220 B1
arboughbridge YO51 ....141 B4
ham cum Oglethorpe
................188 E6
ogate HG2 ....220 B1
Deighton LS22 ....180 D5
esborough HG5 ....221 D4
nghall LS22 ....179 E3
aster LS24 ....189 D6
on LS23 ....180 F2
ton LS22 ....180 B2
YO26 ....227 B3
ercote La YO7 ....67 C1
ands La DL11 ....18 G7
ale Ave YO12 ....212 E8

Weymouth Ave TS8 ....7 A7
Weymouth Rd **1** HG1 ....219 E4
Whaddon Chase TS14 ....8 F6
Whaites La YO7 ....115 C5
Whales La DN14 ....202 E2
Wham La BD24 ....130 F1
Wharfe Dr YO24 ....230 D8
Wharfe Gr **8** LS22 ....180 B3
Wharfe La
Grassington BD23 ....134 D3
Kearby with Netherby
................179 B1
LS22 ....179 B1
Wharfe Pl **2** LS29 ....175 A4
Wharfe View
Grassington BD23 ....134 D3
Kirkby Overblow HG3 ....179 A4
Wharfe View Rd LS29 ....218 B4
Wharfedale YO11 ....101 A3
Wharfedale Ave HG2 ....222 A7
Wharfedale Cl **1** BD23 ....217 B4
Wharfedale Cres
Hazlegate HG2 ....222 A7
Tadcaster LS24 ....189 E6
Wharfedale Dr
Ilkley LS29 ....218 C4
Normanton WF6 ....200 A3
Wharfedale General Hospl
LS21 ....176 F1
Wharfedale Pl HG2 ....222 A7
Wharfedale RUFC
BD23 ....134 D3
Wharfedale View 8
LS29 ....174 F4
Wharfeside Ave BD23 ....134 D3
Wharfeside La LS29 ....218 C5
Wharncliffe Pl **1** YO14 ....101 A3
Wharton Ave YO30 ....224 F2
Wharton Rd **8** YO41 ....168 D2
Whartons The LS21 ....177 A2
Whartons The LS21 ....177 A1
Whashton Rd Aske DL10 ....20 C1
Richmond DL10 ....209 C8
Wheatcroft **6** YO12 ....167 A6
Wheatcroft YO11 ....213 B1
Wheatcroft Cty Prim Sch
YO11 ....213 B1
Wheatdale Rd LS24 ....190 B2
Wheatear La TS17 ....6 A5
Wheatfield La YO32 ....225 C8
Wheatlands
Great Ayton TS9 ....8 A2
Ilkley LS29 ....218 C4
Wheatlands Ave 8
BD20 ....187 E8
York YO26 ....227 C6
Wheatlands Dr
7 Glusburn BD20 ....187 E8
Roecliffe YO51 ....140 E4
Wheatlands Rd HG2 ....222 A7
Wheatlands Rd E HG2 ....222 B7
Wheatlands Way HG2 ....222 B7
Wheatley Ave
Ilkley LS29 ....218 E3
Normanton South WF6 ....200 A1
Wheatley Gdns **2** LS29 ....218 E3
Wheatley Gr LS29 ....218 E3
Wheatley La **2** LS29 ....218 E3
Wheatley Rd LS29 ....218 E3
Wheatley Rise LS29 ....218 E3
Wheeldale Cres TS17 ....6 B7
Wheeldale Rd YO18 ....51 A4
Wheelgate So **7** YO17 ....215 C4
Wheelhouse The 4
YO30 ....224 B5
Wheels La YO8 ....204 F3
Wheelwright Cl
Copmanthorpe YO23 ....230 B2
Sutton upon Derwent
YO41 ....185 C1
Wheldale La WF10 ....201 B5
Wheldon Rd WF10 ....201 A5
Wheldrake CE Prim Sch
YO19 ....193 A8
**Wheldrake Ings Nature
Reserve*** YO19 ....193 C2
Wheldrake La
Deighton YO19 ....184 B1
Escrick YO19 ....192 B5
Whenby Gr YO31 ....225 F1
Whenby La YO60 ....145 C6
Whernside TS7 ....7 C5
Whernside Ave YO31 ....229 A5
Whessoe Rd DL3 ....3 C8
Whin Bank YO12 ....212 D5
Whin Cl
3 Strensall YO32 ....167 B6
York YO24 ....230 F6
Whin Gn YO22 ....32 A6
Whin Hill YO17 ....147 E1
Whin La
South Milford LS25 ....195 C2
Warlaby DL7 ....64 C5
Whin Rd YO24 ....230 F6
Whinbeck Ave WF6 ....200 B1
Whinbush Way DL3 ....3 F8
Whinchat Tail TS14 ....8 D6
Whincup Ave HG5 ....221 B6
Whincup Cl **3** HG5 ....221 B6
Whincup Gr **7** HG5 ....221 B6
Whinfield Rd DL1 ....3 E7

Whinfield Road Jun & Inf Sch
DL1 ....3 F7
Whinfields The **1** HG3 ....138 A1
Whingroves TS17 ....6 C8
Whinmoor Hill YO7 ....66 C2
Whinney La HG3 ....222 A5
Whinney Mire La LA2 ....103 E1
Whinny Bank YO61 ....117 C8
Whinny Gill Rd BD23 ....217 B3
Whinny Hagg La YO8 ....197 A2
Whinny Hill DL9 ....40 E3
Whinny La YO60 ....145 E4
Whinnythwaite La
YO26 ....181 D8
Whins La
Spofforth with Stockeld
HG3 ....179 E4
Thorp Arch LS23 ....180 F1
Whins The YO12 ....212 A7
Whinstone View **8** TS9 ....8 A2
Whinwath La DL8 ....87 F4
Whipley Bank HG3 ....161 A8
Whipley Hill HG3 ....161 A7
Whip-ma-whop-ma-gate
YO1 ....233 C2
Whipperdale Bank DL8 ....60 A8
Whiston Dr **18** YO14 ....101 B3
Whit Moor Rd HG3 ....158 F5
**Whitby Archives & Heritage
Ctr*** YO21 ....208 E7
Whitby Ave
Guisborough TS14 ....8 F6
York YO31 ....229 A7
**Whitby Benedictine Abbey
(rems of)*** YO22 ....208 E7
Whitby Com Coll
YO21 ....208 C5
Whitby Dr YO31 ....229 A7
Whitby Gate YO18 ....96 D6
Whitby Hospl YO21 ....208 D6
Whitby Mus & Art Gall*
................208 C6
Whitby Pavilion & Theatre
................208 C8
Whitby Rd
Guisborough TS14 ....9 A7
Pickering YO18 ....96 B8
Staithes YO21 ....13 K2
Whitby Sta YO21 ....208 D6
Whitby Town Football Club
................208 B7
Whitby Way YO13 ....3 A7
Whitcliffe Cres LS26 ....194 A1
Whitcliffe Dr **1** LS26 ....194 A1
Whitcliffe La **1** LS26 ....194 A1
Whitcliffe Rise LS26 ....194 A1
Whitecote La LS25 ....195 D2
Whitecross Hill DL8 ....87 F3
Whitefield Bglws
................206 F8
Whitefield La DN14 ....202 E1
Whitefields Dr DL10 ....209 E7
Whitefields Gate 1
DL10 ....209 E8
Whitefields Wlk 2
DL10 ....209 E8
Whitefriars Ct **8** BD24 ....131 D2
Whitegate Cl **7** TS13 ....13 K2
Whitegate La HG4 ....114 F1
Whitehill Rd BD22 ....187 A5
Whitehouse Ave LS26 ....200 B8
Whitehouse Cres
LS26 ....200 B8
Whitehouse La
Great & Little Preston
LS26 ....200 B8
Swillington LS26 ....194 B2
Whitelass Cl YO8 ....198 C4
Whiteoak Ave YO61 ....143 C8
Whitepits La LA2 ....129 A5
Whiterose Dr YO41 ....168 D2
Whitethorn Cl YO31 ....225 E2
Whitethorn Cl YO31 ....225 E2
Whitewall YO17 ....215 D1
Whitewall Corner Hill
YO17 ....147 E8
Whiteway Head HG5 ....221 A4
Whitfield Ave YO18 ....96 A6
Whitkirk Pl **17** YO14 ....101 B3
**Whitley & Eggborough Cty
Prim Sch** DN14 ....202 F1
Whitley Bridge Sta
DN14 ....202 F1
Whitley Cl **8** YO30 ....225 A1
Whitley Pl **8** WF10 ....200 E6
Whitley Rd
Elvington YO41 ....185 A3
Norton-le-Clay YO7 ....115 B1
Thornaby TS17 ....6 B6
Whitley Thorpe La
DN14 ....206 F7
Whitsundale Cl **1** HG5 ....221 D5
Whitton Pl YO31 ....229 A6
Whitton Croft Rd **2**
LS29 ....218 B4
Whitton Pl YO10 ....229 C4
Whitwell Rd YO60 ....146 E5
Whitwood Common La
DN14 ....200 C3
Whitwood La WF10 ....200 C3
Whitworth Way BB18 ....171 E2
Whixley Cty Prim Sch
YO26 ....164 B4
Whixley La YO26 ....163 E2
Whorlton Castle (rems of)*
DL6 ....25 D1
Whorlton La DL6 ....45 A8
Whorlton Parochial Sch
DL6 ....45 D8
Wyett Bank YO21 ....28 F6
Wickets The **8** TS15 ....25 C5
Widdale Rd HG5 ....221 D5
Widdale Sch DL8 ....55 E2
Widdowfield St DL3 ....3 C6
Widow Hole **1** YO7 ....114 E8
Wide La YO14 ....127 E5
Widgeon Cl **4** YO14 ....101 A4
Wigby Cl YO10 ....229 C4
Wigginton Prim Sch
YO32 ....166 D5
Wigginton Rd YO31 ....233 B4
Wigginton Terr YO31 ....228 C8
Wigglesworth Sch
BD23 ....153 C3
Wighill Garth LS24 ....189 E6
Wighill La
Healaugh LS24 ....181 F3
Healaugh LS24 ....189 E7
Wighill St **28** BD20 ....187 E7
Wilberforce Ave YO30 ....228 A7
Wilberforce Cl YO41 ....185 E6
Wilcock La AL8 ....173 F2
Wild Rd DL1 ....4 A4
Wilfreds Dr **8** YO8 ....198 B4
Wilfreds Rd **8** YO8 ....198 B4
Wilken Cres TS14 ....8 F6
Wilkinson St TS12 ....9 E7
Wilkinson Way
3 Otley LS21 ....176 F1
3 Strensall YO32 ....167 B6
Willance Gr DL10 ....209 A7
Willaston Cres HG2 ....220 A2
Willaston Rd **1** HG1 ....220 A3
Willerby Carr La YO12 ....99 C3

White Rose Cl continued
Nether Poppleton YO26 ....224 C1
White Rose Cres DL10 ....209 E7
White Rose Gr **5** YO32 ....225 D3
White Rose Way
Nether Poppleton YO26 ....227 C8
Thirsk YO7 ....211 D4
White Sprunt Hill
YO17 ....125 A1
White St YO8 ....232 B6
White Wall La HG3 ....160 D4
White Way YO13 ....54 C1
White Way Heads YO18 ....51 F4
Whitebridge Dr DL1 ....3 D8
Whitecar La YO62 ....95 A5
Whitecliffe Cres LS26 ....194 A1
Whitecliffe Dr **1** LS26 ....194 A1
Whitecliffe Rise LS26 ....194 A1

Willgutter La BD22 ....187 F1
William Crossthwaite
TS17 ....6 B4
William Jacques Dr
YO8 ....198 E2
William Plows Ave
YO10 ....228 E2
William Rd YO8 ....198 B4
William St **18** BB18 ....172 A1
Dilham's Hill Ring & Bailey*
....
Williamson Cl **18** HG4 ....214 C5
Williamson Dr **4** HG4 ....214 C5
Willis St YO10 ....228 E3
Willitoft Rd YO8 ....199 F6
Willoughby Way YO24 ....230 B8
Willow Ave
Catterick Garrison DL9 ....209 B1
Clifford LS23 ....188 E7
Willow Bank YO32 ....225 E4
Willow Beck Rd DL6 ....210 E5
Willow Bridge La YO7 ....115 F8
Willow Chase The TS21 ....4 F7
Willow Cl
20 Burley in Wharfedale
................176 C1
5 Filey YO14 ....101 B4
Willow Cres
Clifford LS23 ....188 E7
Richmond DL10 ....209 D8
Willow Ct Kexby YO41 ....168 C2
2 North Featherstone
WF7 ....200 E1
3 Pickering YO18 ....95 F6
Willow Dr **5** Bedale DL8 ....63 B3
Eston & South Bank TS6 ....7 E8
1 North Duffield YO8 ....199 A7
Willow Garth
Ferrensby HG5 ....162 F7
Scalby YO12 ....212 A7
12 Thornton Dale YO18 ....96 D5
Willow Garth Ave
BD20 ....187 E8
Willow Garth La DN6 ....207 A1
Willow Glade
5 Boston Spa LS23 ....188 E2
York YO31 ....225 F3
Willow Gr
3 Boston Spa LS23 ....188 E2
Earswick YO32 ....226 A7
Harrogate HG1 ....219 E5
York YO31 ....228 F7
Willow La
Boston Spa LS23 ....188 E2
North Featherstone
WF7 ....200 D3
Willow Rd La **4** WF7 ....200 C1
Willow Park Rd WF7 ....185 F5
Willow Rd
10 Campsall DN6 ....206 E1
Darlington DL3 ....3 B6
13 Knottingley WF11 ....202 A3
Northallerton DL7 ....210 D2
Willow Rise
5 Kirkbymoorside YO62 ....70 B1
Tadcaster LS24 ....189 D5
Thorpe Willoughby YO8 ....197 B1
Willow Tree Gdns 10
YO11 ....176 C1
Willow View **1** DL10 ....41 D5
Willow Way **8** BD20 ....187 E6
Willow Wlk TS14 ....214 B2
Willowbank TS8 ....7 A5
Willowbridge Rd WF8 ....206 C3
Willowbridge Way
WF10 ....200 C3
Willowdene La WF8 ....201 B2
Willowgate **24** YO19 ....95 F7
Willows Ave TS8 ....6 E4
Willows The
11 Hambleton YO8 ....196 F1
Middlesbrough TS7 ....7 C6
6 Strensall YO32 ....167 B7
Willmatt Rd LS29 ....218 C4
Wilson St
Castleford WF10 ....200 E4
Guisborough TS14 ....8 F6
Lockwood TS12 ....9 F7
12 Pontefract WF8 ....201 B1
Sutton BD20 ....187 E8
Wilson's La 5 YO13 ....99 A7
Wilsthorpe Gr **1** YO10 ....231 F8
Wilstrop Farm Rd
................230 A2
Wilton Carr La YO18 ....97 A3
Wilton Ings La YO18 ....97 A4
Wilton La TS14 ....8 F7
Wilton Rd TS14 ....8 E1
Wilton Rose YO24 ....227 F3
Wimbledon Cl **2** DL1 ....3 F6
Wimpole Cl **6** YO30 ....225 A1
Winchester Ave 3
YO30 ....227 C4
Winchester Gr **1** YO26 ....227 E4
Winchester Way **1** DL3 ....3 F6
Windermere YO24 ....230 D7
Windermere Ave BB8 ....186 A3
Windermere Dr WF11 ....201 F3
Windgate Hill La YO8 ....197 B6
Windle La BD20 ....173 D1
Windless Dr TS3 ....7 B8
Windmill Rise YO26 ....232 B7

Windmill Gr LS24 ....189 D5
Windmill La
  Norton DN6 ....206 D1
  York YO10 ....229 B2
Windmill Mdw YO41 ......185 E6
Windmill Rd LS23 ....188 F6
Windmill Rise
  Aberford LS25 ....194 F7
  Tadcaster LS24 ....189 D5
  York YO26 ....227 E3
Windrose CI WF6 ....200 A2
Windross Sq YO61 .....143 C8
Windsor Ave
  Richmond DL10 ....209 D8
  Skipton BD23 ....217 A4
Windsor CI WF6 ....200 B1
Windsor Cres
  Middlesbrough TS7 ....7 D6
  7 Whitby YO21 ....208 D6
Windsor Dr
  2 Haxby YO32 ....166 D5
  Lockwood TS12 ....9 F7
Windsor Garth YO24 ....227 D1
Windsor La HG5 ....221 B5
Windsor Pl BB18 ....171 E2
Windsor Rd
  4 Catterick Garrison DL9 ..40 E4
  4 Harrogate HG2 ....220 A1
  Ripon HG4 ....214 C3
  Thornaby TS17 ....6 B7
Windsor St **1** YO23 ...228 B1
Windsor Terr YO21 ......208 D6
Windy Hill LA2 ....129 B8
Winewall La BB8 ....186 B2
Winewall Rd **18** BB8 ..186 A3
Winksley Banks Rd
  HG4 ....112 E2
Winksley Gr HG3 ....219 A4
Winn La YO7 ....115 C6
Winnow La LS23 ....188 D8
Winscar Gr **9** YO30 ...224 E3
Winston Ave BD20 ......187 F8
Winston Ct
  Northallerton DL6 ....210 E6
  Norton YO17 ....215 E3
Winter Gap La BD20 .....186 D8
Winter Gn **2** HG1 ....161 B3
Winterburn BD23 ....155 D5
Winterscale St YO10 ...228 D2
Winthropp CI YO17 .....215 C5
Winton Rd DL6 ....210 E6
Wise House La YO17 ....215 F7
Wisker La YO19 ....228 C2
Wisp Hill **10** BD23 ...134 E3
Wistow Parochial C of E Prim
  Sch YO8 ....197 D6
Wistow Rd YO8 ....232 A8
Wistowgate YO8 ....197 C6
Witch La YO25 ....127 B2
Witham Dr YO32 ....226 A6
Withington Rd **6** YO62 ..92 F7
Witton Cres DL3 ....3 A7
Witton Steeps DL8 ......59 E2
Wobeck La HG4 ....114 B7
Wold La Willerby YO12 ...99 D1
  Willerby YO12 ....125 E8
Wold Newton GM Sch
  YO25 ....126 A4
Wold Newton Rd
  YO25 ....126 E3
Wold Rd YO17 ....149 E8
Wold St YO17 ....215 D3
Wold View YO14 ....100 F2
Wold View Gr **1** YO12 ..99 E6
Woldcroft YO41 ....185 C2
Wolfe Ave YO31 ....228 F5
Wolsey Ave YO8 ....197 B8
Wolsey CI **11** LS25 ...195 F4
Wolsey Croft LS25 ......195 F4
Wolsey Dr YO23 ....231 A3
Wolsey Gdns **12** LS25 ..195 F4
Wolsingham Dr TS5 ......6 F2
Wolsley St YO10 ....228 E3
Wolviston Ave YO10 .....229 C3
Womersley C of E Prim Sch
  DN6 ....206 C6
Womersley Rd WF11 .....202 A2
Wood Acre CI BD23 .....134 C3
Wood Ave LS26 **3** HG3 ..161 B3
Wood CI
  Bradleys Both BD20 ......173 D3
  Skipton BD23 ....216 E5
  7 Strensall YO32 ....167 A7
  4 Thorpe Willoughby
    YO8 ....197 B1
Wood End La DL8 ....59 C5
Wood End Mus *
  YO11 ....213 A5
Wood Gate YO13 ....74 A1
Wood Gn WF10 ....200 C2
Wood Hill CI YO51 ......141 D1
Wood La
  Acaster Selby YO23 ......191 B2
  Austwick LA2 ....131 A8
  Birkin WF11 ....202 D6
  Gainford DL2 ....1 D8
  10 Grassington BD23 .....134 E2
  Great Preston LS26 .....200 C7
  Low Coniscliffe & Merrybent
    DL2 ....2 E4
  Spennithorne DL8 ....61 A4
  Thorp Arch LS23 ....180 F2
  10 Thorpe Willoughby
    YO8 ....197 B1
  Threshfield BD23 ....134 B3

Wood La continued
  Whitwood WF10 ....200 C3
  16 Wood La WF11 ....201 E4
  Wood Park DL8 ....220 B1
  Wood Row LS26 ....200 A6
Wood St
  Castleford WF10 ....200 E4
  Norton YO17 ....215 D3
  York YO31 ....228 E6
Wood View
  Airmyn DN14 ....205 E3
  Embsay BD23 ....217 C7
  Harrogate HG1 ....219 C3
  14 Sherburn in Elmet LS25 ..195 F4
Wood View Ave WF10 ....200 D4
Wood Way YO32 ....226 A4
Woodall Ave YO12 ....212 F7
Woodall Ct **8** YO8 ....197 D6
Woodbine CI **13** TS9 ...8 A2
Woodbine Terr **9** HG1 ..219 D3
Woodburn Dr **3** DL8 ...60 D5
Woodcock CI
  Eston & South Bank TS6 ...7 F8
  6 Haxby YO32 ....166 F5
Woodcock Dr **6** DL9 ....40 F2
Woodcrest Rd DL3 ....3 B4
Wooden Hill La DL7 .....210 B2
Woodend WF10 ....200 C7
Woodend Cres WF10 .....200 C7
Woodfield Ave HG1 ......219 E4
Woodfield CI HG1 ....219 E4
Woodfield CP Sch
  HG1 ....219 F5
Woodfield Gdns **5** HG1 ..219 E4
Woodfield Inf Sch
  HG1 ....219 F5
Woodfield PI **6** HG1 ...219 E4
Woodfield Rd
  Goole DN14 ....205 F3
  Harrogate HG1 ....219 F7
  4 Woodfield Sq HG1 .....219 E4
Woodford PI **8** YO24 ...227 D1
Woodgate YO12 ....212 D5
Woodgate La LS17 ......178 B2
Woodhall Dr HG1 ....219 F6
Woodhall Gr
  Harrogate HG1 ....219 F6
  Mickletown LS26 ....200 B6
  4 Stockton-on-Tees TS18 ...5 D8
Woodhall La
  Hemingbrough YO8 ......199 B3
  Womersley DN6 ....206 D6
Woodhead Field La
  YO62 ....70 A4
Woodhill View **3** LS22 ..180 B3
Woodhouse Gr YO31 ....229 A5
Woodhouse La BD23 ....157 B7
Woodhouse Rd
  Guisborough TS14 ....8 C6
  Thorganby YO19 ....193 A3
Woodland Ave
  Scarborough YO12 ......212 D6
  3 Swillington LS26 .....194 A1
Woodland Chase
  YO30 ....225 B1
Woodland CI YO12 ......212 D6
Woodland Cres **8** LS26 ..194 A1
Woodland Dr DL7 ....63 F3
Woodland Gr
  Scarborough YO12 ......212 C6
  7 Swillington LS26 .....194 A1
Woodland PI
  New Earswick YO32 .....225 E4
  Scarborough YO12 ......212 C6
Woodland Ravine
  YO12 ....212 D6
Woodland Rd DL3 ....3 B6
Woodland Rise YO12 ....212 D6
Woodland St **3** BD22 ...187 B6
Woodland Terr DL3 ....3 A5
Woodland View YO7 ......89 A1
Woodland Way
  6 Airmyn DN14 ....205 E4
  Longnewton TS21 ....4 F7
  York YO32 ....225 B1
Woodlands
  Escrick YO19 ....192 B5
  Ilkley LS29 ....218 D4
Woodlands Ave
  Harrogate HG2 ....220 B1
  Haxby YO32 ....225 C8
  Norton YO17 ....215 E2
  Rillington YO17 ....122 F5
  Tadcaster LS24 ....189 D5
Woodlands CI
  Goldsborough HG5 ......163 A3
  Harrogate HG2 ....220 C2
  18 Ilkley LS29 ....175 C2
  Sherburn in Elmet LS25 ..195 F2
Woodlands Cres HG2 ....220 C2
Woodlands Croft
  LS25 ....200 D8
Woodlands Ct **8** HG2 ...220 B1
Woodlands Cty Jun Sch
  HG2 ....220 B2
Woodlands Dr
  Eggbescliffe TS15 ....5 E3
  Garforth LS25 ....194 D4
  Harrogate HG2 ....220 C1
  Scarborough YO12 ......212 B5
  Skipton BD23 ....216 E5
Woodlands Gn **8** HG2 ...220 D1
Woodlands Gr
  Harrogate HG2 ....220 B1
  6 Ilkley LS29 ....175 C2

Woodlands Gr continued
  Kippax LS25 ....200 E8
  Rillington YO17 ....122 F5
  York YO31 ....229 A7
Woodlands La LS25 ......202 B7
Woodlands Rd
  Harrogate HG2 ....220 C2
  Rillington YO17 ....122 F5
Woodlands Rise
  1 Harrogate HG2 ....220 C2
  14 Ilkley LS29 ....175 C2
  Norton DN6 ....206 E1
Woodlands Sch The
  YO12 ....212 B5
Woodlands The TS7 ....7 D5
Woodlands View
  Barlby with Osgodby
    YO8 ....198 B4
  Kippax LS25 ....200 E8
  3 Tadcaster LS24 ......189 D5
  2 Thornton Dale YO18 ...96 D5
Woodlands Way
  Hurworth DL2 ....3 D1
  2 Hurworth-on-Tees DL2 ..22 D8
Woodlands Wlk
  Harrogate HG2 ....220 C2
  Skipton BD23 ....216 E5
  Stokesley TS9 ....26 C8
Woodlea Ave YO26 ......227 C4
Woodlea Bank YO26 .....227 D4
Woodlea Cres YO26 .....227 D4
Woodlea Gr YO26 ....227 D5
Woodleigh CI YO32 .....167 A6
Woodleigh Sch YO17 ....148 A6
Woodley Gr TS7 ....7 D7
Woodman La LA6 ....102 B6
Woodman Terr **2** BD23 ..216 F4
Woodmanwray La
  HG3 ....159 C8
Woodpark Ave HG5 ......221 A7
Woodpark Dr HG5 ....221 A7
Woodpecker Rd **12**
  LS29 ....176 C1
Woodrow Ave TS7 ....7 B6
Woodrow Cres LS26 .....200 A6
Woodroyd Gdns LS29 ...218 F3
Woodruff CI **27** HG3 ...161 B3
Woodrush TS8 ....7 B4
Wood's CI YO13 ....75 C8
Wood's Gr YO13 ....75 C8
Woods La YO26 ....142 B2
Woods PI LS29 ....218 C4
Woodside
  Castleford WF10 ....201 B4
  Harrogate HG1 ....219 E2
  Hutton Rudby TS15 ......25 C6
  6 Leyburn DL8 ....60 D5
Woodside Ave YO31 .....229 A6
Woodside CI **3** YO61 ...117 D1
Woodside Gr
  Allerton Bywater WF10 ...200 C7
  3 Stockton-on-Tees TS18 ...5 D8
Woodside La BD20 ......173 C2
Woodside Rd
  Garton YO12 ....125 A8
  Sibsden BD20 ....174 B1
Woodside St WF10 ......200 C7
Woodthorpe Prim Sch
  YO24 ....230 C7
Woodville Ave TS8 ....7 A4
Woodville Rd DL8 ....3 B4
Woodville Ave
  Middlesbrough TS4 ......7 A8
  3 Scalby YO12 ....212 A7
Woodville Terr YO8 .....232 C3
Wooldale Dr YO14 ....101 B4
Wooler St YO12 ....212 E5
Woolmoor CI YO7 ....211 D4
Woolnough Ave YO10 ....229 B3
Woolpots La YO41 ....117 B4
Woolsington Dr DL2 .....4 C4
Worcester Dr YO31 .....229 B5
Wordsworth App **2**
  WF8 ....201 B1
Wordsworth Ave **4**
  DN6 ....206 E1
Wordsworth CI YO13 ....75 C5
Wordsworth Cres
  Harrogate HG2 ....222 C8
  York YO24 ....230 C7
Wordsworth Dr WF11 ....201 D3
Workhouse Museum *
  HG4 ....214 C6
Worsall Rd TS15 ....5 D2
Worsall Toll Bar TS15 ...24 B7
Worsendale Rd YO42 ...169 F2
Worsley CI TS16 ....5 E7
Worsley Cres TS7 ....7 B6
Worsley Ct YO17 ....215 A3
Woundales La
  Knayton with Brawith YO7 ..65 F4
  Upsall YO7 ....66 A2
Wrangham Dr **4** YO14 ..127 A8
Wray with Botton Endowed
  Sch LA2 ....128 A5
Wray's Ave YO31 ....229 A7
Wrea Head CI **2** YO13 ..75 D5
Wrea La **1** YO12 ....212 F6
Wreaks La HG4 ....111 E6
Wreaks Rd
  Birstwith HG3 ....160 E6
  Harrogate HG3 ....220 B3
Wrelton Cliff Rd YO18 ...95 B8
Wrelton Hall Gdns
  YO18 ....71 C1
Wren Croft **5** WF8 .....201 B1
Wren Hall La YO8 ....204 E6
Wren La **2** YO8 ....232 D5

Wrenbeck Ave **1** LS21 ..177 A1
Wrenbeck CI **2** LS21 ...177 A1
Wrenbeck Dr LS21 ......177 A1
Wressle Sta YO8 ....199 D2
Wrexham Rd LS29 ....176 B1
Wreyfield Dr YO12 ......212 C7
Wright St **8** BD20 ......187 E7
Wrights La WF11 ....206 B8
Wycar **1** DL8 ....63 A2
Wycliffe Ave
  Northallerton DL7 ....210 C2
  York YO10 ....229 B3
Wycliffe Rd DL7 ....22 B1
Wycoller Ctry Pk *
  ....186 D2
Wydale La YO13 ....98 B6
Wydale Rd YO13 ....98 B6
Wydale Rise YO13 ....98 A5
Wydra La HG3 ....159 F1

Y

Yafforth Rd DL7 ....210 B6
Yall Flat La YO21 ....29 B6
Yan Brow YO62 ....70 C3
Yarborough CI DL10 .....41 B2
Yarburgh CI **4** DN14 ...204 B1
Yarburgh Gr **2** YO26 ...227 E5
Yarburgh Way YO10 .....229 C3
Yarde Ave DL10 ....41 E4
Yarker Bank La DL8 ......60 C6
Yarkside La BD23 ....171 B4
Yarm Back La TS15 ......5 E2
Yarm Cty Jun Sch TS15 ...5 E2
Yarm La TS9 ....7 D1
Yarm Rd Darlington DL1 ...3 E5
  Eaglescliffe TS16 ....5 E5
  Hilton TS15 ....4 C2
  Middleton St George DL2 ...4 B4
Yarm Road Ind Est DL1 ...3 F5
Yarm Sch TS15 ....5 E2
Yarm Sta TS15 ....5 E2
Yarrow Dr HG3 ....161 B3
Yatts Rd YO18 ....96 A8
Yaud Sike La YO18 ....95 E5
Yeadon Wlk **2** DN14 ...204 B4
Yealand Ave BD24 ......131 D3
Yearby CI TS5 ....6 D7
Yearsley Cres YO31 .....228 D7
Yearsley Gr YO31 ....225 E1
Yearsley Grove Jun Sch
  YO32 ....225 F1
Yearsley Moor Bank
  YO62 ....118 B7
Yearsley Swimming Baths
  YO31 ....228 D8
Yedmanslie Rd YO13 .....98 B8
Yedingham Priory (site of) *
  YO17 ....97 D2
Yedmandale Rd
  2 East Ayton/West Ayton
    YO13 ....99 A7
  Hutton Buscel YO13 .....98 F7
Yeomans Mount HG3 ....137 B4
Yew Tree CI
  Acaster Malbis YO23 ....191 C8
  Harrogate HG2 ....222 C4
  11 Low Bradley BD20 ...173 E3
  Rufforth YO23 ....182 C6
  Selby YO8 ....232 C6
  18 Sleights YO22 ....32 A6
Yew Tree Gdns **2** LS25 ..222 B5
Yew Tree La HG2 ....222 B5
Yew Tree Mews YO19 ...229 C5
Yew Tree Pk DN14 ......207 A7
Yew Tree Wlk HG2 ......222 B6
Yew Wlk The TS21 ....4 F7
Yewbank CI **3** LS29 ....218 A4
Yewbank Terr LS29 .....218 A4
Yewdale Rd HG2 ....220 A1
Yiewsley Dr DL3 ....3 A5
YMCA Leisure Ctr
  YO11 ....213 A6
Yoadwath Bank YO62 ....70 C3
Yoredale Ave
  Darlington DL3 ....3 B6
  17 Leyburn DL8 ....60 D5
York Abbey * YO30 ....233 A3
York Barbican Leisure Ctr
  YO10 ....233 C1
York Castle Mus *
  YO1 ....233 B1
York City Art Gall *
  YO30 ....233 B3

York City Football Club
  YO30 233
York CI **2** HG5 221
York Coll of Further & Higher
  Ed YO24 230
York Cricket & RUFC
  YO30 227
York District Hospl
  YO30 233
York Dungeon * YO1 233
York Garth **1** HG5 221
York Ind Pk YO17 121
York La Flaxton YO60 167
  Knaresborough HG5 221
York Minster * YO1 233
York PI Harrogate HG2 ..223
  Knaresborough HG5 221
  Scarborough YO11 213
York Race Course (The
  Knavesmire) * YO24 233
York Rd Bagby YO7 211
  Barlby YO8 190
  Bilbrough YO23 182
  Bilton-in-Ainsty with Bickerton
    LS22 181
  Boroughbridge YO51 141
  10 Burley in Warfedale
    LS29 176
  Cliffe YO8 198
  Cottam YO25 150
  Dunnington YO19 184
  Easingwold YO61 143
  Flaxby HG5 163
  Green Hammerton YO26 ..164
  Harrogate HG1 219
  Haxby YO32 225
  Kilham YO25 150
  Kirk Hammerton YO26 ...164
  Knaresborough HG5 221
  Leavening YO17 147
  Long Marston YO26 182
  Malton YO17 215
  Middlesbrough TS7 7
  Naburn YO19 191
  North Duffield YO8 199
  Riccall YO19 197
  Sledmere YO25 150
  Sowerby YO7 211
  Stillingfleet YO19 191
  Strensall YO32 167
  Sutton-on-the-Forest
    YO61 144
  Sutton-on-the-Forest
    YO61 145
  Tadcaster LS24 189
  Wetherby LS22 180
  York YO26 227
York Rugby League Club
  YO32 226
York Sixth Form Coll
  YO24 230
York St
  Barnoldswick BB18 171
  Castleford WF10 200
  Crathorne TS15 24
  5 Dunnington YO19 184
  12 Glusburn BD20 187
  1 Selby YO8 232
  1 Sitre YO24 233
York Steiner Sch
  YO10 229
York View DL10 41
York Villas WF6 200
Yorkdale CI **1** YO10 228
Yorkdale Dr **8** YO10 228
Yorkersgate YO17 215
York Yorkshire Air Mus *
  YO41 185
Yorkshire Carriage Mus *
  YO12 212
Yorkshire Coast Coll
  YO12 212
Yorkshire Dales National
  Park Ctr * BD24 131
Yorkshire Mus * YO1 233
Yorkshire Mus of Farming *
  YO19 184
Young Bank La YO62 92
Young's Ct LS25 194
Young's Dr **8** HG3 161
Youngs Way **10** DL10 ...41
Ypres Rd DL9 209
Yule La YO26 164

Z

Zetland Dr DL10 209
Zetland St DL6 210

NH	NJ	NK
NN	NO	NP
NS	NT	NU
NX	NY	NZ
SC	SD	SE	TA
SH	SJ	SK	TF	TG
SN	SO	SP	TL	TM
SS	ST	SU	TQ	TR
SX	SY	SZ	TV

Any feature in this atlas can be given a unique reference to help you find the same feature on other Ordnance Survey maps of the area, or to help someone else locate you if they do not have a Street Atlas.

The grid squares in this atlas match the Ordnance Survey National Grid and are at 500 metre intervals. The small figures at the bottom and sides of every other grid line are the National Grid kilometre values (**00** to **99** km) and are repeated across the country every 100 km (see left).

To give a unique National Grid reference you need to locate where in the country you are. The country is divided into 100 km squares with each square given a unique two-letter reference. Use the administrative map to determine in which 100 km square a particular page of this atlas falls.

The bold letters and numbers between each grid line (**A** to **F**, **1** to **8**) are for use within a specific Street Atlas only, and when used with the page number, are a convenient way of referencing these grid squares.

Example   The railway bridge over DARLEY GREEN RD in grid square B1

Step 1: Identify the two-letter reference, in this example the page is in **SP**

Step 2: Identify the 1 km square in which the railway bridge falls. Use the figures in the southwest corner of this square: Eastings **17**, Northings **74**. This gives a unique reference: **SP 17 74**, accurate to 1 km.

Step 3: To give a more precise reference accurate to 100 m you need to estimate how many tenths along and how many tenths up this 1 km square the feature is (to help with this the 1 km square is divided into four 500 m squares). This makes the bridge about **8** tenths along and about **1** tenth up from the southwest corner.

This gives a unique reference: **SP 178 741**, accurate to 100 m.

Eastings (read from left to right along the bottom) come before Northings (read from bottom to top). If you have trouble remembering say to yourself "Along the hall, THEN up the stairs"!

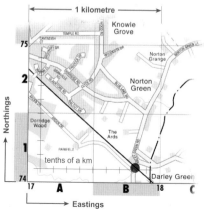

ne and Address	Telephone	Page	Grid reference

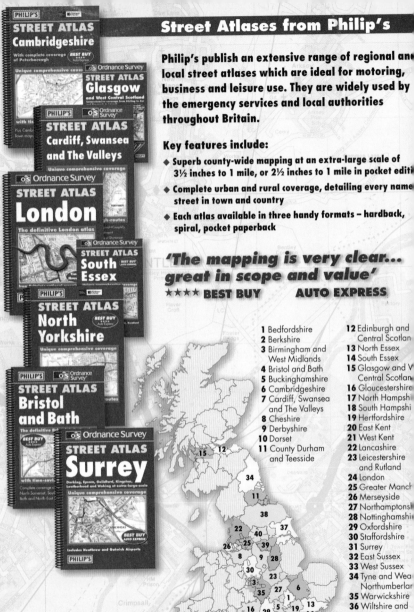